STUDENTS' INTERLINEAR TRANSLATIONS

CAESAR'S
COMMENTARIES
ON THE
GALLIC WAR

Books I—VII

THE ORIGINAL LATIN TEXT
WITH AN INTERLINEAR ENGLISH TRANSLATION
By FREDERICK HOLLAND DEWEY, A.B.

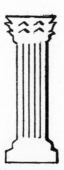

TRANSLATION PUBLISHING CO., INC.
67 Irving Place, New York

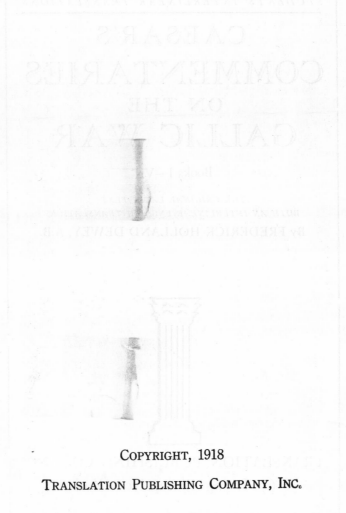

INTRODUCTION

Since Caesar is the first Roman author studied by beginners in Latin, a translation of his work should be practical and helpful for both teacher and student. Such a translation, especially an interlinear, must not be so smooth and polished in English style and diction as to escape the true Latin meaning of word and phrase, or so slavishly literal and exact that the real meaning is clouded by the abuse of English idiom.

Owing to the style and nature of Caesar's work, it is impossible to produce an elegant, polished English rendering, and at the same time indicate the full force and meaning of the original. The Commentaries of Caesar are camp notes, hastily composed, and sent to Rome annually, merely as military reports. The author never considered them a classical production and for that reason never carefully revised and polished them as did Cicero his famous orations.

As Caesar, in early life, devoutly studied and practiced versification, with the secret hope of becoming a famous poet, his writings are occasionally enlivened with poetic terms and expressions. Although his epigrams and lyrics have disappeared, his military notes, hastily written, have become immortal. The poetic element in the Commentaries appearing in many vivid and original uses of words, calls for especial attention in a translation. These Commentaries, little valued as a literary work by the author, were soon adopted as a text by ancient Roman teachers, and ever since have been found indispensable in classical instruction because of their artistic perfection. We have endeavored to indicate these natural touches by following Caesar as closely as possible.

The elements of Caesar's work which render it so suitable as a means of instruction also make it the most difficult to translate into good English. The Commentaries, being mere camp notes, are written with a conciseness, force and teeming thought in a climactic progress, which the English idiom can with difficulty reproduce from the brevity of the Latin. Caesar's command of climax, his fluency, his poetic use of words, together with his philosophic outlook, cause a strictly literal translation to be very inadequate.

The frequent use of indirect discourse is also an added difficulty for the translator. If the rendering of such passages is too free, the translation as a reproduction of the Latin thought and a clue to the Latin construction, will be most misleading to the student. For practical use a translation must be transparent and behind it the original language must be visible. In certain passages where Caesar desires to represent rapid action, he has used a vivid and condensed form of construction, even for Latin. A smooth and easy rendering would fail to reproduce the life and vitality of Caesar's thought.

He will suddenly use a word in a bright and original manner, even as we might expect from the pen of a poet, and unless the feeling and force of the passage is rendered as well as the bare thought, an important element of Caesar's style is entirely lost. Caesar possessed such a command of both the essential and secondary meanings of Latin terms that his brief and cursory notes shine with these gems of thought. The natural Latin order of thought and expression, a style somewhat inverted to the English thinking mind, of course is found in Caesar in all its Roman complexity. Beside Caesar has inverted forms of expression, peculiarly his own.

Translators therefore have found it impracticable to preserve the Latin order of the original and the student after the use of the interlinear must reconstruct his own translation and by comparison with the usual text book, will be able to appreciate the power and beauty of the Latin language, which must in a large degree escape even the most careful translation, as a result of the artificial English order of the Latin words.

Owing to the prevalence of these difficulties throughout the Commentaries of Caesar and the inadequacy of the usual methods of translation, a new system has been adopted in the production of this interlinear. In the reproduction of the Latin words into English it has been the endeavor to render the Latin terms as literally and exactly as possible, consistent with good English idiom. To remedy the crudeness of passages which have been impossible to render exactly into our idiom in an interlinear translation and which would become too wordy beneath the Latin, explanatory notes have been added in many instances providing a freer translation. Notes of this nature are an innovation in an interlinear and taken together with the parallel translation will afford both a free and an exactly literal rendering. In this manner the full meaning, the original and poetic feeling, the strength and rapidity, the artistic completeness of Caesar's style, by comparison of the renderings, can be obtained.

In order to modify exact renderings so that a more pleasing English idiom may be produced, not too far removed from the Latin sense, brackets have been used about these synonymous terms and expressions. In translating, if desired, these bracketed portions may be substituted for the more exact renderings which immediately precede. It has been the endeavor in every instance not to use in brackets any forms which would mislead the student concerning the essential meanings of the Latin text.

Words and expressions which may be entirely omitted or those which may be supplied bodily to suit more nearly the English phraseology, and which are not synonymous, have been inserted in parentheses. Such parenthetical portions may be used or omitted as the student's judgment may decide in order to obtain the best English rendering. In the preparation of this work the standard Latin school text as regards punctuation and orthography in so far as possible has been followed.

THE COMMENTARIES OF

CAIUS JULIUS CAESAR

ON THE

GALLIC WAR

FIRST BOOK

Cæsar, in recounting the events of the war which he waged in.
Gaul, first describes Gaul itself, then tells of two battles against the
Helvetians and then of one against the Germans.

1. Omnis[1] Gallïa est divisa in tres partes: unam
All Gaul is divided into three parts: one

quarum Belgæ incŏlunt; aliam Aquitani; tertiam,
of which the Belgæ inhabit; another the Aquitani; the third,

  qui linguâ ipsorum appellantur
(those) who in (the) language of themselves are called

Celtæ, nostrâ, Galli. Omnes hi diffĕrunt inter
Celtæ, in ours, Gauls. All these differ between

 se linguâ, institutis, legïbus. Flumen
themselves in language, in institutions, (and) in laws. The river

Garumna divĭdit Gallos ab Aquitanis,
Garonne divides the Gauls from the Aquitani,

Matrona et Sequăna à Belgis. Belgæ sunt
the Marne and Seine from the Belgæ. The Belgæ are

fortissïmi omnïum horum, propterĕa quòd absunt
the bravest of all these, because (that) they are distant

longissïmè à cultu atque humanitate
farthest from the cultivation and humanity [refinement]

Provincïæ; que mercatores minïmè sæpe
of the Province [Provence]; and merchants least often

commĕant   ad   ĕos,   atque   important   ĕa,
resort   to   them,   and   import   those (things)

quæ   pertĭnent   ad   anĭmos   effeminandos.
which tend   to   minds   to be effeminated [to enfeeble

        Sunt   proxĭmi   Germanis,   qui
their minds]. They are   nearest   to the Germans,   who

incŏlunt   trans   Rhenum,   cum   quĭbus   gĕrunt
dwell   beyond   the Rhine, with   whom   they carry on

bellum   continenter :   de   quâ   caussâ   Helvetĭi
war   continually :   from   which cause   the Helvetii

quŏque   præcedunt   relĭquos   Gallos   virtute;
also   go before [excel] the remaining Gauls   in valor;

quòd   contendunt   cum   Germanis   fĕrè,   quotidianis
because they contend   with   the Germans almost,   in daily

prœlĭis   quum   aut   prohĭbent   ĕos   suĭs
battles   when   either they prohibit [bar] them   from their own

finĭbus,   aut   ipsi   gĕrunt   bellum   in
borders,   or   they [themselves] carry on   war   in

finĭbus   eorum.[2]   Una   pars   eorum,   quam
the borders of them [their]. One   part   of them,   which

dictum-est   Gallos   obtinere,   căpit   init'ium   à
it has been said the Gauls to hold, [possess] takes   beginning   from

flumĭne   Rhodăno;   continetur   flumĭne   Garumnâ,
the river   Rhone;   it is bounded   by the river Garonne,

Oceăno,   finĭbus   Belgarum;   etĭam   attingit
by the ocean,   by the borders of the Belgæ; also   it touches

          flumen   Rhenum[3]   à   Sequănis   et
[reaches to] the river Rhine   from   the Sequani   and

Helvetĭis;[4]   vergit   ad   Septentriones.
the Helvetii;   it inclines to   the seven stars [the North].

Belgæ   oriuntar   ab   extremis   finĭbus   Gallĭæ;
The Belgæ rise   from the farthest borders   of Gaul;

pertĭnent   ad   inferiorem   partem   flumĭnis   Rheni;
they reach   to   the lower   part   of the river Rhine;

spectant   in   Septentriones   et   orientem   solem.
they look   unto [towards] the North   and   the rising   sun.

Aquitanĭa   pertĭnet   à   flumĭne   Garumnâ   ad
Aquitania   reaches   from   the river   Garonne   to

Pyrenæos   montes,   et   ĕam   partem   Ocĕăni,
the Pyrenees   mountains,   and   that   part   of the Ocean,

quæ est   ad   Hispanĭam,   spectat   inter   occasum
which is [next] to   Spain,   it looks   between the   going down

Solis   et   Septentriones.
of the sun [West] and   the North.

2. Orgetŏrix fŭit   longè   nobilissĭmus et ditissĭmus
Orgetorix   was   by far   the most noble   and   the richest

ăpud   Helvetĭos.   Is, Marco Messalâ   et   Marco
among   the Helvetii.   He, Marcus   Messala   and   Marcus

Pisone   consulĭbus,   inductus   cupiditate   regni,
Piso (being) consuls,   induced   by desire   of the kingdom, [of

        fecit   conjurationem   nobilitatis;   et   persuasit
reigning] made   a conspiracy   of the nobility;   and   persuaded

civitati,   ut   exirent   de   sŭis   finĭbus
(to) the state   that   they should go out   from   their own   borders

cum   omnĭbus   copĭis: esse   perfacĭle,   quum
with   all their   forces: to be [that it was] very easy,   since

præstarent   (imp. subj.)   omnĭbus   virtute,   potiri
they were excelling   (to) all   in valor,   to gain

imperĭo   totius   Gallĭæ.   Persuait   id   ĕis[5]
the empire   of all   Gaul.   He persuaded (to) this   (to) them

hoc   facilĭùs,   quòd   Helvetii   continentur
by this   more easily, because the Helvetii are contained in [hemmed in]

undĭque   natura   lŏci;   ex[6]   unâ   parte,
on every side   by the nature   of the place;   from [on]   one   side,

latissĭmo   atque   altissĭmo   flumĭne   Rheno,
by the widest [very wide] and   very deep   river   Rhine,

qui   divĭdit   Helvetĭum   agrum   à   Germanis:
which   divides   the Helvetian   land   from   the Germans:

ex   altĕrâ parte,   altissĭmo   monte Jurâ,
on   the other side,   by the very high   mountain   Jura, [St. Cloude]

qui est   inter   Sequănos   et   Helvetĭos;
which   is   between   the Sequani   and   the Helvetii; (on the)

tertĭâ,   lăcu Lemano,   et
third (side),   by lake   Lemanus [the lake Geneva],   and

flumĭne   Rhodăno,   qui   divĭdit nostram provincĭam
by the river   Rhone,   which   divides   our   province

ab   Helvetiïs.   Fiebat
[Provence]   from   the Helvetii.   It was made   [it happened]

his   rebus,   ut   et   vagarentur (imp. sub.) mĭnus
by these   things,   that   both   they were roving   less

latè   et   possent (imp. sub.) minùs facĭlè   inferre
widely and   were able   less   easily   to bring on

bellum   finitĭmis.   De[7] quâ caussâ homĭnes
[wage]   war   (on) neighbors.   From   which cause   men

cupĭdi   bellandi   afficiebantur magno dolore.   Autem
desirous   of warring   were affected   with great distress.   But

arbitrabantur[8]   se   habere   angustos fines, pro
they were deeming   themselves to have   narrow   borders, for

multitudĭne   homĭnum   et   pro   glorĭâ belli   atque
the multitude   of men   and   for   the glory of war   and

fortitudĭnis ;   qui   patebant   ducenta   et
of bravery;   which was lying open [extending] two hundred and

quadraginta   millĭa passŭum in longitudĭnem, centum
forty   thousand (of) paces into [in] length,   a hundred

et octoginta in   latitudĭnem.
and eighty   into [in]   width.

3. Adducti   his   rebus,   et   permoti   auctoritate
Induced   by these   things,   and   excited   by the authority

Orgetorĭgis,   constituerunt   comparare   ĕa,
of Orgetorix,   they determined   to prepare   those (things)

quæ   pertinerent (imp. subj.) ad   proficiscendum ;
which   were pertaining   to   setting out;   [the expedition]

coëmĕre quàm   maxĭmum   numĕrum
to buy up   as   the greatest [the greatest possible]   number

jumentorum   et carrorum ;   facĕrĕ[9] quàm
of beasts of burden [cattle] and   of wagons;   to make   as

maxĭmas   sementes, ut   copĭa frumenti   suppetĕret
the greatest   sowings,   that   a supply of corn   might be at hand

in   itinĕre ;   confirmare pacem et amicitĭam cum
on   the way [march]; to confirm   peace   and friendship   wᶦth

proxĭmis   civitatĭbus.   Duxerunt   b025 biennĭum[10]
the nearest   states.   They led [thought]   two years

esse   sătis   sĭbi   ad   ĕas   res
time   to be   enough   for themselves   for   those   things

conficiendas ;   confirmant   lege   profectionem
to be accomplished;   they established   by law   (their) departure

in   tertĭum   annum.   Orgetŏrix[11]   deligitur   ad
upon [for] the third   year.   Orgetorix   is chosen   for

ĕas   res   conficiendas.   Is   suscepit   sĭbi
those   things   to be accomplished. He   undertook   to himself

legationem   ad   civitates.   In   ĕo   itinĕre   persuadet
an embassy   to   the states.   In   this   journey   he persuades

Castĭco,   filĭo   Catamantaledis,   Seqăno,   păter[12]
(to) Casticus, son   of Catamantaledes,   a Sequanian,   the father

cujus   obtinuĕrat   regnum   in   Sequănis   multos
of whom   had held   the kingdom in   the Sequani many

annos,   et   appellatus-ĕrat   amicus   Romani   popŭli
years,   and   had been called   friend   of the Roman people

à   Senatu,   ut   occuparet   regnum   in
by   the Senate,   that   he should occupy   the kingdom   in

sŭâ   civitate,   quod   păter   antè   habuĕrat :   que
his own   state,   which   (his) father before had held: and

item   persuadet   Ædŭo   Dumnorĭgi,   fratri
likewise   he persuades (to) the Æduan Dumnorix,   the brother

Divitiăci,   qui   ĕo   tempŏre obtinebat principatum
of Divitiacus,   who   in this   time   was holding sovereignty

ĭn   sŭâ   civitate,   ac   ĕrat maxĭmè   acceptus
in   his   state,   and   was especially   acceptable

        plebi,   ut   conaretur   ĭdem ;
to the common people,   that   he should attempt   the same (thing);

que   dat   sŭam   filiam   in   matrimonĭum   ĕi.
and   gives   his   daughter   into [in] marriage   to him.

Prŏbat   illis   esse   perfacĭle   factu
He proves   to them   to be [that it was] very easy   to be done

perficĕre   conata,   proptereâ   quòd   ipse
to effect(the things) attempted,   because   (that)   (he) himself

esset (imp.subj.)   obtenturus   imperĭum   sŭæ
was   about to hold [obtain]   the empire   of his

civitatis :   esse   non   dubĭum   quin
state: to be [that it was] not   doubtful   but that

Helvetii   possent (imp.subj.) plurĭmum   totius
the Helvetians   were able   most [most powerful] of all

Gallĭæ;   confirmat,[13]   se   conciliaturum
Gaul;   he confirms [assures],   himself   about to secure

regna   illis   sŭis copĭis   que   sŭo exercĭtu.
the kingdoms   for them   with his stores   and with his   army.

Adducti   hâc   oratione,   dant   inter   se
Induced   by this   speech,   they give   between   themselves

fĭdem   et   jusjurandum;   et   regno
faith   and   oath;   and   the kingdom [government]

occupato   per   tres   potentissĭmos   ac   firmissĭmos
being occupied   by   three   most powerful   and   most steadfast

popŭlos,   sperant[14]   sese   posse   potiri   totius
peoples,   they hope   themselves   to be able   to possess   (of) all

Gallĭæ.
Gaul.

4. Ut   ĕa   res   enuntiata-est   Helvetĭis   per
When   this thing [action]   was declared to   the Helvetii   through

indicĭum,   sŭis morĭbus   coëgerunt   Orgetorĭgem dicĕre
a disclosure, by their   customs   they forced   Orgetorix   to say

caussam   ex   vincŭlis. Oportebat   pœnam
[plead] (his) cause   from [in]   bonds.   It must be   punishment

sĕqui   damnatum,   ut   cremaretur
to [should] follow (him)   condemned,   (viz:) that   he be burnt

igni.   Dĭe   constitutâ   dictionis   caussæ,
with fire.   On the day   appointed   of saying [pleading]   the cause,

Orgetŏrix coëgit   omnem sŭam familĭam,   ad
Orgetorix   collected   all   his   family, [clan]   to [about]

dĕcem   millĭa   homĭnum   ad   judicĭum;   et[15]
ten   thousand   (of) men   to   the trial;   and

conduxit   eòdem   omnes   sŭos   clientes   que
he led together   to the same place   all   his   clients   and

obæratos,   quorum   habebat magnum numĕrum:
debt bondsmen .   of whom   he was having   a great   number;

per   ĕos,   eripŭit   se   ne-dicĕret
by   these,   he rescued   himself   that he might not plead

causam.   Quum   civĭtas,   incitata   ob
the cause.   When   the state,   excited   on account of

ĕam   rem,   conaretur (imp. subj.)   exĕqui   sŭum   jus
this   thing,   was endeavoring   to execute   its   right

armis,   que   magistratus   cogĕrent (imp. subj.)
by arms,   and   the magistrates   were collecting

multitudĭnem homĭnum ex agris, Orgetŏrix mortŭus-est;
a multitude   of men out of the fields, Orgetorix   died;

nĕque[16] suspicĭo ăbest, ut Helvetĭi arbitrantur, quin
nor   suspicion is absent, as the Helvetii think,   but that

ipse   conscivĕrit (perf. subj.) mortem sĭbi.
himself determined   death to himself [committed suicide].

5. Nihĭlomĭnùs   post   mortem   ejus   Helvetĭi
   Nevertheless   after   the death   of him   the Helvetii

conantur   facĕre   id,   quod   constituĕrant,   ut
endeavor   to do   this, which they had determined, that

exĕant   è   sŭis finĭbus. Ubi jam arbitrati-sunt
they may go out from their borders. When now   they deemed

se   paratos-esse ad   ĕam rem,   incendunt
themselves to have been prepared to [for] this thing, they set fire to

omnĭa   sŭa oppĭda, ad   duodĕcim   nuinĕro,   vicos
all   their towns, to [about] twelve   in number, villages

ad   quadringentos,   relĭqua   privata   ædĭficia;
to [about] four hundred,   the remaining private   buildings;

comburunt omne frumentum, præter   quod ĕrant
they burn up   all   the corn,   except (that) which they were

portaturi   cum   se;   ut,   spe   reditionis
about to carry with themselves; that,   the hope of a return

dŏmum   sublatâ,   essent[17]   paratiores   ad
home   being taken away,   they might be more ready   to

omnĭa pericŭla   subeunda: jŭbent   quemque
all   dangers   to be undergone: they order   each

afferre dŏmo   sĭbi   molĭta cibarĭa trĭum
to bring from home for himself ground provisions of [for] three

mensĭum.   Persuadent   Rauracis,   et   Tulingis,
months.   They persuade (to) the Rauraci, and (to) the Tulingi,

et   Latobrĭgis,   finitĭmis,   utì   usi
and (to) the Latobrigi, (their) neighbors,   that   having adopted

eodem   consilĭo,   sŭis   oppĭdis   que   vicis
the same   plan,   their   towns   and   villages

exustis,   proficiscantur   unà   cum   eis:
having been burnt up, they should depart together with   them:

que[18] adsciscunt   receptos   ad   se   socios
and   they vote in   received   to   themselves as allies

sĭbi,   Boĭos,   qui   incoluĕrant   trans   Rhenum
to themselves, the Boii, who   had dwelt   across the Rhine

et   transiĕrant   in   Norĭcum   agrum,   que
and   had passed over into the Norican   land,   and

oppugnârant   Noreiam.
had beseiged   Noreia.

6. Erant   omnino   dŭo   itinĕra,   quĭbus   itinerĭbus
There were in all   two   roads,   by which   roads

possent   exire   dŏmo;   unum   per
they might be able to go forth   from home;   one   through

Sequănos   angustum   et   difficĭle,   inter   montem
the Sequani narrow   and   difficult   between   Mount

Juram   et   flumen   Rhodănum,   qua   singŭli
Jura   and   the river   Rhone,   by [in] which single

carri   vix   ducerentur; autem   altissĭmus
wagons scarcely could be led; but [moreover] the highest [a very

          mons   impendebat,   ut   perpauci   facĭlè
high]   mountain   was overhanging , so that very few   easily

possent   prohibere;   altĕrum   per nostram
would be able [could]   (to) prohibit; the other through our

provincĭam,   multò   facilĭus   atque   expeditĭus;
province,   much   more easy   and   more unimpeded;

proptereă   quòd   inter   fines   Helvetiorum   et
because   (that) between the borders of the Helvetii and

Allobrŏgum, qui   nuper   pacati-ĕrant,
of the Allobroges, who lately had been reduced to peace [subdued]

Rhodănus   flŭit,   que   is   nonnullis lŏcis   transitur
the Rhone flows,   and   this   in some   places   is passed

vădo.   Genava est extremum oppĭdum   Allobrŏgum
by ford. Geneva is   the farthest   town   of the Allobroges

que   proxĭmum   finĭbus   Helvetiorum;   ex   ĕo
and   nearest   to the bordes of the Helvetii; from   that

oppĭdo   pons pertĭnet ad   Helvetĭos. Existimabant[19]
town   a bridge reaches to   the Helvetii. They were thinking

    sese   ve   persuasuros   Allobrogĭbus,(dat.) quòd
themselves either about to persuade the Allobroges,   because

viderentur (imp. subj.) nondum bŏno anĭmo in
they were seeming · not yet · with good mind · towards

Romanum popŭlum; vel coacturos vi,
the Roman · people; · or · about to force · by violence.

ut paterentur ĕos ire per sŭos fines.
that · they should suffer · them · to go · through · their · borders

Omnĭbus rebus comparatis ad profectionem,
All · things · being prepared · for · (their) departure,

dicunt dĭem, quâ dĭe omnes convenĭant,
they say [appoint] a day, · on which · day · all · may assemble

ad ripam Rhodăni. Is dĭes ĕrat ante quintum
at the bank · of the Rhone. · This · day · was · before · the fifth

dĭem kalendarum Aprilis; Lucĭo Pisone,
day · of the Kalends · of April [27th March]; · Lucius · Piso,

Aulo Gabinĭo consulĭbus.
Aulus · Gabinius · (being) consuls.

7. Quum id nuntiatum-esse (pl. perf. subj.) Cæsări,
When · this · had been told · to Cæsar (that),

ĕos conari facĕre ĭter per nostram
them · to [they would] endeavor · to make · a journey · through · our

provincĭam, maturat proficisci ab urbe, et
province, · he hastens · to depart · from · the city, · and

contendit in ulteriorem Gallĭam itinerĭbus[20] quàm
rushes · into · farther · Gaul · by journeys · as

maxĭmis pŏtest, et pervĕnit ad Genavam. Impĕrat
greatest · he can, · and · arrives · at · Geneva. · He orders

toti provincĭæ quàm maxĭmum
(to) the whole · province (to furnish) · as · greatest [the greatest

numĕrum milĭtum (una legĭo ĕrat omnino
possible] number · of soldiers · (one · legion · was · in all

in ulteriore Gailĭâ). Jŭbet pontem, qui ĕrat
in · farther · Gaul). · He orders · the bridge, · which · was

ad Genavam, rescindi. Ubi Helvetĭi facti-sunt
at · Geneva, · to be cut down. · When the Helvetii · were made

certiores de adventu ejus, mittunt nobilissĭmos
more certain [told] · of · the arrival · of him, · they sent · the noblest

civitatis legatos ad ĕum; cujus legationis
of the state (as) · ambassadors · to · him; · of which · embassy

Nummeïus et Verudoctïus obtinebant princïpem lŏcum:
Numeius   and   Verodoctius   were holding   the chief   place:

qui   dicĕrent   esse   sïbi   in anïmo,
who   should say   to be   to themselves   in mind (that they

sïne ullo   maleficïo   facĕre   ïter   per
intended) ,without any   damage   to make   a journey   through

provincïam, propterĕa quòd haberent (imp.subj.) nullum
the province,   because   (that)   they were having   no

aliŭd   ïter: rogare,[21] ut   licĕat   sïbi
other   journey [road]:   to ask,   that   it may be lawful   to themselves

facĕre   id   voluntate   ejus.   Cæsar,[22]   quòd   tenebat
to do   this   by the will   of him.   Cæsar,   because   he held

memorïâ,   Lucïum   Cassïum   consŭlem occisum,   que
in memory,   Lucius   Cassius   the consul being slain,   and

exercïtum ejus   pulsum   ab Helvetïis, et missum
the army   of him   driven [routed]   by the Helvetii, and sent

sub   jŭgum,   putabat   non   concedendum; nĕque
under the yoke,   considered (it)   not   to be granted;   nor

existimabat homïnes   inimico   anïmo,   facultate
did he think   men   with unfriendly   mind,   liberty

faciundi   itinĕris   per   provincïam   dătâ,
of making   a journey   through   the province   being given,

temperaturos   ab injurïâ et maleficïo: Tămen
about to refrain [would refrain] from injury and damage: However

ut spatïum   posset   intercedĕre, dum milïtes,
that a space [period] might be able to intervene, while the soldiers,

quos   imperavĕrat,   convenirent,   respondit,
whom   he had ordered,   might assemble,   he replied,   (to the

se[23] sumpturum dïem   ad deliberandum;
ambassadors) himself about to take a day [time] to   deliberate;

si   vellent   (imp. subj.)   quid   reverterentur   ad
if   they were wishing   any thing   let them return   at

idus   Aprilis.
the ides of April.

8. Interĕa   ĕâ   legione,   quam   habebat
   Meanwhile   with this   legion,   which he   was having

cum   se   que   militïbus   qui convenĕrant   ex
with   himself   and   with the soldiers   who had assembled   from

provincĭâ,   perducit   murum   in   altitudĭnem
the province,   he constructs   a wall   into [in]   height

sexdĕcim   pĕdum,   que   fossam   à   lăcu   Lemanno,
(of) sixteen   feet,   and   a trench   from the lake   Lemanus,

qui   inflŭit   in   flumen   Rhodănum,   ad   montem   Juram,
which   flows   into   the river   Rhone,   to   Mount   Jura,

qui   divĭdit   fines   Sequanorum   ab   Helvetĭis,
which   divides   the borders   of the Sequani   from   the Helvetii,

dĕcem[24]   et   nŏvem   millĭa (pl.) pasŭum.   Eo   opĕre
ten   and nine [nineteen]   thousand   (of) paces.   This   work

perfecto,   disponit   præsidĭa, communit castella;
being completed,   he posts   garrisons, (he) fortifies the redoubts;

quŏ   posset   prohibere   facilĭùs,   si
that   he might be able   to prevent   more easily,   if

conarentur   transire,   se   invito.
they should endeavor   to pass over,   himself   (being) unwilling.

Ubi   ĕa   dĭes   venit,   quam   constituĕrat   cum
When   that   day   came,   which   he had appointed   with

legatis,   et   legati   reverterunt ad ĕum;
the ambassadors,   and   the ambassadors   returned   to   him·

nĕgat[25]   se   more   et   exemplo   Romani
he denies   himself,   by the custom and   example   of the Roman

popŭli,   posse   dăre   ĭter   per   provincĭam ulli;
people,   to be able to give a journey   through   the province   to any;

et   ostendit   prohibiturum,   si   conentur (pres.
and   shows (himself) about to prohibit,   if   they attempt

subj.) facĕre   vim.   Helvetĭi   dejecti   ĕâ
to make   violence.   The Helvetii   cast down   from this

spe,   alĭi,   navĭbus[26]   junctis,   que   complurĭbus
hope,   others [some],   ships   being joined, and   a great many

ratĭbus   factis,   alĭi   vădis   Rhodăni,   quà[27]
rafts   being made,   others   by fords   of the Rhone,   where

minĭma altitudo flumĭnis ĕrat,   nonnunquam interdĭu,
the least   depth   of the river   was;   sometimes   in daytime,

sæplĭùs   noctu,   conati   si   possent (imp.
more often   by night,   having endeavored   if   they were able

subj.) perrumpĕre,   repulsi   munitione (sing.)
to break through   repulsed   by the fortifications

opĕris,   et   concursu   et   telis
of the work,   and   by the charge   and   weapons

milĭtum, destiterunt   hoc   conatu.
of the soldiers, they desisted from this   endeavor.

9. Una   vĭa   per   Sequănos   relinquebatur;
One   way   through the Sequani   was left;

quâ,   Sequănis   invitis,   potĕrant   non
by which the Sequani (being) unwilling,   they were able not

ire   propter   angustĭas.   Quum possent (imp.
to go   on account of   the defiles.   When they were able

subj.) non   persuadere   ĭis (dat.)   sŭâ   sponte,
        not   to persuade   them   by their own accord,

mittunt   legatos   ad   Dumnorĭgem   Ædŭum,
they send   ambassadors   to   Dumnorix   the Æduam,

ut, ĕo   deprecatore,   impetrarent   hoc   à
that, he (being) intercessor,   they might obtain   this   from

Sequănis.   Dumnŏrix   potĕrat   plurĭmum
the Sequani.   Dumnorix   was able   most [had very great in-

        ăpud   Sequănos   gratĭâ   et   largitione,   et
fluence] with   the Sequani by service and (by) lavishness, and

ĕrat   amicus   Helveitĭis,   quòd[28]   duxĕrat   in
was   friendly   to the Helvetii,   because   he had led   into

matrimonĭum   filĭam   Orgetorĭgis   ex   ĕâ   civitate;
marriage   the daughter of Orgetorix   from that   state;

et[29] adductus   cupiditate   regni,   studebat
and   induced   by a desire   of the kingdom,   he was eager

nŏvis   rebus;   et   volebat   habere   quamplurĭmas
for new   things;   and was wishing to have   as many as possible

civitates obstrictas   sŭo   beneficĭo   sĭbi.   Ităque
states   bound   by his   favor   to himself.   Therefore

suscĭpit   rem,   et   impĕtrat   à   Sequănis,
he undertakes the thing,   and obtains   from the Sequani,

ut   patiantur   Helvetĭos   ire   per   sŭos
that   they may suffer the Helvetii   to go   through   their

fines,   que   perfĭcit   ŭtì   dent   obsĭdes   inter
borders,   and   effects   that they may give hostages between

sese;   Sequăni   ne   prohibĕant
themselves; the Sequani lest   they may prohibit [that they may

Helvetĭos   itĭnĕre ;   Helvetĭi,
not prohibit]   the Helvetii   from the journey;   the Helvetii

ut   transĕant   sĭne   maleficĭo   et   injurĭâ.
that   they may pass   without   damage   and   injury.

10. Nuntiatur   Cæsări,   esse   in   anĭmo,
It is announced   to Cæsar,   to be [it is]   in   the mind,

Helvetĭis   facĕre   ĭter   per   agrum
to [of] the Helvetii   to make   the journey   through   the land

Sequanorum   et   Æduorum   in   fines
of the Sequani   and   of the Ædui   into   the borders

Santŏnum,   qui   absunt   non   longè   à
of the Santones,   who   are distant   not   far   from

finĭbus Tolosatĭum, quæ civĭtas est in provincĭâ.
the borders of the Tolosates, which state is in the province.

Si id fĭĕret (imp. subj.) intelligebat   futurum
If this should be[were]done   he understood (it)   about to be[it would

cum magno pericŭlo provincĭæ, ut   haberet
be}   with great   danger of the province, that   it should have

bellicosos   homĭnes,   inimicos   Romani   popŭli,
warlike   men,   enemies   of the Roman   people,

finitĭmos   lŏcis   patentĭbus   et   maxĭmè
neighbors   to places   open   and   especially

frumentarĭis.   Ob   ĕas   caussas   præfecit
abounding in corn.   On account of   these   causes   he appointed

Titum Labienum   legatum   ĕi   munitioni quam
Titus   Labienus   lieutenant   to this   fortification which

fecĕrat: ipse   contendit   in
he had made: (he) himself   hastens   into

Italĭam   magnis   itinerĭbus   que ĭbi conscribit dŭas
Italy   by great   journeys   and there he levies two

legiones;   et   educit ex   hibernis   tres,
legions;   and   he leads from   winter quarters   the three.

quæ   hiemabant   circum   Aquileĭam;   et[30]   quâ
which   were wintering   around   Aquileia;   and   by which

ĭter   ĕrat proxĭmum in ulteriorem Gallĭam
(way) the journey   was   nearest   into   farther   Gaul

per   Alpes,   contendit   ire   cum   his
through   the Alps,   he hastens   to go   with   thes●

quinque legionĭbus. Ibi Centrones et   Graioceli,
five   legions.   There the Centrones and the Graioceli,

et Caturíges, superiorĭbus lŏcis   occupatis
and the Caturiges. the higher   places having been occupied

conantur prohibere exercĭtum   itinĕre.   His
endeavor to check   the army   on the journey. These

    pulsis   complurĭbus prœlĭis, pervenit   ab
having been repulsed in several battles,   he comes   from

Ocĕlo, quod est extremum   citerioris provincĭæ,
Ocelum, which is the extreme(town) of the hither province,

in   fines   Vocontiorum ulterioris   provincĭæ
into the borders of the Vocontii of the farther province

septĭmo   dĭe; inde in   fines   Allobrŏgum;
on the seventh day; thence into the borders of the Allobroges;

ducit exercĭtum ab   Allobrogĭbus in Segusiavos.
he leads the army   from the Allobroges into the Segusiavi.

Hi sunt primi extra provincĭam trans Rhodănum.
These are the first without the province beyond the Rhone.

11. Helvetii   jam   transduxĕrant sŭas copias
    The Helvetii already   had led over   their forces

per   angustĭas   et   fines   Sequanorum et
through the defiles and borders of the Sequani and

pervenĕrant in   fines   Æduorum,   que
had come   into the borders of the Ædui,   and

populabantur   agros   eorum.   Ædŭi,   quum
were laying waste the lands of them. The Ædui when

possent (imp. subj.) non defendĕre   se   que[31]
they were able   not   to defend   themselves and

sŭa   ab   his,   mittunt legatos   ad
their own(effects) from these,   send   ambassadors to

Cæsărem rogatum auxilĭum; "se   omni tempŏre
Cæsar   to ask   aid;   "themselves in all time

merĭtos esse   ita de Romano   popŭlo,   ut,
(to) have deserved so of the Roman people,   that,

penè   conspectu   nostri   exercĭtûs,   ăgri
almost in sight   of our   army,   (their) lands

debuĕrint (perf. subj.) non vastari,   libĕri[32]
ought   not   to be laid waste the children

eorum   abduci   in   servitutem,   oppĭda
of them   to be led away   into   slavery,   the towns

expugnari.''   Eodem   tempŏre,   Ædŭi
to be taken by storm.''   At the same   time,   the Ædui

Ambarri   quŏque,   necessarĭi   et   consanguinĕi
Ambarri   also,   friends   and   kinsmen

Æduorum,   facĭunt Cæsărem   certiorem,
of the Ædui,   make   Cæsar   more certain [inform Cæsar],

"sese,   agris[33] depopulatis,   non facĭlè   prohibere
"themselves,   the lands being depopulated,   not easily   to prohibit

vim   hostĭum   ab   oppĭdis.''   Item
the violence   of the enemy   from   the towns.''   Likewise

Allobrŏges,   qui   habebant   vicos   que
the Allobroges,   who   were having   villages   and

possessiones trans Rhodănum, recipĭunt se   fŭgâ
possessions   beyond the Rhone,   betake   themselves in flight

ad   Cæsărem;   et[34] demonstrant,   nĭhil   relĭqui
to   Cæsar;   and   show,   nothing   of remaining

esse   sĭbi   præter   sŏlum   agri.   Adductus
to be   to themselves beside   the soil   of the land.   Induced

quĭbus   rebus,   Cæsar   statŭit   non   expectandum
by which   things,   Cæsar   resolved   not   to be waited

sĭbi,   num,   omnĭbus
to [by] himself [that he ought not to wait],   until,   all

fortunis   sociorum   consumptis,   Helvetĭi
the fortunes   of the allies   having been consumed,   the Helvetii

pervenirent (imp. subj.)   in   Santŏnes.
should come   into   the Santones.

12. Arar   est   flumen,   quod   inflŭit in
    The Arar [the Saone]   is   a river,   which   flows into

Rhodănum   incredibĭli   lenitate   per   fines
the Rhone   with incredible   smoothness   through   the borders

Æduorum   et   Sequanorum;   ita   ut   possit
of the Ædui   and   of the Sequani;   so   that   it is possible

non   judicari   ocŭlis   in   utram   partem
not   to be judged   by the eyes   in   which   part [direction]

flŭat. (pres. sub.)   Helvetĭi   transibant id,   ratĭbus ac
it flows.   The Helvetii   were crossing this,   rafts   and

lintrĭbus   junctis.   Ubi[35] Cæsar   factus-est   certĭor
boats   being joined.   When Cæsar   was made   more certain

per   exploratores,   Helvetĭos   jam   transduxisse
by   scouts (that),   the Helvetii   already   to have [had] led over

id   flumen   tres   partes   copiarum,   verò   quartam
this   river   three   parts   of (their) forces,   but   the fourth

partem   esse   relĭquam   citra   flumen   Arărim ;
part   to be   remaining   on this side   the river   Arar [Saone];

de   tertĭâ   vigilĭâ   profectus   è
from [at]   the third   watch [midnight]   having set out   from

castris   cum   trĭbus   legionĭbus   pervĕnit   ad   ĕam
the camp   with   three   legions   he arrives [comes]   to   this

partem,   quæ   nondum   transĭĕrat   flumen.
part,   which   not yet   had passed   the river.

Aggressus   ĕos   impeditos   et   inopinantes
Having attacked   them   encumbered   and   unaware

concidit   magnam   partem   eorum ;   relĭqui
he cut up [slew]   a great   part   of them;   the rest

mandârunt   sese   fŭgæ atque abdiderunt   in
committed   themselves to flight and   hid away   into [among]

proxĭmas silvas.   Is   pagus appellabatur   Tigurinus :
the nearest woods.   This   canton was called   the Tigurine:

nam   omnis   Helvetĭa   civĭtas   divisa-est   in
for   all   the Helvetian   state   has been divided   into

quatŭor   pagos.   Hic   unus   pagus,   quum
four   cantons.   This   one   canton,   when

exîsset (pl. pref. subj.)   dŏmo,   memorĭâ
it had gone out   from home,   in the memory

nostrorum   patrum,   interfecĕrat   Lucĭum   Cassĭum
of our   fathers,   had slain   Lucius   Cassius

Consŭlem,   et   misĕrat   exercĭtum   ejus   sub
the Consul,   and   had sent   the army   of him [his army]   under

jŭgum.   Ita   sive   casu,   sive   consilĭo
the yoke.   Thus   whether   by chance,   or   by the plan

immortalĭum   deorum,   pars   Helvetĭæ   civitatis,
of the immortal   gods,   the part   of the Helvetian   state,

quæ   intulĕrat   insignem   calamitatem   Romano
which   had brought on   a remarkable   calamity   to the Roman

popŭlo,   ĕa   princeps   persolvit   pœnas.   In   quâ
people,   this   chief [first]   paid   penalties.   In   which

re   Cæsar   ultus-est   non   solùm   publĭcas   sed   etĭam
thing   Cæsar   avenged   not   only   public   but   also

privatas   injurĭas;   quòd   Tigurini   interfecĕrant
private   injuries;   because   the Tigurini   had slain

Lucĭum   Pisonem   legatum,   ăvum   Lucĭi
Lucius   Piso   the lieutenant, (general)   grandfather   of Lucius

Pisonis   socĕri   ejus,   eodem   prœlĭo,
Piso   father in law   of him [Cæsar],   in the same   battle,

quo   Cassĭum.
in which (they slew)   Cassius.

13. Hoc   prœlĭo   facto,   ut   posset
This   battle   having been made,   that   he might be able

consĕqui   relĭquas   copĭas   Helvetiorum,   curat[36]
to reach   the remaining   forces   of the Helvetii,   he takes care

pontem   faciendum   in Arăre,   atque   ĭta   transducit
a bridge   to be made   on the Arar, [Saone]   and   so   leads over

exercĭtum.   Helvetĭi   commoti   repentino   adventu
the army.   The Helvetii   moved   by the sudden   arrival

ejus,   quum[37]   intelligĕrent (imp. subj.)   illum
of him,   when   they were understanding   him

fecisse   uno   dĭe   id,   quod   ipsi
to have [he had] done   in one   day   that,   which   [they] themselves

confecĕrant   ægerrĭmè   viginti   diebus,   ut
had accomplished   most grievously   in twenty   days,   that

transirent   flumen,   mittunt   legatos   ad
they should pass   the river,   send   ambassadors   to

ĕum;   cujus   legationis   Divĭco   fŭit   princeps,   qui
him;   of which   embassy   Divico   was   chief,   who

fuĕrat   dux   Helvetiorum   Cassiano   belln.
had been   leader   of the Helvetii   in the Cassian   war.

Is   ĭta   egit   cum   Cæsăre;   "si   Romanus
He   thus   acts [treats] with   Cæsar;   "if   the Roman

popŭlus   facĕret   pacem cum   Helvetĭis,   Helvetĭos
people   would make   peace with   the Helvetii,   the Helvetii

ituros   in ĕam   pastem,   atque   futuros
about to go[would go] into that   part,   and   about to [would] be

ĭbi,　　ŭbi　　Cæsar　constituisset　atque　voluissit
there,　where　Cæsar　might appoint　and　might wish (them)

esse;　　sin　　perseveraret　　persĕqui　　bello,
to be;　but if　he should continue　to pursue　with war,

reminisceretur　　vetĕris　　incommŏdi　　Romani
let him remember　(of) the old　misfortune　of the Roman

popŭli,　et　　pristĭnæ　virtutis　Helvetiorum:
people,　and　(of) the ancient　valor　of the Helvetii:

quŏd　　adortus-esset (pl. perf. subj.)　improvisò
because　he had assailed　　　　　　　　　unexpectedly

unum　　pagum,　quum　ĭi,　qui　trans-
one　　canton,　when　these,　who　had

îssent (pl. perf. subj.)　flumen,　possent (imp. subj.)
crossed　　　　　　　　the river,　were able

non　ferre　auxilĭum　sŭis;　　　tribuĕret
not　to bring　aid　to their (people);　let him attribute

ne　aut　magnopĕre　sŭæ　virtuti　ob
not　either　very greatly　to his own　valor　on account of

ĕam　rem,　aut　despicĕret　ipsos.
this　thing,　nor　let him despise　themselves.

　　Se　ĭta　didicisse　à　sŭis　patrĭbus
They themselves　so　(to) have learned　from　their　fathers

que　majorĭbus,　ut　contendĕrent　măgis
and　elders,　that　they should contend　more

virtute　quàm　niterentur　dŏlo,　aut
by valor　than (that)　they should strive　by deceit,　or

insidĭis.　Quare　committĕret　ne,　ut
stratagems.　Wherefore　he should permit　not,　that

is　lŏcus,　ŭbi　constitissent (pl.perf.subj.),
this　place,　where　they had stood

capĕret　nomen　ac　prodĕret　memorĭam
should take　(its) name　and　hand down　the memory

ex　calamitate　Romani　popŭli,　et
from　the calamity　of the Roman　people,　and

internecione　exercĭtûs.
the destruction　of the army.

14. Cæsar　respondit　ĭta　his;　　"ĕò
　　Cæsar　answered　thus　to these (words);　"therefore

mĭnus　　dubitationis　　　dărı　　　sĭbi,　　　quòd
.ess　　　(of) doubt　　to be [was] given　to himself,　because

teneret (imp.subj.) ĕas　　res　　memorĭâ,　　quas
he was holding　　　　these　　things　　in memory,　　which

Helvetĭi　　　legati　　　commemorâssent (pl. perf.
the Helvetian　ambassadors　　　had mentioned

subj.), atque　ferre　　　　　ĕò　　　gravĭus,
　　　and　to bear [he bore it]　for this　the more heavily,

quò　　accidissent　(pl. perf. subj.)　　mĭnùs
that　　they had befallen　　　　　　　　the less

merĭto　　　Romani　　popŭli,　　qui　　si
by the merit　of the Roman　people,　which　if

fuisset (pl. perf. subj.)　conscĭus　sĭbi　alicujus
it had been　　　　　　　conscious　to itself　of some

injurĭæ,　　　　　fuisse　non
injury (done to the Helvetii) to have been　not [it would not have been]

difficĭle　cavere;　　　　sed　　　deceptum
difficult　to beware [to be on guard], but　to have [it was] deceived in

ĕo,　　quòd　nĕque　intelligĕret　(imp. subj.)
this,　because　neither　was it thinking (anything)

commissum　à se,　quare　timeret; nĕque
to have [had] been committed　by itself, wherefore　it should fear; nor

putaret (imp.subj.) timendum　　　sĭne causâ.
was it thinking　　to be feared [it should fear] without cause.

Quòd si vellet (imp.subj.) oblivisci vetĕris contumelĭæ,
But　if　he was wishing　　to forget　(of)the ancient　insult,

num　　posset　etĭam　deponĕre　memorĭam
whether　would he be able　also　to lay aside　the memory

recentĭum　injuriarum,　quòd,　ĕo　　　invito,
of the recent　injuries,　that,　he　(being) unwilling,

tentâssent (pl. perf. subj)　iter　per　Provincĭam
they had attempted　　a march　through　the Province

per vim,　quòd　vexâssent (pl. perf. subj.)　Ædŭos,
by violence,　that　they had harassed　　　　the Ædui,

quòd　Ambbarros,　quòd　Allobrŏges?　Quòd
that (also)　the Ambarri,　that (also)　the Allobroges?　That

gloriarentur (imp.subj.) tam insolenter　sŭâ　victorĭâ;
they were boasting　　so　insolently　in [of] their victory;

que quòd   admirarentur   se   tulisse   injurĭas
and   that   they wonder that   they   (to) have committed   outrages

impunè   tam dĭu,   pertinere   eòdem.
with impunity   so   long,   to pertain [pertains]   to the same thing.

Enim   immortales   dĕos   consuêsse,
For   the immortal   gods   (to) have been accustomed,

quò   homĭnes   dolĕant   gravĭùs   ex
that   men   may grieve   more heavily   from [by]

commutatione rerum,   quos vĕlint (pr. subj.) ulcisci
the change   of things,   whom   they may wish   to punish

pro   scelĕre   eorum,   interdum concedĕre
for   the wickedness of them [their wickedness], sometimes (to) grant

secundiores   res   his,   et   diuturniorem
more prosperous   affairs   to these,   and   more lasting

impunitatem.   Cùm   ĕa   sint (pres. subj.)
impunity.   Although   these (things)   are

Ĭta, tămen si obsĭdes dentur (pres. subj.) sĭbi ab ĭis,
so,   yet   if   hostages   may be [are] given   to himself by them,

ŭtì   intellĭgat   facturos   ĕa
that   he may understand (that they)   about to [will] do   these (things)

quæ   polliceantur (pres. subj.);   et   si   satisfacĭant
which   they promise;   and   if   they satisfy

Æduis   de   injurĭis,   quas
(to) the Ædui   concerning   the wrongs,   which

intulĕrint (perf. subj.)   ipsis   que   socĭis
they have inflicted   on them   and   on the allies

eorum,   ĭtem si Allobrogĭbus, sese esse
of them [their allies], likewise (if) (to) the Allobroges, he himself to be

facturum   pacem cum ĭis." Divĭco respondit:
about to [will] make   peace   with   them."   Divico   answered;

"Helvetĭos   institutos-esse   ĭta à   majorĭbus,
"the Helvetii (to) have been instructed   thus by (their)   ancestors,

ŭtì   consuevĕrint (perf.subj.) accipĕre, non dăre
that   they should be accustomed   to receive,   not   to give

obsĭdes; Romanum popŭlum esse testem ejus rei."
hostages;   the Roman   people to be [are] witness of this thing."

Hoc responso   dăto,   discessit.
This   answer   having been given,   he departed.

15. Postĕro   dĭe   mŏvent   castra   ex   ĕo
     On the next day   they move   the camp   from   that

lŏco.   Cæsar   făcit   ĭdem ;   que   præmittit
place.   Cæsar   does   the same;   and   sends forward

omnem   equitatum   ad   numĕrum   quatüor   millĭum,
all   the cavalry   to   the number   of four   thousand,

quem   habebat   coactum   ex   omni   provincĭâ,
which he   was having   collected   from   all   the province,

et   Ædŭis   atque   socĭis   eorum ;[37a]
and   from the Ædui   and   from the allies   of them ;

qui   vidĕant   in   quas   partes   hostes   facĭant
who   may see   into   what   parts   the enemy   may make

   ĭter :   qui,   insecuti   cupidĭùs
(their) way :   who,   having followed up   more [too] eagerly

novissĭmum   agmen,   committunt   prœlĭum
the last   troop [the rear],   join   battle

cum   equitatu   Helvetiorum   alieno
with   the cavalry   of the Helvetii   in strange [an unfavorable]

lŏco,   et   pauci   de   nostris   cădunt.   Quo   prœlĭo
place,   and   a few   of   our (men)   fall.   By which   battle

Helvetĭi   sublati,   quŏd   quingentis
the Helvetii   being lifted up [elated]   because   with five hundred

equitĭbus   propulĕrant   tantam   multitudĭnum
horsemen   they had repulsed   so great   a multitude

equĭtum,   cœperunt   subsistĕre   audacĭùs ;
of horsemen,   began   to withstand   more boldly;

nonnunquam   ex   novissĭmo   agmĭne   lacessĕre
sometimes   from   the last   troop [the rear]   to challenge

prœlĭo   nostros.   Cæsar   continebat   sŭos
with battle   our (men).   Cæsar   was restraining   his (men)

à   prœlĭo,   ac   habebat   sătis
from   battle,   and   was holding (it)   enough

in   præsentĭâ   prohibere   hostem
in [for]   the present   to prohibit   the enemy

rapinis,   pabulationĭbus,   que   populationĭbus.
from rapines,   from foragings,   and   from devastations.

Ita   circĭter   quindĕcim   dĭes   fecerunt   ĭter,
So   about   fifteen   days   they made   the march.

ŭti   inter   novissĭmum   agmen   hostĭum   et
that   between   the last   troop [rear]   of the enemy   and

nostrum   prizmum,   non   amplĭùs   quinis   aut
our   first [front],   not   more (than)   five   or

senis   millĭbus   passŭum   interesset.
six   thousand   (of) paces   intervened.

16. Intĕrim[38]   Cæsar   quotidĭe   flagitare
Meanwhile   Cæsar   daily   to demand earnestly from

Ædŭos   frumentum,   quod   pollicĭti-essent (pl. perf.
the Ædui   the corn,   which   they had promised

subj.)   publĭcè.   Nam   propter   frigŏra   quòd
publicly.   For   on account of   the cold   because

Gallĭa   posĭta est   sub   Septentrionĭbus (pl.),
Gaul   is situated   under [toward]   the North

(ut   dictum-est   antè,)   non   mŏdò   frumenta
(as   has been said   before,)   not   only   the corn (crops)

ĕrant   non   matura   in   agris   sed   ne
were   not   ripe   in   the fields   but   not

pabŭli[39]   quĭdem   sătis   magna   copĭa,
of forage   even   a sufficiently   great   plenty,

suppetebat.   Autem   potĕrat   mĭnùs ut   ĕo (abl.)
was supplied.   But   he was able   less to use   this

frumento, quod   subvexĕrat   navĭbus   flumĭne
corn,   which   he had carried up   in ships   by the river

Arăre,   propterĕa   quòd   Helvetĭi   avertĕrant
Arar,   because   (that)   the Helvetii   had turned away

ĭter   ab   Arăre,   à   quĭbus   nolebat
the march   from   the Arar,   from   whom   he was unwilling

discedĕre.   Ædŭi[40]   ducerĕ   dĭem
to depart.   The Ædui   to lead [put off]   day

ex   dĭe,   dicĕre   conferri,
from [after]   day,   to say (the corn)   to be brought together

comportari,   adesse.   Ubi   intellexit
to be conveyed,   to be present [ready].   When   he understood

se   duci   diutĭùs,   et   dĭem
(he) himself   to be [is] led [put off]   longer,   and   the day

instare,   quo   dĭe   oporteret   metirĭ
to be [is] at hand,   on which   day   it would be due   to measure out

frumentum   militĭbus ;   principĭbus   corum
corn   to the soldiers;   the chiefs   of them

convocatis,[41]   quorum   habebat   magnum
having been called together,   of whom   he was having   a great

copiam   in   castris,   in   his   Divitiăco
number   in   the camp,   in [among]   these   Divitiacus

et   Lisco, qui   præĕrat   summo magrı̆stratŭi
and   Liscus, who   was over [invested with]   the highest   magistracy

(quem Ædŭi   appellant vergobretum,   qui   creatur
(which the Ædui   name   vergobretus,   which   is created

annŭus   que   hăbet potestatem vitæ   que   nĕcis
annually   and   has   the power   of life   and   of death

in   sŭos),   accusat   ĕos   gravĭter,
over   his own (people)),   he accuses   them   severely,

quòd   quum   posset (imp.subj.) nĕque   emi,
because   when   it was possible   neither   to be bought,

nĕque   sumi   ex   agris,   tempore   tam
nor   to be taken   from   the fields,   in a time   so

necessarĭo,   hostĭbus   tam   propinquis,
necessary,   the enemy (being)   so   near,

sublevetur (pres.subj.) non ab ı̆is;   præsertim quum,
he is succored   not   by them; especially   when,

ex[42]   magna   parte   adductus   precĭbus   eorum
from   a great   part   induced   by the prayers   of them

suscepĕrit (perf.subj.)   bellum,   querı̆tur   etı̆am
he has undertaken   the war,   he complains   also

multò gravı̆ùs   quòd   destitutus-sit (perf.subj.).
much the more severely   that   he had been left destitute (of corn).

17. Tum   demum   Liscus   adductus   oratione
Then   at last   Liscus   induced   by the speech

Cæsăris,   proponit   quod antĕà   tacuĕrat :
of Cæsar,   sets forth   (that) which before   he had kept silent:

"Esse[43]   nonnullos,   auctorı̆tas   quorum
"To be [that there are]   some,   the authority   of whom

valĕat (pres.subj.) plurı̆mùm   ăpud   plebem,
avails   most[very much]   with the common people,

qui   privati   possint (pres.subj.)   plus
who (though)   private (persons)   are powerful   more

quàm   magistratus   ipsi,   hos   seditiosâ
than   the magistrates   themselves,   these   by seditious

et   impröbâ   oratione deterrere   multitudĭne   ne
and   wicked   speech (to) deter   the multitude   lest

confĕrant   frumentum;   quòd   dicant
they may bring together   the corn;   because   they say

(pres.subj.)   præstare,   si   jam   possint
   to be [it is] preferable if   now   they may be able

non   obtinere   principatum   Gallĭæ,   perferre
not   to obtain   the sovereignty   of Gaul,   to indure

imperĭa   Gallorum   quàm   Romanorum;   nĕque
the commands   of the Gauls   than   of the Romans;   nor

debĕant (pres.subj.) dubitare   quin,   si   Romani
ought they   to doubt   but that,   if   the Romans

superavĕrint   Helvetĭos,   sint (pres. subj.)
should overcome   the Helvetii,   they are

erepturi   libertatem   Ædŭis   unà
about to snatch away   libertv   from the Ædui   together

cum   relĭquâ   Gallĭâ: ab   ĭisdem   nostra
with   remaining   Gaul: by   the same (persons)   our

consilĭa, quæque gerantur (pres. subj.) in castris, (pl.)
councils, whatsoever are carried on   in the camp,

enuntiari   hostĭbus;   hos   posse   non
to be [are] announced to the enemy; these to be [are] able   not

coërceri   à   se: Quin-etĭam,   quòd
to be restrained   by   himself: Moreover,   because

enuntiârit (perf. subj.)   rem   necessarĭò   Cæsări,
he has told   the thing   necessarily   to Cæsar,

sese   intelligĕre   cum quanto pericŭlo
himself to understand [that he is aware] with how great danger

fecĕrit (perf. subj.)   id;   et   ob   ĕam   caussam
he has done   it;   and   for   this   cause

tacuisse   quamdĭu   potuĕrit''.   (perf. subj.)
to have [he] kept silent   as long as   he could''.

18. Cæsar   sentiebat   Dumnorĭgem   fratrem
Cæsar   was perceiving   Dumnorix   the brother

Divitiăci   designari   hâc   oratione   Lisci;
of Divitiacus   to be [was] indicated   by this   speech   of Liscus;

sed, quòd nolebat ĕas res
but, since he was not wishing (that) these things to [should]

jactari pluribus præsentĭbus, dimittit
be tossed [debated], more (being) present, he dismisses

concilĭum, celeriter, retĭnet Liscum: quærit ex
the council, quickly, he retains Liscus: he seeks from (him)

solo ĕa, quæ dixĕrat in conventu.
alone those (things), which he had said in the assembly.

Dicit liberĭus, atque audacĭus. Quaerit
He speaks more freely, and more boldly. He inquires

eădem ab aliis secretò, reperiter esse vera:
the same (things) from others apart, he finds to be true:

"Dumnorĭgem ipsum esse summâ audacĭâ,
"Dumnorix himself to be [is] with (of) the highest boldness

magnâ gratĭâ ăpud plebem propter
in great favor with the common people on account of

liberalitatem, cupĭdum novarum rerum;
(his) liberality, desirous of new things [revolution];

habere portorĭa que omnĭa relĭqua
to have [that he had] the customs duties and all the remaining

vectigalĭa Æduorum complures annos redempta
taxes of the Ædui many years purchased

parvo pretĭo; proptereă quòd, ille licente, nemc
for a small price; because (that,) he bidding, no one

audĕat (pres. subj.) liceri contrà; his rebus
dares to bid against (him); by these things

et auxisse[44] sŭam familiarem rem, et
both to have [he] increased his family estate, and

comparâsse magnas facultates ad largiendum
to have [he] procured great means for giving bribes:

semper alĕre magnum
always to maintain [that he always maintained] a great

numĕrum equitatûs sŭo sumptu, et habere
number of horsemen at his own expense, and to have [had] (them)

circum se: nĕque posse largĭter
around himself: nor to be able (to bestow) largely [nor was he powerful]

solùm dŏmi, sed etĭam ăpud finitĭmas civitates;
only at home, but also with the bordering states:

atque   causâ[45]   hujus   potentĭæ,   collocâsse
and   by reason   of this   power,   to have [he had] placed

matrem   in   Biturigĭbus,   homĭni   illĭc
(married]   (his) mother   in   the Bituriges,   to a man   there

nobilissĭmo et potentissĭmo; ipsum habere   uxorem
most noble   and   most powerful;   himself   to have [he had] a wife

ex Helvetĭis: collocâsse   sororem   ex
from the Helvetii: to have placed [he had given]   a sister   from [by]

matre,   et   sŭas propinquas   nuptum   in   alĭas
the mother,   and   his   kinswomen   to be married into   other

civitates.   Favere[45a]   et   cupĕre   Helvetĭis
states.   To favor   and   to desire [wish well]   to the Helvetii

propter   ĕam   affinitatem,   etĭam   odisse
on account of   this   alliance,   also   to hate

Cæsărem   et   Romanos   sŭo   nomĭne,
Cæsar   and   the Romans   from his own   name,

quòd   potentĭa   ejus   diminuta-sit (perf. subj.)
because   the power   of him   had been diminished

adventu   eorum,   et Divitiăcus   frater restitutus
by the arrival   of them,   and   Divitiacus   (his) brother   restored

in   antiquum   lŏcum   gratĭæ   atque   honoris :   si
into   the ancient   place   of favor   and   of honor: if

quid   accĭdat   Romanis,   venire[46]   in
any (thing)   may happen   to the Romans,   to come   into

summan   spem   regni   obtinendi   per
the highest   hope   of the kingdom   to be obtained   through

Helvetĭos ;   imperĭo   Romani   popŭli,   non[47]
the Helvetii;   (under) the empire   of the Roman   people,   not

mŏdò desperare de regno,   sed etĭam de ĕâ
only   to despair   of the kingdom, [of reigning]   but   also   of that

gratĭâ   quam habĕat." (pres. subj.) Cæsar etĭam
favor [influence]   which   he has."   Cæsar   also

reperiebat in quærendo, quòd   adversum prœlĭum
was finding   by   inquiring,   that [how]   the adverse   battle

equestre (adj.)   factum-esset (plup. subj.)   paucis
of cavalry   had been made [occured]   a few

diebus   antè,   initĭum   ejus   fŭgæ
days   before, (that)   the beginning   of this   flight

factum-esse　　　à Dumnorīge atque　　　equitĭbus
to have [had] been made by　　Dumnorix　　and　　by the horsemen

ejus,　　(nam Dumnŏrix prǣĕrat　　　equitatŭi (dat.),
of him,　　(for　　Dumnorix　　was over [commanded]　　the cavalry,

quem Ædŭi misĕrant auxilĭo Cæsări;)　　que　　　fŭgâ
which the Ædui had sent　for aid　to Cæsar;)　and by　the flight

eorum relĭquum　equitatum　　　perterrĭtum-esse.
of them the remaining　cavalry　　to have [had] been dismayed.

19. Quĭbus　　rebus　　cognitis,　　quum[48] certissĭmæ
Which　　things　　being known,　　since　　most certain

res accedĕrent (imp. subj.)　　ad　　has　suspiciones ;
facts were approaching [confirming]　(to)　these　suspicions;

quòd　　traduxisset (pl. perf. subj.) Helvetĭos per
because [that] he [Dumnorix] had led over　　the Helvetii through

fines　　Sequanorum ;　　quòd　　curâsset (pl. perf.
the borders　of the Sequani;　because [that]　he had taken care

subj.) obsĭdes　　dandos　　inter　ĕos :　　quòd
hostages　to be [should] given between　them:　because [that]

fecisset (pl. perf. subj.) omnĭa　ĕa　　non　mŏdŏ
he had done　　all　　those (things) not　only

sŭo　injussu　et　　civitatis,　　sed　etĭam
without　his order　and　(that) of the state,　but　also

ipsis　inscientĭbus ; quòd　　accusaretur (imp.
themselves　not knowing;　because [that]　he was accused

subj.) à　magistratu　Æduorum ;　arbitrabatur[49]
by　a magistrate　of the Ædui;　he [Cæsar] was deeming

sătis caussæ esse　　quare, aut ipse animadvertĕret
enough (of) cause to be [was] wherefore, either himself should attend

in　ĕum, aut juberet civitatem animadvertĕre.
upon [to]　him,　or　should order　the state　to attend (to him).

Unum　　repugnabat omnĭbus his, quòd cognovĕrat
One (thing)　was opposing　(to) all　these,　that　he had known

summum　studĭum　fratris　Divitiăci　in
the highest　zeal　of (his) brother　Divitiacus　unto [towards]

Romanum popŭlum, summam voluntatem in
the Roman　people,　(his) highest　good will　unto [toward]

se,　egregĭam　fĭdem, justitĭam, temperantĭam.
himself,　(his) preeminent　faith.　justice,　temperance.

Nam verebatur, ne   offendĕret   anĭmum   Divitiăci
For he was fearing, lest he should offend the mind   of Divitiacus

supplicĭo   ejus.   Ităque   prĭus   quàm
by the punishment of him Therefore sooner than [before that]

conaretur   quidquam,   jŭbet   Divitiăcum
he should attempt   anything,   he orders   Divitiacus

vocari   ad   se;   et   quotidianis
to be called   to   himself;   and   the daily [usual]

interpretĭbus   remotis,   colloquĭtur   cum   ĕo.
interpreters   having been removed, he converses with   him.

per   Caĭum   Valerĭum   Procillum,   principem
through   Caius   Valerius   Procillus,   chief

provincĭæ   Gallĭæ,   suŭm   familiarem,   cui
of the province of Gaul,   his   intimate (friend), to [in]whom

habebat   summam   fĭdem   omnĭum   rerum;
he was having the highest faith [confidence] of all   things

sĭmul   commonefăcit,   quæ   dicta-sint
at the same time he reminds, (Divitiacus) what (things) were said

de   Dumnorĭge   in   concilĭo   Gallorum,   ipso
of   Dumnorix   in   the council of the Gauls, himself

præsente;   et ostendit   quæ quisque   dixĕrit   (perf
(being)present;   and   shows   what every one has said

subj.)   separatim   de   ĕo   ăpud   se.   Petit
separately   of   him   to   himself [Cæsar]. He asks

atque hortatur   ut,   sĭne offensione   anĭmi   ejus,
and   exhorts   that, without offence   of mind   of him,

vel   ipse   statŭat   de ĕo,
either he himself [Cæsar] may determine of him [pass judgment on him],

caussâ   cognĭtâ;   vĕl   jubĕat
(his) cause being known [the case being tried];   or   may order

civitatem   statuĕre.
the state   to determine.

20. Divitiăcus   complexus   Cæsărem   cum   multis
Divitiacus   having embraced   Cæsar   with   many

lacrymis   cœpit   obsecrare,   "nestatuĕret
tears   began   to beseech,   "that he should not determine

quid   gravĭus   in   fratrem;   se   scire[50]
any thing   more severe   against (his) brother; himself to know

illa   esse vera nec quenquam capĕre
[that he knows] those (things) to be true nor anyone to take

plus   doloris   ex ĕo,   quàm se;   proptĕrĕa quòd
more   (of) grief   from this,   than himself;   because   (that)

(quum ipse   posset (imp. subj.) plurĭmum gratĭă
(when himself   was able (to do)   most   in influence

dŏmi atque in relĭquă Gallĭâ, ille   minĭmum
at home and in the remaining Gaul, he [Dumnorix] the least

paopter   adolescentĭam) crevisset (pl. perf. subj.)
on account of   (his) youth   had increased (in power)

per   se;   quĭbus opĭbus ac nervis[51]
through himself [Divitiacus] ; which means and nerves [strength]

uteretur (imp. subj.) non solùm ad   gratĭam
he was using   not   only   to (Diviaticus) influence

minuendam, sed penè ad sŭam   pernicĭem;
to be diminished, but almost to his [Diviaticus] destruction;

sese   tămen commoveri et fraterno amore
(that) himself however to be [was] moved both by fraternal love

et   existimatione   volgi: quòd si
and   by the esteem   of the common people: because if

quid   gravĭus   accidisset   ĕi
any (thing) more heavy [serious]   should happen   to him

à Cæsăre, cùm ipse   teneret (imp. subj.)
from Cæsar, when he himself   was holding

ĕum lŏcum amicitĭæ ăpud ĕum,   nemĭnem
this place of friendship with him [Cæsar], no one

existimaturum   non factum sŭâ voluntate;
about to think [would think] (the thing) not done with his will;

futurum   ex quâ re, ŭti[52] anĭmi
about to [it would] be from which thing, that the minds

totius Gallĭæ averterentur à   se.''
of the whole of Gaul would be turned away from himself.''

Quum flens   petĕret (imp. subj.) hæc
When weeping   he was seeking   these (things)

à Cæsăre plurĭbus verbis, Cæsar prehendĭt
from Cæsar with many words, Cæsar takes

dextram ejus;   consolatus,   rŏgat (ut)
the right hand of him; having consoled, he asks (that)

faciat finem orandi: ostendit gratiam
he make an end of entreating: he shows (that) the favor

ejus esse tanti ăpud se, ŭtì
of him to be [is] of so much (account) with himself, that

condonet et injuriam rei publïcæ et
he forgives both the injury of the republic and

sŭum dolorem, voluntati ac precïbus
his own grief, for the good will and for the prayers

ejus. Vŏcat Dumnorïgem ad se; adhïbet
of him. He calls Dumnorix to himself; he summons

fratrem; ostendit quæ reprehendat (pres. subj.)
the brother; he shows what he blames

in ĕo; proponit quæ ipse intellïgat,
in him; he sets forth what (he) himself understands,

(pres. subj.), quæ civïtas queratur (pres. subj.);
what the state complains of;

mŏnet, ut[53] vitet omnes suspiciones in
he warns, that he may avoid all suspicions into [for]

relïquum tempus. Dicit[54] se condonare
the remaining time. He says himself to forgive

præterïta fratri Divitiăco; ponit
past (things) for (his) brother Divitiacus; he places

custodes Dumnorïgi, ut possit scire
keepers [spies] to [over] Dumnorix, that he may be able to know

quæ ăgat (pres. subj.) cum quïbus
what (things) he does with whom

loquatur (pres. subj.)
he speaks.

21. Eodem dìe factus certìor ab
On the same day being made more sure [being informed] by

exploratorïbus, hostes consedisse sub
scouts (that), the enemy to have [had] encamped under [at the

montem, octo millïa passŭum ab
foot of] the mountain, eight thousand (of) paces from

castris (pl.) ipsius; misit qui cognoscĕrent,
the camp of himself; he sent (persons) who might learn,

qualis esset natura montis, et
what might be [was] the nature of the mountain, and

qualis   ascensus   in   circuĭtu.   Renuuntiatum-est
what   the ascent   in   a circuit.   It was reported

esse[55]   facĭlem.   De   tertĭâ   vigilĭâ   jŭbet
to be   easy.   About [at]   the third   watch   he orders

Titum Labienuml   legatum   pro   prætore
Titus   Labienus   lieutenant   for   prætor [with prætorian

cum   duaous   legionĭbus,   et   iisdem ducĭbus, qui
powers] with   two   legions,   and the same   guides,   who

cognovĕrant   ĭter,   ascendĕre   summum   jŭgum
had learned   the route,   to ascend   the highest   peak

montis;   ostendit   quid   sit   sŭi   consilĭi.
of the mountain;   he shows   what   may be   (of) his   counsel.

Ipse   de   quartâ   vigilĭâ
[design].   He himself   about   the fourth   watch

eodem   itinĕre,   quo   hostes   iĕrant,
by the same   route,   by which   the enemy   had gone.

contendit ad ĕos, que mittit antĕ omnem equitatum.
hastens   to   them, and   sends   before   all   the cavalry.

Publĭus   Considĭus,   qui   habebatur   peritissĭmus
Publius   Considius,   who   was deemed   most skilled

militaris   rĕi (sing.), et   fuĕrat   in exercĭtu   Lucĭi
of [in]military affairs,   and had been   in   the army   of Lucius

Syllæ,   et   postĕa   in   Marci   Crassi,
Sylla,   and   afterwards   in (that)   of Marcus   Crassus,

præmittĭtur   cum   exploratorĭbus.
is sent forward   with   the scouts.

22. Primâ[56]   luce,   quum   summus   mons
At the first   light [early dawn],   when   the highest   mountain

teneretur (imp subj.)   à   Tito   Labieno,   ipse
was held   by   Titus   Labienus,   he himself

abesset (imp. subj.)   non   longĭus   mille   et
was distant   not   farther (than)   a thousand   and

quingentis   passĭbus   ab   castris (pl.)   hostĭum;
five hundred   paces   from   the camp   of the enemy

nĕque,   ut   compĕrit   postĕa   ex   captivis,
nor.   as   he found   afterwards   from   the captives,

aut   adventus   ipsius,   aut   Labieni
either   the arrival   of himself,   or (that)   of Labienus

cognĭtus-esset (pl. perf. subj.); Cosindĭus, ĕquo
had been known; Considius, (his) horse

admisso, accurrit ad ĕum; dicit.
at full speed, rushes to him [Cæsar]; he says,

montem quem voluĕrit (perf. subj.) occupari
the mountain which he wished to be occupied

à Labieno, teneri ab hostĭbus: se
by Labienus to be [is] held by the enemy: (that) he himself

cognovisse id à Gallĭcis armis atque insignĭbus.
to have known[knew] this from the Gallic arms and ensigns.

Cæsar subducit sŭas copĭas in proxĭmum collem,
Cæsar leads away his forces to the nearest hill,

instrŭit acĭem. Labienus, ut præceptum-ĕrat
he arrays the line. Labienus, as had been directed

ĕi à Cæsăre, ne-committĕret prœlĭum,
to him by Cæsar, that he should not join battle,

nisi copĭæ ipsius visæ-essent (pl. perf. subj.)
unless the forces of himself had been seen

prŏpe castra (pl.) hostĭum, ut impĕtus fiĕret
near the camp of the enemy, that the attack might be made

in hostes undĭque uno tempŏre,
against the enemy on every side at one time,

monte occupato, expectabat nostros, que
the mountain having been occupied, was awaiting our (men), and

abstinebat prœlĭo. Denĭque, multo dĭe Cæsar
was holding from battle. Finally, far in the day Cæsar

cognovit per exploratores, et montem teneri
learned by scouts (that), both the mountain to be [was] held

à sŭis, et hostes movisse castra
by his own (men), and (that) the enemy to have [had] moved camp,

(pl.), et Considĭum perterrĭtum timore renuntiâsse
and Considius dismayed by fear to have [had]

pro viso, quod non vidisset (pl. perf.
announced for [as] seen, (that) which he had not seen.

subj.). Eo dĭe, intervallo quo consuêrat,
On that day, in the interval with which he had been accustomed,

sequĭtur hostes, et ponit castra (pl.) trĭa
he follows the enemy. and places (his) camp three

millĭa   passŭum   ab   castris (pl.) eorum.
thousand   (of) paces   from   the camp   of them [their camp].

23. Postridĭe   ejus   diei,   quòd   bidŭum
The day after   this   day,   because   a period of two days

omnino   superĕrat,   quum   oporteret (imp. subj.)
altogether   was remaining,   when   it was obligatory

metiri   frumentum   exercĭtu (exercitŭi);   et
to measure [deal] out   corn   to the army;   and

quòd   abĕrat   à   Bibracte,   longè
because   he was distant   from   Bibracte,   by far

maxĭmo   ac   copiosissĭmo   oppĭdo   Æduorum,
the greatest   and   most wealthy   town   of the Ædui,

non   amplĭùs   octodĕcim   millĭbus   passŭum ;
not   more (than)   eighteen   thousand   (of) paces ;

existimavit   prospiciendum   frumentarĭæ
he believed   it must be looked out [he must provide] for the grain

rĕi ;   et   avertit   ĭter   ab   Helvetĭis
supply;   and   he turns away   the route   from   the Helvetii

ac   contendit   ire   Bibracte.   Ea⁵⁷   res
and   hastens   to go   (to) Bibracte.   This   thing

nuntiatur   hostĭbus   per   fugitivos   Lucĭi   Æmilĭi,
is announced   to the enemy   by   fugitives   of Lucius   Æmilius.

decurionis   equĭtum   Gallorum.   Helvetĭi,
captain   of the horsemen   of the Gauls.   The Helvetii,

seu   quòd   existimarent (imp. subj.)   Romani
either   because   they were judging (that)   the Romans

discedĕre   à   se perterrĭtos   timore,   ĕo   măgis
(to) withdraw   from them   dismayed   with fear,   by this the more

quòd   pridĭe   superiorĭbus   lŏcis   occupatis,
because   the day before   the higher   places having been occupied,

commisissent (pl. perf. subj.)   non   prœlĭum,   sive
they had joined   not   battle,   or

quòd⁵⁸ confidĕrent (imp. subj) posse   inter-
because   they were trusting (our men)   to be able [could]   (to) be inter-

cludi   frumentorĭâ   re: consilĭo   commutato
cepted   from the corn   supply;   (their) plan   having been altered

atque   itinĕre   converso,   cœperunt   insĕqui   ac
and   the route   having been changed,   they began   to pursue   and

lacessĕre nostros   à   novissĭmo   agmĭne.
to harass our (men) from   the last   marching-line [in the rear].

24. Postquam Cæsar   animadvertit   id,   subducit
    After (that) Cæsar   perceived   this;   he leads up

ĭŭas copĭas in   proxĭmum collem que misit equitatum,
his forces onto the nearest hill and sent   cavalry,

qui   sustineret   impĕtum   hostĭum.   Ipse
which   should meet the attack of the enemy. He himself

ĭntĕrim instruxit triplĭcem acĭem quatŭor veteranarum
meanwhile drew up a triple   line of four   veteran

legionum in medĭo   colle; ita ŭti   collocaret
legions   on the center (of the) hill; so that he might place

supra se, in summo jŭgo, dŭas legiones quas
above himself, on the highest peak, the two legions which

conscripsĕrat proxĭmè in citeriore Gallĭâ, et omnĭâ
he had levied very lately in hither   Gaul, and all

auxilĭa,   et   compleret totum   montem
the aids [auxiliaries], and might fill the whole mount

hominĭbus.   Interĕa   jussit   sarcĭnas
with men. In the mean time he ordered (that) the baggage

          conferri   in unum lĕcum et   ĕum
(to) be brought together into one place and (that) this

     muniri   ab ĭis, qui constitĕrant in superiore
(to) be fortified by those, who took stand in the higher

acĭe.   Helvetĭi,   secuti   cum omnĭbus sŭis
line. The Helvetii, having followed with all   their

carris,   contulerunt   impedimenta in unum
wagons,   brought together the baggage into one

lŏcum; ipsi   confertissĭmâ acĭe, nostro equitatu
place; (they) themselves in a very dense line, our cavalry

    rejecto,   phalange   factâ,   successerunt
having been repulsed, a phalanx having been made, advanced

sub   nostram primam acĭem.
under [to] our   first   line.

25. Cæsar,   sŭo   primùm, deinde ĕquis
    Cæsar,   his own (horse) first,   then the horses

omnĭum   remotis   è conspectu, ut pericŭlo
of all having been removed from sight, that the danger

æquato,   tollĕret   spem   fŭgæ,
having been made equal, he might take away   the hope   of flight.

cohortatus   sŭos,   commisit   prœlĭum.
having encouraged   his (men),   joined   battle.

Milĭtes,   pilis   missis   è superiore lŏco,
The soldiers, javelins having been sent [cast] from the higher place.

facĭlè   perfregerunt   phalangem   hostĭum :   ĕâ
easily   broke through   the phalanx   of the enemy: this

disjectâ,   fecerunt impĕtum in ĕos districtis
having been dispersed. they made an attack upon them with drawn

gladĭis. Erat[59] magno impedimento Gallis ad
swords.   ..was (for) a great   impediment   to the Gauls   for

pugnam, quòd plurĭbus scutis eorum transfixis
the fight, that   many   shields of them having been pierced

et   colĭgatis   uno   ictu   pilorum,   cùm
and bound together by one stroke of the javelins,   when

ferrum inflexisset (pl. perf. subj.) se, potĕrant
the iron   had bent   itself, (in) they were able

nĕque evellĕre, nĕque, sinistrâ impeditâ,
neither to tear (it) out. nor, the left (hand) having been entangled,

pugnare   sătis   commŏdè,   ut multi,   brachĭo
to fight   sufficiently   easily,   so that many,   the arm

dĭu   jactato,   præoptarent (imp. subj.)
a long time having been tossed about, were preferring

emittĕre   scutum   mănu,   et   pugnare
to discard   the shield   from the hand,   and   to fight

nudo corpŏre. Tandem defessi vulnerĭbus cœperunt
with naked body.   At length wearied with wounds they began

et   referre   pĕdem,   et   quòd   mons
both to bear back the foot [to retreat], and because a mountain

subĕrat circĭter mille passŭum recipĕre
was near   about   a thousand (of) paces   to betake

se   ĕò.   Monte   capto,
themselves [withdraw] thither. The mountain having been taken,

et   nostris   succedentĭbus,   Boĭi et Tulingi,
and   our (men)   advancing,   the Boii and Tulingi,

qui claudebant agmen hostĭum circĭter
who were closing the marching line of the enemy (with) about

quindĕcim   millĭbus   homĭnum,   et ĕrant   præsidĭo
fifteen   thousand   (of) men.   and were   (for) a guard

novissĭmis,   agressi[60]   nostros,   ex
to the last [rear], having attacked our (men),   from [upon]

itinĕre   aperto   latĕre   circumvenire ;
the march   on the open   flank ,   (began) to surround (them);

et   Helvetĭi   qui   recepĕrant   se   in
and the Helvetii who had betaken themselves to

montem,   conspicati   id,   cœperunt   rursus
the mountain, having beheld this,   began   again

instare et   redintegrare   prœlĭum.   Romani
to advance and   to renew   the battle.   The Romans

intulerunt   signa   conversa   bipartitò ;
bore on[charged] the standards (having been) turned in two directions:

prima   ac   secunda acĭes,   ut   resistĕret
the first and   second   line,   that   it [they] might resist

victis   et submotis ; tertĭa   ut   excipĕret
to) the conquered and   routed;   the third that   it might receive

venientes.
(those) coming.

26. Ita[61] pugnatum-est   ancipĭti   prœlĭo   dĭu
Thus   it was fought   with doubtful battle a long time

atque   acrĭter.   Quum   possent (imp. subj.)   non
and   sharply.   When   they were able   not

sustinere impĕtum nostrorum diutĭùs, altĕri receperunt
to sustain the attack of our (men) longer, others [some] betook

se   in   montem,   ut   cœpĕrant;   altĕri
themselves unto the mountain, as   they had begun;   others

contulerunt   se   ad   impedimenta et   sŭos
collected   themselves to [at]   the baggage and   their

carros.   Nam hoc   toto   prœlio, quum
wagons.   For   in this whole   battle, when [although]

pugnatum-sit (perf. subj.) ab septĭmâ horâ
it was fought   from the seventh hour [one o'clock]

ad vespĕram, nemo[62]potŭit videre hostem aversum.
to   evening   no one was able to see the enemy turned away.

Pugnatum-est   etĭam   ad   multam   noctem   ad
It was fought   also   to [until] much [late] night   at

impedimenta : proptereă quòd objecĕrant carros pro
the baggage :   because (that) they had opposed   wagons for

vallo,   et conjiciebant tela è superiore lŏco in
a rampart, and were hurling weapons from a higher   place upon

nostros   venientes, et nonnulli subjiciebant matăras
our (men) advancing, and some   were thrusting   spears

ac   tragŭlas inter   carros   que   redas,   que
and javelins between the wagons and   carts,   and

vulnerabant   nostros.   Quum⁶³ pugnatum-esse
were wounding our (men).   When   it had been fought

(pl. perf. subj.)   dĭu,   nostri   potiti-sunt
                     a long time,   our (men)   won [captured]

impedimentis que castris. Ibi   filĭa   Orgetorĭgis,
the baggage   and camp.   There a daughter of Orgetorix,

atque unus è   filĭis captus-est. Superfuerunt
and   one from [of] (his) sons was [were] taken. There survived

ex   ĕo prœlio circĭter centum et triginta millĭâ
from this battle about   a hundred and thirty   thousand

hommum, que ierunt   continenter ĕâ totâ nocte :
(of) men, and they went[traveled] incessantly this whole night;

itinĕre   intermisso   nullam partem noctis,
the march   being interrupted   no   part   of the night,

quarto die pervenerunt in   fines Lingŏnum :
on the fourth day they arrived to[at] the borders of the Lingones;

quum   nostri   morati   tridŭum
since   our (men)   having delayed   the space of three days

et   propter   vulnĕra   militum   et
both   on account of the wounds of the soldiers and

propter   sepulturam   occisorum, potuissent
on account of   the burial   of the slain, had been able

(pl. perf. subj.) non sĕquí   ĕos. Cæsar misit
            not to follow [could not follow] them. Cæsar sent

litĕras que nuntĭos ad Lingŏnes,   ne juvarent
letters and messengers to the Lingones, that they should not assist

ĕos   frumento neve   alĭâ   re: qui   si
them   with corn nor   with (any)other thing: who   if

juvissent,⁶⁴   se   habiturum   illos
they (should have) assisted, ne himself about to [would] hold them

eodem   lŏco,   quo   Helvetĭos.   Ipse,
in the same   place [light],   in which [as]   the Helvetii.   (He) himself,

tridŭo   intermisso,   cœpit   sĕqui
the period of three days   having intervened,   began   to follow

ĕos   cum   omnĭbus   copĭis.
them   with   all   (his) forces.

27. Helvetĭi,   adducti   inopĭâ   omnĭum   rerūm,
  The Helvetii,   induced   by want   of all   things,

miserunt[65]   legatos   qui   cum   convenissent
sent   ambassadors to him   who   when   they had met

(pl. perf. subj.)   ĕum   in   itinĕre,   que
        him   on   the march,   and

projecissent (pl. perf. subj.)   se   ad   pĕdes,   que
had thrown   themselves   at   (his) feet,   and

locuti   supplicĭter,   flentes   petîssent   (pl.
having spoken   suppliantly.   weeping   sought

perf. subj.) pacem, atque   jussisset (pl. perf. subj.)
     peace,   and (when) he had ordered

ĕos   expectare   sŭum   adventum   in   ĕo   lŏco,   quo
them   to await   his   arrival   in that place,   in which

tum   essent (imp. subj.),   paruerunt. Postquam Cæsar
then   they were,   they obeyed.   After (that)   Cæsar

pervenit ĕo,   poposcit   obsĭdes,   arma,   servos,   qui
came   there,   he demanded   hostages,   arms,   the slaves,   who

perfugissent (pl. perf. subj.)   ad   ĕos.   Dum   ĕa
had fled   to   them.   While   these

   conquiruntur   et   conferuntur,
(things)   are sought for   and   are brought together,

nocte   intermissâ,   circĭter   sex   millĭa
a night   having intervened,   about   six   thousand

homĭnum   ejus   pagi,   qui   appellatur
(of) men   of this   canton,   which   is called

Verbigenus,   sive   perterrĭti timore,   ne,   armis
Verbigenus,   either   alarmed   by fear,   lest,   (their) arms

tradĭtis,   afficerentur   supplicĭo ;
having been delivered, they should be affected [visited] with punishment;

sive   inducti   spe   salutis,   quòd   in   tantâ
or   induced   by hope   of safety,   because   in   so great a

multitudĭne   deditieiorum,[66] existimarent (imp. subj.)
multitude   of (those) surrendered,   they were thinking

sŭam fŭgam posse   aut   occultari   aut   ignorari
their   flight to be able either to be concealed or to be disregarded

omnino;   primâ vigilĭâ noctis,   egressi   ex
altogether; in the first   watch of the night, having gone out from

castris (pl.) Helvetiorum, contenderunt ad Rhenum
the camp   of the Helvetii,   hastened   to the Rhine

que   fines   Germanorum.
and   borders   of the Germans.

28. Quod[67] ŭbi Cæsar reseivit,   imperavit   his,
Which when   Cæsar discovered,   he ordered (to) these.

per   fines   quorum   iĕrant,   ŭtì
through   the borders   of whom   they had gone,   that

conquirĕrent   et   reducĕrent,   si[68]
they should search out   and   should lead back,   if

vellent (imp. subj.) esse purgati   sĭbi.   Habŭit[69]
they were wishing   to be blameless to himself. He held

reductos in numĕro hostĭum : accepit omnes
(those) led back in the number of enemies: he received   all

relĭquos   in deditionem, obsidĭbus, armis, perfŭgis
the remaining into   surrender,   hostages,   arms,   deserters

traditis.   Jussit   Helvetĭos, Tulingos,
having been delivered up. He ordered the Helvetii, Tulingi.

Latobrĭgos,   reverti   in   sŭos   fines,   unde
Latobrigi,   to return   into   their   territories, whence

profecti-ĕrant; et quòd, omnĭbus frugĭbus amissis,
they had set out; and because,   all   the crops having been lost.

nĭhil   ĕrat dŏmi,   quo   tolerarent   fămem,
nothing was at home, by which they might bear hunger,

imperavit Allobrogĭbus, ut   facĕrent   copĭam
he ordered   (to) the Allobroges, that they should make plenty

frumenti eis;   jussit   ipsos   restituĕre
[a supply] of corn for them; he ordered themselves to replace

oppĭda que vicos,   quos incĕndĕrant.   Fecit
the towns and villages,   which they had burned. He did

id   maxĭme   ĕâ   ratione,   quòd[70]   nolŭit
this   chiefly with this   reason,   because he was unwilling

ĕum   lŏcum,   unde   Helvetĭi   discessĕrant,   vacare;
this   place,   whence   the Helvetii   had departed,   to be vacant;

ne   propter   bonitatem   agrorum,   Germani,
lest   on account of   the excellence   of the lands,   the Germans

qui   incŏlunt   trans   Rhenum,   transirent   è
who   dwell   beyond   the Rhine,   should cross   from

sŭis finĭbus   in   fines   Helvetiorum,   et   essent
their borders   into   the borders   of the Helvetii,   and   should be

finitĭmi   provincĭæ   Gallĭæ   que   Allobrogĭbus.
neighbors   to the province   of Gaul   and   to the Allobroges.

Concessit   Ædŭis   petentĭbus,   ut   collocarent
He granted   to the Ædui   asking,   that   they should place [settle]

Boĭos   in   sŭis   finĭbus,   quŏd   cognĭtierant
the Boii   in   their   borders,   because   they were known

egregĭâ   virtute: quĭbus   illi   dederunt agros, que
of excellent   valor: to whom   they   gave   lands,   and

quos[71]   receperunt   postĕa   in   părem   conditionem
whom   they received   afterwards   into   equal   condition

juris   que   libertatis   atque   ipsi   ĕrant.
of right   and   of liberty   as   they themselves   were.

29. In   castris (pl.) Helvetiorum   tabŭlæ   confectæ
In   the camp   of the Helvetii   tablets   prepared

Græcis litĕris repertæ-sunt, et perlatæ ad Cæsărem;
with Greek letters   were found,   and brought   to   Cæsar:

in   quĭbus   tabŭlis   ratĭo   confecta-ĕrat
in   which   tablets   a computation   had been made

nominatim,   qui numĕrus eorum exîsset (pl.
name by name. [individually] what number of them had gone forth

perf. subj.) dŏmo, qui possent (imp. subj.) ferre arma,
from home,   who were able   to bear arms

et   ĭtem   separatim   puĕri,   sĕnes   que   muliĕres.
and   likewise   separately   the boys,   old men   and   women.

Summa omnĭumq uarum   rerum   ĕrat,   ducenta
The sum   of all   which   things [items] was,   two hundred

sexaginta et   trĭa   millĭa   capĭtum   Helvetiorum;
sixty   and   three   thousand   (of) heads [souls]   of the Helvetii:

triginta   et   sex   millĭa   Tulingorum;   quatuordĕcim
thirty   and   six   thousand   of the Tulingi;   fourteen

Latobrigorum; Rauracorum viginti et trĭa; Boiorum
of the Latobrigi;   of the Rauraci   twenty and three;   of the Boii

triginta   et   dŭo.   Ex his, qui   possent (imp. subj.)
thirty   and   two.   Of those, who   were able

ferre arma ad   nonaginta et dŭo millĭa.   Summa
to bear arms to [about] ninety   and two thousand.   The sum

omnĭum fuĕrat ad   trecenta sexaginta et
[total] of all   was   at [about] three hundred   sixty   and

octo   millĭa.   Censu   habĭto,   ut   Cæsar
eight   thousand.   A census   having been held,   as   Cæsar

imperavĕrat, numĕrus eorum, qui redierunt domum,
had ordered,   the number of those, who   returned   home,

repertusest   centum   et   dĕcem   millĭa.
was found (to be) a hundred and   ten   thousand.

30. Bello   Helvetiorum   confecto,   legati[72]
The war   of the Helvetii   having been finished,   ambassadors

fĕrè totius Gallĭæ, princĭpes civitatum, convenerunt
almost of the whole of Gaul,   chiefs   of the states,   came together

ad Cæsărem gratulatum: "sese,   intelligĕre,
to   Cæsar   (to) congratulate: "(they) themselves, (to) understand,

tametsi Romanus popŭlus repetîsset (pl. perf. subj.)
although   the Roman   people   had required

pœnas   ab   ĭis   bello   pro   veterĭbus   injurĭis
penalties from them in war   for   the ancient   injuries

Helvetioram; tămen ĕam rem   accidisse   non
of the Helvetii;   yet   this thing to have [had] happened not

mĭnùs ex   usu   terræ   Gallĭæ,
less   from [for] the   use [advantage]   of the land   of Gaul,

quàm   Romani   popŭli; proptereă quòd   ĕo
than   of the Roman   people;   because   (that)   with this

consilĭo, florentissĭmis rebus,   Helvetĭi reliquissent
plan,   in most flourishing affairs,   the Helvetii   had left

(pl. perf. subj.) sŭas   dŏmos,   ut   inferrent
their   homes,   that   they might wage

bellum toti Gallĭæ (dat.) que potirentur imperĭo (abl.);
war   on all Gaul   and   might gain   empire;

que   deligĕrent   lŏcum domicilĭo ex magnâ copĭâ,
and (might) choose   a place for abode from a great supply

quem　　　　　judicâssent　　　　opportunissĭmum　　　ac
which　　　they (might have) judged　　most advantageous　　and

fructuosissĭmum　　ex　　　omni　Gallĭâ;　que　haberent
most fruitful　　from [of]　all　　Gaul;　and　might have

relĭquas　　　civitates stipendiarĭas.　Petierunt,　ŭtĭ
the remaining　　states　　as tributaries.　They asked,　that

liceret　　　　sĭbi　　　　indicĕre　　concilĭum
it might be allowed　(to) themselves　to proclaim　　a council

totius　Gallĭæ　in　certam　dĭem,　que　facĕre　id
of all　　Gaul　upon a certain　day,　and　to do　this

voluntate Cæsărĭs.　　Sese　　habere quasdan res,
with the will of Cæsar.　They themselves (to) have certain　things,

quas　vellent (imp. subj.) petĕre　ab　ĕo　　è
which　they were wishing　to ask　from　him　from [with]

communi　consensu.　Eâ　　re　　　permissâ,
the common　consent.　This　thing　having been permitted,

constituerunt　dĭem　　concilĭo,　et　sanxerunt
they appointed　a day　for the council,　and　ratified

jurejurando　inter　　se,　　　ne　　quis
by oath　　between　themselves.　(that) noᵗ　any one

enuintiaret　　nĭsi　quĭbus　mandatum-esset (pl.
should divulge (it)　unless　to whom　it had been enjoined

perf. subj.) communi consilĭo.
　　　　by common　design.

31 Eo　　concilĭo　dimisso,　iidem　princĭpes
This　　council　having dismissed,　the same　chiefs

civitatum,　qui　fuĕrant　antè,　reverterunt　ad
of the states,　who　had been　before,　returned　to

Cæsărem;　que　petierunt,　ŭtĭ　　liceret
Cæsar;　　and　asked,　　that　it might be allowed

sĭbi　　　agĕre　　secretò　cum　ĕo　de
(to) themselves　to act [treat]　secretly　with　him　about

sŭâ　salute　que　　omnĭum.　Eâ　　re
their　safety　and　(that) of all.　This　thing

impetratâ,　omnes　flentes projecerunt sese
having been obtained,　all　weeping　cast　themselves

ad　pĕdes　Cæsări;　"se　　non　mĭnùs
at　the feet　to [of] Cæsar;　"they themselves　not　less

contendĕre   et   laborare   id,   ne   èa
to strive   and   to labor for   this,   lest   these (things)

quæ   dixssent (pl. perf. subj.)   enuntiarentur,
which   they had said   should be divulged,

quàm   ŭti   impetrarent   ĕa,   quæ
than   that   they might obtain   these (things),   which

vellent (imp. subj.); proptereă   quòd   si   enun-
they were wishing;   because   (that)   if   it

tiatum-esset,   viderent (imp. subj.)   se
was divulged,   they were seeing (that)   (they) themselves

venturos   in   summum   cruciatum." Divitiăcus
about to [would] come   to   the highest   torture."   Divitiacus

Ædŭus[73] locutus-est pro   his :   esse   dŭas
the Æduan   spoke   for   these;   to be [there are]   two

factiones   totius   Gallĭæ ;   Ædŭos   tenere
factions   of all   Gaul;   the Ædui   to hold

principatum   alterĭus   harum,   Arvernos
sovereignty   of the one   of these,   the Arverni

alterĭus.   Quum   hi   contendĕrent (imp. subj.)
of the other.   When   these   were contending

tantopĕre   inter   se   de   potentatu   multos
very greatly   between   themselves   about   dominion   many

annos,   factumesse,   ŭti   Germani
years,   to have been done [it resulted],   that   the Germans

accerserentur (imp. subj.) ab   Avernĭs que   Sequănis
were sent for   by   the Arverni and   Sequani

mercede.   Primò   circĭter   quindĕcim
with [for] hire [as mercenaries].   At first   about   fifteen

millĭa   horum   transîsse   Rhenum ; posteăquam
thousand   of these   (to have) crossed   the Rhine;   after (that)

fĕri   ac   barbări   homĭnes   adamâssent
the wild   and   barbarous   men   had fallen in love with

(pl. perf. subj.) agros,   et   cultum,   et   copĭas
             the lands,   and   cultivation,   and   resources

Gallorum, plures   transductos : nunc   esse
of the Gauls,   more   (were) led over: now   to be [they are]

in   Gallĭâ   ad   numĕrum   centum   et   viginti
in   Gaul   to   the number   of a hundred   and   twenty

millĭum : Ædŭos,[74] que clientes eorum,
thousand: the Ædui, and clients [dependants] of them,

sĕmel atque itĕrum contendisse armis cum
time and again (to) have contended in arms with

his ; pulsos accepisse magnam
these; repulsed to (they) have received a great

calamitatem ; amisisse omnem nobilitatem,
calamity; to (they) have lost all (their) nobility,

omnem senatum, omnen equitatum. Fractos
all the senate, all (their) cavalry. Broken

quĭbus prœlĭis que calamitatĭbus, qui
by which [these] battles and calamities, (they) who

antè potuissent (pl. perf. subj.) plurĭmum
before had been able most [were most powerful]

in Gallĭâ, et sŭâ virtute et
in Gaul, both by their own valor and

hospitĭo atque amicitĭa Romani popŭli,
by the alliance and friendship of the Roman people,

coactos-esse dăre obsĭdes Sequănis,
(to) have been forced to give hostages to the Sequani,

nobilissĭmos civitatis, et obstringĕre civitatem
the most noble (men) of the state, and to bind the state

jurejurando, sese nĕque repetituros
by oath (that they), themselves neither about to [would] ask back

obsĭdes, nĕque imploraturos auxilĭum
the hostages, nor about to [would] implore aid

à Romano popŭlo, nĕque[75] recusaturos, quò
from the Roman people, nor about to [would] refuse, that

mĭnùs-essent perpetŭò sub ditione
they might not be perpetually under the dominion

atque imperĭo illorum. Se esse unum
and empire of them. He himself to be [was] the only one

ex omni civitate Æduorum, qui potuĕrit (perf.
from [of] all the state of the Ædui, who has been able

subj.) non adduci ut juraret, aut
not to be induced that he should swear, or

dăret sŭos libĕros obsĭdes : Ob ĕam rem
should give his children (as) hostages: For this thing

se profugisse ex civitate, et venisse
he himself to have [had] fled from the state, and to have [had] come(to)

Roman ad Senatum postulatum auxilĭum, quŏd
Rome to the Senate to request aid, because

solus teneretur (imp. subj.) nĕque jurjurando.
(he) alone was held neither by oath,

nĕque obsidĭbus. Sed accidisse pejus
nor by hostages. But to have [it had] happened worse

Sequănis victorĭbus, quàm Ædŭis victis:
to the Sequani, the conquerors, than to the Ædui, the conquered;

proptĕrĕa quŏd Ariovistus,[76] rex Germanorum,
because (that) Ariovistus, king of the Germans,

consedisset (pl. perf. subj.) in finĭbus eorum,
had settled in the borders of them,

que occupavisset (pl. perf. subj.) tertiam partem
and had occupied the third part

Sequăni agri, qui esset (imp. subj.) optĭmus
of the Sequanian land, which was the best

totius Gallĭæ; et nunc juberet (imp. subj.)
of all Gaul; and now was ordering

Sequănos decedĕre de altĕrâ tertĭâ parte;
the Sequani to depart from the other third part;

proptĕrĕa quŏd, paucis mensĭbus (abl.) antĕ,
because (that), a few months before,

viginti et quatŭor millĭa hominum Harudum
twenty and four thousand (of) men of the Harudes

venissent (pl. perf. subj.) ad ĕum, quĭbus lŏcus
had come to him, for whom a place

et sedes pararentur: futurum esse
and habitations should be prepared: to be about to be [it would be]

paucis annis, ŭtì omnes pellerentur è
in a few years, that all would be driven from

finĭbus Gallĭæ, atque omnes Germani
the regions of Gaul, and all the Germans

transirent Rhenum: ĕnim nĕque Gallĭcum
would cross the Rhine: for neither (is) the Gallic (land)

esse conferendum[77] cum agro Germanorum,
to be mentioned with the land of the Germans,

nĕque hanc consuetudĭnem victûs comparandam
nor is this custom of life to be compared

cum illâ. Autem Ariovistum, ut sĕmel
with that. But Ariovistus, when once

vicĕrit (perf. subj.) copĭas Gallorum prœlĭo,
he conquered the forces of the Gauls in battle,

quod prœlĭum factum-sit (perf. subj;) ad
which battle was made [fought] at

Magetobrigam, imperare superbè et crudelĭter,
Magetobriga, to command [commands] proudly and cruelly,

poscĕre libĕros cujusque nobilissĭmi
to require [demands] the children of each (of the) most noble

obsĭdes, et edĕre omnĭa exempla cruciatûs in
(as) hostages, and to impose [imposes] all examples of torture upon

ĕos, si qua res facta-sit (perf. subj.) non ad nutum[78]
them, if any thing has been done not at the nod

aut ad voluntatem ejus: homĭnem esse barbărum,
or at the will of him: the man to be [is] barbarous,

iracundum, temerarĭum: imperĭa[79] ejus non posse
irascible, headstrong: the commands of him not to be able

sustineri diutĭùs. Nisi quid auxilĭi
to be sustained longer. Unless some (thing) (of) aid

sit in Cæsăre que Romano popŭlo,
may be [is] in Cæsar and the Roman people,

ĭdem esse faciendum omnĭbus Gallis, quod
the same must (to) be done by all the Gauls, which

Helvetĭi fecĕrant, ut emĭgrent dŏmo;
the Helvetii had done, that they may emigrate from home;

pĕtant alĭud domicilĭum, alĭas sedes remotas
(that) they may seek another abode, others seats remote

à Germanis, que experiantur fortunam, quæcunque
from the Germans, and (that they) may try fortune, whatsoever

accĭdat. Si hæc enunciata-sint
may happen [befall them]. If these (things) were told

Ariovisto, non dubitere,[80] quin sumat
to Ariovistus, not to doubt, but that he may take

gravissĭmum supplicĭum de omnĭbus obsidĭbus, qui
the heaviest punishment upon all the hostages, wha

sint (pres. subj.) ăpud ĕum. Cæsărem, vel sŭâ
are with him. Cæsar, either by his

auctoritate atque exercĭtûs, vel recenti
authority and (that) of (his) army, or by (his) recent

victorĭâ, vel nomĭne Romani popŭli, posse
victory, or by the name of the Roman people, to be [is] able

deterrere, ne major multitudo Germanorum
to prevent, lest a greater multitude of Germans

transducatur Rhenum, que posse defendĕre
(may) be led over the Rhine, and (to) be able to defend

omnem Gallĭam ab injurĭâ Ariovisti.
all Gaul from the injury [wrongs] of Ariovistus.

32. Hâc oratione[81] habĭtâ à Divitiăco, omnes,
This speech having been had[made] by Divitiacus, all,

qui adĕrant, cœperunt petĕre auxilĭum à Cæsăre
who were present, began to ask aid from Cæsar

magno fletu. Cæsar animadvertit Sequănos
with great weeping. Cæsar observed (that) the Sequani

unos ex omnĭbus facĕre nĭhil earum rerum.
alone from [of] all (to) do nothing of those things,

quas cætĕri facĕrent (imp. subj.); sed tristes, capĭte
which the rest were doing; but sad, (with) head

demisso, intueri terram. Miratus,
(being) cast down, (to) look upon the earth. Having wondered,

quæ esset caussa ejus rĕi, quæsivit ex
what was the cause of this thing, he inquired from

ipsis. Sequăni respondêre nĭhil, sed
them. The Sequani answered nothing, but

permansêre tacĭti in eâdem tristitĭâ. Quum quærĕret
remained silent in the same sadness. When he was asking

(imp. subj.) sæpĭùs ab ĭis, nĕque posset (imp.
more often from them, nor was able

subj.) exprimĕre ullam vocem omnino;
to extort any voice [word] at all;

idem Ædŭus Divitiăcus respondit: "Fortunam
the same Æduan Divitiacus answered: "The fortune

Sequanorum, esse hôc miseriorem que graviorem,
of the Sequani, to be [is] in this more wretched and more heavy,

quàm　reliquorum　quòd　　　soli　auderent (imp.
than　of the rest,　because　(they) alone　were daring

subj.)　nec　quĭdem　quĕri　in　occulto,
　　　　neither　indeed　to complain　in　private,

nec　implorare auxilĭum; que horrerent (imp. subj.)
nor　to implore　aid;　　and　were dreading

crudelitatem　absentis　Ariovisti, vĕlut si　adesset
the cruelty　of the absent　Ariovistus,　as　if　he was present

(imp. subj.) coràm; proptereă　quòd　　tămen
　　　　　　in person; because　(that)　notwithstanding

　　　　facultas　　　　　　　fŭgæ　　daretur
[indeed]　an opportunity [a resource]　of flight　was given

(imp. subj.) relĭquis; verò omnes cruciatus essent
　　　　　to the rest;　but　all　tortures　were

(imp. subj.)　perferendi　　Sequănis,　　quɪ
　　　　　to [must] be endured　to [by] the Sequani,　who

recepissent (pl. perf. subj.) Ariovistum intra sŭos fines,
had received　　　　　　Ariovistus　within　their borders,

ɔmnĭa oppĭda quorum　　　　essent (imp.subj.) in
all　the towns of whom [whose towns] were　　　　in

potestate ejus.''
the power of him [his power].''

33. His rebus cognĭtis,　Cæsar confirmavit
These things having been known, Cæsar confirmed [cheered]

anĭmos　Gallorum　verbis,　que pollicĭtus-est
the minds　of the Gauls　with words,　and　promised

''ĕam　rem　futuram　　curæ　sĭbi:
"(that) this thing about to [would] be (for) a care to himself:

　se　habere　magnam spem,　Ariovistum
(he) himself to have [has]　great　hope,　(that) Ariovistus

adductum sŭo beneficĭo et auctoritate,　facturum
induced by his kindness and authority, about to [would] make

finem　injurĭis.''　Hâc oratione　habĭtâ,
an end to [of his] wrongs." This speech having been delivered,

dimisi　concilĭum. Et secundùm ĕa (pl.) multæ
he dismissed the council. And besides this　many

res hortabantur ĕum, quare　putaret　ĕam
things were urging him, wherefore he should think (that) this

rem   cogitandum   et   suscipiendum
thing   to [must] be considered and to [must] be undertaken

sĭbi: imprimis, quòd   videbat   Ædŭos,
to [by] himself: especially, because he was seeing (that) the Ædui,

sæpenumĕro   appellatos   fratres   que
oftentimes   having [who had] been named brothers   and

consanguinĕos ab Senatu,   teneri   in servitute
kinsmen   by the Senate, to be [were] held in slavery

atque in ditione Germanorum, que   intelligebat
and in dominion of the Germans, and he was understanding

obsĭdes eorum   esse   ăpud Ariovistum
hostages of them [their hostages] to be [were] with Ariovistus

ac Sequănos; quod, in tanto imperĭo Romani
and the Sequani; which, in so great empire of the Roman

popŭli, arbitrabatur esse   turpissĭmum sĭbi
people, he was considering to be [was] most disgraceful to himself

et reipublĭcæ. Autem   Germanos[82] consuescĕre
and to the republic. But (that) the Germans to be [are] accustomed

paullatim   transire   Rhenum,   et   magnam
little by little   to cross the Rhine, and a great

multitudĭnem eorum venire in Gallĭam, videbat
multitude   of them to come into Gaul, he was seeing (was)

periculosum Romano popŭlo: neque existimabat
dangerous to the Roman people: nor was he thinking

fĕros ac   barbăros homĭnes   temperaturos
wild and barbarous   men about to [would] restrain

sĭbi,   quin,   quum   occupâssent
(to) themselves, but that, when they had occupied

(pl. perf. subj.) omnem Gallĭam, ut Cimbri que
all   Gaul, as the Cimbri and

Teutŏni fecissent (pl. perf. subj.) antè,   exirent
Teutones had done   before. they would go out

in Provincĭam, atque inde   contendĕrent in
into the Province, and thence would hasten into

Italĭam; præsertim quum Rhodănus dividĕret (imp.
Italy; especially since the Rhone was dividing

subj.) Sequănos à   nostrâ provincĭâ. Quĭbus[83]
the Sequani from our province. (To) which

rebus	putabat	occurrendum	quàm-maturĭmè.
things	he was thinking	to [must] be met	as early as possible.

Autem	Ariovistus	ipse	sumsĕrat[84]	sĭbi	tantos
Moreover	Ariovistus	himself	had taken	to himself	so great

spirĭtus,	tantam	arrogantĭam,	ut	videretur (imp.
spirits, [airs]	so great	arrogance,	that	he was seeming

subj.)	non	ferendus.
	not	to be borne [endured].

34.
Quamŏbrem	placŭit	ĕi,	ut	mittĕret
Wherefore	it pleased	(to) him,	that	he should send

legatos	ad	Ariovistum,	qui	postularent	ab
ambassadors	to	Ariovistus,	who	should demand	from

ĕo,	"ut	deligĕret	alĭquem	lŏcum	medĭum
him,	"that	he should choose	some	place	midway

utriusque	colloquĭo;	sese	velle	agĕre
of each	for a conference;	(he) himself	to will [wishes]	to act [treat]

cum	ĕo	de	re publĭcâ	et	summis	rebus
with	him	about	a public matter	and	the highest	affairs

utriusque."	Ariovistus	respondit	ĕi	legationi:	"Si
of each."	Ariovistus	answered	to this	embassy:	"If

quid[85]	esset	(imp. subj.)	opus	ipsi	à
any (thing)	was		needful	to himself	from

Cæsăre,	sese	fuisse	venturum	ad ĕum;
Cæsar,	(he) hinself	to have been	about to [would] come	to him;

si	ille	vĕlit (pres. subj.)	quid	à	se,
if	he	wishes	any (thing)	from	himself,

oportere	illum	venire	ad	se;	præterĕa,	se
to behoove [it behoves]	him	to come	to himself:		besides,	he

nĕque	audere	venire	sĭne	exercĭtu	in	ĕas
neither	to dare [dares]	to come	without	an army	into	these

partes	Gallĭæ,	quas	Cæsar	possideret (imp. subj.);
parts	of Gaul,	which	Cæsar	was possessing;

nĕque[86]	posse	contrahĕre	exercĭtum	in	unum
nor	to be [is he] able	to gather	an army	into	one

lŏcum	sĭne	magno	commeatu	atque	molimento:
place	without	great	provisions	and	trouble:

autem	videri	mirum	sĭbi,	quid	negotĭi
moreover	to seem [it seems]	wonderful	to himself,	what	(of) business

esset   aut   Cæsări   aut   omnino   Romano
might be   either   to Cæsar   or   at all   to the Roman

popŭlo, in sŭâ Gallĭâ, quam vicĭsset (pl. perf. subj.)
people,   in   his   Gaul,   which   he had conquered

bello.
in war.

35. His responsis   relatis   ad Cæsărem,
These   answers   having been brought back   to   Cæsar,

Cæsar itĕrum mittit legatos ad ĕum cum his
Cæsar   again   sends   ambassadors   to   him   with these

mandatis: "Quonĭam affectus   tanto   beneficĭo
commands: "Since   being affected   with so great kindness

sŭo   que   Romani   popŭli (quum
his own [Cæsar's]   and   (that) of the Roman   people   (since

appellatus-esset (pl. perf. subj.) in sŭo consulatu rex
he had been named   in his own   consulship   king

atque amicus à Senatu,) referret (imp. subj.) hanc
and   friend   by   the Senate,)   he was returning   this

gratĭam sĭbi   que   Romano   popŭlo, ut[87]
favor   to himself   and   to the Roman   people,   that

gravaretur   invitatns   venire   in
he shoud be averse   (though) invited   to come   into

colloquĭum, nĕque   putaret   dicendum
a conference,   nor   should think (it)   to [must] be spoken

sĭbi   et   cognoscendum   de communi
to [by] himself   and [nor]   (to) be investigated   concerning   a common

re; hæc esse,   quæ   postularet (imp. subj.)
matter;   these   to be, [are]   what   he was demanding

ab ĕo: primùm,   ne-traducĕret   quam
from   him: first,   (that) he should not lead over   any

multitudĭnem homĭnum amplĭùs trans Rhenum in
multitude   of men   more   across   the Rhine   into

Gallĭam: deinde   reddĕret   obsĭdes quos
Gaul: then   (that) he should restore   the hostages   that

haberet (imp. subj.) ab Ædŭis; que permittĕret[88]
he was having   from   the Ædui;   and   should permit

Sequănis,   ut   liceret   voluntate
(to) the Sequani,   that   it should be allowed   by the will

ejus   reddĕre illis   quos illi
of him [his will] to restore to them [the Ædui] (those) whom they

haberent (imp. subj.);   nève   lacessĕret   Ædŭos
were having;   nor   should harass the Ædui

injurĭâ;   nève   inferret   bellum   his   ve
with violence nor   should bring on war   to these or

socĭis   eorum;   si   fecisset   id   ĭta,
to the allies of them; if   he should do   this thus,

perpetŭam   gratĭam   atque   amicitĭam   futuram
perpetual   favor   and   friendship   about to [would] be

sĭbi   que   Romano   popŭlo   cum   ĕo.   Si
to himself and   to the Roman people with   him.   If

impetraret (imp. subj.) non, quonĭam, Marco Messalâ,
he was obtaining (it)   not,   since,   Marcus Messala,

Marco   Pisone   consulĭbus, Senatus   censuisset
Marcus   Piso   (being) consuls, the Senate had resolved

(pl. perf. subj.)   ŭtĭ   quicunque   obtineret   Gallĭam
                    that   whosoever   should hold   Gaul

provincĭam,   defendĕret   Ædŭos   que
(as a) province,   should defend   the Ædui   and

cætĕros   amicos   Romani   popŭli,   quod
other   friends   of the Roman people,   which [as]

posset   facĕre   commŏdo   rei publĭcæ,
he might be able to do   to the advantage   of the republic,

se   non   neglecturum   injurias Æduorum."
he) himself not about to [would not] neglect the injuries of the Ædui."

36. Ariovistus   respondit   ad hæc: "esse
    Ariovistus   answered   to these (things): "to be [it was]

jus   belli,   ut   qui vicissent (pl. perf. subj.),
the right of war, that   (they) who had conquered,

imperarent ĭis (dat.), quos   vicissent (pl. perf. subj.),
should rule   those,   whom   they had conquered,

quemadmŏdum   vellent: item   Romanum
in whatsoever manner   they may wish; likewise   the Roman

popŭlum   consuêsse   imperare victis (dat.)
people   to have [had] been accustomed   to rule the conquered

non   ad   præscriptum alterĭus, sed   ad   sŭum
not according to   the edict   of another, but according to their own

arbitrĭum. Si[89] ipse   præscribĕret   (imp. subj.)
will.   If   he (himself) was dictating

non   Romano   popŭlo, quemadmŏdum uteretur
not   to the Roman people,   how   it should use

sŭo jure (abl.), non   oportere   se   impediri
its right, (it was) not (to be) proper (that) himself (to) be hindered

à   Romano   popŭlo in sŭo jure: Ædŭos
by   the Roman   people in his right: the Ædui

     factos-esse   stipendarĭos   sĭbi,   quonĭam
to have [had] been made tributary   to himself,   since

tentâssent   (pl. perf. subj.) fortunam   belli,   et
they had tried   the fortune of war,   and

congressi-essent (pl. perf. sudj.)   armis   ac
had engaged   in arms   and (had been)

superati: Cæsărem facĕre magnam injurĭam, qui
overcome: Cæsar   to do [did] great injury,   who

sŭo adventu facĕret (imp. subj.) vectigalĭa deteriora
by his arrival was making   the taxes worse [less]

sĭbi: se[90]   esse   non   redditurum
for him: (he) himself to be [was] not   about to restore

obsĭdes   Ædŭis; nĕque   illaturum   bellum
the hostages to the Ædui; nor about to [would] bring on war

injurĭâ ĭis, neque socĭis   eorum,   si
with damage to them, nor to the allies of them [their allies], if

manerent   in ĕo,   quod   convenisset (pl.
they should abide in that, which   had been agreed upon,

perf. subj.), que pendĕrent   stipendĭum quotannis:
              and should pay   tribute   yearly:

sì non   fecissent   id,   fraternum   nomem
if they would not do this,   the fraternal name

Romani   popŭli   abfuturum   longè   ab
of the Roman people about to [would] be absent far from

his; quòd Cæsar denuntiaret (imp. subj.) sĭbi,
these; that Cæsar was declaring   to him,

     se   non   neglecturum   injurĭas
(that) he himself not about to [would not] neglect the injuries

Æduorum, nemĭnem   contendisse   cum   se
of the Ædui, no one to have [had] contended with himself

sĭne   sŭâ   pernicĭe   congrederetur   quum
without   his own   destruction   let him come on   when

vellet;   intellecturum,   quid   invicti
he wishes;   about to [he would] understand,   what   the invincible

Germani, exercitatissĭmi in armis, qui subîssent
Germans,   most practiced   in   arms,   who   had gone under

(pl. perf. subj.) non   tectum   intra   quatuordĕcim
                  not [no]   roof   within   fourteen

annos,   possent   virtute.''
years,   might be able (to effect)   by valor.''

37   Eodem   tempŏre   hæc   mandata
    In [at] the same   time   these   charges

referebantur   Cæsărĭ;   et   legati   veniebant
were reported   to Cæsar; and [also] ambassadors   were coming

ab   Æduis   et   Trevĭris: Ædŭi,   questum,
from   the Ædui   and   Treviri: the Ædui,   (to) complain,

quòd   Harudes,   qui   nuper   transportati-essent (pl.
that   the Harudes,   who   lately   had been brought over

perf. subj.)   in   Gallĭam,   popularentur (imp. subj.)
               into   Gaul,   were laying waste

fines[91]   eorum;   sese   potuisse   redimĕre
the borders   of them; themselves   to have [had] been able   to purchase

pacem   Ariovisti,   ne   obsidĭbus   quĭdem
peace   of Ariovistus,   not   hostages   indeed [even]

    dătis.   Autem   Trevĭri,   centum   pagos
having been given.   But   the Treviri, (reported) a hundred   cantons

Suevorum   consedisse   ad   ripam   Rheni,   qui
of the Suevi   to have [had] settled   at   the bank   of the Rhine,   who

conarentur (imp. subj.) transire Rhenum;   fratres
were endeavoring   to cross   the Rhine; (that) the brothers

Nasŭam   et   Cimberĭum   præesse   ĭis (dat.)   Quĭbus
Nasua   and   Cimberius   to be [are] over   these.   By which

rebus   Cæsar   commotus   vehementer   existimavit
things   Cæsar   being moved   greatly   thought

maturandum[92]   sĭbi   ne   si   nŏva mănus
to be [it must be] hastened   to [by] himself,   lest,   if   the new band

Suevorum   conjunxisset (pl. perf. subj.)   sese   cum
of the Suevi   should join   itself   with

veterĭbus   copĭis   Ariovisti,   posset[98]   mĭnùs
the old   forces   of Ariovistus,   it might be able   less

facĭlè   resisti.   Ităque,   frumentarĭâ   re
easily   to be withstood.   Therefore,   the corn   affair [grain]

comparatâ,   quàm-celerrĭmè   potŭit,   contendit
having been procured,   as quickly as   he could,   he hastened

magnis   itinerĭbus   ad   Ariovistum.
by great [forced]   marches   to   Ariovistus.

38. Quum[94]   jam   processisset (pl. perf. subj.)
When   now   he had proceeded

vĭam   tridŭi,   nuntiatum-est   ĕi,
a course   of three days,   it was reported   to him,

Ariovistum[95]   cum omnĭbus sŭis copĭis   contendĕre ad
Ariovistus   with all his forces   to hasten to

occupandum   Vesontionem,   quod est maxĭmum
occupy   Vesontio,   which is the largest

oppĭdum Sequanorum, que   processisse   vĭam
town   of the Sequani, and to have [had] proceeded a course

tridŭi   à   sŭis finĭbus.   Cæsar existimabat
of three days from his borders.   Cæsar was thinking

præcavendum   sĭbi   magnopĕre, ne id
to [it must] be guarded to [by] himself very greatly, lest this

accidĕret: namque   ĕrat   summa   facultas
should happen; for indeed there was the highest [largest] supply

in ĕo oppĭdo omnĭum rerum, quæ ĕrant usŭi ad
in this town of all things, which were for use to

bellum,[96] que idem muniebatur sic naturâ
war, and the same was fortified so by the nature

lŏci, ut dăret (imp. subj.) magnam facultatem
of the place, that it was giving great means

ad[97] ducendum bellum; proptereă quòd flumen
to lead [protract] the war; because (that) the river

Dubis, ut circumductum circĭno, cingit
Dubis [Doux], as (if) led [traced] around by a compass, girds

penè totum oppĭdum; reliquum spatĭum, quod
almost the whole town; the remaining space, which

est non amplĭus sexcentorum pĕdum, quà flumen
is not more (than) (of) six hundred feet, where the river

ıntermittit,   mons   contĭnet,   magnă
ceases,   a mountain   occupies,   with (of) great

altitudĭne, Ita[98] ut radices ejus montis contingant
height,   so   that the roots [foot] of this mountain   reach

(pres. subj.)   ripæ   flnmĭnis   ex   utrâque
[reaches]   to the bank   of the river   from [on]   each

parte.   Murus circumdătus effĭcit hunc
part [side].   A wall thrown around makes this (mountain)

arcem   et   conjungit   cum   oppĭdo.   Huc[99]
a citadel   and   joins (it)   with   the town.   Hither

Cæsar contendit magnis diurnis que nocturnis
Cæsar   hastens   by great   day   and   night

itinerĭbus, que oppĭdo occupato, collŏcat
marches,   and   the town having been occupied, he places

præsidĭum   ĭbi.
a garrison   there.

39. Dum moratur paucos dĭes ad Vescontionem
While   he delays   a few days   at   Vescontio

causâ[100] frumentarĭæ rĕi   que commeatûs, ex
by cause   of corn   affair [grain]   and of provisions, from

percunctatione nostrorum que vocĭbus Gallorum
the inquiry   of our (men) and the expressions of the Gauls

et   mercatorum   qui   prædicabant   Germanos
and   of the merchants   who   were proclaiming   the Germans

esse   ingenti   magnitudĭne   corpŏrum,
to be [were]   with [of] vast   size   of bodies,

incredibĭli   virtute atque exercitatione in armis,
with (of) incredible   valor   and   practice   in   arms,

sese[101] sæpenumĕro congressos cum ĭis,
(they) themselves   oftentimes   having encountered with   them,

potuisse   ferre ne vultum quĭdem atque
to have [had] been able to bear not the look indeed [even] and

acĭem   oculorum,   tantus   tĭmor   subĭtŏ
edge [glance]   of (their) eyes,   so great   fear   suddenly

occupavit omnem exercĭtum, ut perturbaret (imp.
occupied   all   the army,   that   it was disturbing

subj.) non mediocrĭter mentes que anĭmos omnĭum.
in no moderate degree the minds and spirits of all.

Hic   primùm   ortus-est   à   tribunis   milĭtum,
This (fear)   first   arose [started] from   the tribunes   of soldiers

ac   præfectis,   que   relĭquis,   qui   causâ
and   prefects,   and   remaining (persons),   who   by cause [reason]

amicitĭæ   secuti   Cæsărem   ex   urbe,
of friendship   having followed   Cæsar   from   the city,

mĭserebantur   magnum perĭcŭlum, quòd   habebant
were deploring   the great   danger,   because   they were having

non   magnum   usum   in   militari   re (sing.):
not [no]   great   experience   in   military   affairs:

quorum alĭus,[102] alĭâ   causâ   illatâ,
of whom   one,   one   cause   being brought [alleged],   (another,

     quam   dicĕret (imp. subj.) esse   necessarĭam
another) which   he was saying   to be [was]   necessary

sĭbi   ad   proficiscendum,   patebat,   ut   liceret
to himself   for   setting out,   was asking,   that   it might be

     discedĕre   voluntate   ejus;   nonnulli
allowed (him)   to depart   by the will   of him [by his will];   some

adducti   pudore,   ut[103]   vitarent   suspicionem
prompted   by shame,   that   they might avoid   the suspicion

timoris   remanebant.   Hi   potĕrant   nĕque   fingĕre
of fear   were remaining.   These   were able   neither   to form [keep]

     vultum   nĕque   interdum   tenere   lacrymas;
(their) countenance   nor   sometimes   to hold   (their) tears;

abditi   in   tabernacŭlis, aut   querebantur   sŭum
hidden   in   the tents,   either   they were bewailing their own

fatum, aut cum   sŭis   familiarĭbus   mĭserebantur
fate,   or   with   their   confidants   were deploring (their)

commune perĭcŭlum.   Vulgò   testamenta obsignabatur
common   danger.   Everywhere   wills   were sealed

totis   castris (pl.).   Vocĭbus   ac   timore   horum
in the whole   camp.   By the words   and   fear   of these

paullatim etĭam   ĭi,   qui habebant magnum   usum
gradually   also   they, who were having   great   experience

in   castris (pl.), milĭtis que centuriones, que   qui
in   camps,   soldiers and   centurions,   and (those) who

præĕrant   equitatŭi (dat.), perturbabantur. Qui[104]   ex
commanded   the cavalry,   were disturbed.   Whoever   of

his volebant se existimari mĭnùs timĭdos,
these were wishing themselves to be thought less alarmed,

dicebant se non vereri hostem, sed timere
were saying they (did) not (to) dread the enemy, but (to) feaɪ

angustĭas itinĕris et magnitudĭnem silvarum,
the (hard) straits of the way and the vastness of the woods,

quæ intercedĕrent (imp. subj.) inter ĕos ɐtque
which were intervening between them and

Ariovistum, aut frumentarĭam rem, ut
Ariovistus, or the corn affair [supply], that

posset commŏdè sătis supportari.
it might be able [could] (not) conveniently enough (to) be carried up.

Etĭam nonnulli renuntiabant Cæsări, cùm
Also some were reporting to Cæsar, when

jussisset (pl. pref. subj.) castra (pl.) moveri, ac
he had ordered the camp to be moved, and

signa ferri, milĭtes[105] non fŏre
the standards to be borne, the soldiers not to be about to [would not] be

audientes dicto, nĕque laturos
hearing [obedient] to the word, nor about to [would] bear

signa propter timorem.
the standards on account of fear.

40. Quum Cæsar animadvertisset (pl. perf. subj.)
When Cæsar had observed

hæc, concilĭo convocato, que
these (things), a council having been called together, and

centurionĭbus omnĭum ordĭnum adhibĭtis ad
the centurions of all ranks having been admitted to

id concilĭum, incusavit ĕos vehementer; primùm,
this council, he blamed them vehemantly; first,

quòd[106] putarent (imp. subj.) quærendum aut
because they were thinking to [it must] be inquired [investigated] or

cogitandum sĭbi, aut in quam
to [must] be considered to (by) themselves, either into what

partem, aut quo consilĭo ducerentur (imp. subj.).
part, or with what plan they should be led.

Ariovistum, se consŭle, cupidissĭmè
Ariovistus, himself (being) consul, most eagerly

appetîsse   amicitĭam   Romani   popŭli:
to have [had] sought   the friendship   of the Roman   people :

cur   quisquam   judicaret   hunc   discessurum
why   should any one judge   this (man)   about to [would] depart

tam   temĕrè   ab   officĭo?   Quĭdem[107]   persuaderi
so   rashly   from (his) duty?   Indeed   to be [it was] persuaded

sĭbi,   sŭis   postulatis   cognĭtis,   atque   æquĭtate
to himself, his demands   having been known,   and   the justice

conditionum   perspectâ,   ĕum (acc.)   nĕque   repudĭa-
of the conditions being clearly seen, he   neither   about to

turum   sŭam   gratĭam   nĕque   Romani
[would] reject his   favor   nor   (that) of the Roman

popŭli: quòd   si,   impulsus   furore   atque   amentĭâ.
people: but   if,   impelled   by rage   and   by madness,

intulisset   bellum,   quid   tandem   vererentur?
he would wage war,   what,   pray   should they fear

aut   cur   desperarent   de   suâ   virtute,
or   why   should they despair concerning   (their) own valor,

aut   de   diligentĭâ   ipsius?   Perĭcŭlum
or   concerning the diligence of himself [Cæsar]?   Danger [trial]

ejus   hostis   factum   memorĭâ   nostrorum
of this   enemy   (was) made   in the memory   of our

patrum,   quum,   Cimbris   et   Teutŏnis
fathers,   when,   the Cimbri   and   Teutones

pulsis   a   Caio   Marĭo,   exercĭtu.
having been routed by   Caius   Marius,   the army

videbatur[108] merĭtus   non   minorem   laudem,   quàm
was seeming   to have deserved not   less   praise,   than

imperator   ipse: etĭam   factum   nuper   in
the general   himself: also   (a trial was) made   recently   in

Italĭâ,   servili[109]   tumultu,   quos   tămen   alĭquis
Italy,   in the slave   uprising,   whom   however   some

usus   ac   disciplina,   quam   accepissent
experience   and   discipline,   which   they had received

(pl.perf.subj.)   à   nobis,   sublevarent.   Ex[110]   quo
                   from   us,   assisted.   From   which

posse   judicari,   quantum   bŏni   constantĭa
to be able [it can] (to) be judged, how much (of) good   firmness

haberet (imp. subj.)   in   se;   proptereă   quŏd
was having [had]   in   itself; because   (that)

        quos   aliquandĭu   timuissent (pl. perf. subj.)
(those) whom   for some time they had feared

sine   causâ   inermes,   superâssent (pl. perf. sudj.),
without cause,   unarmed,   they had subdued,

hos   posteă   armatos   ac   victores.   Denĭque,
these afterwards armed   and   conquered.   Lastly,

hos   esse   Germanos   cum   quĭbus   Helvetĭi
these to be [are] the Germans with   whom   the Helvetii

sæpenumĕro   congressi   non   solùm   in   sŭis,
oftentimes   having engaged not   only   in   their own,

sed   etĭam   in   finĭbus   illorum   plerumque
but   also   in   the borders of them [their borders] generally

superârint (perf. subj.); qui   tămen   potuĕrint
have overcome;   who   notwithstanding have been able

(perf. subj.) non   esse   păres   nostro   exercitŭi.
              not   to be   equal   to our   army.

Si   adversum   prœlĭum   et   fŭga   Gallorum
If   the adverse   battle   and   flight   of the Gauls

commoveret   quos,   hos   posse   reperire,
might move [affect] any,   these to be able [can] (to) find,

si   quærĕrent (imp. subj.),   Gallis   defatigatis
if   they should inquire,   (that) the Gauls being wearied

        diuturnitate   belli,   Ariovistum,   quum
by the long continuance of the war, Ariovistus,   when

continuisset (pl. perf. subj.)   se   multos   menses
he had kept   himself many   months

castris (pl.)   ac   paludĭbus,   nĕque   fecisset (pl. perf.
in camp   and   marshes,   nor   had made

subj.) potestatem   sŭi,   adortum
       power   of himself [given an opportunity], having attacked

subĭtò   jam   desperantes   de   pugnâ   et
suddenly (those) already despairing   of   battle   and

dispersos,   vicisse   măgis   ratione
scattered,   to have [had] conquered more   by reason [trickery]

ac   consilĭo   quàm   virtue: cui   rationi
and   by counsel [wiles] than   by valor: for which trickery

lŏcus   fuisset   contra   barbăros   atque
a place [chance]   might have been   against   barbarous   and

imperitos   homĭnes: hâc   ne   ipsum   quĭdem
unskilled   men: by this   not   (he) himself   even

sperare   nostros   exercĭtus   posse   căpi.
to expect [expected]   our   armies   to be able [could]   (to) be taken.

   Qui   conferrent (imp. subj.)   sŭum   timorem   in
  (They) who   were assigning   their   fear   upon

simulationem[111] frumentarĭæ   rĕi   que   angustias
  the pretence   of the corn   affair [supply]   and   the difficulties

itinĕrum,   facĕre   arroganter,   quŭm
of the marches,   (to) do (this)   officiously,   since

viderentur (imp. subj.)   aut   desperare   de   officĭo
they were seeming   either   to despair   of   the duty

  imperatoris,   aut   præscribĕre.   Hæc[112]
of the commander,   or   to prescribe.   These (things)

  esse   curæ   sĭbi;   Sequănos,   Leucos,
to be [are]   (for) a care   to himself;   the Sequani,   Leuci,

Lingŏnes   subministrare   frumentum;   que   jam
  Lingones   to [will] supply   corn;   and   now

frumenta (pl.) esse   matura   in   agris.   De   itinĕre
  corn   to be [is] ripe   in   the fields.   Of   the route

    ipsos   judicaturos   brĕvi   tempŏre.
  (they) themselves   about to [would] judge   in a short   time.

Quŏd   dicantur[113] (pres. subj.)   non   fŏre
  That   they are [it is] said   (they would) not   (to be about to) be

audientes   dicto,   nĕque   laturi   signa,
hearing [obedient]   to the word,   nor   (about to) bear   the standards,

   se   commoveri   nĭhil   ĕâ   re; enim
(he) himself   to be [was] moved   nothing [not at all]   by this   thing;   for

scire,   quibuscumque   exercitus   fuĕrit (perf.
to know [he knew],   to whomsoever   an army   has been

subj.)   non   audĭens   dicto,   aut,
     not   hearing [obedient]   to the word,   either,

   re   gestâ   mâlè,   fortunam   defu-
an affair   having been carried on   ill,   fortune   to have

   isse;   aut   alĭquo   facinŏre   comperto,
[had] failed;   or   some   crime   being found out.

avaritĭam　　convictam-esse :　　sŭam[114] innocentĭam
avarice　to have [had] been proved :　his (own) innocence [integrity]

perpetŭâ　　vitâ,　felicitatem　　bello　　Helvetiorum
in (his) whole　　life,　(his) success　in the war　of the Helvetii

　　perspectam-esse.　　Ităque,　　se　　repræ-
to have been [were] clearly seen.　　Therefore,　(he) himself　about to

　　sentaturum　　quod　　fuisset (pl. perf. subj.)
[would] do presently　　(that) which　he had been

　　collaturus　in　longiorem　dĭem ;　et
(otherwise) about to defer　to　a more distant　day ;　and

proxĭmâ　　nocte　de　　quartâ　vigilĭâ
on the nearest [next]　night　from [at]　the fourth　watch

moturum　　castra (pl.), ut　　quam primùm
about to [he would] move　the camp,　in order that　as　soon as

　posset　　intelligĕre,　　utrùm　pŭdor
he might be able　to [he may] understand,　whether　shame

atque　offcĭum,　an　tĭmor　valeret　plùs
and　duty,　or　fear　may prevail　the more

ăpud　ĕos.　Quòd　si　nemo　præterĕa　sequatur
with　them.　But　if　no one　besides　follows,

(pres. subj.), tămen　　se　　iturum　cum
nevertheless　(he) himself　about [would] go　with

decĭmâ　legione　solâ,　de　quâ　non　dubi-
the tenth　legion　alone,　of　which　he was not　doubt-

taret (imp. subj.) que　ĕam　futuram　Prætorĭam
ing　　and　this　about to [would] be　a Prætorian

cohortem　sĭbi.''　Cæsar　et　indulsĕrat　præcipŭe
cohort　for himself.''　Cæsar　both　had favored　especially

huic legioni (dat.) et confidebat,　maxĭmè　propter
this　legion　and was trusting,　(it) very mnch　on account of

virtutem.
(its) valor.

41.　Hâc　oratione　habĭtâ,　　mentes
　　This　speech　having been delivered,　the minds

omnĭum　conversæ-sunt　in　mirum　mŏdum,
of all　were changed　into [in]　a wonderful　manner,

que　summa　alacrĭtas　et　cupidĭtas　belli
and　the highest　eagerness　and　desire　of war

gerendi[115]   innata-est :   que decĭma
to be carried on [of waging war] was born in [inspired] : and the tenth

legĭo princeps egit   gratĭas   ĕi   per   tribunos
legion first   rendered thanks to him through the tribunes

milĭtum,   quòd   fecisset (pl. perf. subj.)   optĭmum
of soldiers,   that   he had made   the best

judicĭum   de   se,   que[116] confirmavit se   esse
judgment concerning itself, and   declared   itself to be

partissĭmam   ad   gerendum   bellum.   Inde
most prepared   for   carrying on   war.   Then

relĭquæ   legiones   egerunt   per   tribunos
the remaining legions   acted   through the tribunes

milĭtum   et   centuriones primorum ordĭnum, ŭtĭ
of soldiers and centurions of the first ranks,   that

satisfacĕrent   Cæsări ;   "se   nĕque unquam
they might satisfy (to) Cæsar ; "(they) themselves neither ever

dubitâsse, nĕque timuisse. nĕque existimavisse
to be [had] doubted, nor to have [had] feared, nor (to) have thought

judicĭum   de   summâ (sing.)   belli   esse
the judgment of the highest (concerns) of war to be [was]

sŭum sed   imperatoris." Satisfactione[117]
their own but (the part) of the commander." The satisfaction [apology]

eorum   acceptâ, et itinĕre   exquisito
of them [their apology] being received, and the way being reconnoitred

per Divitiăcum, quòd   habebat   maxĭmam
by Divitiacus, because he was having the greatest

fĭdem   ĕi   ex   alĭis   ut   ducĕret
faith to [in] him from [of] the others [Gauls] that he might lead

exercĭtum   apertis   lŏcis,   circuĭtu   amplius
the army   in the open places,   by a circuit of more

quadraginta millĭum, profectus-est de   quartâ
(than) forty   miles,   he set out from [at] the fourth

vigilĭâ, ŭtĭ   dixĕrat.   Septĭmo   dĭe,   quum
watch,   as   he had said. On the seventh day,   when

non intermittĕret (imp. subj.) ĭter,   factus-est
he was not ceasing   the march, he was made

certĭor[118]   ab exploratorĭbus,   copĭas
more certain [was informed] by scouts,   (that) the forces

Ariovisti   abesse   à   nostris   quatŭor   et
of Ariovistus to be [were] distant from our (forces) four and

viginti   millĭbus (abl.)   passŭum.
twenty   thousand   (of) paces.

42. Adventu   Cæsăris   cognĭto,   Ariovistus
     The arrival   of Cæsar   being known   Ariovistus

mittit   legatos   ad   ĕum;   "id   licere
sends   ambassadors to   him;   "this   to be [is] allowed

fiĕri   per   se,   quod   antĕa   postulásset
to be done by   himself, which   before   he had demanded

(pl. perf. subj.)   de   colloquĭo,   quonĭam
                     concerning a conference,   since

accessisset (pl. perf. subj.) propĭus; que[119] existimaret
he had approached   nearer;   and   he was thinking

(imp. subj.)   se   posse   facĕre   ĭd   sine
            (he) himself to be able [could] (to) do this without

per\icŭlo.''   Cæsar   non   respŭit   conditionem,   que[120]
danger."   Cæsar   did not   reject   the condition,   and

arbìtrabatur ĕum jam   reverti   ad   sanitatem,
was thinking him [he] now to [would] return to soundness [reason].

quum   polliceretur (imp. subj.)   ultrò   id,   quod
since   he was offering   spontaneously that,   which

antĕa   denegâsset (pl. perf. subj.)   petenti;
before   he had denied   to (him) asking;

que veniebat   in   magnam spem, pro sŭis
and he was coming [entering] into great hope,   for his

tantis   beneficĭis que   Romani   popŭli
(so) great benefits   and   (those) of the Roman people

in   ĕum,   sŭis postulatis   cognĭtis,   fŏre[121]
towards him (that), his demands having been known, to be about to be

ŭtì   desistĕret   pertinacĭâ.   Quintus
[it would be] that he would cease from (his) obstinacy. The fifth

dĭes   ex   ĕo   dĭe dictus-est   colloquĭo.
day   from that day was said [appointed] for the conference.

Intĕrim,   quum   legati   mitterentur (imp. subj.)
Meanwhile, when ambassadors were sent

sæpe   citro que   ultrò   inter   ĕos.   Ariovistus
often hither and thither between them,   Ariovistus

postulavit;   Cæsar   ne adducĕret   quem   pedĭtem
requested;   Cæsar   should not lead up   any   foot soldiers

ad   colloquĭum,   "se   vereri
to   the conference,   "himself   to dread [he feared]

ne   circumveniretur   ab   ĕo   per
lest   he should be circumvented   by   him   through

insidĭas (pl.):   uterque   veniret   cum
ambush: each   should come   with

equitatu,   alĭâ[122]   ratione   se   esse
cavalry,   in other   method [manner]   (he) himself   to be

non   venturum."   Cæsar,   quòd   volebat
not   about to [would not] come."   Cæsar,   because   he was willing

nĕque   colloquĭum   tolli,   causâ
(that) neither   the conference   to [should] be taken away [be lost],   cause

interposĭta;   nĕque   audebat   committĕre   sŭam
being interposed;   nor   was daring   to commit   his

salutem   equitatu   Gallorum,   statŭit   essе
safety   to the cavalry   of the Gauls,   determined   to be

commodissĭmum,   omnĭbus   Gallis   equitĭbus
[it was] most convenient [fitting],   all   the Gallic   horsemen

detractis   ĕquis,   imponĕre   ĕò
having been withdrawn   from the horses,   to place upon   there [them]

legionarĭos   milĭtes   decĭmæ   legionis,   cui (dat.)
the legionary   soldiers   of the tenth   legion,   in which

confidebat   quàm-maxĭmè;   ut   haberet
he was confiding   as much as possible;   that   he might have

præsidĭum   quàm-amicissĭmum,   si   quid   ŏpus
a guard   as friendly as possible,   if   any   need

esset   facto (abl.).   Quum   quod   fiĕret
should be   of deed [action].   When   which [this]   was done,

(imp. subj.),   quidam   ex   militĭbus   decĭmæ
    a certain one   of   the soldiers   of the tenth

legionis   dixit   non   irridicŭlè,   "Cæsărem   facĕre
legion   said   not   unwittily,   "Cæsar   to do [does]

plus   quàm   pollicĭtus-esset   (pl. perf. subj.);
more   than   he had promised;

pollicĭtum   habiturum   decĭmam   legionem
having promised   about to [he would] have   the tenth   legion

in lŏco prætorĭæ cohortis; nunc rescribĕre[123]
in place of a pretorian cohort; now to enroll (it)

ad ĕquum.''
[he enrolls it] to the horse.''

43. Erat magna planitĭes et in ĕâ tumŭlus
(There) was a great plain and on it a hillock

terrĕnus sătis grandis. Hic lŏcus abĕrat
of earth sufficiently large. This place was distant

spatĭo fĕrè æquo ab castris Ariovisti et
by a space nearly equal from the camps of Ariovistus and

Cæsaris. Eò, ut dictum-ĕrat, venerunt ad
Cæsar. Thither, as had been said [appointed], they came to

colloquĭum. Cæsar constitŭit legionem, quam
the conference. Cæsar arranged the legion, which

devexĕrat ĕquis, ducentis passĭbus (abl.)
he had brought down with horses, two hundred paces

ab ĕo tumŭlo. Item equĭtes
from this hillock. Likewise the horsemen

Ariovisti constiterunt pări intervallo.
of Ariovistus took stand with [at] an equal interval.

Ariovistus postulavit, ut colloquerentur ex
Ariovistus demanded, that they should converse from [on]

ĕquis et ut adducĕrent denos præter
horses and that they should lead up ten each besides

se ad colloquĭum. Ubi[124] ventum-est ĕò,
themselves to the conference. When it was come [they came] there,

Cæsar, initĭo orationis, commemoravit
Cæsar, in the beginning of (his) speech, recounted

sŭa que beneficĭa Senatûs in ĕum,
his own and the benefits of the Senate towards him,

quòd appellatus-esset (pl. perf. subj.) rex à
that he had been called king by

Senatu, quòd amicus, quòd
the Senate, that (he had been called) a friend, that

amplissĭma munĕra missa; quam rem,
most ample gifts (had been) sent; which thing,

docebat, et contigisse paucis,
he was showing, both to have [had] happened to few,

et   consuevisse   tribŭi   à
and   to have [had] been accustomed   to be granted   by

Romanis   pro   maxĭmis   officĭis   homĭnum,
the Romans   for   the greatest   services   of men,

illum,   quum   haberet (imp. subj.) nĕque adĭtum,
him [that he], although he was having   neither access,

nĕque   justam causam   postulandi,   beneficĭo
nor   just   cause   of demanding,   by (his) bounty

ac   sŭâ   liberalitate   ac   Senatûs,
and   by his   liberality   and (that) of the Senate,

consecutum   ĕa præmĭa.   Docebat
having [he had] obtained these rewards [honors]. He was showing

etĭam,   quàm   vetĕres,   que   quàm   justæ
also,   how   ancient,   and   how   just

causæ   necessitudĭnis   intercedĕrent[125] (imp. subj.)
causes   of alliance   were existing

ipsis   cum Ædŭis; quæ consulta Senatûs,
to themselves with the Ædui; what decrees of the Senate,

quotĭes, que quàm honorifĭca facta-essent (pl.
how often, and how honorable had been made

perf. subj.) in   ĕos;   ut omni tempŏre,
towards them [in their behalf]: that in all time,

Ædŭi   tenuissent (pl. perf. subj.)   principatum
the Ædui had held   the supremacy

totius   Gallĭæ, etĭam prĭusquàm appetissent
of the whole of Gaul, even before that they had sought

(pl. perf. subj.) nostram amicitĭam. "Hanc esse
      our   friendship. "This to be [was]

consuetudĭnem   Romani popŭli, ut vĕlit
the custom   of the Roman people, that it wished

socĭos atque amicos non mŏdò deperdĕre
(its) allies and friends not only to lose

nĭhil   sŭi,   sed esse auctiores gratĭâ,
nothing of their own, but to be more increased in favor,

dignitate, honore: verò quis posset
in dignity, in honor: but who would be able

pǎti   id   erĭpi
[could] (to) suffer (that) this to be [should be] snatched

Ĭis (dat.),   quod   attulissent (pl. perf. subj.)   ad
from them,   which   they had brought   to

amicitĭam   Romani   popŭli?''   Deinde
the friendship   of the Roman   people?''   Afterwards

postulavit   eădem,   quæ   dedĕrat   in   mandatis
he demanded   the same,   which   he had given   in   the charges

legatis   ne inferret   bellum   aut
to the ambassadors   that he should not bring on   war   either

Ædŭis,   aut   socĭis   eorum;   reddĕret
to the Ædui,   or   to the allies   of them [their allies];   (that) he should

obsĭdes;   si   posset (imp. subj.)
restore   the hostages;   if   he was able

remittĕre   dŏmum   nullam   partem   Germanorum;
to send back   home   no   part   of the Germans;

at   ne pateretur   quos   amplĭus   transire
still   that he should not suffer   any   more   to cross

Rhenum.
the Rhine.

44. Ariovistus respondit pauca   ad   postulata
     Ariovistus   answered   a few (things)   to   the demands

Cæsăris: prædicavit   multa   de   sŭis
of Cæsar: he declaimed   many (things)   of   his own

virtutĭbus;   sese   transîsse   Rhenum
virtues;   (that he) himself   to have [had] crossed   the Rhine

non   sŭâ   sponte, sed   rogatum   et arcessitum
not   on his own accord,   but   (having been) asked   and   sent for

à   Gallis: reliquisse   dŏmum   que   propinquos
by   the Gauls: to have [he had] left   home   and   relations

non   sĭne   magnâ   spe   que   magnis   præmĭis:
not   without   great   hope   and   great   rewards:

habere   sedes   in   Gallĭâ   concessas   ab
to have [he has]   settlements   in   Gaul   granted   by

ipsis,   obsĭdes   ipsorum   dătos   voluntate,
themselves,   hostages   of them   given   by (their) free will,

capĕre   stipendĭum   jure   belli,   quod
to take [he takes]   tribute   by the right   of war,   which

victores   consuevĕrint (perf. subj.)   imponĕre
conquerors   have been accustomed   to impose

victis ;   se   non[126]   intulisse   bellum
to [on] the conquered; (he)himself not to have[has not]brought on war

Gallis,   sed   Gallos   sĭbi ;   omnes civitates
to the Gauls,   but   the Gauls   to himself;   all   the states

Galliæ   venisse   ad   oppugnandum   se,   ac
of Gaul   to have [had] come   for   opposing [to oppose]   himself,   and

habuisse   castra contra   se;   omnes   ĕas   copĭas
to have had [had]   camps   against himself;   all   these   forces

pulsas (esse)   ac superatas esse abs   se   uno
to have [had] been routed   and   overcome   by   himself in one

prœlĭo.   Si   vĕlint (pres. subj.)   experiri   itĕrum,
battle.   If   they wish   to try   again.

se   paratum iterum decertare :   sin   malint
he himself (is) prepared   again   to contend :   but if   they prefer

(pres. subj.)   uti   pace (abl.),   esse   iniquum
to use   peace,   to be [it is]   unjust

recusare   de   stipendĭo, quod   pependĕrint (perf.
to object   concerning   the tribute,   which   they paid

subj.)   sŭâ   voluntate   ad   id   tempus :
by their own   will [volition]   to   this   time :

oportere   amicitĭam   Romani   popŭli
to be [it is] proper (that)   the friendship   of the Roman   people

esse   ornamento   et   præsidĭo   sĭbi,   non
(to) be   (for) an ornament   and   a guard   to himself,   not

detrimento;   que   se   petîsse   id   ĕâ
(for) a detriment ;   and   (he) himself   to have [had] sought   it   in this

spe.   Si   stipendĭum   remittatur (pres. subj.)   per
hope.   If   the tribute   be remitted   by

Romanum   popŭlum,   et   deditĭtĭi   subtrahantur
the Roman   people,   and   the surrendered   be withdrawn,

(pres. sudj.), sese   recusaturum   non mĭnùs libenter
(he) himself about to [would] refuse not   less   willingly

amicitĭam   Romani   populi,   quàm   appetiĕrit
the friendship   of the Roman   people,   than   he sought (it).

(perf. subj.). Quòd   traducat (pres. subj.) multitudĭnem
That   he leads [brings] over   a multitude

Germanorum   in   Gallĭam,   se[127]   facĕre   id
of the Germans   into   Gaul,   he himself   to do [did]   this

causâ	muniendi,	sŭi	non	impugnandæ
for the sake	of protecting,	himself	not	of fighting against

Gallĭæ;	esse	testimonĭum	ejus
Gaul;	to be [it was]	a testimony [proof]	of this

rĕi	quòd	venĕrit (perf. subj.)	non[128]	nĭsi
thing	that	he came	not	except (when)

rogatus,	et	quòd	non	intulĕrit (perf. supj.)
asked,	and	that	he has not	waged

bellum,	sed	defendĕrit (perf. subj.) :	se
war,	but	has defended (himself):	(he)himself

venisse	in	Gallĭam	prĭus	quàm	Romanum
to have [had] come	into	Gaul	earlier	than	the Roman

popŭlum.	Nunquam[129]	ante	hoc	tempus	exercĭtum
people.	Never	before	this	time	an army

Romani	popŭli	egressum	finibus	provincĭæ
of the Roman	people	[has] gone out of	the borders	of the province

Gallĭæ:	quid	vellet (imp. subj.)	sĭbi?	cur
of Gaul:	what	did he wish	for himself?	why

veniret (imp. subj.)	in	sŭas	possessiones?	hanc
did he come	into	his	possessions ?	this

Gallĭam	esse	sŭam	provincĭam,	sicŭti	illam
Gaul	to be [is]	his	province,	even as	that (is)

nostram:	ut	oporteret (imp. subj.)	non
ours:	as	it was proper [it ought]	not

concedi	sĭbi,	si	facĕret	impĕtum	in
to be permitted	to himself,	if	he should make	an attack	upon

nostros	fines:	sic	item,	nos	esse	iniquos,
our	borders ;	so	also,	us	to be [we are]	unjust,

quòd	interpellaremus (imp. subj.)	se	in	sŭo
because	we interfered with	himself	in	his

jure:	quòd	dicĕret (imp. subj.)	Ædŭos	appellatos
right:	that	he was saying (that)	the Ædui	were called

amicos	ex	consulto	Senatŭs,	se	esse
friends	from	[by] a decree	of the Senate,	(he) himself	to be [was]

non	tam	barbarum,	nĕque	tam	imperitum
not	so	barbarous,	nor	so	inexperienced

rerum,	ut	non,	sciret (imp. subj.)	Ædŭos
of [in] affairs,	that	he did not,	know	the Ædui

nĕque   tulisse   auxilĭum   **Romanis**
neither   (to) have brought   aid   to the Romans

proxĭmo   bello   Allobrŏgum,   nĕque
in the nearest [latest]   war   of the Allobroges,   nor (that they)

ipsos   in   his   contentionĭbus,   quas   Ædŭi
themselves   in   these   contests,   which   the Ædui

habuissent (pl. perf. subj.)   cum   se   et   cum
had had   with   himself   and   with

Sequănis,   usos-esse   auxilĭo (abl.)   Romani
the Sequani,   to have [had] used   the aid   of the Roman

popŭli: se   debere[130]   suspicari,   amicitĭā
people: (he) himself   to owe [ought]   to suspect,   friendship

simulatâ,   Cæsărem,   quŏd   habĕat (pres. subj.)
being [was] pretended,   Cæsar,   because   he has

exercĭtum in Gallĭâ,   habere   causâ opprimendi
an army   in   Gaul,   to have[has it]   for the sake   of crushing

sŭi: qui   nĭsi   decedat   (pres. subj.   aut
himself: who   unless   he depart   or

deducat (pres. subj.)   exercĭtum   ex   his   regionĭbus,
lead away   (his) army   from   these   regions,

sese   habiturum   illum   non   pro   amico, sed
he himself   about to [would] hold   him   not   for   a friend,   but

pro   hoste: quod[131]   si   interfecĕrit (perf. subj.) ĕum,
for   an enemy: that   if   he killed   him,

sese   esse   facturum   gratum   multis
he himself   to be   about to [would] do   a grateful (thing)   to many

nobilĭbus   que   principĭbus   Romani   popŭli:
nobles   and   chiefs   of the Roman   people:

se   habere[132]   id   compertum   ab   ipsis
he himself   to have [has]   this thing   found out   from   themselves

per   eorum   nuntĭos;   gratĭam   atque   amicitĭam
by   their   messengers;   the favor   and   friendship

omnĭum   quorum   posset (imp. subj.)   redimĕre
of all   of whom   he was able   to purchase

ejus   morte: quŏd   si   discessisset (pl. perf. subj.)
by his   death: that   if   he should depart

ac   tradidisset (pl. perf. subj.) librăam possessionem
and   should deliver   free   possession

Gallĭæ   sĭbi,   se   remuneraturum
of Gaul   to himself,   (he) himself   about to [would] remunerate

illum   magno   præmĭo,   et   confecturum,
him   with great   reward,   and   about to [would] dispatch,

quæcunque bella   vellet (imp. sudj.)   geri
whatever   wars   he was wishing   to be carried on

sĭne   ullo   labore   et   perĭcŭlo   ejus.
without   any   labor   and   danger   of him [on his part].

45. Multa   dicta-sunt   à   Cæsăre   in   ĕam
    Many (things)   were said   by   Cæsar   upon   this

sententĭam,   quare   posset (imp. subj.)   non
opinion,   wherefore   he was able [could]   not

desistĕre   negotĭo.   Nĕque   sŭam   nĕque
(to) desist   from the business[undertaking].   Neither   his   nor

consuetudĭnem   Romani   popŭli   pătı,   ŭtì
the custom   of the Roman   people   to suffer [permits],   that

    deserĕret   socĭos[133]   merĭtos   optĭmè;
he should desert   allies   having[who have] deserved   the best;

nĕque   se   judicare   Gallĭam   esse
nor (does)   (he)himself   (to) judge(that)   Gaul   to be[is]

    potĭùs   Ariovisti,   quàm   Romani   popŭli.
rather (the possession)   of Ariovistus,   than   of the Roman   people.

Arvernos   et   Rutenos   superatos-esse   bello
The Arverni   and   Ruteni   to have [had] been overcome   in war

à   Quinto   Fabĭo   Maxĭmo;   quĭbus (dat.)   Romanus
by   Quintus   Fabius   Maximus;   whom   the Roman

popŭlus   ignovisset (pl. perf. subj.),   nĕque
people   had pardoned,   nor

redegisset (pl. perf. subj.)   ın   provincĭam   nĕque
had reduced (them)   (in)to   a province   nor

imposuisset (pl. perf. subj.)   stipendĭum: quòd[134]   si
had imposed   tribute: that   ıf

oporteret (imp. subj.) quodque antiquissĭmum tempus
it was proper (that)   every   most ancient   time

    spectari,   imperĭum   Romani   popŭli   in   Gallĭâ
(to) be considered,   the empire   of the Roman   people   in   Gaul

esse   justissĭmum;   si   oporteret (imp. subj.)
to be [was]   most inst: if   it is proper (that)

judicĭum   Senatûs   observari,   Gallĭam   debere
the judgment   of the Senate   (to) be kept,   Gaul   to owe [ought]

esse   libĕram,   quam   victam   bello
to be   free,   which   (though) conquered   in war

voluisset   (pl. perf. subj.)   uti   sŭis
it [the senate] had willed   to [should] use   its own

legĭbus''   (abl.).
laws.''

46. Dum   hæc   geruntur   in   colloquĭo,
While   these (things)   are transpiring   in   the conference,

nⁿntiatum-est   Cæsări,   equĭtes   Ariovisti
it was reported   to Cæsar,   (that) the horsemen   of Ariovistus

accedĕre[135]   propĭus   tumŭlum,   et   adequitare   ad
(to) approach   nearer   the hillock,   and   (to) ride up   to

nostros,   conjicĕre   lapĭdes   que   tela   in
our (men),   (to) throw   stones   and   weapons   against

nostros.   Cæsar fecit   finem   loquendi   que recepit
our (men).   Cæsar made   an end   of speaking   and   betook

se   ad   sŭos,   que   imperavit   sŭis (dat.)
himself   to   his own (men),   and   ordered   his own (men)

ne rejicĕrent   quod   telum   omnino
that they should not throw back   any   weapon   at all

in   hostes :   nam   etsi   videbat
against   the enemy: for   although   he was seeing (that)

prœlĭum   fŏre   cum   equitatu   sĭne
a battle   to be about to [would] be   with   the cavalry   without

ullo periculo   delectæ   legionis;   tămen   putabat[136]
any   danger   of (his) chosen   legion ;   yet   he was thinking (it)

non,   committendum   ut,   hostĭbus   pulsis,
not,   [must not] be permitted   that,   the enemy   having been routed

posset   dici,   ĕos   circumventos à
it might be able [it could] (to) be said,   them [they were] circumvented by

se   per   fĭdem   in   colloquĭo.   Posteăquam
himself   through (broken)   faith   in   the conference.   After that

elatum-est   in   volgus   milĭtum,   qua[137]
it was published   among   the mass   of soldiers,   what

arrogantĭâ (abl.)   Ariovistus   usus   in   colloquio
arrogance   Ariovistus   having used   in   the conference

interdixisset (pl. perf. subj)   Romanis (dat.)   omni
he had forbidden   the Romans   from all

Galliâ;   que   equïtes   ejus   fecissent
Gaul;   and that the horsemen of him [his horsemen] had made

(pl. perf. subj.)   impĕtum   in   nostros;
                           an attack   upon   our men;

que   ĕa   res   diremisset (pl. perf. subj.) colloquïum;
and   this thing had broken up   the conference;

multò   major   alacrïtas que   majus   studïum
much   greater activity   and   a greater   desire

pugnandi   injectum-est   exercituĭ.
of fighting was incited   to [in] the army.

47.   Bidŭo   pòst   Ariovistus   mittit   legatos
       Two days afterwards Ariovistus   sends   ambassadors

ad   Cæsarem,   "se   velle   agĕre   cum
to   Cæsar, (to say), "he himself to wish [wishes] to treat with

ĕo   de   his rebus, quæ   cœptæ-essent (pl. perf. subj.)
him about these things, which had been begun

ăgi   inter   ĕos,   nĕque   perfectæ-essent
to be treated between them,   nor   had been completed:

(pl.perf.subj.):   ŭtì   aut   constituĕret   itĕrum
                   that   either he would determine [fix] again

dïem   colloquïo,   aut   si   vellet (imp. subj.)
a day   for a conference, or   if   he was wishing

mïnùs   id,   mittĕret   alïquem   ex   sŭis
less   (for) this (that), he would send some one from   his

legatis   ad   se.   Causa[138] colloquendi   visa-est
lieutenants to himself. A cause   of conferring seemed

non   Cæsări;   et   ĕò   măgis,   quòd   pridïe,
not   to Cæsar; and   for this the more,   that   the day before,

ejus diei, Germani   potuĕrant   non   retineri
this day, the Germans had been able [could] not (to) be restrained,

quin   conjicĕrent   tela   in   nostros.
but that   they should throw weapons   against our (men).

Existimabat   sese   missurum
He was thinking (that he) himself   about to [would] send

legatum   ex   sŭis   cum   magno   pericŭlo ad
an ambassador from his own (men) with   great   danger   to

ĕum,   et   objecturum   fĕris   hominĭbus.
him,   and   about to [would] expose   (him) to savage   men.

Visum-est   commodissĭmum   mittĕre ad   ĕum   Caĭum
It seemed   most convenient   to send   to   him   Caius

Valerĭum   Procillum,   filĭum   Caĭi   Valerĭi
Valerius   Procillus,   a son   of Caius   Valerius

Caburi,   adolescentem   summâ   virtute   et
Caburus,   a young man   with [of] the highest   virtue   and

humanitate,   (păter   cujus   donatus-ĕrat
politeness,   (the father   of whom   had been presented

civitate   à   Caĭo   Valerĭo   Flacco   et
with citizenship   by   Caius   Valerius   Flaccus   both

propter   fĭdem   et   propter   scientĭam
on account of   (his) fidelity   and   on account of   (his) knowledge

Gallĭcæ   linguæ,   quâ (abl.)   Ariovistus   utebatur
of the Gallic   tongue,   which   Ariovistus   was using

multâ (adj.)   jam   longinquâ   consuetudĭne,   et
much [fluently]   now   by long   custom,   and

quòd   causa[139]   peccandi   esset   non
because   a cause   of transgressing [offense]   was   not

Germanis   in   ĕo);   et   Marcum   Mettĭum,   qui
to the Germans   in   him);   and   Marcus   Mettius,   who

utebâtur   hospitĭo (abl.)   Ariovisti.   Mandavit
was enjoying   the hospitality   of Ariovistus.   He charged

his (dat.),   ut   quæ   Ariovistus   dicĕret,
these,   that   what (things)   Ariovistus   might say,

cognoscĕrent   et   referrent   ad   se.   Quos
they should learn   and   should bring back   to   himself.   Whom

quum[140]   Ariovistus   conspexisset (pl. perf. subj.)   in
when   Ariovistus   had beheld   in

castris (pl.)   ăpud   se,   sŭo   exercĭtu
(his) camp   with   himself,   his   army (being)

præsente,   conclamavit: "Quid   venirent (imp. subj.)
present,   he cried out: "Why   did they come

ad   se?   an   causâ   speculandi?"   Prohibŭit
to   himself?   (was it)   for the sake   of spying?"   He stopped

conantes   dicĕre,   et   conjecit   in   catenas.
(them) endeavoring   to speak,   and   cast (them)   into   chains.

48. Eodem dïe promovit castra (pl.),
On the same day he moved forward (his) camp,

et consedit sub monte sex millïbus (abl.)
and pitched (it) under a mountain six thousand

passŭum à castris (pl.) Cæsăris. Postridïe
(of) paces from the camp of Cæsar. The day after

ejus diei traduxit sŭas copïas præter castra (pl.)
this day he led over his forces beyond the camp

Cæsăris et fecit castra (pl.) duobus
of Cæsar and made a camp (by) two

millïbus (abl.) passŭum ultra ĕum, ĕo
thousand (of) paces beyond him, with this

consilïo, ŭtì intercludĕret Cæsărem frumento
design, that he might shut off Cæsar from corn

que commeatu, qui supportaretur[141] ex
and provisions, which was [were] brought from

Sequănis et Ædŭis. Ex èo dïe Cæsar
the Sequani and the Ædui. From this day Cæsar

produxit sŭas copïas quinque continŭos
led forth his forces five continual [successive]

dïes pro castris (pl.), et habŭit aciem
days before the camp, and had (his) battle line

instructam, ut si Ariovistus vellet contendĕre
drawn up, that if Ariovistus might wish to contend

prœlïo, potestas[142] non deesset ĕi.
in battle, the power [opportunity] might not be wanting to him.

Ariovistus omnïbus his diebus continŭit exercïtum
Ariovistus on all these days kept (his) army

castris (pl.); contendit quotidïe equestri prœlïo.[143]
in camp; he contended daily in a cavalry battle

Hoc ĕrat gĕnus pugnæ, quo Germani
This was the kind of fight, in which the Germans

exercuĕrant se. Erant sex millïa
had exercised themselves. (There) were six thousand

equïtum, totïdem pedïtes numĕro velocissïmi
(of) horsemen, as many foot soldiers in number most swift

ac fortissimi, singŭlos quos singŭli
and most brave, each (of), whom (the horsemen) each

delegĕrant	ex	omni	copĭa,	causâ
had chosen	from	all	the force,	for the sake of

sŭæ	salutis (gen.).	Versabantur	cum
their own	safety.	They were engaged	with

his	in	prœlĭis;	equĭtes	recipiebant
these	in	the battles;	the horsemen	were betaking

se	ad	hos:	hi,	si	quid
themselves	to	these:	these,	if	any (thing)

ĕrat	dŭrĭus,	concurrebant:	si	qui,	graviore
was	more difficult,	were rushing up:	if	any,	a heavier

volnĕre	accepto,	decidĕrant
[rather severe] wound	having been received,	had fallen down

ĕquo,	circumsistebant:	si	ĕrat[144]
from (his) horse,	they were rallying around:	if	it was

prodeundum	longĭus	aut	recipiendum
to be advanced	farther	or	to be retreated

celerĭus	quò,	tanta	ĕrat	celerĭtas
more quickly	any where,	so great	was	the speed

horum	exercitatione,	ut,	sublevati	jŭbis
of these	by exercise,	that,	supported	by the manes

equorum,	adæquarent	cursum.
of the horses,	they would equal	(their) course [speed].

49.

Ubi	Cæsar	intellexit	ĕum	tenere
When	Cæsar	learned (that)	him [he]	to hold

se	castris (pl.),	ne	prohiberetur
[was holding] himself	in camp,	(that) he might not be prohibited

diutĭus	commeatu,	delegit	lŏcum	idonĕum
longer	from provision,	he chose	a place	suitable

castris (pl.),	circĭter	sex-centos	passus	ab
for camp,	about	six hundred	paces	from

his	ultra	ĕum	lŏcum,	in	quo	lŏco
them	beyond	this	place,	in	which	place

Germani	consedĕrant,	que	triplĭci	acĭe
the Germans	had encamped,	and	a triple	battle line

instructâ,	venit	ad	ĕum	lŏcum.	Jussit
having been drawn up,	he came	to	this	place.	He ordered

primam	et	secundam	acĭem	esse	in	armis,
the first	and	second	line	to be	in	arms,

tertĭam   munire   castra (pl.).   Hic   lŏcus,   ŭtĭ
the third   to fortify   the camp.   This   place,   as

dictum-est,   abĕrat   ab   hoste   circĭter
has been said,   was distant   from   the enemy   about

sex-centos   passus.   Eò   Ariovistus   misit
six-hundred   paces.   Thither   Ariovistus   sent

numĕrum   homĭnum   circĭter   sexdĕcim   millĭa
a number   of men   about   sixteen   thousand

expedita,   cum   omni   equitatu;   quæ   copĭæ
light armed,   with   all   the cavalry;   which   forces

perterrerent nostros,   et prohiberent   munitione.
should alarm   our (men), and   should check (them)   from fortifying.

Nihĭlo secĭùs,   Cæsar,   ut   constituĕrat   antè,
Nevertheless,   Cæsar,   as   he had determined   before,

jussit   dŭas   acĭes   propulsare   hostem,
ordered   the two   lines   to repel   the enemy,

tertĭam   perficĕre   ŏpus.   Castris (pl.)   munitis,
the third   to complete   the work.   The camp   having been fortified,

reliquit   ĭbi   dŭas   legiones   et   partem   auxil-
he left   there   two   legions   and   part   of the aux-

iorum;   reduxit   quatŭor   relĭquas   in
iliaries;   he led back   the four   remaining (legions)   into

majora   castra (pl.).
the greater   camp.

50. Proxĭmo   dĭe,   Cæsar   sŭo   instituo
On the next   day,   Cæsar   by his   practice

eduxit   sŭas   copĭas   ex   utrisque   castris;   que
led forth   his   forces   from   both   camps;   and

progressus   paullŭlum   à   majorĭbus,   instruxit
having advanced   very little   from   the greater,   drew up

acĭem   que   fecit   hostĭbus   potestatem
(his) line   and   made [gave]   (to) the enemy   an opportunity

pugnandi.   Ubi   intellexit   ĕos   ne
of fighting.   When   he understood (that)   them [they]   not

tum   quĭdem   prodire,   circĭter meridĭem
then   indeed (even)   to [would] come forth,   about   midday

reduxit   exercĭtum   in   castra (pl.).   Tum   demum
he led back   the army   into   camp.   Then   at last

Ariovistus   misit   partem   suarum   copiarum,   quæ
Ariovistus   sent   part   of his   troops,   which

oppugnaret[145]   minora   castra (pl.).   Pugnatum-est
might assault   the lesser   camp.   It was fought

acrĭter   utrimque   usque   ad   vespĕrum.   Occasu
sharply   on both sides quite   to   [till] evening.   With the setting

solis   Ariovistus   reduxit   sŭas   copĭas   in
of the sun   Ariovistus   led back   his   troops   into

castra (pl.), multis   volnerĭbus   et   illatis
camp,   many   wounds   both   having been inflicted

et   acceptis.   Quum   Cæsar   quærĕret (imp. subj.)
and   received.   When   Cæsar   was inquiring

ex   captivis,   quamŏbrem Ariovistus   decertaret
from   the captives,   wherefore   Ariovistus   was contending

(imp. subj.)   non   prœlĭo,   reperiebat   hanc
               not   in battle,   he was ascertaining   this

causam,   quòd   ĕa   consuetudo   esset (imp.
was the cause,   because   this   custom   was common

subj.) ăpud Germanos,   ut   matresfamilĭâs
        with   the Germans,   that   the mothers of family [matrons]

eorum   declararent   sortĭbus   et   vaticinationĭbus,
of them   should declare   by lots   and   by divination,

utrùm   esset   ex   usu prœlĭum   committi
whether   it might be   from [of] use that battle to [should] be joined

necne: ĕas   dicĕre[147] ĭta. "Non esse   fas
or not: them [they] (to) say   thus.   "Not to be [it is not] right

Germanos   superare,   si   contendissent   prœlĭo
the Germans to [should] conquer,   if   they should contend   in battle

ante   nŏvam   lunam."
before   the new   moon."

51. Postridĭe   ejus   diei,   præsidĭo   relicto
    The day after   (of) this day,   a guard   having been left

utrisque castris,   quod visum-est   sâtis,   constitŭit
for both   camps,   which   seemed   sufficient,   he arranged

omnes   alarĭos   in   conspectu   hostĭum   pro
all   the auxiliaries in   sight   of the enemy before

minorĭbus castris (pl.),   quod   valebat[148]
the lesser   camp,   because   he did avail [was strong]

mĭnùs multitudĭne legionariorum milĭtum pro
less in the multitude of legionary soldiers for

numĕro hostĭum; ut uteretur alarĭis (abl.)
the number of the enemy; that he might use the auxiliaries

ad specĭem. Ipse, triplĭci acĭe instructâ,
foɪ a show. (He) himself, a triple battle line having been arrayed,

accessit usque ad castra (pl.) hostĭum. Tum
approached quite to the camp of the enemy. Then

demum Germani necessarĭò eduxerunt sŭas
at last the Germans necessarily led out their

copĭas è castris (pl.); que constituerunt
forces from the camp; and arranged (them)

generatim; que parĭbus intervallis, Harudes,
by nations; and at equal intervals, the Harudes,

Marcomannos, Triboces, Vangiŏnes, Nemetes,
Marcomanni, Triboces, Vangiones, Nemetes,

Sedusĭos, Suevos; que circumdederunt omnem
Sedusii, Suevi; and surrounded all

sŭam acĭem rhedis et carris. Eò
their line with carriages and wagons. There

imposuerunt muliĕres, quæ, manibus passis,
they consigned the women, who, (their) hands (having been) spread,

flentes implorabant milĭtes proficiscentes
weeping were imploring the soldiers setting out

ɪd prœlĭum, nĕ tradĕrent se in
to battle, that they should not deliver themselves into

ᴤervitutem Romanis.
slavery to the Romans.

52. Cæsar præfecit[149] legatos singŭlos
Cæsar appointed lieutenants one each

et quæstorem singŭlis legionĭbus (pl.), ŭtì quisque
and a quæstor to each legion, that every one

haberet ĕos testes sŭæ virtutis. Ipse
might have them (as) witnesses of his valor. (He) himself

à dextro cornu, quòd animadvertĕrat
from [on] the right horn [wing], because he had observed

ĕam partem hostĭum esse minĭmè firmam,
(that) this part of the enemy to be [was] least firm,

commisit   prœlium.   Nostri,   signo   dăto,
joined   battle.   Our (men), the signal (having been) given,

fecerunt   impĕtum   ita   acrĭter   in   hostes: que
made   an attack so   sharply   upon the enemy: and

hostes   procurrerunt ĭta   repentè que celerĭter, ut
the enemy charged   so   suddenly and quickly,   that

spatĭum   conjĭciendi   pila   in   hostes   non
space [time] of [for] throwing javelins against the enemy was not

daretur.   Pilis   rejectis,[150]   pugnatum-est
given.   The javelins (having been) thrown aside, it was fought

comĭnus   gladĭis.   At   Germani   celerĭter
hand to hand with swords. But the Germans quickly

ex   sŭâ consuetudĭne, phalange   factâ,
from [after] their custom,   a phalanx having been formed,

exceperunt impĕtus   gladiorum. Complures nostri
received   the attacks of the swords. Very many (of) our

milĭtes(nom.) reperti-sunt, qui insilirent in phalanges
soldiers   were found, who would leap up upon the phlanxes

et   revellĕrent   scuta   manĭbus,   et
and   would tear away the shields with (their) hands, and

vulnerarent desŭper.   Quum   acĭes   hostĭum
would wound from above. When   the line   of the enemy

pulsa-esset (pl. perf. subj.)   à   sinistro cornu,
had been routed   from [on] the left horn [wing],

atque   conversa   in   fŭgam,   premebant
and   turned   into   flight,   they were pressing

nostram acĭem   vehementer   à   dextro
our   line   urgently   from (on) the right

cornu   multitudĭne   suorum.   Quum
horn [wing] by the multitude   of their (men). When

Publĭus   Crassus   adolescens,   qui   præĕrat
Publius   Crassus   a young man,   who   commanded

equitatŭi (dat.) animadvertisset (pl. perf. subj.)   id
the cavalry,   had perceived   this

quòd   ĕrat[151]   expeditĭor   quàm   hi,   qui
because he was   more disengaged than   these, who

versabantur   inter   acĭem,   misit   tertĭam
were employed among [within] the line, he sent the third

acĭem   nostris   laborantĭbus   subsidĭo.
line   to our (men)   toiling [struggling]   for [as] a reinforcement.

53. Ita   prœlĭum   restitutum-est   atque   omnes
Thus   the battle   was restored   and   all

hostes   verterunt   terga,   nĕque   destiterunt
the enemy   turned   (their) backs,   nor   ceased

fugĕre,   prĭus   quàm   pervenerunt   ad   flumen
to flee,   before   that   they arrived   at   the river

Rhenum,   circĭter   quinque   millĭa   passŭum   ex ĕo
Rhine,   about   five   thousand (of) paces   from this

lŏco.   Ibi   perpauci, aut   confisi   virĭbus
place.   There   very few,   either   having trusted   their strength,

(dat. pl.), contenderunt   transnatare; aut, lintrĭbus
strove   to swim over;   or,   boats

inventis,   reppererunt   salutem   sĭbi.
having been discovered.   found   safety   for themselves.

In   his   fŭit   Ariovistus,   qui,   nactus
In [among] these   was   Ariovistus,   who,   having found

navicŭlam   deligatam   ad   ripam,   profugit   ĕâ:
a small skiff   fastened   at   the bank,   escaped   in it:

nostri   equĭtes   consecuti   interfecerunt   omnes
our   horsemen   having overtaken   slew   all

relĭquos.   Uxores   Ariovisti   fuerunt   dŭæ,
the remaining.   The wives   of Ariovistus   were   two,

una   Sueva[152]   natione,   quam
one   a Suevian (woman)   by nation [nationality],   whom

adduxĕrat   secum   dŏmo;   altĕra
he had brought up   with himself   from home;   the other

Norĭca,   soror   regis   Voccionĭs,
a Norican (woman),   sister   of king   Voccio,

quam   duxĕrat   Gallĭâ,   missam   à
whom   he had led [married]   in Gaul,   sent   by

fratre: utrăque   perĭit   in   ĕâ
(her) brother: each   perished   in   this

fŭgâ: dŭæ   filĭæ   harum,   altĕra
fight: (there were) two   daughters   of these,   the one

occisa-est,   altĕra   capta.   Caĭus   Valerĭus
was slain,   the other   taken [captured].   Caius   Valerius

Procillus, quum traheretur (imp. subj.) in
Procillus, when he was dragged in (their)

fŭgâ vinctus trinis catenis à custodĭbus,
flight bound with triple chains by (his) keepers,

incĭdit in Cæsărem ipsum persequentem
fell upon [fell in with] Cæsar himself pursuing

equitatum hostĭum. Quæ res quĭdem
the cavalry of the enemy. Which thing [circumstance] indeed

attŭlit non minorem voluptatem Cæsări, quàm
brought not less pleasure to Cæsar, than

victorĭa ipsa; quòd videbat honestissĭmum
the victory itself; because he was seeing a most honorable

homĭnem provincĭæ Gallĭæ, sŭum familiarem
man of the province of Gaul, his acquaintance

et hospĭtem, ereptum è manĭbus hostĭum,
and host, rescued from the hands of the enemy,

restitutum sĭbi: nĕque fortuna diminuĕrat
restored to himself: nor [and] fortune had [not] diminished

quidquam de tantâ voluptate et gratulatione
any thing from so great pleasure and congratulation

calamitate ejus. Is dicebât
by a disaster of [to] him. He was saying

consultum (-esse) sortibus ter, se
to have [it had] been consulted by lots thrice, himself

præsente, de se, utrùm necaretur
(being) present, about himself, whether he should be put to death

stătim igni, an reservaretur in alĭud
immediately with fire, or should be reserved unto [for] another

tempus: se esse incolúmen beneficĭo
time: (that he) himself to be [was] safe by the favor

sortĭum. Item Marcus Mettĭus repertus-est
of the lots. Likewise Marcus Mettius was found

et reductus ad ĕum.
and led back to him.

54. Hoc prœlĭo nuntiato trans Rhenum,
This battle having been reported beyond the Rhine,

Suevi, qui venĕrant ad ripas Rheni,
the Suevi, who had come to the banks of the Rhine

cœperunt reverti dŏmum: quos Ubĭi, qui
began to return home: whom the Ubii, who

incŏlunt[153] proxĭmè Rhenum, insecuti
dwell nearest the Rhine, having followed up

perterrĭtos, occiderunt magnum numĕrum ex his.
dismayed, slew a great number from [of] these.

Cæsar, duobus maxĭmas bellis confectis
Cæsar, two very great wars having been finished

unâ æstate, deduxit paullo maturĭùs, quàm
in one summer, conducted a little earlier, than

tempus anni postulabat, exercĭtum in
the time of the year was demanding [requiring] the army into

hiberna in Sequănos: præposŭit
winter quarters into [among] the Sequani: he appointed

Labienum hibernis: ipse profectus-est
Labienus for the winter quarters: (he) himself departed

in citeriorem Gallĭam ad agendos conventus.[154]
into hither Gaul for holding assemb'ies.

SECOND BOOK

The second book contains an account of Cæsar's expeditions aganist the Belgæ, the Nervii. the Aduatuci, and the Amorici, in the six hundred and ninety seventh year after the founding of Rome, B. C. 57. Learning that the Belgæ had entered with the other tribes into a confederacy against the Roman people, Cæsar immediately moves with his army against them. First the Remi are conquered, from whom valuable information is gained relating to the movements of the Belgæ. Crossing the Aisne, Cæsar relieves Bibrax then under attack by the Belgæ. It is not long before the Belgæ and the Suessiones are forced to surrender. The war then turns against the Nervii, who in spite of their extraordinary courage, are at last subdued. The Aduatuci then through sheer treachery seek to overthrow Cæsar's troops. But they like the other tribes are quickly brought under Roman rule. Cæsar returns to Italy and a Thanksgiving is voted by the senate.

1. Quum	Cæsar	esset	in	citeriore	Gallĭâ
When	Cæsar	was	in	hither	Gaul,

Ïta	ŭtì	suprà	demonstravĭmus,	crebri
just	as	above	we have shown,	frequent

rumores	afferebantur	ad	ĕum,	que
rumors	were brought	to	him,	and

Ïtem[1]	fiebat	certĭor	litĕris (pl.) Labieni,
likewise	he was made	more sure [informed]	by letters of Labienus,

omnes	Belgas,	quam	dixeramus	esse	tertĭam
(that) all	the Belgæ,	which	we have said	to be [are]	the third

partem Gallĭæ,	conjurare	contra	Romanum	popŭlum,
part	of Gaul,	(to) conspire	against	the Roman people,

que	dăre	obsĭdes	inter	se.	Has	esse
and	(to) give	hostages	between	themselves.	These	to be [are]

causas	conjurandi:	primùm,	quòd	vererentur
the causes	of conspiring:	first,	because	they were fearing

(imp.subj.)	ne,	omni	Gallĭâ	pacatâ,	noster
	lest	all	Gaul	having been subdued,	our

exercĭtus　adduceretur　ad　ĕos;　deinde,　quŏd
army　　　should be led up　to　them;　then,　　because

sollicitarentur (imp. subj.) ab nonnullis Gallis,　partim
they were solicited　　　　　by　some　　Gauls,　partly

　qui,　　ut　　nollent (imp. subj.)　Germanos
(those) who,　as　they were unwilling that　the Germans

　　versari　　　diutĭus　in　Gallĭâ,　　Ĭta
to be [should] be employed　longer　in　Gaul,　　so

ferebant　　moleste　　exercĭtum　Romani
were bearing (it)　uneasily (that)　the army　of the Roman

popŭli　hiemare　atque　inveterascĕre　in
people　to [should] winter　and　to grow old [continue]　in

Gallĭâ; partim　qui,　mobilitate　et　levitate
Gaul:　partly (those)　who,　by fickleness　and　lightness

anĭmi,　studebant　nŏvis　imperĭis;　etĭam
of mind,　were eager　for new　governments;　also

ab nonnullis,　quŏd　in　Gallĭâ　regna
by　some,　　because　in　Gaul　the kingdoms [the thrones]

vulgŏ　occupabantur　à　　potentiorĭbus　atque
commonly　were occupied　by　the more powerful　and

ĭis,　　qui　habebant　facultates　ad　conducendos
by those,　who　were having　means　for　hiring

homĭnes,[2]　qui　potĕrant　mĭnùs　facĭle　consĕqui
men,　　who　were able　less　easily　to attain

ĕam rem　　nostro　imperĭo.
this thing　(under) our　government.

2.　Cæsar　commotus　　ĭis　　nuntĭis　que
　　Cæsar　　moved　　by these　messages　and

litĕris　conscripsit　duas　nŏvas　legiones　in　citeriore
letters　levied　　two　new　legions　in　hither

Gallĭâ,　et　æstate　inĭtâ,　　misit　Quintum
Gaul,　and　summer　having begun,　he sent　Quintus

Pedĭum　lègatum　qui　　deducĕret　　in
Pedius　(his) lieutenant　who　might lead (them) down　into

interiŏrem Gallĭam.　Ipse,　quum[3] primùm incip-
inner　　　Gaul.　(He) himself,　when　first there was

ĕret (imp. subj.)　esse,　copĭa　pabŭli　venit　ađ
beginning　　　to be,　plenty　of forage　came　to

exercĭtum.   Dat   negotĭum   Senonĭbus
the army.   He gives   the business [task]   to the Senones

que   relĭquis   Gallis,   qui   ĕrant   finitĭmi
and   to the remaining   Gauls,   who   were   neighbors

Belgis,   ŭtì   cognoscant[4]   ĕa,   quæ
to the Belgæ,   that   they learn [ascertain]   these (things),   which

gerantur (pres. subj.)   ăpud   ĕos,   et   facĭant
are carried on [transpiring]   with   them,   and   may make

se   certiorem   de   his   rebus.   Omnes
himself   more certain [inform him]   about   these   things.   All

hi   constanter   nunciaverunt,   mănus
these   continually   reported,   (that)   bands

cogi,   exercĭtum   conduci
to be [were being] brought together,   an army   to be [was being]

in   unum   lŏcum.   Tum   verò
assembled   to   one   place.   Then   indeed

existimavit   non   dubitandum,[5]   quin
he thought (it) [he must]   not   to be hesitated [hesitate],   but that

proficisceretur   ad   ĕos.   Re   frumentariâ
he should set out   to   them.   The   grain supply

provisâ,   mŏvet   castra (pl.)   que
having been provided,   he moves (his)   camp   and

circĭter   quindĕcim   diebus   pervĕnit   ad
in about   fifteen   days   arrives   to [at]

fines   Belgarum.
the borders   of the Belgæ.

3. Quum   venisset (pl. perf. subj.)   ĕò   de
When   he had come   there   from

improviso   que   celerĭùs   opinione
unforseen [unexpectedly]   and   more quickly (than)   the opinion [belief]

omnĭum,   Remi,   qni   sunt   proxĭmi   ex
of all,   the Remi,   who   are   nearest   from [of]

Belgis   Gallĭæ,   miserunt   ad   ĕum   legatos,
the Belgæ   to Gaul,   sent   to   him   ambassadors,

Iccĭum   et   Andocombogĭum   primos   sŭæ
Iccius   and   Andocombogius   nrst (men)   of their

civitatis,   qui   dicĕrent,   "permittĕre[6]   se
state,   who   should say,   "to [that they] entrust   themselves

que omnĭa sŭa in fĭdem atque potestatem
and all their (effects) into [to] the faith and power

Romani popŭli, nĕque   se
of the Roman people, (that) neither (they) themselves

consensisse cum relĭquis Belgæ, nĕque
(to) have combined with the remaining Belgæ, nor

conjurâsse contra Romanum popŭlum, que
(to) have conspired against the Roman people, and (that)

esse paratos et dăre obsĭdes, et
to be [they are] prepared both to give hostages, and

facĕre imperata, et recipĕre oppĭdis
to do (the things) commanded, and to receive (them) in the towns

et juvare frumento que cætĕris rebus;
and to aid with corn and in other things [matters];

omnes relĭquos Belgas esse in armis:
(that) all the remaining Belgæ to be [are] in arms:

que Germanos, qui incŏlunt cis Rhenum
and the Germans, who dwell on this side the Rhine

conjunxisse sese cum his;   que
(to) have united themselves with these [Belgæ]; and

tantum esse furorem omnĭum eorum, ut[7]
so great to be [is] the fury of all of them, that

poturĕrint (perf. subj) deterrere ne Suessiones
they have been able to restrain not the Suessiones

quĭdem, sŭos fratres que consanguinĕos, qui
even, their brothers and kinsmen, who

utantur (pres. subj.) eodem jure, iisdem
use the same right, the same

legĭbus, habĕant (pres. subj.) unum imperĭum, que
laws, have one government, and

unum magistratum cum ipsis, quin
one magistracy with themselves, but that

consentirent cum his.
they should conspire with these.

4. Quum quærĕret (imp. subj.) ab his, quæ
When he was inquiring from these, what

civitates que quantæ essent (imp. subj.) in armis,
states and how great were in arms,

et   quid   possent (imp. subj.) in   bello,
and what   they were able   in   war,

reperiebat   sic;   plerosque   Belgas
he was acertaining thus; (that) the most of   the Belgæ

ortos-esse   Germanis   que   antiquĭtùs
(to) have sprung from the Germans and   of old

traductos Rhenum,   consedisse   ĭbi
(were) led over the Rhine, to [that they] have settled there

propter fertilitatem agri; que   expulisse
on account of the fertility of the land; and (to) have driven out

Gallos, qui incolĕrent (imp. subj.) ĕa lŏca; que
the Gauls, who were inhabiting   these places; and

esse solos,[8] qui, memorĭâ nostrorum patrum,
to be [are] alone, (those) who, in the memory of our fathers,

omni Gallĭâ vexatâ, prohibuĕrint (perf. subj.)
all Gaul having been harassed, prohibited

Teutŏnes que Cimbros ingrĕdi intra sŭos
the Teutones and Cimbri to enter within their

fines. Ex quâ re fiĕri ŭtì
borders. From which thing to be done [it resulted] that

sumĕrent (imp. subj.) magnam auctoritatem que
they were taking [assuming] great authority and

magnos spirĭtus in militari re sĭbi,
great spirits [airs] in military matters to themselves,

memorĭâ earum rerum. Remi dicebant
by the memory of these things. The Remi were saying

se habere omnĭa explorata de
(that) they themselves (to) have all (things) investigated about

numĕro eorum, proptereă quòd conjuncti
the number of them [their number], because (that) joined together

propinquitatĭbus (pl.) atque affinitatĭbus,
by kindship   and by marriage alliances,

cognovĕrint (perf. subj.) quantam multitudĭnem
they knew   how great a multitude

quisque pollicĭtus-sit (perf. subj.) in communi
each promised   in the common

concilĭo Belgarum ad id bellum. Bellovăcos[9]
council of the Belgæ to [for] this war. The Bellovacı

valere   plurĭmum   inter   ĕos,   et   virtute,   et
(to) prevail   most   among   them,   both   in valor,   and

auctoritate,   et   numĕro   homĭnum;   hos   posse
in authority,   and   in the number   of men;   these   to be [are] able

conficĕre   centum   millĭa   armata;
to convene [muster]   a hundred   thousand   armed (men);

pollicĭtos   sexaginta   millĭa   electa
having [that they had] promised   sixty   thousand   chosen

ex   ĕo   numĕro,   que   postulare
from   this   number,   and   to demand [demanded]

imperĭum   belli   sĭbi.   Suessiones   esse
the control   of the war   for themselves.   The Suessiones   to be [are]

sŭos   finitĭmos;   possidere   latissĭmos   que
their   neighbors;   to (they) possess   the most broad   and

feracissĭmos   agros;   Divitiăcum   fuisse   rĕgem
most productive   lands;   Divitiacus   to have [has] been   king

ăpud   ĕos,   potentissĭmum   totius   Gallĭæ,
with [over]   them,   the most powerful   of entire   Gaul,

etĭam   nostrâ   memorĭâ,   qui   cùm   obtinuĕrit
even   in our   memory,   who   not only   had held

(perf. subj.)   imperĭum   magnæ   partis   harum
the empire   of a great   part   of these

regionum,   tum   etĭam   Britannĭæ;   Galbam
regions,   but also   even   of Britain;   Galba

nunc   esse   regem;   summam
now   to be [is]   (their) king;   the sum [chief command]

totius   belli   deferri   ad   hunc
of the whole   war   to be [was] conferred   to (on)   this (man)

voluntate   omnĭum;   habere   duodĕcim   oppĭda
by the will   of all;   to have [they have]   twelve   towns

numĕro,   polliceri   quinquaginta   millĭa
in number,   and (to) promise   fifty   thousand

armata: Nervĭos,   totĭdem,   qui   habeantur
armed (men):   the Nervii,   just as many,   who   are held [deemed]

(pres. subj.)   maxĭmè fĕri   inter   ipsos   que   absint
the most fierce   among   them   and   are distant

(pres. subj.)   longissĭmè;   Atrebătes,   quindĕcim
farthest;   the Atrebates,   fifteen

millĭa;   Ambianos,   decem   millĭa;   Morĭnos,
thousand;   the Ambiani,   ten   thousand;   the Morini,

viginti quinque millĭa: Menapĭos, novem millĭa;
twenty   five   thousand: the Menapii, nine thousand;

Calĕtos   decem   millĭa;   Veliocasses   et
the Caleti   ten   thousand;   the Veliocasses   and

Veromandŭos totĭdem; Aduatucos, viginti nŏvem
Veromandui just as many; the Aduatuci, twenty nine

millĭa;   arbitrari Condrusos, Eburones, Cærosos,
thousand; to [they] believe the Condrusi, Eburones, Cærosi,

Pæmanos, qui appellantur uno nomĭne Germani,
Pæmani, who are called by one name German,

ad   quadraginta millĭa.
(promise), to [about] forty thousand.

5. Cæsar, cohortatus[10]   Remos,   que
Cæsar, having encouraged the Remi, and

prosecutus liberalĭter oratione, jussit
having followed up liberally [kindly] with a speech, ordered

omnem senatum convenire ad se, que
all (their) senate to assemble to himse'f and

libĕros princĭpum adduci obsĭdes ad
(that) the children of the chiefs (to) be brought (as) hostages to

se. Omnĭa quæ facta-sunt diligenter
him(self). All which (things) were done exactly

ab his ad dĭem. Ipse cohortatus
by these to the day. He himself having encouraged

magnopĕre Ædŭum Divitiacum, dŏcet
very greatly [earnestly] the Æduan Diviiacus, shows

quantopĕre intersit (pres. subj.) rei publĭcæ (gen.)
how greatly it concerns the republic

que communis salutis, manus hostĭum
and the common safety, (that) the bands of the enemy

distineri, ne sit[11] configendum uno tempŏre
(to) be separated, lest it must be fought at one time

cum tantâ multitudĭne; id posse
with so great a multitude; that it to be able [could

fiĕri, si Ædŭi introduxĕrint (perf. subj.)
to) be done, if the Ædui should introduce

sŭas   copĭas   in   fines   Bellovacorum   et
their   forces   into   the borders   of the Bellovaci   and

cœpĕrint (perf. subj.) populari agros eorum.
should begin   to ravage the lands of them [their lands].

His   mandatis,   dimittit[12]   ĕum   ab
These (things)   having been enjoined,   he dismisses   him   from

se.   Postquam   cognovit   ab   his exploratorĭbus,
himself.   After that   he knew   from   these   scouts,

quos   misĕrat,   et   ab   Remis,   omnes   copĭas
whom   he had sent,   and   from   the Remi,   (that) all   the forces

Belgarum   coactas   in   unum   lŏcum
of the Belgæ   (having been) collected   into   one   place

venire   ad   se,   nĕque   jam
to come [were coming]   to   him(self),   nor   now

abesse[13]   longè;   maturavit   traducĕre
to be [were] distant   far;   he hastened   to take over

flumen   Axŏnam,   quod   est   in   extremis
the river   Axona,   which   is   in   the extreme [remotest]

finibus   Remorum,   exercĭtum,   atque   ĭbi
borders   of the Remi,   the army,   and   there

posŭit   castra (pl.).   Quæ   res   et
pitched   (his) camp.   Which   thing [action]   both

muniebat   unum   lătus   castrorum (pl.)   ripĭs
was fortifying   one   side   of the camp   by the banks

flumĭnis   et   reddebat   ĕa
of the river   and   was rendering   these (things)

quæ   ĕrant   pòst,   tuta   ab   hostĭbus,   et
which   were   behind,   safe   from   the enemy,   and

efficiebat   ut   commeatus   possent
was effecting   that   provisions   might be able [could]

portari   ad   ĕum   ab   Remis,   que
(to) be carried   to   him   from   the Remi,   and

relĭquis   civitatĭbus   sĭne   pericŭlo.   Pons   ĕrat
the remaining   states   without   danger.   A bridge   was

in   ĕo   flumĭne;   ĭbi   ponit   præsidĭum,
on   this   river;   there   he places   a guard,

et   reliquit   Quintum Titurĭum Sabinum   legatum
and   left   Quintus   Titurius   Sabinus   (his) lieutenant

in   altĕrâ   parte   flumĭnis   cum   sex cohortĭbus;
on   the other part [side] of the river with   six   cohorts;

jŭbet   munire   castra (pl.)   vallo   in
he orders (him) to fortify   the camp   with a rampart   into [in]

altitudĭnem   duodĕcim   pĕdum   que   fossâ
height   (of) twelve   feet   and   with a trench

duodeviginti   pĕdum.
(of) eighteen   feet (deep).

6. Oppĭdum   Remorum,   nomĭne   Bibrax,   abĕrat
   A town   of the Remi,   by name   Bibrax,   was distant

octo   millĭa   passŭum   ab   castris   ipsis (pl.);
eight   thousand   (of) paces   from   the camp   itself;

Belgæ   cœperunt oppugnare id   magno   impĕtu
the Belgæ   began   to assault   it   with great   violence

ex   itinĕre: sustentatum est   ægrè
from [on] the march: it [the assault] was sustained   hardly

ĕo   dĭe.   Eădem   oppugnatĭo   Gallorum   atque
on this   day.   The same   assault   of the Gauls   and

Belgarum   est   haec: Hi,   ŭbi,   multitudĭne
of the Belgæ   is   this: These,   when,   a multitude

homĭnum   circumjectâ   totis   mœnĭbus (dat.),
of men   having been thrown around the whole   wall,

lapĭdes   cœpti-sunt   jăci   in   murum
stones   were begun   to be thrown   against   the wall

undĭque   que   murus   nudatus-est   defensorĭbus;
on all sides   and   the wall   was stripped   from defenders

testudĭne   factâ,   succedunt   portis (dat.)
a testudo   having been formed,   approach   the gates

que   subrŭunt   murum.   Quod   tum   fiebat
and   undermine   the wall.   Which   then   was done

facĭlè.   Nam   cum   tanta[14]   multitudo   conjiciebant
easily.   For   when   so great   a multitude   were hurling

lapĭdes   ac   tela,   protestas   consistendi   in
stones   and   darts,   a power [ability]   of standing   on

muro   erat   nulli.   Quum   nox   fecisset
the wall   was   to none.   When   night   had made

(pl. perf. subj.) finem   oppugnandi,   Remus   Iccĭus,
                an end   of assaulting ,   the Remian   Iccius,

summâ   nobilitate   et   gratîâ   inter
with [of the] highest   nobility   and   favor   among

sŭos,   qui tum præĕrat   oppĭdo,   unus   ex
his own (people),   who then commanded (to) the town,   one   from [of]

Iis,   qui venĕrant ad   Cæsărem   legati
those,   who   had come   to   Cæsar   (as) ambassadors

de   pace,   mittit   nuntĭos   ad   ĕum,   nĭsi
about   peace,   sends   messengers   to   him,   unless

subsidĭum   submittatur (pres. subj.)   sĭbi,   se
aid   is sent   to him(self),   he himself

posse   nor   sustinere diutĭùs.
to be able [could]   not   (to) hold out   longer.

7. Eò   de medĭâ nocte, Cæsar   usus
   Thither about mid   night,   Cæsar   having used

iisdem   ducĭbus, qui venĕrant   nuntĭi   ab
the same   guides,   who   had come   (as) messengers   from

Iccĭo,   mittit   Numĭdas   et   Cretas sagittarĭos
'ccir,   sends   the Numidian   and   Cretan   archers

et Baleares funditores   subsidĭo   oppidanıs.
and   Balearic   slingers for a reinforcement   to the townsmen.

Adventu   quorum,   et   studĭum   propugnandi
By the arrival   of whom,   both   a zeal   of resisting

cum   spe   defensionis   accessit
with   a hope   of defence   approached

Remis (dat.),   et   de   eâdem   causâ   spes
the Remi,   and   from   the same   cause   the hope

potiundi   oppĭdi   discessit   hostĭbus.
of gaining   the town   departed from [left]   the enemy.

Ităque   morati   paulisper   ăpud   oppĭdum
Therefore   having delayed   a little while   at   the town

que   depopulati   agros   Remorum,   omnĭbus
and   having laid waste   the lands   of the Remi,   all

vicis   que   ædificĭis   incensis,   quò
the villages   and   buildings   having been burnt,   where

potĕrant   adire,   contenderunt
they were able   to approach,   they strove [hastened]

ad castra (pl.) Cæsăris cum omnĭbus   copĭis,
to   the camp   of Cæsar   with   all   (their) forces.

et   posuerunt   castra (pl.)   à   mĭnùs   duobus
and   pitched (their)   camp   from [at] less   than two

millĭbus   passŭum,   quæ   castra (pl.)   ut
thousand   (of) paces,   which   camp   as

significabatur   fumo   atque   ignĭbus,   patebant
was indicated   by smoke   and   by fires,   was extending

in   latitudĭnem   amplĭus   octo   millĭbus
into [in]   breadth   more   (than) eight thousand

passŭum.
(of) paces.

8. Cæsar   primò   statŭit   supersedĕre
Cæsar   at first   determined   to defer

prœlĭo (abl.)   et   propter   multitudĭnem
a battle   both   on account of   the multitude

hostĭum   et   propter   eximĭam   opinionem
of the enemy   and   on account of   the extraordinary   reputation

virtutis ;   tămen   periclitabatur   quotidĭe
of (their) valor ;   yet   he was making trial   daily

equestrĭbus   prœlĭis,   quid   hostis   posset
in cavalry   battles,   what   the enemy might be able

virtute,   et   quid   nostri   auderent.   Ubi
in valor,   and   what   our (men) might dare.   When

intellexit   nostros   esse   non   inferiores,
he understood (that) our (men) to be [were] not   inferior,

lŏco   pro   castris (pl.)   opportuno   atque
the place   before   the camp   (being) favorable   and

idonĕo[15]   naturâ   ad   instruendam   acĭem ;   quòd
suitable   by nature   for   drawing up   the line ;   because

is   collis   ŭbi   castra (pl.)   posita-ĕrant,   edĭtus
this   hill   where   the camp   had been placed,   being raised

paullŭlum   ex   planitĭe,   patebat   in
a little   from   the plain,   was extending   into [in]

latitudĭnem   adversus   tantum   lŏci,   quantum
breadth   opposite   so much   of place [distance]   as

acĭes   instructa   potĕrat   occupare   atque
the line (of battle),   arrayed,   was able   to occupy,   and

habebat   dejectus   latĕris   ex   utrâque
was having   descents   of the side   from [on]   either

parte, et lenĭter fastigiatus in fronte, paullatim
part [hand], and gently sloping in front, gradually

redibat ad planitĭem : ab utroque latĕre
was returning to the plain : from each side

ejus collis obduxit transversam fossam circĭter
of this hill he led over a transverse trench about

quadringentorum passŭum, et ad extremas
(of) four hundred paces, and at the extreme [both ends of]

fossas constitŭit castella, que ĭbi collocavit
the trenches he planted redoubts, and there placed

tormenta; ne, quum instruxisset (pl. perf. subj.)
engines; lest, when he had arrayed

acĭem, hostes (quòd potĕrant tantum
(his) battle line, the enemy (because they were able so much

multitudĭne) possent circumvenire à
by (their) multitude) might be able [could] (to) surround from [on]

laterĭbus sŭos pugnantes. Hoc facto,
the flanks his (men) fighting. This having been done,

duabus legionĭbus, quas conscripsĕrat proxĭmè,
two legions, which he had levied last,

relictis in castris (pl.), ut, si quid ŏpus
having been left in camp, that, if any need

esset possent duci subsidĭo,[16] constitŭit
should be, they might be able to be led for reinforcement, he formed

relĭquas sex legiones in acĭe pro castris (pl.).
the remaining six legions in battle line before the camp.

Item hostes instruxĕrant sŭas copĭas eductas
Likewise the enemy had drawn up their forces led forth

ex castris (pl.).
from the camp.

9. Pălus non magna ĕrat inter nostrum atque
A marsh not great was between our (men) and

exercĭtum hostĭum; hostes expectabant, si
the army of the enemy; the enemy were awaiting, if

nostri transirent hanc; autem nostri ĕrant
our (men) would cross over this; but our (men) were

parati in armis ut, si initĭum transeundi
prepared in arms that, if a beginning of crossing

fĭĕret   ab   illis,[17]   aggrederentur   impeditos.
should be made   by   those (forces)   they might attack (them)   entangled.

Intĕrim   contendebatur[18]   equestri   prœlĭo
Meanwhile   there was fighting   in a cavalry   battle

inter   dŭas   acĭes.   Ubi   neutri   facĭunt
between   the two   lines.   When   neither   make

initĭum   transeundi,   prœlĭo   nostrorum   equĭtum
a beginning   of crossing,   the battle   of our   horsemen

secundiore,   Cæsar   reduxit   sŭos   in
(being) more successful,   Cæsar   led back   his (men)   into

castra (pl.).   Hostes   protĭnus   contenderunt
the camp.   The enemy   forthwith   strained [hastened]

ex   ĕo   lŏco   ad   flumen   Axŏnam,   quod
from   that   place   to   the river   Axona,   which it

demonstratum-est   esse   post   nostra   castra (pl.);   ibi
has been shown   to be [is]   behind   our   camp;   there

vadis   repertis,   conati-sunt   traducĕre
fords   being found,   they endeavored   to lead over

partem   suarum   copiarum,   ĕo   consilĭo,   ut,
part   of their   forces,   with this   design,   that,

si   possent,   expugnarent   castellum,
if   they should be able,   they might storm   the fortress,

cui   Q. Titurĭus   legatus   præĕrat,   que
over which   Q. Titurius   the lieutenant   held command,   and

interscindĕrent   pontem: si   mĭnùs,   popula-
might cut down   the bridge: if   less [not],   they might

rentur   agros   Remorum,   qui   ĕrat   magno
ravage   the lands   of the Remi,   which   were   for [of] great

usŭi   nobis   ad   gerendum   bellum[19]   que
use   to us   for   carrying on   the war   and

prohibĕrent[20]   nostrŏs   commeătŭ.
were cutting off   our (men)   from supplies.

10. Cæsar   factus   certĭor   à Titurĭo,
Cæsar   being made   more certain [informed]   by   Titurius,

traducit   pontem   omnem   equitatum,   et   Numĭdas
leads over   the bridge   all   the cavalry,   and   Numidians

lĕvis[21]   armaturæ,   funditores   que   sagittarĭos,   atque
of light   armor   the slingers   and   archers,   and

contendit   ad   ĕos.   Pugnatum-est   acrĭter[22]   in
strains [hastens]   to   them.   It was fought   sharply   in

ĕo   lŏco: nostri   aggressi   hostes
this   place: our (men)   having attacked   the enemy

impeditos in flumĭne, occiderunt magnum numĕrum
entangled in the river.   slew   a great   number

eorum: repulerunt   multitudĭne   telorum
of them;   they [our men] repulsed with a multitude of weapons

relĭquos   conantes   audacissĭmè   transire
the remaining (men) endeavoring   most boldly   to cross

per   corpŏra eorum: interfecerunt primos, qui
among   the bodies of those (slain);   they killed   the first, who

transiĕrant, circumventos   equitatu.   Hostes (pl.),
had passed,   surrounded   by cavalry.   The enemy

ŭbi intellexerunt spem[23]   fefellisse   se
when they understood hope to have [had] deceived themselves [them]

et de expugnando oppĭdo, et de transeundo
both of   storming   the town,   and of   crossing

flumĭne, nĕque   viderunt   nostros   progrĕdi
the river,   nor   saw   our (men)   advance

in   iniquiorem   lŏcum   causâ
into   a more unequal (disadvantageous)   place   for the sake

pugnandi, atque frumentarĭa   res   cœpit
of fighting,   and   corn   thing [provisions] began

deficĕre ĕos; concilĭo   convocato,   constituto fail   them; a council   having been convened,   they

erunt   esse optĭmum quemque reverti sŭam
resolved it was best (for)   each   to return   (to) his

dŏmum: et   convenire   undĭque   ad   defend-
home: and   to assemble   from all sides for   defend-

endos,[24]   ĕos   in   fines   quorum   Romani
ing,   those into the borders of whom the Romans

primùm introduxissent exercĭtum; ut   decertarent
first   should lead on   the army;   that they might contend

potĭùs in   sŭis,   quàm alienis   finĭbus, et
rather   in   their own,   than in foreign borders,   and

uterentur domesticis copĭis (abl.) frumentarĭæ rĕi.
might use   domestic   supplies   of corn   thing

Quŏque　hæc　ratĭo,　cum　relĭquis
[provisions].　Also　this　reason,　with　remaining [other]

causis,　deduxit　ĕos　ad　ĕam　sententĭam,
causes,　led　them　to　this　opinion [resolution],

quŏd　cognovĕrant　Divitiăcum　atque　Ædŭos
because　they had known　Divitiacus　and　the Ædui

appropinquare[25]　finĭbus　Bellovacorum.　Potĕrat
(to) approach　(to) the borders　of the Bellovaci.　It was possible

non　persuaderi　his,　ut　morarentur
not　to (be) persuaded [persuade]　(to) these,　that　they should delay

diutĭùs,　neque　ferrent　auxilĭum　suis. [26]
longer,　nor　should bring　aid　to their (countrymen).

11. Eâ　re　constitutâ,　secundâ　vigilĭâ,
This　thing　being resolved,　in the second　watch,

egressi　castris　cum　magno　strepĭtu
having gone out　from camp　with　great　noise

ac　tumultu,　nullo　certo　ordĭne　nĕque　imperĭo,
and　tumult,　with no　certain　order　nor　command,

quum　quisque　petĕret (imp. subj.)　primum
since　each　was seeking　the first

lŏcum　itinĕris　sĭbi,　et　properaret (imp. subj.)
place　of the road for　himself,　and　was hastening

pervenire　dŏmum,　fecerunt,　ut　profectĭo
to reach　(to) home,　they did [acted] so,　that　(their) departure

videretur (imp. subj.)　consimĭlis　fŭgæ.　Hâc
was seeming　very like　(to) a flight.　This

re　stătim　cognĭta　per　speculatores,
thing　immediately　being known　through　scouts,

Cæsar　verĭtus　insidĭas,　quŏd　per-
Cæsar　having feared　snares,　because　he had

spexĕrat[27]　nondum　de　quâ　causâ　disced-
seen clearly　not yet　on [for]　what　cause　they were

ĕrent (imp. subj.)　continŭit　exercĭtum,　qœe
departing　held　the army,　and

equitatum　castris.　Primâ　luce,[28]　re
cavalry　in camp.　At the first　light　the thing [fact]

confirmatâ　ab　exploratorĭbus,　præmisit
being confirmed　by　scouts,　he sent before

omnem	equitatum,	qui	moraretur
all	the cavalry,	which	should delay [detain]

novissĭmum	agmen.	His	præfecit	Quintum
the last	troop [rear].	Over them	(he) appointed	Quintus

Pedĭum,	et	Lucĭum	Aurunculeĭum	Cottam
Pedius,	and	Lucius	Aurunculeius	Cotta

legatos	ĕi :		jussit Titum Labienum
lieutenants	to him [his lieutenants]:	he ordered	Titus Labienus

legatum	subsĕqui	cum	trĭbus	legionĭbus.
the lieutenant	to follow close	with	three	legions.

Hi	adorti	novissimos	et	prosecuti
These,	having attacked	the last [rear]	and	having pursued

	multa	millĭa	passŭum,	conciderunt	magnam
(them)	many	thousand	(of) paces,	cut up	a great

multitudĭnem	eorum	fugentĭum.	Quum	hi	ab
multitude	of them	fleeing	When	those	from [on]

extremo	agmĭne,	ad	quos	ventum-ĕrat,[29]
the last	troop [rear],	to	whom	it had been [they had] come,

consistĕrent (imp. subj.),	que	sustinerent (imp. subj.)
were standing together	and	were sustaining

fortĭter	impĕtum	nostrorum	milĭtum ;	priores,
bravely	the attack	of our	soldiers ;	the former [the

	quòd	viderentur (imp. subj.)	abesse	à
van].	because	they seemed	to be distant	from

pericŭlo,	nĕque	continerentur (imp. subj.)	ullâ
danger,	nor	were held together	by any

necessitate	nĕque	imperĭo,	clamore	exaudito,
necessity	nor	command,	the din	being heard,

ordinĭbus	perturbatis,		omnes	ponerent
the ranks	being disturbed [confused],		all	put

præsidĭum	sĭbi	in	fŭgâ.	Ita	sĭne	ullo
protection	for themselves	in	flight.	Thus	without	any

pericŭlo	nostri	interfecerunt	tantam	multitudĭnem
danger	our (men)	killed	so great	a multitude

eorum,	quantum	spatĭum[30]	diei	fŭit ;	que
of them,	as	the space	of the day	was [permitted];	and

sub	occasum	solis	destiterunt
under [just before]	the going down	of the sun	they ceased

sequi,   que receperunt   se   in   castra,   ŭtĭ
to follow,   and   betook   themselves   into   camp,   as

imperatum-ĕrat.
it had been commanded.

12. Postridĭe   ejus   diei, priùs-quàm   hostes (pl.)
     The day after   this   day,   before (that)   the enemy

recipĕrent   se   ex   terrore   ac   fŭgâ,
might recover   themselves   from   terror   and   flight,

Cæsar   duxit   exercĭtum   in   fines   Suessi-
Cæsar   led   (his) army   into   the borders   of the Suessi-

onum,   qui   ĕrat   proxĭmi   Remis;   et
ones,   who   were   nearest   to the Remi;   and

magno   itinĕre   confecto,   contendit   ad
a great   march   having been completed,   he hastened   to

oppĭdum,   Noviodunum.   Conatus   oppugnare
the town,   Noviodunum.   Having attempted   to storm

id   ex   itinĕre,   quòd   audiebat
this   from   the way [on his march],   because   he was hearing

esse   vacŭum   ab   defensorĭbus,   potŭit[31]
(it) to be [was]   clear   from [of]   defenders,   he was able

non   expugnare   propter   latitudĭnem   fossæ,
not   to storm (it)   on account of   the breadth   of the ditch,

que   altitudĭnem   muri,   paucis   defendentĭbus.[32]
and   the height   of the wall,   few (men)   defending (it).

Castris (pl.)   munitis   cœpit   agĕre   vinĕas,
The camp   having been fortified   he began   to drive [push]   the sheds,

que   comparare   quæ   ĕrant   usŭi
and   to prepare   (the things) which   were   for use

ad   oppugnandum.[33]   Intĕrim   omnis   multitudo
for   storming.   Meanwhile   all   the multitude

Suessionum   convĕnit   ex   fŭgâ   in
of the Suessiones   comes together [gathers]   from   flight   into

oppĭdum   proxĭmâ   nocte. Vinĕis   actis
the town   on the nearest [next] night. The sheds   having been pushed

celerĭter   ad   oppĭdum, aggĕre   jacto,   que
quickly   to   the town,   a mound   having been thrown up,   and

turrĭbus   constitutis, Galli   permoti
towers   (having been) erected,   the Gauls   much moved [alarmed]

magnitudĭne — by the vastness | opĕrum, — of the works, | quæ — which | nĕque — neither | vidĕrant — they had seen

antè — before | nĕque — nor | audiĕ⸳ant, — had heard (of), | et — and | celeritate — by the quickness

Romanorum, — of the Romans, | mittunt — send | legatos — ambassadors | ad — to | Cæsărem — Cæsar

de — about | deditione; — a surrender; | et, — and, | Remis — the Remi | petentĭbus, — seeking [petitioning],

ut — that | conservarentur,[34] — they may be preserved, | impĕtrant. — they obtain (it).

13. Cæsar — Cæsar | obsidĭbus — hostages | acceptis — having been received | primis — the first (men)

civitatis, — of the state, | atque — and | duobus — two | filĭis — sons | regis — of king | Galbæ — Galba

ipsius que — himself and | omnĭbus — all | armis — arms | tradĭtis — having been delivered | ex — from | oppĭdo, — the town,

Cæsar — Cæsar | accipit — received | Suessiones — the Suessiones | in — into | deditionem;[35] — a surrender; | que — and

duxit — led | exercĭtum — the army | in — among | Bellovăcos: — the Bellovaci: | qui — and | quum — when

contulissent (pl. perf. subj.) — they had brought together | se — themselves | que — and | omnĭa — all

sŭa — their (things) | in — into | oppĭdum — the town | Bratuspantĭum, — Bratuspantium, | atque — and

Cæsar, — Cæsar, | cum — with | exercĭtu, — the army, | abesset (imp. subj.) — was distant | ab — from

ĕo — this | oppĭdo — town | circĭter — about | quinque — five | millĭa — thousand | passŭum, — (of) paces,

omnes — all | majores — (the) greater | natu — by birth [the elders] | egressi — having gone out | ex — from

oppĭdo, — the town, | cœperunt — began | tendĕre — to stretch | mănus — (their) hands | ad — to

Cæsărem, — Cæsar, | significare — to signify | voce, — by voice, | sese — (that they) themselves | venire — (to) come

in — into | ejus — his | fĭdem — faith [protection] | ac — and | potestatem — power | nĕque — nor

contendĕre — (to) contend | contra — against | Romanum — the Roman | popŭlum — people | armis:[36] — with arms:

Ĭtem,   quum   accessisset (pl. perf. subj.) ad oppĭdum,
also,   when   he had approached   to   the town,

que   ponĕret (imp. subj.) castra (pl.) ĭbi,   puĕri que
and   was placing [pitching]   (his) camp   there,   the boys   and

mulieres   ex   muro,   manĭbus   passis,   sŭo
women   from   the wall.   (with) hands   stretched out,   by their

more,   petierunt   pacem   à   Romanis.
custom,   sought   peace   from   the Romans.

14. Divitiăcus   făcit   verba   pro   his   (nam
    Divitiacus   makes   words [intercedes] for   these   (for

post   discessum   Belgarum,   copĭis   Æduorum
after   the departure   of the Belgæ,   the forces   of the Ædui

    dimissis,   revertĕrat   ad   ĕum):
having been sent away,   he had returned   to   him [Cæsar]);

Bellovăcos omni tempŏre   fuisse   in   fĭde
the Bellovaci   in [for] all   time   (to) have been   in   the faith [confidence]

atque   amicitĭâ   Ædŭæ   civitatis;   impulsos à
and   friendship   of the Æduan   state;   impelled by

sŭis   principĭbus,   qui   dicĕrent (imp. subj.)   Ædŭos
their   chiefs,   who   were saying   the Ædui,

redactos   in   servitutem à Cæsăre,   perferre   omnes
reduced   into   servitude   by   Cæsar,   (to) endure   all

indignitates   que contumelĭas, et   defecisse   ab
indignities   and   outrages,   (both)   (to) have revolted   from

Ædŭis, et   intulisse   bellum   Romano   popŭlo.[37]
the Ædui,   and   have waged   war   upon the Roman   people.

    Qui   fuissent (pl. perf. subj.)   prĭncipes   hujus
(Those) who   had been   chiefs [authors]   of this

consilĭi,   quòd   intelligĕrent (imp. subj.)   quantam
counsel,   because   they understood   how great

calamitatem   intulissent (pl. perf. subj.) civitati (dat),
a calamity   they had brought on   the state,

profugisse   in Britannĭam. Non solùm Bellovăcos
to have [had] fled   into   Britain.   Not   only   the Bellovaci

    petĕre,   sed   etĭam   Ædŭos,   pro   his,
to seek [entreated]   but   also   the Ædui,   for   these

ut   utatur   sŭâ   clementĭâ   ac   mansuetudĭne (abl.)
that   he may use his   clemency   and   mildness

in   ĕos :   quod   si   fecĕrit,   amplificaturum
towards   them :   which if   he shall have done, about to [it would]

        auctoritatem   Æduorum   ăpud   omnes
enlarge the authority   of the Ædui at [among]   all

Belgas,   auxilis   atque   opĭbus   quorum
the Belgæ,   by the troops and   resources   of whom

        consuevĕrint (perf. subj.)   sustentare,[38]   si
they have been accustomed   to endure,   if

qua   bella   incidĕrint.
any   wars   may have happened [occurred].

15. Cæsar,   causâ   honoris   Divi-
     Cæsar,   for the sake   of the honor   of Divi-

tiăci   atque   Æduorum,   dixit   sese
tiacus and   of the Ædui, said   (that he) himself

recepturum   ĕos   in   fĭdem   et
about to [would] receive them into faith [allegiance]   and

conservaturum;   et   quòd   civĭtas   ĕrat
about to [would] preserve (them); and because the state was

magna   et   præstabat   inter Belgas   auctoritate
great   and   it was excelling among the Belgæ   in authority

ac   multitudĭne homĭnum,   proposcit   sex-centos
and in multitude of men,   he required   six hundred

obsĭdes : his   tradĭtis   que omnĭbus   armis
hostages : these having been delivered and   all   (their) arms

        collatis   ex   oppĭdo, pervenit ab   ĕo
(having been) brought together out of the town, he passed from this

lŏco   in   fines   Ambianorum,   qui   dediderunt
place into   the borders of the Ambiani,   who   surrendered

se   que   omnĭa   sŭa   sĭne   mŏrâ.
themselves and   all   their (possessions)   without delay.

Nervĭi   attingebant   fines   eorum :   de
The Nervii were touching upon the borders of them [their borders]: con-

        naturâ   que   morĭbus quorum,   quum   Cæsar
cerning the nature   and   manners of whom,   when   Cæsar

quærĕret (imp. subj.),   reperiebat   sic ;   nullum
was inquiring,   he ascertained thus :   no

adĭtum   esse   mercatorĭbus   ad   ĕos :   pằti
access   to be [was] for merchants   to   them :   to (they) suffer

nĭhil   vini,   que reliquarum rerum pertinentĭum
nothing [no]   (of) wine,   and (of) remaining   things   tending

ad   luxurĭam,   inferri :   quòd
to   luxury,   to be brought in [imported]:   because

existimarent (imp. subj.)   anĭmos   eorum
they thought (that)   the minds   of them [their minds]

relanguescĕre,   que   virtutem   remitti
(to) grow feeble,   and   (their) virtue [valor]   to be [is] relaxed

his   rebus :   homĭnes   esse   fĕros,   que   magnæ
by these   things :   the men   to be [are]   fierce,   and   of great

virtutis :   increpitare   atque   incusare   relĭquos
valor :   to (they) upbraid   and   (to) blame   the remaining

Belgas,   qui   dedissent   (pl. perf. subj.)   se
Belgæ,   who   had surrendered   themselves

Romano   popŭlo,   que projecissent (pl. perf. subj.)
to the Roman   people,   and   had cast aside

patrĭam   virtutem ;   confirmare,
(their) native   virtue [national honor];   to (they) affirm (that they),

se   nĕque   missuros   legatos,   nĕque
themselves   neither   about to [would] send   ambassadors,   nor

accepturos   ullam   conditionem   pacis.[39]
about to [would] receive   any   condition   of peace.

16. Quum   fecisset (pl. perf. subj.)   ĭter   tridŭo
    When   he had made   a journey   of three days

per   fines   eorum,   inveniebat
through   the borders   of them [their borders],   he was learning

ex   captivis,   flumen   Sabin   abesse   ab
from   the captives,   (that) the river   Sabis   to be [was] distant   from

sŭis   castris   non   amplĭùs   decem   millĭa
his   camp   not   more   (than)   ten   thousand

passŭum :   omnes   Nervĭos   consedisse
(of) paces :   (that) all   the Nervii   to have [had] halted

trans   id   flumen,   que   ĭbi   unà   cum
beyond   this   river,   and   there   together   with

Atrebatĭbus   et   Veromandŭis,   sŭis   finitĭmis,
the Atrebates   and   Veromandui,   their   neighbors,

expectare   adventum   Romanorum ;   nam
to [were] awaiting   the arrival   of the Romans ;   for

persuasĕrant   utrisque   his,[40]   ut   experirentur
they had persuaded   both   these,   that   they should try

eandem   fortunam   belli;   etĭam   copĭas
the same   fortune   of war: also   (that) the forces

Aduatucorum   expectari   ab   his,
of the Aduatuci   to be waited for [were expected]   by   these,

atque   esse   in   ĭtinĕre:
and (that they)   to be [were]   on   the way [march]:

conjecisse   mulĭĕres,   que
to have [that they had] thrown [put] together   the women,   and

qui   per   ætatem   viderentur (imp. subj.)
(those) who   through   age   were seeming

inutĭles   ad   pugnam,   in   ĕum   lŏcum,   quŏ
useless   for   a battle,   into   this   place,   in which

propter   paludes   adĭtus   non   esset   exercitŭi.[41]
on account of   the marshes   access   might not   be   for an army.

17. His   rebus   cognĭtis,   Cæsar   præmittit
These   things   having been known,   Cæsar   sends forward

exploratores,   que   centuriones,   qui   delĭgant
scouts,   and   centurions,   who   may choose

lŏcum   idonĕum   castris: que   quum   complures
a place   suitable   for camp: and   since   many

ex   Belgis   que   relĭquis   Gallis
from   the Belgæ   and   remaining   Gauls

deditĭtĭis,   secuti   Cæsărem,   facĕrent
(who had) surrendered,   having followed   Cæsar,   made

(imp. subj.)   ĭter   unà: quidam   ex
(their) way   together: certain ones   from [among]

his,   ut   postĕa   cognĭtum-est   ex   captivis,
these,   as   afterwards   it was known   from   the captives,

consuetudĭne   itinĕris   nostri   exercĭtûs
the custom   of the journey [march]   of our   army

eorum   dierum   perspectâ,   pervenerunt   nocte
of those   days   being fully seen.   repaired   by night

ad   Nervĭos   atque   demonstraverunt   ĭis
to   the Nervii   and   showed   to them (that)

magnum   numĕrum   impedimentorum   intercedĕre
a great   number   of baggage wagons   (to) come between

inter   singŭlas   legiones;   nĕque
[intervened]   between   the several   legions;   nor

esse   quidquam   negotĭi,[42]   cùm   prima
to be [was] (there) any thing   of business [any difficulty],   when   the first

legĭo   venisset   in   castris,   que   relĭquæ
legion   had come   into   camp,   and   the remaining

legiones   abessent   magnum   spatĭum,   adoriri
legions   were distant   a great   space [way],   to attack

hanc   sub   sarcĭnis: quâ   pulsâ,   que
this (one)   under   packs [baggage]:   which   being routed,   and

impedimentis   direptis,   futurum,[43]
the baggage wagons   having been plundered,   about to [it would] be,

ut   relĭquæ   non   auderent consistĕre
that   the remaining (legions)   would not   dare   to stand

contrà.   Etĭam adjuvabat consilĭum eorum,
against [in opposition].   Also   it was aiding   the design   of these,

qui   deferebant   rem,   quòd   Nervĭi
who   were proffering   the thing [plan],   because   the Nervii

antiquĭtùs,   quum   possent (imp. subj.) nĭhil
anciently,   since   they were able (to do)   nothing

equitatu,   (ĕnim   nĕque   ad   hoc   tempus
with cavalry,   (for   neither   to   this   time

stŭdent   ĕi   rĕi,   sed,   quidquid   possunt,
are they zealous   for this   thing,   but, (in) whatever   they are able.

vălent   pedestrĭbus copĭis,)   quò   impedirent
they are strong   in foot   forces,)   that   they might hinder

facilĭùs   equitatum   finitimorum,   si   venissent
more easily   the cavalry   of (their) neighbors,   if   they might come

ad   ĕos   causâ   prædandi,   tenĕris arborĭbus
to   them   for the sake of   robbing,   pliant   trees

incisis   atque   inflexis,   que   crebris   ramis
being cut   and   bent in,   and   thick   boughs

enatis   in   latitudĭnem,   et   rŭbis
having sprouted forth   into   breadth [sidewise],   and   brambles

que   sentĭbus   interjectis,   effecĕrant,
and   thorns   having been cast between,   they had brought to pass,

ut   hæ   sæpes   præberent (imp. subj.) munimenta
that   these   hedges   were affording   fortifications

instar muri; quò posset (imp. subj.) non mŏdò
like a wall; where it was possible not only

non intrari, sed ne perspĭci[44] quĭdem.
not to be entered, but not to be seen through even.

Quum ĭter nostri agmĭnis impediretur
When the march of our army should be hindered

(imp. subj.) his rebus Nervĭi
by these things [conditions] the Nervii

existimaverunt consilium non omittendum
thought the advice (must) not (to) be omitted

sĭbi (dat.).
[neglected] by themselves.

18. Hæc ĕrat natura lŏci, quem
This was the nature of the place, which

nostri delegĕrant castris. Collis æqualĭter
(our) men had chosen for camp. A hill equally

declivis ab summo vergebat ad
sloping from the highest (point) was receding to

flumen Sabim, quod nominavĭmus supra :
the river Sabis [Sambre], which we have named [mentioned] above:

ab ĕo flumĭne pări acclivitate collis
from this river with equal ascent a hill

nascebatur advĕrsus et contrarĭus huic, infĭmus
was rising opposite and facing this, the lowest

circĭter ducentos passus apertus,
(portion) about two hundred paces (being) clear.

silvestris ab superiore parte; ut posset (imp.
woody from [on] the higher part; so that it was possible

subj.) non perspĭci facĭlè introrsus.[45] Intra
not to be seen through [to see] easily within. Inside

ĕas silvas hostes continebant se in
these woods the enemy were holding themselves in

occulto. In aperto lŏco, secundùm flumen,
secret [hiding]. In the open place, near [along] the river,

paucæ stationes equĭtum videbantur. Altitudo
a few pickets of horsemen were seen. The depth

flumĭnis ĕrat circĭter trĭum pĕdum.
f the river was about (of) three feet.

19. Cæsar, equitatu   præmisso,   subsequebatur
Cæsar, the cavalry having been sent before, was following closely

omnĭbus   copĭis : sed   ratĭo   que   ordo
with all   (his) forces;   but   the manner   and   order

agmĭnis   habebat   se   alīter   ac
of the marching line   was keeping itself   otherwise   and   [than]

Belgæ   detulĕrant   ad   Nervios. Nam,
the Belgæ   had carried [reported]   to   the Nervii. For,

quŏd   hostis   appropinquabat,   Cæsar   sŭâ
because   the enemy   was approaching,   Cæsar   by his

consuetudĭne ducebat   sex   expeditas   legiones :[46]
custom   was leading   six   light armed   legions:

post   ĕas   collocabat   impedimenta
after [behind]   these   he was putting   the baggage

totius   exercītûs;   inde   dŭæ   legiones,
of the whole   army;   then   (the) two   legions,

quæ   conscriptæ-ĕrant   proxĭmè,   claudebant
which   had been enrolled   last,   were closing up

totum   agmen,   que   ĕrant   præsidĭo
the whole   line of march,   and   were   (for) a safeguard

impedimentis.   Nostri   equĭtes   cum   fundi-
to the baggage.   Our   horsemen   with   the

torĭbus   que   sagittarĭis   transgressi   flumen,
slingers   and   archers   having passed   the river,

commiserunt   prœlĭum   cum   equitatu   hostĭum.
joined   battle   with   the cavalry   of the enemy.

Quum   illi   identĭdem   recipĕrent (imp. subj.)
When   they   now and then   were betaking

se   in   silvas   ad   sŭos,   ac   rursus
themselves   into   the woods   to   their (men),   and   again

facĕrent (imp. subj) impĕtum   in   nostros   ex
were making   an attack   upon   our (men)   out of

silvâ;   neque   nostri   auderent (imp. subj.) insĕqui
the wood;   nor   our (men)   were daring   to pursue

cedentes longĭùs, quam   ad   quem   finem
(those) yielding farther,   than   to   which   end [the limit]

porrecta   ac   aperta   lŏca   pertinebant :[47]
the extended   and   open   places   were reaching:

intĕrim sex legiones, quæ venĕrant primæ,
meanwhile the six legions, which had come first,

opĕre dimenso, cœperunt munire castra.
the work having been measured, began to fortify (the) camp.

Ubi prima impedimenta nostri exercĭtûs visa-
When the first baggage wagons of our army were

sunt ab eis, qui latebant abdĭti in silvis,
seen by these, who were lying concealed in the woods,

quod tempus convenĕrat inter ĕos
which time had been agreed upon between them

committendi prœlĭum: ut constituĕrant intra
of [for] joining battle: as they had stationed within

silvas acĭem que ordĭnes, atque
the woods the battle line and ranks, and

ipsi confirmavĕrant sese,[48] subĭtò
they themselves had encouraged themselves, suddenly

provolaverunt omnĭbus copĭis, que fecerunt
they flew forth with all (their) forces [troops], and made

impĕtum in nostros equĭtes. His pulsis
an attack upon our horsemen. These having been routed

facĭlè ac proturbatis, decucurrerunt incredibĭli
easily and disordered, they ran down, with incredible

celeritate ad flumen; ut pænè uno tempŏre
speed to the river; so that almost at one time

hostes viderentur (imp. subj.) et ad silvas,
the enemy were seen both at the woods,

et in flumĭne, et jam in nostris
and in the river, and now in our

manĭbus. Autem contenderunt eâdem
hands [close at hand]. But they hastened with the same

celeritate adverso colle ad nostra castra, atque ĕos
speed on the opposite hill to our camp, and (to) these

qui ĕrant occupati in opĕre.
who were occupied in the work.

20. Omnĭa ĕrant agenda Cæsări (dat.) uno
All (things) were to be acted [managed] by Cæsar at one

tempŏre: vexillum proponendum, quod ĕrat
time: the standard to [must] be set up, which was

insigne,   quum   opporteret   concurri (passive verb)
the sign,   when   it was proper   to make a rush

ad   arma :   signum   dandum   tŭbâ :
to   arms :   the signal   to [must] be given   with the trumpet :

milĭtes   revocandi   ab   opĕre :   qui
the soldiers   to [must] be recalled   from   the work :   (those) who

processĕrant   paulò   longĭus,   causâ   aggĕris
had proceded   a little   farther,   for the sake   of the rampart

                petendi   arcessendi,[49]   acĭes
[materials]   to [must] be sought,   to [must] be summoned,   the line

            instruenda :   milĭtes   cohortandi :
(of battle)   to [must] be arranged :   the soldiers   to [must] be exhorted :

signum   dandum.   Magnam partem quarum rerum
the signal   to [must]be given.   A great   part   of which   things

brevĭtas   tempŏris,   et   successus   et   incursus
the shortness   of the time,   and   the approach   and   charge

hostĭum   impediebat (sing.).   Dŭæ   res   ĕrant   subsidĭo
of the enemy were hindering.   Two   things   were (for) an aid

his   difficultatĭbus,   scientĭa   atque   usus
to these   difficulties,   the knowledge   and   experience

milĭtum,   quòd,   exercitati   superiorĭbus
of the soldiers,   because,   having been exercised   in former

prœlĭis,   potĕrant   ipsi   præscribĕre
battles,   they were able   themselves   to prescribe [assign]

sĭbi   quid   oporteret   fiĕri,   non   mĭnùs
to themselves   what   was proper   to be done,   not   less

commŏdè   quàm   doceri   ab   alĭis :
conveniently [fitly],   than   to be shown   by   others ;

et   quòd   Cæsar   vetuĕrat   singŭlos   legatos
and   because   Cæsar   had forbidden   the several   lieutenants

discedĕre   ab   opĕre   que   singŭlis   legionĭbus,
to depart   from   the work   and   (their) several   legions,

nĭsi   castris (pl.)   munitis.   Hi,   propter
unless the camp   having been [was] fortified.   These,   on account of

propinquitatem   et   celeritatem   hostĭum,
the nearness   and   swiftness   of the enemy,

spectabant   nĭhil   jam   imperĭum   Cæsăris ;
were awaiting   not at all   now   the command   of Cæsar ;

sed	per	se,	administrabant	quæ
but	by	themselves,	were managing	what (things)

videbantur.
seemed (best).

21.
Necessariis	rebus	imperatis,	Cæsar
The necessary	things	having been commanded,	Cæsar

decucurrit	ad	cohortandos[50]	milites	in partem,
ran down	for	exhorting [to exhort]	the soldiers	into the part,

quam	fors	obtŭlit;	et	devenit	ad	decĭmam
which	chance	presented;	and	came down	to	the tenth

legionem.	Cohortatus-est	milites	non	longiore
legion.	He exhorted	the soldiers	not	with longer

oratione,	quàm	ŭtì	retinerent	memorĭam
speech,	than	that	they should retain	the memory

suæ	pristĭnæ	virtutis,	neu	perturbarentur	anĭmo
of their	former	valor,	nor	should be confused	in mind

que	sustinerent	fortĭter	impĕtum	hostĭum;
and	should sustain	bravely	the attack	of the enemy;

et,	quòd	hostes	abĕrant	non	longĭùs,
and,	because	the enemy	were distant	not	farther,

quàm	quò	telum	posset	adjĭci,	dĕdit
than	where	a weapon	might be able [could]	(to) be cast,	he gave

signum	committendi[51]	prœlĭi	atque	profectus
the signal	of [for] joining	battle	and	having set out

Ĭtem	in	altĕram	partem,	causâ	cohortandi,
likewise	into	another	part,	for the sake	of exhorting,

occurrit	pugnantĭbus.	Tanta	fŭit	exig-
he meets (them)	fighting.	So great [such]	was	the brief-

uĭtas	tempŏris,	que	tam	paratus	anĭmus	hostĭum
ness	of the time,	and	so	prepared	the mind	of the enemy

ad	dimicandum,	ut	tempus	defŭĕrit (perf. subj;)
for	battling,	that	time	failed

non	mŏdò	ad	accommodanda	insignĭa,
not	only	for	fitting on	the ensigns [badges],

sed	etĭam	ad	ĭnduendas	galĕas,	que	detrahenda
but	even	for	putting on	the helmets,	and	(for) drawing off

tegmenta	scutis.[52]	In	quam	partem
the coverings	from the shields.	Into	what [whatever]	part

quisque devenit casu ab opĕre, que
each came down by chance from the work, and

quæ signa conspexit prima, constĭtit
what (whatever) standards he beheld first, he took stand

ad hæc, ne dimittĕret tempus pugnandi
at these, lest he might let pass [lose] the time of fighting

in quærendo sŭos.
in seeking his own (comrades).

22. Exercĭtu instructo, măgis ut natura
The army having been drawn up, rather as the nature

lŏci que dejectus collis, et necessĭtas
of the place and the declivity of the hill, and the necessity

tempŏris postulabat (sing.), quàm ut ratĭo
of the time were requiring, than as [according to] the plan

atque ordo militaris rĕi (sing.); quum alĭæ
and arrangement of military affairs; since some

legiones in alĭâ parte resistĕrent (imp.
legions in one part (others in another) were resisting

subj.) hostĭbus (dat.) diversis lŏcis, que densissĭmis
the enemy in different places, and very thick

sepĭbus interjectis, ut demonstravĭmus
hedges having been interposed [intervening], as we have shown

antè, prospectus impediretur (imp. subj.): nĕque
before, the view was impeded: neither

certa subsidĭa potĕrant collocari, nĕque
sure reserves were able [could] (to) be placed, nor

provideri, quid esset ŏpus in quâque
(to) [could it] be foreseen, what might be needful in each

parte; nĕque omnĭa imperĭa administrari
part; nor all the orders to [could] be managed [given]

ab uno.[53] Ităque, in tantâ iniquitate
by one. Therefore, in so great an irregularity

rerum, varii eventus fortunæ quŏque sequebantur.
of things, various events of fortune also were following.

23. Milĭtes nonæ et decĭmæ legionis,
The soldiers of the ninth and tenth legions,

ut constitĕrant in sinistrâ parte acie,
as they had stood in the left part of the battle line, (their)

pilis emissis, celerĭter compulerunt ex
javelins having been thrown, quickly forced from

superiore lŏco in flumen Atrebates, (nam
the higher place into the river the Atrebates, (for

ĕa pars obvenĕrat his) exanimatos cursu
this part had fallen to these) exhausted [spent] with running

ac lassitudĭne, que confectos vulnerĭbus;
and fatigue, and worn out with wounds:

et insecuti gladĭis conantes
and having pursued (them) with swords endeavoring

transire, interfecerunt magnam partem eorum
to cross over, they killed a great part of them

impeditam. Ipsi dubitaverunt non transire
encumbered. They hesitated not to cross

flumen;[54] et progressi in iniquum lŏcum,
the river ; and having advanced into an unfavorable place,

conjecerunt in fŭgam hostes rursus resistentes,
cast into flight the enemy again resisting,

prœlĭo redintegrato. Item in alĭâ parte, dŭæ
the battle having been renewed Also in another part, two

diversæ legiones, undecĭma et octava, Verom-
different legions, the eleventh and eighth, the Verom-

andŭis profligatis, cum quĭbus congressi-ĕrant,
andui having been routed, with whom they had joined,

prœliabantur ex superiore lŏco in ripis
were fighting from the higher place in [on] the banks

ipsis flumĭnis.[55] At totis castris (pl.)
themselves [the very banks] of the river. But the whole camp

fĕrè nudatis à fronte et à sinĭstrâ
nearly being exposed from [on] the front and from [on] the left

parte, cùm duodecĭma legĭo et septĭma
part [side], when the twelfth legion and the seventh

non magno intervallo ab ĕâ, constitisset
not at a great distance from it, had taken stand

(pl. perf. subĭ.) in dextro cornu, omnes Nevĭi
        upon the right wing, all the Nervii

confertissĭmo agmĭne duce Boduognato,
in closest marching line the leader (being) Boduognatus,

qui   tenebat   summam   imperĭi,   contenderunt
whȝ   was holding   the chief place   of command,   hastened

ad   ĕum   lŏcum :   pars   quorum   cœpit   circumvenire
to   this   place :   part   of whom   began   to surround

legiones   aperto   latĕre   pars   petĕre
the legions   (on) the open   flank,   part   to seek [attack]

summum   lŏcum   castrorum.
the highest   place [portion]   of the camp.

24.   Eodem   tempŏre   nostri   equĭtes   que
    At the same   time   our   cavalry   and

pedĭtes   lĕvis   armaturæ,   qui   fuĕrant   unà
infantry   of light   armor,   who   had been [were]   together

cum his,   quos   dixĕram   pulsos(-esse)   primo
with these,   whom   I had said   to have [had] been routed   in the first

impĕtu   hostĭum,   cùm   recipĕrent (imp. subj.)
attack   of the enemy,   when   they were betaking

se   in   castra,   occurrebant   hostĭbus (dat.)
themselves   into   camp,   were meeting   the enemy

adversis   ac   rursus   petebant   fŭgam   in   alĭam
opposite   and   again   were seeking   flight   into   another

partem.   Et   calones,   qui conspexĕrant   à
part [direction].   And   the camp followers,   who   had beheld   from

Decumanâ   portâ,   ac   summo   jŭgo   collis
the Decuman   gate,   and   the highest   ridge   of the hill

nostros   victores   transire   flumen,   egressi
our (men)   conquerors   (to) cross   the river,   having gone out

causâ   prædandi,   quum   respexissent (pl. perf.
for the sake   of plundering,   when   they had looked back

subj.)   et   vidissent (pl. perf. subj.)   hostes
    and   had seen   the enemy (to be)

versari   in   nostris   castrĭs,   præcipĭtes   mandabant
engaged   in   our   camp,   headlong   were consigning

sese   fŭgæ :   sĭmul   clamor   que
themselves   to flight :   at the same time   the shout   and

fremĭtus   eorum   qui   veniebant   cum   impedimentis
uproar   of those   who   were coming   with   the baggage wagons

oriebatur,   que   alĭi   perterrĭti   ferebantur in   alĭam
was arising,   and   some   dismayed   were borne   into   one

partem.[56]   Omnĭbus   quĭbus   rebus   Trevĭri
part (others into another). By all which [these] things, the Trevirian

equĭtes   permoti,   virtutis   quorum   est
cavalry   having been alarmed, of the valor of whom there is

singularis   opinĭo   inter   Gallos,   qui
a singular [very high] opinion among the Gauls, who

missi   causâ   auxilĭi   à   civitate,
(having been) sent for the sake of aid by the state,

venĕrant ad Cæsàrem, quum vidissent (pl. perf. subj.)
had come to Cæsar, when they had seen (that)

nostra castra   compleri   multitudĭne   hostĭum,
our   camp to be [was] filled with a multitude of the enemy

legiones   prĕmi,   et   teneri
(that) the legions to be [were] pressed, and to be [were] held

pænè circumventas,   calones,   equĭtes,
almost surrounded, (that) the camp followers, the cavalry,

Numĭdas funditores, diversos que   dissipatos
the Numidian slingers, separated and scattered

fugĕre   in   omnes   partes, nostris rebus
to flee [were fleeing] into all parts, our affairs

disperatis, contenderunt dŏmum; renuntiaverunt
being despaired of, hastened home; they announced

civitati,   Romanos   pulsos   que
to the state (that) the Romans (had been) routed and

superatos,   hostes   potitos   eorum[57]
overcome, (that) the enemy to have [had] got possession of their

castris que impedimentis (abl.).
camp and baggage.

25. Cæsar   profectus   ab   cohortatione
    Cæsar   having set out from the exhortation

decĭmæ legionis ad dextrum cornu, ŭbi vidit
of the tenth legion to the right wing, where he saw

sŭos   urgeri,   que   signis
his (men) to be [were] pressed hard, and the standards

collatis   in   unum   lŏcum,   milĭtes
having been assembled into one place, the soldiers

duodecĭmæ legionis   confertos esse
of the twelfth legion to have been [were] crowded together

impedimento	sĭbi ipsis	ad	pugnam,	omnĭbus
for [as] an impediment	to themselves	for	the battle,	all

centurionĭbus	quartæ	cohortis	occisis,	que
the centurions	of the fourth	cohort	having been killed,	and

signifĕro	interfecto,	signo
the standard bearer	(having been) slain,	the standard

amisso,	fĕrè	omnĭbus	centurionĭbus
(having been) lost,	almost	all	the centurions

reliquarum	cohortĭum,	aut	vulneratis	aut
of the remaining	cohorts,	either	having been wounded	or

occisis,	in	his	primopilo	Publĭo	Sextĭo
killed,	in [among]	these	the first centurion	Publius	Sextius

Bacŭlo,	fortissĭmo	vĭro,	confecto	multis
Baculus,	a very brave	man,	(having been) worn out	with many

que	gravĭbus	vulnerĭbus,	ut	jam	non
and	heavy [severe]	wounds,	(so) that	now	he was not

posset (imp. subj.)	sustinere	se;	relĭquos
able	to support	himself;	the rest

esse	tardiores,	et	nonnullos	desertos	à
to be [were]	more slow,	and	some	(being) deserted	by

novissĭmis	excedĕre	prœlĭo,	ac
the rear	to depart [were withdrawing]	from the battle,	and

vitare	tela;	hostes	nĕque
to avoid [were avoiding]	the weapons;	(that) the enemy	neither

intermittĕre,	subeuntes	à	fronte	ex
to intermit [ceased],	advancing	on	the front	from

inferiore	lŏco,	et	instare	ab
the lower	place [ground],	and	to press [pressed] on	from [at]

utroque	latĕre,	et	rem	esse	in
each	flank,	and (that)	the affair	to be [was]	in

angusto,	nĕque	esse	ullum	subsid-
a narrow [critical state],	nor	to be [was there]	any	reinforce-

ĭum,	quod	posset	submitti;[58]	scuto
ment,	which	might be able [could]	(to) be sent up;	(with) a shield

detracto (abl. abs.)	uni	milĭti (dat.)
(having been) snatched away	from one	soldier

ab	novissĭmis	(quòd	ipse	venĕrat	ĕŏ
from [in]	the latest [rear]	(because	(he) himself	had come	there

sĭne   scuto)   processit   in   primâm   acĭem;
without   a shield)   he advanced   into   the first   battle line;

que   centurionĭbus   appellatis   nominatim,
and   the centurions   having been called   by name,

cohortatus   relĭquos,   jussit   milĭtes   inferre
having encouraged   the rest,   he ordered   the soldiers   to bear on

signa,   et   laxare   manipŭlos,   quò
the standards,   and   to loosen [open]   the companies,   in order that

possent   uti   gladĭis (abl.)   facilĭùs.   Spe
they might be able   to use   the swords   more easily.   Hope

illatâ   militĭbus   ejus,   adventu   ac
having been brought in   to the soldiers   by his,   arrival   and

anĭmo (sing.)   redintegrato,   quum   quisque
(their) spirits   having been renewed,   since   every one

pro   se   cupĕret (imp. subj.)   navare   opĕram
for   himself   was desiring   to ply [do well]   (his) task

in   conspectu   Imperatoris,   etĭam   in   sŭis
in   the sight   of the General,   even   in   his

extremis   rebus,   impĕtus   hostĭum   tardatus-est
most critical   affairs,   the violence   of the enemy   was retarded

paulùm.⁵⁹
a little.

26.   Quum   Cæsar   vidisset (pl. perf. subj.)   septĭmam
        When   Cæsar   had seen   (that) the seventh

legionem,   quæ   constitĕrat   juxtà,   urgeri
legion,   which   had stood   near,   to be [was] pressed

Ĭtem   ab   hoste,   monŭit   tribŭnos   milĭtum,
likewise   by   the enemy,   he advised   the tribunes   of the soldiers,

ut   legiones   conjungĕrent   sese   paullatim,   et
that   the legions   should join   themselves   gradually,   and

inferrent   signa   conversa   in   hostes.⁶⁰
should bear on   the standards   turned   against   the enemy.

Quo   facto,   quum   alĭi   ferrent (imp. subj.)
Which   having been done   when   some   were bringing

subsidĭum   alĭis   nĕque   timerent (imp.
aid   to some (others to others)   nor   were fearing

subj.)⁶¹ ne   aversi   circumvenirentur
lest   having been turned about   they might be surrounded

ab   hoste,   cœperunt   resistĕre   audacĭŭs   ac
by   the enemy,   they began   to resist   more boldly   and

pugnare   fortĭŭs.   Intĕrim   milĭtes   duarum
to fight   more bravely. Meanwhile the soldiers   of the two

legionum,   quæ   fuĕrant   in   novissĭmo   agmĭne
legions,   which   had been   in   the rear   marching line

præsidĭo   impedimentis,   prœlĭo   nuntiato,
for protection to the baggage,   the battle   having been reported,

cursu   incitato,   conspiciebantur   in
(their) course having been increased,   were beheld   on

summo   colle (abl.) ab   hostĭbus :   et
the highest [the summit] (of the) hill by   the enemy :   and

Titus Labienus   potitus   castris (abl.) hostĭum,
Titus Labienus   having possessed   the camp   of the enemy,

et   conspicatus   ex   superiore   lŏco,   quæ   res
and   having beheld   from   the higher   place,   what   things

gererentur (imp. subj.)   in   nostris   castris,   misit
were transpiring   in   our   camp,   sent

decĭmam   legionem   subsidĭo   nostris ;   qui
the tenth   legion   for [as] aid to our (men) ; who

quum   cognovissent (pl. perf. subj)   ex   fŭgâ
when   they had ascertained   from   the flight

equĭtum   et   calonum,   in quo   lŏco
of the cavalry and of the camp followers in what   place [condition]

res   esset (imp. subj.),   que   quanto
the affair [action] was,   and   in how great

pericŭlo   et   castra   et   legiones   et
danger   both   camp,   and   the legions   and

Imperator   versaretur,   fecerunt   nĭhil
the Commander   were involved,   made [left]   nothing

relĭqui (gen.)   sĭbi   ad   celeritatem.[62]
left [wanting]   to themselves   for   speed.

27.   Tanta   commutatĭo   rerum   facta-est
        So great   a change   of things [conditions]   was made

adventu   horum,   ut   nostri   etĭam   qui
by the arrival of these,   that   our (men)   even   those who

procubuissent (pl. perf. subj.)   confecti   vulnerĭbus,
had lain down   spent   with wounds·

innixi   scutis (dat.), redintegrarent (imp. subj.)
having leaned on   the shields,   were renewing

prœlĭum.   Tum   calones   conspicati
the battle.   Then   the camp followers   having beheld

hostes   perterrĭtos,   etĭam   inermes   occurrĕrent
the enemy   dismayed,   even   unarmed   were assailing

(imp. subj.)   armatis :   equĭtes   verò,
            the armed (enemy):   the cavalry   indeed,

ut   delerent   turpitudĭnem   fŭgæ   virtute,
that   they might blot out   the disgrace   of flight   by valor,

pugnabant   in   omnĭbus   lŏcis,   quò   præ-
were fighting   in   all   places,   in order that   they might

ferrent   se   legionarĭis militĭbus
show better   themselves than [might surpass]   the legionary   soldiers.

(dat.).   At   hostes,   etĭăm   in   extremâ
        But   the enemy,   even   in   the extreme [last]

spe   salutis,   præstiterunt   tantam   virtutem,   ut,
hope   of safety,   displayed   so great   valor,   that.

quum   primi   eorum   cecidissent   proxĭmi
when   the first   of them   had fallen   the nearest [next]

insistĕrent   jacentĭbus,   atque   pugnarent
would stand upon   (those) lying prostrate,   and   would fight

ex   eorum   corporĭbus :   his   dejectis,
from   their   bodies :   these   having been thrown down.

et   cadavĕribus   coacervatis[63]   quï
and   the dead bodies   having been heaped up   (those) who

superessent,   conjicerent   tela   in   nostros   ut
survived,   would hurl   weapons   upon   our (men)   as

ex   tumŭlo,   que   remittĕrent   intercepta
from   a mound,   and   would return   the intercepted

pila :   ut   deberet (imp. subj.)   judicari   non
javelins :   so that   it ought   to be judged   (that) not

nequidquam homĭnes tantæ virtutis[64]   ausos-esse
in vain   men   of so great   valor   (to have) [had] dared

transire   latissĭmum   flumen,   ascendĕre   altissĭmas
to cross   a very broad   river,   to ascend   very high

ripas,   subire   iniquissĭmum   lŏcum :   quæ
banks.   to mount   a most unfavorable   place :   which (things)

magnitudo   anĭmi   redegĕrat   facilĭa   ex
a greatness   of soul   had rendered   easy   from

difficilimis.
the most difficult (conditions).

28. Hoc   proelĭo   facto,   et   gente
This   battle   having been done [fought], and the nation

ac   nomĭne   Nerviorum   redacto   prŏpè   ad
and   name   of the Nervii   having been reduced   nearly   to

internecionem :   majores   natu,
extermination :   (those) greater   by birth [the elders],

quod   dixeramus   collectos[65]   unà
whom   we had said   to have [had been] collected   together

cum   puĕris   que   mulierĭbus   in   æstuariâ
with   the boys   and   women   into [among[the inlets

ac   palŭdes,   hac   pugnâ   nuntiatâ,   quum
and   marshes,   this   battle   having been reported,   when

arbitrarentur (imp. subj.)   nihil   impeditum
they were considering (that)   nothing   was difficult

victorĭbus,   nĭhil   tutum   victis ;
for the conquerors,   nothing   safe   for the conquered,

consensu   omnĭum,   qui   superĕrant,   miserunt
by consent   of all,   (those) who   survived,   sent

legatos   ad   Cæsărem   que   dediderunt
ambassadors   to   Cæsar   and   surrendered

se   ĕi :   et   in   commemorandâ,
themselves   to him :   and   in   to be recounted

calamitate   civitatis   dixerunt :
[recounting],   the calamity   of the state   they said (that they):

sese   esse   redactos   ex   sexcentis
themselves   to be [were]   reduced   from   six-hundred

ad   tres   senatores ;   ex   sexaginta   millĭa
to   three   senators ;   from   sixty   thousand

homĭnum,   ad   vix   quingentos,   qui   possent
(of) men,   to   scarcely   five-hundred,   who   were able

ferre   arma ;   quos   Cæsar   conservavit   diligent-
ᴠᴏ bear   arms ;   whom   Casar   preserved   most care-

issĭmè,   que   jussit   uti   sŭis
fully,   and   commanded (them)   to use   their own

finĭbus atque oppĭdis, ut videretur usus[66]
territories and towns, that he might seem to have used

misericordĭâ (abl.) in misĕros ac supplĭces;
compassion toward the wretched and suppliant;

et imperavit finitĭmis (dat.) ut prohiberent
and ordered the neighbors that they should check

se que sŭos ab injurĭâ et
themselves and their own (people) from injury and

maleficĭo.
trouble (to them).

29. Aduatuci, de quĭbus scripsĭmus suprà,
The Aduatuci, of whom we have written above,

quum venirent (imp. subj.) omnĭbus copĭis
when they came with all (their) forces

auxilĭo Nervĭis, hâc pugnâ nuntiatâ,
for aid to the Nervii, this battle having been reported,

reverterunt dŏmum ex itinĕre; cunctis
returned home from the march; all

oppĭdis que castellis desertis, contulerunt
the towns and fortresses having been deserted, they brought together

omnĭa sŭa in unum oppĭdum egregĭè
all their (effects) into one town excellently

munitum naturâ: quum quod habere
fortified by nature: since which [this] had

(imp. subj.) altissĭmas rupes que despectus
very high rocks and outlooks

ex omnĭbus partĭbus in circuĭtu,[67]
from [on] all parts [sides] in compass [round about],

adĭtus lenĭter acclivis relinquebatur, ex
an approach gently sloping was left, from [on]

unâ parte, non amplĭùs ducentis pĕdum
one side, not more (than) two hundred (of) feet

in latitudĭnem: quem lŏcum muniĕrant
in breadth: which place they had fortified

altssĭmo duplĭci muro: tum collocârant
with a very high double wall: besides they had placed

saxa magni pondĕris, et præacutas trăbes
stones of great weight, and sharpened beams

in   muro.   Ipsi   ĕrant   prognati   ex   Cimbris
on   the wall. They   were   descended   from   the Cimbri

que   Teutŏnis: qui,   quum   facĕrent (imp. subj.)
and   Teutones: who,   when   they were making

       Iter   in   nostram   Provincĭam   atque   Italĭam,
(their) march into our   Province   and   Italy,

his   impedimentis (pl.),   quæ   potĕrant   non
this   baggage,   which   they were able not

agĕre   ac   portare   secum,   deposĭtis
to bring   and   to carry   with them,   having been deposited

citra   flumen   Rhenum,   reliquerunt   unà
on this side   the river   Rhine,   they left   together

sex   millĭa   homĭnum   ex   sŭis   custodĭam
six   thousand   (of) men   from [of]   their own   as a guard

ac   præsidĭum.   Hi,   post   obĭtum
and   protection.   These [the latter], after   the destruction

eorum,   exagitati   multos   annos   à
of those,   having been harassed   many   years   by

       finitĭmis,   quum   alĭàs   inferrent (imp. subj.)
(their) neighbors,   when   sometimes   they were waging

bellum,   alĭàs   defendĕrent (imp. subj.)   illatum,
war,   at other times were repelling (it)   (when) waged,

pace[68]   factâ   consensu   omnĭum,   delegerunt
a peace   having been made   by consent   of all,   chose

hunc   lŏcum   domicilĭo.
this   place   for an abode.

30. Ac   primo   adventu   nostri   exercĭtûs,
    And   at the first   approach   of our   army,

faciebant   crebras   excursiones   ex   oppĭdo,
they were making   frequent   sallies   from   the town,

que   contendebant   parvŭlis   prœlĭis   cum
and   were contending   in trifling   battles   with

nostris.   Postĕa   circummuniti   vallo
our (men).   Afterwards   having been fortified around with a rampart

duodĕcim   pĕdum,   quindĕcim   millĭum   in
of twelve   feet,   fifteen   thousand (feet)   in

circuĭtu,   que   crebris   castellis,   continebant
compass,   and   with frequent   fortresses,   they were holding

sese   oppĭdo.   Ubi,   vinĕis   actis,
themselves in the town. When, the sheds having been driven on,

aggĕre   exstructo,   viderunt turrim   constitŭi
a mound having been constructed, they saw a tower (to be) erected

prŏcul,   primùm   irridere   ex
at a distance,   (they began) first   to mock   from

muro   atque   increpitare   vocĭbus: quò
the wall   and   to call out   with voices [cries]: wherefore

tanta   machinatĭo   institueretur   ab   tanto
so great a machine   was constructed from [at] so great

spatĭo !   quibusnam   manĭbus,   aut   quĭbus
a space [distance]! with what   hands,   or   with what

virĭbus,   confidĕrent   sese   collocare
forces,   did they trust (that they) themselves to [would] place

turrim   tanti   onĕris   in   muros,   præsertim
a tower of so great burden against the walls, especially

homĭnes   tantŭlæ   staturæ,   (nom   nostra   brevĭtas
men   of so little statue,   (for   our   shortness

est   contemptŭi   plerisque   Gallĭs   hominĭbus,
is   (for) a contempt to most   Gallic   men,

præ   magnitudĭue   suorum
before [in comparison with]   the hugeness   of their own

corpŏrum).
bodies).

31. Verò   ŭbi   viderunt   moveri,   et
     But   when   they saw (it)   (to be) moved,   and

appropinquare   mœnĭbus,[69]   commoti   nŏvâ
(to) approach   (to) the walls, being alarmed by the new

et   inusitatâ   specĭe,   miserunt   legatos   ad
and   unusual   sight,   they sent   ambassadors to

Cæsărem   de   pace: qui   locuti (-sunt) ad   hunc
Cæsar   about peace: who   spoke   to [after] this

mŏdum: Se   existimare   Romanos
manner :   (They) themselves (to) think   the Romans

gerere   bellum   non   sĭne   ŏpe   deorum,
(to) carry on war   not   without the assistance of the gods,

qui   possent   promovere   machinationes   tantæ
who   are able   to move forward   machines   of so great

altitudĭnis   tantâ   celeritate,   et   pugnare   ex
   height   with so great   speed,   and   to fight   from [at]

propinquitate: dixerunt   permittĕre
   nearness [close quarters]:   they said   (they)   (to) give up

se   que   omnĭâ   sŭa   eorum
   themselves   and   all   their   (effects)   to their

potestati   petĕre   ac   deprecari   unum,[70]   si
   power   to (they) seek   and   (to) beg   one (thing),   if

pro   sŭâ   clementĭâ   ac   mansuetudĭne,   quam
   for [according to]   his   clemency   and   mildness,   which

ipsi audîssent (pl. perf. subj.) ab alĭis,   statuisset
   they had heard   from others,   he should decree that

fortè   Aduatucos   conservandos-esse,
   perchance   the Aduatuci   should be preserved,

ne despoliaret   se   armis (abl.):   omnes
   that he would not deprive   themselves   of arms: all

finitĭmos   fĕrè   esse   inimicos   sĭbi,   ac
   the neighbors   nearly   to be [are]   hostile   to themselves,   and

invidere   sŭæ   virtuti (dat.),   à   quĭbus   possent
   (to) envy   their   valor,   from   whom   they could

non defendĕre   se,   armis   tradĭtis;
   not (to) defend   themselves,   (their) arms   having been surrendered;

præstare   sĭbi   păti   quamvis
   to be [it is] better   for themselves   to endure   any

fortunam   à   Romano   popŭlo,   si   deducerentur
   fortune   from   the Roman   people,   if   they should be led

in   ĕum   casum,   quàm   interfĭci   per   cruciatum
   into   this   calamity,   than   to be slain   with   torture

ab   his   inter   quos   consuêssent (pl. perf. subj.)
   by   those   among   whom   they had been accustomed

dominari.
   to rule.

32. Cæsar   respondit   ad   hæc: Se
   Cæsar   answered   to   these (words):   He himself

conservaturum   civĭtatem   măgis   sŭâ
   about to [would] preserve   the state   rather   by his

consuetudĭne   quàm   eorum   merĭto,   si
   custom   than   by their   merit [deserts],   if

dedidissent   se,   prĭùs-quàm   arĭes
they should surrender   themselves,   before (that)   the battering ram

attigisset   murum :   sed   esse   nullam
should touch   the wall :   but   to be [there was]   no

conditionem   deditionis,   nĭsi   armis   tradĭ-
condition   of surrender,   unless   the arms   having been

tis :   se   facturum[71]   id,   quod
[were] delivered up :   (he) himself   about to [would] do   that,   which

fecisset (pl. perf. subj.)   in   Nervĭos ;   que
he had done   to   the Nervii ;   and

imperaturum   finitĭmis (dat.),   ne-inferrent
about to [would] order   the neighbors,   that they should not inflict

quam   injurĭam   deditĭtĭis (dat.)   Romani
any   injury   upon the surrendered (subjects)   of the Roman

popŭli.   Re   nuntiatâ   ad   sŭos,   illi
people.   The matter   having been reported   to   their own (people),   they

dixerunt   se   facĕre,   quæ   imperarentur.
said (that they)   themselves   to [would] do,   what   was ordered.

Magnâ   multitudĭne   armorum   jactâ   de
A great   multitude   of arms   having been thrown   from

muro   in   fossam,   quæ   ĕrat   ante   oppĭdum,
the wall   into   the ditch,   which   was   before   the town,

sic   ut   acervi   armorum   adæquarent (imp. subj.)
so   that   the heaps   of arms   were equalling

propè   summam   altitudĭnem   muri   que
nearly   the highest [greatest]   height   of the wall   and

aggĕris :   et   tămen   circĭter   tertĭâ   parte
of the mound :   and   yet   about   a third   part

celatâ,   (ut   perspectum-est   postĕa,)
having been concealed,   (as   was ascertained   afterwards,)

atque   retentâ   in   oppĭdo,   portis
and   having been retained   in   the town,   the gates

patefactis,   usi-sunt   pace (abl.)
having been thrown open,   they used [obtained]   peace

ĕo   dĭe.
on that   day.

33.   Sub   vespĕrum   Cæsar   jussit   portas
     Towards   evening   Cæsar   ordered   the gates

claudi,	que	milĭtes	exire	ex	oppĭdo,
to be shut,	and	the soldiers	to go out	from	the town,

ne	oppidani	accipĕrent	quam	injurĭam	à
lest	the townsmen	might receive	any	injury	from

militĭbus	noctu.	Illi,	consilio	inĭto
the soldiers	by night.	They,	a plan	having been formed

antè,	ut	intellectum-est,	quòd,	deditione
before,	as	it was understood,	because,	the surrender

factâ,	credidĕrant	nostros	non
having been made,	they had believed	our (men)	not

inducturos	præsidĭa,	aut	denĭque
about to [would not] introduce	garrisons,	or,	finally,

servaturos	indiligentĭùs :	partim	cum	his
[would] watch	somewhat carelessly :	partly	with	these

armis,	quæ	retinuĕrant	et	celavĕrant,
arms,	which	they had retained	and	had concealed,

partim	scutis	factis	ex	cortĭce,	aut	intextis
partly	with shields	made	from	barks,	or	woven

viminĭbus,	quæ	induxĕrant	pellĭbus	subĭtò
twigs,	which	they had overlaid	with hides	suddenly

(ut	exĭguĭtas	tempŏris	postulabat),	fecerunt
(as	the briefness	of the time	was demanding),	(they) made

eruptionem	repentè	ex	oppĭdo	omnĭbus
a sally	unexpectedly	from	the town	with all

copĭis,	tertĭâ	vigilĭâ,	quà	ascensus	ad
the forces,	in the third	watch,	where	the ascent	to

nostros	munitiones	videbatur	minĭmè	ardŭus.
our	fortifications	was seeming	least	difficult.

Significatione	factâ	celerĭter	ignĭbus,	ut	Cæsar
A signal	having been made	quickly	by fires,	as	Cæsar

imperavĕrat	antè,	concursum-est	eò	ex
had ordered	before,	it was [they] run together	there	from

proxĭmis	castellis;	que	pugnatum (-est)	ab
the nearest	fortresses;	and	it was fought	by

hostĭbus[72]	ĭta	acrĭter,	ut	debŭit	pugnari
the enemy	so	vigorously,	as	it ought	to be fought

à	fortĭbus	vĭris	in	extremâ	spe	salutis,
by	brave	men	in	the last	hope	of safety

iniquo lŏco, contra ĕos, qui jacĕrent
in an unfavorable place, against those, who were casting

(imp. subj.) tela ex vallo que turrĭbus, quum
weapons from a rampart and towers, when

omnis spes salutis consistĕret (imp. subj.) in
all hope of safety was resting in

virtute unâ. Ad quartŭor millĭbus homĭnum
valor alone. About four thousand (of) men

occisis, relĭqui rejecti-sunt in oppĭdum.
having been killed the rest were thrown back into the town.

Postridĭe ejus diei (gen.), portis refractis,
The day after this day, the gates having been broken down,

quum nemo jam defendĕret (imp. subj.), atque
when no one now was defending, and

nostris militĭbus intromissis, Cæsar vendĭdit
our soldiers having been sent within, Cæsar sold

universam sectionem ejus oppĭdi. Numĕrus
the entire section [booty] of this town. The number

quinquaginta trĭum millĭum capĭtum relatus-est
of fifty three thousand (of) heads [souls] was reported

ad eum ab his qui emĕrant.
to him by those who had bought (them).

34. Eodem tempŏre factus-est certĭor
At the same time he was made more sure [was

à Publio Crasso, quem misĕrat cum
informed] by Publius Crassus, whom he had sent with

unâ legione ad Venĕtos, Unellos, Osismĭos,
one legion to the Veneti, Unelli, Osismii,

Curiosolitas, Esuvĭos, Aulercos, Redŏnes, quæ
Curiosolitæ, Esuvii, Aulerci, Redones, which

sunt maritĭmæ civitates, que attingunt Oceănum,
are maritime states, and touch on the ocean,

omnes ĕas civitates redactas-esse in
(that) all those states to have [had] been reduced into

ditionem que potestatem Romani popŭli.
the authority and power of the Roman people.

35. His rebus gestis, omni Gallĭâ
These things having been accomplished, all Gaul

pacatâ   tantâ   opinĭo   hujus   bellĭ
having been subdued,   so great   an opinion   of this   war

perlata-est   ad   barbăros,   ut   legati
was carried   to   the barbarians,   that   ambassadors

mitterentur (imp. subj.)   ad   Cæsărem   ab   nationĭbus,
were sent   to   Cæsar   by   the nations,

quæ   incolĕrent (imp. subj.)   trans   Rhenum,   quæ
which   were dwelling   across   the Rhine,   who

pollicerentur (imp. subj.)   se   daturas
were promising   (that they)   themselves   about to [would] give

obsĭdes,   facturas   imperata: quas
hostages,   about to [and would] do (the things)   commanded: which

legationes   Cæsar   jussit   reverti   ad   se,
embassies   Cæsar   commanded   to return   to   himself,

proxĭmâ   æstate   inĭtâ,   quòd
(when) the next   summer   having begun [began],   because

properabat   in   Italĭam,   que   Illyrĭcum.   Ipse
he was hastening   into   Italy,   and   Illyricum.   He himself

profectus-est   in   Italĭam,   legionĭbus   deductis
set out   into   Italy,   the legions   having been conducted

in   hiberna   in   Carnutes,   Andes,
into   winter quarters   into [among]   the Carnutes,   Andes,

Turŏnes,   quæ   civĭtates   ĕrant   propinquæ   his
Turones,   which   states   were   neighboring   to these

lŏcis,   ŭbi   gessĕrat   bellum.   Ex   litĕris
places,   where   he had carried on   war.   From   the letters

Cæsăris,   supplicatĭo   quindĕcim   dĭes
of Cæsar,   a general thanksgiving   (for) fifteen   days

decreta-est   ob   ĕas   res: quod
was decreed   on account of   these   things: which

accidĕrat   nuʼli   ante   id   tempus.
had happened   to no one   before   this   time.

THIRD BOOK

This book describes the principal events of five wars which were carried on against the various nations of Gaul in the six hundred and ninety-eighth year after the founding of Rome, B. C. 56: the first, against the Nantuates, the Veragri and the Seduni, is successfully conducted by the lieutenant, Galba; the second, against the Veneti, though fought at a disadvantage by the Roman forces because of the position of the Venetic towns, finally ends through the strategy of Cæsar, himself, in a naval engagement; the third results in a victory by Titurius Sabinus, a lieutenant, over the Venelli, the Auberci, the Eburovices, and the Lexovii; the fourth is conducted by Crassus against the Sotiates and other Aquitanian tribes, the greatest part of Aquitania being subdued; and the fifth, Cæsar's campaign against the Morini and the Menapii closes with the army entering into winter quarters after brilliantly repelling the offensive attack of the enemy.

1. Quum   Cæsar   proficisceretur (imp. subj.)   in
When   Cæsar   was setting out   into

Italĭam,   misit   Sergĭum   Galbam   cum   duodecĭmâ
Italy,   he sent   Sergius   Galba   with   the twelfth

legione   et   parte   equitatûs   in   Nantuates,
legion,   and   part   of the cavalry   into   the Nantuates,

Veragros,   que   Sedunos;   qui   pertĭnent   à
Veragri,   and   Seduni;   who   reach [extend]   from

finĭbus   Allobrŏgum,   et   lăcu   Lemanno
the borders   of the Allobroges,   and   the lake   Lemannus

et   flumĭne   Rhodăno,   ad   summas
and   the river   Rhone,   to   the highest [summit of the]

Alpes.   Causa   mittendi   fŭit,   quòd
Alps.   The cause   of sending (him)   was,   because

volebat   Ĭter   patefĭĕri   per   Alpes,
he was desiring (that)   the passage   (to) be opened   through   the Alps,

quo   mercatores   consuevĕrant   ire   cum
by which   merchants   had been accustomed   to go   with

magno pericŭlo que magnis portorĭis. Permisit
great danger, and great tolls. He permitted

huic (dat.), si arbitraretur esse opus,
him if he should think (it) to be [was] necessary,

ŭti collocaret legionem in ĭis lŏcis,
that he might place a legion in in these places,

causâ hĭemandi. Galba, alĭquot secundis
for the sake of wintering. Galba, some successful

prœlĭis factis, que complurĭbus eorum
battles having been made [completed], and several of their

castellis expugnatis, legatis missis
strongholds having been stormed, ambassadors having been sent

undĭque ad ĕum, que obsidĭbus dătis,
from every side to him, and hostages having been given,

et pace factâ, constitŭit collocare dŭas
and peace having been made, resolved to place two

cohortes in Nantuatĭbus; ipse hiemare cum
cohorts in [among] the Nantuates; himself to winter with

relĭquis cohortĭbus ejus legionis, in vico
the remaining cohorts of this legion, in a village

Veragrorum, qui appellatur Octodurus: qui[1]
of the Veragri, which is called Octodurus: which

vicus posĭtus in valle, planitĭe non magnâ
village being placed [situated] in a valley, a plain not large

adjectâ, continetur undĭque altissĭmis
being adjacent, is bounded on every side by very high

montĭbus. Quum hic divideretur (imp. subj.) in
mountains. Since this was divided into

lŭas partes flumĭne, concessit altĕram partem
two parts by the river, he granted the one part

ejus vici Gallis; attribŭit altĕram
of this village to the Gauls; he assigned the other

relictam vacŭam ab illis cohortĭbus ad
left vacant by them to the cohorts for win-

hiemandum: munivit ĕum lŏcum vallo
tering [to winter]: he fortified this place with a rampart

que fossâ.
and (with) a trench.

2. Quùm complùres dĭes hibernorum
  When several days of the winter quarters

transîssent (pl. perf. subj.) que jussisset (pl. perf.
had passed   and he had ordered

subj.) frumentum comportari ĕò, factus-est
    corn to be brought there, he was made

certĭor   subĭtò per exploratores,
more sure [was informed] suddenly by scouts, (that)

omnes discessisse noctu ex ĕâ
 all to have [had] departed by night from this

parte vici, quam concessĕrat Gallis; que
part of the village, which he had granted to the Gauls; and

  montes, qui impenderent (imp. subj.),
(that) the mountains, which were overhanging

 teneri à maxĭmâ multitudĭne Sedunorum
to be [were] held by a very great multitude of the Seduni

et Veragrorum. Id accidĕrat de alĭquot
and of (the) Veragri. This had happened from several

causis, ut Galli capĕrat (imp. subj.) subĭtò
causes, that the Gauls were taking   suddenly

consilĭum renovandi belli que opprimendæ
the purpose of renewing the war and of overwhelming

legionis. Primùm, quòd despiciebant legionem,
the legion. First, because they were despising the legion,

propter paucitatem, nĕque ĕam
on account of the fewness (of soldiers), nor (was) this

plenissĭmam, duabus cohortĭbus detractis
very full, two cohorts having been drawn out (of it)

et complurĭbus singillatim absentĭbus, qui
and very many individually (being) absent, who

missi-ĕrant causâ petendi commeatûs; tum
had been sent for the purpose of seeking provisions; then

etĭam, quòd propter iniquitatem loci
also, because, on account of the unfavorableness of the place,

existimabant ne quĭdem primum impĕtum
they were thinking (that) not even the first attack [shock]

posse sustineri, quum
to be able [could] (to) be withstood (by the Romans), when

ipsi   decurrĕrent   ex   montĭbus   in
(they) themselves   should run down   from   the mountains   into

vallem,   et   conjicĕrent   tela.   Accedebat,
the valley,   and   should hurl   (their) weapons.   It was added,

quòd   dolebant   sŭos   libĕros   abs-
because [that]   they were mourning for   their   children   (having

tractos   ab   se   nomĭne   obsĭdum;   et
been) taken   from   themselves   in the name   of hostages ;   and

habebant[2]   persuasum   sĭbi
they were having (it)   persuaded   to themselves [were persuaded]

Romanos   conari   occupare   culmĭna
(that) the Romans   to endeavor [endeavored]   to occupy   the tops

Alpĭum   non   solùm   causâ   itinĕrum,   sed
of the Alps   not   only   for the sake   of the passes,   but

etĭam   perpetŭæ   possessionis,   et   adjungĕre   ĕa
also   of perpetual   possession,   and   to unite   these

lŏca   finitĭmæ   provinciæ.
places   to the neighboring   province.

3. His   nuntĭis   acceptis,   quum[3]   nĕque
These   messages   having been received,   since   neither

ŏpus   hibernorum,   que   munitiones
the work   of the winter quarters,   and   the fortifications

essent (imp. subj.)   plenè   perfectæ,   nĕque
were   fully   finished,   nor

esset (imp. subj.) provisum   sătis   de   frumento,
was   (there)   provided   enough   from [of]   corn,

que   relĭquo   commeatu,   quŏd,   deditione
and   the other   provisions,   because,   a surrender

factâ,   que   obsidĭbus   acceptis,   Galba
having been made,   and   hostages   having been received,   Galba

existimavĕrat   nĭhil   timendum   de   bello:
had thought   nothing   to [must] be feared   about   war :

concilĭo   convocato   celerĭter, cœpit exquirĕre
a council having been called together   quickly,   he began   to seek

sententĭas.   In   quo   concilĭo,   quum
the opinions.   In   which   council,   since

tantum   repentini   perĭculi   accidisset (pl. perf.
so much   (of) sudden   danger   had happened

subj.) præter opinionem, ac jam fĕrè omnĭa
contrary to opinion [expectation], and now nearly all

superiora lŏca conspicerentur (imp. subj.) completa
the higher places were seen (to be) filled

multitudĭne armatorum, nĕque
with a multitude of armed (men), neither (could it) [any one]

veniri, subsidĭo[4] nĕque commeatus posset
(to be) come, to (their) aid nor were provisions able

supportari, itinerĭbus interclusis: jam
to be brought up, the ways having been shut up [closed]: now

salute prŏpè desperatâ, nonnullæ sententĭæ
safety nearly having been despaired of some opinions

hujasmŏdi dicebantur; ut, impedimentis (pl.)
of this kind were said [delivered]: that, the baggage

relictis, eruptione factâ, contendĕrent
having been left a sally having been made, they should hasten

ad salutem, iisdem itinerĭbus, quĭbus
to safety, by the same ways, by which

pervenissent (pl. perf. subj.) ĕò. Tămen placŭit
they had arrived there. However it pleased

majori parti (dat.), hoc consilĭo reservato
(to) the greater part, this counsel having been reserved

ad extremum, experiri eventum reĭ
to the last, to try the issue of the thing [matter]

intĕrim, et defendĕre castra.
meanwhile, and to defend the camp.

4. Brĕvi spatio interjecto, vix ut
A short space [period] having intervened, scarcely that

tempus daretur collocandis[5] atque administrandis
time might be given for arranging and for managing

his rebus, quas constituissent (pl. perf.
these things, which they had resolved,

subj.), hostes decurrĕre[6] ex omnĭbus
the enemy (to) run down from all

partĭbus, signo dăto, conjicĕre
sides, a signal having been given, (and) (to) hurl

lapĭdes que gæsa in vallum. Nostri[7]
stones and heavy darts upon the rampart. Our (men)

primò   repugnare   fortīter   intĕgris
at first   (to) repulse (them)   bravely   (when) with whole [fresh]

virĭbus   nĕque   mittĕre   ullum   telum
power [strength]   nor   (to) send [cast]   any   weapon

frustrà   ex   superiore   lŏco: ut   quæque   pars
in vain   from   the higher   place: as   each   part

castrorum   nudata   defensorĭbus   videbatur
of the camps   stripped   from [of] defenders   was seeming

premi,   occurrĕre   ĕò,   et   ferre   auxilĭum:
to be pressed.   to (they) run   there   and   (to) bring   aid:

sed   superari   hoc,   quòd
but   to be (they are) surpassed [overcome]   in this (manner),   because

hostes   defessi   diuturnitate   pugnæ   excedebant
the enemy   wearied   by the length   of the fight   were retiring

prœlĭo,   alĭi   succedebant   intĕgris   virĭbus:
from battle,   others   were succeeding   with whole [fresh]   powers

          nĭhil   quarum   rerum   potĕrat
[strength]:   nothing   of which [these]   things   was able [could]

fiĕri   à   nostris   propter   paucitatem;   ac
(to) be done   by   our (men)   on account of   (their) fewness: and

non   mŏdò   facultâs   dabatur   defesso
not   only   (no) opportunity   was given   to a wearied (man)

excedendi   ex   pugnâ,   sed   ne   saucĭo   quĭdem
of retiring   from   the fight,   but   not   to a wounded   even

relinquendi   ejus   lŏci (gen.),   ŭbi   constitĕrat,   âc
of leaving   his   place,   where   he had stood,   and

recipiendi   sŭi (gen.).
of recovering   himself.

5. Quum   pugnaretur[8]   jam   continenter   amplĭùs
  When   it was fought   now   unceasingly   more (than)

sex   horis,   ac   non   solùm   vires (pl.)   sed   etĭam
six   hours,   and   not   only   strength   but   also

tela   deficĕrent (imp. subj.)   nostris (dat.),   atque
the weapons   were failing   our (men),   and

hostes   instarent (imp. subj.)   acrĭùs,   que
the enemy   were pressing on   more vigorously,   and

nostris[9]   languidiorĭbus,   cœpissent (pl. perf. subj.)
our (men)   having become more faint,   they began

scindĕre   vallum   et   complere   fossas,   que
to tear down   the rampart   and   to fill up   the ditches,   and

res   esset (imp. subj.) jam   deducta   ad
the affair [action]   was   now   led [brought]   to

extremum   casum;   Publĭus   Sextĭus   Becŭlus,
the last   chance;   Publius   Sextius   Baculus,

centurĭo   primipili   quem[10]   dixĭmus
a centurion   of the first rank   whom [who]   we have said

confectum (-esse)   complurĭbus   vulnerĭbus
to have [had] been overcome   with many   wounds

Nervĭco   prœlĭo,   et   ĭtem   Caĭus   Volusenus,
in the Nervian   battle,   and   also   Caius   Volusenus,

tribunus   milĭtum,   vir   et   magni   consilĭi
a tribune   of the soldiers,   a man   both   of great   counsel [prudence]

et   virtutis,   accurrunt   ad   Galbam,   atque   dŏcent
and   valor,   run up   to   Galba,   and   show

esse[11]   unam   spem   salutis,   si   eruptione
(that) to be [there is]   one   hope   of safety,   if   a sally

factâ,   experirentur   extremum   auxilĭum.
having been made,   they should try   the last   aid [resort].

Ităque   centurionĭbus   convocatis,   făcit
Therefore   the centurions   having been called together,   he makes

milĭtes   certiores   intermittĕrent
the soldiers more sure [informs them]   (that) they should intermit [moder-

prœlĭum   paullisper,   ac   excipĕrent   tantummŏdo
ate]   the battle   a little while,   and   should deliver   only

tela   missa,   que   reficĕrunt   se   ex
the weapons   sent [thrown],   and   should refresh   themselves   from

labore;   pòst,   signo   dăto,   erum-
labor;   afterwards,   the signal   having been given,   they should

pĕrent   è   castris,   atque   ponĕrent   omnem
burst forth   from   the camp,   and   should put   all

spem   salutis   in   virtute.
hope   of safety   in   (their) valor.

6. Facĭunt,   quod   jussi-sunt;   ac   eruptione
They do,   what   they were ordered;   and   a sally

factâ   subĭtò   omnĭbus   portis,   relinquunt
having been made   suddenly   from all   the gates,   they leave

facultatem	hostĭbus	nĕque	cognoscendi	quid
opportunity	to the enemy	neither	of knowing	what

fiĕret,	nĕque	colligendi[12]	sŭi.	Ita,
should be done,	nor	of collecting	themselves.	Thus,

fortunâ	commutatâ,	interficĭunt	ĕos[13]
fortune	having been changed,	'hey slay	these

circumvetos	undĭque,	qui	venĕrant in	spem
surrounded	on every side,	who	had come into	the hope

potiundorum	castrorum;	et	ex	amplĭus
of possessing	the camps;	and	from	more (than)

triginta	millĭbus	homĭnum,	(quem	numĕrum
thirty	thousand	(of) men,	(which	number

barbarorum	constabat	venisse ad	castra)
of the barbarians	it was manifest	to have [had] come to	the camp)

plus	tertĭâ parte	interfectâ,	conjicĭunt
more (than)	the third part	having been killed,	they throw

in fŭgam	relĭquos	perterrĭtos; ac	patiuntur
into flight	the rest	affrighted; and	suffer (them)

consistĕre	ne	quĭdem[14] in superiorĭbus	lŏcis.
to take stand	not	even in the higher	places.

Sic omnĭbus	copĭis	hostĭum	fusis,
Thus all	the forces	of the enemy	having been routed,

que	armis	exutis,	recipĭunt se
and	(their) arms	having been stripped off,	they betake themselves

in castra (pl.)	que sŭas	munitiones.	Quo prœlĭo
into the camp	and their	fortifications.	Which battle

facto,	quòd Galba	nolebat
having been done [completed],	because Galba	was unwilling

tentare fortunam	sæpĭùs, atque	meminĕrat[15]
to try fortune	too often, and	(he had) remembered

sese	venisse	alĭo
(that) he himself	to have [had] come	with another [a different]

consilĭo in	hiberna,	videbat
design into	winter quarters,	he was seeing (that he)

occurrisse alĭis rebus (dat.);	permotus maxĭmè
to have [had] met with other things;	being moved principally

inopĭâ frumenti que commeatûs:	postĕro
by the want of corn and of provisions:	on the following [next]

dĭe, omnĭbus ædificĭis ejus vici
day, all the buildings of this village

incensis, contendit reverti in provincĭam:
having been burned, he hastened to return into the province;

ac nullo hoste prohibente, aut demorante
and no enemy preventing, or delaying

ĭter, perduxit legionem incolŭmem in
the march, he conducted the legion safe into

Nantuates, inde in Allobrŏges, que
the Nantuates, thence into the Allobroges, and

hiemavit ĭbi.
wintered there.

7. His rebus gestis, quum Cæsar
These things having been performed, when Cæsar

existimaret (imp subj.) Gallĭam pacatam de
was thinking that Gaul (was) subdued from

omnĭbus causis; Belgis superatis,
all (these) reasons; the Belgæ having been overcome,

Germanis expulsis, Sedunis victis
the Germans having been expelled, the Seduni having been conquered

in Alpĭbus, atque ĭta hiĕme[16]
in the Alps, and so the winter

inĭtâ profectus-esset (pl. perf. subj.) in
having begun he had set out into

Illyrĭcum, quòd volebat adire ĕas nationes
Illyricum, because he was wishing to visit these nations

quŏque et cognoscĕre regiones; subĭtum
also and to know [investigate] the countries; a sudden

bellum coortum-est in Gallĭâ. Hæc fŭit causa
war arose in Gaul. This was the cause

ejus belli. Publĭus Crassus adolescens hiemabat
of this war. Publius Crassus a young man was wintering

cum septĭmâ legione in Andĭbus proxĭmus
with the seventh legion among the Andes nearest

Oceănum măre.[17] Is dimisit complures præfectos
the Ocean (sea). He dispatched very many prefects

que tribunos milĭtum in finitĭmas civtates,
and tribunes of soldiers into the neighboring states,

causâ   frumenti,   quòd   inopĭa   frumenti   ĕrat
for the sake   of corn,   because   a want   of corn   was

in   his   lŏcis: in   quo   numĕro   Titus
in   these   places: in   which   number   Titus

Terrasidĭus   missus ĕrat   in   Eusubĭos;   Marcus
Terrasidius   had been [was] sent   into   the Eusubii;   Marcus

Trebĭus   Gallus   in   Curiosolitas;   Quintus
Trabius   Gallus   into   the Curiosolitæ;   Quintus

Velanĭus   cum   Tito   Silĭo   in   Venĕtos.
Velanius   with   Titus   Silius   into   the Veneti.

8. Auctorĭtas   hujus   civitatis   est   longè
The authority   of this   state   is   by far

amplissĭma   omnis   maritĭmæ   oræ   earum
the most extensive   of all   the maritime   coast   of these

regionum;   quòd   Venĕti   habent   et   plurĭmas
countries;   because   the Veneti   have   both   very many

naves,   quĭbus   consueverunt   navigare   in
ships,   with which   they have been accustomed   to sail   into

Britannĭam;   et   antecedunt   cætĕros   scientĭâ
Britain;   and   they excel   the rest   in the knowledge

atque   usu   nauticarum   rerum;   et   in   magno
and   use [practice]   of naval   matters;   and   in   the great

impĕtu   vasti   atque   operti   măris,   paucis
violence   of the vast   and   open   sea,   few

portŭbus   interjectis,   quos   ipsi   tĕnent,
harbors   intervening,   which (they)   themselves   hold,

hăbent   fĕrè   omnes   vectigales,   qui   consue-
they have   nearly   all (those)   tributary,   who   have been

verunt   uti   eodem   mări (abl.).   Initĭum
accustomed   to use   the same   sea.   A beginning

fit   ab   ĭis,   retinendi   Silĭi   atque   Velanĭi,
was made   by   these,   of retaining   Silius   and   of Velanius,

quòd   per   ĕos   existimabant   se
because   through   them   they were thinking   (that they) themselves

recuperaturos   sŭos   obsĭdes,   quos   dedissent
about to [would] recover   their   hostages,   whom   they had given

(pl. perf. subj.)   Crasso.   Finitĭmi   adducti
   to Crassus.   (Their) neighbors   induced

auctoritate horum (ut consilĭa Gallorum sunt
by the authority of these (as the councils of the Gauls are

subĭta et repentina) retĭnent Trebĭum que
sudden and immediate) detain Trebius and

Terrasidĭum de eâdem causâ: et legatis
Terrasidius on the same cause: and ambassadors

missis celerĭter, conjurant[18] inter se
having been sent quickly, they conspire among themselves

per sŭos princĭpes; esse acturos
through their chiefs; (that they) to be about to [would] act

nĭhil nĭsi communi consilĭo, que laturos
in nothing unless by common counsel, and about to [would] bear

eundem exĭtum omnis fortunæ; que sollicĭtant
the same issue of every fortune; and they solicit

relĭquas civitates, ut mallent permanere
the remaining states, that they should prefer to remain

in ĕâ libertate, quam accepĕrant à
in this liberty, which they have received from

majorĭbus, quàm perferre servitutem Romanorum.
(their) ancestors, than to endure the slavery of the Romans.

Omni maritĭmâ orâ perductâ celerĭter
All the maritime coast having been brought over quickly

ad sŭam sententĭam, mittunt communem
to their opinion, they send a common

legationem ad Publĭum Crassum, "Si vĕlit
embassy to Publius Crassus, "If he wishes

recipĕre sŭos, remittat obsĭdes
to receive his (ambassadors), let him send back (the) hostages

sĭbi."
to themselves."

9. De quĭbus rebus Cæsar factus
Concerning which things Cæsar having been made

certĭor à Crasso, jŭbet
more certain [having been informed] by Crasso, he orders

longas naves ædificari intĕrim in
long ships [war ships] to be built meanwhile on

flumĭne Ligĕri, quod influĭt Oceănum,
the river Liger [Loire], which flows into the Ocean,

remĭges	instĭtŭi	ex	Provincĭâ,	nautas
rowers	to be provided	from	the Province,	sailors

que	gubernatores	comparari,	quòd	ipse
and	pilots	to be procured,	because	he himself

abĕrat	longĭus.	His	rebus	administratis
was distant	farther [too far].	These	things	having been managed,

ipse	contendit	celerĭter	ad	exercĭtum,	quàm-
he himself	hastened	quickly	to	the army,	as soon

primùm	potŭit	per	tempus	anni.
as	he was able	through [for]	the time	of the year.

Venĕti	que	ĭtem	relĭquæ	civitates,	adventu
The Veneti	and	also	the other	states,	the arrival

Cæsaris	cognito,	sĭmul	quòd
of Cæsar	having been known,	at the same time	because

intelligebant	quantum	facĭnus	admisissen.
they were understanding	how great	a crime	they had committed

(pl. perf. subj.) in	se,	legatos,[19]	nomen
	against	themselves, the ambassadors,	a name

quod	semper	fuisset (pl. perf. subj.)	sanctum	que
which	always	had been	holy	and

inviolatum	ăpud	omnes	nationes,	retentos
inviolate	at [among]	all	nations,	to have [had] been

ab	se	et	conjectos	in	vincŭla;
detained	by	themselves	and	cast	into	chains;

instĭtŭunt	parare	bellum	pro
resolve	to prepare	a war	for [in proportion to]

magnitudĭne	pericŭli,	et	maxĭmè	providere
the greatness	of the danger,	and	especially	to provide

ĕa	quæ	pertinerent	(imp. subj.)
these (things)	which	were pertaining	

ad	usum	navĭum;	hôc,	majore
to	the use	of ships;	from this [on this account],	with greater

spe,	quòd	confidebant	multùm	naturâ
hope,	because	they were relying	much	in [on] the nature

lŏci.	Sciebant	pedestrĭa	itinĕra
of the place.	They were knowing	(that)	the foot	ways

concisa-esse	æstuarĭis;	navigationem
to have [had] been cut up	by æstuaries;	navigation

impeditam[20]   propter   inscientĭam   locorum
prevented   on accout of   (our) ignorance   of the places

que paucitatem   portŭum: confidebant   nostros
and   the fewness   of the harbors: they were trusting   (that) our

exercĭtus   nĕque   posse   morari   diutĭŭs[21]
armies   neither   to [would] be able   to delay   longer

ăpud   se,   propter   inopĭam   frumenti.
at [among]   themselves,   on account of   the want   of corn.

Ac jam,   ut   omnĭa   accidĕrent   contra
And   now,   though   all (things)   might happen   against [contrary to]

opinionem,   tămen   se   posse
(their) opinion,   yet   (they) themselves   to [would] be able (to do)

plurĭmum navĭbus: Romanos habere   nĕque ullam
very much   by ships: the Romans to have [had]   neither   any

facultatem navĭum, nĕque   novisse   văda,
power [supply]   of ships,   nor   to have known [knew]   the shallows,

ɔortus,   insŭlas   eorum   locorum,   ŭbi   essent (imp.
harbors,   islands   of these   places,   where   they were

subj.)   gesturi   bellum: ac   perspiciebant
about to carry on   war: and   they were perceiving

navigationem   in   concluso   mări,   atque   in
(that) navigation   in   an inclosed   sea,   and   in

vastissĭmo   atque apertissĭmo Oceano, esse   longè
a very immense   and   very open   Ocean,   to be [is]   far

alĭam.   His   consilĭis   inĭtis,
other [different],   These   counsels   having been entered into,

munĭunt   oppĭda,   comportant   frumenta (pl.)[22]
they fortify   the towns,   they bring together   corn

ex   agris   in   oppĭda;   cogunt   naves
from   the fields   into   the towns: they collect   (their) ships

quàm-plurĭmas   possunt,   in   Venetĭam,   ŭbi
as many as   they can,   into   Venetia,   where

constabat   Cæsărem primum   gesturum
it was evident   Cæsar   first   to be about to [would] carry on

bellum.   Adsciscunt   socĭos   sĭbi   ad   id
the war.   They unite   (as) allies   to themselves   for   this

bellum   Osismĭos,   Lexovĭos, Nannetes, Ambialites,
war   the Osismii.   Lexovii.   Nannetes.   Ambialites.

Morĭnos, Diablintes, Menapĭos; accersunt auxilĭa
Morini, Diablintes, Menapii; they send for auxiliaries

ex Britannĭâ, quæ est posĭta contra
from Britain, which is located over against

eas regiones.
these countries.

10. Hæ ĕrant difficultates gerendi,[23] belli
These were the difficulties of carrying on, a war

quas ostendĭmus suprà: sed tămen multa
which we have shown above: but yet many (things)

incitabant Cæsărem ad id bellum: injurĭæ (pl.)
were urging Cæsar to this war: the injuries [wrong]

retentorum Romanorum equĭtum; rebellĭo
of detaining Roman knights; an uprising

facta post deditionem: defectio, obsidĭbus
having been made after a surrender: the revolt, hostages

dătis: conjuratĭo tot civitatum:
having been given: the conspiracy of so many states:

in-primis, ne, hâc parte neglectâ,
in particular, lest, this part [region] having been neglected

relĭquæ nationes arbitrarentur ĭdem
the remaining nations might think the same (thing)

licere sĭbi. Ităque quum
to [would] be allowed to themselves. Therefore since

intelligĕret (imp. subj.) fĕrè omnes Gallos
he understood (that) nearly all the Gauls

studere novis rebus, et
to be [were] eager for new things [revolution], and

excitari mobilĭter que celerĭter ad
to be [were] aroused readily and quickly to

bellum; autem omnes homĭnes naturâ
war; moreover (that) all men by nature

studere libertati, et odisse
to be [are] eager for liberty, and (to) have hated

conditionem servitutis; prĭùs-quam plures civitates
the condition of slavery; before (that) more states

conspirarent, putavit exercitum partiendum,
should conspire, he thought the army to [must] be divided.

ac	distribuendum	latĭus	sĭbi(dat.).
and	to [must] be distributed	more widely	by himself.

11. Ităque mittit Titum Labienum legatum
Therefore he sent Titus Labienus (his) lieutenant

cum	equitatu	in	Trevĭros,	qui	sunt	proxĭmi
with	the cavalry	among	the Treviri,	who	are	nearest

flumĭni	Rheno.	Mandat	huic (dat.),	adĕat
to the river	Rhine.	He charges	him,	(that) he go to

Remos	que	relĭquos	Belgas,	atque	continĕat
the Remi	and	the remaining	Belgæ,	and	keep (them)

in	officĭo;	que	prohibĕat	Germanos,	qui
in	duty;	and	prevent	the Germans,	who

dicebantur	arcessiti[24]	auxilĭo	à	Belgis,	si
were said	(to have) been summoned	for aid	by	the Belgæ,	if

conentur	per	vim	transire	flumen
they may attempt	by	force	to cross	the river

navĭbus.	Jŭbet	Publĭum	Crassum	cum
with ships.	He orders	Publius	Crassus	with

duodĕcim	legionarĭis	cohortĭbus,	et	magno	numĕro
twelve	legionary	cohorts,	and	a great	number

equitatûs	proficĭsci	in	Aquitanĭam,	ne	auxilĭa
of cavalry	to set out	into	Aquitania,	lest	auxiliaries

mittantur	ex	his	nationĭbus	in	Gallĭam,	ac
may be sent	from	these	nations	into	Gaul,	and

tantæ	nationes	conjungantur.	Mittit	Quintum
so great	nations	may be united.	He sends	Quintus

Titurĭum	Sabinum	legatum	cum	trĭbus	legionĭbus
Titurius	Sabinus	(his) lieutenant	with	three	legions

in	Unellos,	Curiolitas,	que	Lexovĭos;	qui
among	the Unelli,	the Curiosolitæ,	and	the Lexovii;	who

curet	ĕam	mănum	distinendam.
may take care	(that) this	band (of people)	(to) be kept apart.

Præfecit	Decĭum	Brutum	adolescentem	classi,
He appointed	Decius	Brutus	a young man	to the fleet,

que	Gallĭcis	navĭbus,	quas	jussĕrat
and	to the Gallic	ships,	which	he had ordered

convenire	ex	Pictonĭbus	que	Santŏnis,	et
to assemble	from	the Pictones	and	Santoni.	and

relĭquis   pacatis   regionĭbus ;   et   jŭbet
the remaining   subdued   countries ;   and   he orders

proficisci   quàm-primùm   posset,   in
(him) to set out   as soon as   he may be able,   among

Venĕtos.   Ipse   contendit   ĕò   pedestrĭbus
the Veneti.   He himself   hastens   thither   with the foot

copĭis.
forces.

12. Sĭtus   oppidorum   ĕrant   fĕrè
     The situations   of (their) towns   were   nearly

ejusmŏdi,   ut   posĭta   in   extremis
of this sort,   that   having been placed [located]   on   extreme

lingŭlis   que   promontorĭis,   haberent (imp.
little tongues (of land)   and   promontories,   they were having

subj.)   nĕque   adĭtum   pedĭbus,   quum   æstus
         neither   access   by feet [foot],   when   the tide

incitavisset   se   ex   alto,   quod   accĭdit
may have aroused   itself   from   the deep,   which   occurs

semper   bis   spatĭo   duodĕcim   horarum :
always   twice   in the space [period]   of twelve   hours :

nĕque   navĭbus,   quòd   æstu   rursus   minuente
nor   by ships,   because   the tide   again   diminishing

              naves   afflictarentur   in   vădis.   Ita
[ebbing]   the ships   may be dashed   on   the shoals.   Thus

utrâque   re   oppugnatĭo   oppidorum
by each   thing [condition]   a siege   of the towns

impediebatur.   Ac,   si   quando   fortè   sup-
was hampered.   And,   if   at any time   by chance   having

erati   magnitudĭne   opĕris,   mări
been overcome   by the greatness   of a work.   the sea

extruso   aggĕre   ac   molĭbus,   atque
having been shut out   by a mound   and   by moles,   and

his   adæquatis   mœnĭbus   oppĭdi,
these   having been made equal   to the walls   of the town,

cœpĕrant[25]   desperare   sŭis   fortunis ;   magno
they had begun   to despair of   their   fortunes ;   a great

numĕro   navĭum   appulso,   cujus   rĕi
number   of ships   having been landed,   of which   thing [means]

habêbant summam facultatem, deport-
they were having the highest [greatest] power [supply], they were

abant omnĭa sŭa que recipiebant se
removing all their (effects) and were betaking themselves

in proxĭma oppĭda : ĭbi defendebant se
into the nearest towns : there they were defending themselves

rursus iisdem opportunitatĭbus lŏci. Facie-
again by the same favorableness of place. They were

bant hæc ĕò facilĭus magnam partem
doing these (things) for this reason more easily a great part

æstatis, quòd nostræ naves detinebantur
of the summer, because our ships were detained

tempestatĭbus; que ĕrat summa difficultas
by storms; and (there) was the highest [greatest] difficulty

navigandi vasto atque aperto mări, magnis
of sailing in an immense and open sea, with great

æstĭbus, raris ac prŏpè nullis portŭbus.
tides, with few and nearly no harbors,

13. Namque ipsorum naves factæ-ĕrant que
For indeed their ships had been made and

armatæ ad hunc mŏdum : carinæ
armed [equipped] according to this manner: the keels (were)

aliquanto planiores quàm nostrarum navĭum ;
considerably more flat than (those) of our ships ;

quò²⁶ possent excipĕre
in order that they might be able [could] (to) receive [endure]

văda ac decessum æstûs facilĭus :
the shoals and the departure [ebb] of the tide more easily :

proræ admŏdum erectæ, atque ĭtem puppes,
the prows (were) very upright, and also the sterns

accommodatæ ad magnitudĭnem fluctŭum que
suited to the greatness of the waves and

tempestatum. Totæ naves factæ ex
storms. The whole ships (were) made from

robŏre, ad perferendam²⁷ quamvis vim et
oak, for bearing [enduring] any force and

contumelĭam; transtra ex trabĭbus
violence; the benches (were made) from [of] beams

pedalĭbus in latitudĭnem (acc), confixa   ferrĕis
  a foot   in   width,   fixed [fastened] together with iron

clavis,   crassitudĭne   pollĭcis   digĭti:
  nails,   with [of] the thickness   of the thumb   (finger):

anchŏræ   revinctæ   ferrĕis   catenis,   pro
the anchors (were) fastened with iron chains,   instead of

funĭbus. Pelles que   alutæ (pl.)   tenuĭter
  ropes.   Hides   and   fine leathers   (were)   thinly

confectæ   pro   velis;   sive   propter   inopĭam
 dressed   for   sails; whether on account of   the want

linì,   atque   inscientĭam   usûs   ejus;   sive,
of flax,   and   ignorance   of the use   of it;   or,

quod est   măgis   verisimĭle,   quŏd   arbitrabantur
what   is   more   likely,   because they were thinking

   tantas   tempestates   oceăni   que   tantos[28]
(that) so great   storms   of the ocean   and   so great

impĕtus ventorum   posse   non   sustineri,
violence   of winds to be able [could] not (to) be supported.

ac   tanta   onĕra   navĭum   rĕgi   velis
and so great burdens of ships (to) be governed by sails

  sătis   commŏdè.   Congressus   nostræ   classi
sufficiently conveniently. The encounter to [of] our   fleet

cum his navĭbus ĕrat   ejusmŏdi ut   præstaret
with these ships   was   of this kind that it was excelling

(imp. subj.) celeritate unâ,   et   pulsu   remorum;
        in speed   alone, and the beat [stroke] of oars;

  reliqua   essent (imp. subj.) aptiora   et
the remaining (conditions) were   more suitable   and

accommodatiora   illis   pro   naturâ
more accommodated to them for [in view of]   the nature

  lŏci,   pro   vi   tempestatum: ĕnim
of the place (and),   (for)   the violence   of the storms: for

nostræ   nĕque   potĕrant   nocere   his (dat.)
our (ships) neither   were able   to injure   them

  rostro,   (tanta   ĕrat   firmitude   in   his)
with the beak [prow], (so great was   the strength in   them)

nĕque   telum   adjiciebatur[29] facĭlè   propter
  nor   a weapon   was hurled   easily   on account of

altitudĭnem;　　et　　de　　eâdem　　causâ　　continebantur
(their) height ;　and　from　the same　cause　they were held fast

scopŭlis　　　　　mĭnùs　　commŏdè.　　Accedebat
by grappling hooks　　less　　conveniently.　　It was added,

ut　　quum　　ventus　　cœpisset (pl. perf. subj.)
that　when　the wind　had begun

sævire　et　　dedidissent (pl. perf. subj.)　　se
to rage　and　they had given [committed]　　themselves

vento,　　et　　ferrent　　tempestatem　　facilĭùs,
to the wind,　both　they would bear　a storm　more easily,

et　consistĕrent　tutĭùs　in　vădis,　ct
and　would stop　more safely　in　the shoals,　and

derelictæ　ab　æstu,　　timerent　　nĭhil
having been left　by　the tide,　they would fear　nothing

saxa　et　cautes:　casus　omnĭum
[in no wise]　the rocks　and　reefs :　accidents　of all

quarum　rerum　ĕrant extimescendi　nostris
which [these]　things [kinds]　were　to be dreaded　by our

navĭbus (dat.).
ships,

14. Complurĭbus　oppĭdis　expugnatis,　ŭbi
Several　towns　having been stormed,　when

Cæsar　intellexit　tantum　laborem　sumi
Cæsar　understood　so great　labor　to be [was] taken

frustrà,　nĕque　fŭgam　hostĭum　reprĭmi,
in vain,　neither　the flight　of the enemy　to be [was] checked,

oppĭdis　captis,　nĕque　posse[30]
the towns　having been taken,　nor　to be able [could he]

noceri　his (dat.),　statŭit　classem
to be injured [injure]　them,　he resolved　(that) the fleet

exspectandam,　Ubi　quæ　convenit　ac
to [must] be awaited.　When　which [this]　assembled　and

primùm　visa-est　ab　hostĭbus,　circĭter　ducentæ[31]
first　was seen　by　the enemy,　about　two hundred

viginti　paratissĭmæ　eorum,　naves　atque
twenty　most prepared [equipped]　of their,　ships　and

ornatissĭmæ　omni　genĕre　armorum,
most furnished　with all [every]　kind　of arms,

profectæ	è	portu,	constiterunt	adversæ
having set out	from	port,	stood	opposite

nostris.	Nĕque	satis constabat	Bruto,
(to) our (ships).	Neither	was it sufficiently clear	to Brutus,

qui	præĕrat	classi (dat.),	nĕque	tribunis
who	commanded	the fleet,	nor	to the tribunes

milĭtum	que	centurionĭbus,	quĭbus	singŭlæ
of the soldiers	and	to the centurions,	to whom	single

	naves	attributæ-ĕrant,	quid	agĕrent,
[particular]	ships	had been assigned,	what	they should do,

aut	quam	rationem	pugnæ	insistĕrent:	ĕnim
or	what	plan	of battle	they should adopt:	for

cognovĕrant[32]	posse	non	noceri
they had known	to be able [they could]	not	(to) be injured

rostro:	autem	turrĭbus	excitatis,
by the beak [prow]:	but	towers	having been raised,

tămen	altitudo	puppĭum	ex	barbăris
yet	the height	of the sterns	from [of]	the barbarian

navĭbus	superabat	has;	ut	nĕque	tela
ships	was overtopping	these;	(so) that	neither	weapons

	possent	adjĭci	commŏdè	sătis	ex
might be able [could]	(to) be thrown	conveniently	enough	from

inferiore	lŏco,	et	missa	à	Gallis
the lower	place,	and	(those) sent	by	the Gauls

accidĕrent	gravĭùs.	Una	res	præparata	à
would fall	more heavily.	One	thing	prepared	by

nostris	ĕrat	magno	usŭi;	præacutæ	falces,
our (men)	was	for [of] great	use;	sharp-pointed	scythes.

insertæ	que	affixæ	longurĭis,	formâ	non
inserted in	and	fastened	to long poles,	with a shape	not

absimĭli	muralĭum	falcĭum:[33]	quum	funes,	qui
unlike	(that) of wall	scythes:	when	the ropes,	which

destinabant	antennas	ad	malos,	comprehensi-ĕrant
were bracing	the yards	to	the masts,	had been seized

que	adducti	his,	navigĭo	incitato
and	drawn taut	by these,	the vessel	having been urged forward

remis,	prærumpebantur:	quĭbus
with the oars,	they were broken apart:	which

abscissis,   antennæ   necessariò   concidebant;
having been cut away,   the yards   necessarily   were falling;

ut   quum   omnis spes   consistĕret (imp. subj.)
(so) that   since   all   hope   was resting

Gallĭcis   navĭbus in   velis   que   armamentis,
for the Gallic   ships   in   (their) sails   and   riggings,

his   ereptis,   omnis   usus[34]   navĭum
these   having been torn away,   all   use   of (their) ships

eriperetur (imp. subj.)   uno   tempŏre.   Relĭquum
was wrested away   at one   time.   The remaining

certamen   ĕrat   posĭtum   in   virtute;   quâ
contest   was   placed   in   valor;   in which

nostri   milĭtes   facĭlè   superabant;   atque   măgis
our   soldiers   easily   were excelling;   and   the more

ĕò,   quòd   res   gerebatur   in
for this reason,   because   the action   was carried on   in

conspecto   Cæsăris   atque   omnis   exercĭtûs,   ut
sight   of Cæsar   and   of all   the army,   that

nullum factum   paulò   fortĭus   posset   latere;
no   deed   a little   more brave   was able   to be hid;

ĕnim   omnes   coles   ac   superiora   lŏca,   unde
for   all   the hills   and   higher   places,   whence

ĕrat   propinquus   despectus   in   măre,   tenebantur
was   a near   view   upon   the sea,   were held

ab   exercĭtu.
by   the army.

15. Antennis   disjectis,   ut   dixĭmus,
The yards   having been thrown down,   as   we have said,

quum binæ   aut   ternæ   naves   circumsisterent (imp.
when   two   or   three   ships   were surrounding

subj.)   singŭlas   naves,   milĭtes   contendebant
(our) individual   ships,   the soldiers   were striving

summâ   vi   transcendĕre in   naves
with highest [utmost]   force [exertion]   to climb over   into   the ship⸱

hostĭum.   Quod[35]   postquam   barbări
of the enemy.   Which   after (that)   the barbarians

animadverterunt   fiĕri,   complurĭbus   navĭbus
perceived   to be [was] done,   several   ships

expugnatis,   quum   nullum   auxilĭum
having been stormed [boarded],   since   no   aid

reperiretur   ĕi   rĕi,   contenderunt   petere
was found   for this   thing [crisis],   they hastened   to seek

salutem   fŭgâ: ac jam navĭbus   conversis   in
safety   by flight: and now the ships   having been turned   to

ĕam   partem,   quò   ventus   ferebat,   tanta
that   part [direction]   where   the wind   was bearing,   so great

malacĭa   ac   tranquillĭtas   subĭtò   exstĭtit,   ut
a calm   and   stillness   suddenly   occurred,   that

possent (imp. subj.)   non movere   se   ex
they were able   not to move   themselves   from

lŏco: quæ res[36]   quĭdem   fŭit   maxĭmè   opportuna
the place: which thing   indeed   was   most   seasonable

ad conficiendum   negotĭnm,   nam   nostri
for   completing   the business [engagement],   for   our (men)

consectati   singŭlas   expugnaverunt,   ut
having pursued   individual (ships)   stormed [boarded] (them),   so that

perpaucæ   ex   omni   numĕro   pervenĕrint   ad
very few   from [of]   all   the number   arrived   to

terram,   interventu   noctis,   quum   pug-
land,   by the interposition   of night,   since   it was

naretur[37] (imp. subj.)   ab   quartâ   horâ   usque
[they] fought   from   the fourth   hour   until

ad   occasum   solis.
(to)   the setting   of the sun.

16. Quo   prœlĭo   bellum   Venetorum   que
By which   battle   the war   of the Veneti   and

totius   maritĭmæ   oræ   confectum-est.   Nam
of the whole   maritime   coast   was finished.   For

quum   omnis   juventus,   etĭam omnes   gravioris
not only   all   (their) youth,   also   all   of more mature

ætatis, in   quĭbus[38]   fŭit,   alĭquid   consilĭi   aut
age, in   whom   (there) was,   something [some]   (of) counsel   or

dignitatis   convenĕrant   ĕò;   tum   coēgĕrant
(of) dignity   had assembled   there;   but also   they had collected

in   unum   lŏcum,   quod   navĭum   fŭĕrat
into   one   place,   what [whatever]   (of) ships   had been

ubique:	quĭbus	amissis,	relĭqui	habebant
everywhere:	which	having been lost,	the rest	were having

nĕque	quò	recipĕrent	se,	nĕque
neither	where	they might betake	themselves,	nor

quemadmŏdum	defendĕrent	oppĭda.	Ităque
how	they might defend	(their) towns.	Therefore

dediderunt	se	que	omnĭa	sŭa
they surrendered	themselves	and	all	their (effects)

Cæsări:	in	quos	Cæsar	statŭit	vindicandum
to Cæsar:	against	whom	Cæsar	resolved	to be avenged

gravĭùs	ĕò	quò	jus	legat-
more severely	for this reason	in order that	the right	of ambas-

orum	conservaretur	diligentĭùs	à	barbăris
sadors	might be observed	more carefully	by	the barbarians

in	reliquum	tempus.	Ităque,	omni
for	the remaining [future]	time.	Therefore,	all

senatu	necato,	vendĭdit	relĭquos	sub
the senate	having been put to death,	he sold	the rest	under

coronâ.[39]
the crown [at auction].

17. Dum   hæc   geruntur   in
While   these (things)   are carried on   in [among]

Venĕtis,	Quintus	Titurĭus	Sabinus	pervenit	in
the Veneti,	Quintus	Titurius	Sabinus	passed	into

fines	Venellorum,	cum	his	copĭis,	quas
the borders	of the Venelli,	with	these	forces,	which

accepĕrat	à	Cæsăre.	Viridŏvix	præĕrat
he had received	from	Cæsar.	Viridovix	commanded

his (dat.),	ac	tenebat	summam	imperĭi
these,	and	was holding	the height	(of) [the chief] power

omnĭum	earum	civitatum,	quæ	defecĕrant;	ex
of all	of these	states,	which	had revolted;	from

quĭbus	coĕgĕrat	exercĭtum	que	magnas
which	he had collected	an army	and	great

copĭas.	Atque	his	paucis	diebus,	Aulerci,
resources.	And	in these	few	days,	the Aulerci,

Eburovices,	que	Lexovĭi,	sŭo	senatu	inter-
Eburovices,	and	Lexovii,	their	senate	having been put

fecto,   quòd   nolebant   esse auctores   belli,
to death, because they were unwilling to be advisers of war,

clauserunt   portas,   que conjunxerunt   se
shut   (their) gates,   and joined   themselves

cum Viridovice: que præterĕa magna   multitudo
with Viridovix: and besides   a great multitude

perditorum   homĭnum que latronum   convenĕrat
of abandoned men   and robbers   had assembled

undĭque   ex   Gallĭâ,   quos   spes
from every side from Gaul,   whom   the hope

prædandi   que studĭum[40]   bellandi   revoc-
of plundering and an inclination of warrıng were calling

abat   ab   agri culturâ   et   quotidiano labore.
away   from agriculture   and daily   labor.

Sabinus   tenebat   sese   castris (pl.) lŏco
Sabinus   was holding himself in camp   ın a place

idonĕo   omnĭbus   rebus: quum   Viridŏvix
suitable   for all   things: when   Viridovix

considisset (pl. perf. subj.) contrâ   ĕum   spatĭo
had pitched camp   opposite him   (to) a space

              dŭûm   millĭum,   que   copĭis
[distance]   of two   miles,   and   (his) forces

productis   quotidĭe   facĕret (imp. subj.)
having been led forth daily   he was making

potestatem   pugnandi;   ut   Sabinus jam
power [an opportunity]   of fighting; so that Sabinus already

veniret (imp. subj.) in   contemptionem non solùm
was coming   into contempt   not only

       hostĭbus,   sed etĭam carperetur (imp. subj.)
to [as regards] the enemy, but also   was censured

nonnĭhil   vocĭbus   nostrorum milĭtum: que
somewhat   by the expressions of our   soldıers: and

præbŭit   tantam   opinionem   timoris, ut
he exhibited so great an opinion [a sentiment] of fear, that

hostes   auderent   jam   accedĕre   ad   vallum
the enemy   would dare at length to approach to   the rampart

castrorum (pl.). Faciebat   id   ĕâ   causâ,
of the camp.   He was doing this from this cause [reasor]

quòd existimabat[41] non dimicandum
because he was thinking (it) not to [must not] be contended

legato (dat.) cum tantâ multitudĭne hostĭum,
by a lieutenant with so great a multitude of the enemy,

præsertim ĕo absente, qui teneret (imp. subj.)
especially he (being) absent, who was holding

summam imperĭi, nĭsi æquo lŏco,
the height [chief] (of) command, unless on equal place [ground],

aut alĭquâ opportunitate dătâ.
or some opportunity having [had] been given.

18. Hâc opinione timoris confirmâtâ,
This opinion of fear having been strengthened,

delegit quandam Gallum idonĕum et callĭdum
he selected a certain Gaul a suitable and shrewd

homĭnem, ex ĭis, quos habebat secum
man, from those, whom he was having with him

causâ auxilĭi (sing.). Persuadet huic (dat.)
for the sake of reinforcements. He persuades him

magnis præmĭis que pollicitationĭbus, ŭtì
by great rewards and promises, that

transĕat[42] ad hostes: edŏcet quod
he go over to the enemy: he shows (him) what

vĕlit fieri. Qui, ŭbi venit ad ĕos
he wishes to be done. Who, when he came to them

pro perfŭgâ, proponit timorem Romanorun :
for [as] a deserter, exposed the fear of the Romans

dŏcet quĭbus angustĭis Cæsar ipse
he shows (them) with what straits [difficulties] Cæsar himself

prematur (pres. subj.) à Venĕtis: nĕque[43] longĭus
is pressed by the Veneti: nor farther

abesse, quin Sabinus educat
to be [was it] distant (from fact), but that Sabinus may lead out

exercĭtum clàm ex castris (pl.) proxĭmâ
(his) army secretly from the camp on the next

nocte, et proficiscatur ad Cæsărem, causâ
night, and (may) set out to Cæsar, for the sake

ferendi auxilĭi. Ubì quod auditum-est,
of bearing aid, When which (this report) was heard,

omnes conclamant, occasionem gerendi ne-
all cry out (that), an opportunity of performing the

gotĭi bĕnè non amittendam-esse: oportere
business [task] well not to [must not] be lost: to be fitting

iri ad castra (pl.). Multæ
'they ought] to be gone [to go] to the camp. Many

res hortabantur Gallos ad hoc consilĭum:
things were encouraging the Gauls to this plan:

cunctatĭo Sabini superiorum dierum;
the hesitation of Sabinus of [on] the former days;

confirmatĭo perfŭgæ; inopĭa⁴⁴ cibariorum (pl.),
the assurance of the deserter; the want of food,

cui provisum-ĕrat ab his parùm
for which it had been provided by them not very

diligenter; spes Venetĭci belli; et quòd
carefully; the hopes of the Venetian war; and because

homĭnes fĕrè credunt libenter id quod
men generally believe willingly that which

vŏlunt. Adducti⁴⁵ ĭis rebus, dimittunt
they desire. Induced by these things, they dismiss

Viridovicem que relĭquos dŭces ex
Viridovix and the rest of the generals from

concilĭo non prĭùs quàm concessum-sit ab
the council not sooner than it has been [was] granted by

his, ŭtì capĭant arma et contendant ad
them, that they may take arms and may hasten to

castra (pl.). Quâ re concessâ, læti,
the camp. Which thing having been granted, (they) joyful,

vĕlut victorĭâ exploratâ, sarmentis que
as if the victory having been [were] assured, fagots and

virgultis collectis, quĭbus complĕant
bushes having been collected, with which they may fill up

fossas Romanorum, pergunt ad castra (pl.).
the ditches of the Romans, they press on to the camp.

19. Lŏcus castrorum (pl.) ĕrat edĭtus, et
The situation of the camp was elevated, and

paullatim acclivis ab imo, circĭter
gradually sloping from the lowest [from below] about

mille   passus :   huc   contenderunt   magno
a thousand   paces :   hither   they hastened   with great

cursu,[46]   ut   quàm   minĭmum   spatĭi
running,   that   as   least [little as possible]   (of) space [time]

datur   Romanis   ad   colligendos,
might be given   to the Romans   for   collecting,

que   armandos,   se   que   exanimati
and   arming   themselves   and   breathless

pervenerunt.   Sabinus,   hortatus   sŭos,
they arrived (there).   Sabinus,   having encouraged   his (men),

dat   signum   cupientĭbus :   hostĭbus
gives   the signal   to (them) being eager for (it):   the enemy

impeditis   propter   ĕa   onĕra,   quæ
having been encumbered   on account of   these   burdens,   which

ferebant,   jŭbet   eruptionem   fiĕri   subĭtò
they were bearing,   he orders   a sally   to be made   suddenly

duabus   portis.   Fǎctum-est[47]   opportunitate
from the two   gates.   It was done   by the convenience

lŏci,   inscientĭa   ac defatigatione   hostĭum,
of the place,   by the ignorance   and   exhaustion   of the enemy.

virtute   milĭtum   ac   exercitatione   superiorum
by the valor   of the soldiers   and   the practice   of former

pugnarum,   ut   ferrent (imp. subj.)   ne   quĭdem
battles,   that   they were bearing   not   even

primum   impĕtum   nostrorum ;   ac   stătim
the first   charge   of our (men);   and   immediately

vertĕrent (imp. subj.)   terga :   quos[48]   impeditos
they were turning   (their) backs: whom   encumbered

nostri   milĭtes   consecuti   intĕgris   virĭbus (pl.),
our   soldiers   having pursued   with fresh   strength,

occiderunt   magnum   numĕrum   eorum :   equĭtes
slew   a great   number   of them :   the cavalry

consectati   relĭquos   reliquerunt   paucos,   qui
having pursued   the rest   left   few,   who

evasĕrant   ex   fŭgâ.   Sic   Cæsar   factus-est
had escaped   from   flight.   Thus   Cæsar   was made

certĭor   uno   tempŏre   et   de
more sure [was informed]   in [at] one   time   both   of

navali   pugnâ,   et   de   victorĭâ   Sabini:
the naval   battle,   and   of   the victory   of Sabinus:

que omnes   civitates   dediderunt   se   stătim
and   all   the states   surrendered   themselves   immediately

Titurĭo.   Nam   ut   anĭmus   Gallorum   est
to Titurius.   For   as   the spirit   of the Gauls   is

alăcer   ac   promptus   ad   suscipienda[49]   bella,
alert   and   ready   for   undertaking   wars,

sic   eorum   mens   est   mollis   ac   minĭmè
so   their   mind   is   soft [weak]   and   by no means

resistens   ad   perferendas   calamitates.
resistant   for   bearing   misfortunes.

20. Fĕrè   eodem   tempŏre,   quum   Publĭus
Nearly   at the same   time,   when   Publius

Crassus   pervenisset (pl. perf. subj.) in   Aquitanĭam,
Crassus   had arrived   into [at]   Aquitania,

quæ   pars,   ut   dictum-est   antè,   est
which   part,   as   has been said   before,   is

æstimanda   ex   tertĭâ   parte   Gallĭæ,   et
to [must] be regarded   from [as]   the third   part   of Gaul,   both

latitudĭne   regionum   et   multitudĭne
by the breadth [extent]   of countries   and   by the multitude

homĭnum;   quum   intelligĕret (imp. subj.) bellum
of men;   when   he was understanding   (that)   war

gerendum   sĭbi (dat.)   in   eis   lŏcis,
to [must] be carried on   by himself   in   these   places,

ŭbi   paucis (abl.)   annis   antè   Lucĭus
where   a few   years   before   Lucius

Valerĭus   Præconinus   legatus   interfectus-esset
Valerius   Præconinus   the lieutenant   had been killed,

(pl. perf. subj.),   exercĭtu   pulso;   atque
    (his) army   having been routed;   and

unde   Lucĭus   Manilĭus   Proconsul,   impedi-
whence   Lucius   Manilius   the Proconsul,   (his)

mentis   amissis,   profugisset (pl. perf. subj.),
baggage   having been lost,   had escaped,

intelligebat   non   mediocrem   diligentĭam
he was understanding (that)   not [no]   moderate   diligence

adhibendam   sĭbi (dat.). Ităque, frumentarĭâ
to [must] be employed by himself. Therefore, corn

re   provisâ,   auxilĭis que equitatu
affair [grain] having been provided, auxiliaries and cavalry

comparato,   præterĕa multis fortĭbus vĭris
having been prepared, moreover many brave men

Tolosâ   et   Narbone (quæ sunt civitates
from Tolosa and Narbo (which are cities

provincĭæ Gallĭæ, finitĭmæ   his   regionĭbus)
of the province of Gaul, neighboring to these countries)

evocatis   nominatim, introduxit exercĭtum
having been called out by name, he led forth (his) army

in   fines   Sotiatĭum.   Cujus   adventu
into the territories of the Sotiates. Whose arrival

cognĭto,   Sotiates,   magnis copĭis   coac-
having been known, the Sotiates, great forces having been

tis,   que   equitatu,   quo   valebant
collected, and cavalry, in which they were availing

plurĭmum,   adorti   nostrum agmen in itinĕre,
most,   having attacked our   army on the march.

primùm commiserunt equestre prœlĭum; deinde
first   engaged   (in) a cavalry fight;   afterwards

sŭo   equitatu   pulso,   atque nostris
their cavalry having been routed, and our (men)

insequentĭbus, ostenderunt   subĭtò pedestres
pursuing,   they showed [revealed] suddenly the foot

copĭas, quas   collocavĕrant in   convalle   in
forces, which they had placed in a valley basin in

insidĭis,   Hi   adorti   nostros disjectos,
ambuscades. These having attacked our (men) scattered,

renovârunt   prœlĭum.
renewed   the battle.

21. Pugnatum-est[50]   dĭu   atque acrĭter, quum
     It was fought   long   and   sharply,   since

Sotiates,   freti   superiorĭbus victorĭis,
the Sotiates, having relied on former   victories,

putarent (imp. subj.) salutem[51] totius   Aquitanĭæ
were thinking (that)   the safety of the whole of Aquitania

posĭtam   in   sŭâ   virtute;   autem   nostri
was placed   in   their own   valor;   but   our (men)

cupĕrent (imp. subj.)   perspĭci,[52]   quid   pos-
were desiring   (that it)   to [should] be seen,   what   they might be

sent   efficĕre   sĭne   imperatore,
able [could]   (to) accomplish   without   the commander in chief,

et   sĭne   relĭquis   legionĭbus,   adolescentŭlo
and   withc ut   the remaining   legions,   a very young man

duce.   Tămen   hostes   tandem   confecti
(being) general.   However   the enemy   at length   having been spent

vulnerĭbus   vertêrunt   terga :   magno   numĕro
with wounds   turned   (their) backs: a great   number

quorum   interfecto,   Crassus   cœpit   oppugnare
of whom   having been slain,   Crassus   began   to storm

oppĭdum   Sotiatĭum   ex   itinĕre;   quĭbus
the town   of the Sotiates   from [on]   (his) march;   who [they]

resistentĭbus[53]   fortĭter,   egit   vinĕas   que
opposing   bravely,   he pushed   the sheds   and

turres.   Illi,   alĭas   eruptione   tentatâ,
towers.   They   at one time   a sally   having been tried,

alĭas   cunicŭlis   actis   ad   aggĕrem
at another time   mines   having been pushed   to   the rampart

que   vinĕas;   cujus   rĕi   Aquitani   sunt   longè
and   sheds;   of which   thing   the Aquitani   are   by far

peritissĭmi,   proptere̊a-quòd   ærarĭæ   que   secturæ
most skillful,   because (that)   copper mines   and   quarries

sunt   ăpud   ĕos   multis   lŏcis;   ŭbi   intellexerunt
are   among   them   in many   places;   when   they understood

nĭhĭl   posse   profĭci   his   rebus,
nothing   to be able [could]   (to) be accomplished   by these   things

diligentĭâ   nostrorum,   mittunt   legatos
[tactics],   from the activity   of our (men),   they send   ambassadors

ad   Crassum   que   pĕtunt,   ut   recipĭat   se
to   Crassus   and   request,   that   he may receive   themselves

in   deditionem.   Quâ   re   impetratâ,
into   a surrender.   Which   thing   having been obtained,

jussi   tradĕre   arma,   facĭunt
having been ordered   to deliver   (their) arms,   they do (it)

22. Atque   anĭmis   omnĭum   nostrorum   intentis
        And   the minds   of all   our (men)   being engaged

in   ĕâ   re,   Adiatŏmus   qui   tenebat   summam
on   this   thing,   Adiatomas   who   was holding   the height

            imperĭi,   ex   alĭâ   parte   oppĭdi,   cum
(of) [the chief] command,   from   another   part   of the town,   with

sexcentis   devotis,   quos   illi   appellant
six hundred   devoted (men),   whom   they   call

Soldurĭos: quorum   hæc   est   condĭtĭo   ut
Soldurii: of whom   this   is   the estate   that

fruantur (pres. subj.)   omnĭbus   commŏdis (abl.)   in
they enjoy   all   advantages   in

vitâ   unà   cum   his,   amicitĭæ   quorum
life   together   with   those,   to the friendship   of whom

        dedĭdĕrint   se: si   quid
they may have given up [devoted]   themselves: if   any (thing)

accĭdat   ĭis   per   vim,   aut
may happen   to these   through   violence,   (that) either

fĕrant   eundem   casum   unà,   aut   consciscant[54]
they may bear   the same   calamity   together, or   inflict

mortem   sĭbi (dat.)   nĕque   quisquam   repertus-est
death   upon themselves   nor   has any one   been found

adhuc   memorĭâ   homĭnum,   qui   recusaret
as yet   in the memory   of men,   who   would refuse

mŏri,   ĕo   interfecto,   amicitĭæ   cujus
to die,   he   having been killed,   to the friendship   of whom

        devovisset   se.   Cum   his   Adiatŏmus
he might have devoted   himself.   With   these   Adiatomus

conatus   făcĕre   eruptionem,   clamore
having endeavored   to make   a sally,   a shout

        sublato   ab   ĕâ   parte   munitionis,
having been raised   from   that   part   of the fortification,

quum   milĭtes   concurrissent (pl. perf. subj.)   ad
when   the soldiers   had run together   to

arma,   que   pugnatum-esset[55] (pl. perf. subj.)   ĭbi
arms,   and   it had been [they had] fought   there

vehementer,   repulsus-est   in   oppĭdum;   tămen
violently,   he was forced back   into   the town;   however

impetravit   à   Crasso,   ŭtì   uteretur[56]
he obtained   from   Crassus,   that   he might use

eâdem   conditione (abl.)   deditionis.
the same   condition [terms]   of surrender.

23. Armis   que   obsidĭbus   acceptis,   Crassus
The arms and   hostages   having been received   Crassus

profectus-est   in   fines   Vocatĭum   et
set out   into   the territories of the Vocates and

Tarusatĭum.   Tum   verò   barbări
of the Tarusates. Then   indeed   the barbarians (were)

commoti, quòd   cognovĕrant   oppĭdum munitum
alarmed,   because they had learned (that) a town   fortified

et   naturâ   lŏci   et   mănu
both   by the nature of the place and   by hand [by art]

expugnatum[57]   paucis   diebus, quĭbus   ven-
having been stormed in the few days,   in which   it had been

tum fuĕrat   ĕò;   cœperunt dimittĕre   legatos
[they had] come there; they began to send   ambassadors

quoqueversus,   conjurare,   dăre   obsĭdes   inter
in every direction, to take oaths, to give hostages between

se,   parare   copĭas.   Legati   mittuntur
themselves, to prepare forces.   Ambassadors are sent

etĭam   ad   ĕas   civitates,   quæ   sunt   citerioris
also   to   these   states,   which   are   in nearer

Hispanĭæ (gen.)   finitĭmæ   Aquitanĭæ: inde
Spain   neighboring to Aquitania: thence

auxilĭa   que   dŭces   arcessuntur;   adventu
auxiliaries and   generals are summoned;   on the arrival

quorum   conantur   gerĕre   bellum cum   magnâ
of whom   they endeavor to wage   war   with   great

auctoritate et   cum   magnâ   multitudĭne homĭnum.
authority   and with a great   multitude   of men.

Verò   ĭi   deliguntur   dŭces,   qui   fuĕrant
Moreover these are chosen (as) generals, who   had been

unà   cum   Quinto   Sertorĭo   omnes   annos,   que
together with   Quintus Sertorius   all   the years, and

existimabantur habere   summam   scientĭam militaris
were thought   to have the highest knowledge of military

rĕi Hi consuetudĭne Romani popŭli
affair [tactics] These by the custom of the Roman people

institŭunt capĕre lŏca, munire
resolve to take [choose] places [ground], to fortify

castra (pl.), intercludĕre nostros commeatĭbus.
the camp, to shut off our (men) from provisions.

Quod ŭbi Crassus animadvertit, sŭas
Which when Crassus perceived, (and that) his own

copĭas non facĭlè diduci propter
forces not easily to be [were] divided on account of

exiguitatem, et hostem vagari
(their) scantiness [fewness], and (that) the enemy (to) wander about

et obsidere vĭas, et relinquĕre sătis
and (to) block up the ways, and (to) leave enough

præidĭi castris (pl.); ob ĕam causam
of protection to (their) camp; on account of this cause (that)

frumentum que commeatum supportari
corn and provision to be [were] brought up

sĭbi mĭnùs commŏdè, numĕrum hostĭum
to himself less conveniently, (that) the number of the enemy

augeri in dĭes; existimavit[58] non cunctan-
(to be) increased daily; he considered (it) not to [he must not] be

dum, quin decertaret pugnâ. Hâc re
delayed [delay], but that he should contend in battle. This thing

delatâ ad concilĭum, ŭbi intellexit
having been referred to a council, when he understood (that)

omnes[59] sentire ĭdem, constitŭit postĕrum
all (to) think the same, he appointed the following

dĭem pugnæ.
day for the battle.

24. Omnĭbus copĭis productis primâ
All (his) forces having been drawn out at the first

luce, duplĭci acĭe institutâ, que
light [early dawn], a double line having been formed, and

auxilĭis conjectis in medĭam acĭem,
the auxiliaries having been thrown into the middle line,

exspectabat quid consilĭi (gen.) hostes capĕrent.
he was awaiting what plan the enemy might take.

Illi,   etsi   propter   multitudĭnem,   et
They,   although   on account of   (their) multitude,   and

vetĕrem   glorĭam   belli   que paucitatem nostrorum
ancient   glory   of war and the fewness   of our (men)

existimabant   se   dimicaturos   tutô;
were considering (that) themselves about to [would] contend safely;

tămen   arbitrabantur   esse   tutĭus   potiri
however   they were judging (it)   to be [was]   safer   to possess

victorĭâ   sĭne   vulnĕre,   vĭis
a victory   without   a wound,   the ways [roads]   having

obsessis,   commeatu   intercluso: et si
been blocked up,   provisions   having been intercepted: and if

  propter   inopiam   rei   frumentariae   Romani
on account of   the want   of   provisions   the Romans

cœpissent (pl. perf. subj.)   recipĕre   sese,
should begin   to take away   themselves [to re-

            cogitabant   adoriri   impeditos
treat],   they were thinking to [they would] attack (them) encumbered

agmĭne   et   sub   sarcĭnis (pl.), inferiores anĭmo.
on the march and   under   baggage, (and)   weaker   in spirit.

Hoc   consilĭo[60]   probato   ab   ducĭbus,
This   plan   having been approved   by (their) generals,

copĭis   Romanorum   productis,   tenebant
the forces   of the Romans having been drawn out, they were keep-

        sese   castris (pl.). Hâc   re   perspectâ
ing themselves   in camp.   This   thing   being clearly seen

Crassus,   quum   hostes   effecissent (pl. perf. subj.)
Crassus,   since   the enemy   had rendered

sŭâ   cunctatione   atque   opinione   timoris,
by their   delay   and   the belief   of fear,

nostros   milĭtes   alacriores   ad pugnandum,
our   soldiers   more eager   to fight [for fighting],

atque   voces   omnĭum   audirentur (imp. subj.),
and   the expressions   of all   were heard,   (that it)

oportere[61]   non   exspectari   diutĭus,   quin
to be [was] fitting   not   to be waited [to wait]   longer,   but that

    iretur   ad   castra (pl.); cohortatus
it should be gone [they should go] to   the camp;   having exorted

sŭos,   omnĭbus   cupientĭbus,   contendit   ad
his (men),   all   desiring,   he hastens   to

castra (pl.)   hostium.
the camp   of the enemy.

25. Ibi   quum   alĭi   complerent (imp. subj.) fossas
There when some   were filling   the ditches

alĭi   depellĕrent (imp. subj.) defensores   vallo
others were dislodging   the defenders from the rampart

que   munitionĭbus,   multis   telis   conjectis,   que
and   fortifications,   many   weapons having been thrown, and

auxiliares,   quĭbus (dat.) Crassus   confidebat   non
the auxiliaries,   [in] whom   Crassus   was confiding   not

multùm   ab   pugnam,   præberent (imp. subj.)
much   for   the battle,   were exhibiting

specĭem   atque   opinionem   pugnantĭum
the appearance   and   impression   of fighting (men)

subministrandis lapidĭbus que telis, et comportandis
by supplying   stones   and weapons, and by collecting

cespitĭbus ad aggĕrem;   quum ĭtem   pugnaretur
turfs   for a mound;   since likewise it was fought

(imp. subj.) constanter ac non timĭdè ab hostĭbus,
            steadily   and not timidly by   the enemy,

que   tela   missa   ex   superiore   lŏco,
and   the weapons sent [thrown] from the higher   place,

accidĕrent (imp. subj.) non frustrà; equĭtes, castris
were falling   not in vain; horsemen, the camp

(pl.) hostĭum   circumĭtis, renuntiaverunt Crasso
of the enemy   having encircled, announced   to Crassus

        castra (pl.) non   esse   munita   eâdem
(that) the camp   not to be [was not] fortified with the same

diligentĭâ   ab   Decumanâ portâ, que habere
diligence   from [at]   the Decuman gate, and to have

        facĭlem   adĭtum.
[had]   an easy   access.

26. Crassus   cohortatus   præfectos   equĭtum
    Crassus   having encouraged the perfects of the horsemen

ut   excitarent   sŭos   magnis   præmĭis
that   they should stimulate their (men) by great   rewards

que   pollicitationĭbus,   ostendit   quid   vĕlit
and   promises,   shows (them)   what   he wishes

fiĕri.   Illi,   ut   imperatum ĕrat,   eis
to be done.   They,   as   it had been commanded,   these

cohortĭbus   devectis,   quæ   relictæ
cohorts   having been brought forth,   which   having been left

præsidĭo   castris (pl.),   ĕrant   intritæ   ab
for a guard   to the camp,   were   unworn [fresh]   from

labore: et   circumductis   longiore   itinĕre,
labor: and   having been led round   by a longer   route,

ne   possent   conspĭci   ex   castris
lest   they might be able [should]   (to) be seen   from   the camp

hostĭum;   ocŭlis   que   mentĭbus   omnĭum
of the enemy;   the eyes   and   minds   of all

intentis   ad   pugnam,   pervenerunt   celerĭter
being engaged   to [on]   the fight,   they arrived   quickly

ad   ĕas   munitiones,   quas   dixĭmus;   atque
to [at]   these   fortifications,   which   we have mentioned;   and

his   prorutis,   constiterunt   in   castris
these   having been demolished,   they stood   in   the camp

(pl.)   hostĭum   prĭus   quàm   posset
   of the enemy   before   that   it might be able [could]

vidĕri   planè   ab   his   aut   cognosci,   quid
(to) be seen   plainly   by   these   or   (to) be known,   what

rĕi   gereretur.   Tum   verò   clamore
(of) thing   was transpiring.   Then   indeed   a shout

audito   ab   ĕâ   parte,   nostri,   virĭbus (pl.)
having been heard   from   this   part,   our (men),   their strength

redintegratis,   quod   plerumque   consuevit
having been renewed,   which   generally   has been accustomed

accidĕre   in   spe   victorĭæ,   cœperunt   impugnare
to occur   in   the hope   of victory,   began   to assault

acrĭùs.   Hostes   circumventi   undĭque,
more vigorously.   The enemy   surrounded   on every side,

omnĭbus   rebus   desperatis,   contenderunt
all   things   having been despaired of,   hastened

dejicĕre   se   per   munitones,   et
to hurl   themselves   through   the fortifications,   and

petĕre   salutem   fŭgâ   Quos   equitatus
to seek   safety   by flight.   Whom   the cavalry

consectatus   apertissĭmis   campis,   recepit
having pursued   in the most open   plains,   betook

se   in   castra (pl.)   mŭltâ   nocte,[62]
itself   into   camp   in much   night [late at night],

vix   quartâ   parte   relictâ   ex
scarcely   a fourth   part   having been left   from

numĕro   quinquaginta   millĭum,   quæ
the number   of fifty   thousand,   which

constabat   venisse   ex   Aquitanĭâ
it was evident   to have [had] come   from   Aquitania

que   Cantăbris.
and   the Cantabri.

27. Hâc   pugnâ   auditâ,   maxĭma   pars
This   battle   having been heard of,   the greatest   part

Aquitanĭæ   dedĭdit   sese   Crasso,   que   misit
of Aquitania   surrendered   itself   to Crassus,   and   sent

obsĭdes   ultrò: in   quo   numĕro   fuerunt
hostages   voluntarily: in   which   number   were

Tarbelli,   Bigerriŏnes,   Ptianii,   Vocates,   Tarusates,
the Tarbelli,   Bigerriones,   Ptianii,   Vocates,   Tarusates,

Elusătes,   Gates,   Ausci,   Garumni,   Sibusates,   que
Elusates,   Gates,   Ausci,   Garumni,   Sibusates,   and

Cocosates.   Paucæ   ultĭmæ   nationes,   confisæ
Cocosates.   A few   remotest   nations,   having relied

tempŏre   anni,   quòd   hĭems   subĕrat,
on the time   of the year,   because   winter   was near,

neglexerunt   facĕre   id.
neglected   to do   this.

28. Fĕrè   eodem   tempŏre,   etsi   æstas
Nearly   at the same   time,   although   the summer

ĕrat   jam   prŏpè   exacta,   tămen   quòd,   omni
was   already   almost   finished,   still   because,   all

Gallĭâ   pacatâ,   Morĭni   que   Menapĭi
Gaul   having been subdued,   the Morini   and   Menapii

superĕrant,   qui   essent (imp. subj.)   in   armis
were remaining,   who   were   in   arms

nĕque   unquam   misissent[63] (pl. perf. subj.) ad   ĕum
nor   had ever   sent   to   him

lĕgatos   de   pace,   Cæsar   arbitratus
ambassadors about   peace,   Cæsar   having thought (that)

id   bellum   posse   confĭci   celerĭter,   duxit
this   war   to be able [could] (to) be finished quickly,   led

exercĭtum   ĕò :   qui   cœpĕrunt   agĕre   bellum
the army   thither: who   began   to conduct   the war

ratione   longè   alĭâ   ac   relĭqui   Galli :
in a manner   far   otherwise   than   the remaining   Gauls:

nam,   quòd   intelligebant   maxĭmas
for,   because   they were understanding (that)   the greatest

nationes,   quæ   contendissent (pl. perf. subj.) prœlĭo
nations,   which   had contended   in battle

      pulsas-esse   que   superatas,   que   habebant
to have [had] been routed and   overcome,   and   they were having

continentes   silvas   ac   paludes,   contulerunt   ĕò
extended   woods   and   marshes,   they bore away thither

se   que   omnĭa   sŭa.   Ad   initĭun
themselves   and   all   their (effects).   At   the beginning

quarum[64]   silvarum,   quum   Cæsar   pervenisset (pl.
of which   woods,   when   Cæsar   had arrived,

perf. subj.),   que   instituisset (pl. perf. subj.) munire
                and   had resolved   to fortify

castra (pl.),   nĕque   intĕrim   hostis   visus esset
the camp,   nor   meanwhile   the enemy   had been seen ;

(pl. perf. subj.);   nostris   dispersis   in
                     our (men)   having been scattered   in

opĕre,   evolaverunt   subĭtò   ex   omnĭbus   partĭbus
the work, they flew out suddenly   from   all   parts

silvæ,   et   fecerunt   impĕtum   in   nostros.
of the wood, and   made   an attack   upon   our (men).

Nostri   celeriter   ceperunt   arma,   que
Our (men)   quickly   took   arms,   and

repulerunt   ĕos   in   silvas ;   et   complur-
forced   them   into   the woods ;   and   very

ĭbus   interfectis,   secuti   longĭùs
many   having been killed,   having followed (them)   rather far

impeditiorĭbus   lŏcis,   deperdiderunt   paucos
in more entangled   places,   they lost   a few

ex   sŭis.
from [of]   their own (men).

29.   Cæsar   institŭit   cædĕre   silvas   deinceps
      Cæsar   resolved   to cut   the woods   in succession

relĭquis   diebus;   et   ne   quis   impĕtus
on the remaining   days;   and   lest   any   attack

posset   fiĕri   ab   latĕre   militĭbus
might be able [couid]   (to) be made   from   the flank   on the soldiers

(dat.)   inermĭbus   que   imprudentĭbus,   collocabat
       unarmed   and   unaware,   he was placing

omnem   ĕam   materĭam,   quæ   cæsa ĕrat,
all   this   materal [timber],   which   had been cut,

conversam   ad   hostem,   que   exstruebat   pro
turned   to   the enemy,   and   was building (it)   for

vallo   ad   utrumque   lătus.   Magno   spatĭo
a rampart   to [on]   each   flank.   A great   space

confecto   paucis   diebus   incredibĭli
having been finished [cleared]   in a few   days   with incredible

celeritate,   quum   pĕcus   atque   extrema   imped-
speed,   when   the cattle   and   the farthest   bag-

imenta (pl.)   tenerentur (imp. subj.)   jam   ab   nostris,
gage   was possessed   now   by   our (men),

ipsi   petĕrent (imp. subj.)   densiores   silvas;
(they) themselves   were seeking   the thicker   woods:

tempestates   ejusmŏdi   consecutæ sunt,   ŭti   ŏpus
storms   of such kind   followed,   that   the work

intermitteretur (imp. subj.)   necessarĭò;   et   contin-
was interrupted   necessarily;   and   by the

uatione   imbrĭum,   milĭtes   possent (imp. subj.)
continuance   of the rains,   the soldiers   were able

non   contineri   diutĭùs   sub   pellĭbus.   Ităque,
not   to be kept   longer   under   hides [tents].   Therefore,

omnĭbus   eorum   agris   vastatis,[65]   vicis
all   their   lands   having been ravaged,   the villages

que   ædificĭis   incensis,   Cæsar   reduxit   exercĭtum
and   buildings   having been burned,   Cæsar   led back   the army

et   collocavit   in   hibernis   in   Aulereis
and   placed (it)   in   winter quarters   among   the Aulerci

que   Lexovïis,   Ïtem   relïquis   civitatibus,   quæ
and   the Lexovii,   also   the remaining   states,   which

facerant   bellum   proxïmè.
had made   war   last.

FOURTH BOOK

The fourth book contains the description of Cæsar's campaign against the Germans and of his first invasion of Britain, B. C. 55. The German tribes, the Usipetes Germani and the Tencteri, pressed by the Suevi, had crossed the Rhine near its mouth and conquered the Menapii. Cæsar, fearing complications and a possible alliance of the Gauls and Germans, orders the Germans to withdraw from Gaul. He then advances with the army and a protracted parley takes place between him and the Germans. After a treacherous attack by the German cavalry Cæsar assaults the camp of the Germans and puts them to flight. The Rhine is bridged by Cæsar, who invades Germany and after a stay of 18 days returns. He sends a reconnoitering fleet to Britain, and after assembling a large fleet, himself, sails and lands on the British coast. A storm disables the fleet, whereupon the Britons attack him and are defeated. Cæsar returns to Gaul. The Morini rebel and are subdued. For that winter the legions are quartered among the Belgæ and the Senate appoints a thanksgiving of 20 days.

1. Eâ hiĕme quæ secuta est, qui fŭit annus,
In this winter which followed, which was the year,

Cneĭo Pompeĭo, Marco Crasso consulĭbus,
(when) Cneius Pompey, Marcus Crassus (were) counsuls,

Germani Usipĕtes, et Ĭtem Tenctĕri transiêrunt
the German Usipetes, and also the Tencteri crossed

flumen Rhenum cum magnâ multitudĭne homĭnum,
the river Rhine with a great multitude of men,

non longè à mări, quò Rhenus inflŭit.
not far from the sea, where the Rhine flows in.

Causa transeundi fŭit, quòd exagitati ab
The cause of crossing was, because having been harassed by

Suevis complures annos, premebantur bello,
the Suevi many years, they were crushed by war,

et prohibebantur agri culturâ. Gens
and were prevented from agriculture. The nation

Suevorum est longè maxĭma et bellicosissĭma
of the Suevi is by far the greatest and most warlike

omnĭum Germanorum. Hi dicuntur habere
of all the Germans. These are said to have

centum pagos; ex quĭbus[1] educunt
a hundred cantons; from which they lead forth

quotannis singŭla (pl.) millĭa armatorum
yearly single thousands of armed (men)

ex sŭis finĭbus, causâ bellandi: relĭqui
from their borders, for the sake of warring: the rest

qui mănsĕrunt dŏmi (gen.), alunt se atque
who remained at home, support themselves and

illos. Hi rursus sunt in armis invĭcem
those. These again are in arms in turn

anno pòst; illi remănent dŏmi (gen.).
in the year after; they [those] remain at home.

Sic nĕque agri cultura, nĕque ratĭo atque
Thus neither agriculture, nor the theory and

usus belli intermittĭtur. Sed est nĭhil
practice of war is interrupted. But (there) is nothing

privati ac separati agri ăpud
[not any] (of) private and separate land at [among]

ĕos: nĕque lĭcet remanere longĭùs anno
them: neither is it lawful to remain longer (than) a year

in uno lŏco, causă colendi. Nĕque
in one place, for the sake of tilling [farming]. Neither

vivunt multum frumento, sed maxĭmam[2]
do they live much by [on] corn, but the greatest

partem lacte atque pecŏre; que sunt
part by [on] milk and cattle; and they are

multum in venationĭbus (pl.); quæ res et
much in huntings [in the chase]; which thing both

ălit vires et effĭcit homines
nourishes the forces [strength] and produces men

immani magnitudĭne corpŏrum et genĕre
with [of] huge size of bodies and by the kind

cĭbi, et quotidianâ exercitatione, et libertate
of food, and daily exercise. and freedom

vitæ,   quòd   âssuefacti   nullo   officĭo   aut
of life,   because   having been accustomed   to no   duty   or

disciplinâ   à   puĕris,   facĭant (pres. subj.)
discipline   from   boys [boyhood],   they do

nĭhil   omnino   contra   voluntatem.   Atque
nothing   at all   against   (their) will.   And

adduxerunt   se   in   ĕam   consuetudĭnem,
they have brought   themselves   into   this   habit,

ut   habĕant (pres. subj.)   nĕque   quidquam
that   they have   neither   any (thing)

vestitûs   frigidissĭmis   lŏcis,   præter   pelles;
(of) clothing   in the coldest   places,   except   skins;

propter   exiguitatem   quarum,   magna   pars
on account of   the scantiness   of which,   a great   part

corpŏris   est   aperta;   et   laventur (pres. subj.)
of the body   is   uncovered;   and   they are washed [bathe]

in   fluminĭbus.
in   the rivers.

2. Adĭtus   est   mercatorĭbus   ad   ĕos,   măgis
   Access   is   for merchants   to   them,   more

ĕò,   ut   habĕant   quĭbus
by this [on this account],   that   they may have (those)   to whom

vendant,   quæ   cepĕrint   bello,   quàm
they may sell,   what   they may have taken   in war,   than

quò   desidĕrent   ullam   rem   importari
that   they may desire   any   thing   to be imported

ad   se.   Quinetĭam   Germani   utuntur   non
to   themselves.   Moreover   the Germans   use   not

importatis   jumentis,   quĭbus   Galli   maxĭmè
imported   beasts of burden,   with which   the Gauls   especially

delectantur   que   quæ   părant   impenso
are delighted   and   which   they procure   at expensive [a high]

pretĭo;   sed   efficĭunt   hæc,   quæ   sunt   nata
price;   but   they render   these,   which   are   born

prava   atque   deformĭa   ăpud   ĕos,   quotidianâ
mis-shapen   and   deformed   among   them,   by daily

exercitatione   ut   sint   summi
exercise   that   they may be (capable)   of the highest [greatest]

*l*aboris.   Equestrĭbus   prœlĭis   desilĭunt   sæpe
labor.   In cavalry   fights   they leap down   often

ex   ĕquis,   ac   prœliantur[3]   pedĭbus;   qu.e
from   the horses,   and   fight   on feet [on foot];   and

assuefacĭunt   ĕquos   remanere   eodem   vestigĭo,
they accustom   the horses   to remain   in the same   footstep [spot],

ad   quos   recipĭunt   se   celerĭter,   quum   usus
to   which   they betake   themselves   quickly,   when   need

poscit: nĕque   quidquam   habetur   turpĭus
requires: nor   is any thing   held   more shameful

aut   inertĭus   eorum   morĭbus   quàm   uti
or   more lazy   by their   customs   than   to use

ephippĭis (abl.).   Ităque,[4]   quamvis   pauci   audent
saddles.   Therefore,   however   few,   they dare

adire   ad   quemvis   numĕrum   ephippiatorum
to approach   to   any   number   of saddled

equĭtum.   Non   sĭnunt   vinum   importari
horsemen.   They do not   permit   wine   to be imported

omnino   ad   se,   quòd[5]   arbitrantur
a: all   to   themselves,   because   they think (that)

homĭnes   remollescĕre   ĕâ   re   ad   ferendum,
men   (to) become enfeebled   by this   thing   for   bearing,

laborem   atque   effœminari.
labor   and   to be [are] effeminated.

3. Publĭcè   pŭtant   esse   maxĭmam
   Publicly [as a nation]   they think (it)   to be [is]   the greatest

laudem,   agros   vacare   quàm   latis-
praise (that),   the lands   to be [are] vacant   as   most exten-

sĭmè   à   sŭis   finĭbus.
sively [as extensively as possible]   from   their   borders.   (That)

Sıgnificari   hâc   re,   magnum   numĕrum
to be [it is] indicated   by this   thing (that),   a great   number

civitatum   non   potuisse   sustinere
of states   not   (to) have been able   to [could not] withstand

sŭam   vim.   Ităque   circ:ter   sexcenta   millĭa
their   force [power].   Therefore   about   six hundred   thousands

passŭum   agri   dicuntur[6]   vacare   à
(of) paces   of land [country]   are said   to be vacant   from

Suevis ex unâ parte. Ubïi succedunt
the Suevi from [on] one part [side]. The Ubii come next

ad altĕram partem, quorum civĭtas fŭit
at the other part [side], whose state has been

ampla atque florens, ut captus Germanorum
extensive and flourishing, as the nature of the Germans

est; ei sunt paulò humaniores cætĕris,
is; they are a little more civilized than the rest,

quamquam sunt ejusdem genĕris: propterĕa
although (they) are of the same race; because

quòd attingunt Rhenum, que mercatores ventĭtant
(that) they touch on the Rhine, and merchants travel

multùm ad ĕos, et ipsi sunt assuefacti
much to them, and they are accustomed

Gallĭcis morĭbus propter propinquitatem. Quum
to Gallic manners on account of (their) nearness. When

Suevi, experti hos (acc.) sæpè multis
the Suevi, having made trial of these often in many

bellis, potuissent (pl. perf. subj.) non expellĕre
wars, had been able [could] not (to) expel (them)

finĭbus, propter amplitudĭnem que
from (their) borders, on account of the extent and

gravitatem civitatis, tămen fecerunt
weight [influence] of the state, at length they made

vectigales sĭbi, ac redegerunt multò
(them) tributary to themselves, and rendered (them) much

humiliores que infirmiores.
lower [poorer] and weaker.

4. Usipĕtes et Tenctĕri, quos dixĭmus
The Usipetes and Tencteri, whom we have said

suprà, fuerunt in eâdem causâ: qui
above, were in the same cause [condition]: who

sustinuerunt vim Suevorum complures annos:
withstood the violence of the Suevi many years:

tămen ad extremum expulsi
however at last having been driven out from (their)

agris, et vagati multis lŏcis Germanïæ
lands, and having wandered in many places of Germany

triennĭum,   pervenerunt[7]   ad   Rhenum:
(during)   three years time,   they arrived   at   the Rhine:

quas   regiones   Menapĭi   incolebant,   Hi
which   countries   the Menapii   were inhabiting,   These

habebant   agros,   ædificĭa,   qua   vicos   ad
were holding   lands,   buildings,   and   villages   at [along]

utramque   ripam   flumĭnis: sed   perterrĭtis
each   bank   of the river: but   alarmed

adventu   tantæ   multitudĭnis,   demigraverunt
by the arrival   of so great   a multitude,   they emigrated

ex   his   ædificĭis,   quæ   habuĕrant   trans   flumen:
from   these   buildings,   which   they had had   beyond   the river:

et   præsidĭis   disposĭtis   cis   Rhenum,
and   garrisons   having been posted   on this side   the Rhine,

prohibebant[8]   Germanos   transire.
they were checking   the Germans   to cross [from crossing] over.

Illi   experti   omnĭa,   quum   possent (imp.
They,   having tried   all (things)   when   they were able

subj.)   nĕque   contendĕre   vi,   propter
neither   to contend   by force,   on account of

inopĭam   navĭum,   nĕque   transire   clàm,
the want   of ships,   nor   to cross over   secretly,

propter   custodĭas   Menapiorum,   simulaverunt[9]
on account of   the guards   of the Menapii,   pretended

se   reverti   in   sŭas   sedes
(that they)   themselves   (to) return   into   their   seats

que   regiones;   et   progressi   vĭam
[settlements]   and   countries;   and   having advanced   a way

tridŭi,   reverterunt   rursus;   atque
[distance]   of three days,   they return   again   and

omni   hoc   itinĕre   confecto   unâ   nocte
all   this   march   having been finished   in one   night

equitatu,   oppresserunt   Menapĭos   inscĭos   que
by cavalry,   they overwhelmed   the Menapii   ignorant   and

inopinantes;   qui[10]   facti   certiores
unaware;   who   having been made   more sure [having been

de   discessu   Germanorum   per
informed]   of   the departure   of the Germans   by

exploratores,　　remigravĕrant　　sĭne　　mĕtu　　in
　spies,　　　　　had moved back　without　fear　　into

sŭos　　vicos　　trans　　Rhenum.　　His　　interfectis
their　villages　beyond　the Rhine.　These　having been slain

que　　eorum　　navĭbus　　occupatis,　　priùs-quam[11]
and　　their　　ships　　having been seized,　before (that)

ĕa　　pars　　Menapiorum,　　quæ　　ĕrat　　citra
this　part　of the Menapii,　which　was　on this side

Rhenum,　　fiĕret (imp. subj.)　　certĭor,
the Rhine,　was made　　more sure [was informed],

transierunt　　flumen;　　atque　　omnĭbus　　eorum
they crossed　the river;　and　　all　　their

ædificĭis　　occupatis,　　aluerunt　　se
buildings　having been seized,　they supported　themselves

eorum　　copĭis　　relĭquam　　partem　　hiĕmis.
with their　supplies [stores]　the remaining　part　of the winter.

5. Cæar　　factus　　certĭor　　　　de
　Cæsar　being made　more sure [having been informed]　of

his　rebus,　et　verĭtus　infirmitatem　Gallorum.
these　things,　both　having feared　the weakness　of the Gauls,

quòd　sunt　mobĭles　in　capiendis　consilĭis,　et
because　they are　changeable　in　taking　councils,　and

plerumque　　stŭdent　　nŏvis　　rebus,
generally　are zealous　for new　things [a revolution],

existimavit　nĭhil　committendum　　his.　Autem
thought　nothing　to [should] be entrusted　to these.　But

hoc　est　Gallĭcæ　consuetudĭnis;　　ut　et
this　is　(of) the Gallic　custom;　　that　both

cogant (pres. subj.)　viatores,　etĭam　invitos,
they compel　　travellers,　even　unwilling,

consistĕre;　et　quærant (pres. subj.)　quod　quisque
to stop;　and　they inquire　　what　each

eorum　audiĕrit　aut　cognovĕrit　de
of them　may have heard　or　may have learned　about

quâque　re:　et　vulgus　circumsistat
each　thing:　and　the common people　stand about

(pres. subj.)　mercatores　in　oppĭdis:　cogant
　　the merchants　in　the towns:　they compel

(pres. subj.)   pronuntiare   ex   quĭbus   regionĭbus
(them)   to declare   from   what   countries

venĭant,   que   quas   res   cognovĕrint   ĭbi.
they come,   and   what   things   they have learned   there.

Permoti   his   rumorĭbus   atque   auditionĭbus,
Aroused   by these   reports   and   hearsays,

inĕunt   consilĭa   sæpè   de   summis
they enter upon   plans   often   concerning   the most important

rebus: quorum   est   necesse   ĕos   pœnitere
things: of which   it is   necessary   (for) them   to repent

in   vestigĭo,   quum   servĭant (pres. subj.)
on   the track [spot],   since   they are slaves

incertis   rumorĭbus,   et   plerique[12]   respondĕant
to uncertain   reports,   and   very many   answer

(pers. subj.)   ficta   ad   eorum   voluntatem.
feigned (things)   to   their   wish.

6. Quâ   consuetudĭne   cognĭtâ,   Cæsar
Which   custom   having been known,   Cæsar

proficiscĭtur   ad   exercĭtum   maturĭùs   quàm
sets out   to   the army   sooner   than

consuevĕrat,   ne[13]   occurrĕret   grav, iori
he had been accustomed,   lest   he might meet   a heavier [more serious]

bello (dat.).   Quum   venisset (pl. perf. subj.)   ĕò
war.   When   he had come   there

cognovit[14]   ĕa   facta,   quæ
he learned (that)   these (things)   (had been) done,   which

suspicatus-ĕrat   fŏre: legationes   mis-
he had suspected   to be about to [would] be: embassies   to have

sas   à   nonnullis   civitatĭbus   ad   Germanos,
[had] been sent   by   some   states   to   the Germans.

que   ĕos   invitatos   ŭti   discedĕrent
and   these   to have [had] been invited   that   they should depart

ab   Rheno: que   omnĭa   quæ
from   the Rhine: and   all (things)   which

postulâssent   fŏre   parata   ab
they had demanded   to be about to [would] be   prepared   by

se.   Quâ[15]   spe   Germani   adducti,
themselves.   By which   hope   the Germans   being induced [moved]

vagabantur   jam   latĭùs,   et   pervenĕrant
were wandering   now   more widely,   and   had arrived

in   fines   Eburonum   et   Condrusorum,
into [at]   the borders   of the Eburones   and   of the Condrusi,

qui   sunt   clientes   Trevirorum.   Principĭbus
who   are   dependents   of the Treviri.   The chiefs

Gallĭæ   evocatis,   Cæsar   existimavit
of Gaul   having been summoned,   Cæsar   thought   (that)

ĕa,   quæ   cognovĕrat,   dissimulanda
these (things),   which   he had learned,   to [must] be concealed

sĭbi (dat.);   que   eorum   anĭmis   permulsis
by himself;   and   their   minds   having been soothed

et   confirmatis,   que   equitatu   imperato,
and   strengthened,   and   cavalry   having been demanded,

constitŭit   gerĕre   bellum   cum   Germanis.
he resolved   to carry on   war   with   the Germans.

7. Frumentarĭâ   re   comparatâ,   que
The grain   supply   having been prepared,   and

equitĭbus   delectis,   cœpit   facĕre   ĭter
the cavalry   having been chosen,   he began   to make   (his) march

in   ĕa   lŏca,   in   quĭbus   lŏcis   audiebat
into   these   places,   in   which   places   he was hearing

Germanos   esse.   A   quĭbus[16]   quum
the Germans   to be [were].   From   whom [them]   when

abesset (imp. subj.)   ĭter   paucorum   dierum,
he was distant   a journey   of a few   days,

legati   venerunt   ab   ĭis,   quorum[17]   hæc
ambassadors   came   from   them,   of whom   this

fŭit   oratĭo: "Germanos   nĕque   inferre   bellum
was   the speech: "The Germans   neither   (to) wage   war

Romano   popŭlo   priores,   nĕque[18]   tămen
to [on] the Roman   people   the first,   nor   however

recusare,   quin   contendant   armis,   si
to refuse,   but that   they may contend   in arms,   if

lacessantur: quòd   hæc consuetudo Germanorum
they shoul be attacked: because   this   custom   of the Germans

tradĭta-sit (perf. subj.)   à   majorĭbus,   resistĕre,
has been delivered   by   (their) ancestors,   to oppose,

nĕque deprecari, quicumque infĕrant
nor to beg off [ask quarter of], whosoever may bring on

bellum: tămen dicĕre hoc: venisse
war: however to [they] say this: to (that they) have come

invitos, ejectos dŏmo: si Romani vĕlint
unwilling, having been driven from home: if the Romans wish

sŭam gratĭam, posse esse utĭles amicos
their favor, to be [they are] able to be useful friends

ĕis: vel attribŭant agros sĭbi, vel
to them: either let them assign lands to themselves, or

patiantur tenere ĕos, quos possedĕrint
let them permit (them) to hold these, which they have possessed

armis: sese concedĕre Suevis
by arms: (that they) themselves (to) yield to the Suevi

unis; quĭbus ne quĭdem immortales dii
one [alone]; to whom not even the immortal gods

possint esse păres: nemĭnem reliquum
are able to be equal: (that) no one remaining [else]

quĭdem esse in terris, quem
indeed to be [is] in the lands [on earth], whom

non-possint superare."
they are not able to overcome."

8. Cæsar respondit ad hæc quæ
Cæsar answered to these (words), what (things)

visum-est; sed exĭtus orationis fŭit:
seemed (best); but the conclusion of (his) speech was:

"Nullam amicitĭam posse esse sĭbi
"No friendship to be able [can] (to) be for himself

cum his, si remanerent in Gallĭâ: nĕque
with them, if they should remain in Gaul: neither

esse verum occupare alienos, qui
to be [is it] true [just] to seize others' (lands), who

potuĕrint non tueri sŭos fines:
may have been able not to defend their own borders:

nĕque ullos agros vacare in Gallĭâ, qui
nor (are) any lands (to be) vacant in Gaul, which

possint dări sĭne injurĭâ, præsertim
may be able to be given without injury, especially

tantæ   multitudĭni: sed   licere,   si
to so great   a multitude: but   (that) to be [it is] permitted,   if

vĕlint,   considere   in   finĭbus   Ubiorum;
they wish,   to settle   in   the territories   of the Ubii:

legati   quorum   sint (pres. subj.) ăpud   se,
ambassadors of whom   are   at [with] himself,

et   querantur (pres. subj.) de   injurĭis   Suevorum,
and   complain   of   the injuries of the Suevi,

et   pĕtant (pres. subj.) auxilĭum   à   se :
and   ask   aid   from   himself: (he)

se   impetraturum   hoc   ab   Ubĭis."
himself   about to [would] obtain this   from   the Ubii."

9.   Legati   dixerunt   se   rela-
     The ambassadors   said (that they)   themselves   about to

turos   hæc   ad   sŭos,   et
[would] carry back these (words) to   their own (people),   and

re   deliberatâ,   reversuros
the thing   having been considered,   (to be) about to [would] return

ad   Cæsărem   post   tertĭum   dĭem: interéa
to   Cæsar   after   the third   day: meantime

petiêrunt   ne moveret   castra (pl.) propĭus
they requested   (that) he would not move (his) camp   nearer

se.   Cæsar   dixit   ne   id   quĭdem   posse
themselves.   Cæsar   said   not   this   even   to be able

impetrari   ab   se.   Enim   cognovĕrat
[could]   (to) be obtained from   himself.   For   he had known

magnam   partem   equitatûs   missam   ab
a great   part   of (their) cavalry having [had] been sent by

ĭis   ad   Ambivaritos   trans   Mŏsam,   alĭquot
them   to   the Ambivariti   across   the Meuse,   some

diebus antè,   causâ   prædandi   que frumentandi:
days   before,   for the sake of plundering and of providing corn:

arbitrabatur   hos   equĭtes   expectari,
he was thinking (that)   these   horsemen   to be [were] awaited,

atque   mŏram   interponi   causâ
and   the delay   to be [was] interposed   for the sake

ejus   rĕi.
of this   thing.

10.   Mŏsa   proflŭit   ex   monte   Vogĕso,
The Mosa [Meuse]   flows   from   mount   Vogesus

   qui   est   in   finĭbus   Lingŏnum;
[Vosges],   which   is   in   the territories   of the Lingones;

et   quâdam   parte   ex   Rheni   receptâ,
and   a certain   part   from   [of] the Rhine   having been received,

quæ   appellatur   Vahălis,   effĭcit   insŭlam
which (part)   is called   Vahalis [Waal],   it forms   the island

Batâvorum: nĕque   longĭus   ab   ĕo
of the Batavi: and not farther   from   this (than)

octoginta   millĭbus   passŭum   influit   in   Oceănum.
eighty   thousand   (of) paces   it empties   into   the Ocean.

Autem   Rhenus   orĭtur   ex   Lepontīis,   qui
But   the Rhine   rises   from   the Lepontii,   who

incŏlunt   Alpes,   et   fertur   citatus   longo   spatĭo
inhabit   the Alps,   and   is borne   rapid   in a long   distance

per   fines   Nantuatĭum,   Helvetiorum,
through   the territories   of the Nantuates,   of the Helvetii,

Sequanorum,   Mediomatricorum,   Tribocorum,   que
of the Sequani,   of the Mediomatrici,   of the Triboci,   and

Treverorum;   et   ŭbi   appropinquat   Oceăno,
of the Treveri;   and   when   it approaches   (to) the Ocean,

diffiŭit   in   plures   partes;   multis[19]
it flows apart   into   more [several]   parts [estuaries];   many

que   ingentĭbus   insŭlis   effectis;   magna
and   great   islands   having been formed;   a large

pars   quarum   incolĭtur   à   fĕris   que   barbăris
part   of which   is inhabited   by   wild   and   barbarous

natiŏnĭbus;   (ex   quĭbus   sunt   qui
nations;   (from [of]   which   (there) are   (some) who

existimantur   vīvĕre   piscĭbus   atque   ovis
are thought   to live   (on) fishes   and   the eggs

avĭum);   que   inflŭit   in   Oceănum   multis
of birds);   and   it empties   into   the Ocean   by many

capitĭbus.
heads [outlets].

11. Quum   Cæsar   abesset (imp. subj.)   ab
     When   Cæsar   was distant   from

hoste	non	amplĭus	duodĕcĭm	millĭbus
the enemy	not	more	(than) twelve	thousand

passŭum,	legati	revertuntur	ad	ĕum,
(of) paces,	the ambassadors	returned	to	him,

ut	constitutum-ĕrat:	qui	congressi	in
as	it had been appointed:	who	having met (him)	on

itinĕre,	orabant	magnopĕrè,	ne progrederetur
the march,	were praying	very much,	that he would not advance

longĭus.	Quum	non	impetrâssent (pl. perf.
farther.	When	they had not	obtained

subj.)	id,	petebant,	"ŭtì	præmittĕret
	this,	they were asking,	"that	he would send before

ad	ĕos	equĭtes,	qui	antecessissent (pl. perf. subj.)
to	these	horsemen,	who	had preceded

agmen,	que	prohiberet	ĕos	pugnâ:	que
the marching line,	and	would prohibit	them	from battle:	and

uti	faceret	potestatem	sĭbi	mittendi
that	he would make	an opportunity	to themselves	of sending

legatos	in	Ubĭos:	si	quorum	princĭpes	que
ambassadors	unto	Ubii:	if	their	chiefs	and

senatus	fecissent	fidem[20]	sĭbi
senate	would make	faith [give pledge]	to themselves

jurejurando,	ostendebant	se
by oath,	they were showing	(that they) themselves

usuros	ĕâ conditione,	quæ	ferretur
about to use [would accept]	this condition,	which	was offered

à	Cæsăre;	dăret	sĭbi	spatĭum	tridŭi
by	Cæsar:	let him give	to themselves	the period	of three days

ad	conficiendas	has	res."	Cæsar	arbitrabatur
for	accomplishing	these	things."	Cæsar	was thinking (that)

ᴐmnĭa	hæc	pertinere	eòdem-illò,	ut,
all	these (things)	(to) tend	to this same (point),	that,

mŏrâ	tridŭi	interposĭtâ,	eorum
the delay	of three days	having been interposed,	their

equĭtes	qui	abessent (imp. subj.)	reverterentur:
horsemen	who	were absent	might return:

tămen	dixit	sese	processurum	non
however	he said (that he)	himself	about to [would] advance	not

longiùs   quatŭor   millĭbus   passŭum   ĕo   dĭe
farther   (than) four thousand   (of) paces   on this   day

causâ   aquationis: convenirent[21]   huc   quàm
for the sake of watering: let them assemble   hither   as

ſrequentissĭmi   postĕro   dĭe,
most numerous [as many as possible]   on the following   day,

ut   cognoscĕret   de   eorum   postulatis.
that   he might learn   concerning   their   requests.

Intĕrim   mittit   ad   præfectos,   qui
Meanwhile   he sends (persons)   to   the commander,   who

antecessĕrant   cum   omni   equitatu,   qui
had advanced   with   all   the cavalry,   who

nuntiarent,   ne lacessĕrent   hostes
should announce [instruct],   that they should not provoke   the enemy

prœlĭo; et, si   ipsi   lacesserentur,
to battle; and, if (they) themselves   should be provoked, [attacked],

sustinerent   quŏad   ipse   accessisset
they should hold out   until   (he) himself   should approach

propĭus   cum   exercĭtu.
nearer   with   the army.

12. At   hostes,[22]   ŭbi   primùm   conspexerunt
    But   the enemy,   when   first [as soon as]   they beheld

nostros equĭtes,   numĕrus   quorum   ĕrat   quinque
our   cavalry,   the number   of whom   was   (of) five

millĭum,   quum   ipsi   haberent (imp. subj.)
thousand,   although   (they) themselves   were having

non   amplĭus   octongentos   equĭtes,   quŏd
not   more (than)   eight hundred   cavalry,   because

ĭi,   qui   iĕrant   trans   Mŏsam   causâ
those, who had gone   beyond   the Meuse   for the sake

frumentandi,   nondum   rediĕrant;   nostris
of foraging,   had not yet   returned;   our (men)

timentĭbus   nĭhil,   quŏd   eorum   legati
fearing   nothing,   because   their   ambassadors

discessĕrant   paulò   antè   à   Cæsăre,   atque   is
had departed   a little before from   Cæsar,   and   this

dĭes   petitus-ĕrat   ab   ĭis   indutĭis (pl.),[23]
day   had been sought   by   them   for a truce,

impĕtu   facto,   perturbaverunt   celerĭter
an attack   having been made,   confused   quickly

nostros.   Nostris rursus resistentĭbus, desiliêrunt
our (men).   Our (men) again resisting,   they leaped down

ad pĕdes,   sŭâ consuetudĭne, que   ĕquis
to   feet, [on foot] by their   custom,   and the horses

suffossis,   que   complurĭbus   nostris
having been stabbed,   and   very many   (of) our (men)

dejectis,   conjecerunt relĭquos in fŭgam;
having been cast down,   they hurled the rest into flight;

atque egerunt   ĭta perterrĭtos, ut   desistĕrent
and drove (them) so panicstricken, that they were ceasing

(imp. subj.) non   fŭgâ   prĭùs quàm venissent
not   from flight before that they had come

(pl. perf. subj.) in conspectum nostri   agmĭnis.
into   sight of our marching line

Quatŭor et septuaginta ex   nostris   equitĭbus
Four   and seventy out of our cavalry

interficiuntur in ĕo prœlĭo; in his   Piso,
are killed in this battle; among these (was) Piso,

fortissĭmus vir, Aquitanus, natus amplissĭmo
a most brave man, an Aquitanian, born from [of a] most distin-

genĕre, cujus ăvus obtinuĕrat regnum
guished family, whose grandfather had obtained the sovereignty

in sŭâ civitate,   appellatus amicus à nostro
in his own state, having been called a friend by our

senatu. Quum hic ferret (imp. subj.) auxilĭum
senate. When he was bearing   aid

fratri   intercluso ab hostĭbus,   eripŭit
to (his) brother cut off   by the enemy, he rescued

illum ex pericŭlo; ipse,   ĕquo   vulnerato,
him from danger; (he) himself, (his) horse having been

dejectus   restĭtit fortissĭme   quŏad
wounded. thrown down, resisted most bravely as long as

potŭit. Quum   circumventus   cecidisset
he was able. When having been surrounded he had fallen;

(pl. perf. subj.); multis vulnerĭbus   acceptis,
many   wounds having been received,

atque   frater,   qui jam excessĕrat   prœlĭo
and   (his) brother, who already had departed   from the battle

animadvertisset (pl. perf. subj.) id   prŏcul,   ĕquo
(had) perceived   this   afar off,   (his) horse

incitato   obtŭlit   sese   hostĭbus,
having been urged on   he threw   himself   to [upon] the enemy,

atque   interfectus-est.
and   was slain.

13. Hoc prœlĭo   facto,   Cæsar   jam
    This   battle   having been done [fought], Cæsar   now

arbitrabatur   nĕque   legatos   audiendos
ɪ was thinking (that) neither ambassadors   (ought) to be heard

sĭbi (dat.),   neque conditiones   accipiendas
by himself,   nor   conditions   (ought) to be received

ab   ĭs,   qui,   pace   petitâ,   intulissent
from   these, who, peace having been sought, had brought on

(pl. perf. subj.) bellum   ultrŏ,   per   dŏlum
                   war   voluntarily, through   deceit

atque   insidĭas (pl.). Verŏ   judicabat   esse
and   treachery.   But   he was judging (that)   to be

              summæ   dementĭæ expectare,   dum
[it was]   (of) the highest   madness   to wait,   until

copĭæ   hostĭum   augerentur   que
the forces   of the enemy   should be increased and   (their)

equitatus reverteretur et   infirmitate   Gallorum
cavaɪry   should return and   the weakness   of the Gauls

cognĭtâ,   sentiebat   quantum   auctoritatis
having been known,   he was perceiving how much   (of) prestige

hostes   consecuti-essent (pl. perf. subj.) ăpud   ĕos
the enemy   had obtained   among them

uno   prœlĭo;   quĭbus   existimabat   nĭhil[24]
by one   battle; to whom   he was judging   nothing [not any]

spatĭi   dandum   ad   capienda   consilĭa.
of space [time]   to [must] be given for   taking   counsels

His rebus   constĭtutis,   et   consilĭo
These things   having been determined, and   (his) plan

communicato   cum   legatis   et
having been communicated   with [to] the lieutenants   and

quæstore,   opportunissĭma   res   accĭdit,
the quæstor,   a most advantageous   thing [incident]   occurred,

ne prætermittĕret   quem   dĭem   pugnæ,   quòd
that he might not omit   any   day   of [for] a battle,   because

   manè   postridĭe   ejus   diei,   Germani
in the morning   the day after   (of) this   day,   the Germans,

frequentes,   usi   et   eâdem   perfidĭâ   et
in numbers,   having used   both   the same   treachery   and

simulatione,   omnĭbus   principĭbus   que
pretence,   all   (their) chiefs   and   (those)

majorĭbus-natu   adhibĭtis,   venerunt   ad
greater by birth [the elders]   having been brought,   came   to

ĕum   in   castra (pl.);   sĭmul,[25]   ut   dicebatur,
him   into   the camp;   as well,   as   it was said,

   causâ   purgandi   sŭi,   quòd   commisissent
for the sake   of clearing   themselves,   because   they had joined

(pl. perf. subj.)   prœlĭum   pridĭe,   (contrà[26]   atque
                    battle   the day before,   (contrary   as

dictum-esset (pl. perf. subj.),   et   ipsi
(it) had been said,   and (they)   themselves

petîssent (pl. perf. subj.)): sĭmul   ut   impetrarent
had requested):   as   that   they might obtain

quid,   si   possent (imp. subj.),   fallendo
some (thing),   if   they could,   by deceiving

   de   indutĭis (pl.).   Quos   oblatos
concerning   the truce.   (When) whom [they] (were) presented

sĭbi   Cæsar   gavisus,[27]   jussit   illos
to himself   Cæsar,   having rejoiced,   commanded   them

retineri: ipse   eduxit   omnes   copĭas
to be detained: he himself   led out   all   (his) forces

castris (pl.);   jussit   equitatum   subsĕqui
from the camp;   he ordered   the cavalry   to follow near

   agmen,   quòd   existimabat   perterrĭtum-
the marching line,   because   he was thinking   (it) to have [had]

esse   recenti   prœlĭo.
been alarmed   by the late   battle.

14.   Triplĭci   acĭe   institutâ,   et   itinĕre
      A tripple battle   line   having been arranged,   and   a march

octo   millĭum   confecto   celerĭter,   pervenit
of eight   miles   having been completed   quickly,   he arrived

ad   castra (pl.)   hostĭum,   prĭùs   quàm   Germani
at   the camp   of the enemy,   before   (that)   the Germans

possent   sentire   quid   ageretur: qui[28]   per-
were able   to perceive   what   was transpiring: who   having

terrĭti   subĭtò   omnĭbus   rebus,   et
been panicstricken   suddenly   by all   the things,   both

celeritate   nostri   adventûs,   et   discessu
by the quickness   of our   arrival,   and   by the departure

suorum,   nĕque   spatĭo[29]   dăto
of their own (people),   neither   space [time]   having been given

habendi,   consilĭi   nĕque   capiendi   arma,
of having [forming].   a plan   nor   of taking   arms,

perturbantur,   ne   præstaret   educĕre
are confused (as to)   whether   it would be better   to lead out

copĭas   adversùs   hostem,   an   defendĕre
(their) troops   against   the enemy,   or   to defend

castra,   an   petĕret   salutem   fŭgâ.   Quum
the camp,   or   to seek   safety   by flight.   When

quorum   tĭmor[30]   significaretur (imp. subj.)   fremĭtu
their   fear   was signified   by the noise

et   concursu,   nostri   milĭtes   incitati   perfidĭa
and   running,   our   soldiers   impelled   by the treachery

pristĭni   diei,   irruperunt   in   castra (pl):   in
of the former   day,   broke in   upon   the camp   in

quo   lŏco,   qui   potuerunt   capĕre   arma
which   place,   (those) who   were able   to take   arms

celerĭter,   restiterunt   nostris (dat.)   paulisper,
quickly,   resisted   our (men)   a little while,

atque   commiserunt   prœlĭum   inter
and   joined   battle   between [among]

carros   que   impedimenta.   At   relĭqua
the wagons   and   baggage.   But   the remaining

multitudo   **puerorum**   que   muliĕrum   (nam
multitude   **of boys**   and   (of) women   (for

excessĕrant   dŏmo   cum   omnĭbus   sŭis
they had departed   from home   with   all   their

que	transiĕrant	Rhenum,)	cœpit	fugĕre
(people) and	had crossed	the Rhine,)	began	to flee

passim,	ad consectandos	quos	Cæsar	misit
everywhere,	for pursuing	whom	Cæsar	sent

equitatum.
the cavalry.

15. Germani, clamore audito post
    The Germans, a shout having been heard behind [in]

tergum, quum viderent (imp. subj.) sŭos
the back [the rear], when they were beholding their

interfĭci, armis abjectis
(people) (to be) slaughtered, (their) arms having been cast away

que militarĭbus signis relictis, ejecerunt
and the military standards having been left, hurled

se ex castris (pl.); et quum perven-
themselves from the camp; and when they had

issent (pl. perf. subj.) ad confluentem Mŏsæ
arrived at the junction of the Meuse

et Rheni, relĭquâ fŭgâ des-
and (of) the Rhine, remaining [further] flight having

peratâ, magno numĕro interfecto,
been despaired of, a great number having been killed,

relĭqui præcipitaverunt se in
the rest dashed themselves headlong into

flumen, atque oppressi ĭbi timore
the river, and having been overpowered there by fear

lassitudĭne et vi flumĭnis,
by weariness and by the force of the river,

periêrunt. Omnes nostri incolŭmes ad
they perished. All our (men) safe to

unum, perpaucis vulneratis, receperunt
one [to a man], very few having been wounded, betook

se in castris (pl.) ex timore
themselves into camp (freed) from the fear

tanti belli, quum numĕrus hostium fuisset
of so great a war, since the number of the enemy was

quadringentorum triginta millĭum capĭtum.
(of) four hundred thirty thousand of heads [souls].

Cæsar   fecit   potestem   discedendi   ĭis,
Cæsar   made   power [an opportunity]   of departing   to those,

quos   retinŭĕrat   in   castris (pl.).   Illi   ver-
whom   he had detained   in   the camp.   They   having

ĭti   supplicĭa   que   cruciatus   Gallorum,
feared   the punishments   and   tortures   of the Gauls,

quorum   agros   vexavĕrant,   dīxerunt
whose   lands   they had harassed,   said (that they)

se   velle   remanere   ăpud   ĕum.   Cæsar
themselves   (to) wish   to remain   at [with]   him.   Cæsar

conces∂it   libertatem   his.
granted   the liberty [privilege]   to them.

16. Germanĭco   bello   confecto,   Cæsar   de
The German   war   having been finished,   Cæsar   from

multis   causis   statŭit   Rhenum   transeundum-esse
many   causes   resolved (that)   the Rhine   to [must] be crossed

sĭbi (dat.);   quarum   illa   fŭit   justissĭma ;³¹
by himself   of which   that [this]   was   the most just

quŏd,   quum   videret (imp. subj.)   Germanos
[strongest] because,   when   he was seeing (that)   the Germans

impelli   tam facĭlè, ut   venirent
to be [were] incited [impelled]   so   easily, that   they should come

in   Gallĭam,   volŭit   ĕos   timere   sŭis
into   Gaul,   he wished   them   to fear   for their own

rebus   quŏque,   quum   intelligĕrent
things [possessions]   also,   when   they should understand (that)

exercitum   Romani   popŭli   et   posse
the army   of the Roman   people   both   to be [was] able

et   audere   transire   Rhenum.   Accessit³²
and   to dare [dared]   to cross   the Rhine.   It was added

etĭam,   quŏd   illa   pars   equitatûs   Usipĕtum
also,   that   that   part   of the cavalry   of the Usipetes

et   Tencterorum,   quam   commemoravi   suprà
and   of the Tencteri,   which   I have mentioned   above

transîsse   Mŏsam   causâ   prædandi   que
(to have) crossed   the Meuse   for the sake   of plundering   and

frumentandi,   nĕque   interfuisse   prœlĭo,
of providing corn,   nor   (to have) [had] been present   to [at] the bat-

recepĕrat se trans Rhenum, post
tle, had betaken itself across the Rhine, after

fŭgam suorum in fines Sugambrorum,
the flight of their own (people) into the borders of the Sugambri,

que conjunxĕrat se cum ĭis. Ad quos[33]
and had united itself with them. To whom

quum Cæsar misisset (pl. perf. subj.) nuncĭos, qui
when Cæsar had sent messengers, who

postularent, ŭti dedĕrent sĭbi ĕos,
should demand, that they should surrender to himself those,

qui intulissent (pl. perf. subj.) bellum sĭbi
who had borne war to [on] himself

que Gallĭæ, responderunt: "Rhenum finire
and to [on] Gaul, they answered: "the Rhine to end [terminates]

imperĭum Romani popŭli: si existimaret[34]
the empire of the Roman people; if he should judge (it)

non æquum Germanos transire in Gallĭam,
not just (that) the Germans to [should] cross over into Gaul,

se invito, cur postularet
he himself (being) unwilling. why should he require (that)

quidquam sŭi imperĭi aut potestatis esse
any of his empire or power to [should] be

trans Rhenum? Autem Ubĭi, qui uni ex
across the Rhine? But the Ubii, who one [alone] from [of]

Transrhenanis misĕrant legatos ad Cæsarem,
the Over-Rhine (nations) had sent ambassadors to Cæsar,

fecĕrant amicitĭam, dedĕrant obsĭdes, orbant
had made friendship, had given hostages, were praying

magnopĕrè, ut ferret auxilĭum sĭbi,
very greatly, that he would bear aid to themselves,

quòd premerentur (imp. subj.) gravĭter ab Suevis:
because they were oppressed grievously by the Suevi:

vel, si prohiberetur facĕre id occupationĭbus
or. if he should be hindered to [from] doing this by the engagements

rei publĭcæ, mŏdò transportaret Rhenum
of the state, only (that) he would carry over the Rhine

exercĭtum: id futurum sătis sĭbi
(his) army: that about to [would] be enough to themselves

ad   auxilĭum   que   spem   relĭqui   tempŏris:
for   aid   and   hope   of [for] the remaining   time:

tantum   esse   nomen   atque   opinionem
so great   to be [is]   the name   and   opinion [repute]

Romani   exercĭtûs,   Ariovisto   pulso,[35]
of a Roman   army,   Ariovistus   having been routed,

et   hoc   novissĭmo   prœlĭo   facto,
and   this   newest [last]   battle   having been done [fought],

etĭam   ad   ultĭmas   nationes   Germanorum,   ŭtì
even   to   the remotest   nations   of the Germans,   that

possint   esse   tuti   opinione   et
they may be able   to be   safe   by the opinion [repute]   and

amicitĭâ   Romani   popŭli.''   Pollicebantur
friendship   of the Roman   people.''   They were promising

magnam   copĭam   navĭum   ad   transportandum
a great   supply   of ships   for   transporting

exercĭtum.
the army.

17. Cæsar   de   his   causis,   quas   commemoravi,
Cæsar   from   these   causes,   which   I have mentioned,

decrevĕrat   transire   Rhenum: sed   arbitrabatur
had resolved   to cross   the Rhine: but   he was judging (that)

nĕque   esse   sătis   tutum   transire   navĭbus,
neither (it)   to be [was]   sufficiently   safe   to cross   with ships,

nĕque   statuebat   esse   sŭæ
nor   was he considering (that)   to be [it was] (worthy)   of his own

dignitatis,   nĕque   Romani   popŭli: ităque,
dignity,   nor   (that) of the Roman   people: therefore,

etsi   summa   difficultas   faciundi   pontis
although   the highest [greatest]   difficulty   of making   a bridge

proponebatur,   propter   latitudĭnem,   rapiditatem,
was confronting (him),   on account of   the breadth,   swiftness,

que   altitudĭnem   flumĭnis;   tămen   existimabat
and   depth   of the river: yet   he was thinking

id   contendendum   sĭbi,   aut   alĭter
this   to [must] be attempted   by himself,   or   otherwise

exercĭtum   non   transducendum.   Igĭtur
the army   not   to [must not] be led over.   Therefore

instituit hanc rationem pontis. Jungebat
he formed this plan of the bridge. He was joining

bina sesquipedalia tigna, paulùm præacuta
double [two] foot and half thick beams, a little sharp pointed

ab imo, dimensa ad
from [at] the lowest (part), measured to [according to]

altitudinem fluminis, intervallo duorum pedum
the depth of the river, with a distance of two feet

inter se: cùm defixerat hæc
between themselves [them]; when he had fastened these

demissa in flumen machinationibus que adegerat
let down into the river by machines and had driven

fistucis, non directa ad perpendiculum
(them) with pile drivers, not straight to a perpendicular

modo sublicæ, sed prone ac fastigate,
in the manner of a pile, but inclining and sloping,

ut procumberent secundùm naturam
that they might lean forward according to the nature [flow]

fluminis: statuebat item duo contraria
of the river: he was setting up also two (beams) opposite

his juncta ad eundem modum intervallo
(to) these joined to [after] the same manner with an interval

quadragenûm pedum ab inferiore parte conversa
of forty feet from the lower part turned

contra vim atque impetum fluminis: utraque
against the force and pressure of the river: both

hæc distinebantur binis fibulis utrimque
these were separated by two clamps on either side

ab extremâ parte, bipedalibus trabibus
from [at] the extreme part [the top], two foot wide beams

immissis, quantum junctura eorum
having been let in (to them), as much as the joint of these

tignorum distabat: quibus³⁶ disclusis,
beams was apart: which having been separated,

atque revinctis in contrariam partem
and having been fastened on the opposite part [side]

tanta erat firmitudo operis, atque ea
so great was the firmness of the work, and this [such]

natura   rerum,   ut   quŏ-major   vis
the nature   of the things [parts],   that   the greater   the force

ăquæ   incitavisset   se,   hŏc   arctĭus
of the water   roused   itself [increased],   so much   the more closely

tenerentur (imp. subj.)   illigata: hæc   directa
they were kept   fastened: these   laid straight

contexebantur   materĭâ   injectâ,
were interwoven   with material [timber]   thrown on (them),

ac   consternebante   longurĭis   que   cratĭbus:
and   were strewed   with long poles   and   hurdles:

ac   nihĭlo secĭus   sublĭcæ   adigebantur   oblique
and   in no wise [likewise]   piles   were driven   obliquely

əd   inferiorem   partem   flumĭnis,[37]   quæ   sub-
at   the lower   part   of the river,   which   having been

jectæ   pro   parĭĕte,   et   conjunctæ   cum
put below   for [as]   a wall,   and   united   with

omni   opĕre,   excipĕrent   vim   flumĭnis:
all   the work,   [would] receive   the force   of the river:

et   ĭtem   alĭæ   mediocri   spatĭo   supra
and   also   other (piles)   at a moderate   distance   above

pontem,   ut   si   trunci   arbŏrum   sive   naves
the bridge,   so that   if   trunks   of trees   or   ships

essent   missæ   à   barbăris,   causâ
should be   sent   by   the barbarians,   for the sake

dejiciendi,   opĕris   vis   earum   rerum
of casting down,   the work   the force   of these   things

minueretur   his   defensorĭbus,   neu
would be diminished   by these   defenses,   nor

nocerent   ponti (dat).
would they injure   the bridge.

18. Omni   opĕre   effecto   dĕcem
    All   the work   having been completed   in ten

diebus,   quĭbus   materĭa   cœpta-ĕrat   comportari,
days,   in which   the material   had been begun   to be gathered,

exercĭtus   transducĭtur.   Cæsar,   firmo   præsidĭo
the army   is led over.   Cæsar,   a strong   guard

relicto   ad   utramque   partem   pontis,
having been left   at   each   part [end]   of the bridge.

contendit in fines Sugambrorum. Intĕrim
hastened into the territories of the Sugambri. Meantime

legati à complurĭbus civitatĭbus venĭunt
ambassadors from very many states come

ad ĕum, quĭbus petentĭbus pacem atque
to him, to whom seeking peace and

amicitĭam respondit liberalĭter, que jŭbet obsĭdes
friendship he answered generously, and orders hostages

adduci ad se. Sugambri, ex ĕo
to be brought to himself. The Sugambri, from this [that]

tempŏre, quŏ pons cœptus-est institŭi,
time, in which the bridge was begun to be built,

fŭgâ comparatâ, ĭis hortantĭbus,
flight having been prepared, these exhorting (them),

quos habebant ex Tenctĕris atque Usipetĭbus
whom they were having from the Tencteri and Usipetes

ăpud se, excessĕrant sŭis finĭbus,
at [among] themselves, had departed from their territories,

que exportavĕrant omnĭa sŭa, que
and had carried away all their (effects), and

abdidĕrant se in solitudĭnem ac
had concealed themselves in the desert and

silvas.
woods.

19. Cæsar moratus paucos dĭes in eorum
Cæsar having delayed a few days in their

finĭbus omnĭbus vicis que ædificĭis
territories all the villages and buildings

incensis, que frumentis (pl.) succissis,
having been bʏɾned, and the corn (having been) cut down.

recepit se in fines Ubiorum; atque
betook himself into the territories of the Ubii; and

pollicĭtus sŭum auxilĭum his, si preme-
having promised his aid to them, if they should

rentur à Suevis, cognovit hæc ab
be oppressed by the Suevi, he learned these (things) from

ĭis; Suevos, postquam comperissent (pl. perf.
them; (that) the Suevi, after (that) they had found

subj.)   per   exploratores   pontem   fĭĕri,
      by   spies   (that)   a bridge   to be [was] made,

concilĭo   habĭto,   sŭo   more,   dimisis-
a council   having been held,   in their manner,   to have [had]

se   nuntĭos   in   onnes   partes,   ŭtì   demig-
sent   messengers into   all   parts,   that   they might

rarent   de   oppĭdis,   deponĕrent   libĕros,
emigrate   from   the towns   might deposit   (their) children,

uxores,   que   omnĭa   sŭa   in   silvas,
wives,   and   all   their (effects) into [in] the woods.

atque   omnes,   qui   possent   ferre   arma,
and   all,   who   were able   to bear   arms

convenirent   in   unum   lŏcum :   hunc
should assemble into [in] one   place: (that)   this (place)

delectum-esse   fĕrè   medĭum   earum
to have [had] been chosen   nearly   the middle   of these

regionum,   quas   Suevi   obtinerent (imp. subj.):
countries,   which   the Suevi   were possessing: (that)

exspectare   hĭc   adventum   Romanorum,   atque
to [they] await   here   the approach   of the Romans,   and

constituisse   decertare   ĭbi.   Quod   ŭbi
to have [had] resolved   to fight   there.   Which   when

Cæsar   compĕrit,   omnĭbus   his   rebus
Cæsar   discovered,   all   these   things [matters]

confectis,   causâ   quarum   rerum   con-
having been completed   for the sake   of which   things   he had

stituĕrat transducŏre   exercĭtum,   ut   injicĕret
resolved   to lead over   (his) army,   that   he might arouse

mĕtum   Germanis,   ut   ulcisceretur
fear   to [in] the Germans,   that   he might punish

Sugambros,   ut   liberaret   Ubĭos   obsidione,
the Sugambri.   that   he might deliver   the Ubii   from a blockade.

octodĕcim   diebus   omnino   consumptis   trans
eighteen   days   altogether   being spent   across

Rhenum,   arbitratus   profectum (esse)
the Rhine,   having thought (that)   to have [he had] accomplished

sătis   et   ad   laudem   et   ad
enough   both   to [for]   praise   and   to [for]

utilitatem, recepit se in Gallĭam que
advantage [utility], he betook himself into Gaul and

rescĭdit pontem.
cut down the bridge.

20. Exigŭâ parte æstatis relĭquâ,
A small part of the summer having been left,

Cæsar, etsi hiĕmes in his lŏcis sunt
Cæsar, although the winters in these places are

maturæ, (quòd omnis Gallĭa vergit ad
early, (because all Gaul lies to

Septentrionem), tămen contendit proficisci in
the North), yet hastened to set out into

Britannĭam; quòd intelligebat auxilĭa
Britain; because he was understanding (that) auxiliaries

submınistrata (esse) inde nostris hostĭbus,
to have [had] been supplied from there to our enemies,

fĕrè omnĭbus Gallĭcis bellis: et, si tempus
in nearly all the Gallic wars: and, if the time

anni deficĕret ad gerendum bellum; tămen
of the year should fail to carry on war; yet

arbitrabatur fŏre magno usŭi
he was thinking (it) to be about to [would] be for [of] great use [ad-

sĭbi, si mŏdò adîsset insŭlam,
vantage] to himself, if only he should visit the island,

perspexisset gĕnus homĭnum, cognovisset lŏca,
should observe the kind of men, should learn the places,

portus, adĭtus: quæ fĕrè omnĭa ĕrant
harbors. approaches; which nearly all were

incognĭta Gallis. Enim nĕque quisquam ădit
unknown to the Gauls. For neither any one goes

illò temĕrè præter mercatores; nĕque est
thither rashly except merchants; nor is

quidquam notum ĭis ipsis, præter
any (thing) known to these themselves, except

maritĭmam oram, atque ĕas regiones, quæ
the maritime coast, and these countries, which

sunt contra Gallĭam. Ităque, mercatorĭbus
are opposite Gaul. Therefore, the merchants

convocatis undĭque ad se,
having been called together from every side to himself,

potĕrat reperire nĕque quanta esset
he was able to find neither how great might be

magnitudo insŭlæ, nĕque quæ aut quantæ
the size of the island, nor what or how great

nationes incolĕrent, nĕque quem usum
nations might inhabit (it), nor what method

belli haberent, aut quĭbus (abl.) institutis
of warfare they might have, or what customs

uterentur, nĕque qui portus essent idonĕi
they might use, nor what harbors might be suitable

ad multitudĭnem majorum navĭum.
for a number of the larger ships.

21. Arbitratus esse idonĕum, prĭus quàm
Having thought (it) to be [was] proper, before (that)

facĕret pericŭlum, præmittit Caĭum
he should make the trial, he sends before (him) Caius

Volusenum cum longâ navi, ad
Volusenus with a long ship [war ship], for

cognoscenda hæc. Mandat huic (dat.) ut,
ascertaining these (things). He charges him that,

omnĭbus rebus exploratis, revertatur
all things having been reconoitered, he should return

ad se quam primùm. Ipse proficiscĭtur
to himself as soon as possible. He himself sets out

cum omnĭbus copĭis in Morĭnos, quŏd
with all (his) forces into the Morini, because

trajectus inde in Britannĭam ĕrat brevissĭmus.
the passage from there into Britain was the shortest.

Jŭbet naves convenire huc undĭque ex
He orders ships to assemble hither from everywhere from

finitĭmis regionĭbus, et classem, quam
the neighboring countries, and the fleet, which

fecĕrat ad Venetĭcum bellum superiore
he had made for the Venetian war in the preceding

æstate. Intĕrim ejus consilĭo cognĭto,
summer. Meantime his design having been known [learned],

et   perlato   ad   Britannos   per
and   having been reported   to   the Britons   through

mercatores,   legati   venĭunt   ad   ĕum   à
the merchants,   ambassadors   came   to   him   from

complurĭbus   civitatĭbus   ejus   insŭlæ,   qui
very many   states   of this   island,   who

polliceantur   dăre   obsĭdes,   atque   obtemperare
promise   to give   hostages,   and   to obey

imperĭo (dat.)   Romani   popŭli.   Quĭbus   auditis,
the empire   of the Roman people.   Whom   having been heard,

pollicĭtus   liberalĭter,   que   hortatus
having promised   generously,   and   having exhorted (them)

ut   permanerent   in   ĕâ   sententĭâ   remisit
that   they should continue in   this   determination   he sent

ĕos   dŏmum: et   unà   cum   his   mittit
them (back)   home: and   together   with   these   he sends

Commĭum,   quem   ipse   contituĕrat   regem
Commius,   whom   (he) himself had appointed   king

Ibi,   Atrebatĭbus   superatis,   et   cujus
there,   the Atrebates   having been overcome,   and   whose

virtutem   et   consilĭum   probabat,   et   quem
valor   and   discretion   he was approving, and   whom

arbitrabatur   fidelem   sĭbi,   que   cujus auctorĭtas
he was thinking   faithful   to himself, and   whose   authority

habebatur   magna   in   his   regionĭbus:
was held [considered]   great   in   these   countries:

impĕrat   huic (dat.),   adĕat   quas   civitates
he commands   him,   (that) he should visit what   states

possit,   que   hortetur   ut   sequantur
he may be able,   and   should exhort (them) that   they follow

fĭdem   Romani   popŭli,   que   nun-
[accept]   the faith   of the Roman   people,   and   he should

tĭet   se   venturum   ĕò   celerĭter.
announce (that he)   himself   about [was] to come   there   quickly.

Volusenus,   regionĭbus[38]   perspectis,   quantum
Volusenus,   the countries   having been reconnoitered,   as much

facultatis   potŭit   dări   ĕi,   qui
(of) opportunity (as)   was able   to be given   to him,   who

non	auderet	egredi	navi,	ac
might not	dare	to disembark	from the ship,	and

committĕre	se	barbăris,	revertĭtur	quinto
to entrust	himself	to the barbarians,	returns	on the fifth

dĭe	ad	Cæsărem,	que	renuntĭat	quæ
day	to	Cæsar,	and	announces	what (things)

perspexisset (pl. perf. subj.)	ĭbi.
he had discovered	there.

22.
Dum	Cæsar	commoratur	in	his	lŏcis
While	Cæsar	delays	in	these	places

causâ	parandarum	navĭum,	lĕgati	venerunt
for the sake	of preparing	ships,	ambassadors	came

ad	ĕum	ex	magnâ	parte	Morinorum,	que
to	him	from	a great	part	of the Morini,	who

excusarent	se	de	consilĭo[39]	superioris
excused	themselves	concerning	the design	of the former

tempŏris;	quòd	barbări	homĭnes	que
time;	because	(being) barbarous	men	and

imperiti	nostræ	consuetudĭnis (gen.),	fecis-
unacquainted	with our	custom,	they had

sent (pl. perf. subj.)	bellum	Romano	popŭlo;
made	war	[on] the Roman	people;

que	pollicerentur	se	facturos
and	promised (that they)	themselves	about to [would] do

ĕa,	quæ	imperâsset.	Cæsar	arbitratus
these (things),	which	he commanded.	Cæsar	having thought

hoc	accidisse	opportunè	sătis	sĭbi;
this	to have [had] happened	conveniently	enough	for himself;

quòd	volebat	nĕque	relinquĕre	hostem
because	he was wishing	neither	to leave	an enemy

post	tergum,	nĕque	habebat	facultatem
behind	(his) back,	nor	was he having	the means

gerendi	belli	propter	tempus	anni;
of carrying on	war	on account of	the time	of the year;

nĕque	judicabat	has	occupationes	tan-
nor	was he judging (that)	these	engagements	of so

tularum	rerum	anteponendas	sĭbi (dat.)
trifling	things [matters]	to [should] be preferred	by himself

Britannĭæ: impĕrat his magnum numĕrum
to Britain: he demands from them a great number

obsĭdum. Quĭbus[40] adductis, recepit ĕos
of hostages. Whom having been brought, he received them

in fĭdem. Circĭter octoginta onerarĭis
into allegiance. About eighty burden [transport]

navĭbus coactis que contractis,
ships having been collected and brought together,

quot existimabat esse sătis ad
as many as he was thinking to be [was] sufficient for

transportandas dŭas legiones, distribŭit quæs-
transporting two legions, he distributed to the

tori, legatis que præfectis quod
quæstor, to the lieutenants and perfects what(ever)

longarum navĭum præterĕa habebat: huc
(of) long ships [war ships] besides he was having: hither

accedebant octodĕcim onerarĭæ naves,
[to these] were added eighteen burden [transport] ships,

quas tenebantur vento octo millĭbus
which were detained by the wind eight thousand

passŭum ex ĕo lŏco, quŏ mĭnùs possent
(of) paces from this place, that they were the less [not] able

pervenire in eundem portum: distribŭit
to arrive into [at] the same harbor: he distributed

has equitĭbus; dĕdit relĭquum exercĭtum
these to the horsemen; he gave the rest of the army

Quinto Titurĭo Sabino, et Lucĭo Aurunculeĭo
to Quintus Titurius Sabinus, and to Lucius Aurunculeius

Cottæ, legatis, deducendum in Menapĭos
Cotta, (his) lieutenants. to be led down into the Menapii

atque in ĕos pagos Morinorum, ab
and into these cantons of the Morini, from;

quĭbus legati non venĕrant ad ĕum;
which ambassadors had not come to him;

jussit Publĭum Sulpicĭum Rufum legatum
he ordered Publius Sulpicius Rufus (his) lieutenant

tenere portum cum ĕo præsidĭo,
to hold the harbor with this guard,

quod   arbitrabatur   esse   sătis.
which   he was thinking   to be [was]   sufficient.

23. His rebus   constitutis,   nactus   idonĕam
     These things having been arranged, having got suitable

tempestatem   navigandum,   solvit   fĕrè
weather   for sailing,   he cast loose   nearly

tertĭâ   vigilĭâ,   que   jussit   equĭtes   progrĕdi
at the third watch, and   commanded   the cavalry   to proceed

in   ulteriorem   portum,   et   conscendĕre   naves,
to   the farther   harbor,   and   to board   the ships,

ac   sĕqui   se: ab   quĭbus[41]   cùm   adminis-
and   to follow himself: by   whom   when   it had been

tratum-esset (pl. perf. subj)   paulò   tardĭùs,
performed   a little   more slowly

ipse   attĭgit   Britannĭam   cum   primis
(he) himself touched [reached]   Britain   with   the first

navĭbus   circĭter   quartâ   horâ (abl.) diei: atque
ships   about   the fourth hour   of the day: and

ĭbi   conspexit   copĭas   hostĭum   armatas,
there   he beheld   the forces   of the enemy   armed,

exposĭtas   in   omnĭbus   collĭbus.   Cujus   lŏci
drawn up   on   all   the hills.   Of which   place

hæc   ĕrat   natura :   mărе   continebatur
this was   the nature: the sea   was bounded

montĭbus   ita   anguste,   ut   telum   posset
by heights so   closely,   that a weapon   might be able

         adjĭci   ex   superiorĭbus   lŏcis   in
[could] (to) be cast from   the higher   places upon

littus.   Arbitratus   hunc   lŏcum   nequaquam
the shore.   Having thought   this   place   by no means

idonĕum   ad egrediendum   expectavit   in   anchŏri
suitable   for disembarking he waited   in [at] anchor

(pl.)   ad   nonam   horam,   dum   relĭquæ
        to   the ninth hour,   until   the remaining

naves   convenirent   ĕò.   Intĕrim   legatis
ships   should assemble   there.   Meantime   the lieutenants

que   tribunis   milĭtum   convocatis,
and   tribunes   of soldiers   having been called together,

ostendit　　et　　quæ　　cognovisset (pl. perf.
he showed (them)　both　what (things)　he had learned

subj.)　　ex　　Voluseno,　　et　　quæ　　vellet
　　　　from　　Volusenus,　　and　　what　　he wished

fĭĕri :　　que　　monŭit　　omnes　　res
to be done:　　and　　he warned (that)　　all　　things

administrarentur　ab　ĭis　ad　nutum　et　ad
should be managed　by　them　at　the nod　and　to [on]

tempus　ut　ratĭo⁴²　militaris　rĕi (sing),
time　as　the method　of military　affairs,

maxĭmè　ut　maritĭmæ　res　postularent
(and) especially　as　maritime　affairs　were demanding,

(imp. subj.),　(ut　quæ　haberent (imp. subj.)
　　　　　　(as　which [they]　were having

celĕrem　atque　instabĭlem　motum.)　His
a quick　and　unsteady　movement.)　These

dimissis,　　et　　nactus　　et　　secundum
having been dismissed,　and　having got　both　a favorable

ventum　et　æstum　uno　tempŏre,　signo
wind　and　tide　at one　time,　a signal

dăto,　　et　　anchŏris　　sublatis,
having been given,　and　the anchors　having been taken up

progressus　circĭter　octo　millĭa
[weighed],　having advanced　about　eight　thousand

passùum　ab　ĕo　lŏco,　constitŭit　naves
(of) paces　from　this　place,　he stood [stationed]　the ships

aperto　ac　plano　littŏre.
against an open　and　level　shore.

24. At　　barbări,　　consilĭo　　Romanorum
　　But　　the barbarians,　　the design　　of the Romans

cognĭto,　　equitatu　　præmisso,　　et
having been known.　the cavalry　having been sent before, and

essedarĭis ;　quo　genĕre (abl.)　consueverunt
the charioteers;　which　kind [means]　they have been accustomed

plerumque　uti　in　prœlĭis,　subsecuti
generally　to use　in　battles,　having followed near

relĭquis　copĭis,　prohibebant　nostros
with the rest of　(their) forces,　they were hindering　our (men)

egrĕdi · navĭbus. · Erat
to come out [from disembarking] · from the ships. · (There) was

summa · difficultas ob · has · causas, · quòd
the highest [greatest] · difficulty · for · these · reasons, · because

naves, · propter · magnitudĭnem · non · potĕrant
the ships, · on account of · (their) size · were not · able

constitŭti · nĭsi · in · alto: · autem · et · ĕrat
to be stationed · unless · in · the deep: · moreover · both · it was

desiliendum[43] · sĭmul · de · navĭbus,
to [it must] be leaped down · at the same time · from · the ships,

et · consistendum · fluctĭbus, · et · pugnandum
and · to [must] be stood · in the waves, · and · to [must] be fought

cum · hostĭbus · militĭbus, · ignotis · lŏcis,
with · the enemy · by the soldiers, · in unknown · places,

impeditis · manĭbus, · pressis · magno · et
with encumered · hands, · oppressed · with a great · and

grăvi onĕre armorum; quum illi[44] conjicĕrent (imp.
heavy · load · of arms: · while they · were hurling

subj.) · tela · audacter · aut · ex · arĭdo · aut
weapons · boldly · either · from · dry (ground) · or

progressi · paulum · in · ăquam, · expediti
having advanced · a little · into · the water, · unencumbered

omnĭbus · membris, · notissĭmis · lŏcis, · et
in all · (their) limbs, · in very well known · places, · and

incitarent (imp. subj.) · ĕquos · insuefactos.
were urging on · the horses · accustomed to (it).

Quĭbus · rebus · nostri · perterrĭti, · atque
By which · things · our (men) · being dismayed, · and

imperiti · omnino · hujus · genĕris · pugnæ, · omnes
unskilled · altogether · of [in] this · kind · of battle, · all

nitebantur · non · eâdem · alacritate · ac · studĭo,
were striving · not · with the same · eagerness · and · zeal,

(abl.), · quo (abl.) · consuevĕrant · uti · in
which · they had been accustomed · to use · in

pedestribus · prœlĭis.
infantry · battles.

25. Quŏd[45] · ŭbi · Cæsar · animadvertit, · jussit
Which · when · Cæsar · perceived, · he ordered

longas	naves	species	quarum	et
the long	ships [war ships],	the appearance	of which	both

ĕrat	inusitatĭor	barbăris,	et	motus
was	more unusual	to the barbarians,	and	the motion

expeditĭor	ad	usum,	removeri	paulum	ab
more easily	for	use,	to be removed	a little	from

onerarĭis	navĭbus,	et	incitari
the burden [transport]	ships,	and	to be impelled

remis,	et	constitŭi	ad	apertum	lătus
with oars,	and	to be stationed	at	the open	flank

hostĭum,	atque	hostes	propelli	ac
of the enemy,	and	the enemy	to be repulsed	and

submoveri	inde	fundis,	tormentis,
to be removed	from there	by slings,	shooting engines,

sagittis;	quæ	res	fŭit	magno	usŭi
arrows;	which	thing [means]	was	for [of] great	use

nostris.	Nam	barbări	permoti	et
to our (men).	For	the barbarians	much alarmed	both

figurâ	navĭum,	et	motu	remorum,
by the shape	of the ships,	and	by the motion	of the oars,

et	inusitato	genĕre	tormentorum,	constit-
and	by the unusual	kind	of the shooting engines,	halt-

erunt,	ac	retulerunt	pĕdem	paulùm.	Ac,
ed,	and	retraced (their)	foot [steps]	a little.	And,

nostris	militĭbus	cunctantĭbus,	maxĭmè	propter
our	soldiers	delaying,	chiefly	on account of

altitudĭnem	măris,	qui	ferebat	aquĭlam
the depth	of the sea,	(he) who	was bearing	the eagle

decĭmæ	legionis,	obtestatus	dĕos,	ut	ĕa
of the tenth	legion,	having implored	the gods,	that	this

res	eveniret	felicĭter	legioni:	inquit,
thing	might happen	fortunately	to the legion:	says,

"Desilite,	commilitones,	nĭsi	vultis	prodĕre
"Jump down!	fellow soldiers,	unless	you wish	to betray

aquĭlam	hostĭbus;	ĕgo	certè	præstitĕro
the eagle	to the enemy;	I	certainly	shall have performed

mĕum	officĭum	rei publĭcæ	atque	Imperatori."
my	duty	to the republic	and to	(my) Commander."

Quum   dixisset (pl. perf. subj.)   hoc   magnâ
When he   had said   this   with a great [loud]

voce,   projecit   se   ex   navi,   atque
voice.   he cast   himself (forth)   from   the ship,   and

cœpit   ferre   aquĭlam   in   hostes.   Tum
began   to bear   the eagle   against   the enemy.   Then

nostri   cohortati   inter   se,
our (men)   having encouraged   among   themselves [each other],

universi   desilierunt   ex   navi,   ne   tantum
every one   leaped down   from   the ship,   lest   so great

dedĕcus   admitteretur.   Quum   alĭi   ĭtem   ex
a disgrace   should be allowed.   When   others   also   from

proxĭmis   navĭbus   conspexissent (pl. perf. subj.)   hos,
the nearest   ships   beheld   these,

subsecuti   appropinquârunt   hostĭbus (dat.).
having followed close   they approached   the enemy.

26. Pugnatum-est[46]   acrĭter   ab   utrisque (plur.)
It was fought   vigorously   by   each

Tămen   nostri   perturbabantur   magnopĕre, quŏd
However   our (men)   were disordered [confused]   very greatly,   because

potĕrant   nĕque   servare   ordĭnes,   nĕque
they were able   neither   to keep   (their) ranks,   nor

insistĕre firmĭter,   nĕque   subsĕqui   signa,
to stand   firmly,   nor   to follow   the standards (closely),

atque   alĭus   ex   alĭâ   navi
and   one   from   one (another from another)   ship

aggregabat   se   quibuscumque   signis   occurrĕret.
was attaching   himself   to whatever   standards   he should meet.

Verò   hostes,   omnĭbus   vădis   notis,
But   the enemy,   all   the shallows   having been [being] known,

ŭbi   conspexĕrant   ex   littŏre   alĭquos
when   they had beheld   from   the shore   some

egredientes   singulares   ex   navi,   ĕquis
coming out   single [singly]   from   a ship,   (their) horses

incitatis,   adoriebantur   impeditos.
(having been) urged on,   were attacking   (them) encumbered.

Plures   circumsistebant   paucos :   alĭi
More [several]   were surrounding   a few :   others

conjiciebant   tela   in   universos   ab aperto
were hurling (their) weapons upon the whole [the mass] from the open

latĕre.   Quod   quum   Cæsar   animadvertisset (pl.
flank.   Which   when   Cæsar   had observed,

perf. subj.),   jussit   scăphas   longarum   navĭum,
              he ordered   the skiffs   of the long   ships,

            ĭtem   speculatorĭa-navigia   compleri
[war ships],   likewise   the spy-boats   to be filled

militĭbus;   et   submittebat   subsidĭa   his,
with soldiers,   and   he was sending   aid   to these.

quos   conspexĕrat   laborantes.   Nostri   sĭmul-
whom   he had beheld   laboring.   Our (men)   as soon

atque   constiterunt   in   arĭdo,   omnĭbus
as   they stood   on   dry (ground),   all

sŭis   consecutis,   fecerunt   impĕtum
their (comrades)   having followed,   made   a charge

in   hostes,   atque   dederunt   ĕos   in
upon   the enemy,   and   gave [put]   them   to

fŭgam: nĕque   potuerunt   prosĕqui   longĭus
flight: nor   were they able   to pursue   rather far

quòd   equĭtes   non   potuĕrant   tenere
because   the horsemen   had not   been able   to hold

     cursum,   atque   capĕre   insŭlam.   Hoc
(their)   course,   and   to take [reach] the island.   This

unum   defŭit   Cæsări   ad   pristĭnam
one (thing)   was wanting   to Cæsar   for   (his) former

fortunam.
good fortune.

27.   Hostes,   superati   prœlĭo,
     The enemy,   having been overcome   in the battle.

miserunt   stătim   legatos   ad   Cæsărem   de
sent   immediately   ambassadors   to   Cæsar   about

pace,   sĭmul-atque   receperunt   se   ex
peace,   as soon as   they recovered   themselves   from

fŭgâ;   poilicĭti-sunt   sese   daturos
flight: they promised (that they) themselves about to [would] give

obsĭdes,   que   facturos   quæ   imperâsset.
hostages.   and   about to [would] do   what   he might command.

Commĭus   Atrĕbas   venit   unà   cum   his
Commius   the Atrebatian   came   together   with   these

legatis,   quem   demonstravĕram   suprà   præmiss-
ambassadors.   whom   I had shown   above   to have [had]

um (-esse)   in   Britannĭam :   illi   comprehendĕrant
been sent before   into   Britain: they   had seized

hunc   egressum   è   navi,   quum   deferret
him   having disembarked   from   the ships,   when   he was bearing,

(imp. subj.)   modo   oratoris   mandata
in the character   of an envoy,   the commands

Cæsaris   ad   ĕos,   atque   conjecĕrant   in
of Cæsar   to   them,   and   had thrown (him)   into

vincula.   Tum   prœlĭo   facto,
chains.   Then   the battle   having been done [fought],

remiserunt   et   in   petenda   pace   contulerunt
they sent (him) back   and   in   seeking   peace   they laid

culpam   ejus   rĕi   in   multitudĭnem,   et
the blame   of this   thing   upon   the multitude.   and

petiverunt,   ut   ignosceretur   propter
sought,   that   it might be pardoned   on account of

imprudentĭam.   Cæsar   questus   quòd   quum
ignorance.   Cæsar,   having complained   that   when

petîssent (pl. perf. subj.)   pacem   à   se,
they had sought   peace   from   himself,

legatis   missis   ultrò   in   continentem,
ambassadors   having been sent   voluntarily   into [to]   the continent,

intulissent (pl. perf. subj.)   bellum   sĭne   causâ,
they had waged   war   without   cause,

dixit   ignoscĕre   imprudentĭæ,[47]   que
said   to [he would] pardon   (their) indiscretion,   and

imperavit   obsĭdes :   partem   quorum   illi   dederunt
demanded   hostages: part   of whom   they   gave

stătim :   dixerunt   sese   daturos
immediately: they said (that they)   themselves   about to [would] give

paucis   diebus   partem   arcessitam   ex   longinqui-
in a few   days   a part   sent for   from   more

orĭbus   lŏcis.   Interĕa   jusserunt   sŭos
distant   places.   Meantime   they ordered   their (people)

remigrare　in　　　　agros ;　　　　　que　　princĭpes
to return　into [to]　the lands [country] ;　and　　the chiefs

cœpĕrunt　convenêre　undĭque　　et　commendâre
began　　to assemble　from every side　and　to recommend

se　　　que　sŭas　civitates　Cæsări.
themselves　and　their　states　to Cæsar.

28. Pace　　　　　firmatâ　　　　his　　rebus,
　　　Peace　　having been established　by these　things,

octodĕcim　naves　de　　quĭbus demonstratum-est
the eighteen　ships　concerning　which　it had been shown

suprà, quæ sustulĕrant　　　equĭtes, solverunt
above,　which had taken up [embarked]　the cavalry,　cast loose

ex　superiore　portu　leni　vento,　quar-
from　the upper　harbor　with a gentle　wind,　the

tum　dĭem　post[48]　quàm　ventum-est　　　in
fourth　day　after　that　it was come [they came]　into

Britannĭam :　quum　quæ　　　appropinquarent
　Britain :　when　which [these]　were approaching

(imp. subj.)　Britannĕæ (dat),　et　viderentur (imp.
　　　　　Britain,　　　　and　were seen

subj.)　ex　　castris (pl.),　tanta　tempestas
　　　from　the camp,　so great　a storm

subĭtò　coorta-est,　ut　nulla　earum　posset (imp.
suddenly　arose,　that　no one　of them　was able

subj.)　tenere　cursum,　sed　alĭæ　referrentur
　　　to hold　the course,　but　some　were carried back

(imp. subj.)　eòdem　　　unde　profectæ ĕrant ;
　　　to the same (place)　whence　they had set out ;

alĭæ　dejicerentur (imp. subj.)　ad　inferiorem
others　were cast down [driven]　to　the lower

partem　insŭlæ,　quæ　est　propĭus　occasum
part　of the island,　which　is　nearer　the setting

solis　　　cum　suo magno　pericŭlo quæ[49]
of the sun [the west]　with　their great　danger　which [they]

tămen,　ânchŏris　jactis,　cùm　complerentur
however,　anchors　having been cast,　when　they were filled

(imp. subj.)　fluctĭbus,　provectæ　necessarĭò
　　　with the waves,　having been borne out　necessarily

in	altum	adversâ	nocte,	petiverunt
into	the deep	in an unfavorable	night,	they sought

continentem.
the continent.

29. Accĭdit   eâdem   nocte,   ut   luna
It happened   in the same   night,   that   the moon

esset (imp. subj.)	plena,	quæ	dĭes	con-
was	full,	which	day	has been

suevit	efficĕre	maxĭmos	maritĭmos	æstus
accustomed	to produce	the greatest	maritime	tides

in	oceăno;	que	id	ĕrat	incognĭtum	nostris.
in	the ocean;	and	this	was	unknown	to our

Ita   æstus   complebat   uno   tempŏre
(men).   Thus   the tide   was filling   at one   time

et	longas	naves,	(quĭbus[50]	Cæsar
both	the long	ships [war ships],	(in which	Cæsar

curavĕrat   exercĭtum   transportandum)
had taken care (that)   the army   to [should] be carried over)

quas	Cæsar	subduxĕrat	in	arĭdum;	et
which	Cæsar	had drawn up	on	dry (ground);	and

tempestas	afflictabat	onerarĭas,	quæ	deligatæ-
the storm	was shattering	the transports,	which	had been

ĕrant	ad	anchŏras (pl.):	nĕque	ulla	facultas
fastened	at	anchor	nor	any	opportunity

aut	administrandi	aut	auxiliandi	dabatur
either	of managing	or	of aiding	was given

nostris.	Complurĭbus	navibus	fractis,
to our (men).	Very many	ships	having been broken

quum   relĭquæ   essent (imp. subj.)   inutĭles
[wrecked],   since   the rest   were   useless

ad navigandum,	funĭbus,	anchŏris,	que
for sailing,	ropes [cables],	anchors,	and

relĭquis	armamentis (pl.)	amissis,	magna
the remaining	rigging	having been lost,	a great

perturbatĭo	totius	exercĭtûs	facta-est,	(id
alarm	of the whole	army	was occasioned,	(this

quod	ĕrat	necesse	accidĕre).	Enim	nĕque
which	was	inevitable	to happen).	For	neither

ĕrant   alĭæ   naves,   quĭbus   possent (imp.
were (there)   other   ships,   by which   they were able

subj.)   reportari;   et   omnĭa[51]   deĕrant,
       to be carried back;   and   all (things)   were wanting,

quæ   essent   usŭi   ad   reficiendas;   naves
which   would be   for [of] use   for   repairing;   ship

et   quòd   constabat   omnĭbus   oportere
and   because   it was evident   to all   (it) to be [was] expedient

hiemare   in   Gallĭâ,   frumentum   non   provisum
to winter   in   Gaul,   corn   had not   been

ĕrat   in   his   lŏcis   in   hiĕmem.
provided   in   these   places   against   the winter.

30. Quĭbus rebus   cognĭtis,   princĭpes Britannĭæ,
    Which   things   having been known,   the chiefs   of Britain,

qui   post   prœlĭum   convenĕrant   ad   Cæsarem[52]
who   after   the battle   had come together   to   Cæsar

collocuti   inter   se;   quum   intelligĕrent
having conferred   among   themselves;   when   they were understanding

(imp. subj.)   ĕquĭtes,   et   naves   et   frumentum
       (that) horsemen,   and   ships   and   corn

    deesse   Romanis,   et   cognoscĕrent (imp.
to be [were] wanting   to the Romans,   and   were ascertaining

subj.)   paucitatem   nostrorum milĭtum ex   exiguitate
      the fewness   of our   soldiers   from   the smallness

castrorum (pl.);   quæ   etĭam   ĕrant (pl.)   angustiora
of the camp;   which   also   was   more narrow

   hôc,   quòd   Cæsar   transportavĕrat
from this fact,   because   Cæsar   had brought over

legiones   sĭne   impedimentis;   duxerunt   esse
the legions   without   baggage;   considered (this)   to be [was]

optĭmum   factu,   rebellione   factâ,   prohibere
best   to be done,   a revolt   having been made,   to prevent

nostros   frumento   que   commeatu,   et   producĕre
our (men)   from corn   and   provisions,   and   to prolong

rem   in   hiĕmem;   quòd   his   superatis
the thing [campaign] into   the winter;   because   these   having been

    aut interclusis   redĭtu,   confidebant
overcome.   or   intercepted   from a return,   they were trusting (that)

nemĭnem   postĕa   transĭturum   in
no one   afterwards   about to [would] cross over   into

Britannĭam   causâ   inferendi   belli.   Ităque,
Britain   for the sake   of waging   war.   Therefore,

conjuratione   factâ   rursus,   cœperunt
a conspiracy   having been made   again,   they began

discedĕre   paulatim   ex   castris (pl.),   ac
to depart   little by little from   the camp,   and

deducĕre   clam   sŭos   ex   agris.
to lead out   secretly their (men)   from   the fields.

31. At   Cæsar,   etsi   nondum,   cognovĕrat
But   Cæsar,   although   he had not yet,   known

eorum   consilĭa   tămen   suspicabatur   id
their   plans   however   he was suspecting   (that) this

fŏre,   quod   accĭdit,   et   ex   eventu
to be about to [would] be,   which   happened,   both   from   the fate

suarum   navĭum,   et   ex   ĕo,   quòd
of his   ships,   and   from   this (fact),   because

intermisĕrant   dăre   obsides.   Ităque
they had omitted [failed]   to give   hostages.   Therefore

comparabat   subsidĭa (pl.)   ad   omnes   casus:
he was preparing   aid [remedies]   for   all   crises:

nam   et   conferebat   frumentum   quotidĭe   ex
for   both   he was bringing   corn   daily   from

agris   in   castra; (pl.) et   utebatur   materĭâ
the fields   into   the camp;   and   was using   the material

(abl.)   atque   ære   earum   naves,   quæ   afflictæ
[timber]   and   copper of these ships,   which   had been

ĕrant   gravissĭmè,   ad   reficiendas   relĭquas
shattered   most severely [seriously],   for   repairing   the rest

et   jubebat   comportari   ex   continenti,
and   was ordering   to be brought   from   the continent,

quæ   ĕrant   usŭi   ad   ĕas   res.   Ităque,
what   were   for [of] use for   these   things.   Therefore

quum   id   administraretur (imp. subj.)   summo
since   this   was performed   with the highest

studĭo   à   militĭbus,   duodĕcim   navĭbus
[greatest]   zeal   by   the soldiers,   twelve   ships

amissis,   offecit,[53]   ut   posset
having been lost,   he accomplished,   that   it [they] might be able

navigari   commŏdè   relĭquis.
;o be sailed [to sail]   readily   in the rest.

32. Dum   ĕa   geruntur,   unâ   legione,
While   these (things)   are transpiring,   one   legion,

quæ   appellabatur   septĭma,   missâ   frumen-
which   was called   the seventh,   havⁱng been sent   to bring

tatum   ex   consuetudĭne,   nĕque   ullâ   suspicione
corn   according to   custom,   nor   any   suspicion

belli   interposĭtâ   ad   id   tempus,   quum
cf war   having been offered [shown]   to   this   time,   when

pars   homĭnum   remaneret (imp. subj.)   iⁿ
a part   of the men   were remaining   iᴠ

agris,   pars   etĭam   ventitaret (imp. subj.)
the fields,   a part   also   were coming often

in   castra (pl.);   ĭi,   qui   ĕrant   in   statione
to   the camp;   those,   who   where   on   guard

pro   portis   castrorum (pl.),   renunciaverunt
before   the gates   of the camp,   announced

Cæsări,   majorem   pulvĕrem,   quàm   con-
to Cæsar,   (that)   a greater   dust,   than   cus-

suetudo   ferret,   videri   in   ĕâ
tom   bore [warranted],   to be [was] seen   in   this

parte,   in   quam   partem   legĭo   fecisset
part,   into   which   part   the legion   had made

(pl. perf. subj.)   ĭter.   Cæsar   suspicatus,
the march.   Cæsar   having suspected,

id   quod   ĕrat,   alĭquid   nŏvi   consilĭi
this   which   was,   (that)   some (thing)   (of) new   plan

            inĭtum(esse)   à   barbăris.   jussit
to have [had] been entered on   by   the barbarians,   ordered

cohortes,   quæ   ĕrant   in   statyonĭbus (pl.),   pro-
the cohorts,   which   were   on   guard,   to

ficisci   secum   in   ĕam   partem,   dŭas
set out   with himself   into   this   part,   two (cohⁿrts)

succedĕre   in   stationem,   relĭquas   armari,   et
to succeed   on   guard,   the rest   to be armed,   and

se   subsĕqui   confestim.   Quum   proces-
to follow himself   closely   immediately.   When   he had

sisset (pl. perf. subj.)   paulò   longĭùs   à   castris
advanced   a little   farther   from   the camp,

(pl.),   animadvertit   sŭos   prĕmi
        he perceived   (that)   his own (men)   to be [were] pressed

ab   hostĭbus,   atque   ægrè   sustinere,   ct
by   the enemy,   and   hardly   (to) withstand,   and

legione   confertâ,   tela
the legion   having been crowded together,   (that)   weapons

conjĭci   ex   omnĭbus   partĭbus.   Nam,
to be [were] thrown   from   all   parts [sides].   For,

quòd   omni   frumento   demesso   ex
because   all   the corn   having been cut down [reaped]   from

relĭquis   partĭbus,   una   pars   ĕrat   relĭqua,
the remaining   parts,   one   part   was   left,

hostes,   suspicati   nostros   esse
the enemy,   having suspected   (that)   our (men)   to be [were]

venturos   huc,   delituĕrant   noctu   in   silvis.
about to come   hither,   had lurked   by night   in   the woods.

Tum   subĭtò   adorti   dispersos,
Then   suddenly   having attacked   (them)   dispersed,

occupatos   in   metendo,   armis   deposĭtis,
engaged   in   reaping,   (their) arms   having been laid aside,

paucis   interfectis,   perturbavĕrant   relĭquos
a few   having been slain,   they had disordered   the rest

incertis   ordinĭbus;   sĭmul   circum-
in uncertain [confused]   ranks;   at the same time   they had

dedĕrant   equitatu   atque   essĕdis.
surrounded (them)   with cavalry   and   with chariots.

33. Hoc   est   gĕnus   pugnæ   ex   essĕdis :
This   is   the kind   of battle   from   the chariots.

primò,   perequĭtant   per   omnes   partes,   et
first,   they ride   through   all   parts,   and

conjicĭunt   tela :   atque   perturbant[54]   ordĭnes
hurl   (their) weapons :   and   they disorder   the ranks

plerumque   terrore   ipso   equorum,   et
generally   by the terror   itself   of the horses.   and

strepĭtu   rotarum :   et   quum   insinuavêre
rattling   of the wheels: and   when   they have introduced

se   inter   turmas   equĭtum,   desilĭunt
themselves   among   the troops   of the horsemen,   they leap down

ex   essĕdis   et   prœliantur[55]   pedĭbus.
from   the chariots   and   fight   on feet [on foot].

Intĕrim   aurigæ   excedunt   paulùm   è
Meantime   the charioters   retire   a little   from

prœlĭo,   atque   collŏcant   se   ĭta,   ut   si
the battle,   and   place   themselves   so,   that   if

illi   premantur   à   multitudĭne   hostĭum,   hab-
those   are pressed   by   the multitude   of the enemy,   they

ĕant   expeditum   receptum   ad   sŭos.   Ita
may have   an unhindered   retreat   to   their own (men).   Thus

præstant   mobilitatem   equĭtum,   stabilitem
they display   the activity   of cavalry,   the steadiness

pedĭtum   in   prœlĭis ;   ac   efficĭunt   tantum
of infantry   in   battles;   and   they accomplish   so much

quotidiano   usu   et   exercitatione,   ut   con-
by daily   practice   and   exercise,   that   they have

suevĕrint (perf. subj.)   in   declivi   ac   præcipĭti
been accustomed   in   a sloping   and   steep

lŏco, sustinere   ĕquos   incĭtatos,   et   moderari
place,   to rein in   (their) horses   spurred on,   and   to control

ac   flectĕre   brĕvi,   et   percurrĕre
and   (to) turn (them)   shortly [sharply],   and   to run along

per   temonem,   et   insistĕre   in   jugo,
though [on]   the pole,   and   to stand   on   the yoke,

et   recipĕre   se   inde   citissĭmè   in
and   to betake   themselves   thence   most quickly   into

currus.
the chariots.

34. Nostris   perturbatis   quĭbus
     To our (men)   having been disordered   by which [these]

rebus,   novitate   pugnæ,   Cæsar   tŭlit
things,   by the novelty [strangeness]   of the battle,   Cæsar   brought

auxilĭum   opportunissĭmo   tempŏre : namque   hostes
aid   at a most seasonable   time :   for   the enemy

constiterunt   ejus,   adventu   nostri   receperunt
halted   on his,   arrival   our (men)   recovered

se   ex   timore.   Quo   facto,
themselves   from   fear.   Which   having been done,

arbitratus[56]   tempus   esse   alienum   ad
having thought   the time   to be [was]   improper   for

lacessendum   hostem   et   committendum   prœlĭum,
attacking   the enemy   and   for engaging in   battle,

continŭit   se   sŭo   lŏco;   et   brĕvi
he kept   himself   in his own   place;   and   a short

tempŏre   intermisso,[57]   reduxit   legiones
time   having been passed [spent],   he led back   the legions

in   castra.   Dum   hæc   geruntur,   omnĭbus
into   the camp.   While   these (things)   are passing,   all

nostris   occupatis,   qui   ĕrant   in   agris
our (men)   having been engaged,   who   were   in   the fields

relĭqui[58]   discesserunt.   Tempestates   secutæ-sunt
the rest   departed.   Storms   followed

complures   continŭos   dĭes,   quæ   et   continerent
many   successive   days,   which   both   were restraining

(imp. subj.)   nostros   in   castris (pl.),   et   prohib-
  our (men)   in   camp,   and   were

erent (imp. subj.)   hostem   à   pugnâ.   Intĕrim,
hindering   the enemy   from   battle.   Meantime

barbări   dimiserunt   nuncios   in   omnes
the barbarians   dispatched   messengers   into   all

partes,   que   prædicaverunt   sŭis   pau-
parts,   and   proclaimed   to their own (people)   the

citatem   nostrorum   milĭtum;   et   demonstraverunt
fewness   of our   soldiers;   and   showed

quanta   facultas[59]   daretur (imp. subj.)   faciendæ
how great   an opportunity   was given   of making

prædæ   atque   liberandi   sŭi   in   perpetŭum,
plunder   and   of freeing   themselves   forever,

si   expulissent   Romanos   castris (pl.).   Magnâ
if   they should drive   the Romans   from the camp.   A great

multitudĭne   peditatûs   que   equitatûs   co-
multitude   of infantry   and   of cavalry   having been

actâ   celerĭter   his   rebus,   venerunt
assembled   quickly   with these   things [objects],   they came

ad   castra (pl.).
to   the camp.

35. Etsi   Cæsar   videbat   ĭdem
    Although Cæsar   was seeing   (that) the same (things)

fŏre,   quod   accidĕrat   superiorĭbus
to be about to [would] be,   which   had happened   in former

diebus;   ut,   si   hostes   essent   pulsi,
days;   that,   if   the enemy   should be   routed,

effugĕrent   periculum   celeritate;   tămen
they would escape   danger   by speed;   nevertheless

nactus   circĭter   triginta   equĭtes,   quos   Commĭus
having got   about   thirty   horsemen,   whom   Commius

Atrĕbas,   (de   quo   dictum-est   antè)
the Atrebatian,   (of   whom   it has been mentioned   before)

transportavĕrat   secum,   constituĭt   legiones
had brought over   with himself,   he drew up   the legions

in   acĭe   pro   castris (pl.).   Prœlĭo
in   battle line   before   the camp.   The battle

commisso,   hostes   potuerunt   non   ferre
having been joined,   the enemy   were able   not   to bear

impĕtum   nostrorum   milĭtum   diutĭus   ac   verterunt
the charge   of our   soldiers   longer   and   turned

terga: quos   secuti   tanto   spatĭo,
(their) backs [retreated]:   whom   having followed   for so great a distance,

quantum   potuerunt   efficĕre   cursu   et
as   they were able   to accomplish   by running   and

virĭbus (pl.),   occiderunt   complures   ex   ĭis:
by exertion,   they killed   many   from [of]   them:

deinde   omnĭbus   ædificĭis   incensis   longè
then   all   the buildings   having been burned   far

que   latè,   receperunt   se   in   castra (pl.).
and   wide,   they betook   themselves   into   the camp.

36. Eodem   dĭe   legati   missi   ab
    On the same   day   ambassadors   (having been) sent   by

hostĭbus   venerunt   ad   Cæsărem   de   pace.
the enemy   came   to   Cæsar   concerning   peace.

Cæsar — duplicavit — his — numĕrum — obsĭdum,
Cæsar — doubled — for these [them] — the number — of hostages

quem — imperavĕrat — antĕa; — que — jussit — ĕos
which — he had ordered — before; — and — commanded — them

adduci — in — continentem; — quòd, — dĭe
to be conducted — to — the continent; — because, — the day

æquinoctĭ — propinquâ, — existĭmabat — navigationem[60]
of the equinox — (being) near, — he was thinking — the voyage

non — subjiciendam — hiĕmi — infirmis — navĭbus:
not — to [would not] be exposed — to winter — with weak — ships:

ipse — nactus — idonĕam — tempestatem — solvit
he himself — having gained — suitable — weather — cast loose

naves — paulò — post — medĭam — noctem; — omnes
the ships — a little — after — mid — night; — all

quæ — pervenerunt — incolŭmes — ad — continentem.
which [these] — passed — safe — to — the continent.

Ex — his, — dŭæ — onerarĭæ — potuerunt
From [of] — these. — two — burden [transport ships] — were able

non — capĕre — eosdem — portus, — quos
not — to take [reach] — the same — harbors, — which [as]

relĭquæ; — sed — delatæ-sunt — paulò — infrà.
the rest; — but — were carried down — a little — below.

37. Ex — quĭbus[61] — navĭbus, — quum — circĭter
From — which — ships, — when — about

trecenti — milĭtes — exposĭti-essent (pl. perf. subj.),
three hundred — soldiers — had been landed,

atque — contendĕrent (imp. subj.) — in — castra (pl.),
and — were hastening — into — camp,

Morĭni, — quos — Cæsar — reliquĕrat — pacatos
the Morini, — whom — Cæsar — had left — subdued

proficiscens — in — Britannĭam, — adducti — spe
setting out — into — Britain, — induced — by hope

prædæ, — primò — circumsteterunt — numĕro
of plunder, — first — surrounded (them) — with a number

suorum — non — ĭta — magno, — ac — jusserunt
of their own (men), — not — so — large, — and — ordered

ponĕre — arma, — si — nollent[62]
(them) to lay down — (their) arms, — if — they were unwilling

	sese	interfĭci.	Quum illi,
(that they)	themselves	to [should] be slain.	When they,

orbe	facto,	defendĕrent (imp. subj.)
a circle	having been formed,	were defending

sese,	circĭter	sex	millĭa	celerĭter	convenerunt
themselves,	about	six	thousand	quickly	assembled

ad	clamorem	homĭnum.	Quâ	re	nun-
at	the shout	of the men.	Which	thing	having been

tiatâ,	Cæsar	misit	omnem	equitatum	ex
announced,	Cæsar	sent	all	the cavalry	from

sŭis	castris (pl,)	auxilĭo	sŭis.	Intĕrim	nostri
his	camp	for aid	to his (men).	Meantime	our

milĭtes	sustinuerunt	impĕtum	hostĭum,	atque
soldiers	bore	the attack	of the enemy,	and

pugnaverunt	fortissĭmè	amplĭùs	quatŭor	horis;
fought	most bravely	more (than)	four	hours;

et,	paucis	vulnerĭbus	acceptis,	occiderunt
and,	a few	wounds	having been received,	killed

complures	ex	ĭis.	Verò	posteăquàm	noster
many	from	them.	But	after (that)	our

equitatus	venit	in	conspectum,	hostes,	
cavalry	came	into	sight,	the enemy,	(their)

armis	abjectis,	verterunt	terga,
arms	having been thrown away,	turned	(their) backs,

	que	magnus	numĕrus	eorum	occisus-est.
[retreated] and		a great	number	of them	was killed.

38. Cæsar	misit	legatum	Titum	Labienum
Cæsar	sent	(his) lieutenant	Titus	Labienus

postĕro	dĭe,	cum	ĭis	legionĭbus,	quas
the following	day,	with	these	legions,	which

reduxĕrat	ex	Britannĭâ,	in	Morĭnos,
he had brought back	from	Britain,	into	the Morini,

qui	fecerant	rebellionem.	Qui,	quum	habe-
who	had made	a rebellion.	Who,	when	they were

rent (imp. subj.)	non	quò	recipĕrent
having	not [no]	where	they might betake

se	propter	siccitates (pl.)	paludum,
themselves	on account of	the dryness	of the marshes,

quo   perfugĭo (abl.)   usi-fuĕrant   superiore   anno,
which   refuge   they had used   in the former   year,

fĕrè   omnes prevenerunt in potestatem Labieni.
nearlv   all   came   into the power of Labienus.

At   Quintus Titurĭus et Lucĭus Cotta,   legati,
But   Quintus Titurius and Lucius Cotta,   the lieutenants,

qui   duxĕrant legiones in   fines   Me-
who   had led   the legions into the territories of the

napiorum, omnĭbus eorum agris   vastatis,
Menapii,   all   their   lands having been devastated.

frumentis (pl.)   succisis,   que   ædificĭis
the corn   having been cut down, and the buildings

incensis,   quòd omnes Menapĭi abdidĕrant
having been fired, because all the Menapii had hid

se   in   densissĭmas silvas, receperunt
themselves among the thickest   woods,   betook

se   ad Cæsărem. Cæsar constitŭit   hi-
themselves to Cæsar.   Cæsar established the winter

berna omnĭum legionum in Belgis.   Eò
quarters of all   the legions among the Belgæ. There

dŭæ civitates omninc ex Britannĭâ miserunt
two   states   altogether from Britain   sent

obsĭdes: relĭquæ neglexerunt. His   rebus
hostages: the rest   neglected (it). These things

gestis,   supplicatĭo   viginti
having been acⁿomplished. a general thanksgiving of twenty

dierum decreta-est à senatu, ex
days   was decreed by the senate, from [because of]

litĕris (abl.) Cæsăris.
the letters   of Cæsar.

FIFTH BOOK

The fifth book includes the description of Cæsar's second campaign against the Britons and an account of certain internal trouble and revolts which endangered several Roman encampments. Cæsar in preparing to leave his winter quarters ordered a huge fleet of specially constructed ships to be made ready. A second expedition against Britain is undertaken, and boldly resisted by the tribesmen of the island. The Roman fleet suffers severe losses through storms. The Britons throw a fresh offensive against the Romans ; but they are defeated. Cæsar with hostages returns to Gaul. There the tribes are involved in an internal war, and a revolution under Indutiomarus and Ambiorix is attempted. Contrary to his custom, Cæsar quarters his army in divisions and Gaul is finally brought again to a peaceful state.

1. Lucio   Domitio,   Appio   Claudio
  Lucius   Domitius,   Appius   Claudius   (being)

Consulibus,   Cæsar   discendens   ab   hibernis
  Consuls.   Cæsar   departing   from   winter quarters

in   Italiain,   ut   consuerat   facĕre
into   Italy,   as   he had been accustomed   to do

quotannis,   impĕrat   legatis (dat.),   quos
yearly [every year],   orders   the lieutenants,   whom

præfecĕrat   legionibus (dat.),   uti
he had appointed over   the legions,   that

curent   quam plurimas[1]   naves
they should take care   (that)   as many   ships

possent   ædificandas   hiĕme,   que
as might be possible   to [should] be built   in the winter,   and

vetĕres   reficiendas.   Demonstrat eorum mŏdum
the old (ships) to [should] be repaired.   He shows   their   size

que   formam;   făcit   paulò humiliores quàm
and   form;   he makes (them)   a little   lower   than

quibus (abl.)   consuevimus   uti   in
(those) which   we have been accustomed   to use   in

nostro   mări,   ad   celeritatem   onerandi,   que
our   sea,   for   quickness   of loading,   and

subductionis;   atque   id   măgis   ĕò,
of drawing up [beaching];   and   this   the more   for this reason,

quòd   cognovĕrat   mĭnùs   magnos
because   he had learned   (that)   less [not so]   great

fluctus²   fiĕri   ĭbi   propter   crebras
waves   to be [are] found   there   on account of   the frequent

commutationes   æstuum;   paulò   latiores   quàm
changes   of the tides: a little   wider   than

quĭbus (abl.)   utĭmur   in   relĭquis   marĭbus,   ad
what   we use   in   the other   seas,   for

onĕra³   et   ad   transportandum   multitudĭnem
loads   and   for   transferring   a multitude

jumentorum.   Impĕrat   omnes   has   fiĕri
of beasts of burden.   He commands   all   these   to be made

actuarĭas :   ad   quam⁴   rem   humilĭtas   adjŭvat
fast sailing: for   which   thing [object]   the lowness   aids

multùm.   Jŭbet   ea,   quæ   sunt   usŭi   ad
much.   He orders   these things,   which   are   for use   for

armandas⁵   naves   apportari   ex   Hispanĭâ.
rigging   ships   to be brought   from   Spain.

Ipse,   conventĭbus   citerioris   Gallĭæ   peractis,
He himself,   the assemblies   of nearer   Gaul   having been finished,

proficiscĭtur   in   Illyrĭcum;   quòd   audiebat
sets out   into   Illyricum;   because   he was hearing (that)

finitĭmam   partem   Provincĭæ   vastari
the neighboring   part   of the Province   to be [was] ravaged

incursionĭbus   à   Pirustis.   Quum   venisset
with incursions   by   the Pirustæ.   When   he had come

(pl. perf. subj.)   ĕò,   impĕrat⁶   civitatĭbus (dat.)
there.   he demands   (of) the states

milĭtes, que   jŭbet   convenire   in   certum   lŏcum
soldiers,   and   orders (them)   to assemble   to [into] a certain   place.

Quâ   re   nuntiatâ,   Pirustæ
Which [This]   thing   having been announced.   the Pirustæ

mittunt   legatos   ad   ĕum,   qui   docĕant   nĭhil
send   ambassadors   to   him,   who   may show   that nothing

earum rerum factum (-esse) publĭco
of these things [acts] to have [had] been done by public

concilĭo: que demonstrant sese esse
council: and they show (that they) themselves to be

paratos satisfacĕre omnĭbus rationĭbus de
[are] prepared to satisfy by all means regarding

injurĭis. Eorum oratione acceptâ,
the injuries. Their speech having been received [heard],

Cæsar impĕrat obsĭdes, que jŭbet ĕos adduci
Cæsar demands hostages, and orders them to be brought

ad certam dĭem: nĭsi fecĕrant ĭta,
to [on] a certain day: unless they should do so.

demonstrat[7] sese persecuturum
he shows (that he) himself about to [would] pursue

civitatem bello. Iis adductis ad
the state by war These having been brought on the

dĭem, ut imperavĕrat, dat arbĭtros
day. as he had commanded, he gives [appoints] arbitrators

inter civitates, qui æstĭment litem
among the states, who may value the suit [the damage]

que constitŭant pœnam.
and may determine the penalty

2. His rebus confectis, que
These things having been accomplished, and

conventĭbus peractis, revertĭtur in
the assemblies having been concluded, he returns into

citeriorem Gallĭam, atque inde proficiscĭtur ad
hither Gaul, and thence sets out to

exercĭtum. Quum venisset (pl perf subj.) ĕò,
the army. When he had come there.

omnĭbus hibernis circuĭtis, invenit
all the winter quarters having been visited, he found

circĭter sexcentas naves ejus genĕris, cujus
about six hundred ships of this kind, (of) which

demonstravĭmus supra, et viginti octo longas
we have shown above. and twenty eight long

constructas, singulari studĭo milĭtum,
[•var ships] built, by the singular zeal of the soldiers

in   summâ   inopĭâ   omnĭum rerum,   neque   multum
in   the highest   want   of all   things,   nor   much

abesse[8]   ab   ĕo,   quin
to be [was] wanting   from   this (condition),   but that

possent   deduci   paucis   diebus.
they might be able [could]   (to) be launched   in a few   days.

Milĭtĭbus   collaudatis,   atque   ĭis,   qui
The soldiers   having been commended   and   to those,   who

præfuĕrant   negotĭo,   ostendit   quid
had presided   in the business [undertaking],   he shows   what

vĕlĭt   fiĕri;   atque   jŭbet   omnes   convenire
he wishes   to be done;   and   orders   all   to assemble

ad   portum   Itĭum: ex   quo   portu
to[at]   the port   Itius [Boulogne]:   from   which   port

cognovĕrat   trajectum   in   Britannĭam   esse
he had learned   the passage   into   Britain   to be [was]

commodissĭmum,   circĭter   triginta   millĭum
the most convenient,   about   thirty   (of) thousand

passŭum   à   continenti.   Relinquit   quod
paces   from   the continent.   He leaves   what

visum-est   esse   sătis   milĭtum   huic   rĕi:
seemed   to be   enough   (of) soldiers   for this   thing

ipse   proficiscĭtur   cum   quatŭor
[expedition]:   (he) himself   sets out   with   four

expeditis   legionĭbus,   et   octingentis   equitĭbus,
light-armed   legions,   and   eight hundred   cavalry,

in   fines   Trevirorum;   quòd   hi   nĕque
into   the territories   of the Treviri: because   these   neither

veniebant   ad   concilĭa,   nĕque   parebant
were coming   to   the councils,   nor   were obeying

imperĭo (dat.),   que   dicebantur   sollicitare
(his) command,   and   were said   to be inciting

Germanos   transrhenanos.
the Germans   beyond the Rhine.

3. Hæc   civĭtas   vălet[9]   longè   plurimùm
This   state   prevails   by far   the most

totius   Galĭĭæ   equitatu,   que   hăbet   magnas
of the whole   of Gaul   in cavalry,   and   has   great

copĭas   pedĭtum;   que   tangıt   Rhenum,   ut
forces   of ınfantry ;   and   borders   the Rhıne,   4s

demonstravīmus   suprà.   In   ĕâ   civitate   dŭo,
we have shown   above   In   thıs   state   two (men),

Indutiomărus   et   Cingetŏrix,   contendebant[10]   inter
Indutiomarus   and   Cıngetorıx,   were strıving   among

        se   de   principatu :   alter ex
[between] themselves   about   the supreme authorıty :   one   from [of]

quĭbus,   sīmul atque   cognitum-est   de   adventu
whom,   as soon as   it was known   concerning   the approach

Cæsăris   que   legionum,   venit   ad   ĕum;   confirmavit
of Cæsar   and   of the legions,   came   to   him ;   he declared

        se   que   omnes   sŭos   futuros
(that he) himself   and   all   his (people)   about to [would] be

in   officĭo,   nĕque   defecturos   ab
in   duty [allegıance],   nor   about to [would] revolt   from

amicitĭâ   Romani   popŭli ;   que   ostendit,
the friendship   of the Roman   people ;   and   he shows,

quæ   gererentur (imp. subj.)   in   Trevīris.
what (things)   were transpırıng   among   the Trevıri.

At   Indutiomărus   instĭtŭit   cogĕre   equitatum   que
But   Indutiomarus   began   to collect   cavalry   and

peditatum ;   que   īis,   qui   per   ætatem   potĕrant
infantry ;   and   those,   who   through   age   were able

non   esse   in   armis,   abdĭtis   in   silvam
not   to be   in   arms,   having been hıd   within   the forest

Arduennam,   (quæ   ingenti   magnitudīne
of Arduenna [Ardennes],   (which   of great   extent

pertĭnet   à   flumīne   Rheno   ad   initĭum
reaches   from   the rıver   Rhine   ¦to   the beginning

Rhemorum   per   medĭos   fines   Trevirorum)
of the Rhemi   through   the central   territories   of the Trevıri)

parare[11]   bellum.   Sed   posteăquàm   nonnulli
[to] prepare [prepares]   war.   But   after (that)   some

princĭpes   ex   ĕâ   civitate,   et   adductı   familiaritate
chıefs   from   thıs   state,   ˈoth   ınduced   by the ıntımacy

Cingetorĭgis,   et   perterrĭti   adventu   nostri
of Cingetorıx,   and   alarmed   by the approach   of our

exercĭtûs, venerunt ad Cæsărem, et cœperunt petĕre
army,   came   to   Cæsar   and   began   to seek

ab   eo   de   sŭis   privatıs rebus, quonĭam
from him about their own prıvate affaırs,   since

possent (imp. subj.)   non   consulĕre   civitati :
they were able   not   to consult   for the state :

Indutiomărus   verĭtus   ne   desereretur
Indutiomarus   having feared   lest   he mıght be abandoned

ab omnĭbus, mittit   legatos   ad   Cæsărem ;
by all.   sends ambassadors to   Cæsar ;   (to say)

        se[12]   discĕdere   idcircò   à
(that he) himself to withdraw [withdraws] for this reason   from

sŭis,   atque   noluısse   venire ad
his own (people). and to have [had] been unwilling to come to

ĕum,   quò   contineret   civitatem   facilĭus
him, in order that he might restrain the state more easily

in   officĭo ;   ne   discċ..su   omnis
in   duty [allegiance] : lest   by the departure   of all

nobilitatis,   plebs   laberetur   propter
the nobility,   the common people   might slıp   through   (their)

imprudentĭam :   ităque   civitatem esse   in   sŭâ
indıscretion :   therefore   the state to be [was] in   his

potestate ;   que   se   venturum
power ;   and (that he) himself (to be) about to [would] come

ad   ĕum   in   castra (pl.), si   Cæsar permittĕret ;
to   hım ınto   the camp.   if   Cæsar would permit

et   permissurum   sŭas   fortunas   que
and   (to be) about to [would] consign his own   fortunes   and

        civitatis   ejus   fidĕi.
(those) of the state to his   faith.

4. Etsi   Cæsar   intelligebat   de   quà causâ[13]
    Although   Cæsar was understandıng from   what   cause

    ĕa   dicerentur (imp. subj.),   que   quæ   res
these things   were said,   and   what   thing

deterreret (imp. subj.)   ĕum   ab   instituto
was deterring   hım   from   (his) determined

consilĭo ;   tămen,   ne   cogeretur   consumĕre
purpose :   however, lest   he might be compelled   to waste

æstatem	in	Trevĭris,	omnĭbus	rebus
the summer	among	the Treviri,	all	things

comparatis	ad	Britannĭcum	bellum,	jussit
having been prepared	for	the Britannic	war,	he ordered

Indutiomărum	venire	ad	se	cum	ducentis
Indutiomarus	to come	to	himself	with	two hundred

obsidĭbus.	His	adductis,	et	filĭo
hostages.	These	having been brought,	and	(his) son

in	ĭis,	que omnĭbus	ejus	propinquis,	quos
among	them,	and all	his	relations,	whom

evocavĕrat	nominatim,	consolatus est	que
he had called out	by name,	he consoled	and

hortatus (est)	Indutiomărum,	ŭtĭ	permaneret
encouraged	Indutiomarus,	that	he might continue

in	officĭo.	Tămen, nihĭlo secĭùs principĭbus
in	duty [allegiance].	Yet,	nevertheless	the chiefs

Trevirorum	convocatis	ad	se,
of the Treviri	having been called together	to	himself,

conciliavit	ĕos	singillatim	Cingetorĭgi:	quod[14]
he reconciled	them	individually	to Cingetorix:	which

intelligebat	cùm	fiĕri	à	se
(thing) he was understanding	not only	to be [was] done	by	himself

ejus	merĭto (sing.)	tum	arbitrabatur	interesse
by his	deserts	but also	he was judging	to concern

magni,	ejus auctoritatem
[it concerned] (him)	of great [greatly],	(that)	his	authority

valere	quam plurĭmùm	inter	sŭos,
to [should] prevail	as much as possible	among	his own (people),

cujus	voluntatem	perspexisset (pl. perf. subj.)
whose	(good) will	he had perceived	(was)

tam	egregĭam	in	se.	Indutiomărus	tŭlit
so	excellent	toward	himself.	Indutiomarus	bore

id	factum	gravĭter,	sŭam	gratĭam
this	act	heavily [bitterly].	his own	favor

minŭi	inter	sŭos :	et	qui
to be [was] diminished	among	his own (people) :	and	(he) who

fuisset (pl. perf. subj.)	inimico	anĭmo	antè
had been	in [of] unfriendly	spirit	before

in   nos   exarsit   multò   gravĭus   hoc
toward   us   blazed forth [raged]   much   more violently   by this

dolore.
vexation.

5. Iis   rebus   constitutis,   Cæsar   pervenit
    Those   things   having been settled,   Cæsar   arrived

ad   portum   Itĭum   cum   legionĭbus.   Cognoscit
at   the harbor   Itus   with   the legions.   He learns

ĭbi,   quadraginta   naves,   quæ   factæ ĕrant
there,   (that)   forty   ships,   which   had been made

in   Meldis,   rejectas   tempestate,   non
among   the Meldi,   thrown back   by a storm.   not

potuisse[15]   tenere   cursum,   atque
to have [had not] been able   to hold   (their) course.   and

relatas   eŏdem,   unde   profectæ ĕrant:
(were) carried back   to the same (place)   whence   they had set out:

invĕnit   relĭquas   paratas   ad navigandum,   atque
he finds   the rest   prepared   for sailing,   and

instructas   omnĭbus   rebus.   Equitatus   totius
furnished   with all   things.   The cavalry   of the whole

Gallĭæ convenit   eŏdem,   numĕro   quatŭor
of Gaul   assembled   in the same (place)   to the number   of four

millĭum,   que   princĭpes   ex   omnĭbus   civitatĭbus;
thousand,   and   the chiefs   from [of]   all   the states,

perpaucos   ex   quĭbus,   quorum   fĭdem   in
a very few   from [of]   whom.   whose   fidelity   toward

se   perspexĕrat,   decrevĕrat   relinquĕre   in
himself   he had clearly seen.   he had resolved   to leave   in

Gallĭâ;   ducĕre   relĭquos   secum   lŏco
Gaul;   (and) to lead [take]   the rest   with him   in the place

obsĭdum;   quòd   verebatur   motum   Gallĭæ,
of hostages;   because   he was fearing   a disturbance   of Gaul,

quum   ipse   abesset.
when   (he) himself   was absent.

6. Dumnŏrix   Ædŭus   ĕrat   una   cum
   Dumnorix   the Æduan   was   together   with

cætĕris   de   quo   dictum est
the rest   concerning   whom   it has been spoken

à   nobis   antĕa.   Constituĕrat
[mention was made]   by   us   before   He had resolved

ducĕre   hunc   secum   inprimis,   quòd
to conduct   him   with him   in particular,   because

cognovĕrat   ĕum   cupĭdum   novarum   rerum,
he had known   him   desirous   of new   things

cupĭdum   imperii,   magni   anĭmi,   magnæ
[revolution].   desirous   of power.   of high   spirit,   of great

auctoritatis   inter   Gallos.   Accedebat   huc,[16]
authority   among   the Gauls.   It was added   to this,

quòd   Dumnŏrix   dixĕrat   jam   in   concilĭo
that   Dumnorix   had said   already   in   a council

Æduorum,   regnum   civitatis
of the Ædui,   (that)   the government   of the state

deferri   sĭbi   à   Cæsâre.   Quod
to be [was] conferred   to [on] himself   by   Cæsar.   Which

dictum   Ædŭi   ferebant   gravĭter,   nĕque
saying   the Ædui   were bearing   heavily [ill].   nor

audebant   mittĕre   legatos   ad   Cæsărem
were they daring   to send   ambassadors   to   Cæsar

causâ   recusandi   nĕque   deprecandi.   Cæsa.
for the sake   of objecting   nor   of protesting.   Cæsar

cognovĕrat   id   factum (esse)   ex
had known   (that) this   to have been [was] done   from

sŭis[17]   hospitĭbus.   Ille   primò   contendit   petĕre
his   guests.   He   at first   strove   to seek

omnĭbus   precĭbus,   ut   relinqueretur   in   Gallĭâ;
by all   entreaties,   that   he might be left   in   Gaul;

partim   quòd   insuetus   navigandi   timeret (imp.
partly   because   unused   of [to] voyaging   he was fearing

subj.)   mări a;   partim   quòd   dicĕret (imp. subj.)
the sea;   partly   because   he was saying

sese   impediri   religionĭbus.
(that he) himself   to be [was] hindered   by religious scruples.

Posteăquam   vidit   id   negari[18]   obstĭnatè
After (that)   he saw   this   to be [was] denied   obstinately

sĭbi,   omni   spe impetrandi   ademptâ,
to himself,   all   hope   of obtaining (it)   having been taken away

cœpit   sollicitare   princĭpes   Gallĭæ,   sevocare
he began   to instigate   the chiefs   of Gaul,   to call apart

singŭlos   que   hortari,   ut   remanerent   in
individuals   and   to exhort,   that   they should remain   on

contincnti;   territare[19]   mĕtu
the continent;   (saying) he to be [was] alarmed with the fear (that this)

fiĕri   non   sīne   causâ,   ut   Gallĭa
to be [was] done   not   without   reason,   that   Gaul

spoliaretur   omni   nobilitate.   Id   esse
might be stripped   from [of] all   the nobility.   (That) this   to be [was]

consilĭum   Cæsăris,   ut   necaret   omnes
the plan   of Cæsar,   that   he might destroy   all

hos   transductos   in   Britannĭam,   quos
these   conveyed over   into   Britain,   whom

vereretur (imp. subj.)   interficĕre   in   conspectu
he was fearing   to slay   in   the sight

Gallĭæ.   Interponĕre[20]   fĭdem   relĭquis;
of Gaul.   To suggest [He suggests]   a pledge   to the rest;

poscĕre   jusjurandum,   ut   administrarent
to demand [he demands]   an oath,   that   they would perform

communi   consilĭo,   quod   intellexissent   esse
with common   design,   what   they should understand   to be

ex   usu   Gallĭæ.
[was]   from [for]   the use [advantage]   of Gaul.

7. Hæc   deferebantur   ad   Cæsărem   à
These (matters)   were reported   to   Cæsar   by

complurĭbus. Quâ   re   cognĭtâ,   Cæsar,   quòd
very many. Which   thing   having been known,   Cæsar,   because

tribuebat   tantum   dignitatis   Ædŭæ   civitati,
he was granting   so much   (of) honor   to the Æduan   state,

statuebat   Dumnorĭgem   coërcendum
was determining   (that) Dumnorix   to [should] be restrained

atque   deterrendum   quibuscunque   rebus
and   to [should] be checked   by whatever   things [means]

posset;   quòd   videbat   ejus   amentĭam
he might be able;   because   he was seeing   his   madness

progrĕdi   longĭus,   prospiciendum,[21]   ne
to [would] proceed   further.   (it was) to be provided,   lest

posset — nocere — sĭbi (dat.) — ac
he might be able [should] — (to) injure — himself — and

rei publĭcæ (dat.). — Ităque — commoratus — in — ĕo
the republic. — Therefore — having delayed — in — this

lŏco — circĭter — viginti — quinque — dĭes, — quòd — ventus
place — about — twenty — five — days, — because — the wind

Corus — impediebat — navigationem, — qui
Corus (North West wind) — was hindering — the passage, — which

consuevit — flare — in — his — lŏcis — magnam — partem
is accustomed — to blow — in — these — places — a great — part

omnis — tempŏris, — dăbat — opĕram,²² — ut
of every — season. — he was giving — work [attention]. — that

contĭneret — Dumnorĭgem — in — officĭo; — tămen
he might keep — Dumnorix — in — (his) duty; — yet (that)

cognoscĕret — nĭhĭlò-secĭus — omnĭa — ejus — consilĭa.
he should learn — nevertheless — all — his — designs.

Tandem — nactus — idonĕam — tempestatem, — jŭbet
At length — having got — favorable — weather, — he orders

miltes — que — equĭtes — conscendĕre — in — naves. — Aϲ
the soldiers — and — cavalry — to embark — on — the ships. — But

anĭmis — omnĭum — impedĭtis, — Dumnorix — cum
the minds — of all — having been occupied. — Dumnorix — with

equitĭbus — Æduorum, — Cæsăre — insciente, — cœpit
the cavalry — of the Ædui. — Cæsar — not knowing, — began

discedĕre — dŏmum — à — castris (pl.). — Quâ — re
to depart — home — from — the camp. — Which [This] — thing

nuntiatâ, — Cæsar, — profectione — inter-
having been announced — Cæsar — the departure — having been

missâ — atque — omnĭbus — rebus — postposĭtis,
discontinued — and — all — things — having been postponed,

mittit — magnam — partem — equitatûs — ad insequendum
sends — a large — part — of the cavalry — to pursue

ĕum, — que — impĕrat — retrăhi: — si — facĭat²³
him, — and — orders (him) — to be dragged back: — if — he may do

vim, — nĕque — parĕat, — jŭbet — interfĭci:
violence, — nor — may obey, — he commands (him) — to be killed:

arbitratus — hunc — facturum — nĭhil
having considered — him (that he) — about to [would] do — nothing

pro   sano,   qui neglexisset (pluperf. subj.)
for [as] a sound [sane] (man), who had disregarded

imperĭum   præsentis.   Enim ille   revocatus
the command of (him) present. For he having been summoned

cœpit resistĕre, ac defendĕre se   mănu,
began to resist, and to defend himself by hand [force],

que   implorare   fĭdem   suorum ;
and   to entreat   the faith [support] of his own (people);

clamĭtans sæpè,   se   esse   libĕrum,
crying out often, (that he) himself to be [was] a free (man),

que   libĕræ   civitatis.   Isti   circumsistunt
and   of a free   state.   They   surround

que   interficĭunt   homĭnem,   ut   imperatum ĕrat :
and   slay   the man,   as   it had been ordered :

at   omnes   Ædŭi   equĭtes   revertuntŭr ad
but   all   the Æduan horsemen   return   to

Cæsărem.
Cæsar.

8. His   rebus   gestis,   Labieno
These   things   having been performed,   Labienus

relicto   in   continente cum trĭbus legionĭbus
having been left on the continent with three   legions

et duobus   millĭbus   equitum,   ut   tueretur
and   two   thousand   (of) cavalry, that he might defend

pŏrtus,   et   provideret   frumentarĭæ rĕi,   que
the harbors, and might provide for the grain supply, and

cognoscĕret   quæ   gererentur   in Gallĭâ, et
might ascertain what   might be transpiring in Gaul,   and

capĕret consilĭum pro[24]   tempŏre et pro
might take counsel   for [according to] time   and for

re :   ipse   cum quinque legionĭbus et
the affair : (he) himself with   five   legions   and

pări   numĕro   equĭtum,   quem relinquĕrat in
an equal number   of cavalry, which he had left   on

continente,   solvit   naves   ad   occasum
the continent, cast loose   the ships at [about] the setting

solıs ;   et   provectus   leni
of the sun ;   and   having been carried forward by a gentle

Afrĭco, vento intermisso circĭter
South West wind, the wind having discontinued about

medĭâ nocte, tenŭit non cursum: et
mid night, he held not the course: and

delatus longĭùs æstu, luce
being carried away farther by the tide, the light [day]

ortâ, conspexit Britannĭam relictam sub
having risen, he beheld Britain left [lying] under [on]

sinistrâ. Tum rursus secutus commutationem
the left. Then again having followed the change

æstûs, contendit remis, ut capĕret
of the tide, he strove with oars, that he might take [reach]

ĕam partem insŭlæ, quâ cognovĕrat
this part of the island. on which he had known

superiore æstate esse optimum egressum. In
in the former summer to be [was] the best landing. In

quâ re virtus milĭtum fŭit
which [this] thing [attempt] the merit of the soldiers was

admŏdum laudanda, qui, labore remigandi non
very much to be praised, who, the labor of rowing not

intermisso, adæquaverunt cursum longarum
having been interrupted. equalled the course of the long

navĭum, vectorĭis que gravĭbus navigĭis.
ships [war-ships], with transports and heavy vessels.

Accessum est[25] ad Britannĭam omnĭbus navĭbus
It was [They] approached to Britain with all the ships

fĕrè meridiano tempŏre. Nĕque[26] hostis visus est
nearly at noon time. Nor an enemy was seen

in ĕo lŏco. Sed, ut Cæsar postĕa compĕrit
in this place. But, as Cæsar afterwards discovered

ex captivis, quum magnæ mănus convenissent
from the prisoners, when a great band had assembled

(pl. perf. subj.) ĕò, perterrĭtæ multitudĭne
there, having been alarmed by the multidude

navĭum, quæ amplĭus octingentæ visæ ĕrant
of ships, which more (than) eight-hundred had been seen

unà cum annotĭnis que privatis,
together with last year's (ships) and the private (ones),

quas   quisque   fecĕrat   causâ   sŭi
which   each   had made   for the sake   of his own

commŏdi,   discessĕrant   timore   à   littŏre,
convenience,   they had departed   in fear   from   the shore,

ac   abdidĕrant   se   in   superiora   lŏca.
and   had concealed   themselves   in   the higher   places.

9. Cæsar,   exercĭtu   exposĭto,   ac
    Cæsar,   the army   having been disembarked,   and

lŏco   idonĕo   castris (pl.)   capto,   ŭbi
a place   suitable   for a camp   having been taken,   when

cognovit   ex   captivis,   in   quo   lŏco   copĭæ
he learned   from   the prisoners,   in   what   place   the forces

hostĭum   consedissent (pl. perf. subj.),   dĕcem
of the enemy   had encamped,   ten

cohortĭbus   relictis   ad   măre,   et   trecentis
cohorts   having been left   at [near]   the sea,   and   three-hundred

equitĭbus,   qui   essent   præsidĭo   navĭbus,
horsemen,   who   were   (for) a guard   to the ships,

contendit   ad   hostes   de   tertĭâ   vigilĭâ;
hastened   to   the enemy   on   the third   watch;

verĭtus   ĕò   mĭnùs   navĭbus,   quòd
having feared   for this reason   the less   for the ships,   because

relinquebat   deligatas   ad   anchŏras (pl.)   in   molli
he was leaving (them)   fastened   at   anchor   on   a soft

atque   aperto   littŏre;   et   præfecit   Quintum
and   open   shore;   and   he put in command   Quintus

Atrĭum   præsidĭo   navĭbus.   Ipse   progressus
Altrius   for protection   to the ships.   He himself   having advanced

noctu   circĭter   duodĕcim   millĭa   passŭum
by night   about   twelve   thousand   (of) paces

conspicatus est   copĭas   hostĭum.   Illi
discovered   the forces   of the enemy.   They

progressi   ad   flumen   equitatu   atque
having advanced   to   the river   with the cavalry   and

essĕdis,   cœperunt   prohibere   nostros   ex
chariots,   began   to check   our (men)   from

superiore   lŏco   et   committĕre   prœlĭum.
the higher   place   and   to engage   battle.

Repulsi ab equitatu, nacti lŏcum
Having been repulsed by the cavalry, having got a place

egregĭè munitum et naturâ et opĕre,
excellently fortified both by nature and by work [art],

quem, (ut videbantur,) præparvĕrant jam
which, (as it was seeming,) they had prepared already

antè, causâ domestĭci belli, abdiderunt
before, for the sake of domestic war they hid

se in silvas: nam crebris arborĭbus
themselves in the woods: for the thick trees

succissis, omnes introĭtus præcĭusi-ĕrant.
having been cut down, all the entrances had been shut up.

Ipsi rari propugnabant ex
They themselves, few [in squads], were charging from

silvis, que prohibebant nostros ingrĕdi[27]
the woods, and were preventing our (men) to enter

intra munitiones. At milĭtes
[from entering] within the fortifications. But the soldiers

septĭmæ legionis, testudĭne factâ, et
of the seventh legion, a testudo having been made, and

aggĕre adjecto ad munitiones,
a mound having been thrown up against the fortifications,

ceperunt lŏcum, que expulerunt ĕos ex silvis,
took the place, and drove them from the woods,

paucis vulnerĭbus acceptis. Sed Cæsar
a few wounds having been received. But Cæsar

vetŭit persĕqui ĕos fugientes longĭùs, et quòd
forbade to pursue them fleeing farther, both because

ignorabat naturam lŏci, et quòd
he was not knowing the nature of the place, and because

magnâ parte diei consumptâ, volebat
a great part of the day having been spent, he was wishing

tempus relinqui munitioni
(that) time to [should] be left for the fortification

castrorum (pl.).
of the camp

10. Postridĭe ejus diei, misit manè
The day after this day, he sent in the morning

milĭtes que equĭtes tripartitò in
the soldiers and cavalry in three divisions on

expeditionem, ut persequerentur ĕos, qui
an expedition, that they might pursue these, who

fugĕrant. Iis progressi aliquantum
had fled. These having advanced a considerable part

itinĕris, quum jam extremi essent
of the march, when already the last [the rear] were

(imp. subj.) in conspectu, equĭtes venerunt à
in sight, horsemen came from

Quinto Atrĭo ad Cæsărem, qui nuntiarent
Quintus Atrius to Cæsar, who announced (that)

maxĭmâ tempestate coortâ superiori nocte,
a very great storm having arisen on the former night,

omnes naves propè afflictas-esse atque
all the ships nearly to have [had] been dashed and

ejectas in litŏre; quòd neque anchŏræ
thrown up on the shore; because neither the anchors

que funes subsistĕrent (imp. subj.), neque nautæ
and cables were holding, nor the sailors

que gubernatores possent (imp. subj.) păti
and pilots were able to endure

vim tempestatis.Ităque magnum
the violence of the storm. Therefore great

incommŏdum acceptum esse ex ĕo
damage to have [had] been received from this

concursu navĭum.
collision of the ships.

11. His rebus cognĭtis, Cæsar jŭbet
These things having been known, Cæsar orders

legiones que equitatum revocari, atque
the legions and the cavalry to be recalled, and

desistĕre itinĕre, ipse revertitur ad
to halt from the march, he himself returns to

naves: perspĭcit coràm fĕrè eadem,
the ships: he observes when present nearly the same (things),

quæ cognovĕrat ex nuntĭis (litĕris[28] (pl.));
which he had known from the messengers (the letters);

sic   ut,   circĭter quadraginta navĭbus   amissis,
so   that,   about   forty   ships   having been lost,

tămen   relĭquæ   viderentur (imp. subj.)   posse
however   the rest   were seeming   to be able

refĭci   magno   negotĭo.   Itaque   deligit
to be repaired with great   trouble.   Therefore   he selects

fabros   ex   legionĭbus,   et   jŭbet   alĭos
mechanics   from   the legions,   and   orders   others

arcessi   ex   continenti: scribit   Labieno,
to be summoned   from   the continent: he writes   to Labienus,

ut   institŭat   quàm-plurĭmas   naves (acc.)
that   he construct   the greatest number   (of) ships

posset   ĭis   legionĭbus,   quæ   sunt   ăpud
he may be able   with those   legions.   which   are   with

eum.   Ipse,   etsi   res   ĕrat   multæ
him.   He himself,   although   the thing   was   (of) much

opĕræ   ac   laboris,   tămen   statŭit   esse
trouble   and   labor.   however   determined (that)   to be

commodissĭmum,   omnes   naves
[it was]   most convenient.   (that)   all   the ships

subduci,   et   conjungi   unâ   munitione
(to) be drawn up,   and   (to) be united   in one   fortification

eum   castris (pl.).   Consumit   circĭter   dĕcem   dies
with   the camp.   He spends   about   ten   days

in   his   rebus,   ne   nocturnis[29]   temporĭbus
in   these   things [matters],   not   the night   time

(pl.)   quĭdem   intermissis   ad   laborem
even   having been intermitted [lost]   for   the labor

milĭtum.   Navĭbus   subductis   que
of the soldiers.   The ships   having been drawn up   and

castris (pl.)   egregĭè   munitis,   relinquit   easdem
the camp   excellently   fortified,   he leaves   the same

copĭas   quas   antè,   præsidĭo   navĭbus:
forces   which [as]   before,   for a guard   to the ships:

ipse   proficiscĭtur   eòdem,   unde
'he) himself   sets out   to the same (place),   whence

rediĕrat.   Quum   venisset (plup. subj.)   ĕò,
he had returned.   When   he had come   there,

majores copĭæ Britannorum jam convenĕrant
greater forces of the Britons now had assembled

undĭque in ĕum lŏcum. Summa[30]
from every side into this place. The supreme authority

imperĭi que administrandi belli permissa-est,
of command and of managing the war was assigned,

communi consilĭo, Cassivellauno, fines
by a common counsel, to Cassivellaunus, the territories

cujus flumen, quod appellatur Tamĕsis,
of whom a river, which is called Tamesis [Thames],

divĭdit à maritĭmis civitatĭbus, circĭter octoginta
divides from the maritime states, about eighty

millĭa passŭm à mări. Continentĭa bella
thousand (of) paces from the sea. Continual, wars

intercessĕrant huic (dat.) cum relĭquis civitatĭbus,
had involved him with the rest of the states,

superiori tempŏre; sed Britanni, permoti
in former times; but the Britons, alarmed

nostro adventu, præfecĕrant hunc toti bello
by our arrival, had appointed him over the whole war

que imperĭo (dat.).
and command.

12. Interĭor pars Britannĭæ incolĭtur ab ĭis,
The interior part of Britain is inhabited by those,

quos dicunt prodĭtum[31] memoriâ
whom they say (to have [it has] been) handed down by memory

natos in insŭlâ ipsâ; maritĭma pars
(to) have been born in the island itself: the maritime part

ab ĭis, qui transiĕrant ex
(is inhabited) by those, who had crossed over from

Belgis causâ prædæ ac inferendi, belli
the Belgæ for the sake of plunder and of waging, war

qui omnes fĕre appellantur ĭis nominĭbus
who all nearly are called by those names

civitatum, ex quĭbus civitatĭbus orti
of states, from which states having sprung

pervenerunt ĕò, ex bello illato
they arrived there, and war having been waged

remanserunt   ĭbi,   atque   cœperunt colĕre   agros.
remained   there,   and   began   to till   the lands.

Multitudo   homĭnum   est   infinĭta,   que
The multitude   of men [inhabitants]   is   boundless,   and

ædificĭa   creberrĭma   fĕre   consimilĭa   Gallĭcis:
the buildings   most numerous   nearly   similar   to the Gallic:

numĕrus   pecŏris   magnus.   Utuntur   aut
the number   of the cattle (is)   great.   They use   either

ære (abl.),   aut   æreo   numnio   aut   ferrĕis   taleis
brass,   or   brass   coin   or   iron   bars

(abl.) examinatis[32]   ad   certum   pondus,   pro nummo.
regulated   to   a certain   weight,   for   coin.

Album plumbum   nascĭtur   ĭdi   in mediterranĕis
White   lead [tin]   is procured   there   in   the midland

regionĭbus;   ferrum   in   maritĭmis;   sed
countries;   iron   in   the maritime (parts),   but

copia   ejus   est   exigŭa: utuntur   importato
the quantity   of it   is   small: they use   imported

ære.   Est   materĭa   cujusque   genĕris,   ut   in
brass.   (There) is   timber   of every   kind.   as   in

Gallĭâ, præter   fagum   atque   abiĕtem.   Pŭtant
Gaul.   except   the beech   and   the fir tree.   They think (it)

non   fas   gustare   lepŏrem   et   gallinam   et
not   right   to taste   the hare   and   the hen   and

ansĕrem: tămen   ălunt   hæc   causâ
the goose: however   they breed   these   for the sake

anĭmi   que   voluptatis.   Lŏca   sunt
of mind [the interest]   and   of pleasure   The places   are

temperatĭora   quàm   in   Gallĭâ,   frigorĭbus (pl.)
more temperate   than   in   Gaul.   the cold

remissiorĭbus.
(being) more mild.

13.   Insŭla   naturâ   triquĕtra,   unum   lătus
The island (is)   by nature   triangular.   one   side

cujus   est   contra   Gallĭam.   Alter   angŭlus
of which   is   opposite   Gaul.   The one   angle

hujus   latĕris,   qui   est   ad   Cantĭum,
of this   side,   which   is   near   Cantium [Kent].

quò   naves   ex   Gallĭâ   fĕre   appelluntur,
where   ships   from   Gaul   generally   are landed,

ad   orientem   solem;   inferĭor
(is) toward   the rising   sun [the East] ;   the lower (angle)

spectat   ad meridĭem. Hoc lătus   tĕnet
looks [is directed] to   the south. This   side   holds [extends]

circĭter   quingenta   millĭa   passŭum.   Altĕrum
about   five hundred   thousand   (of) paces   The other (side)

vergit   ad   Hispanĭam,   atque   occidentem   solem:
inclines   toward   Spain,   and   the setting   sun:

ex   quâ   parte   est   Hibernia,   mĭnor
from [on]   which   side   is   Hibernia [Ireland].   less

dimidĭo   quàm   Britannĭa,   ut   existimatur;   sed
by half   than   Britain.   as   it is thought .   but

transmissus   est   pări   spatĭo   atque   ex
the passage across   is   with [of an] equal   distance   as   from

Gallĭâ   in   Britannĭam.   In   medĭo   hoc   cursu
Gaul   to   Britain.   In   the middle of   this   course

est   insŭla,   quæ   appellatur   Mŏna.   Complures
is   an island,   which   is called   Mona [Man].   Several

minores   insŭlæ   præterĕa   existimantur   objectæ,
lesser [smaller] islands   besides   are thought (to be)   interposed,

de   quĭbus   insŭlis   nonnulli   scripserunt,   noctem
of   which   islands   some   have written.   (that)   the night

esse   triginta   continŭos   dĭes   sub   bruma.
to be [is]   thirty   successive   days   under [during]   winter.

Nos   reperiebamus   nĭhil   de   ĕo
We   were discovering   nothing   concerning   this

percunctationĭbus,   nĭsi   videbamus   certis
by inquiries.   except   we were seeing   by certain

mensuris   ex   ăquâ,   noctes   esse
measures   of   water.   (that)   the nights   to be [were]

breviores   quàm   in   continente.   Longitudo   hujus
shorter   than   on   the continent.   The length   of this

latĕris est   septingentorum   millĭum   passŭum,
side   is   (of) seven hundred   thousand   (of) paces,

ut   opinĭo   illorum   fert.   Tertĭum
as   the opinion   of them [their opinion]   reports.   The third (side)

est   contra   Septentrionem ;   cui   parti   nulla
is   opposite   the North ;   to which   part   no

terra   est   objecta,   sed   angŭlus   ejus   latĕris
land   is   opposed,   but   the angle   of that   side

spectat   maxĭmè   ad   Germanĭam.
looks [is directed]   chiefly   toward   Germany.

Existimatur   octingenta   millĭa   passŭum
It is thought   (that)   eight hundred   thousand   (of) paces

in   longitudĭnem   esse   huic.   Ita
in   length   to be [is]   to [on] this (side).   Thus

omnis   insŭla   est   vicĭes   centena   millĭa
all   the island   is   twenty times   a hundred   thousand

passŭum   in   circuĭtu.³³
(of) paces   in   compass.

14. Ex   omnĭbus   his,   qui   incŏlunt
From [Of]   all   these,   (those) who   inhabit

Cantĭum,   sunt   longè   humanissĭmi ;   omnis
Cantium [Kent],   are   by far   the most civilized ;   all

quæ   regĭo   est   maritĭma,   nĕque   diffĕrunt   multùm
which   tract   is   maritime,   nor   do they differ   much

à   Gallĭcâ   consuetudĭne.   Plerique   interiores
from   the Gallic   custom.   Most of   the interior

sĕrunt   non   frumenta (pl.),   sed   vivunt
(inhabitants)   sow [plant]   not   corn,   but   live

lacte   et   carne,   que   sunt   vestiti   pellĭbus.
on milk   and   flesh [meat],   and   are   clad   with skins.

Verò   omnes   Britanni   inficĭunt   se   vitro,
But   all   the Britons   stain   themselves   with woad,

quod   effĭcit   cærulĕum   colorem,   atque   hôc
which   forms   a bluish   color,   and   by this

sunt   horribiliores   adspectu   in   pugnâ :
they are   more frightful   in appearance   in   battle :

que   sunt³⁴   promisso   capillo, atque   omni   parte
and   they are   with long   hair,   and   every   part

corpŏris   rasâ,   præter   căput   et   superĭus
of the body   shaved,   except   the head   and   upper

labrum.   Deni   que   duodeni   hăbent   uxores
lip.   Ten   and   twelve (men)   have   wives

communes   inter   se,   et   maxĭmè   fratres
common   among   themselves.   and   chiefly   brothers

cum   fratrĭbus,   et   parentes   cum   libĕris.   Sed   si
with   brothers.   and   parents   with   children.   But   if

qui   sunt   nati   ex   his,   habentur
any   are   born   from [of]   these.   they are considered

libĕri   eorum,   quo   quæque   virgo   primum
the children   of those.   to whom   each   virgin   first

deducta est.
was married.

15. Equĭtes   que   essedarĭi   hostium
The cavalry   and   charioteers   of the enemy

conflixerunt   acrĭter   prœlĭo   cum   nostro   equitatu
engaged   sharply   in battle   with   our   cavalry

in   itinĕre,   ita   tămen,   ut   nostri   fuĕrint
on   the march,   so,   nevertheless,   that   our (men)   were

(perf. subj.) superiores   omnĭbus   partĭbus,   atque
superior   in [on] all   parts [sides],   and

compulĕrint (perf. subj.)   ĕos   in   silvas   que
drove   them   into   the woods   and

colles; sed,   complurĭbus   interfectis,   insecuti
hills,   but,   very many   having been killed,   having pursued

cupidĭùs,   amiserunt   nonnullos   ex
(them)   rather eagerly.   they lost   some   from [of]

sŭis.   At   illi,   spatĭo   intermisso,
their own.   But   they,   an interval   having been interposed,

subĭtò   ejecerunt   se   ex   silvis,   nostris
suddenly   cast   themselves   from   the woods,   our

imprudentĭbus   atque   occupatis   in
(men)   (being) unaware   and   engaged   in

munitione   castrorum (pl.);   que   impĕtu
the fortification   of the camp;   and   an attack

facto   in   ĕos,   qui   collocati ĕrant
having been made   upon   these,   who   had been stationed

in statione   pro   castris (pl.),   pugnaverunt acrĭter:
on   picket   before   the camp,   they fought   sharply:

que   duabus   cohortĭbus   missis   subsidĭo   à
and   two   cohorts   having been sent   for aid   by

Cæsăre,   atque   his   primis   duarum   legionum,
Cæsar,   and   these   the first   of two   legions,

quum   hæ   constitissent (pluperf. subj.), perexigŭo
when   these   had taken stand,   a very small

spatĭo   lŏci   intermisso   inter   se,
space   of ground having been left between   themselves.

nostris   perterrĭtis   nŏvo   genĕre   pugnæ,
our (men)   having been alarmed by the new   kind   of battle,

proruperunt   audacissĭmè   per   medĭos
they burst   most daringly   through   the midst (of our men)

que receperunt   se   inde   incolŭmes.
and betook   themselves   from there   safe [safely].

Eo   dĭe   Quintus   Laberĭus   Durus,   tribunus
On this   day   Quintus   Laberius   Durus,   a tribune

milĭtum   interficĭtur: illi   repelluntur,   plurĭbus
of soldiers is slain: they   are repulsed,   more

cohortĭbus   submissis.
cohorts   having been sent up.

16. In   hoc   toto   genĕre   pugnæ,   quum
In   this   whole   kind   of battle,   since

dimicaretur (imp. subj.)   sub   ocŭlis   omnĭum   ac
it was fought   under   the eyes   of all   and

pro   castris (pl.),   intellectum est,   nostros
before   the camp,   it was understood.   (that)   our (men)

esse   minùs   aptos   ad   hostem   hujus   genĕris,
to be [were]   less   adapted   to   an enemy   of this   kind,

propter   gravitatem armorum,   quòd   possent
on account of   the weight   of the arms,   because   they were able

(imp. subj.)   nĕque   insĕqui   cedentes,   nĕque
neither   to pursue   (them) yielding.   nor

auderent (imp. subj.) discedĕre   ab   signis;
(did) they dare   to depart   from   the standards ;

autem   equĭtes   dimicare   prœlio   cum   magno
but   the cavalry   (to) contend   in battle   with   great

periculo,   proptereă quòd illi etĭam cedĕrent (imp.
danger.   because   (that) they   also   were giving way

subj.) plerumque consultò;   et   quum   removissent
very often   purposely ;   and   when   they had removed

(pluperf. subj.) nostros   paulum   ab   legionĭbus.
         our (men)   a little   from   the legions.

desilirent   ex   essĕdis   et   contendĕrent
they would leap down   from   the chariots   and   would contend

pedĭbus   dispări   prœlĭo.   (Autem   ratĭo
with feet [on foot]   in an equal   fight.   (But   the method

equestris   prœlĭi,   et   cedentĭbus   et
of the cavalry   fight,   (they) both   yielding   and

insequentĭbus,   inferebat   par   atque   ĭdem
pursuing,   was offering   an equal   and   the same

periculum.)   Accedebat   huc,[35]   ut
[a like]   danger.)   It was added   to this,   that

prœliarentur (imp. subj.) nunquam   conferti,   sed
they were fighting   never   in close order,   but

rari   que   magnis   intervallis,   que
few [in open ranks]   and   at great   distances,   and

haberent (imp. subj.) stationes disposĭtas; atque alii[36]
were having   pickets   posted ;   and   some

excipĕrent (imp. subj.) alĭos   deinceps,   que
were relieving   others   in succession,   and

intĕgri   et   recentes   succedĕrent (imp. subj.)
fresh   and   new (men)   were replacing

defatigatis.
the exhausted

17.   Postĕro   dĭe   hostes   constiterunt
    On the following   day   the enemy   took stand

prŏcul   à   castris (pl.) in collĭbus; que rari
far   from   the camp   on   the hills,   and   squads

cœperunt ostendĕre   se,   et   lacessĕre nostros
began   to show   themselves,   and   to provoke   our

equĭtes   prœlĭo   lentĭùs,   quàm   pridĭe.
cavalry   to battle   more slowly,   than   the day before.

Sed   meridie,   quum   Cæsar misisset (pluperf. subj.)
But   at noon,   when   Cæsar   had sent

tres   legiones   atque omnem   equitatum   cum   Caĭo
three   legions   and   all   the cavalry   with   Caius

Trebonĭo   legato   causâ   pabulandi,
Trebonius   the lieutenant   for the sake   of foraging.

advolaverunt repentè ad pabulatores ex
they flew suddenly to the foragers from

omnĭbus partĭbus, sic ŭti non
all parts [sides], so that they were not

ıbsistĕrent[37] (imp. subj.) ab signis que
ʇeeping apart from the standards and

legionĭbus. Nostri, impĕtu facto acrĭter
the legions Our (men) an attack having been made sharply

in ĕos, repulerunt, nĕque fecerunt finem
ȝpon them, repulsed (them). nor did they make an end

ınsequendi, quŏad equĭtes, confisi subsidĭo,
of pursuing. while the cavalry. relying on aid.

quum viderent (imp subj.) legiones post
since they were seeing the legions behind

se, egerunt hostes præcipĭtes: que magno
themselves, drove the enemy headlong. and a great

numĕro eorum interfecto, nĕque dederunt
number of them having been killed neither they gave

facultatem[38] colligendi sŭi nĕque
the power [the chance] of collecting themselves nor

consistendi, aut desiliendi ex essĕdis.
of halting, or [nor] of leaping down from the chariots.

Auxilĭa, quæ convenĕrant undĭque,
The auxiliaries which had assembled from every side,

discesserunt protĭnus ex hâc fŭgâ; nĕque
departed immediately after this flight. nor

post id tempus hostes unquam contenderunt
after this time (did) the enemy ever contended

nobiscum summis copĭis
[contend] with us with (their) highest [entire] forces.

18. Cæsar, eorum consilĭo cognĭto, duxit
Cæsar, their design having been known. led

exercĭtum ad flumen Tamĕsin in
the army to the river Tamesis [Thames] into

fines Cassivellauni: quod flumen pŏtest
ʇhe territories of Cassivellaunus· which river is able

transiri pedĭbus (pl.) omnino uno lŏco, atque
to be crossed on foot only in one place, and

hoc   ægrè.   **Quum**   venisset (pluperf. subj.)
in this   with difficulty   When   he had come

ĕŏ,   animadvertit   magnas copĭas   hostĭum
there.   he perceived   (that)   great   forces   of the enemy

esse   instructas   ad   altĕram rĭpam flumĭnis.
to be [were]   drawn up   at [near]   the other   bank   of the river.

Autem   rĭpa   ĕrat   munita   acutĭs   sudĭbus
But   the bank   was   fortified   with sharp   stakes

præfixĭs,   que   sŭdes   ejusdem   genĕris   defixæ
fixed in front.   and   stakes   of the same   kind   driven

sub   ăquâ   tegebantur   flumĭne.   Iis   rebus
under   water   were covered   by the river   These   things

cognĭtis   à   captivis   que   perfŭgis,
having been learned   from   the prisoners   and   deserters,

Cæsar,   equitatu   præmisso,   jussit
Cæsar   the cavalry   having been sent before,   ordered

legiones   subsĕqui   confestim.   Sed   milĭtes
the legions   to follow   immediately.   But   the soldiers

iĕrunt   ĕâ   celeritate atque   eo
went   with this [such]   speed   and   with this [such]

impĕtu,   quum   exstarent (imp. subj.)   ex
force.   when   they were standing out   from

ăquâ   capĭte   solo,   ut   hostes   possent
the water   with the head   alone,   that   the enemy   were able

(imp. subj.) non   sustinere   impĕtum   legionum
non   to withstand   the attack   of the legions

que   equĭtum,   que   dimittĕrent (imp. subj.)
and   of the cavalry.   and   were abandoning

ripas   ac   mandarent (imp. subj.)   se
the banks   and   were consigning   themselves

fŭgæ.
to flight,

19. Cassivellaunus, omni   spe contentionis   de-
Cassivellaunus   all   hope   of a contest   having been

posĭtâ,   ut   demonstravĭmus   suprà,   amplorĭbus
abandoned.   as   we have shown   above.   (his) larger

copĭis   dimissis,   circĭter quatŭor millĭbus
forces   having been dismissed,   about   four   thousand

essedariorum relicitis, servabat nostra
(of) charioteers having been left was watching our

itĭnĕra, que excedebat paulum ex vĭâ,
marches. and was withdrawing a little from the way,

que occultabat sese impeditis atque
and was concealing himself in entangled and

silvestrĭbus lŏcis, atque compellebat pecŏra (pl.)
woody places. and was driving the cattle

atque homĭnes ex agris in silvas ĭis
and men from the fields into the woods from these

regionĭbus, quĭbus cognovĕrat nos fac-
regions, in which he had known us [we] about to [would]

turos ĭter: et quum noster equitatus ejecerat
make the march and when our cavalry cast

se liberĭùs in agros causâ vastandi
itself more freely into the fields for the sake of ravaging

que prædandi, emittebat essedarĭos ex
and of plundering. he was dispatching the charioteers from

silvis omnĭbus vĭis que semĭtis; et confligebat
the woods by all ways and paths and was combatting

cum ĭis cum magno pericŭlo nostrorum equĭtum;
with them with great danger of [to] our horsemen:

atque hoc mĕtu prohibebat vagari
and by this fear was hindering (them) to rove [from roving]

latĭùs. Relinquebatur, ut Cæsar nĕque
more widely. It was left that Cæsar neither

pateretur discedi[39] longĭus ab
would allow (it) to be departed [them to depart] farther from

agmĭne legionum: et noceretur
the marching-line of the legions: and it might be injured [they

hostĭbus in vastandis agris, que
might injure] (to) the enemy in ravaging the fields. and

faciendis incendĭis tantum quantum legionarĭi
in making burnings [fires] as much as the legionary

milĭtes potĕrant efficĕre labore atque itĭnĕre.
soldiers were able to effect by labor and on the march.

20. Intĕrim Trinobantes, propè firmissĭma
Meanwhile the Trinobantes, nearly the strongest

civĭtas	earum	regionum,	ex	quâ	Mandubraciu⸗
state	of these	countries.	from	which	Mandubracius

adolescens,		secutus	fĭdem	Cæsăris,
a youth.		having secured	the good faith	of Cæsar,

venĕrat	ad	ĕum	in	continentem	(Gallĭam),	(cujus
had come	to	him	to	the continent	(Gaul),	(whose

pater	obtinuĕrat	regnum		in	ĕâ
father	had obtained	the kingdom [the throne]		in	this

civitate,	que	interfectus ĕrat	à	Cassivellauno ·
state.	and	had been slain	by	Cassivellaunus:

ipse	vitavĕrat	mortem	fŭgâ,)	mittunt
he himself	had avoided	death	by flight,)	send

legatos	ad	Cæsărem,	que	pollicentur	dedit-
ambassadors	to	Cæsar,	and	promise	(that) to be about to

uros	(esse)	sese	ĕi	et	facturos
[they would] surrender		themselves	to him	and	about to [would] do

imperata.	Pĕtunt	ut	defendat
(his) commands.	They request	that	he may defend

Mandubratĭum	ab	injurĭâ	Cassivellauni,	atque
Mandubracius	from	the injustice	of Cassivellaunus.	and

mittat	in	civitatem,	qui	præsit
may send (him)	into	(their) state.	who	may preside [be over it]

que	obtinĕat	imperĭum.	Cæsar	impĕrat	his(dat.)
and	may obtain	the authority.	Cæsar	orders	these

	quadraginta	obsĭdes	que	frumentum
(to furnish)	forty	hostages	and	corn

exercitŭi;	que	mittit	Mandubratĭum	ad	ĕos.
for the army.	and	sends	Mandubracius	to	them.

Illi	fecerunt	imperata	celerĭter;	miserunt
They	did	(his) commands	quickly;	they sent

obsides	ad	numĕrum,	que	frumentum.
hostages	to	the number (stated).	and	corn.

21. | Trinobantĭbus | | defensis, | | atque |
|---|---|---|---|---|
| The Trinobantes | | having been protected, | | and |

prohibĭtis	ab	∂mni	injurĭâ	milĭtum,
having been kept	from	all	injury	of the soldiers.

Cenimagni,	Segontiăci,	Ancalites,	Bibrŏci,	Cassi,
the Cenimagni,	Segontiaci,	Ancalites,	Bibroci,	Cassi,

legationĭbus missis, dedĭderunt sese
embassies having been sent, surrendered themselves

Cæsări. Cognoscit ab his, oppĭdum
to Cæsar. He understands from these, (that) the town

Cassivellauni abesse non longè ex ĕo
of Cassivellaunus to be [is] distant not far from this

lŏco, munitum silvis que paludĭbus, quŏ
place. fortified by woods and by marshes, whither

numĕrus sătis magnus homĭnum que pecŏris
a number sufficiently great of men and of cattle

convenĕrit (perf. subj.). Autem Britanni vŏcant
has assembled. But the Britons call

oppĭdum, quŏ consueverunt convenire,
(that) a town, where they have been accustomed to assemble.

causâ vitandæ incursionis hostĭum, quum
for the sake of avoiding an invasion of the enemy. when

munîerunt impeditas silvas vallo
they have fortified the entangled woods with a rampart

atque fossâ. Eŏ proficiscĭtur cum legionĭbus:
and a trench. Thither he sets out with the legions:

repĕrit lŏcum egregĭè munitum naturâ atque
he finds the place excellently fortified by nature and

opĕre ; tămen contendit oppugnare hunc
by work [art]: however he endeavors to storm this

ex duabus partĭbus. Hostes morati
from [on] two sides. The enemy having delayed

paulisper, non tulerunt impĕtum nostrorum
a little while, did not bear the attack of our

milĭtum, que ejecerunt sese ex aliâ parte
soldiers, and cast out themselves from another part

oppĭdi. Magnus numĕrus pecŏris repertus (est)
of the town. A great number of cattle was found

ĭbi ; que multi[40] comprehensi sunt atque interfecti
there ; and many were seized and killed

in fŭgâ.
in the flight.

22. Dum hæc geruntur in his
While these (things) are transpiring in these

lŏcis,   Cassivellaunus mittit   nuntĭos   ad   Cantĭum,
places,   Cassivellaunus   sends   messengers   to   Cantium

   quod   demonstravĭmus   suprà   esse   ad
[Kent],   which   we have shown   above   to be [is]   at [near]

mare,   quĭbus   regionĭbus   quatŭor   reges   præĕrant,
the sea,   which   countries   four   kings   ruled.

Cingetôrix,   Carvilĭus,   Taximagŭlus,   Segŏnax;   atque
Cingetorix,   Carvilius.   Taximagulus.   Segonax: and

  impĕrat   his,   ut   omnĭbus   copĭis
he commands   these.   that   all   (their) forces

   coactis,   adoriantur   navalĭa   castra (pl.)
having been collected,   they attack   the naval   camp

de improviso,   atque   oppugnent.   Quum   hi
unexpectedly,   and   storm (it).   When   these

venissent (pl. perf.subj.)   ad   castra (pl.),   nostri,
had come   to   the camp,   our (men),

eruptione   factâ,   multis   eorum   inter-
a sally   having been made   many   of these   having been

fectis,   etĭam   nobĭli   dŭce   Lugotorĭge
killed.   also   (their) noble   leader   Lugotorix

capto,   reduxerunt   sŭos   incolŭmes,
having been taken   (they) led back   their (men)   safe.

Cassivellaunus,   hoc prœlĭo   nuntiato,   tot
Cassivellaunus,   this   battle   having been announced   so many

detrimentis   acceptis,   finĭbus
reverses   having been received.   (his) territories   (having been)

vastatis,   etĭam   maxĭmè   permotus   defectione
ravaged   also   chiefly   alarmed   by the revolt

civitatum,   mittĭt   legatos   ad   Cæsărem   per
of the states.   sends   ambassadors   to   Cæsar   through

Commĭum   Atrebătem   de   deditione.   Quum
Commius   the Atrebatian   about   a surrender.   Since

Cæsar   statuisset (pl. perf subj.)   agĕre   hiĕmem
Cæsar   had resolved   to spend   the winter

in   continente   propter   repentinos   motus
on   the continent   on account of   the sudden   commotions

Gallĭæ;   nĕque   multum   æstatis   superesset
of Gaul;   nor   much   of the summer   was remaining;

(imp. subj.); atque intelligĕret (imp. subj.), id
     and he was understanding (that), this

posse   extrăhi facĭlè, impĕrat
to be abJe [could] (to) be protracted easily, he demands

obsĭdes; et constitŭit quid vectigalis Britannĭa
hostages; and decreed what (of) tribute Britain

pendĕret Romano popŭlo in singŭlos annos
should pay to the Roman people (on) each year.

(pl.). Interdicit[41] atque impĕrat Cassivellauno
   He prohibits and commands Cassivellaunus,

(dat.),   ne nocĕat Mandubracĭo (dat.), neu
  (that) he may not injure Mandubracius, nor

Trinobantĭbus.
the Trinobantes.

23. Obsidĭbus acceptis, reducit
  The hostages having been received, he leads back

exercĭtum ad măre: invenit naves refectas.
the army to the sea: he finds the ships repaired.

His   deductis,   constitŭit reportare
These having been launched he resolved to carry back

exercĭtum duobus commeatĭbus, et quòd
the army by two passages, both because

habebat magnum numĕrum captivorum, et
he was having a great number of prisoners, and

nonnullæ naves deperiĕrant tempestate. Ac
some ships had perished by the storm. And

accĭdit sic, ut ex tanto numĕro navĭum
it happened so. that from so great a number of ships

tot navigationĭbus, nĕque hoc nĕque
in so many voyages. neither in this nor

superiore anno, ulla navis omnino, quæ
in the foregoing year, any ship at all which

portaret (imp. subj.) milĭtes, desideraretur (imp.
was carrying the soldiers, was missing

subj.), at ex iis, quæ remitterentur
  but from [of] these. which were sent back

(imp. subj.) inanes ad ĕum ex continente, et[42]
   empty to him from the continent, (and)

militĭbus	prioris	commeatûs	exposĭtis,
the soldiers	of the former [first]	passage	having been landed,

et	quas[43]	Labienus	postĕa	curavĕrat
and	which	Labienus	afterwards	nad taken care

faciendas,	numĕro	sexaginta,	perpaucæ
to [should] be made.	in number	sixty,	very few

capĕrent (imp. sudj.)	lŏcum,	fĕrè	omnes
were taking [reaching]	the place,	nearly	all

relĭquæ	rejicerentur (imp. subj.).	Quas[44]	quum
the rest	were thrown back.	Which	when

Cæsar exspectâsset (pl. perf subj.)	aliquandĭu	frustrà,
Cæsar had awaited	some time	in vain,

ne	excluderetur	navigatione	tempŏre
lest	he might be prevented	from the voyage	by the time

anni,	quŏd	æquinoctĭum subĕrat,	necessarĭò
of the year.	because	the equinox was near	(he) necessarily

collocavit	milĭtes	angustĭùs.	Ac	consecutus
stowed	the soldiers	more closely.	And	having secured

summam	tranquillitatem	quum	solvisset
the utmost	calm	when	he had cast loose.

(pl. perf. subj),	secundâ	vigilĭâ	initâ,
	the second	watch	having been begun,

attĭgit	terram	primâ	luce,	que
he touched	land	in the first	light [early dawn].	and

perduxit	omnes	naves	incolŭmes.
brought in	all	the ships	safe

24. Navĭbus	subductis,	que	concilĭo
The ships	having been drawn up	and	a council

Gallorum	Samarobrivæ	peractò,
of the Gauls	at Samarobriva	having been completed.

coactus est	collocare	exercĭtum	in	hibernis
he was compelled	to place	the army	in	winter quarters

alĭter	ac	superiorĭbus	annis,	que	distribuĕre
otherwise	than	in former	years	and	distribute

legiones	in	plures civitates,	quŏd	èo	anno
the legions	into	more states	because	in this	year

frumentum	provenĕrat	angustĭùs	in
the corn	had yielded	more narrowly [scantily]	in

Gallĭâ,   propter   siccĭtates :   ex   quĭbus[45]
Gaul,   on account of   the droughts·   from [of]   which

dĕdit   unam   Caĭo   Fabĭo   legato   ducendam
he gave   one   to Caius   Fabius   the lieutenant   to be led

in   Morĭnos,   altĕram   Quinto   Ciceroni   in
among   the Morini.   another   to Quintus   Cicero   among

Nervĭos,   tertĭam   Lucĭo   Roscĭo   in   Esuvĭos ;
the Nervii,   the third   to Lucius   Roscius   among   the Esuvii ;

jussit   quartam   hiemare in confinĭo   Trevirorum,
he ordered   the fourth   to winter   on the border   of the Treviri,

in   Remis   cum   Tĭto   Labieno: collocavit   tres
among   the Remi   with   Titus   Labienus :   he placed   three

in   Belgĭo :   præfecit   his   Marcum   Crassum
in   Belgium :   he appointed over   these   Marcus   Crassus

quæstorem,   et   Lucĭum Munatĭum Plancum,   et
(as) quæstor   and   Lucius   Munatius   Plancus.   and

Caĭum   Trebonĭum   legatos.   Misit   unam
Caius   Trebonius   (as) lieutenants.   He sent   one

legionem, quam conscripsĕrat proxĭmè trans Pădum,
legion.   which   he had levied   very lately   across   the Po,

et   quinque cohortes,   in   Eburones,   maxĭma
and   five   cohorts,   into   the Eburones,   the greatest

pars quorum   est   inter   Mŏsam   et   Rhenum,
part   of whom   is   between   the Mense   and   the Rhine.

qui   ĕrant   sub   imperĭo   Ambiorĭgis   et
who   were   under   the authority   of Ambiorix   and

Catuvolci.   Jussit   legatos   Quintum Titurĭum
of Catuvolcus.   He ordered   the lieutenants   Quintus   Titurius

Sabinum   et   Lucĭum   Aurunculeĭum   Cottam
Sabinus   and   Lucius   Aurunculeius   Cotta

præesse   his   militĭbus (dat.).   Legionĭbus   distri-
to command   these   soldiers.   The legions   having been

butis   ad   hunc modum, existimavit
distributed   according to   this   manner,   he thought   (that he)

sese   posse   mederi facillĭmè   frumentarĭæ
himself   to be able [could]   (to) relieve   most easily   (to) the corn

inopĭæ: atque   tămen   hiberna   omnĭum
scarcity :   and   moreover   the winter quarters   of all

harum legionum continebantur   centum   millĭbus
of these   legions   were contained   in a hundred   thousand

passŭum (præter ĕam,   quam   dedĕrat   Lucĭo
(of) paces (except   this (one),   which   he had given   to Lucius

Roscĭo   ducendam   in   pacatissĭmam   et
Roscius   to be led   into   the most peaceful   and

quietissĭmam partem). Interĕa   ipse   constitŭit
calmest   portion).   Meanwhile (he) himself   resolved

morari   in Gallĭâ, quŏad   cognovisset (pl. perf. subj.)
to tarry   in   Gaul,   until   he had known

legiones   collocatas,   que   hiberna
(that) the legions   being [were] settled,   and   the winter quarters

munita.
fortified.

25. Erat   in   Carnutĭbus Tasgetĭus   natus
There was   among   the Carnutes   Tasgetius   born

summo   lŏco;   cujus   majores   obtinuĕrant
in the highest   place [rank];   whose   ancestors   had obtained

regnum   in   sŭâ   civitate.   Cæsar
the kingdom [sovereignty] in   their own   state.   Cæsar

restituĕrat   lŏcum   majorum   huic   pro
had restored   the position   of (his) ancestors   to him   for

ejus   virtute   atque   benevolentĭâ   in   se,
his   valor   and   (his) good will   toward   himself,

quòd   usus fuĕrat   ejus   singulari (abl.)   opĕrâ
because   he had used   his   remarkable   works

in omnĭbus   bellis.   Inimici interfecerunt
[efforts] in   all   the wars.   (His) enemies   slew

hunc pălàm, regnantem jam tertium annum, multis
him   openly,   reigning   now   the third   year,   many

etĭam   ex   civitate   auctorĭbus.   Ea
also   from [of]   the state   (being) authors (of the deed).   This

res   defertur   ad   Cæsărem. Ille   verĭtus,
matter   is reported   to   Cæsar.   He   having feared,

ne   civĭtas   deficĕret   impulsu   eorum,
lest   the state   might revolt   by the instigation   of these,

quòd   res   pertinebat   ad   plures,   celerĭter
because   the affair   was relating   to   several,   quickly

jŭbet Lucĭum Plancum proficisci in Carnutes
orders Lucius Plancus to set out among the Carnutes

cum legione ex Belgĭo, que hiemare ĭbi;
with a legion from Belgium, and to winter there,

que mittĕre hos comprehensos ad se,
and to send those arrested to himself,

opĕrâ⁴⁶ quorum cognovĕrit Tasgetĭum
by the work of whom he may have learned Tasgetius

interfectum. Intĕrim factus est certĭor
(to have [had] been) killed Meantime he was made more sure

ab omnĭbus legatis que
[was informed] by all the lieutenants and

quæstorĭbus, quĭbus tradidĕrat legiones,
quæstors. to whom he had delivered the legions.

perventum esse in hĭberna, que
to have been [that they had] arrived into winter quarters, and

lŏcum munitum hibernis.
the place (to have [had] been) fortified for winter quarters

26. Quindĕcim diebus circĭter quĭbus
In fifteen days about in which [since]

ventum est in hiberna, inĭtĭum
it was come [they came] into winter quarters. the beginning

repentĭni tumultûs ac defectĭonis ortum est ab
of a sudden tumult and revolt arose by

Ambiorĭge et Catuvolco: qui quum fuissent
Ambiorix and Catuvolcus: who although they had been

(pl. perf subj.) præstò Sabino que Cottæ
near (to) Sabinus and (to) Cotta

ad fines sŭi regni, que comportavissent
at the borders of their kingdom and had carried

(plup. subj.) frumentum in hiberna, impul-
corn into winter quarters, having been

si nuntĭis Indutiomări Trevĭri,
instigated by the messengers of Indutiomarus the Treviri,

concitaverunt sŭos que lignatorĭbus
incited their own (people); and the wood cutters

oppressis subĭtò, venerunt magnâ
having been overwhelmed suddenly, they came with a great

mănu oppugnatum castra (pl.). Quum nostri
band to assault the camp. When our (men)

cepissent (pl. perf. subj.) arma celerĭter, que
had taken arms quickly, and

adscendissent (pl. perf. subj.) vallum, atque
had ascended the rampart. and

Hispanis equitĭbus emissis ex unâ
the Spanish cavalry having been sent out from one

parte, fuissent (pl. perf. subj.) superiores
part [side]. had been superior

equestri prœlĭo, re desperatâ,
in the cavalry fight. the thing [action] having been despaired of.

hostes reduxerunt sŭos ab oppugnatione
the enemy led back their (men) from the assault

Tum conclamaverunt sŭo more, ŭtì alĭqui
Then they cried out in their manner, that some

ex nostris prodirent ad colloquĭum;
from [of] our (people) should come forth to a conference;

sese habere, quæ vellent
(that they) themselves (to) have (things). which they wish

(imp. subj.) dicĕre de communi re, quĭbus
to say about a common matter. by which

sperarent (imp. subj.) controversĭas posse
they were hoping (that) the disputes to be able [could]

minŭi.
(to) be diminished

27. Caĭus Arpineius, Romanus ĕques, familiaris
Caius Arpineius, a Roman knight. an acquaintance

Quinti Titurĭi mittĭtur ad ĕos causâ
of Quintus Titurius is sent to them for the sake

colloquendi; que Quintus Junĭus, quidam ex
of conferring; and Quintus Junius, a certain (one) from

Hispanĭâ, qui jam antè consuevĕrat
Spain. who already before had been accustomed

ventitare ad Ambiorĭgem, missu Cæsăris.
to come often to Ambiorix, on the mission of Cæsar.

Apud quos Ambiŏrix locutus est in hunc
Before whom Ambiorix spoke after this

mŏdum: "Sese   confiteri   debere
manner: " He himself to confess [confesses] to owe [that he owed]

plurĭmum   ĕi,   pro   beneficĭis   Cæsăris   in
very much   to him,   for   the kindnesses   of Cæsar   toward

se,   quòd   ejus   opĕrâ   liberatus esset (pl. perf.
himself,   because   by his   efforts   he had been freed

subj.)   stipendĭo,   quod   consuêsset (pl. perf.
from the tribute,   which   he had been accustomed

subj.)   pendĕre   sŭis   finitĭmis   Aduatucis;   que
to pay   to his   neighbors   the Aduatuci ;   and

quòd   et   filĭus   et   filĭus   fratris,
because   both   (his) son   and   the son   of (his) brother,

quos   Aduatuci   tenuissent (pl. perf. subj.)   in
whom   the Aduatuci   had held   in

servitute   et   catenis   ăpud   se,   missos
slavery   and   chains   among   themselves,   having been sent

numĕro   obsĭdum,   remissi essent (pl. perf. subj.)
in the number   of hostages.   had been returned

ab   Cæsăre: nĕque   fecisse   id,
by   Cæsar: nor   (that he)   to have [had] done   this

quod   fecĕrit (perf. subj.)   de   oppugnatione
which   he had done   in the storming

castrorum (pl.),   aut   judicĭo   aut
of the camp,   either   by (his own) judgment   or

sŭâ   voluntate,   sed   coactu   civitatis: que
his own   will,   but   by compulsion   of the state: and

sŭa   imperĭa (pl.)   esse   ejusmodi,   ut
his own   authority   to be [was]   of this sort,   that

multitudo   haberet (imp. subj.)   non   mĭnus
the multitude   were having   not   less

juris   in   se,   quàm   ipse   in
(of) jurisdiction   towards   himself   than   (he) himself   towards

multitudĭnem.   Porrò   hanc   fuisse   causam
the multitude.   Moreover   this   to have [had] been   the cause

belli   civitati: quòd   potuĕrit (perf. subj.)
of war   for the state: because   he was able

non   resistĕre   repentinæ   conjurationi   Gallorum;
not   to withstand   (to) the sudden   conspiracy   of the Gauls;

se   posse   probare   id   facĭlĕ   ex
he himself   to be [was] able   to prove   this   easily   from

sŭâ   humĭlĭtate;   quòd   sit   non adĕò
his own   humbleness [weakness] ;   because   he is   not   so

imperitus   rerum (gen.),   ut   confidat
unacquainted   with things,   that   he may trust   (that he)

se   posse   superare Romanum popŭlum
himself   to be able [can]   (to) overcome   the Roman   people

sŭis   copĭis;   sed   esse   commune consĭlĭum
with his   forces;   but   to be [it is]   the common   design

Gallĭæ. Hunc esse   dictum   dĭem omnĭbus
of Gaul.   This   to be [is]   the said [appointed]   day   of all

hibernis   Cæsăris   oppugnandis,   ne   qua
the winter quarters   of Cæsar   to be assaulted   lest   any

legĭo   posset   venire   subsidĭo   altĕri
legion   might be able [should]   (to) come   for aid   to another

legioni: Gallos[47] non facĭlè   potuisse   negare
legion ·   **Gauls**   not   easily   to have been [are] able   to refuse

Gallis (dat.);   præsertim   quum   consĭlĭum   videretur
Gauls;   especially   when   a design   was seeming

(imp. subj.)   inĭtum   de   recuperandâ
entered into   concerning   regaining

communi lĭbertate. Quĭbus quoniam   satisfecĕrit
(the) common   liberty.   Whom   since   he has satisfied

(perf. subj.)   pro   pietate,   se
for [as regarded]   patriotism,   (he) himself

habere   nunc   rationem   officĭi;   monere[48]
to have [had]   now   a regard   of moral duty;   to advise

Cæsărem pro   beneficĭis,   orare   Tĭturĭum   pro
Cæsar   for   (his) kindnesses.   to beseech   Titurius   for

hospitĭo,   ut   consŭlat   sŭæ   saluti
(his) hospitality.   that   he may consult   for his own   safety

ac   milĭtum: magnam mănum Germanorum
and (that)   of the soldiers: a great   band   of Germans

conductam   transisse   Rhenum;   hanc
having been hired   (to) have crossed   the Rhine;   this

affŏre   bidŭo: esse[49]   ipsorum
to be about to [would] be   in two days: to be [it is]   their

consilĭum   vĕlint ne   deducĕre   milĭtes   eductos
counsel   whether they wish   to conduct the soldiers led out

ex   hibernis   aut   ad   Cĭceronem   aut   ad
from   winter quarters   either   to   Cicero   or   to

Labienum,   prĭus quàm   finitĭmi   sentĭant;
Labienus,   before (that) (their) neighbors may perceive (it):

alter quorum   absĭt (pres. subj.) circĭter quinquaginta
the one of whom is distant   about   fifty

millĭa   passŭum,   alter   paulò   amplĭùs:
thousand   (of) paces,   the other   a little   more:

        se   polliceri   illud   et
(that he) himself   to promise [promises]   that [this]   and

confirmare   jurejurando,   se   dat-
to affirm [affirms]   by oath,   (that he) himself   about to

urum   tutum   ĭter   per   sŭos   fines:
[would] give   a safe   journey   through   his   territories:

quod[50]   quum   facĭat   sese   et   consulĕre
which   when   he does   (he) himself   both   to consult

            civitati,   quòd   levetur
[consults]   for the state,   because   it may be relieved

hibernis,   et   referre   gratĭam Cæsări
from winter quarters, and   to return [returns]   a favor   to Cæsar

pro ejus   merĭtis."   Hâc   oratione   habĭtâ,
for   his   services."   This   speech   having been delivered,

Ambiŏrix   discedit.
Ambiorix   departs.

28. Caĭus   Arpineius   et   Junĭus   defĕrunt   ad
     Caius   Arpineius   and   Junius   report   to

legatos   quæ   audiĕrant.   Illi   perturbati
the lieutenants what   they had heard.   They,   much disturbed

repentinâ   re,   etsi   ĕa
by the sudden   affair [condition],   although   these (things)

dicebantur ab   hoste,   tămen   existimabant
were said   by   an enemy.   however   were thinking (that

        non   negligenda: que   maxĭmè
they)   not   to [must not] be neglected.   and   especially

permovebantur   hâc   re,   quòd   ĕrat
were much alarmed   by this   affair [condition]. because   it was

vix   credendum   ignobĭlem   atque   humĭlem
hardly   to be believed   (that)   the mean   and   humble

civitatem   Eburonum   ausam (esse)   facĕre
state   of the Eburones   to [would] have dared   to make

bellum   sŭâ   sponte   Romano   popŭlo.
war   by [of] its own   accord   on the Roman   people

Ităque   defĕrunt   rem   ad   concilĭum,   que
Therefore   they report   the matter   to   a council   and

magna   controversĭa   existit   inter   ĕos   Lucĭus
a great   controversy   arises   among   them.   Lucius

Aurunculeĭus   que   complures   tribuni   milĭtum   et
Aurunculeius   and   very many   tribunes   of soldiers   and

centuriones   primorum   ordĭnum   existimabant   "nĭhil[51]
centurions   of the first   ranks   were thinking   "nothing

agendum   temĕrè,   nĕque   discedendum
to [must] be acted   rashly   nor   to be departed [must they

ex   hibernis   injussu   Cæsăris.
depart]   from   winter quarters   without the command   of Cæsar.

Docebant   quantasvis   magnas   copĭas
They were showing   (that)   howsoever   great   the forces

etĭam   Germanorum   posse   sustineri,
even   of the Germans   to be able [they could]   (to) be withstood.

hibernis   munitis.   Rem[52]
the winter quarters   having been fortified   The thing [fact]

esse   testimonĭo,   quòd   sustinuĕrint (perf.
to be [is]   for a testimony   that   they have withstood

subj.)   fortissĭmè   primum   impĕtum   hostĭum,
      most bravely   the first   attack   of the enemy.

multis   vulnerĭbus   illatis   ultrò.   Non
many   wounds   having been inflicted   besides.   Not

prĕmi   frumentarĭâ   re.   Interĕa[53]
to be [They are not] pressed   by the corn   supply   Meantime

subsidĭa   conventura   et   ex   proxĭmis
aids   (to be) [are]   about to assemble   both   from   the nearest

hibernis   et   à   Cæsăre.   Postremò,   quid
winter quarters   and   from   Cæsar   Lastly   what

esse   levĭus   aut   turpĭus,   quàm   capĕre
to be [is]   lighter   or   more base   than   to take

consilĭum   de   summ<del>i</del>s   rebus,   hoste
counsel   about   the most important   matters,   an enemy

     auctore?
(being) the adviser?

29. Contra   ĕa   Titurĭus   clamitabat,
   Against   those (reasonings)   Titurius   was exclaiming,

   "facturos   serò,   quum   majores   mănus
"about to [they would] act   late,   when   greater   bands

hostĭum,   Germanis   adjunctıs,   conven-
of the enemy.   the Germans   having been united,   should have

issent;   aut   quum   alĭquid (neuter)   calamıtatıs
assembled;   or   when   some   (of) calamıty

acceptum essent   in   proxĭmis   hibernis.
might have [had] been received   in   the nearest   winter quarters.

Occasıonem   consulendı   esse   brĕvem   Arbıtrari
The opportunity   of consulting   to be [was]   short.   To believe

     Cæsărem   profectum (esse)   in   Italĭam:
[He believes]   Cæsar   to have [had] set out   ınto   Italy:

nĕque[54]   Carnutes   alĭter   fuisse
neither   the Carnutes   otherwise   to have been [would have]

capturos   consilĭum   interficiendı   Tasgetĭı;
about to form [formed]   the design   of slaying   Tasgetius;

nĕque   Eburones   esse   venturos   ad   castra
nor   the Eburones   to be   about to [would] come   to   the camp

(pl.) cum   tantâ   contemptione   nostri,   si   ılle
     with   so great   contempt   of [for] us.   ıf   he

adesset (imp. subj.).   Non   spectare   hostem
were near.   He does not   (to) regard   the enemy

auctorem   sed   rem   Rhenum   subesse:
(as) an adviser   but   the fact.   The Rhıne   to be [ıs] near:

mortem   Ariovisti   et   nostras superiores   victorĭas,
the death   of Ariovistus   and   our   former   victories,

esse   magno   dolorı   Germanis: Gallĭam
to be [are]   a (for) great   grief   to the Germans;   Gaul

ardere   tot   contumellĭis   acceptıs,   reductam
is aflame   so many   insults   havıng been received.   reduced

sub   imperĭum   Romani   popŭlı,   superiore
under   the authority   of the Roman   people.   the former

glorĭâ   mĭlĭtaris   rĕi (sing.)   extinctâ.
glory   of (its) military   affairs   having been extinguished.

Postremò, quis   persuaderet[55]   hoc   sĭbi,
Lastly.   who   should persuade   this   to himself,   (that)

Ambiorĭgem   descendisse   ad   consilĭum
Ambiorix   to have [had] descended   to   advice

ejusmŏdi   sĭne   certâ   re?   Sŭam
of this kind   without   a sure   thing [reason]?   His

sententĭam   esse   tutam   in   utramque
opinion   to be [was]   safe   for   either

partem :   si   sit   nĭl   durĭus,
part [case].   if   there may be   nothing   harder [worse].

perventuros (esse)   ad   proxĭmam   legionem
to be about to [they would] arrive   at   the nearest   legion

cum   nullo   perĭcŭlo ;   si   omnis   Gallĭa   consentĭat
with   no   danger ;   if   all   Gaul   conspires

cum   Germanıs,   unam   salutem   esse   posĭtam
with   the Germans   the one   safety   to be [is]   placed

in   celeritate.   Quĭdem   quem   exĭtum   consilĭum
in   speed   Indeed   what   result   [would] the advice

Cottæ   atque   eorum,   qui   dissentirent,   haberet?
of Cotta   and   of those   who   might disagree,   have?

In   quo[56]   si   non   præsens   perĭcŭlum,   at   certè
In   which   if   not   present   danger.   still   certainly

fămes   esset   pertimescenda   longinquâ   obsidione."
famine   would be   to [must] be dreaded   in a long   siege."

30. Hâc   dısputatıone   habĭtâ   in utramque
This   dispute   having been kept up   on   both

partem (sıng.)   quum   resısteretur (ımp. subj.)   acrĭter
sides   since   it was opposed   sharply

à   Cottâ   que   prımıs   ordınĭbus ;   Sabınus   inquıt,
by   Cotta   and   the first   ranks.   Sabınus   says.

"Vıncĭte,   si   vultıs   ıta,"   et   id   clariore
"Conquer   if   ye wish   so "   and   this   with a louder

voce,   ut   magna   pars   mılĭtum   exaudiret :
voice   that   a great   part   of the soldiers   might hear :

"nĕque   sum   is,"   inquıt,   "ex   vobis,
"neither   am I   this (man) "   says he   " from [of]   you

qui	terrĕar	gravissĭmè	pericŭlo	mortis.
who	is frightened	most severely	by the danger	of death.

Hi		sapĭent;	et,	si	quid	gravĭus
These (men)		will know;	and.	if	any (thing)	more severe

accidĕrit,		reposcent	rationem	abs	te:
shall have happened		they will demand	an account	from	thee;

qui,	si	licĕat	per	te,	conjuncti	cum
who,	if	it were allowed	by	thee.	being united	with

proxĭmis	hibernis	dĭe	perendĭno,
the nearest	winter quarters	on the day	after to-morrow.

sustinĕant	communem	casum	cum	relĭquis;	nec
would endure	a common	chance	with	the rest	nor

rejecti	et	relegati	longè	ab	cætĕris,
driven back	and	separated	far	from	the rest.

intereant	aut	ferro	aut	fămĕ."
would perish	either	by iron [the sword]	or	by famine "

Consurgĭtur		ex	concilĭo:	comprehendunt
It is risen [They rise]		from	the council ·	they seize

utrumque	et	orant;	"ne deducant	rem
both	and	beseech.	" they may not bring	the thing

	in	summum	pericŭlum	sŭâ	dissensione
[situation]	into	the highest	danger	by their	dissension

et	pertinacĭâ:	rem	esse	facĭlem,	seu
and	obstinacy ·	the matter	to be [is]	easy.	whether

manĕant	seu	proficiscantur,	si	mŏdŏ	omnes
they remain	or	set out.	if	only	all

sentĭant	ac	prŏbent	unum	Contrà,
may think	and	may approve	one (thing)	On the other hand.

	se	perspicĕre	nullam	salutem	in
(they) themselves		(to) perceive	no	safety	in

dissensione."	Res	perducĭtur	disputatione	ad
dissension."	The matter	is protracted	in dispute	to

medĭam	noctem.
mid	night

31. Tandem	Cotta	permotus	dat	mănus:
At length	Cotta	having been moved	gives	hands

	sent017entĭa	Sabini	supĕrat	Pronuntiatur
[yields]:	the opinion	of Sabinus	prevails	It is announced

ituros   primâ   luce.
about to (that they) [would] go   at the first   light [day-break].

Relĭqua   pars   noctis   consumĭtur   vigilīis (pl.);
The remaining   part   of the night   is spent   in sleeplessness :

quum   quisque   miles   circumspĭcĕret (imp. subj.)
since   each   soldier   was examining

sŭa,   quid   posset   portare   cum
his own (things)   what   he might be able   to carry   with

se,   quid   cogeretur   relinquĕre   ex
himself   what   he might be compelled   to leave   from

instrumento   hibernorum   Omnĭa⁵⁷
the equipment   of the winter quarters   All (things)

excogitantur,   quare   maneatur
are devised   wherefore   it may be remained [they may remain]

ne   sīne   pericŭlo,   et   perĭcŭlum   augeatur
not   without   danger   and   the danger   may be increased

languore   et   vigilīis (pl)   milĭtum.
by the weariness   and   by the sleeplessness   of the soldiers.

Proficiscuntur⁵⁸   primâ   luce   ex
They set out   at the first   light [early dawn]   from

castris (pl)   sic,   ut   quĭbus   esset (imp.
the camp   so [just]   as (they)   to whom   it was

subj) persuasum   consilĭum   dătum esse
persuaded   (that)   the advice   to have [had] been given

non   ab   hoste,   sed⁵⁹   ab   amicissĭmo   homĭne
not   by   an enemy   but   by   a most friendly   man

Ambiorīge,   longissĭmo   agmĭne   que   magnis
Ambiorix   in a very long   marching line   and   with great

impedimentis (pl.).
baggage

32 At   posteăquàm   hostes   senserunt   de
But   after (that)   the enemy   learned   about

eorum   profectione   ex   nocturno   fremĭtu   que
their   departure   from   the night   din   and

vigilīis,   insidĭis   collocatis   bipartitò
sleeplessness.   ambuscades   having been placed   in two divisions

in   silvis,   opportuno   atque   occulto   lŏco,
ir   the woods.   in a convenient   and   secret   place.

expectabant   adventum   Romanorum   à   circĭter
they were waiting   the approach   of the Romans   at   about

duobus   millĭbus   passŭum :   et   quum   major
two   thousand   (of) paces: and   when   the greater

pars   agmĭnis   demisisset (pl. perf. subj.)
part   of the marching-line   had sent down

se   in   magnam convallem,   ostenderunt
itself [descended]   into   a great   valley,   they showed

sese   subĭtò   ex   utrâque parte   ejus   vallis ;
themselves   suddenly   on   each   side   of this   valley ,

que cœperunt premĕre novissĭmos   et   prohĭbere
and   began   to press   the newest [rear]   and   to hinder

prìmos   adscensu,   atque committĕre prœlĭum
the first [van]   from the ascent,   and   to engage   battle

lŏco   iniquissĭmo   nostris.
in a place   most unfavorable   to our (men).

33. Tum   demum   Titurĭus   trepidare,
Then   at last   Titurius   to bustle [bustled],

concursare   que   disponĕre   cohortes,   ŭtì
to run [ran] about   and   to arrange [arranged]   the cohorts,   as

qui   providisset (pl. perf. subj.)   nĭhil   antè,
(one) who   had foreseen   nothing   before,

tămen,   hæc   ipsa   timĭdè,   atque
however,   (he did) these (things)   themselves   timidly,   and

ut   omnĭa   viderentur (imp. subj.)   deficĕre
as (if)   all (things)   were seeming   to fail (him)

quod   plĕrumque   cŏnsuĕvit   accidere   iis   qui
which   usually   is accustomed   to happen   to those   who

coguntur   capere   consilium   in   negotio   ipso.
are forced   to take   counsel   in   the business   itself.

At   Cotta,   qui   cogitàsset (pl. perf. subj.)   hæc
But   Cotta,   who   had thought   these

posse   accidĕre   in   itinĕre,   atque
(things)   to be able   to [could] happen   on   the march.   and

ob   ĕam   causam   non   fuisset (pl. perf.
on account of   this   reason   had not   been

subj.)   auctor   profectionis,   deĕrat   communi
    the adviser   of the departure,   was failing   for the common

saluti in nullâ re; et præstabat[60] officĭa
safety in no thing; and was performing the duties

imperatoris in appellandis que cohortandis militĭbus
of a general in addressing and exhorting the soldiers

et milĭtis in pugnâ. Que quum propter
and of a soldier in the battle. And when on account of

longitudĭnem agmĭnis, possent (imp. subj.)
the length of the marching-line, they were able

mĭnùs facĭlè obire omnĭa per se,
less easily to perform all (things) by themselves.

et providere, quid esset faciendum quoque
and to provide, what might be to [must] be done in every

lŏco; jusserunt pronuntiari, ut relinquĕrent
place; they ordered (it) to be proclaimed that they should leave

impedimenta atque consistĕrent ın orbem.
the baggage and should take stand ın a circle.

Quod consilĭum, etsi est non
Which [This] plan although it is not

reprehendendum in casu ejusmŏdi, tămen
to be blamed in a case of this kind however

accĭdit incommŏdè· nam minŭit spem nostris
happened badly: for it diminished hope to [in] our

militĭbus, et effecıt hostes alacriores
soldiers. and rendered the enemy more eager

ad pugnandum; quòd id videbatur[61] factum (esse)
for fighting: because this was seeming to have been done

non sĭne summo timore et
not without the highest [utmost] fear and

desperatione. Præterĕa accĭdit, quod ĕrat
despaır Besides it happened. what was

necesse fiĕri, ut milĭtes
necessary to be done [to occur] that the soldiers

discedĕrent (imp subj) volgò ab signis;
were withdrawıng generally from the standards:

que quisque eorum properaret (ımp subj.) petĕre
and every one of them was hastening to seek

atque arripĕre ab impedimentis, quæ
and to seize from the baggage. what

haberet   carissima;   et   omnia   complerentur
he might hold   most dear;   and   all (places)   were filled

(imp. subj.)   clamore   ac   fletu.
                 with noise   and   with bewailing [lamentation]

34. At   consilium   defuit   non   barbaris.
     But   prudence   was wanting   not   to the barbarians

Nam   duces   eorum   jusserunt
For   the leaders   of them [their leaders]   commanded (it)

pronuntiari   totâ   acie,   ne   quis
to be announced   in the whole   battle-line.   that not   any (one)

discederet   ab   loco: quæcunque   Romani
should depart   from   (his) place: whatsoever   the Romans

reliquissent,   esse   illorum   prædam,   atque
might have left.   to be [was]   their   plunder,   and

reservari   illis: proinde   existimarent
to be [was] reserved   for them: wherefore   they should think

omnia   posita   in   victoriâ.   Nostri
(that) all (things)   (were) placed [hung]   on   victory.   Our (men)

erant   pares   pugnando   et   virtute   et   numero:
were   equal   in fighting   both   in valor   and   in number·

tametsi   deserebantur   è   duce   et
although   they were deserted   by   (their) general   and   by

fortunâ,   tamen   ponebant   omnem spem   salutis
fortune,   however   they were putting   all   hope   of safety

in   virtute;   et   quoties   quæque   cohors
in   valor: and   as often as   every   cohort

procurreret (imp. subj.),   magnus   numerus   hostium
was charging,   a great   number   of the enemy

cadebat   ab   eâ   parte.   Quâ   re
were falling   on   that   side.   Which   thing

animadversâ,   Ambiorix   jussit   pronuntiari,
having been observed,   Ambiorix   ordered (it)   to be announced.

ut   conjiciant   tela   procul   neu
that   they cast   (their) weapons   from a distance.   nor

accedant   propius;   et   in   quam   partem
approach   nearer: and   on   what (-ever)   side

Romani   fecerint   impetum,   cedant:
the Romans   made   an attack.   (that) they give way;

nĭhĭl[62]   posse   noceri   ĭis
nothing to be able [could] (to) be injured [injure] to them [them]

levĭtate   armorum   et quotidianâ exercitatione:
by the lightness of (their) arms and by daily   exercise:

insequantur   recipientes   se   rursus
(that) they pursue   (them) betaking   themselves again

ad   signa
to   the standards.

35   Quo præcepto   observato   dĭligentissĭmè
    Which direction having been observed most carefully

ab ĭis, quum quæpĭam cŏhors excessĕrat ex
by them, when any   cohort had gone out from

orbe, atque fecĕrat   impĕtum,   hostes
the circle and had made an attack,   the enemy

refugiebant velocissĭmè; intĕrim ĕrat necesse
were retiring most swiftly meantime it was necessary

nudari   ĕâ   parte,   et   tela
to be exposed on this side and (that) weapons

recĭpi   ab aperto latĕre. Rursus, quum
to [would] be received on the open flank Again, when

cœpĕrant   adverti in ĕum lŏcum, unde
they had begun to return into this place, whence

egressi ĕrant, circumveniebantur et ab ĭis,
they had gone out, they were surrounded both by those

qui cessĕrant et ab ĭis, qui stetĕrant
who had given way and by those. who had stood

proxĭmi; autem sin vellent (imp. subj.) tenere
nearest: but if they wished to hold

lŏcum,   nĕque lŏcus   relinquebatur
(their) place [ground]. neither a place [opportunity] was left

virtuti, nĕque conferti potĕrant vitare tela
for valor nor crowded were they able to avoid the weapons

conjecta à tantâ multitudĭne. Tămen conflictati
hurled by so great a multitude However having struggled

tam multis incommŏdis, multis vulnerĭbus
with so many disadvantages. many wounds

acceptis,   resistebant;   et magnâ
having been received, they were withstanding; and a great

parte	diei	consumptâ,	committebant	nĭhil,
part	of the day	having been spent.	they were doing	nothing,

quod	esset	indignum	ipsis (abl.),	quum
which	would be	unworthy	themselves,	although

pugnaretur (ĭmp. subj.)	à	primâ	luce
it was fought [they fought]	from	the first	light [early dawn]

ad	octavam horam.	Tum[63]	utrumque	fĕmur
to	the eighth hour [two o'clock]	Then	each	thigh

transjicĭtur	tragŭlâ	Tĭto	Balventĭo,	forti
is pierced	with a javelin	to [of] Titus	Balventius,	a brave

vĭro,	et	magnæ auctorĭtatĭs,	quĭ[64]	duxĕrat	prĭmum
man	and	of great authority	who	had led	the first

pilum	superiore	anno.	Quĭntus	Lucanĭus
century	in the former	year.	Quintus	Lucanius

ejusdem	ordĭnĭs	pugnans	fortissĭmè	interficĭtur,
of the same	rank	fighting	most bravely	is slain,

dum	subvĕnit	filĭo (dat.)	circumvento.
while	he aids	(his) son	having been surrounded.

Lucĭus	Cotta,	legatus	adhortans	omnes
Lucius	Cotta.	the lieutenant	encouraging	all

cohortes	que	ordĭnes,	vulneratur	fundâ	in
the cohorts	and	ranks	is wounded	with a sling	on

adversum	os.
the front	face [squarely in the face].

36	Quĭntus	Tĭturĭus	permotus	his	rebus,
	Quintus	Titurius	much alarmed	by these	things

quum	conspexĭsset (pl. perf. subj.)	Ambiorĭgem
when	he had beheld	Ambiorix

prŏcul	cohortantem	sŭos,	mittĭt	sŭum
at a distance	exhorting	his (men)	sends	his

interprĕtem,	Cnæĭum	Pompeĭum	ad	ĕum,	rogatum,
interpreter	Cnæius	Pompey	to	him,	to beseech.

ut	parcat	sĭbĭ (dat.)	que	milĭtĭbus (dat.).	Ilie
that he may spare	himself	and	the soldiers	He

appellatus	respondĭt,	"licere
having been addressed	answered,	" to be [it is] allowed

collŏqui	secum,	si	vĕlit;	sperare
to confer	with himself.	if he	wishes	to hope [he hopes it]

posse   impetrari   à   multitudĭne,
to be able [can]   (to) be obtained   from   the multidude,

quod   pertinĕat   ad   salutem   milĭtum: verò
what   may relate   to   the safety   of the soldiers: but

nĭhil   nocĭtum ıri   ipsi: que
nothing   to be about to be hurt [should harm]   (to) himself: and

          se   interponĕre   sŭam   fĭdem   ın   ĕam
(he) himself   to put [puts]   his own   good faith   on   this

rem."   Ille   communĭcat   cum   sauciŏ   Cottâ;
thing."   He   communicates   with   the wounded   Cotta:

"si   videatur,   ut   excedant   pugnâ,
"if   it may seem (best),   that   they retire   from the battle,

et   colloquantur   unà   cum   Ambiorĭge;   se
and   confer   together   with   Ambiorix: (he) himself

sperare   posse   impetrari   ab   ĕo
to hope [hopes]   to be able   to [that it can] be obtained   from   him

de   sŭâ   salute   ac   milĭtum."   Cotta
about   his own safety   and   (that) of the soldiers."   Cotta

nĕgat   se   iturum   ad   armatum
refuses   (that he) himself   (about) to [should] go   to   an armed

hostem   atque   persevĕrat   in   ĕo.   (37.) Sabinus   jŭbet
enemy   and   persists   in   this.   Sabınus   orders

tribuno   milĭtum,   quos   habebat   circum
the tribunes   of soldiers,   whom   he was having   about

se   in   præsentĭâ,   et   centuriones   primorum
himself   at present,   and   the centurions   of the first

ordĭnum,   sĕqui   se;   et   quum   accessisset
ranks,   to follow   himself;   and   when   he had approached

(pl. perf. subj.) propĭùs   Ambiorĭgem,   jussus
                   nearer   Ambiorix,   having been ordered

abjicĕre   arma,   fâcit   imperatum,   que
to throw aside (his) arms,   he performs   the command.   and

impĕrat   sŭis (dat.),   ut   faciant   ĭdem.   Intĕrım,
commands   his (men),   that   they do   the same.   Meantime.

dum   ăgunt   inter   se   de   conditionĭbus,
while   they treat between themselves   about   conditions,

que   longĭor   sermo   instituĭtur   consultò   ah
and   a rather long   speech   ıs undertaken   designedly   by

Ambıorĭge, circumventus paulatim, interficĭtur.
Ambıorix. having been surrounded gradually he is killed

Tum verò conclamant victorĭam atque tollunt
Then indeed they shout victory and raise

ululatum sŭo more que impĕtu facto
a whoop in their manner and an attack having been made

in nostros, perturbant ordĭnes. Ibi
upon our (men) they disorder the ranks There

Lucıus Cotta pugnans interficĭtur, cum maxĭmâ
Lucıus Cotta fighting is killed with the greatest

parte milĭtum: relĭqui recipĭunt se in
part of the soldıers: the rest betake themselves into

castra (pl.), unde egressı ĕrant. Ex
the camp. whence they had gone out From [Of]

quıbus Lucĭus Petrosidĭus aquilĭfer projecit
whom Lucıus Petrosıdius the eagle bearer [ensıgn] cast

aquĭlam intra vallum, cum premeretur (ımp.
the eagle within the rampart when he was pressed

subj) magnâ multĭtudĭne hostĭum; ıpse
by a great multitude of the enemy: (he) himself

pugnans fortissĭmè pro castris (pl) occidĭtur.
fighting most bravely before the camp is slain.

Alıi ægrè sustĭnent oppugnationem ad
The others hardly [barely] support the assault until

noctem; ipsi omnes ad unum, salute
night (they) themselves all to one [to a man] safety

desperatâ, ınterficĭunt se noctu
having been despaired of. kıll themselves by nıght.

Pauci elapsi ex prœlĭo pervenĭunt
A few having escaped from the battle arrıve

incertis ıtınerĭbus per sılvas ad Tıtum
by uncertain routes through the woods to Tıtus

Labienum legatum in hıberna; atque
Labienus the lieutenant into wınter quarters and

facıunt ĕum certiorem de rebus
make him more sure [inform him] of the things

gestis.
carried ɔ

38. Ambĭŏrĭx sublatus hâc victorĭâ, stătim
    Ambiorix   elated   by this   victory,   immediately

proficĭscĭtur cum equitatu in Aduatucos,
   sets out   with   (his) cavalry   unto   the Aduatuci.

qui ĕrant finitĭmi ejus regno; nĕque
who   were   neighbors   to his   kingdom.   neither

intermĭttĭt dĭem nĕque noctem; que jŭbet
does he pause   day   nor   night.   and   he orders

pedĭtatum subsĕqui se. Re demonstrâtâ,
the infantry   to follow   himself.   The affair   having been explained.

que Aduatucis concĭtatĭs, pervĕnĭt postĕro
and   the Aduatuci   having been incited   he arrives   on the following

dĭe in Nervĭos, que hortatur
day   among   the Nervii.   and   exhorts (them)   "(that)

"ne dimittant occasionem lĭberandĭ sŭi
they may not let slip [lose]   the opportunity   of freeing   themselves

in perpetŭum, atque ulciscendi Romanos pro
forever.   and   of punishing   the Romans   for

ĭis injurĭis, quas accepĕrĭnt (perf. subj.);
those   injuries,   which   they have received

demonstrat dŭos legatos interfectos esse,
he shows (that)   two   lieutenants   (to) have been killed,

que magnam partem exercĭtûs interisse: esse,
and   a great   part   of the army   (to) have perished ·   to be

nĭhĭl[65] negotĭi legionem
[that there is]   nothing   of business [no trouble]   the legion

subĭtò oppressam, quæ hiĕmet (pres. subj.)
suddenly   having been overwhelmed.   which   winters

cum Cicerone interfĭci: profitetur se
with   Cicero   (that it) to [should] be slain: he declares   himself

adjutorem ad ĕam rem.
a helper   for   this   thing.

39 Persuadet Nervĭis (dat.) facĭlè hâc oratione.
He persuades   the Nervii   easily   by this   speech.

Ităque nuncĭis dimissis confestim ad
Therefore   messengers   having been dispatched   immediately   to

Centrones, Grudĭos Levăcos, Pleumoxios, Geidumnos,
the Centrones.   Grudii.   Levaci,   Pleumoxii,   Geidumni.

qui   omnes   sunt   sub   eorum   imperĭo,   cogunt
who   all   are   under   their   authority,   they collect

mănus   quàm   maxĭmas[66]   possunt;   et
bands   as   greatest [great as]   they can.   and

advŏlant   de improviso   ad   hiberna   Ciceronis,
fly   unexpectedly   to   the winter quarters   of Cicero.

famâ   de   morte   Titurĭi   nondum
the report   about   the death   of Titurius   not yet

perlatâ   ad ĕum.   Accĭdit   quŏque   huic,
having been brought   to   him.   It happened   also   to him,

quŏd   fŭit   necesse,[67]   ut   nonnulli   milĭtes,
which [as]   was   necessary.   that   some   soldiers,

qui   discessissent (pl. perf. subj.)   in   silvas
who   had departed   into   the woods

causâ   lignationis   que   munitionis
for the sake   of wood cutting   and   of fortification

interciperentur (imp. subj.)   repentino   adventu
were cut off   by the sudden   arrival

equĭtum.   His   circumventis,   Eburones,
of the cavalry.   These   having been surrounded.   the Eburones,

Aduatuci,   Nervĭi,   atque   socĭi   et   clientes
Aduatuci.   Nervii.   and   the allies   and   dependents

omnĭum   horum,   incipĭunt   oppugnare   legionem
of all   these.   begin   to assault   the legion

magnâ   mănu.   Nostri   celerĭter   concurrunt
with a great   throng.   Our (men)   quickly   run together

ad   arma;   conscendunt   vallum.   Is   dĭes
to   arms;   they mount   the rampart.   This   day

sustentatur   ægrè,   quŏd   hostes
is supported   hardly [with difficulty].   because   the enemy

ponebant   omnem   spem   in   celeritate,   atque
were placing   all   hope   in   haste,   and

adepti   hanc   victorĭam,   confidebant
having obtained   this   victory,   they were trusting

se   fŏre   victores
(that they) themselves   to be about to [would] be   conqueror

in perpetŭum.
forever.

40. Lĭtĕræ (pl.) mittuntur (pl.) confestim ad
A letter   is sent   immediately to

Cæsărem à Cicerone, magnis præmĭis pro-
Cæsar   by Cicero,   great   rewards   having been

posĭtis, si pertulissent. Omnĭbus vĭis
offered, if they should carry (it). All   the ways

obsessis, missi intercipiuntur. Centum
having been blockaded, (those) sent are intercepted. A hundred

et viginti turres excitantur incredibĭli celeritate
and twenty towers are raised with incredible speed

noctu ex ĕâ materĭâ, quam comportavĕrant[68]
by night from this material, which they had brought together

causâ munitionis. Quæ videbantur
for the sake of fortification. What (things) were appearing

deesse opĕri perficiuntur. Hostes, multĉ
to be wanting to the work are completed. The enemy. much

majorĭbus copĭis coactis, oppugnant
greater forces having been collected, assault

castra (pl.) postĕro dĭe, complent fossam.
the camp on the following day they fill up the trench.

Resistĭtur à nostris eâdem ratione,
It is withstood by our (men) in the same manner,

quâ pridĭe: hoc ĭdem fit
in which [as] the day before: this same (thing) is done

deinceps relĭquis diebus. Nulla pars
afterwards on the remaining days. No   part

nocturni tempŏris intermittĭtur ad laborem:
of the night time is discontinued for the labor:

facultas quietis dătur non ægris, non
an opportunity of [for] rest is given not to the sick, nor

vulneratis Quæcunque sunt ŏpus
to the wounded. Whatever (things) are necessary

ad oppugnationem proxĭmi diei, comparantur
for the assault of the next day are prepared

noctu. Multæ sŭdes præustæ, magnus
by night. Many stakes burnt at the point. a great

numĕrus muralĭum pilorum instituĭtur; turres
number of mural [wall-] javelins is prepared. towers

contabulantur;[69] pinnæ que loricæ attexuntur
are built up; battlements and parapets are woven

ex cratĭbus. Cicĕro ispe, quum esset
from [of] hurdles. Cicero himself, although he was

(imp. subj.) tenuissĭmâ valetudĭne, relinquebat
in very delicate health, was leaving

ne nocturnum[70] tempus quĭdem sĭbi ad
not the night time even to himself for

quietem; ut cogeretur (imp. subj.) parcĕre
rest; so that he was compelled to spare

sĭbi (dat.) ultrò concursu
himself beyond [contrary to] (his wishes) by the running

ac vocĭbus milĭtum.
[thronging] (to him) and voices [words] of the soldiers.

41. Tunc dŭces que princĭpes Nerviorum,
Then the leaders and chiefs of the Nervii,

qui habebant alĭquem adĭtum sermonis que
who were having some access of speech and

causam amicitĭæ cum Cicerone, dicunt
cause of friendship with Cicero, say

sese velle collŏqui. Potestate
(that they) themselves (to) wish to parley. The opportunity

factâ, commemŏrant eădem, quæ
having been made, they relate the same (things), which

Ambiŏrix egĕrat cum Titurĭo: "Omnem
Ambiorix had treated with Titurius; "All

Gallĭam esse in armis: Germanos transîsse
Gaul to be [is] in arms: the Germans (to) have crossed

Rhenum: hiberna Cæsăris que reliquorum
the Rhine. the winter quarters of Cæsar and of the rest

oppugnari." Addunt etĭam de morte
to be [are] stormed." They add also about the death

Sabini. Ostentant[71] Ambiorĭgem causâ
of Sabinus. They display Ambiorix for the sake

faciundæ fidĕi. Dicunt ĕos
of making faith [credit]. They say (that) these

errare, si sperent quidquam præsidĭi ab
(to) mistake, if they hope any (of) protection from

īis,   qui   diffīdant (pres. subj)   sŭis   rebus:
those.   who   distrust   (to) their own   affairs

tămen   sese   esse   hoc   anīmo
however   (they) themselves   to be [are]   with [of] this   mind

in   Cicĕronem   que   Romanum   popŭlum,   ut
towards   Cicero   and   the Roman   people.   that

recusent   nīhil,   nīsi   hiberna,   atque
they may refuse   nothing,   except   the winter quarters,   and

nolint   hanc   consuetudĭnem   inveter-
are unwilling (that)   this   custom   to [should] be

ascĕre;[72]   licere   per   se   illis
established;   (it) to be [is] allowed   by   themselves   to them

discedĕre   incolumĭbus   ex   hibernis,   et
to depart   safe   from   the winter quarters,   and

proficisci   sīne   mĕtu   in   quascunque   partes
to set out   without   fear   into   whatever   parts

vĕlint.   Cicĕro   respondit   mŏdò   unum
they may wish.   Cicero   answered   only   one (thing)

ad   hæc: "Non   esse   consuetudĭnem
to   these: "Not   to be [It is not]   the custom

Romani   popŭli   accipĕre   ullam   conditionem   ab
of the Roman   people   to receive   any   condition   from

armato   hoste: si   vĕlint   discedĕre   ab
an armed   enemy.   if   they wish   to withdraw   from

armis,   utantur   se   adjutore,   que
arms,   they may use   himself   (as) a helper.   and

mittant   legatos   ad   Cæsărem: se
may send   ambassadors   to   Cæsar .   (he) himself

sperare   impetraturos,   quæ
to hope [hopes]   them (to be) about to [they may] obtain,   what

petiĕrint,   pro[73]   ejus   justitĭâ."
they may have sought,   on account of   his   justice."

42   Nervĭi   repulsi   ab   hâc   spe,
The Nervii   having been repulsed   from   this   hope,

cingunt   hiberna   ∖allo   undĕcim
surround   the winter quarters   with a rampart   of eleven

pĕdum   et   fossâ   quindĕcim   pĕdum.   Cognovĕrant
feet   and   a ditch   of fifteen   feet.   They had learned

hæc et à nostris consuetudĭne
these (things) also from our (men) by the custom

superiorum annorum; et nacti quosdam
of former years: and having got some

captivos de exercĭtu, docebantur ab his.
prisoners of (our) army. they were taught by these.

Sed nulla copĭa ferramentorum his,
But (there was) no supply of iron tools for them,

quæ esset idonĕa ad hunc usum.
which might be suitable for this use.

Cogebantur circumcidĕre cæspĭtem gladĭis,
They were forced to cut round the sod with swords,

exhaurire terram manĭbus que
to draw out the earth with (their) hands and (carry it)

sagŭlis. Ex quâ re quĭdem, multĭtudo
in cloaks. From which thing indeed, the multitude

homĭnum potŭit cognosci. Nam mĭnùs
of men was able to be known. For in less (than)

trĭbus horis perfecerunt munitionem quindĕcim
three hours they finished a fortification of fifteen

millĭum passŭum in circuĭtu. Que cœperunt
thousand (of) paces in compass. And they began

parare ac facĕre turres relĭquis diebus
to prepare and to make towers on the remaining days

ad altitudĭnem valli, falces que
to the height of the rampart, wall hooks and

testudĭnes, quas iidem captivi docuĕrant.
shelters, which the same prisoners had taught (them).

43. Septĭmo dĭe oppugnationis, maxĭmo
On the seventh day of the siege. a very great

vento coorto, cœperunt jacĕre fundĭs
wind having arisen, they began to throw with slings

ferventes glandes ex fusĭli argillâ, et fervefacta
hot balls of fusible clay. and heated

jacŭla in căsas, quæ tectæ ĕrant stramentis
javelins on the cottages, which had been covered with straw

(pl.) Gallĭco more. Hæ comprehenderunt
in the Gallic manner. These caught

ignem celerĭter, et magnitudĭne venti,
fire quickly, and from the greatness of the wind,

distulerunt[74] in omnem lŏcum castrorum (pl.).
spread (it) into every place of the camp.

Hostes insecuti maxĭmo clamore,
The enemy having followed with a very great shout,

quăsi victorĭâ partâ atque exploratâ
as if the victory (had) been obtained and assured

jam, cœperunt agĕre turres que
already, began to drive the towers and

testudĭnes et ascendĕre vallum scalis.
shelters and to mount the rampart with ladders.

At tanta fŭit virtus atque præsentĭa anĭmi
But so great was the valor and the presence of mind

milĭtum, ut, quum torrerentur (imp. subj.)
of the soldiers, that, although they were scorched

flammâ undĭsque, que premerentur (imp. subj.)
by the flame on every side, and were pressed

maxĭmâ multitudĭne telorum, que
with a very great multitude of weapons, and

intellĭgĕrent (imp. subj.) omnĭa sŭa impedimenta
were understanding (that) all their baggage

atque omnes fortunas conflagrare, non
and all (their) fortunes to be [were] on fire, not

mŏdò nemo decedĕret (imp. subj.) de vallo
only no one was withdrawing from the rampart

causâ demigrandĭ, sed[75] ne quĭsquam pæne
for the sake of going away, but not any one hardly

respĭcĕret (imp. subj.) quĭdem; ac tum
was looking back even; and besides

omnes pugnarent (imp. subj.) acerrĭmè que
all were fighting most vigorously and

fortissĭmè. Hĭc dĭes fŭit longè gravissĭmus
most bravely. This day was by far the most severe

nostris; sed tămen habŭit hunc eventum, ut
for our (men); but however it had this issue, that

ĕo dĭe maxĭmus numĕrus hostĭum vulneraretur
on this day the greatest number of the enemy was wounded

(im p subj)   atque   interficeretur (imp. subj);   ut
                 and   was killed .   as

constipavĕrant   se   sub   vallo   ipso,
they had crowded themselves under   the rampart itself

                que   ultĭmi   dăbant   non recessum
[the very rampart[and the last were giving no   retreat

primis. Quĭdem   flammâ   intermissâ   paulùm,
to the first. Indeed the flame [fire] having ceased a little,

et   turri   adactâ   quodam   lŏco,   et
and   a tower having been forced up in a certain place. and

contingente   vallum,   centuriones   tertĭæ
touching   the rampart.   the centurions   of the third

cohortis recesserunt   ex   ĕo   lŏco,   quo
cohort   retired   from   this place.   in which

      stabant,   que   removerunt omnes   sŭos;
they were standing. and   removed   all   their (men);

'œperunt vocare   hostes   nutu   que vocĭbus,
they began to call the enemy by nod [sign] and   by voices,

       si   vellent   introïre,   nemo   quorum
[words]. if   they wished   to enter   no one   of whom

ausus est   progrĕdi.   Tum   deturbati (sunt)
dared   to advance   Then   they were beaten off

lapidĭbus conjectis   ex   omni parte, que   turris
by stones   thrown   from   every side. and   the tower

succensa est.
was set on fire.

44.   Erant   in   ĕâ   legione   fortissĭmi
       (There) were in   this   legion   (two) very brave

vĭri,   centuriones, Titus Pullo et   Lucĭus Varenus,
men.   centurions. Titus Pullo and Lucius Varenus,

qui   jam   appropinquarent (imp. subj.)   primis
who   now   were approaching   (to) the first

ordinĭbus.   Hi   habebant   perpetŭas
ranks (of centurions). These   were having   constant

controversĭas   inter   se,   ŭter
controversies   between themselves. (as to) which of the two

anteferretur   altĕri;   que   contendebant
should be preferred to the other; and   they were striving

summis simultatĭbus de lŏco
with the highest [greatest] bickerings about place [precedence]

omnĭbus annis. Ex ĭis Pullo inquit,
in all the years. (One) from [of] these, Pullo. says,

quum pugnaretur[76] (imp. subj.—pass. sing.)
when they were fighting

acerrĭmè ad munitones, "Quid dubĭtas,
most vigorously at the fortifications, "Why dost thou hesitate

Varene? aut quem lŏcum[77] probandæ tŭæ virtutis
O Varenus? or what place of proving thy valor

exspactas? Hic dĭes, hic dĭes judicabit
dost thou wait for? This day, this day shall decide

de nostris controversĭis." Quum dixisset (pl. perf.
about our disputes." When he had said

subj.) hæc, procedĭt extra munitiones, et
these (words), he advances outside the fortifications, and

quæ pars hostĭum visa est confertissĭma,
what part of the enemy seems most dense [most crowded]

irrumpit in ĕam. Nec Varenus quĭdem tum
he dashes upon this. Nor Varenus indeed then

contĭnet sese vallo; sed verĭtus
restrains himself on the rampart; but having feared

existimationem omnĭum, subsequitur mediocri
the opinion of all. he follows closely, a moderate

spatĭo relicto. Pullo mittit pilum in
distance being left. Pullo sends (his) javelin against

hostes, atque transjĭcit unum ex multitudĭne
the enemy, and transfixes one from [of] the multitude

procurrentem: quo percusso et exanimato,
running forward: who having been struck and laid senseless

hostes protĕgunt hunc secutis, et
the enemy protect him with (their) shields, and

universi conjicĭunt tela ĭn illum,
all hurl (their) weapons upon him [Pullo]

nĕque dant facultatem regrediendi,
nor do they give (him) a chance of returning.

Scutum[78] Pulloni transfigĭtur et verŭtum
The shield for [of] Pullo is pierced and a javelin

defigĭtur   in   baltĕo.   Hic   casus   avertit
is fixed   in   (his) belt.   This   mishap   turns away

vaginam   et   moratur   dextram   mănum
the scabbard   and   retards   (his) right   hand

conantis   educĕre   gladĭum,   que   hostes
endeavoring   to draw out   (his) sword,   and   the enemy

circumsistunt   impedĭtum.   Varenus   inimicus
surround   (him) entangled.   Varenus   (his) rival

succurrit   illi(dat.), et   subvĕnit
succours [runs to help] him,   and   comes up [brings aid] (to him)

laboranti.   Omnis   multitudo   fonfestim   convertit
laboring   All   the multitude   immediately   turns

se   à   Pullone   ad   hunc.   Arbitrantur   illum
itself   from   Pullo   to   him.   They think   him

transfixum   verŭto.   Illic   verò
[Pullo]   run through [pierced]   with the javelin.   There,   however

Varenus   occursat   ocĭùs   gladĭo   que
Varenus   runs up   very quickly   with (his) sword   and

gĕrit   rem   comĭnùs;   atque   uno
carries on   the affair   hand to hand ,   and   one

interfecto,   propellit   relĭquos   paullùm.   Dum
having been killed.   he repulses   the rest   a little   While

instat   cupidĭùs   dejectus   concĭdit
he presses on   more eagerly.   having been thrown down   he fell

in   inferiorem   lŏcum.   Pullo   rursus   fert
upon   a lower   place   Pullo   again   brings

subsidĭum   huic   circumvento; atque ambo incolŭmes,
aid   to him   surrounded,   and   both   safe.

complurĭbus   interfectis,   recipĭunt   sese
several   having been killed   betake   themselves

cum   summâ   laude   intra
with   the highest [greatest]   praise [applause]   within

munitiones.   Sic   fortuna   versavit   utrumque
the fortifications.   Thus   fortune   turned [treated]   each

in   contentione   et   certamĭne,   ut   alter
in   (their) strife   and   contest,   (so) that   the one

inimicus   esset (imp. subj.)   auxilĭo   que   saluti
rival   was   (for) an aid   and   safety

altĕri ;   nĕque   posset (imp. subj.)   dijudicari,
to the other,   nor   was it possible   to be decided,

ŭter   videretur   anteferendus   ŭtri
which of the two   should seem   to be preferred   to the other

virtute.
in valor.

45. Quantò   gravĭor   atque   asperĭor
As much   more severe   and   more ardous

oppugnatĭo   ĕrat   indĭes,   et   maxĭmè   quòd,
the siege   was   daily,   and   chiefly   because

magnâ   parte   milĭtum   confectâ   vulnerĭbus,
a great   part   of the soldiers   having been spent   with wounds

res   pervenĕrat   ad   paucitatem
the case   had come   to   a fewness [scarcity]

defensorum ;   tantò   crebriores   litĕræ   que
of defenders ;   so much   more frequent   letters   and

nuncĭi   mittebantur   ad   Cæsărem ;   pars   quorum
messengers   were sent   to   Cæsar ;   a part   of whom

deprehensa   necabatur   cum   cruciatu   in
having been caught   was put to death   with   torture   in

conspectu   nostrorum   milĭtum.   Erat   unus
sight   of our   soldiers.   There was   one

Nervĭus   intùs,   nomĭne Vertĭco, natus   honesto
Nervian   within,   by name Vertico,   born   in an honorable

lŏco,   qui   profugĕrat   ad   Ciceronem   à
place [rank],   who   had fled   to   Cicero   from

primâ   obsidiɔne,   que   præstitĕrat   sŭam   fĭdem
the first   siege,   and   had exhibited   his   fidelity

ĕi.   Hic   persuadet servo (dat.),   spe
to him.   This (man)   persuades   a slave,   with the hope

libertatis   que   magnis   præmĭis,   ut   defĕrat
of liberty   and   by great   rewards,   that   he carry

litĕras (pl.)   ad   Cæsărem.   Ille   affert   has (pl.)
a letter   to   Cæsar.   He   bears   this

illigatas   in   jacŭlo ;   et   Gallus   versatus
tied up   in   a javelin ;   and   the Gaul   having mingled

inter   Gallos   sĭne   ullû   suspicĭone,   pervenit
among   the Gauls   without   any   suspicion,   comes

ad　Cæsărem.　Cognoscit　ab　ĕo　de　pericŭlo
to　Cæsar　He learns　from　him　of　the danger

Ciceronis　que　legiŏnis.
of Cicero　and　of the legion.

46. Cæsar,　litĕris (pl.)　acceptis　circĭter
Cæsar.　the letter　having been received　about

undecĭmâ　horâ　diei,　mittit　nuncĭum
the eleventh　hour　of the day.　sends　a messenger

statim　ad　Marcum Crassum　quæstorem　in
immediately　to　Marcus　Crassus　the quæstor　among

Bellovăcos,　cujus　hiberna　abĕrant　ab
the Bellovaci,　whose　winter quarters　were distant　from

ĕo　viginti quinque　millĭa　passŭum　Jŭbet
him　twenty　five　thousand　(of) paces.　He orders

legiŏnem　proficisci　medĭâ　nocte,　que　venire
the legion　to set out　at mid-　night.　and　to come

celerĭter　ad　se.　Crassus　exĭit　cum
speedily [quickly]　to　himself.　Crassus　came out　with

nuncĭo.　Mittit　altĕrum　ad　Caïum
the messenger.　He sends　another (messenger)　to　Caius

Fabĭum　legatum,　ut　adducat　legiŏnem
Fabius　the lieutenant,　that　he lead　(his) legion

in　fines　Atrebatĭum,　quâ　sciebat
into　the territories　of the Atrebates,　where　he was knowing

ĭter　faciendum　sĭbi (dat.).　Scribit
the march　to [would] be made　by himself.　He writes

Labieno,　si　posset　facĕre　commŏdo
to Labienus,　if　he might be able　to do (it)　with the advantage

rei publĭcæ,　venĭat　cum　legione　ad
of the state,　(that) he come　with　(his) legion　to

fines　Nerviorum.　Pŭtat　relĭquam
the territories　of the Nervii.　He thinks　the remaining

partem　exercĭtûs　non　exspectandam,
part　of the army　(must) not　(to) be waited for,

quŏd　abĕrat　paulŏ longĭùs:　cogit　circĭter
because　it was distant　a little farther,　he collects　about

quadringentos　equĭtes　ex　proxĭmis　hibernis.
four hundred　cavalry　from　the nearest　winter quarters.

47. Factus est   certĭor   de   adventu
     He was made   more sure [was informed]   of   the arrival

Crassi   ab   antecursorĭbus   circĭter   tertĭâ   horâ
of Crassus   by   scouts   about   the third   hour.

(abl.):   progredĭtur   viginti   millĭa   passŭum
       he advances   twenty   thousand   (of) paces

ĕo   dĭe.   Præfĭcit   Cassum   Samarobrivæ,
on this   day.   He appoints   Crassus   to Samarobriva,

que   attribŭit   legionem   ĕi;   quòd   relinquebat
and   assigns   a legion   to him;   because   he was leaving

Ĭbi   impedimenta   exercĭtûs,   obsĭdes   civitatum,
there   the baggage   of the army,   the hostages   of the states,

publĭcas   litĕras,   que   omne   frumentum,   quod
the public   letters,   and   all   the corn,   which

devexĕrat   ĕò   causâ[79]   tolerandæ
he had conveyed down   there   for the sake   of enduring

hiemis.   Fabĭus,   ut   imperatum ĕrat,   moratus
the winter.   Fabius,   as   it had been commanded,   having delayed

non   ĭta   multùm,   occurrit   cum   legione   in
not   so   (very) much,   meets (him)   with   a legion   on

itinĕre.   Labienus,   interĭtu   Sabini,   et
the march.   Labienus,   the destruction   of Sacinus,   and

cæde   cohortĭum   cognĭtâ,   quum   omnes
the slaughter   of the cohorts   having been known,   when   all

copĭæ   Trevirorum   venissent (pl. perf. subj.)   ad
the forces   of the Treviri   had come   to

ĕum,   verĭtus   ne,   si   fecisset
[against] him,   having feared   lest,   if   he should make

profectionem   ex   hibernis   simĭlem   fŭgæ,
the departure   from   winter quarters   like   (to) a flight,

ut   posset   non   sustinere   impĕtum
that   he might be able   not   to support   the attack

hostĭum,   præsertim   quos   sciret (imp. subj.)
of the enemy.   especially   whom   he was knowing

efferri   recenti   victorĭâ,   dimittit   litĕras
to be [were] elated   by the late   victory,   despatches   a letter

(pl.)   Cæsări,   cum   quanto   pericŭlo   esset
     to Cæsar.   (to say) with   how great   danger   he was

(imp. subj.)　　　　　educturus　　　legionem　　　ex
　　　　　　　about to [he would] lead out　　the legion　　from

hibernis:　　perscribit　　rem　　　gestam　　　in
winter quarters:　he details　　the affair　carried on　　among

Eburonĭbus:　　dŏcet　　omnes　　copĭas　　peditatûs
the Eburones:　he shows (that)　　all　　the forces　of infantry

que　　equitatûs　　Trevirorum　　consedisse　　trĭa
and　　of cavalry　　of the Treviri　(to) have halted　　three

millĭa　　passŭum　　longè　　ab　　sŭis　castris (pl.).
thousand　(of) paces　　away　　from　　his　camp.

48. Cæsar,　ejus　consilĭo　　probato,　　etsi
　　　Cæsar,　his　　plan　　having been approved,　although

　　　　　　dejectus　　　opinione　　　trĭum
　　(having been) disappointed　in the expectation　of three

legionum,　recidĕrat[80]　ad　dŭas,　tămen　ponebat
legions,　　was reduced　　to　two,　however　he was putting

unum　auxilĭum　communis　salutis　in　celeritate.
the one　aid　　of the common　safety　in　　haste.

Vĕnit　　magnis　　itinerĭbus　　in　　　fines
He comes　by great　　marches　　into　the territories

Nerviorum.　　Ibi　　cognoscit　　ex　　captivis,
of the Nervii.　There　　he learns　　from　the prisoners,

quæ　　gerantur (pres. subj.)　ăpud　Ciceronem,
what (things)　are transpiring　　with　　Cicero,

que　in　quanto　pericŭlo　res　　sit (pres. subj.).
and　in　how great　danger　the case [matter]　is.

Tum　persuadet　　cuidam　　　ex　　Gallis
Then　he persuades　(to) a certain (person)　from [of]　the Gallic

equitĭbus　magnis　præmĭis,　ŭti　defĕrat　epistŏlam
horsemen　by great　rewards.　that　he carry　a letter

ad　Ciceronem.　Mittit　hanc　conscriptam　Græcis
to　　Cicero.　He sends　this　　written　　in Greek

litĕris;　ne,　epistŏlâ　interceptâ,　　nostra
letters,　lest,　the letter　having been intercepted,　our

consilĭa　cognoscantur　ab　hostĭbus.　Mŏnet,
plans　　may be learned　by　the enemy.　He advises (him).

si　non　posset　adire,　　　ut　objicĭat
if　he may not　be able　to approach to (Cicero),　that　he cast

tragŭlam   cum   epistŏlâ   deligatâ   ad   amentum
a javelin   with   the letter   tied   to   the thong

intra   munitiones   castorum (pl.).   Scribit
within   the fortifications   of the camp   He writes

in   litĕris (pl.),   se   profectum
in   the letter,   (that he) himself   having set out   to be about

affŏre   celerĭter   cum   legionĭbus,
to [would] be present   speedily [quickly]   with   the legions,

hortatur   ut   retinĕat   pristĭnam   virtutem.
he encourages (him)   that   he retain   (his) ancient   valor.

Gallus   verĭtus   pericŭlum,   mittit
The Gaul   having feared   danger,   sends [throws]

tragŭlam,   ut   præceptum ĕrat.   Hæc   adhæsit
the javelin,   as   it had been ordered.   This   stuck

ad   turrim   casu,   nĕque   animadversa (est)
to   a tower   by chance,   nor   was perceived

bidŭo   ab   nostris;   tertĭo   dĭe
for two days   by   our (men),   on the third   day

conspicĭtur   à   quodam   milĭte;   dempta
it is seen   by   a certain   soldier,   having been taken down

defertur   ad Cĭceronem.   Ille   recĭtat   per-
it is carried   to   Cicero.   He   reads aloud.   (it) having

lectam   in   conventu   milĭtum,   que
been read through,   in   an assembly   of the soldiers,   and

affĭcit   omnes   maxĭmâ   lætitĭâ.   Tum
affects   all   with the greatest   gladness   Then

fumi (pl.)   incendiorum   videbantur (pl.)   prŏcul,
the smoke   of the fires   was seen   afar off,

quæ   res   expŭlit omnem dubitationem   adventûs
which   thing   banished   all   doubt   of the approach

legionum.
of the legions.

49.   Galli,   re   cognĭtâ   per
The Gauls,   the fact   having been learned   by

exploratores,   relinquunt   obsidionem; contendunt
spies,   leave [raise]   the siege,   they set out

ad   Cæsărem   omnĭbus   copĭis: ĕæ   ĕrant
to   Cæsar   with all   (their) forces;   these   were

circĭter sexaginta millĭa armatorum. Cĭcĕro,
about sixty thousand (of) armed (men) Cicero,

facultate dătâ, repĕtit Gallum ab
the opportunity having been given. requests the Gaul from

eodem Vertĭcone, quem demonstravĭmus suprà,
the same Vertico. whom we have pointed out above,

qui defĕrat lĭtĕras (pl.) ad Cæsărem. Admŏnet
who carried a letter to Cæsar He admonishes

hunc, facĭat ĭter cautè que
him, (that) he make the journey cautiously and

dilĭgenter. Perscribit in lĭtĕris (pl.),
carefully He writes in the letter, (that)

hostes discessisse ab se, que omnem
the enemy (to) have departed from himself and all

multĭtudĭnem convertisse ad ĕum. Quĭbus
the multitude (to) have turned to him. Which

lĭtĕris (pl.) allatis Cæsări circĭter medĭâ
letter having been brought to Cæsar about mid

nocte, făcit certiores sŭos que
night, he makes more sure [informs] his (men) and

confirmat ĕos anĭmo ad dimicandum. Postĕro
strengthens them in mind for fighting On the following

dĭe mŏvet cast˞a (pl.) primâ luce,
day he moves the camp at the first light [early dawn],

et progressus circĭter quatŭor millĭa
and having advanced about four thousand

passŭum, conspicatur multĭtudĭnem hostĭum
(of) paces. he discovers the multitude of the enemy

trans magnam vallem et rivum. Erat res
beyond a great valley and rivulet. It was a matter

magni perĭcŭli dimicare cum tantulis copĭis
of great danger to contend with such small forces

iniquo lŏco. Tămen quonĭam sciebat
in an unfavorable place However since he was knowing

Ciceronem liberatum (fuisse) obsidione,
(that) Cicero to have [had] been delivered from the siege

que ĕò existimabat remittendum[81]
and therefore was thinking (it) to be [he must relax] relaxed

æquŏ animŏ   de   celeritate,   consedit,   et
with an easy mind   from   speed,   he halted,   and

communit   castra (pl.)   lŏco   quàm   æquissĭmo
fortifies   the camp   in a place   as   (most) favorable

pŏtest: atque   etsi   hæc   ĕrant (pl.)
(as) he is able [possible] :   and   although   this   was

exigŭa   per   se (pl.),   vis   septem
small   by   itself,   scarcely   (of) [for] seven

millĭum   homĭnum,   præsertim   cum   nullis
thousand   men,   especially   with   no

impedimentis;   tămen   contrăhit   quàm maxĭmè
baggage;   yet   he contracts (it)   as much as

pŏtest,   angustüs   viarum   ĕo   consilĭo,   ut
he is able,   by narrow   passages,   with this   design,   that

venĭat   in   summam   contemptionem
he may come   into   the highest   contempt

hostĭbus.   Intĕrim speculatorĭbus   dimissis
to [with] the enemy.   Meantime   scouts   having been sent

in   omnes   partes,   explorat   quo   itinĕre
into   all   parts,   he examines   by what   route

posset   transire   vallem   commodissĭnè.
he may be able   to cross   the valley   most conveniently.

50. Eo   dĭe,   parvŭlis   equestrĭbus   prœlĭis
On this   day,   trifling   cavalry   battles

factis   ad   ăquam,   utrique   contĭnent
having been made   at   the water,   each [both]   keep

sese   sŭo   lŏco.   Galli,   quòd   exspectabant
themselves   in their   place.   The Gauls,   because   they were awaiting

ampliores   copĭas,   quæ   nondum   convenĕrant:
more extensive   forces,   which   had not yet   assembled :

Cæsar,   si   fortè   posset   elicĕre   hostes
Cæsar.   if   perhaps   he might be able   to entice   the enemy

in   sŭum   lŏcum   citra   vallem
into   his own   place   on this side   the valley

simulatione   timoris,   ut   contendĕret
by a pretence   of fear.   (so) that   he might contend

prœlĭo   pro   castris (pl):   si   posset   non
in battle   before   the camp: if   he would be able   not

efficĕre   id,   ut.   itinerĭbus   exploratis,
to effect   this,   that   the routes   having been examined,

transiret   vallem   que   rivum   cum   minore
he might cross   the valley   and   rivulet   with   less

pericŭlo.   Primâ   luce,   equitatus
danger.   At the first   light [early dawn],   the cavalry

hostĭum   accedit   ad   castra (pl.),   que
of the enemy   approaches   to   the camp,   and

committit   prœlĭum   cum   nostris   equitĭbus.   Cæsar
joins   battle   with   our   cavalry.   Cæsar

consultò   jŭbet   equĭtes   cedĕre   que   recipĕre
designedly   orders   the horse men   to yield   and   to betake

se   in   castra (pl.),   sĭmul   jŭbet
themselves   into   the camp,   at the same time   he orders

castra (pl.)   muniri   altiore   vallo   ex
the camp   to be fortified   with a higher   rampart   from [on]

omnĭbus   partĭbus,   que   portas   obstrŭi,
all   parts [sides],   and   the gates   (to be) barricaded,

atque   concursari[82]   quàm maxĭmà   in
and   to be hurried [to hurry]   as much as possible   in

administrandis   ĭis   rebus,   et   ăgi
performing   these   things,   and   to be acted [to act]

cum   simulatione   timoris.
with   a pretence   of fear.

51. Omnĭbus quĭbus rebus hostes   invĭtati
By all   which   things   the enemy   having been induced

transducunt   copĭas,   que   constĭtŭunt   acĭem
lead over   (their) forces,   and   station   the battle-line

iniquo   lŏco.   Verò   nostris   etĭam
in an unfavorable   place.   But   our (men)   also

deductis   de   vallo,   accedunt[83]
having been led down   from   the rampart.   they approach

propĭùs;   et   conjicĭunt   tela   ex   omnĭbus
nearer;   and   throw   (their) weapons   from   all

partĭbus   intra   munitionem: que   præconĭbus
sides   within   the fortification: and   criers

circummissis,   jŭbent   pronuntiari;   seu
having been sent about,   they order (it)   to be declared;   whether

quis   Gallus seu Romanus   vĕlit   transire ad
anyone.   Gaul   or   Roman,   may wish   to pass over   to

se   ante   tertĭam   horam,   licere
themselves   before   the third   hour,   to be [it is] allowed

sĭne   pericŭlo: post[84]   id   tempus,   potestatem
without   danger: after   this   time,   the opportunity

non   fŏre: ac   contempserunt
not   to be about to [will not] be: and   they despised

nostros   sic,   ut,   portis   obstructis
our (men)   so.   that.   the gates   having been barricaded

in   speciem   singŭlis   ordinĭbus   cæspĭtum,
in [for]   appearance   with single   rows   of sods,

quòd   videbantur   non   posse   introrumpĕre
because   they were seeming   not   to be able   to burst in

ĕâ,   alĭi   incipĕrent (imp. subj.)   scandĕre
by that (way),   some   were beginning   to climb

vallum   mănu,   alĭi   complere   fossas.
the rampart   by hand,   others   to fill up   the trenches.

Tunc   Cæsar,   eruptione   factâ   omnĭbus
Then   Cæsar,   a sally   having been made   from all

portis   que   equitatu   emisso,   dat
the gates   and   the cavalry   having been sent out,   gives [puts]

hostes   celerĭter   in   fŭgam;   sic   ut   nemo
the enemy   quickly   to   flight,   so   that   no one

omnino   resistĕret (imp. subj.)   causâ   pugnandi,
of all   was withstanding   for the sake   of fighting,

que   occidit   magnum   numĕrum   ex   his,
and   he slew   a great   number   from [of]   these,

atque   exŭit   omnes   armis (abl.).
and   stripped off   all   (their) arms.

52.   Verĭtus   prosĕqui   longĭùs,   quòd
Having feared   to pursue (them)   farther.   because

silvæ   que   paludes   intercedebant;   (nĕque[85]
woods   and   marshes   were intervening;   (nor,

videbat   lŏcum   relinqui   parvŭlo
(was) he was seeing   the place   (to be) left   with trifling

detrimento   illorum);   omnĭbus   sŭis   copĭis
loss   of them [on their part]),   all   his   forces

incolumĭbus, pervĕnit eodem dĭe ad Cĭceronem.
safe, he comes on the same day to Cicero.

Admiratur turres, testudĭnes, que munitiones
He admires the towers, shelters, and the fortifications

hostĭum, institutas Legione
of the enemy, (which they) prepared. The legion

productâ, cognoscit quemque decĭmum
having been drawn out, he learns (that) every tenth

milĭtem non relictum esse sine
soldier (was) not (to have been) left without

vulnĕre. Ex omnĭbus his rebus, judicat,
a wound. From [Of] all these things, he judges,

cum quanto pericŭlo, et cum quantâ virtute,
with how great danger, and with how great valor,

res administratæ sint (perf. subj.). Collaudat
affairs were managed. He commends

Ciceronem pro ejus merĭto (sing.), que
Cicero according to his deserts, and

legionem: appellat sigillatim centuriones que
the legion: he addresses individually the centurions and

tribunos milĭtum, quorum virtutem cognovĕrat
tribunes of the soldiers. whose valor he had known

fuisse egregĭam testimonĭo Ciceronis.
to have [had] been excellent by the testimony of Cicero.

Cognoscit certĭùs de casu Sabini
He learns more surely of the calamity of Sabinus

et Cottæ ex captivis. Postĕro dĭe,
and of Cotta from the prisoners. On the following day,

concione habĭtâ, proponit rem
an assembly having been held, he sets before (them) the affair

gestam: consolatur et confirmat
(as it) transpired: he consoles and encourages

milĭtes: dŏcet detrimentum, quod
the soldiers: he shows (that) the loss, which

acceptum sit (perf. subj.) culpâ et temeritate
has been received by the fault and rashness

legati, ferendum æquiore anĭmo
of the lieutenant to [must] be borne with more even mind

hoc;   quòd   beneficĭo
from this [on this account]:   because   by the kindness

immortalĭum   deorum,   et   eorum   virtute,
of the immortal   gods,   and   by their   valor,

incommŏdo   expiato,   nĕque   diutĭna
the disadvantage   having been atoned for.   neither   a lasting

lætatĭo   relinquatur (pres. subj.)   hostĭbus,   nĕque
rejoicing   is left   to the enemy,   nor

longĭor   dŏlor   ipsis.
longer   grief   to themselves.

53. Intĕrim   fama   de   victorĭâ   Cæsaris
    Meantime   the report   of   the victory   of Cæsar

perfertur   ad   Labienum   per   Remos   incredibĭli
is carried   to   Labienus   by   the Remi   with incredible

celeritate;   ut,   quum   abesset (imp. subj.)
expedition ,   (so) that,   though   he was distant

quinquaginta   millĭa   passŭum   ab   hibernis
fifty   thousand   (of) paces   from   the winter quarters

Ciceronis,   que   Cæsar   pervenisset (pl. subj.)   eò
of Cicero.   and   Cæsar   had arrived   there

post   nonam   horam   diei,   clamor   oriretur
after   the ninth   hour   of the day   a shout   was rising

(imp. subj.)   ante   medĭam   noctem   ad   portas
    before   mid   night   at   the gates

castrorum (pl);   quo   clamore   significatĭo
of the camp;   by which   shout   an indication

victorĭæ   que   gratulatĭo   fĭeret (imp. subj.)
of victory   and   congratulation   was made

Labieno   ab   Remis.   Hâc   famâ   perlatâ
to Labienus   by   the Remi.   This   report   having been carried

ad   Trevĭros,   Indutĭomărus,   qui   decrevĕrat
to   the Treviri.   Indutiomarus.   who   had resolved

oppugnăre   castra (pl.)   Labieni   postĕro
to assault   the camp   of Labienus   on the following

dĭe,   profŭgit   noctu   que   reducit   omnes
day,   flees   by night   and   leads back   all

copĭas   in   Trevĭros.   Cæsar   remittit
(his) forces   among   the Treviri.   Cæsar   sends back

Fabĭum cum legione in sŭa hiberna.
Fabius with the legion into their winter quarters.

Ipse constitŭit hiemare trinis hibernis
He himself resolved to winter in triple winter quarters

cum trĭbus legionĭbus circum Samarobrivam: et
with three legions about Samarobriva; and

quòd tanti motus Gallĭæ exstitĕrant
because so great disturbances of Gaul had arisen

ipse decrevit manere totam hiĕmem
(he) himself determined to remain the whole winter

ad exercĭtum. Nam, illo incommŏdo de
at [with] the army. For, that calamity from

morte Sabini perlato, fĕrè
the death of Sabinus having been carried through (them), nearly

omnes civitates Gallĭæ consultabant de
all the states of Gaul were deliberating about

bello: dimittebant nuntĭos que legationes
war: they were dispatching messengers and embassies

in omnes partes; et explorabant, quid
into all parts, and were searching out, what

consilĭi relĭqui capĕrent, atque unde inĭtĭum
(of) counsel the rest might take, and whence a beginning

belli fĭĕret; que habebant nocturna
of war might be made, and they were holding night

concilĭa in desertis lŏcis: nĕque ullum
assemblies in desert places: nor (did) any

tempus fĕrè totius hĭĕmis intercessit sine
time nearly of the whole winter pass without

sollicitudĭne Cæsăris,[86] quin accipĕret (imp.
the anxiety of Cæsar, but that he was receiving

subj.) alĭquem nuntĭum de concilĭis
some messenger concerning the assemblies

et motu Gallorum. In his factus est
and disturbance of the Gauls. Among these he was made

certĭoi ab Lucĭo Roscĭo legato,
more sure [was informed] by Lucius Roscius the lieutenant,

quem præfecĕrat decĭmæ tertĭæ legioni,
whom he had appointed to the thirteenth legion, (that)

magnas   copĭas   Gallorum   earum   civitatum,   quæ
great   forces   of the Gauls   of these   states,   which

appellantur Armorĭcæ,   convenisse   causâ
are called   Armoricæ,   to have [had] assembled   for the sake

oppugnandi   sŭi;   nĕque   abfuisse
of assaulting   himself;   nor   to have [had] been distant

longĭus   octo   millĭa   passŭum   ab   sŭis
farther   (than) eight   thousand   (of) paces   from   his

  hibernis;   sed,   nuntio   allato   de
winter quarters;   but,   a message   having been brought   about

victorĭâ   Cæsăris,   discessisse,   adĕo
the victory   of Cæsar,   to have (that they) departed,   so

ut   discessus   videretur (imp. subj.)   simĭlis
that   (their)   departure   was seeming   like

  fŭgæ.
(to) a flight.

24. At   Cæsar,   principĭbus   cujusque   civitatis
  But   Cæsar,   the chiefs   of each   state

  vocatis   ad   se,   tenŭit magnam partem
having been called   to   himself,   kept   a great   part

Gallĭæ   in   officĭo,   alĭas   territando,   quum
of Gaul   in   duty,   at one time   by alarming,   when

  denuntiaret (imp. subj.),   se   scire
he was announcing,   (that he) himself   to know

        quæ   fiĕrent (imp. subj.),   alĭas
[knew]   what (things)   were done,   at another time

cohortando.   Tămen   Senŏnes,   quæ   est   civĭtas
by encouraging.   However   the Senones,   which   is   a state

in primis   firma,   et   magnæ   auctoritatis   inter
particularly   strong,   and   of great   authority   among

Gallos,   conati (sunt)   interficĕre   publĭco   consilĭo
the Gauls,   attempted   to slay   by public   counsel

Cavarinum,   quem   Cæsar   constituĕrat   regem
Cavarinus,   whom   Cæsar   had appointed   king

ăpud   ĕos,   (cujus   frater   Moritasgus,   adventu
among   them,   (whose   brother   Moritasgus,   at the coming

Cæsăris   in   Gallĭam,   que   cujus   majores
of Cæsar   into   Gaul,   and   whose   ancestors

obtinuĕrant regnum); quum ille præsensisset
had held the sovereignty; when he had forknown

(pl. perf. subj.) ac profugisset (pl. perf. subj.),
and had escaped.

insecuti usque ad fines, expulerunt
having pursued (him) even to the borders. they expelled

dŏmo que regno; et legatis
(him) from home and the kingdom; and ambassadors

missis ad Cæsărem causâ satis-
having been sent to Cæsar for the sake of making

faciendi, quum is jussisset (pl. perf. subj.) omnem
satisfaction. when he had ordered all

senatum venire ad se, fuerunt non
(their) senate to come to himself. they were not

audientes[87] dicto (dat.). Valŭit tantum
hearing [obedient] to the word It availed so much

ăpud barbăros homĭnes, alĭquos
among barbarian men. (that) some

repertos esse princĭpes inferendi belli,
to have been [were] found leaders of [in] waging war,

que attŭlit tantam commutationem voluntatum
and it brought so great a change of wills

omnĭbus, ut fĕre nulla civĭtas fuĕrit
[heart] to all that scarcely no [any] state was

non suspecta nobis, præter Ædŭos et
not suspected by us, except the Ædui and

Remos, quos Cæsar semper habŭit præcipŭo
Remi. whom Cæsar always had in particular

honore, altĕros pro vetĕre ac perpetŭâ fĭde
honor. the former for ancient and constant faith

erga Romanum popŭlum; altĕros pro recentĭbus
toward the Roman people; the latter for the recent

officiis Gallĭci belli: que scĭo haud, ne
duties of the Gallic war; and I know not. whether

id sit mirandum adĕò, cùm
this may be (to be) wondered at so not only from

complurĭbus aliis causis, tum maxĭmè quòd
many other causes, but also chiefly because

qui præferebantur omnĭbus gentĭbus (dat.)
(those) who were surpassing all nations

virtute belli, dolebant gravissĭmè,
in bravery in war, were grieving most severely. (that they)

se deperdidisse tantum opinionis ejus,
themselves to have [had] lost so much of the reputation of it,

ut perferrent imperĭa Romani
that they should endure the commands of the Roman

popŭli.
people.

55. Verò Trevĭri atque Indutiomărus
But the Treviri and Indutiomarus

intermiserunt[88] nullum tempus totius hiĕmis,
omitted no time of the whole winter,

quin mittĕrent legatos trans Rhenum;
but that they might send ambassadors across the Rhine;

sollicitarent civitates; pollicerentur
(that) they might solicit the states; (that) they might promise

pecunĭas (pl.): dicĕrent, magnâ
money: (that) they might say. (that) a great

parte nostri exercĭtûs interfectâ, multò
part of our army having been slain, by far

minorem partem superesse. Nĕque tămen
the lesser part to remain [remains]. Nor yet

potŭit persuaderi[89] ulli
was it possible to be persuaded to any [to persuade any]

civitati Germanorum, ut transiret Rhenum;
state of the Germans, that it should cross the Rhine;

quum dicĕrent (imp. subj.) se
since they were saying (that they) themselves,

expertos bis, bello Ariovisti, et
having tried twice in the war of Ariovistus, and

transĭtu Tencterorum, non esse
in the crossing of the Tencteri. not to be [are not]

tentaturos fortunam amplius. Indutiomărus
about [going] to try fortune further. Indutiomarus

lapsus hâc spe, nihĭlo mĭnùs cœpit
having slipped [failed], in this hope, nevertheless began

cogĕre copĭas, exigĕre   à   finitĭmis,
to collect   forces,   to demand (them)   from   the neighboring

 parare   ĕquos, allicĕre exŭles que damnatos
(states),   to procure   horses,   to entice   exiles   and   condemned

  ad   se   magnis præmĭis   totâ Gallĭâ:
(persons)   to   himself   by great   rewards   in all   Gaul:

ac comparavĕrat jam tantam auctoritatem   sĭbi
and   he procured   now   so great   authority   for himself

ĭis   rebus   in   Gallĭâ,   ut   legationes
by these   things   in   Gaul,   that   embassies

concurrĕrent (imp. subj.)   undĭque   ad   ĕum;
were assembling   from every side   to   him;

petĕrent (imp. subj.)   gratĭam atque amicitĭam
they were seeking   (his) favor   and   friendship

publĭcè que privatim.
publicly   and   privately.

56. Ubi   intellexit   veniri
 When   he understood (it)   to be come [that they came]

ultrò   ad   se;   Senŏnes   que Carnutes
voluntarily   to   himself;   (that) the Senones   and   Carnutes

 instigatos   conscientĭâ   facinŏris   ex altĕrâ
to be [were] instigated   by a consciousness   of crime   on   one

parte,   Nervĭos que Aduatĭcos   parare
side,   (that) the Nervii   and   Aduatuci   (to) prepare

bellum   Romanis (dat.)   altĕrâ   nĕque
war   against the Romans   on the other side   nor (that)

copĭas voluntariorum   defŏre
forces   of volunteers   to be about to [would] be wanting

sĭbi,   si   cœpisset (pl. subj.)   progrĕdi   ex
to himself,   if   he was beginning   to advance   from

sŭis   finĭbus;   indicit   armatum   concilĭum.
his own   borders;   he proclaims   an armed   council.

Hoc,   more   Gallorum,   est   initĭum
This,   by the custom   of the Gauls.   is   a commencement

belli; quò omnes pubĕres   coguntur
of war;   where   all   full grown (persons)   are compelled

convenire armati,   communi lege; et qui
to assemble   armed.   by a common   law.   and   who

ex   ĭis   vĕnit novissĭmus,   effectus
[whoever] from [of] them   comes   last,   having been visited

omnĭbus   cruciatĭbus   necatur   in   conspectu
with all   tortures   is put to death   in   sight

multitudĭnis.   In   ĕo   concilĭo   curat
of the multitude.   In   this   council   he takes care

Cingetorĭgem, princĭpem   alterĭus   factionis,   sŭum
Cingetorix,   the chief   of the other   party,   his own

genĕrum, judicandum   hostem (quem demonstravĭmus
son in law, to be [is] judged   an enemy (whom   we have shown

suprà,   secutum   fĭdem   Cæsăris,   non
above,   having secured   the good-faith   of Cæsar,   not

discessisse   ab   ĕo),   que   publĭcat
to have [had not] departed   from   him),   and   he confiscates

ejus   bŏna.   His   rebus   confectis,
his   goods.   These   things   having been finished.

pronuncĭat   in   concilĭo   se
he declares   in   the council   (that he) himself

accersitum (esse)   à   Senonĭbus,   et   Carnutĭbus,
to have [has] been sent for   by   the Senones   and   Carnutes,

que   complurĭbus   alĭis   civitatĭbus   Gallĭæ:
and   by very many   other   states   of Gaul:

facturum (esse)   ĭter   huc   per
to be [that he is] about to make   (his) march   hither   through

fines   Remorum,   que   populaturum   eorum
the territories   of the Remi   and   [is] about to ravage   their

agros;   ac   oppugnaturum   castra (pl.)   Labĭeni
lands,   and   [is] about to assault   the camp   of Labienus

prĭùs quàm   facĭat   id,   que   præcĭpit,
before (that)   he may do   this   and   he prescribes.

quæ   vĕlit   fiĕri.
what   he wishes   to be done.

57. Labienus   tĭmebat   nĭhil   de   sŭo
      Labienus   was fearing   nothing   about   his own

perĭcŭlo   ac   legionis,   quum   contineret
danger   and   (that) of the legion,   since   he was keeping

sese   castris (pl.)   munitissĭmis   et   naturâ
himself   in a camp   most fortified   both   by the nature

lŏci, et mănu; sed cogitabat[90]
of the place, and by hand [art]. but he was thinking

ne dimittĕret quam occasionem gerendæ
he should not lose any opportunity of carrying on

rĕi bĕnè. Ităque oratione Indutiomări,
a matter well. Therefore the speech of Indutiomarus,

quam habuĕrat in concilĭo, cognĭtâ
which he had delivered in the council. having been known

à Cingetorĭge atque ejus propinquis, mittĭt
from Cingetorix and his relations. he sends

nuntĭos ad finitĭmas civĭtates, que
messengers to the neighboring states, and

convŏcat equĭtes undĭque. Dĭcit
calls together cavalry from every side. He says [fixes]

certam dĭem conveniendi ĭis. Intĕrĭm
a certain day of meeting for them. Meantime

Indutiomărus vagabatur prŏpè quotĭdĭe cum omni
Indutiomarus was roving almost daily with all

equitatu sub ejus castris (pl.); alĭàs ut
(his) cavalry near his camp; at one time that

cognosceret sĭtum castrorum (pl.); alĭàs
he might learm the situation of the camp. at another time

causâ colloquendi aut territandi: omnes
for the sake of parleying or of alarming · all

equĭtes plerumque conjiciebant tela ĭntra
(his) cavalry generally were hurling weapons within

vallum. Labienus continebant sŭos ĭntra
the rampart. Labienus was keeping his (men) withir

ınunitiones, que augebat opinionem timoris
the fortifications, and was increasing the supposition of fear

quibuscunque rebus potĕrat.
by whatsoever things [means] he was able

58. Qaum Indutiomărus accedĕret (imp. subj.)
When Indutiomarus was approaching

indĭes ad castra (pl.) majore contemptione,
daily to the camp with greater contempt.

equitĭbus omnĭum finitimarum civitatum, quos
the cavalry of all the neighboring states, which

curavĕrat accessendos, intromissis unâ
he had taken care to be sent for. having been admitted in one

nocte, contĭnŭit omnes sŭos custodĭis (pl.) intra
night, he kept all his (men) on guard within

castra (pl.) tantâ diligentĭâ, ut ĕa res
the camp with so great diligence. that this thing

posset enuntĭari nullâ ratione, aut
might be able to [could] be told by no means. or

perferri ad Trevĭros. Intĕrim, ex
(to) be carried to the Treviri. Meantime. according to

quotĭdianâ consuetudĭne, Indutiomărus accedit
daily custom. Indutiomarus approaches

ad castra (pl.), atque consumit magnam partem
(to) the camp. and spends a great part

diei ĭbi. Equĭtes conjicĭunt tela, et
of the day there (His) cavalry hurl weapons. and

evŏcant nostros ad pugnam magnâ[91]
call out our (men) to battle with great

contumelĭâ verborum. Nullo responso dăto
insult of words No answer having been given

à castris (pl.), ŭbi visum est, discedunt
from the camp when it seemed (weil). they depart

dispersi ac dissĭpati sub vespĕrum. Labĭenus
dispersed and scattered about evening. Labienus

subĭtò emittit omnem equitatum duabus
suddenly sends forth all the cavalry from two

portis: præcĭpit atque interdicit,[92] hostĭbus
gates he prescribes and enjoins. the enemy

perterrĭtis, atque conjectis in fŭgam,
having been dismayed and thrown into flight.

(quod videbat fŏre, sicut
(which he was seeing to be about to [would] be. just as

accĭdit) omnes petĕrent Indutiomărum
it happened) (that) all should seek Indutiomarus

unum, neu quis vulneraret quemquam,
one [alone] nor any (man) should wound any one.

prĭus quàm videret illum interfectum: quòd
before (that) he should see him killed. because

nolebat   illum,   nactum   spatĭum
he was unwilling   (that) him [he], having got   space [time]

mŏrâ   reliquorum,   effugĕre.   Proponit
by delay of [with] the rest, to [should] escape. He offers

magna   præmĭa   ĭis,   qui occidĕrint: submittit
great   rewards   to those, who should kill (him). he sends up

cohortes subsidĭo   equitĭbus.   Fortuna comprŏbat
cohorts for aid   to the cavalry. Fortune   approves

             consilĭum   homĭnis;   et   quum   omnes
[favors]   the plan   of the men; and since all

petĕrent (imp. subj.)   unum,   Indutiomărus
were seeking   one,   Indutiomarus

deprehensus   in   vădo   ipso   flumĭnis
having been caught in   the ford itself [the very ford] of the river

interficĭtur,   que   ejus   căput   refertur   in
is slain.   and   his   head   is carried back   into

castra (pl.).   Equĭtes redeuntes consectantur atque
the camp   The cavalry returning   pursue   and

occĭdunt,   quos   possunt. Hâc re   cognĭtâ,
slay (those), whom   they can This thing having been known,

omnes   copĭæ   Eburonum   et   Nerviorum,
all   the forces of the Eburones and   of the Nervii,

quæ convenĕrant, discedunt; que paulò   post   id
which had assembled, depart,   and   a little after this

factum,   Cæsar habŭit Gallĭam quietiorem.
deed [action], Cæsar had   Gaul   more tranquil.

SIXTH BOOK

———

The sixth book begins with a description of Cæsar's rapid and success
ful campaign against the Senonnes and Carnutes. The Triveri attack
Labienus who conquers them in battle after luring them by a stratagem
into an unfavorable place. Cæsar builds another bridge across the Rhine
He enters Germany and receives the surrender of the Ubii. He learns
that the Suevi have taken refuge in the Bacenis forest. Cæsar makes a
digression in his narrative and compares the Gauls and Germans in a
long descriptive passage. He returns to Gaul, having demolished the
farther end of the bridge and fortified the Gallic approach to it. He
marches in pursuit of Ambiorix into the Ardennes forest. Meantime the
Sugambri cross the Rhine, attack Cicero and return. During this period
the Eburones are being plundered and exterminated by a general procla-
mation as punishment for their treachery of the previous year. Ambiorix
is pursued continuously but with a few horsemen succeeds in evading
capture. After condemning Acco for the conspiracy of the Senones and
Carnutes. Cæsar quarters the legions for winter and departs for Italy to
hold assemblies.

1. Cæsar   de   multis   causis   expectans   majorem
   Cæsar   for   many   reasons   expecting (a) greater

motum   Galliæ   instituit   per   legatos,
commotion of Gaul   determines through (his) Lieutenants,

M. Silanum, C. Antistium Reginum,   T. Sextium,
N. Silanus,   C. Antistius Reginus. (and) T. Sextius,

habere delectum.   Simul   petit   ab   Cneio
to hold a levy.   At the same time he requests from Cneius

Pompeio, proconsule,   quoniam ipse   maneret
Pompey,   proconsul, (that) because he   was remaining

ad   urbem   cum   imperio,   causâ
near   the city   with (military) command. for the sake of

rei publicæ,   juberet   quos
the public business, (that) he should order (those) whom

rogavisset (pl. perf. subj.) sacramento   consul ex
he had enrolled   by oath   (as) consul in

Cisalpinâ　Galliâ　convenire　ad　signa　et
Cisalpine　Gaul　to assemble　at　the standards　and

proficisci　ad　se;　existimans　interesse　magni
march　to　him:　deeming　(it)　to be　of great

ad　opinionem　Galliæ
(importance)　regarding　the opinion　of Gaul (which they might

etiam　in　reliquum　tempus
have)　even　for　remaining [future]　time　(that the)

facultates　Italiæ　videri　tantas　ut　si
resources　of Italy　to [should] be seen　so great　that　if

quid (neut.)　detrimenti　acceptum esset　in bello,
any　(of) detriment [harm]　should be received　in　war.

id　non modò　posset　sarciri　brĕvi　tempŏre, sed
this　not　only　could be　repaired　in a short　time,　but

posset　etiam　augeri[1]　majoribus　copiis. Quod
could　also　be supplemented　by greater　forces.　Which

quum　Pompeius　tribuisset　et　rei publicæ　et
when　Pompey　had granted　both　for the republic　and

amicitiæ;　delectu　celeriter　confecto
for (his) friendship.　a levy　quickly　having been made

per　suos,　tribus　legionibus　et
through　his (lieutenants)　three　legions　both

constitutis　et　adductis　ante　hiemem　exactum;
having been raised　and　brought on　before　the winter　had passed ;

et　numero　earum cohortium,　quas　amisĕrat　cum
and　the number　of these　cohorts,　which　he had lost　under

Q. Titurio,　duplicato,　docuit　et
Q. Titurius,　having been doubled.　he showed　both

celeritate　et　copiis,　quid　disciplina
by (his) promptness　and　by (his) forces,　what　the discipline

atque　opes　Romani　populi　posset.
and　resources　of the Roman　people　were able (to do).

2. Indutiomaro　interfecto　ut　docuimus,
Indutiomarus　having been slain　as　we have shown,

imperium　defertur　à Treviris　ad ejus propinquos.
the government　is conferred by the Treviri　on　his　relations.

Illi　non desistunt sollicitare finitimos Germanos
They (do) not　cease　to invite　the neighboring　Germans

et   polliceri pecuniam. Quum possent non impetrare
and   to promise   money.   When   they could   not   obtain

ab   proximis,[2]   tentant   ulteriores.[3]
(this)   from   the neighboring,   they try   the more remote.

Nonnullis,   civitatibus   inventis,
Some.   states   having been found (compliant),

confirmant[4]   jurejurando   inter   se,   que
they pledge   by an oath   among   themselves,   and

cavent   obsidibus   de   pecuniâ;   adjungunt
give security   by hostages   for   the money.   they unite

sibi   Ambiorigem societate et   fœdere. Quibus
to themselves   Ambiorix   by alliance and by treaty   Which

rebus   cognitis,   Cæsar quum   videret bellum
things   having been known.   Cæsar   as   he perceived   war

parari[5]   undique;   Nervios, Aduatucos
to be [was] preparing   on all sides.   (that)   the Nervii,   the Aduatuci

ac   Menapios,   omnibus   cisrhenanis   Germanis
and   the Menapii.   all   the hither-Rhine   Germans

adjunctis   esse in armis;   Senones   non
having been added   were   in   arms;   (that) the Senones   (did) not

venire ad   imperatum,   et   communicare
come   at   (his) command,   and   (that)   they exchange

consilia cum Carnutibus que   finitimis   civitatibus:
counsel   with   the Carnutes and   neighboring   states;

Germanos   sollicitari   a   Treviris   crĕbris
(that)   the Germans   were invited   by   the Treviri   in frequent

legationibus;   putavit   cogitandum,
embassies;   he thought   to [it must] be considered [he must

sibi (dat.)   maturiùs   de   bello.
consider]   by himself   earlier   regarding   the war.

3. Itaque   hieme   nondum   confectâ,
Therefore   the winter   not yet   having been completed

quatuor   proximis   legionibus   coactis,
the four   nearest   legions   having been assembled.

contendit improviso in   fines   Nerviorum;   et
he marched   suddenly   into   the territories   of the Nervii;   and

priùs quàm   illi   aut   possent convenire, aut
before   (that)   they   either   could   assemble,   or

profugere   magno   numero   pecoris   atque   hominum
escape   a great number   of cattle and   of men

capto,   atque   ĕâ   prædâ   concessâ
having been captured   and   this   booty   having been given up

militibus,   que   agris   vastatis,   coëgit
to the soldiers, and   (their) fields having been laid waste he forced

venire   in   deditionem,   atque   dare
(them) to come into   a surrender,   and   to give

obsides   sibi.   Eo negotio   celeriter
hostages   to himself. This business [campaign] having been quickly

confecto,   reduxit   rursus   legiones   in   hiberna.
performed,   he led back   again   the legions into winter quarters.

Concilio   Galliæ   indicto   primo   vere,   ut
A council   of Gaul   having been called   in early   spring, as

instituĕrat,   quum   reliqui   præter   Senones,
he had determined,   since   the rest   except   the Senones,

Carnutes   que   Treviros   venissent,   arbitratus
the Carnutes   and   Treviri   had come,   having judged (that)

hoc   esse   initium   belli   ac   defectionis,
this   to be [was]   the beginning   of war   and   of revolt.

ut   videretur   postponere   omnia,   transfert
although   he might seem   to postpone   every thing. he transfers

concilium   in   Lutetiam   Parisiorum.   Hi   ĕrant
the council   to   Lutetia   of the Parisii (Paris). These   were

confines   Senonibus,   que   memoriâ   patrum
neighbors   to the Senones,   and   in the memory   of the fathers

conjunxĕrant[6]   civitatem,   sed   existimabantur
had united   their state with (them),   but   they were thought

abfuisse   ab   hoc   concilio.   Hâc   re
to have been absent   from   this   council.   This   thing

pronunciatâ   pro   suggestu,   proficiscitur
having been proclaimed   from   the tribunal,   he marches

eodem   die   cum   legionibus   in   Senones,   que
on the same   day   with   the legions   into   the Senones,   and

pervenit   eò   magnis   itineribus.
arrives   there   by long [forced] marches.

4. Ejus   adventu   cognito,   Acco,   qui   fuerat
His   arrival   having been learned.   Acco,   who   had been

princeps ejus concilii, jubet multitudinem convenire
the author of this council. orders the people to assemble

in oppida. Nuntiatur conantibus,
in the towns. It is announced to (those) attempting. (and)

prius quàm id posset effici Romanos
before (that) it could be accomplished (that) the Romans

adesse. Necessariò desistunt sententiâ, que
to have [had] come. Necessarily they desist from the design, and

mittunt legatos ad Cæsarem causâ deprecandi;[7]
send ambassadors to Cæsar for the purpose of imploring;

adeunt per Æduos, in fide
they approach (him) through the Ædui. under the protection

quorum civitas erat antiquitùs. Æduis
of whom (their) state was formerly The Ædui

petentibus Cæsar libenter dat veniam, que accipit
petitioning Cæsar readily gives pardon. and receives

excusationem, quòd arbitrabatur æstivum
(their) excuse. because he was judging (that) the summer

tempus esse instantis belli non
time to be [was] (one) of [for] impending war (and) not

quæstionis. Centum obsidibus imperatis,
of [for] investigation A hundred hostages having been ordered,

tradit hos Æduis custodiendos. Carnutes
he delivers these to the Ædui to be guarded. The Carnutes

mittunt legatos que obsides eòdem,
send ambassadors and hostages to the same place.

usi Remis deprecatoribus, in clientelâ
having made use of the Remi as intercessors. under the protection

quorum erant; ferunt eadem responsa.
of whom they were. they carry (back) the same answer.

Cæsar peragit concilium, que imperat equites
Cæsar held the council. and orders horsemen

civitatibus (dat.).
(of) the states.

5. Hâc parte Galliæ pacatâ, insistit
This part of Gaul having been pacified, he applied

totus et mente et animo in bellum
(himself) altogether both in mind and soul to the war

Trevirorum   et   Ambiorigis.   Jubet   Cavarinum
of the Treviri   and   Ambiorix.   He orders   Cavarinus

proficisci secum cum   equitatu   Senonum,   ne   quis
to march   with him   with   the cavalry   of the Senones,   lest   any

motus   civitatis   existat   aut   ex   hujus
commotion   of the state   may arise   either   from   his

iracundiâ, aut ex   ĕo,   quod   meruĕrat   odio.
irascibility,   or from   this (fact),   that   he had merited   hatred.

His   rebus   constitutis,   quòd   habebat   pro
These   things   having been settled,   because   he was holding   for

explorato   Ambiorigem non esse certaturum[8]
[as] well known   (that)   Ambiorix   would not contend

prœlio,   circumspiciebat animo ejus reliqua consilia.
in battle,   he was considering   in mind   his   other   plans.

Menapii   ĕrant propinqui   finibus   Eburonum,
The Menapii   were   neighboring   to the frontiers   of the Eburones,

muniti   perpetuis   paludibus que silvis; qui   uni ex
protected   by continuous   marshes   and woods;   who   alone of

Galliâ nunquam misĕrant   legatos   ad   Cæsarem
Gaul   never   had sent   ambassadors   to   Cæsar

de   pace;   sciebat   hospitium esse
concerning   peace;   he was knowing   (that) hospitality   was [existed]

cum   iis   Ambiorigi (dat.);   item
with [between]   them   (and)   Ambiorix,   also

cognoverat   venisse   in   amicitiam
he had discovered   (that he) to have [had] come   into   friendship

Germanis   per   Treviros.   Existimabat
to [with] the Germans   through   the Treviri.   He was thinking   (that)

hæc   auxilia   detrahenda   illi,   priùs quàm
these   auxiliaries   to [must] be detached   from him,   before   (that)

ipsum   lacessendum   bello; ne   salute   des-
(he) himself   to be [was] assailed   in war;   lest   safety   having been

peratâ,   aut   abderet   se   in   Menapios,
despaired of,   either   he might hide   himself   among   the Menapii,

aut   cogeretur   congredi   cum   transrhenanis.
or   be forced   to unite   with   the over—Rhine (Germans).

Hoc   consilio   inito,   mittit   impedimenta
This   plan   having been formed,   he sends   the baggage

totius exercitûs ad Labienum in Treviros, que
of all   the army to Labienus among the Treviri, and

jubet duas legiones proficisci ad eum. Ipse
orders two legions to proceed to him. (He) himself

proficiscitur cum quinque expeditis legionibus in
marches with five light armed legions against

Menapios. Illi, nullâ mănu coactâ,
the Menapii They. no force having been assembled.

freti præsidio lŏci, confugiunt in silvas
trusting to the protection of the place. retreat to the woods

que paludes, que conferunt eòdem sŭa.
and marshes and convey to the same place their property

6. Cæsar, copiis partitis cum C. Fabio,
Cæsar, the forces having been divided with C. Fabius.

legato, et M. Crasso, quæstore, que pontibus
the lieutenant. and M. Crassus. the quæstor. and bridges

effectis celeriter, adiit tripartitò;
having been constructed hastily. he invades in three divisions:

incendit ædificia que vicos, potitur magno
he burns the houses and villages (and) gets posession of a great

numero pecŏris, atque hominum. Coacti
number of cattle and of men Having been forced

quibus rebus, Menapii mittunt legatos ad
by which [these] things. the Menapii send ambassadors to

eum, causâ petendæ[9] pacis. Ille, obsidibus,
him. for the purpose of seeking peace He, the hostages.

acceptis confirmat se habit-
having been received declares (that he) himself about to

urum numero hostium, si recepissent
[would] hold (them) in the number of enemies. if they received

aut Ambiorigem, aut ejus legatos sŭis finibus.
either Ambiorix. or his ambassadors in their territories.

His rebus confirmatis, relinquit Commium,
These things having been settled. he leaves Commius,

Atrebatem, cum equitatu in Menapiis lŏco
the Atrebatian. with the cavalry among the Menapii in place

custodis; ipse proficiscitur in Treviros.
of a guard; he himself marches into the Treviri.

7. Dum hæc   geruntur   à Cæsare,   Treviri,
While these (things) are performed by Cæsar. the Treviri,

magnis copiis   peditatûs,   que equitatûs   coac-
a great   force   of foot soldiers, and of cavalry   having been

tis,   parabant   adoriri Labienum   cum unâ
assembled,   were preparing to attack Labienus   with   one

legione, quæ hiemaverat in eorum   finibus.   Que
legion.   which had wintered in their   territories.   And

jam   aberant   ab   ĕo   non   longius
already they were distant from him   not   farther   (than)

viâ   bidui,   quum cognoscunt   duas
a journey of two days. when   they learn   (that)   two

legiones venisse   missu   Cæsaris.
legions   had arrived by the sending [dispatched] of [by] Cæsar.

Castris   positis   à quindecim[10] millibus
Their camp   having been pitched by   fifteen   thousand

passŭum   constituunt   expectare   auxilia (pl.)
(of) paces   they determine to wait for   the aid [auxiliaries]

Germanorum. Labienus, consilĭo hostium   cog-
of the Germans.   Labienus   the plan of the enemy   having

nito   sperans   temeritate   eorum
been learned   (and)   hoping   (that) by the rashness of them

              fore   aliquam
[by their rashness]   to be about to [there would] be   some

facultatem dimicandi, præsidio quinque cohortium
opportunity   of fighting.   a guard   of five   cohorts

relicto   impedimentis, proficiscitur contra hostem
having been left for the baggage,   he marches against the enemy

cum   viginti quinque cohortibus,   que   magno
with   twenty   five   cohorts,   and   a great [much]

equitatu, et communit   castra, spatio   mille
cavalry,   and he fortifies (his) camp, an interval of a thousand

passŭum   intermisso.   Erat,   inter Labienus
paces   having intervened. There was, between Labienus

atque hostem, flumen   difficili   transitu, que
and   the enemy, a river with a difficult crossing and

præruptis ripis. Neque   ipse   habebat in animo
with steep   banks. Neither he himself had   in   mind

transire   hoc,   neque   existimabat   hostes
to cross   this.   nor   was he thinking (that) the enemy

transituros.   Spes   auxiliorum augebatur quotidie.
would cross.   The hope of auxiliaries was increased daily.

Loquitur   palàm   in   concilio,   "quoniam   Germani
It was said openly   in   council.   "because   the Germans

dicuntur   appropinquare   sese   non
are said   to be approaching   (that he) himself   (would)   not

    devocaturum in dubium   suas   que fortunas
(about to) call   into doubt [hazard] his own and the fortunes

exercitûs,   et   moturum   castra
of the army.   and   (that he) about to [would] move   the camp

primâ luce[11] postero die."   Hæc   deferuntur
at early dawn   on the next day."   These (words) are carried

celeriter ad   hostes,   ut   ex   magno numero
quickly   to   the enemy, as   from [of]   the great number

equitatûs   Gallorum,   natura   cogebat   nonnullos
of cavalry   of the Gauls,   nature   was forcing   some

favere Gallicis rebus.   Noctù Labienus,   tribunis
to favor the Gallic   affairs.   At night Labienus,   the tribunes

   militum   que   primis   ordinibus   coac-
of the soldiers   and   the first   orders (of centurions)   having been

tis,   proponit   quid   sit   sui
assembled.   propounds [proposes]   what   may be (of)   his

consilii;   et   quò   faciliùs   det   hostibus
plan ;   and   that   the more easily he may give   to the enemy

suspicionem   timoris,   jubet   castra   moveri
a suspicion   of fear   he orders   the camp   to be moved

majore   strepitu et tumultu, quàm fert consuetudo
with greater   noise   and confusion.   than   was   the custom

Romani   populi.   His   rebus   efficit   profectionem
of the Roman   people.   By these   things   he makes   the departure

similem   fugæ.   Hæc   quoque deferuntur   ad
like   to a flight.   These (things)   also   are announced   to

hostes   per   exploratores   ante   lucem,   in
the enemy   through   spies   before   light,   in

tanta   propinquitate castrorum.
so great [such]   nearness   of the camps.

8. Vix   novissium agmen   processerat   extra
    Scarcely   the rear marching-line   had proceeded   beyond

munitiones, cum Galli   cohortati   inter   se[12]
the fortifications, when the Gauls   having encouraged   one   another

            ne   dimittĕrent speratam prædam ex
(that)   they should not   lose   the hope for   booty   from

        manibus;   esse   longum   expectare
(their) hands.   (that) it would be   long [tedious]   to wait for

auxilium   Germanorum, Romanis   perterritis;
the assistance   of the Germans,   the Romans   having been terrified:

        neque suam dignitatem pati   ut   non
(that)   neither   their   dignity   suffers   that   they should not

audeant adoriri   tantis   copiis, tam exiguam
dare   to attack   with so great   forces,   so   small

manum,   præsertim fugientem atque   impeditam;
a band,   especially   fleeing   and   encumbered;

non   dubitant transire flumen et committere
they do not   hesitate   to cross   the river   and   to join

prœlium   iniquo   lŏco.   Quæ   Labienus
battle   in an unfavorable   place.   Which   Labienus

suspicatus   fŏre,   ut   elicĕret
having suspected   to be about to [would] be,   that   he would lure

omnes   cĭtra   flumen,   progrediebatur   placidè
all   to this side   the river,   he was marching on   quietly

usus   eâdem simulatione (abl.) itineris. Tum,
having used   the same   pretence   of a march.   Then,

impedimentis   præmissis   paulum,   atque
the baggage   having been sent forward   a little.   and

collocatis   quodam tumulo; "habetis," inquit,
having been placed   on a certain   eminence: "you have"   says he.

"milites,   facultatem   quam   petistis;   tenetis
"soldiers,   the opportunity   which   you have sought: you hold

hostem   impedito   atque   iniquo   lŏco;
the enemy   in an encumbered   and   unfavorable   place.

præstate eandem virtutem nobis   ducibus, quam
exhibit   the same   courage   to us   (your) generals   which

sæpenumero præstitistis   imperatori; existimate
so often   you have displayed   to your commander: suppose

ĕum   adesse,   et   cernere   hæc
him   to be present,   and   to observe   these   (deeds as if)

coràm."   Simul   jubet   signa   con-
in his presence. "   At the same time   he orders   the standards   to be

verti   ad   hostem,   que   aciem   dirigi ;   et
turned   to   the enemy,   and   the battle-line   to be formed ,   and

paucis   turmis   dimissis   præsidio   ad
a few   troops of horsemen   having been sent   for [as] a guard   to

impedimenta,   disponit   reliquos   equites ad   latera.
the baggage,   he stations   the remaining   cavalry on   the wings.

Nostri,   clamore   sublato,   celeriter   jaciunt
Our men,   a shout   having been raised.   quickly   throw

pila   in   hostes.   Illi,   ubi,   præter
(their) weapons   at   the enemy.   They,   when,   contrary

spem,   viderunt   quos   credebant   fugĕre
to expectation,   they saw   those whom   they believed   to flee

ire   ad   se   infestis   signis,   non   ferre
come   at   them   with hostile   standards,   (to) [could] not   sustain

impetum   nostrorum ;   ac   primo   concursu,
the attack   of our   (men) :   and   on the first   encounter.

conjecti   in   fŭgam,   petiverunt   proximas
having been thrown   into   flight,   they sought   the nearest

silvas ;   quos   Labienus   consectatus   equitatu
woods ;   whom   Labienus   having followed   with (his) cavalry

magno   numero   interfecto,   compluribus
(and) a great   number   having been slain.   and very many

captis,   recepit   civitatem,   paucis
having been captured   he received   the state (in submission),   a few

diebus   pòst.   Nam   Germani,   qui   veniebant
days   afterwards.   For   the Germans,   who   were coming

auxilio,   fugâ   Trevirorum   perceptâ
for [as] aid,   the flight   of the Treviri   having been known

contulerunt   sese   domum. Cum   iis   propinqui
betook   themselves   home.   With   them   the relations

Indutiomari,   qui   fuĕrant   auctores   defectionis
of Indutiomaris,   who   had been   the authors   of the revolt

comitati   ĕos   excessere   ex   civitate.
having accompanied   them   departed   from   the state.

Principatus atque imperium tradıtum est Cıngetorıgi,
The leadership and command was assigned to Cıngetorıx.

quem demonstravimus permansisse in
whom [who] we have shown to have [had] remaıned ın

officio ab ınitio
allegiance from the beginning

9. Cæsar, postquam venit ex Menapııs in
   Cæsar after he came from the Menapıı ınto

Treviros constıtuit de duabus causıs transıre Rhenum;
the Trevırı resolved for two reasons to cross the Rhıne.

altera quarum ĕrat, quod (Germanı) misĕrant
the one of whıch was because (the Germans) had sent

auxılia Trevırıs contra se; altera
auxılıaries to the Trevırı against hımself the other (that)

Ambiorix ne haberet receptum ad ĕos. Hıs
Ambıorıx might not have a refuge among them. These

rebus constıtutıs, instıtuit facere pontem
thıngs having been determıned he resolved to make a brıdge

paulum supra eum locum, quo antea trans-
a lıttle above thıs place. at whıch before he had

duxĕrat exercitum Ratione notâ atque
transported the army. The plan having been known and

instıtutâ, opus effıcıtur, paucis dıebus, magno
adopted. the work is completed, in a few days by the great

studıo mılıtum. Fırmo præsidıo relıcto ad
zeal of the soldıers A strong guard having been left at

pontem ın Trevirıs, ne quıs motus orıretur
the brıdge among the Trevırı lest any commotion mıght arıse

subıtò ab iis. transducıt reliquas copıas que
suddenly among them. he leads across the remaınıng forces and

equıtatum Ubii, quı antè dederant obsıdes,
the cavalry The Ubıi who before had gıven hostages

atque venerant in deditionem, mittunt legatos ad
and had come to a surrender send ambassadors to

ĕum causâ purgandı sui,[13] quı doceant,
hım for the purpose of clearıng themselves who may show

neque auxılia missa in Treviros ex
(that) neıther auxılıaries had been sent to the Trevırı from

suâ civitate, neque fidem   læsam ab se;
their state,   nor   faith   (had been) violated by them

petunt atque orant   ut   parcat   sibi,   ne
they beg and   pray that he may spare them.   lest

communi   odio Germanorum innocentes pendant
in (his) common hatred of the Germans the innocent pay

pœnas   pro nocentibus; si velit amplius obsidum,
the penalties for the guilty. if he desires more hostages,

pollicentur dare.   Causâ   cognitâ,
they promise to give (them). The case having been investigated.

Cæsar reperit auxilia   missa esse   ab
Cæsar   finds the auxiliaries to have [had] been sent by

Suevis;   accepit satisfactionem Ubiorum;
the Suevi. he accepts the excuses of the Ubii.   and

perquirit aditus que vias in Suevos.
carefully seeks out the approaches and roads into the Suevi.

10.   Interim   fit certior[14] ab Ubiis, paucis
In the meanwhile he is informed by the Ubii. a few

diebus pòst,   Suevos cogĕre   omnes
days   after (that) the Suevi to collect [were collecting] all

copias in unum locum, atque denuntiare
(their) forces into one place.   and also to warn [were

iis nationibus quæ sunt sub eorum imperio,
warning] these nations who are under their command.

ut mittant auxilia peditatûs que equitatûs.
that they should send auxiliaries of foot [infantry] and of cavalry.

His rebus cognitis   providet rem frumentaria,
These things having been known he provides a corn supply.

deligit idoneum lŏcum castris;   imperat
he selects a suitable place for the camp. he commands

Ubiis, ut deducant pecŏra, que conferant
the Ubii that they drive away the cattle, and collect

omnia sua   ex agris in oppida; sperans
all their (property) from the fields into the towns. hoping

barbăros atque imperitos homines adductos
(that) the barbarous and ignorant men led

inopiâ cibariorum posse   deduci ad
by the want of food to be able [might] (to) be brought int

iniquam   conditionem   pugnandi.   Mandat
an unfavorable   condition   of fighting.   He orders (the Ubii)

ut   mittant   crebros   exploratores   in   Suevos,
that   they send   frequent   scouts   among   the Suevi.

cognoscant   quæque   gerantur (pl.)   apud   ĕos.
that they may learn   whatever   is carried on   among   them.

Illi   faciunt   imperata,   et,   paucis   diebus   intermissis,
They   execute   the orders   and,   a few   days   having passed.

referunt;   "omnes   Suevos,   posteaquam   certiores
report: "all   the Suevi   after (that)   more certain

nuncii   venerant   de   exercitû
messengers [news]   had come   concerning   the army

Romanorum,   recepisse   sese   penitus   ad
of the Romans   to have [had] betaken   themselves   quite   to

extremos   fines   cum omnibus suis copiis   que
the extreme   boundaries   with   all   their   forces   and (those)

sociorum,   quas   coëgissent.   Esse
of (their) allies.   which   they had collected.   To be [There is]

silvam   ibi   infinitæ   magnitudinis,   quæ
a forest   there   of boundless   extent,   which

appellatur   Bacenis,   hanc   pertinere   longè
is called   Bacenis.   this   to extend [extends]   far

introrsus,   et objectam pro   nativo   muro,
into the interior   and   is opposed   for [as]   a natural   wall [defence]

prohibĕre   injuriis   que incursionibus Cheruscos
to check [it checks]   from injuries   and   incursions   the Cherusci

à   Suevis,   que   Suevos   à   Cheruscis;   Suevos
from   the Suevi   and   the Suevi   from   the Cherusci.   the Suevi

constituisse   exspectare adventum Romanorum,
to have [had] resolved   to await   the arrival   of the Romans.

ad   initĭum   ejus   silvæ
at   the entrance   of this   forest

11   Quoniam   perventum est   ad   hunc   lŏcum,
Because   it has come   to   this   place.

videtur   non   esse   alienum   proponere
it seems   not   to be   foreign [improper]   to present (an account)

de   moribus   Galliæ   que   Germaniæ,   et
of   the manners   of Gaul   and   of Germany   and

quo   hæ   nationes   differant   inter
in what (respects)   these   nations   may differ   among

sese.[15]   In   Galliâ   sunt   factiones,
themselves   In   Gaul   (there)   are   factions.

non   solum   in   omnibus   civitatibus   atque
not   only   in   all   the states   and

pagis   que partibus, sed   etiam   pæne   in   singulis
cantons   and   parts.   but   also   almost   in   the several

domibus; que principes earum fâctionum sunt
houses   and   the chiefs of those   factions   are   (those)

qui   existimantur habere,   judicio   eorum
who   are considered   to have.   in the judgement   of them [their

summam auctoritatem; ad   arbitrium que
judgement]   the highest   authority   to   the will   and

judicium quorum,   summa   omnium rerum que
judgement   of whom.   the management   of all   affairs   and

consiliorum   redeat.   Que   id   videtur
counsels   may return   And   this   seems   (to have been.

institutum (esse) antiquitùs   causâ   ejus   rei,
instituted   anciently   for the sake   of this   thing

ne quis ex   plebe   egěret   auxilii (gen.)
(that) no   one   from [of]   the people   should want   assistance

contra potentiorem,   enim   quisque   non   patitur
against   the more powerful.   for   each one   does not   suffer

suos   opprimi   que circumveniri; neque si faciat
his own   to be oppressed   and   overreached :   nor   if   he do

aliter   habeat ullam auctoritatem inter   suos.
otherwise   has he   any   authority   among   his (people).

Hæc ěadem ratio   est in   summâ
This   same   plan [system]   is   in   the management [authority]

totius Galliæ.   Namque omnes civitates divsæ sunt
of all   Gaul   For indeed   all   the states   are divided

in   duas partes.
into   two   parties.

12   Quum Cæsar venit in   Galliam,   Ædui   ěrant
     When   Cæsar   came   into   Gaul.   the Ædui   were

principes alterius factionis,   Sequani   alterius   Hi,
the chiefs   of one   faction.   the Sequani   of the other   These

        quum   valerent   minus   per   se,
[The latter]   as   they prevailed   less   by   themselves,

(quòd   summa   auctoritas   ĕrat   in   Ædui
(because   the supreme   authority   was   among   the Ædui

antiquitùs,   que   magnæ   erant   eorum
anciently [of old].   and   great   (states)   were   their

clientelæ),   adjunxĕrant   Germanos   atque
tributaries).   they [the Sequani] had united   the Germans   and

Ariovistum   sibi,   que   perduxĕrant eos   ad
Ariovistus   to themselves,   and   had brought them over   to

   se   magnis jacturis que pollicitationibus.   Verò
themselves   by great   sacrifices   and   promises.   Indeed

compluribus   secundis   prœliis   factis,   atque
very many   successful   battles   having been fought,   and

omni   mobilitate   Æduorum   interfectâ,
all   the nobility   of the Ædui   having been slain,

   antecesserant   tantum   potentiâ,   ut
they [the Sequani] had surpassed   so much   in power.   that

transducerent ad   se   magnam partem clientium
they brought over   to   themselves   a great   part   of the clients

       ab   Æduis,   que   acciperent   ab   iis
[tributaries]   from   the Ædui,   and   received   from   these

filios   principum   obsides,   et   cogĕrent   jurare
the sons   of the chiefs   as hostages.   and   forced   (them) to swear

publicè,   se   inituros[16]   nihil   consilii
publicly,   (that) they   would enter (into)   nothing   of [no] design

contra   Sequanos ;   et   possiderent   partem
against   the Sequani .   and   they kept   a part

   finitimi   agri   occupatam   per   vim,   que
of the neighboring   territories   seized   by   force,   and

obtinerent   principatum   totius   Galliæ.   Divitiacus
obtained   the sovereignty   of all   Gaul.   Divitiacus

adductus   quâ   necessitate,   profectus   Romam
led   by which [this]   necessity.   having proceeded   to Rome

ad   senatum   causâ   petendi   auxilia,   re
to   the senate   for the purpose   of asking   aid.   the thing

         infectâ   redierat.   Adventu
[purpose]   having been accomplished   had returned   By the arrival

Cæsaris,   commutatione   rerum   factâ,
ıf Cæsar,   a change   of affairs   having been effected,

obsidıbus   reddıtis   Æduis,   veterıbus
the hostages   having been returned   to the Ædui,   old

clıentelıs   restitutis,   nŏvis   comparatis
tributaries   having been restored, (and)   new   having been acquired

per   Cæsarem,   (quòd   ii,   qui aggregaverant
through   Cæsar,   (because   these,   who   had united

se   ad   eorum   amicitiam,   videbant   se
themselves   to   their   friendship,   were seeing   (that) they

uti[17]   meliore   conditione   atque   æquiore
to use [possessed]   a better   condition   and   more equitable

imperio)   reliquis   rebus   eorum   gratiâ
government)   (their) other   affairs,   their   authority

que   dignitate   amplificatâ,   Sequani
and   dignity [influence]   having been enlarged,   the Sequani

dımisserant   principatum,   Remi   successerant
had lost   the sovereignty,   the Remi   succeeded

in   eorum   lŏcum;   quos[18]   quòd
ın   their   place;   whom [who]   as

intelligebatur   adæquare   gratiâ   apud
it was perceived   equaled (the Ædui)   in favor   with

Cæsarem,   ii,   qui   propter   veteres inimicitias
Cæsar,   these,   who   on account of   old   hostilities

potĕrant nullo   modo   conjungi   cum   Æduis,
could   ın no   manner   be united   with   the Ædui,

dicabant   se   in   clientelam   Remis.
were declaring   themselves   under   the protection   of the Remi.

Illı   tuebantur   hos   diligenter;   et   ita tenebant
They   were protecting   them   carefully,   and   so   they held

nŏvam   et   repentè collectam auctoritatem.   Res
a new   and   suddenly   acquired   influence.   Affairs

erat   tum   ĕo   statu,   ut   Ædui   haberentur
were   then   in this   state,   that   the Ædui   were held

longè   principes,   Remi obtinerent secundum
by far   as the principal (people),   the Remi   obtained   the second

lŏcum   dignitatis.
place   of dignity [influence].

13. In omni Galliâ eorum hominum, qui sunt
    In   all   Gaul   of these   men   who   are

aliquo numero atque honore, sunt duo genera.
of any   account   and   honor.   there are   two   classes.

Nam plebs habetur pæne lŏco servorum,
For   the common people   are held   almost   in place   of slaves.

quæ audet nihil per se, et adhibetur nulli
who   dare   nothing   by   themselves,   and   are admitted   to no

concilio. Plerique quum premuntur aut ære alieno,
council.   Many,   when   they are oppressed   either   by   debt,

aut magnitudine tributorum, aut injuriâ
or   by the greatness   of the tributes.   or   by the injury [violence]

potentiorum, dicant sese in servitutem
of the more powerful.   declare   themselves   in   servitude

nobilibus; omnia eadem jura sunt in hos, quæ
to the nobles.   all   the same   rights   are   over   these.   which

dominis in servos. Sed de his duobus
[as]   to masters   over   slaves.   But   of   these   two

generibus, alterum est Druidum, alterum
classes,   the one   is   (that) of the Druids.   the other (that)

Equitum. Illi intersunt divinis rebus,
of the knights.   They (the Druids) are occupied   with sacred   things,

procurant publica ac privata sacrificia, inter-
they have charge   of public   and   private   sacrifices.   (and)   inter-

pretantur religiones Magnus numerus adolescentium
pret   religion.   A great   number   of youths

concurrit ad hos causâ disciplinæ, que ii,
resort   to   these   for the purpose   of training.   and   they

sunt magno honore apud ĕos. Nam
(the Druids)   are   in great   honor   among   them   For

constituunt de ferè omnibus controversiis
they decide   concerning almost   all   controversies (both)

publicis que privatis; et si quod facinus est
public   and   private;   and   if   any   crime   had been

admissum, si cædes facta, si est
committed.   if (any)   murder   had been done.   if   (there)   is

controversia de hæreditate, si de finibus, iidem
a dispute   about   inheritance,   if about   boundaries.   the same

decernunt; que constituunt   præmia   que   pœnas.
decide (it), and determine   the recompenses and punishments.

Si quis,   aut   privatus aut publicus,   non
If any (person). either a private   or   public,   should not

steterit eorum decreto,   interdicunt   sacrificiis.
submit to their decree,   they forbid   (him) the sacrifices.

Hæc est gravissima   pœna   apud   ĕos.   Hi
This is a very great punishment among them.   These

quibus[19] est ita   interdictum, habentur   numero
who are thus interdicted,   are held   in number

impiorum   ac   sceleratorum; omnes decedunt   iis,
of the impious and   wicked   all   avoid   them,

que defugiunt eorum aditum que sermonem; ne
and   flee from   their approach and conversation; lest

accipiant   quid (neut.) incommodi   ex
they might receive   some   (of) evil   from (their)

contagione;   neque   jus   redditur   eis
contagion;   neither (is) justice administered to them

petentibus neque ullus hŏnos communicatur.   Autem
petitioning nor any honor is attributed.   But

omnibus   his   Druidibus unus præest,   qui   habet
over all   these   Druids   one presides, who   has

summam auctoritatem inter êos. Hoc   mortuo,
supreme   authority   among them. This (chief) being dead.

si quis   ex   reliquis excellit dignitate succedit.
if any one from [of] the others excels in dignity he succeeds

At si plures sunt pares deligitur   suffragio
But if many   are equal he is elected by the suffrage

Druidum; etiam nonnunquam contendunt   armis
of the Druids, also   sometimes   they contend   with arms

de principatu.   Hi   considunt in consecrato
for the chieftainship. These (Druids) assemble in a consecrated

lŏco,   certo   tempŏre anni   in   finibus
place. at a certain time of the year in   the territories

Carnutum, quæ regĭo habetur media totius Galliæ.
of the Carnutes, which region is held as the center of all   Gaul.

Huc omnes   undique,   qui habent controversias,
Here all from all sides, who have   disputes,

conveniunt, que parent eorum judiciis que decretis.
assemble, and submit to their judgment and decrees

Disciplina existimatur reperta in Britanniâ,
(This) institution [cu't] is supposed (to have) originated in Britain

atque inde (esse) translata in Galliam. Et
and from thence (to have been) transferred into Gaul And

nunc, qui volunt diligentiùs cognoscere ĕam
now those who wish more perfectly to know this

rem, plerumque proficiscuntur illò causâ
thing [sect] often go there for the purpose

discendi
of learning (it)

14. Druides consueverunt abesse à bello, neque
The Druids are accustomed to be absent from war nor

pendunt tributa unà cum reliquis; (habent vaca-
do they pay tribute together with the rest (they have an exemp-

tionem militiæ, que immunitatem omnium
tion from military service and immunity of [in] all

rerum.) Excitati tantis præmiis, et multi suâ
things) Excited by such advantages and many of their

sponte conveniunt in disciplinam, et mittuntur à
own accord assemble for instruction, and they are sent by

parentibus que propinquis Dicuntur ediscere
parents and relations They are said to learn by heart

magnum numerum versuum ibi Itaque nonnulli
a great number of verses there Therefore many

permanent vicenos annos in disciplinâ; neque
remain twenty years under instruction nor

existimant esse fas mandare ăa
do they consider (it) to be lawful to commit these (things)

litteris, quum utantur Græcis litteris, in ferè
to writing although they use the Greek letters in nearly

reliquis rebus, publicis que privatis rationibus.
(all) other affairs, in public and in private transactions.

Id videtur mihi instituisse de duabus causis;
This seems to me to have been established for two reasons

quòd neque velint disciplinam efferi in
because they neither wish their discipline to be divulged to

volgos,   neque   ĕos   qui discunt,   confisos
the common people   nor   (that) those   who   learn   relying

litteris,   studere   memoriæ minùs.
on writing   should cultivate (their)   memory   the less [too little].

Quod   ferè   accidit   plerisque,   ut   præsidio
Which   ordinarily   happens   to the most   so that   by the aid

litterarum remittant   diligentiam in   perdiscendo,
of writing   they relax (their)   application in   thoroughly learning.

ac   memoriam. In   primis   volunt   persuadere
and   (their) memory. In   particular   they wish   to inculcate

hoc: animas   non   interire,   sed   post   mortem
this (that):   souls   [do] not   (to) die,   but   after   death

transire   ab aliis   ad   alios;[20]   atque   putant
(to) pass   from one (body)   to   another;   and   they think

hôc   maximè   exicitari   ad   virtutem,
(that) by this (men)   greatly   to be [are] excited   to   courage,

mĕtu mortis   neglecto.   Præterea   disputant,
the fear of death   having been disregarded.   Moreover   they discuss,

et tradunt juventuti,   multa,   de   sideribus,
and impart to the youths,   many things,   concerning   the stars,

atque eorum motu,   de   magnitudine   mundi
and their motion,   concerning   the size   of the world

ac terrarum,   de   naturâ   rerum,   de
and the earth,   concerning   the nature   of things,   concerning

vi ac potestate immortalium deorum.
the power and majesty of the immortal gods.

15. Alterum genus est equitum. Hi, quum
The other class is the knights. These, when there

est usus, atque aliquod bellum incidit, (quod ante
is need, and any war occurs, (which before

adventum Cæsaris solebat accidere ferè quotannis,
the arrival of Cæear was wont to happen nearly every year,

uti aut ipsi inferrent injurias, aut
as either they themselves inflicted injuries, or

propulsarent illatas) omnes versantur in
repelled (them) inflicted) all are employed in

bello, atque ut quisque eorum est amplissimus
war, and as any one of them is most noble

genere   que   copiis,   ita   habet   plurimos   ambactos
by family   and   resources.   so   he has   very many   vassals

que   clientes   circum   se.   Noverunt   hanc
and   clients   about   himself [him]   They have known   this

gratiam   que   potentiam   unam.
authority   and   power   only

16.   Omnis   natio   Gallorum   est   admodum   dedita
The whole   nation   of the Gauls   is   very much   given

religionibus,   atque   ob   ĕam   causam,
to religion [superstitions]   and   for   this   reason   (those)

qui   sunt   affecti   gravioribus   morbis,   que   qui
who   are   afflicted   with very severe   diseases   and   (those) who

versantur   in   prœliis   que   periculis,   aut   immolant
are engaged   in   war   and   dangers   either   sacrifice

homines   pro   victimis,   aut   vovent   se
men   for [as]   victims   or   they vow   (that they) themselves

immolaturos ;[21]   que   utuntur   Druidibus
to be about to [will] sacrifice (them).   and   they use   the Druids

(abl.)   administris   ad   ĕa   sacrificia ;   quòd   arbitrantur,
as performers   of   these   sacrifices.   because   they think.

nisi   vita   hominis   reddatur   pro   vitâ
(that)   unless   the life   of a man   be rendered   for   the life

hominis,   numen   immortalium   deorum
of a man,   the divine will [divinity]   of the immortal   gods

non posse   aliter   placari ;   que   habent   sacrificia
could not be   otherwise   appeased   and   they have   sacrifices

ejusdem   generis   instituta   publicè   Alii   habent
of the same   kind   performed   publicly   Others   have

simulacra   immani   magnitudine,   membra   quorum
images   with [of] vast   size   the limbs   of which

contexta   viminibus   complent   vivis   hominibus,
woven   with twigs   they fill   with living   men

quibus   succensis   homines   exanimantur
which   having been set on fire   the men   are put to death

circumventi   flammâ   Arbitrantur   supplicia
by the surrounding   flame.   They think   (that)   the sacrifices

eorum,   qui   sint   comprehensi   in   furto   aut   in
of those,   who   may be   taken   in   theft   or   in

latrocinia,   aut   aliquâ   noxâ   esse   gratiora
robbery   or   in any culpable act to be [are] more acceptable

immortalibus   diis,   sed   quum   copia   ejus
to the immortal   gods   but   when   a supply   of this

generis   deficit,   etiam   descendunt   ad   supplicia
kind   is wanting   also   they descend   to   the sacrifice

innocentium
of the innocent

17   Maximè   colunt   deum Mercurium ·   sunt
They principally   worship   the god   Mercury   there are

plurima simulacra hujus;   ferunt   hunc   inventorem
many   images   of him   they regard   him   (as) the inventor

omnium artium;   hunc ducem   viarum
of all   arts   (they consider) him   the guide   of their journeys

atque itinĕrum;   arbitrantur hunc habere maximam
and   marches   they believe   him   to have   very great

vim   ad   quæstus   pecuniæ que mercaturas (pl).
power for   the acquisition of money and   (for) trade

Post hunc   Apollinem   et   Martem, et
After him   (they worship)   Apollo   and   Mars   and

Jovem,   et   Minervam   De   his   habent   ferè
Jupiter   and   Minerva   About these they have   nearly

ĕandem opinionem,   quam   reliquæ gentes;
the same   opinion   which (as)   other   nations   (that)

Apollinem depellĕre[22] morbos,   Minervam tradĕre
Apollo   drives away   diseases   (that)   Minerva   imparts

initia   operum   atque artificiorum;   Jovem
the principles of crafts   and   of arts   (that)   Jupiter

tenere imperium   cœlestium;   Martem regĕre
holds   the empire of the celestials   (that)   Mars   rules

bella   Huic, quum constituerunt dimicare prœlio,
wars   To him   when   they have resolved   to engage   in battle.

plerumque devovent,   ĕa   quæ   ceperint
they often   vow   these (things) which   they may take

bello; animalia   quæ   superaverint,   capta
in war   the animals which may have survived   (when) captured

immolant,   conferunt   reliquas   res   in
they sacrifice.   they bring together   the remaining   things   into

unum locum. In multis civitatibus licet conspicari
one place. In many states there may be seen

tumulos exstructos harum rerum, consecratis lŏcis.
piles built of these things. in consecrated places.

Neque sæpe accĭdit, ut quisqĭam, religione
Nor does it often happen. that any one, religion

neglectâ, auderet aut occultare capta,
being disregarded. should dare either to conceal the things captured,

apud se, aut tollĕre posita, que
at his home, or to take away the things deposited, and

gravissimum supplicium cum cruciatu constitutum est
the most grievous punishment with torture has been ordained

ei rei.
for this thing.

18. Omnes Galli prædicant se prognatos
All the Gauls assert (that) they are descended

ab Dite patre, que dicunt id
from Dis [Pluto] as progenitor, and they say (that) this

prodĭtum[23] ab Druidibus Ob ĕam causam
has been handed down by the Druids. For this reason

finiunt spatia (pl) omnis tempŏris non
they determine the duration of all time not

numero dierum, sed noctium: et sic observant
by the number of days, but of nights and so observe

natales dies, et initĭa (pl.) mensium et
birth days, and the commencement of the month and

annorum, ut dies subsequatur noctem. In
of years, so that the day may follow the night. In

reliquis institutis vitæ differunt hôc ab ferè
other usages of life they differ in this from nearly all

reliquis, quòd non patiantur suos liberos adire
others. that they do not suffer their children to approach

se palàm, nisi quum adoleverint, ut
them publicly. unless when they may have grown up, so that

possint sustinere munus militiæ; que
they may be able to bear the duty of military service, and

ducunt turpe filium in puerili ætate
they consider (it) shameful (for) a son in boyish age

assistĕre   in   conspectu   patris,   in   publĭco.
to attend   in   the presence   of his father.   in   public.

19. Quantas pecunĭas   vĭrı   acceperunt   ab
As much   money   (as) the husbands   may receive   from

uxorıbus,   nomıne,   dotıs,   tantas,   æstimatıone
wives.   in the name.   of dower.   so much.   an estimate

factâ,   communıcant cum dotıbus   ex   suis
having been made,   they join   with   the dower   from their own

bonis. Omnıs hujus pecunıæ   ratīo   conjunctim
goods.   Of all   this   money   an account   in common

habetur, que   fructus   servantur;   uter   ĕorum
is kept,   and   the profits   are reserved.   whoever   of them

superârit   vitâ,   pars utrıusque cum fructıbus
may have survived   in life.   the part   of both   with   the profits

superiorum   tempŏrum (pl.) pervenit ad ĕum.   Viri
to the previous   time   reverts   to   him.   Husbands

habent potestatem vıtæ que nĕcis   in   uxores,
have   the power   of life and death against [over]   the wives,

sicuti   in   libĕros.   Et quum   pater-
as well as   against [over]   the children.   And   when   the fatheı

famılıas natus   ıllustrıore   lŏco   decessit,
of a family   born   in a more illustrious   place [rank]   has died,

ejus propınquı conveniunt, et   si   res   venit
his   relations   assemble,   and   if   the event   has come

in   suspıcıonem, habent de   morte   quæstionem
into   suspicion.   they hold about   his death   an examination

de uxorıbus   in   servilem modum,[24] et   si   est
of   his wives   after   the slave   manner   and   if   it is

compertum interfıcıunt   excrucıatas igni atque
discovered   they kill   (them)   tortured   by fire   and

omnıbus tormentıs.   Funera,   pro   cultu
all   torments.   The funerals,   for   the civilizatioı

Gallorum, sunt magnifica et sumptuosa, que omnia,
of the Gauls,   are   magnificent and   costly.   and   all.

quæ arbıtrantur   fuisse   cordi[25] vivis,   inferunt
which   they judge   to have been   dear   to the living,   they casł

in   ignem, etīam   animalia; ac   paulò supra hanĉ
into   the fire.   even   animals,   and   a little before   this

memoriam,　　　servi　et　clientes,　quos　　　constabat
memory [time],　slaves　and　clients,　whom　it was understood

　dilectos esse　　　ab　iis,　cremabantur　　unà,
to have [had] been beloved　by　them,　were burnt　　together

　　　　justis　funeribus　　　confectis.
(with them),　the proper　funeral rites　having been performed.

20. Quæ　civitates　　　　existimantur administrare
　　　Those　states　(which)　are believed　to administer

suam　rem publicam (sing.)　commodiùs,　　habent
their　public affairs　　more advantageously,　have

sanctum　legibus　　　si　quis　　acceperit
established　by law　(that)　if　any one　shall have heard

　quid　à　finitimis　de　re publicâ　rumore　aut
any thing　from　neighbors　about　the state　by rumor　or

famâ,　uti　　deferat　　ad magistratum,　neve
by report,　that　he should bring (it)　to　the magistrate,　nor

communicet　cum quo　alio;　quòd　cognitum est
communicate　with　any　other,　because　it has been known

　　　sæpe　temerarios　atque　imperitos　homines
(that)　often　rash　　and　inexperienced　men

　terreri　falsis　rumoribus,　et　impelli
to be [are] terrified　by false　rumors,　and　to be [are] impelled

ad facinus,　et　capĕre consilium　de　summis
to　crime,　and　to form　plans　about　the most important

rebus.　Magistratus　occultant　quæ　visa sunt　que
things.　The magistrates　conceal　what　seem best　and

produnt multitudini,　quæ　judicavĕrint esse ex　usu
disclose　to the people,　what　they judge　to be　of　use.

Non　conceditur　loqui　de　re publicâ　nisi
It is not　allowed　to speak　concerning　a public matter　unless

per　concilium.
in　the council.

21. Germani　differunt multùm　ab　hâc　consue-
　　　The Germans　differ　much　from　these　cus-

tudine; nam habent　neque Druides,　qui　præsint
toms,　for　they have　neither　Druids,　who　preside over

divinis rebus; neque　student　sacrificiis　Ducunt
sacred　things;　nor　do they regard　sacrifices　They hold

ĕos   solos   numĕro   deorum,   quos   cernunt,
those   only   in the number   of the gods,   whom   they perceive,

et   quorum   opibus (pl.)   juvantur   apertè,
and   by whose   assistance   they are benefitted   obviously,

Solem,   et Vulcanum,   et   Lunam;   acceperunt
as the Sun,   and   Vulcan, (fire)   and   the Moon ;   they are heard

reliquos   ne   famâ   quidem. Omnis   vita
(of) the others   not   by report   even.   All   (their)   life

consistit   in venationibus (pl.)   atque   in   studĭis
is employed   in   hunting   and   in   the pursuits

militaris   rei (sing);   ab parvulis   student
of military   affairs,   from   children   they accustom themselves

labori   ac   durĭtĭæ.   Qui   permanserunt   diutissimè
to labor   and   hardships.   Those who   have remained   the longest

impuberes,   ferunt maximam laudem   inter   sŭos.
chaste,   obtain   the greatest   praise   among   their (people)

Putant   hôc   staturam   ali,
(They) believe (that)   by this   the statue   to be [is] increased,

hôc   vires   ali,   que   nervos
by this   the strength   to be [is] increased.   and   the nerves

confirmari.   Verò   habuisse   notitiam
to be [are] strengthened.   Indeed   to have had   the knowledge

feminæ   intra   vicesimum annum habent   in
of a woman   within [under]   the twentieth   year   they hold   among

turpissimis   rebus;   cujus   rĕi   est   nulla
the most shameful   things,   of this   thing   there is   no

occultatio,   et   quòd   perluuntur   promiscuè   in
concealment,   both   because   they bathe   promiscuously   in

fluminibus,   et utuntur pellibus,   aut parvis tegimentis
the rivers,   and   use   skins,   or   small   coverings

(abl.) renonum,   magnâ parte   corpŏris   nudâ.
of deer hides,   a great   part   of the body   being naked.

22.   Non   student agri culturæ;   que   major
They do not   attend   to agriculture,   and   the greater

pars   ĕorum   victûs consistit   in   lacte   et   casĕo
part   of their   food   consists   in [of]   milk   and   cheese

et   carne   Neque habet quisquam   certum   mŏdum
and   meat.   Nor   has   any one   a fixed   portion

agri,   aut   proprios   fines;   sed   magistratus ac
of land,   or   proper   boundaries.   but   the magistrates and

principes,   in   singŭlos annos,   attribŭunt   quantum
chiefs,   in   each   year.   assign   as much

   agri,   et   quo   lŏco   visum est,   gentibus   que
(of) land, and in what place it seems best, to the tribes   and

cognationibus hominum,   qui   coierunt   unà,
to the families   of men.   who   may have united   together,

atque anno pòst   cogunt   transire   aliò
and   the year after they compel (them) to go   somewhere else.

Adferunt multas causas   ejus   rei (gen); ne   capti
They offer   many   reasons for this thing.   lest captivated

assiduâ   consuetudine   commutent   studium
by continued   custom   they may change (their)   zeal

   gerendi   belli   agri culturâ;   ne   student
of [for] waging   war   for agriculture.   lest   they may be eager

parare   latos   fines, que   potentiores   expellant
to acquire extensive estates, and   the more powerful   may expel

humiliores   possessionibus;   ne   ædificent
the more humble   from possessions.   lest   they may build

accuratiùs ad vitandos frigŏra atque æstus; ne qua
with more care for avoiding   cold   and   heat,   lest any

cupiditas pecuniæ oriatur,   ex quâ re factiones
desire   of money   may arise, from which thing   factions

que   dissensiones   nascuntur;   ut   contineant
and   dissensions   originate.   that   they may keep

   plebem   æquitate   animi, quum   quisque
the common people   in peace   of mind,   since   each one

videat   sŭas   opes   æquari   cum
may see (that) his own   means   to be [are] equaled   with

potentissimis.
the most powerful.

23. Est   maxima   laus civitatibus,   habere
    It is   the greatest praise   to the states,   to have

solitudines quàm latissimas[26]   circum   se,
deserts   as   (most) wide (as possible) about   themselves,

finibus   vastatis.   Existimant   hoc
their frontiers   having been laid waste.   They consider   this

proprium   virtutis,   finitimos   expulsos
a peculiar   (evidence)   of valor,   (that) their neighbors   expelled

agris   cedĕre,   neque   quemquam
from (their) lands   (to) abandon (them),   nor   (that)   any

(sing)   audere   consistĕre   se   prope.
          (to) dare   (to) settle   themselves   near.

Simul   arbitrantur   se
At the same time   they think   (that)   they themselves

fŏre   tutiores   hôc,   timŏre   repentinæ
to be about to [will] be   more safe   by this,   the fear   of sudden

incursionis   sublato.   Quum   civitas   aut
raids   having been removed.   When   the state   either

defendit   bellum   illatum,   aut   infert;
repels   war   waged against it,   or   wages war;

magistratus   deliguntur,   qui   præsint   ĕi   bello,
magistrates   are chosen,   who   preside   over this   war,

ut   habeant   potestatem   vitæ   que   nĕcis.
so that   they may have   the power   of life   and   death.

In   pace   est   nullum communis magistratus,   sed
In   peace   there is   no   general   magistrate,   but

principes   regionum   atque   pagorum   dicunt
the chiefs   of the provinces   and   cantons   say [administer]

jus   inter   sŭos,   que minŭunt controversias.
justice   among   their (people),   and   settle   disputes.

Habent latrocinĭa nullam infamiam, quæ   fiunt
They hold   robberies   as no   disgrace,   which   are comitted

extra   fines   cujusque   civitatis; atque   prædicant
beyond   the boundaries   of any   state;   and   they assert

ĕa   fieri   causâ   exercendæ
(that)   this   to be [is] done   for the purpose   of exercising

juventutis;   ac   minuendæ   desidiæ.   Atque   ubi
the youth;   and   of preventing   sloth.   And   when

quis   ex   principibus   dixit   in   concilĭo,   "se
any one   from [of]   the chiefs   has said   in   council,

fŏre   ducem,   ut   qui   velint
"he to be about to [will] be   the leader,   that   those who   may wish

sequi   profiteantur;"   ĭi   qui   probant   et
to follow   let them volunteer;"   those   who   approve   both

causam   et   homĭnem consurgunt,   que pollĭcentur
the cause   and   the man   rise up,   and   promise

suum auxĭlium, atque collaudantur ab multĭtudine
their   aid,   and   are applauded   by   the multitude.

Qui   ex   iĭs,   non secuti sunt,   ducuntur
Those   of   them,   (who)   have not followed,   are reckoned

ĭn   numĕro   desertorum   ac   prodĭtorum ,   que
ĭn   the number   of deserters   and   of traitors ,   and

postĕa   fides   abrogatur   iĭs   omnium
afterwards   credit   is taken away   from them   ĭn all

rerum (gen.)   Putant   non   fas   violare
things   They consider   ĭt not   lawful   to injure

hospĭtes ;   qui   venerunt ad   ĕos   de quâque
their guests ,   those who   have come   to   them   for   any

causâ,   prohibent   ab   injuriâ, que   habent
reason.   they defend   from   harm,   and   they hold   (them)

sanctos ;   domus   omnium patent   iĭs,   que
inviolable ;   the houses   of all   are open   to them,   and

victus   communicatur.
food   is shared   (with them).

24. Ac   antĕa   fuit   tempus,   quum   Galli
And   formerly (there)   was   a time,   when   the Gauls

superarent Germanos   virtute,   et   ultro
excelled   the Germans   in bravery,   and   of their own accord

inferrent (imp. subj.)   bella   ac   propter
were waging   war   and   on account of

multitudĭnem   hominum,   que   inopĭam   agri
the multitude   of men,   and   the scarcity   of land

mittĕrent (imp. subj.)   colonĭas   trans   Rhenum.
they were sending   colonies   across   the Rhine.

Itaque   Volcæ   Tectosages occupârunt   ĕa   lŏca
Therefore   the Volcæ   Tectosages   occupied   those   places

Germaniæ,   quæ sunt   fertilissima,   atque consederunt
of Germany,   which are   the most fruitful,   and   settled

ĭbi,   circum   Hercyniam   silvam,   (quam   video
there,   about   the Hercynian   forest,   [which   I perceive

esse   notam   Eratostheni   et   quibusdam
to have been [was]   known   to Eratosthenes   and   some other

Græcis   famâ;   quam   illi   appellant Orcyniam).
Greeks   by report,   which   they   call   Orcynia).

Quæ   gens   continet   se   iis   sedibus
Which [This]   nation   maintains   itself   in these   settlements

ad   hoc   tempus,   que   habet   summam   opinionem
to   this   time,   and   has   the highest   reputation

justitiæ   et   bellicæ   laudis;   que   nunc
of [for] justice   and   (of) warlike   praise,   and   now

permanent   in   eâdem   inopiâ,   egestate,
they remain   in   the same   privation [want],   poverty [need],

patientiâ,   quâ   Germani;   utuntur
(and)   patience,   in which [as]   the Germans,   they use

ĕodem   victu   et   cultu   corpŏris.   Propinquitas
the same   food   and   care   of the body.   The proximity

provinciæ   Gallis,   et   notitia   transmarinarum
of (our) province   to the Gauls,   and   the knowledge   of transmarine

rerum   largitur (sing.)   multa   ad   copiam
things   provides   many (things)   for   supply [wealth]

atque   usus.   Paulatim   assuefacti   superari,   que
and   use.   By degrees   accustomed   to be overcome,   and

victi   multis   prœliis   ipsi   ne   se
conquered   in many   battles   they   do not   themselves

quidem[27]   comparant   virtute   cum   illis.
indeed   compare   in valor   with   them [the Germans].

25.   Latitudo   hujus   Hercyniæ   silvæ,   quæ
The breadth   of this   Hercynian   forest,   which

demonstrata est   suprà,   patet   iter   novem   dierum
has been mentioned   above,   extends   a journey   of nine   days

expedito   Enim   potest   non   finiri   aliter,
to an active (man)   For   it can   not   be bounded   otherwise,

neque   noverunt   mensuras   itinerum.   Oritur
nor   do they know   measures   of roads.   It begins

ab   finibus   Helvetiorum,   et   Nemetum,   et
at   the frontiers   of the Helvetii,   and   of the Nemetes,   and

Rauracorum,   que   rectâ   regione   flumĭnis
of the Rauraci,   and   in a straight   direction (along)   the river

Danuvi,   pertinet   ad   fines   Dacorum   et
Danube,   it extends   to   the territories   of the Daci   and

Anartium; hinc flectit se sinistrorsus diversis
of the Anartes: thence it bends itself to the left in different

regionibus à flumĭne, que attingit fines
directions from the river. and it touches the boundaries

multarum gentium propter magnitudinem. Neque
of many nations on account of the great extent. Nor

est quisquam hujus Germanĭæ, qui dicat
is (there) any one of this (part) of Germany, who may say

(aut audisse) aut adisse
(that) (either to have [he had] heard) or to have [had] gone

ad initium ejus silvæ, quum processerit
to the beginning of this forest, though he may have proceeded

iter sexaginta dierum; aut acceperit ex quo
a journey of sixty days; or may have heard from what

lŏco oriatur. Constat multa genera
place it may take its origin It is certain (that) many kinds

ferarum nasci in ĕa, quæ sint non visa in
of wild beasts are born in it, which are not seen in

reliquis lŏcis; ex quibus quæ maximè differant
other places: from which (those) that greatly differ

ab cæteris, et videantur prodenda
from others, and may seem worthy to be handed down

memoriæ, sunt hæc.
to memory, are these.

26. Est bos figurâ cervi, à mediâ
There is an ox [animal] in the shape of a stag, from the mid

fronte cujus, inter aures, unum cornu existit
forehead of which, between the ears. a horn grows

excelsius, que măgis directum his cornibus,
higher, and more straight (than) these horns,

quæ sunt nota nobis. Ab summo ejus rami
which are known to us. From the top of this branches

diffunduntur latè sicut palmæ. Natura
are spread out broadly like palm (leaves) The nature

femĭnæ que maris est eădem, eădem forma
of the female and male is the same, the same form

que magnitudo cornuum.
and size of the horns.

27. Sunt   item,   quæ appellantur alces.
There are   also (animals),   which   are called   elks.

Figura   harum,   et   variĕtas   pellium   est
The shape   of these,   and   the variety   of the skins   is

consimĭlis   capris,   sed   magnitudĭne   antecedunt
very like   to goats,   but   in size   they surpass

paulo;   que   sunt   multilæ cornĭbus,   et   habent
a little.   and   they are   devoid   of horns,   and   (they) have

cɪura   sine   nodis   que   artɪculis;   neque
legs   without   articulations   and   joints;   neither

procumbunt   causâ   quietis, neque   si   afflictæ
do they lie down   for the purpose   of rest,   nor,   if   afflicted

quo   casu   concidĕrint,   possunt   erɪgĕre
by any   accident   they may fall down,   can they   raise

sese   aut sublevare. Arbores sunt   his   pro
themselves   or   get up.   The trees   are   to them   for [as]

cubilĭbus;   applɪcant   se   ad   ĕas,   atque
beds,   they support   themselves   against   these,   and

ita   reclɪnatæ   modò   paulùm   capiunt   quietem;
so   reclined   merely   a little   they take   rest.

quum   ex   vestigĭis   quarum   animadversum est
when   from   the footsteps   of which [these]   it has been discovered

à   venatoribus,   quò   consuevĕrint   recipĕre
by   the hunters,   where   they have been accustomed   to betake

se,   aut   subrŭunt   omnes   ĕo
themselves,   either   they undermine   all   (the trees)   in that

lŏco,   à radicĭbus,   aut accidunt   arbores tantum   ut
place,   at   the roots,   or   they cut   the trees   so   that

summa   specĭes   earum stantium relinquatur.
the total [mere]   appearance   of them   standing   may be left.

Hùc   quum   ex consuetudine   reclinaverint   se,
Here   when   by   custom   they have reclined   themselves,

affligunt   infirmas arbores   pondĕre,   atque ipsæ
they overturn   the weak   trees   by (their) weight,   and   they

concɪdunt   unà.
fall down   together (with them).

28. Est   tertium   genus   eorum,   qui
There is   a third   kind   of these (animals).   which

appellantur uri. Hi sunt magnitudine paulo
are called the wild ox. These are in size a little

infrà elephantos, specīe et colore et
below the elephant, with the appearance and color and

figurâ tauri. Forum vis est magna, et
form of the bull. Their strength is great, and (their)

velocitas magna; parcunt neque homĭni neque feræ
speed great: they spare neither man nor beast

quam conspexĕrint; hos interficiunt captos
that they may have seen; these they kill captured

studiose foveis. Adolescentes durant se
with much zeal in pits. The youths harden themselves

hôc labore; atque exercent hôc genĕre
by this task; and they exercise by this kind

venationis; et qui interfecerunt plurimos
of hunting; and (those) who have killed the most

ex his, ferunt magnam laudem, cornibus
from [of] these, obtain great praise. the horns

relatis in publicum quæ sint
having been brought into public which may be (as)

testimonĭo. Sed ne parvuli quidem excepti
evidence. But not the young even (when) taken

possunt assuescĕre ad homĭnes, et
[captured] can be accustomed to men. and

mansuefieri. Amplĭtudo et figura et specĭes
tamed. The size and shape and appearance

cornŭum differt multum à cornibus nostrorum
of (their) horns differs much from the horns of our

bŏum. Hæc studiosè conquisita,
oxen. These having been carefully sought.

circumcludunt ab labris argento, atque
they enclose (them) from [on] the brims with silver, and

utuntur in amplissîmis epŭlis pro
use (them) in (their) most splendid feasts for

pocŭlis.
cups.

29. Cæsar postquam compĕrit per Ubios
Cæsar after he discovered through the Ubian

exploratores,   Suevos   recepisse   sese   in
scouts,   (that)   the Suevi   had withdrawn   themselves   into

silvas,   verĭtus   inopĭam   frumenti,   (quòd,   ut
the forests,   fearing   a scarcity   of corn,   (because.   as

demonstravimus   suprà,   omnes   Germani   student
we have shown   above.   all   the Germans   attend

minimè   agri culturæ),   constituit   non   progredi
very little   to agriculture),   he resolved   not   to proceed

longiùs;   sed   ne   tolleret   omnino   metum
further.   but   that   he might not take away   altogether   the fear

sŭi   reditûs   barbăris,   atque ut   tardaret
of his   return   from the barbarians.   and   that   he might retard

eorum   auxilia,   reducto   exercitu,   rescindit
their   auxiliaries,   having led back   the army.   he breaks down

ultimam   partem   pontis,   quæ   contingebat
the farthest   part   of the bridge.   which   was touching

ripas   Ubiorum,   in   longitudinem   ducentorum
the shores   of the Ubii,   to   the length   of two hundred

pedum,   atque   in   extremo   ponte (abl.)
feet,   and   on   the extreme [end]   (of the) bridge

constituit   turrim quatŭor tabulatorum,   que   ponit
he constructs   a tower   of four   stories.   and   places

præsidium   duodĕcim   cohortium   causâ   tuendi
a guard   of twelve   cohorts   for the purpose   of defending

pontis,   que   firmat   ĕum   lŏcum   magnis
the bridge.   and   strengthens   this   place   with great

munitionibus.   Præfecit   ĕi   loco   que   præsidio,
fortifications.   He placed over   this   place   and   garrison

C. Volcatium Tullum, adolescentem;   ipse,   quum
C.   Volcatius   Tullus.   a young man :   he himself.   when

frumenta incipĕrent maturescĕre,   profectus   ad
the corn   began   to ripen.   having set out   to

bellum   Ambiorigis,   per   Arduennam
the war   of [with] Ambiorix.   through   the Arduennian [Ardennes]

silvam,   quæ   est   maxĭma   totius   Galliæ,   atque
forest,   which   is   the largest   of all   Gaul,   and

pertinet   ab   ripis   Rheni   que   finibus
extends   from   the shores   of the Rhine   and   the territories

Trevirorum ad Nervios. que patet ampliùs
of the Treviri to the Nervii, and reaches more than

quingentis millibus in longitudinem; præmittit
five hundred miles in length, he sends forward

L. Minucium Basilium, cum omni equitatu, si
L. Minucius Basilius, with all the cavalry, if

possit proficĕre quid celeritate itinĕris,
he may be able to gain anything by quickness of march,

atque opportunitate tempŏris; monet ut
and by the favorableness of the time, he warns that

prohibeat ignes fieri in castris (pl.), ne
he should prohibit fires to be made in the camp, lest

qua significatio fiat prŏcul ejus
any intimation [sign] might be made at a distance of his

adventûs; dicit sese subsequi confestim.
coming; he says that he himself to [would] follow speedily.

30. Basilius facit ut imperatum est; itinere
Basilius does as he was commanded, the march

confecto celerĭter, que contra opinionem
having been performed quickly, and contrary to the opinion

omnium, deprehendit multos inopinantes in agris;
of all, he captures many unaware in the fields;

eorum indicĭo contendit ad Ambiorigem ipsum,
by their information he marches to Ambiorix himself,

in lŏco quo dicebatur esse cum paucis
in the place in which he was said to be with a few

equitibus. Fortuna potest multum, quum in
horsemen. Fortune can do much, not only in

omnibus rebus, tum in militari re (sing.),
all things, but also in military affairs.

Nam sicut accidit magno casu, ut incideret
For as it happened by great chance, that he fell

in ipsum incautum atque imparatum, que ejus
on him off his guard and unprepared, and his

adventus videretur ab hominĭbus priùs quàm
arrival was seen by the men before (that)

afferretur famâ ac nunciis; sic fuit
it was brought by report and messengers, so it was

magnæ fortunæ, omni militari instrumento, quod
(of) great   fortune,   all   the military   implements,   that

habebat   circum   se   erepto,   rhedis
he was having   about   him   having been seized,   his chariots

que   equis   comprehensis,   ipsum
and   horses   having been captured,   (that)   he himself

effugĕre   mortem.   Sed hoc   factum est   ĕo
should escape   death.   But   this   was effected   in this

quòd ædificĭo   circumdato   silvâ
(manner)   for   the house   (having been) surrounded   by a wood

ut domicilĭa Gallorum ferè sunt, qui causâ
as   the dwellings   of the Gauls   generally   are,   who   for the sake

vitandi   æstûs,   plerumque petunt propinquitates
of avoiding   the heat,   often   seek   the vicinity

silvarum   ac fluminum, ejus comites que familiares
of woods   and   rivers,   his   attendants   and   friends

sustinuerunt   paulisper   vim   nostrorum equitum
sustained   for a little while   the force   of our   cavalry

in angusto   lŏco.   His   pugnantibus (abl.
in   a narrow   place.   (While) these (are)   fighting,

abs.), quidam   ex   sŭis   intulit illum   in
some one   from [of]   his (men)   placed   him   on

equum; silvæ texerunt fugientem; sic fortuna
a horse;   the woods   covered   (him)   fleeing;   thus   fortune

valuit multum,   et   ad   subeundum pericŭlum,   et
availed   much,   botn   for   encountering   danger.   and

ad vitandum.
for   avoiding (it).

31. Ne Ambiorix non conduxĕrit sŭas copĭas
Whether   Ambiorix   did not   assemble   his   forces

judicio, quòd existimavĕrit   non   dimicandum[28]
on purpose,   because   he thought   (it) not   to [must not] be engaged

prœlio; an   exclusus   tempŏre, et   prohibitus
in battle,   or   he had been cut off by   time,   and   had been

fuerit   repentino   adventu   equitum,   quum
prevented   by the sudden   arrival   of the cavalry.   when

credĕret   reliqŭum   exercitum   subsequi,
he believed   (that) the remainder   of the army   was following

est   dubium,   sed   certè   nunclis   dimissis
is   doubtful,   but   certainly   messengers   having been sent

clàm   per   agros   jussit
secretly   through   the fields   [country]   he ordered

quemque   consulĕre   sibi;   quorum   pars
that each one   should take care   of himself;   of whom   a part

profugit   in   Arduennam   silvam,
fled   into   the Arduennan   [Ardunes]   forest,

pars   in   continentes   paludes.   Qui
a part   into   the continuous   marshes.   (Those) who

fuerunt   proxĭmi   Oceanum,   hi   occultaverunt
were   nearest   the Ocean,   these   hid

sese   in   insulis,   quas   æstus
themselves   in   the islands,   which   the tides

consuêrunt   efficĕre.   Multi   egressi   ex   sŭis
are accustomed   to form.   Many   having emigrated   from   their

finibus   crediderunt   se   que   omnia
territories   confided [consigned]   themselves   and   all

sŭa   alienissĭmis.   Catuvolcus   rex   dimidĭæ
their (property)   to entire strangers   Catuvolcus   king   of the half

partis   Eburonum   qui   inierat   consilĭum
part   of the Eburones   who   had   entered into counsel

unà   cum   Ambiorĭge,   jam   confectus   ætate,
together   with   Ambiorix.   now   worn out   with age,

quum   posset   non   ferre   laborem   aut   belli   aut
since   he could   not   bear   the fatigue   either   of war   or

fugæ,   detestatus   Ambiorĭgem   omnĭbus
of flight,   having cursed   Ambiorix   with all   (kinds of)

precĭbus   qui   fuisset   auctor   ejus   consilĭi,
imprecations   who   was   the author   of this   plan [design],

exanimavit   se   taxo,   (cujus   est
killed   himself   by yew (leaves).   (of which (tree)   there is

magna   copĭa   in   Gallĭâ que   Germanĭâ).
a great   abundance   in   Gaul   and   in Germany).

32. Segni   que Condrusi,   ex   gente   et
The Segni   and   Condrusi,   from [of]   the nation   and

numĕro   Germanorum,   qui   sunt   inter   Eburones
the number   of the Germans,   who   are   between   the Eburones

que Treviros, miserunt legatos ad Cæsarem,
and Treviri, sent ambassadors to Cæsar,

oratum "ne ducĕret se in numĕro
to pray " that he would not place them in the numbe

hostium, neve judicaret causam omnium
of enemies, nor should he 'udge (that) the cause of all

Germanorum, qui essent citra Rhenum esse
the Germans, who might be on this side of the Rhine to be

unam; se cogitâsse nihil
[was] one [the same], (that) they to have [had] thought nothing

de bello, misisse nulla auxilia
about war. (that) they to have [had] sent no auxiliaries

Ambiorĭgi." Cæsar, re exploratâ
to Ambiorix." Cæsar, the thing [matter] having been investigated

quæstione captivorum, imperavit si qui
by the questioning of the prisoners, commanded (that) if any

Eburones convenissent ad ĕos ex fugâ ut
Eburones had come to them from flight that

reducerentur ad se. Si fecissent ita,
they should be brought back to him. If they did so,

negavit se violaturum eorum
he disavowed (that) himself [he] about to [would] harm their

fines. Tum copiis distributis in
territories. Then (his) forces having been distributed into

tres partes, contŭlit impedimenta omnium legionum
three parts, he removed the baggage of all the legions

Aduatucam. Id est nomen castelli. Hoc est
to Aduatuca. This is the name of a fortress. This is

ferè in mediis finibus Eburonum, ubi
nearly in the middle (of the) territories of the Eburones, where

Titurius atque Aurunculeius consederunt causâ
Titurius and Aurunculeius had encamped for the purpose

hiemandi. Cæsar probat hunc lŏcum quum
of wintering. Cæsar approves this place not only

reliquis rebus, tum quòd munitiones
for other things, but also because the fortifications

superioris anni manebant integræ, ut
of the preceding year were remaining entire. (so) that

sublevaret   laborem   mīlitum :   reliquit quatuor-
he might relieve   the labor   of the soldiers;   he left   the

decĭmam   legionem   præsidĭo   impedimentis unam
fourteenth   legion   for [as] a guard   to the baggage   one

ex   īis   tribus,   quas proximè   conscrĭptas,
of   those   three.   which   lately   (having been) enrolled,

transduxerat   ex Italiâ.   Præfecit   ĕi   legioni
he had brought over   from   Italy.   He appointed over   this   legion

que   castris,   Q. Tullium Ciceronem, que attribuit
and   the camp,   Q.   Tullius   Cicero.   and   assigned

          ducentos   equites.
(him)   two hundred   horsemen.

33. Exercĭtu   partito,   jubet   T. Labienum
    The army   having been divided,   he orders   T.   Labienus

proficisci   cum   tribus   legionibus   ad   versùs
to march   with   three   legions   in   the direction

Oceanum,   in   ĕas partes quæ attingunt Menapios.
of the Ocean,   into   these   parts which   touch on   the Menapii

Mittit   C. Trebonium cum   pari   numĕro legionum
He sends   C.   Trebonius   with   a like   number   of legions

ad   depopulandum   ĕam regionem,[29]   quæ   adjacet
for   to be laid [laying] waste   this   district,   which   borders on

Aduatucis.   Ipse   cum   tribus   reliquis
the Aduatuci.   (He) himself   with   the three   remaining (legions)

constituit   ire   ad   flumen   Scaldim,   quod
resolves   to go   to   the river   Scaldis [Scheldt].   which

influit   in   Mosam,   que   extremas partes
flows   into   the Mosa [Meuse],   and   (to) the extreme   parts

Arduennæ,   quò   audiebat
of the Arduennian [Ardennes] (forest),   whither   he heard

Ambiorĭgem   profectum   cum   paucis   equitibus.
Ambiorix   had gone   with   a few   horsemen.

Discedens confirmat   sese   reversurum
On departing   he promises (that) (he) himself   about to [would] return

post   septĭmum   diem; ad   quam diem   sciebat
after   the seventh   day,   on   which   day   he was knowing

    frumentum   deberi   ĕi   legioni,   quæ
(that)   corn   to be [was] due   to this   legion,   which

relinquebatur in præsidĭo. Horatur Labienum que
was left   in   garrison.   He exhorts   Labienus   and

Trebonĭum   revertantur   ad ĕam diem, si
Trebonius   that they should return   on this day,   it

possint facĕre   commodo   rei publicæ, ut,
they could do (it) to the advantage of the republic, that,

concilĭo   communicato   rursus, que rationibus
counsel   having been communicated mutually, and the plans

hostium   exploratis,   possint capĕre
of the enemy having been ascertained. they might take [adopt]

aliud initĭum   belli.
another start [beginning] of [in] the war.

34.   Erat, ut demonstravimus suprà, nulla certa
     There was, as we have shown above, no fixed

mănus, non præsidĭum, non oppĭdum, quod
body of men, not a garrison, not a town, that

defendĕret se armis, sed multitudo dispersa in
could defend itself by arms, but a multitude scattered in

omnes partes. Ubi cuique aut abdĭta vallis, aut
all parts. Where to any one either a hidden valley. or

silvestris lŏcus, aut impedita pălus, offerebat
a woody place, or a difficult swamp. was offering

aliquam spem præsidĭi aut salutis, consedĕrat.
some hope of protection or of safety. he had settled

Hæc lŏca ĕrant nota vicinitatibus, que res
These places were known to the neighbors. and the thing

      requirebat magnam diligentĭam, non in
[condition] was requiring great care not in

tuendâ summâ (abl.) exercitûs (enim nullum
protecting the total of the army (for no

periculum, universis, potĕrat accidĕre ab
danger, to the whole, could happen from (them,

perterrĭtis ac dispersis), sed in conservandis singŭlis
terrified and dispersed), but in preserving individual

militibus; quæ res tamen ex parte pertinebat
soldiers; which thing however in part was appertaining

ad salutem exercitûs. Nam et cupidĭtas prædæ
to the safety of the army. For both the desire of booty

evocabat   multos   longĭus, ac   silvæ   incertĭs
was enticing   many   too far   and   the woods   by their uncertain

que occultis itinerĭbus   prohibebant   confertos
and   hidden   paths   were preventing   (them)   collected

adire.   Si   vellet   confici   negotĭum,   que
to advance.   If   he wished   to finish   the business,   and

interfici   stirpem   sceleratorum   homĭnum,
to exterminate   a race   of infamous   men,

plures   mănus   dimittendæ,   que   milĭtes
great many   bands   to [must] be sent out,   and   the soldiers

diducendi ĕrant;   si   vellet   continere   manipŭlos
to [must] be detached;   if   he desired   to keep   the companies

ad   signa,   ut   instituta   ratĭo et   consuetudo
to   the ensigns,   as   the constituted   order and   custom

Romani   exercitûs   postulabat,   lŏcus   ipse   ĕrat
of the Roman   army   was demanding,   the place   itself   was

præsidio   barbăris;   neque   dĕerat
(for) a protection   to the barbarians;   neither   was there wanting

audacĭa   singŭlis   insidiandi   ex   occulto,   et
the daring   to individuals   of ambushing   in   secret,   and

circumveniendi   dispersos.   At   in   difficultatibus
of surrounding   dispersed (soldiers).   But   in   difficulties

ejusmodi   quantum   diligentiâ   potĕrat   provideri
of this nature   whatever   by diligence   could   be provided

providebatur;   ut   potiùs   aliquid   omitteretur
was provided: so that   rather   something   might be omitted

in   nocendo,   etsi   animi   omnium
in   injuring (the enemy),   although   the minds   of all

ardebant   ad ulciscendum,   quàm   nocere-
were burning   to   be avenged   than   that (the enemy) might

tur   cum   aliquo   detrimento   milĭtum.
be injured   with   any   loss   of soldiers.

Cæsar   dimittit   nuncĭos   ad   finitimas   civitates;
Cæsar   sends off   messengers   to   the neighboring   states;

evocat   omnes   ad   se,   spe   prædæ,   ad
he invites   all   to   himself,   by the hope   of plunder   for

diripiendos   Eburones;   ut   potiùs   vita   Gallorum
ravaging   the Eburones;   that   rather   the life   of the Gauls

periclitetur   in   silvis,   quàm   legionariorum;
might be hazarded   in   the woods,   than   (that)   of the legionary

            sĭmul,   ut   magnâ   multitudine
(soldiers);   at the same time.   that   a great   multitude

    circumfusâ,   stirps   ac   nomen   civitatis
having been sent abroad,   the race   and   name   of the state

    tollatur   pro   tali   facinŏre.   Magnus numĕrus
might be destroyed   for   such   a crime.   A great   number

celerĭter   convenit   undĭque.
quickly   assembled   from all places.

35. Hæc   gerebatur   in omnibus partibus
    These (things)   were carried on   in   all   parts

Eburonum,   que   septĭmus   dĭes   appetebat,
of the Eburones,   and   the seventh   day   was approaching

ad   quem   dĭem   Cæsar   constituerat   reverti   ad
on   which   day   Cæsar   had resolved   to return   to

impedimenta que   legionem.   Hic   potuit   cognosci,
the baggage   and   the legion   Here   it might   be learned,

quantum   fortuna   possit   in   bello,   et   quantov
how much   fortune   can do   in   war.   and   how great

    casus   affĕrat.   Hostibus   dissipatis
mischances   it may bring.   The enemy   having been dispersed

ac   perterrĭtis,   ut   demonstravimus,   ĕrat   nulla
and   terrified,   as   we have shown,   there was   no

mănus,   quæ   affĕret   mŏdò   parvam causam
body of men,   which   might create   only   a slight   cause

timŏris.   Fama   pervenit   trans   Rhenum   ad
of fear.   The report   spread   beyond   the Rhine   to

Germanos,   Eburones   dirĭpi,   atque
the Germans,   (that)   the Eburones   to be [were] pillaged,   and

        omnes   evocari   ultrò   ad   prædam.
(that)   all   to be [were] invited   freely   to   the booty

        Sugambri   cogunt duo   millĭa   equitum,
[plunder].   The Sugambri   collect   two   thousand   horse,

quı   sunt   proxĭmi   Rheno,   à   quibus Tencteros
they   are   the nearest   to the Rhine.   by   whom   the Teucteri

atque   Usipetes   receptos   ex   fugâ,
and   Usipetes   were received   in   (their)   flight,   (as,

suprà   docŭimus; transeuntes   Rhenum   navibus
we have above   shown,   crossing   the Rhine   in ships

que   ratibus   triginta   millibus passŭum   infra   ĕum
and   boats   thirty   thousand   paces   below   this

lŏcum   ubi   pons   ĕrat perfectus,   que   præsidĭum
place   where   the bridge   was   made   and   the garrison

relictum ab Cæsare,   adeunt   primos   fines
left   by   Cæsar   they enter   the first [nearest]   territories

Eburonum;   excipiunt   multos dispersos ex fugâ;
of the Eburones: they surprise   many   dispersed   in   flight :

potiuntur   magno   numĕro   pecŏris,   cujus
they obtain possesion   of a great   number   of cattle.   of which

barbări   sunt   cupidissĭmi.   Invitati   prædâ
the barbarians   are   very covetous   Enticed   by booty

procedunt longĭùs.   Non   pălus,   non   silvæ,
they proceed   farther   Neither   swamps   nor   woods

morantur   hos   natos   in   bello,   que   latrocĭnis.
impede   these men   born   in   war   and   plundering

Quærunt   ex   captivis   in   quibus   lŏcis   Cæsar
They inquire   of   the prisoners   in   what   place   Cæsar

sit;   reperĭunt   profectum   longiùs,   que
may be :   they find   (that)   he has gone   further.   and

cognoscunt   omnem exercĭtum   discessisse.
learn   (that)   all   the army   to have [has] departed

Atque   unus   ex   captivis   inquit, "quid   vos
Moreover   one   from [of]   the captives   said   "why   do you

sectamĭni hanc   misĕram   et   tenŭem prædam, quibus
follow   these   wretched   and   trifling   spoils   to whom

jam   licet   esse fortunatissĭmis?   Tribus   horis
it is now   allowed   to be   most fortunate?   In three   hours

potestis venire Aduatucam, huc exercĭtus Romanorum
you can   come to   Aduatuca   there   the army   of the Romans

contŭlit   omnes   sŭas   fortunas;   est   tantum
has collected   all   its   property: there is   so little

præsidĭi,   ut   ne   murus quĭdem possit cingi,
(of a) garrison,   that   not   the wall   even   could   be manned

neque audĕat quisquam egredi   extra   munitĭones."
nor   dares   any one   go   beyond   the fortifications "

(Hac)   spe   oblatâ,   Germani   relinquunt
(This)   hope   having been offered.   the Germans   leave

in   occulto   prædam   quam   nacti ĕrant;
in   hiding   the booty   which   they had obtained;

ipsi   contendunt   Aduatucam,   usi   eodem
they   proceed to   Aduatuca,   using   the same

dŭce   cujus   indiclo   cognovĕrant
(person)   as guide   by whose   information   they had learned

hæc.
these things

36. Cicĕro,   (qui   per   omnes   superiores   dies,
Cicero.   (who   through   all   the former   days,

præceptis   Cæsaris   continuisset   milites   in
according to   the orders   of Cæsar   had kept   the soldiers   in

castris   summâ   diligentiâ,   ac   passus est   ne
camp   with the greatest   diligence,   and   allowed   not

quemquam   calonem   quidem   egredi   extra
any   camp follower   even   to go   beyond

munitionem);   septimo   die   diffidens   Cæsarem
the fortification) ·   on the seventh   day   distrusting (that)   Cæsar

servaturum   fidem   de   numĕro   dierum,
about to [would] keep   faith   about   the number   of days,

quòd   audiebat   eum   progressum   longius,
because   he was hearing   (that)   he   had proceeded   further,

neque   ulla   fama   de   ejus   reditu   afferebatur,
nor   was any   report   of   his   return   brought.

simul   permotus   vocibus   eorum,   qui
at the same time   moved   by the voices   of those,   who

appellabant   illius   patientiam   pænè   obsessionem si
were calling   his   endurance   nearly   a siege   if

quidem   non   licĕret   egredi   ex   castris;
indeed   it was not   allowed   to go out   from   camp;

expectans   nullum   casum   hujusmodi   quo
expecting   no   event   of such kind   by which [that]

posset   offendi,   in   tribus   milibus,
he could   be injured.   within   three   miles (of the camp)

nŏvem   legionibus   oppositis,   que   maximo
nine   legions   having been opposed   and   a numerous

equitatu,	hostĭbus,	dispersis	ac	pænĕ
cavalry.	the enemy.	having been dispersed	and	almost

deletis,	misit	quinque	cohortes	frumentatum	in
annihilated.	he sent	five	cohorts	to forage	in

proxĭmas	segĕtes,	inter	quas	et	castra
the neighboring	corn-fields.	between	which	and	the camp

unus	collis	omnino	intererat.	Complures	ex
one	hill	in all [alone]	intervened.	Many	from

legionibus	ĕrant	relicti	ægri in	castris; ex	quibus,
the legions	had	been left	sick in	the camp; of	whom

	qui,	hôc	spatĭo	dierum,	convalŭerant,
(those)	who.	in this	period	of time.	had recovered

circĭter	trecenti,	mittuntur	sub	vexillo	unà;
about	three hundred	are sent	under	a standard	together

præterĕa	magna	multitudo	calonum		magna
besides	a great	multitude	of camp followers	(and)	a great

vis	jumentorum,	quæ	subsederat	in	castris,
orce	of beasts of burden.	that	remained	in	the camp.

sequitur,	potestate	factâ.		
followed (them).	permission	having been given.

37. Hoc	ipso	tempŏre	et	casu	Germani
At this	very	time	and	by chance	the German

equĭtes	intervenĭunt,	que	protĭnùs	eodem	illo
horsemen	arrived.	and	immediately	with that	same

cursu,	quo	venĕrant,	conantur	irrumpĕre	in
speed,	with which	they had come.	try	to break	into

castra	ab	decumanâ	portâ;	nec	sunt	visi,
the camp	at	the decuman	gate.	nor	were they	seen.

silvis	objectis	ab	eâ	parte,	prĭus
a wood	being interposed	at [on]	this	part [side],	before

quàm	appropinquarent	castris,	usque	eò,	ut
(that)	they had approached	the camp.	even	so.	that

mercatores,	qui	tendĕrent	sub	vallo,
the merchants (sutlers),	who	encamped	under	the rampart.

habĕrent	facultatem	recipiendi	sŭi.
had not	an opportunity	of taking	themselves away

Nostri		inopinantes	perturbantur	novâ
Our	(men)	taken unawares	are confused	with this new

re,   ac   cohors   in statione   vix   sustinet
condition.   and   the cohort on   guard   scarcely sustains

primum   impĕtum;   hostes   circumfunduntur   ex
the first   attack :   the enemy   are spread out   on

reliquis partibus, si possent reperire quem adĭtum;
the other   sides,   if   they could   find   some   approach :

nostri   ægre   tuentur   portas;   lŏcus
our   (men) with difficulty defend the gates : the place

ipse   per   se   que   munitĭo   defendit
itself through itself and by the fortification defends

reliquos   adĭtus,   totis   castris   trepidatur, atque
the other approaches, in all the camp there is alarm.   and

alius quærit ex   alĭo   causam   tumultûs;   neque
one   inquires of   an other the cause of the confusion : neither

provident   quò   signa   ferantur,   neque in
do they provide   where   the ensigns may be carried.   nor   into

quam partem quisque   conveniat.   Alius pronunciat
what   part   each one   may assemble.   One   declares

castra   jam   capta, alius   contendit,
(that) the camp to be [is] already taken, another   affirms (that),

exercitu   atque   imperatore   delecto,
the army   and   the commander   having been destroyed.

victores   barbăros   venisse;   plerique fingun
the victorious barbarians (to) have come . the greater part form

novas religiones   sibi   ex   loco.   Que
strange superstitions for themselves from the place.   And

ponunt ante   oculos calamitatem Cottæ   et
they put   before (their) eyes   the calamity   of Cottæ and

Titurii, qui occiderint in eodem castello. Omnibus
Titurius, who had fallen in   the same fortress.   All

perterrĭtis   tali   timore,   opinĭo
(having been) alarmed by such   fear.   the opinion

confirmatur   barbaris,   ut   audierant ex
is confirmed   to [among] the barbarians, as   they had heard from

captivo   nullum præsidĭum   esse   intùs;
the captive   (that)   no   garrison   to be [was] within:

nituntur   perrumpĕre,   que   ipsi adhortantur
they endeavor   to force an entrance.   and   they   exhort

se, ne dimittant tantam fortunam ex
one another, 'est they may let go so great a prize from

manibus.
their hands.

38. P. Sextĭus Bacŭlus, qui duxĕrat primum
P. Sextius Baculus, who led the first

pilum apud Cæsarem cujus fecĭmus mentionem
company under Cæsar of whom we have made mention

superioribus prœlĭis, ĕrat relictus æger in præsidĭo,
in former battles, was left sick in the garrison,

ac carŭerat cĭbo jam quintum dĭem. Hic,
and had been without food now the fifth day. He,

diffisus sŭæ saluti ac omnium, inermis
mistrusting his safety and (that) of all, unarmed

prodit ex tabernacŭlo, videt hostes
goes out from the tent, he sees (that) the enemy

imminere, atque rem esse in
to be [were] pressing on, and that the affair to be [was] in

summo discrimĭne; capit arma à proxĭmis,
the greatest danger; he seizes arms from the nearest,

atque consistit in portâ. Centuriones ejus
and places himself in the gate. The centurions of this

cohortis quæ ĕrat in statione sequuntur hunc;
cohort which was on guard follow him;

paulisper sustinent prœlium unà; anĭmus
for a little while they sustain the battle together; the mind

relinquit Sextĭum[30] grăvis vulneribus acceptis;
leaves Sextius severe wounds having been received;

tractus per mănus (pl.) ægrè servatur.
drawn away by hand with difficulty he is saved.

Hoc spatĭo interposito, reliqui confirmant
This period having been interposed, the others encourage

sese tantum, ut audeant consistĕre
one another so much that they dare take stand

in munitionibus, que præbĕant specĭem
on the fortifications, and show the appearance

defensorum.
of defenders.

39.   Intĕrim   frumentatione   confectâ,
In the mean time   the foraging   having been completed,

nostri   milĭtes   exaudĭunt   clamorem,   equĭtes
our   soldiers   hear   the shout,   the horsemen

præcurrunt   cognoscunt   in   quanto   pericŭlo
hasten on before,   they ascertain   in   what   great danger

res   sit.   Verò   hìc   est   nulla   munitĭo,
the matter   is.   But   here   there is   no   fortification,

quæ   recipiat   perterritos.   Modò conscriptĭ
which   may receive   (those) affrighted.   (Those) lately   enrolled

atque   imperiti militaris   usûs   convertunt   ora   ad
and   unskilled   in military   practice   turn   faces   to

tribunum   milĭtum   que   centuriones;   expectant
the tribunes   of the soldiers   and   centurions: they await

quid   præcipiatur   ab   his.   Nemo   est   tam
what   may be commanded   by   them.   No one   is   so

fortis, quin   perturbĕtur   novitate   rĕi.
brave,   but   (that) he is disconcerted   by the novelty   of the affair

Barbări,   conspicati   signa   prŏcul,
[condition].   The barbarians,   having seen   the standard   at a distance.

d sistunt   ab   oppugnatione; primò   credunt
desist   from   the attack;   at first   they believe   (that)

legiones   redisse,   quas   cognovĕrant   ex
the legions   had returned,   which   they had learned   from

captivis   discessisse   longiùs;   postĕa,   paucitate
the captives   had gone   further;   afterwards,   the fewness

despectâ,   facĭunt   impĕtum,   ex
having been perceived,   they make   an attack,   from [on]

omnibus   partibus.
all   parts [sides].

40.   Calones   procurrunt in proxĭmum tumŭlum
The camp followers   run   to   the nearest   eminence

celerĭter   dejecti   hinc,   conjicĭunt   se
having been quickly   driven   thence,   they throw   themselves

in   signa   que manipŭlos;   ĕò   mãgis
among   the standards   and   companies,   so   much the more

perterrent   timidos   milites.   Alii   censent
they alarm   the affrighted   soldiers.   Some   are of the opinion

cunĕo   facto   celeriter
(that)   a wedge   having been formed   they may   quickly

perrumpant, quoniam   castra   sint   tam   propinqua,
break through,   and as   the camp   is   so   near

etsi   aliqua   pars   circumventa   ceciderit,
although   some   part   having been surrounded   might fall,

at   confidunt   reliquos   posse
still   they trust   (that)   the remainder   to be able [can]

servari.   Alii   ut   consistant   in
(to) be saved.   Others (advise)   that   they take stand   on

jigo,   atque   omnes   ferant   eundem   casum.
the hill-top.   and   (that)   all   undergo   the same   fate.

Veteres   milites,   quos   documus
The veteran   soldiers,   whom [who]   we have mentioned

perfectos   unà   sub   vexillo   non
(to have) marched out   together   under   a standard   do not

probant   hoc.   Itaque   cohortati   inter   se,
approve   this   Therefore   having encouraged   one   another,

C. Trebonio, Romano equite, qui erat præpositus
C. Trebonius.   a Roman   knight,   who   had   been placed over

eis,   duce,   perrumpunt   per   medios[31]
them.   being their   commander,   they break   through   the middle

hostes   que   omnes   ad   unum   perveniunt
[central] enemies   and   all   to   one [a man]   arrive

incolumnes   in   castra (acc.).   Calones   que
safe   in   the camp   The camp followers   and

equites   subsecuti   hos   eodem   impetu,
the horsemen   having followed   these   with the same   dash,

servantur   virtute   militum.   At   ii,   qui
are saved   by the bravery   of the soldiers.   But   those,   who

constiterant   in   jugo,   etiam   nunc   nullo
had taken stand   on   the hill-top,   even   now   no

usu   militaris   rei (sing.)   percepto,
experience   of military   affairs   having been acquired,

neque permanere   in   eo   consilio,   quod   proba-
neither   persisted   in   this   design,   which   they have

verant,   ut   defenderent   se   superiore
approved.   that   they should defend   themselves   in the higher

lŏco,   neque   potuerunt   imitari   ĕam   vim   que
position,   nor   were able to   imitate   this   vigor   and

celeritatem,   quam   vidĕrant   profuisse
speed,   which   they had seen   to have [had] availed

aliis;   sed   conati   recipere   se   in
the others;   but   having attempted   to betake   themselves   into

castra   demiserant   in   iniqŭum   lŏcum.
the camp   they descended   into   a disadvantageous   place.

Centuriones,   nonnulli   quorum   transducti   erant
The centurions,   some   of whom   had   been transferred

ex   inferioribus   ordinibus   reliquarum   legionum,
from   the lower   ranks   of the other   legions,

causâ   virtutis,   in   superiores   ordines   hujus
by reason of   bravery,   into   the higher   ranks   of this

legionis,   ne   amittĕrent   laudem   militaris
legion,   lest   they might lose   renown   in military

rĕi (sing.)   partam   antè   conciderunt   pugnantes
affairs   acquired   before,   fell   fighting

fortissimè.   Pars   militum,   hostibus
most valiantly.   A part   of (these) soldiers,   the enemy

summotis   virtute   horum,
having been removed   by the bravery   of these [by their bravery],

pervenit   in   castra   incolŭmis,   præter   spem,
arrived   in   the camp   safe,   beyond   expectation,

pars   circumventa   à   barbăris   periit.
a part   surrounded   by   the barbarians   perished.

41. Germani,   expugnatione   castrorum   des-
The Germans,   the storming   of the camp   having

peratâ,   quòd   videbant   nostros
been despaired of,   because   they saw   (that)   our men

jam   constitisse   in   munitionibus   receperunt
had now   taken stand   on   the fortifications   betook

sese   trans   Rhenum,   cum   ĕâ   prædâ   quam
themselves   beyond   the Rhine,   with   this   booty   which

deposuerant   in   silvis.   Ac   tantus   fuit
they had deposited   in   the woods.   And   so great   was

terror,   etiam   post   discessum   hostium,   ut
the alarm,   even   after   the departure   of the enemy,   that

ĕâ nocte, quum C. Volusenus venisset ad
this night, when C. Volusenus had come to

castra, missus cum equitatu, non
the camp having been sent with the cavalry. he could not

facĕret fidem Cæsarem adesse cum
make [create] confidence (that) Cæsar was near with

exercĭtu incolŭmi. Timor præoccupavĕrat animos
the army safe Fear had preoccupied the souls

omnium sic, ut mente pæne alienatâ,
of all so that with a mind almost unbalanced.

dicerent, equitatum tantum recepisse se
they were saying, (that) the cavalry only to have [had] returned

ex fugâ, omnibus copiis deletis,
from the flight, all the forces having been destroyed.

que contendĕrent Germanos ne fuisse
and they asserted (that) the Germans not to have been

oppugnaturos[32] castra exercĭtu
about to assault [had not assaulted] the camp (if) the army

incolŭmi; quem timorem Cæsaris adventus
being [was] safe; which fear Cæsar's arrival

sustŭlit.
removed.

42. Ille reversus, non ignarus eventûs
He [Cæsar] having returned, not ignorant of the casualty

belli, questus unum quòd cohortes essent
of war, complained (of) one (thing) that the cohorts had been

emissæ ex statione et præsidio; indicavit
sent from the post and from the garrison; he pointed out

lŏcum ne minimum quidem debuisse
(that) the place not the least even ought

relinqui casui, fortuna potuisse
to be left to chance fortune might have been able [done]

multum in repentino advetu hostium; etiam multò
much by the sudden arival of the enemy; also much

ampliùs, quòd avertisset barbăros ab
more, because she had turned away the barbarians from

vallo ipso que portis castrorum. Omnium
the rampart itself and the gates of the camp Of all

quarum   rerum   videbatur   maximè   admirandum,
which   things   it seemed   most   to be wondered at.

quòd   Germani,   qui   transiĕrant   Rhenum   ĕo
that   the Germans.   who   had crossed   the Rhine   with this

consilio, ut   depopularentur   fines   Ambiorigis,
design.   that   they might lay waste   the territories   of Ambiorix.

delati   ad   castra   Romanorum,   obtulerunt
having been led   to   the camp   of the Romans   brought

Ambiorigi   optatissimum   beneficium.
to Ambiorix   a most desirable   benefit.

43. Cæsar   rursus   profectus   ad   vexandos[33]
Cæsar   having again   departed   to   harass

hostes;   magno   numĕro   coacto   ex
the enemy :   a great   number   having been assembled   from

finitimis   civitatibus   dimittit   in   omnes
the neighboring   states   he sends   (them)   into   all

partes.   Omnes   vici   atque   omnia   ædificia,
parts   All   the villages   and   all   the buildings

quæ   quisque   conspexĕrat,   incendebantur;   præda
which   any one   might see   were set on fire :   spoils

agebatur   ex   omnibus   lŏcis;   frumenta   non
were driven off   from   all   places   the corn   not

solùm   consumebantur (pl)   à   tantâ   multitudine
only   was consumed   by   such   a multitude

jumentorum atque hominum; sed   etiam procubuĕrant
of cattle   and   men :   but   also   had fallen down

tempŏre   anni   atque   imbribus;   ut   si   qui
by the time   of year   and   the rains   so that   if   any

etiam in   præsentiâ occultâssent   se,   tamen
even   in [for]   the present   had concealed   themselves   yet

videretur   his   perendum[34]   inopiâ   omnium
it would seem (that) they   must perish   through want   of all

rerum   exercĭtu   deducto.   Ac   sæpe
things   the army   having been withdrawn.   And   often

ventum est   in ĕum   lŏcum,   equitatu   diviso
it came   to this   pass.   the cavalry   having been divided

tanto   in   omnes   partes,   ut   captiv.
so much   into [in]   all   directions   that   the prisoners

contenderunt   Ambiorigem   non   modò visum
  declared   (that)   Ambiorix   was not only seen

ab   se   in fugâ, sed etiam   nec abisse
by   them in flight, but also (that) he had not gone

planè ex conspectu;   ut   spe consequendi
clearly out of sight; (so) that the hope of overtaking

    illatâ,   atque   infinito   labore
(him) having been raised, and an immense   labor

  suscepto,   qui   putarent   se
having been undertaken, those who thought (that) they

ituros   summam gratiam à Cæsare, pænè
would obtain the highest favor from Cæsar, nearly

vincĕrent naturam   studio,   que sempèr paulum
conquered nature by (their) efforts, and always a little

videretur defuisse ad summam felicitatem,
seemed to be wanting to complete   success;

atque ille eripĕret se   latebris ac silvis
but he   rescued himself by hiding places and woods

aut saltibus, et occultatus noctu peteret alias
or forests, and concealed by night he sought other

regiones, que partes, non majore præsidio
regions, and places, with no greater guard

equitum quàm quatuor, quibus solis audebat
of horsemen than four, to whom alone he was daring

committere suam vitam.
to commit   his   life.

44. Regionibus   vastatis   tali   modo,
   The country having been laid waste in such manner.

Cæsar reducit   exercitum damno   duarum
Cæsar marches back the army with the loss of two

cohortium Durocortorum Rhemorum; que concilĭo
cohorts to Durocortorum of the Rhemi; and a council

  indicto   in ĕum lŏcum Galliæ, instituit
having been convoked in this part of Gaul, he resolved

habere quæstionem de conjuratione Senonum
to have an investigation about the conspiracy of the Senones

et Carnutum; et graviore sententiâ pronun-
and Carnutes; and a very severe sentence having been

ciatâ   de   Accone,   qui   fuerat   princeps
pronounced   on   Acco,   who   had been   the chief

ejus consilii,   sumpsit   supplicium,   more
of this   counsel,   he took [inflicted]   punishment,   after the custom

majorum.[35]   Nonnulli   veriti   judicium   profugerunt,
of our ancestors.   Some   afraid of   a trial   fled.

quum   interdixisset   aquâ   atque   igni   quibus,
when   he had interdicted   water   and   fire   to them,

collocavit in   hibernis   dŭas   legiones   ad   fines
he stationed in   winter quarters   two   legions   on   the frontiers

Trevirorum,   dŭas   in   Lingonibus,   reliquas
of the Treviri,   two   among   the Lingones,   the remaining

sex   Agendici   in   finibus   Senonum,   que
six   at Agendicum   in   the territories   of the Senones   and

frumento   proviso   exercitŭi,   ut
corn   having been provided   for the army   as

instituĕrat,   profectus est   in   Italiam   ad   agendos
he had resolved.   he departed   for   Italy   to   hold

conventus.
the assemblies.

SEVENTH BOOK

The seventh book opens with a statement of the rising of the Gauls upon knowledge of civil disturbances in Rome which might detain Cæsar in the city. Cæsar at length sets out for his province and unexpectedly crosses the Alps with an army through deep snows. Meantime Vercingetorix, an Arvernian, had been chosen leader of the revolution. Cæsar by rapid marches here and there holds the people in check. He captures Velaunodunum, Cenavum, Noviodunum and Avaricum. Labienus goes on an expedition to the north as far as Lutetia, which the Gauls burn, and after defeating tne Gauls in battle he rejoins Cæsar. In spite of Cæsar's efforts the Ædni join the revolt. Cæsar obtains cavalry from Germany and with their aid defeats Vercingetorix in several battles. He is forced to raise the seige of Gergovia on account of the increasing activity of the Gallic nations. Cæsar concentrates his forces against Vercingetorix and drives him to Alesia. The investment of Alesia and a general upriring of all Gaul now follow. Cæsar is attacked by an army of a quarter of a million from without and holds eighty thousand within the city. After having built extensive works and conquering in fierce contests, he defeats the outside forces, repulses the beseiged and compels the surrender of the city. Vercingetorix is sent to Rome in chains, and six years later takes part in Cæsar's triumph, after which he is executed. The nations make peace with Cæsar who quarters his troops in various places in Gaul. He himself winters at Bibracte. On receiving Cæsar's letters the senate decrees a thanksgiving of twenty days.

1. Galliâ   quietâ,   Cæsar   ut   constituĕrat
   Gaul   being at peace,   Cæsar   as   he had resolved

   proficiscitur   in   Italiam   ad   agendos   conventus;
   proceeded   to   Italy   to   hold   the assemblies;

   ŭbi   cognoscit   de   cæde   P. Clodii,   que
   there   he learned   of   the murder   of P. Clodius,   and

   factus   certior   de   consulto   Senatûs,
   having been made   acquainted   with   the decree   of the Senate.

ut   omnes   juniores   Italiæ   conjurarent,
that   all   the young men   of Italy   should take military oath.

instituit   habere   delectum   totâ   provinciâ.   Eæ
he resolved   to hold   a levy   in all   the province.   These

res   celerĭter perferuntur in Transalpinam Galliam.
things   quickly   are spread   into   Transalpine   Gaul.

Galli   ipsi   addunt   et   affingunt rumoribus,
The Gauls   themselves   add to   and   enlarge   the rumors,

(quod   res   videbatur   poscĕre,)   Cæsarem
(what   the case   seemed   to demand,)   (that)   Cæsar

retineri   urbano   motu (sing.),   neque   posse
was detained   by the city   commotions.   nor   could

venire ad exercitum in tantis dissentionibus. Impulsi
come   to   the army   in   such   dissensions.   Incited

hâc   occasione,   qui   jam   antè   dolĕrent
by this   opportunity,   those who   even   before   lamented

    se   subjectos   imperio   Romani   populi,
(that)   they   were subjected   to the dominion   of the Roman   people.

incipiunt   inire   consilĭa   de   bello   liberiùs
begin   to enter into   plans   concerning   war   more freely

atque   audaciùs.   Principes   Galliæ,
and   more daringly.   The principal men   of Gaul,

concilĭis   indictis   inter   se   silvestribus
councils   having been convoked   among   themselves   in woody

ac   remotis   lŏcis,   queruntur   de   morte
and   remote   places.   complain   concerning   the death

Acconis;   demonstrant   hunc   casum   posse
of Acco;   they represent   (that)   this   fate   might

recidere   ad   ipsos;   miserantur   communem
occur   to   themselves;   they bewail   the common

fortunam Galliæ; deposcunt omnibus pollicitationibus
lot   of Gaul;   they demand   by all   promises

ac   præmiis,   qui   faciant   initium   belli,
and   rewards,   (that)   some   make   a beginning   of war,

et   vindicent   Galliam   in   libertatem
and   defend   Gaul   into [for]   (its)   freedom

pericŭlo   sŭi   capĭtis.[1]   Dicunt   in   primis
at the peril   of their   lives.   They say   especially

ut   rationem   habendam   ejus,   ut
that   care   was to [must] be had   of [for] this,   that

Cæsar intercludatur   ab   exercĭtu, priusquàm ĕorum
Cæsar should be cut off   from   the army,   before   their

clandestina consilĭa efferantur.   Id   essc facile,
secret   designs   are reported.   (That) this was   easy.

quòd   neque   legiones,   imperatore   absente,
because   neither   the legions,   the commander   being absent,

audeant   egrĕdi   ex   hibernis,   neque possit
dare   to come forth   from   winter quarters,   nor   could

imperator   pervenire ad   legiones sine   præsidio.
the commander   arrive   at   the legions without   a guard.

Postremò   præstare   interfici in   acĭe,
Finally   (that) it was better   to be killed in the   battle-line,

quàm   non   recuperare   vetĕrem   glorĭam
than   not   to recover   (their) ancient   glory

belli   que libertatem quam   accepĕrint   à
of [in] war   and   the liberty   which   they have received   from

majoribus.
the forefathers.

2. His rebus   agitatis,   Carnutes profitentur
These things having been discussed,   the Carnutes   proclaim

se   recusare nullum pericŭlum   causâ
(that) they   to [will] refuse   no   danger   for the sake

commŭnis   salutis: pollicentur   se   principes
of the common   safety ,   they promise   (that) they   the first

ex   omnibus   facturos   bellum;   et
from [of]   all   about to [would] make   war ;   and

quoniam in   præsentiâ   possent non   cavere
since   at   the present (time)   they could   not   give security

inter   se   obsidibus,   ne   res   efferatur,
among   themselves   by hostages,   lest   the matter   be divulged,

petunt   ut   sanciatur jurejurando   ac   fide,
they request   that   it be ratified   by oath   and   pledge,

militaribus   signis   collatis,   (quo
the military   standards   having been stacked together,   (by which

more eorum gravissima cærimonia continetur
usage   their   most solemn   ceremony   is guarded [confirmed]

ne initĭo belli facto,
lest the commencement of the war having been made,

deserantur à reliquis. Tunc, Carnutibus
they might be deserted by the others. Then, the Carnutes

collaudatis, jurejurando dato ab
having been applauded, the oath having been given by

omnibus qui adĕrant, tempŏre ejus
all who were present, (and) the time of [for] this

rĕi constituto, disceditur[2] ab
movement having been determined, they departed from

concilĭo.
the council.

3. Ubi ĕa dies venit, Carnutes, Cotuato et
When this day came, the Carnutes, Cotuatus and

Conconnetodumno ducibus, desperatis hominibus,
Conconnetodumnus as leaders, desperate men,

concurrunt Cenabum, signo
assembled hastily at Cenabum [Orleans], the signal

dato, que interficiunt Romanos cives,
having been given, and kill the Roman citizens,

qui constitĕrant ĭbi causâ negotiandi, in
who had settled there for the purpose of trading, among

ĭis C. Fufium Citam, honestum Romanum equĭtem,
them C. Fufius Cita, an honorable Roman knight,

qui præerat frumentariæ rĕi, jussu Cæsaris;
who presided over the grain supply, by order of Cæsar;

que diripiunt eorum bona. Fama celeriter
and they plunder their property. The report quickly

perfertur ad omnes civitates Galliæ. Nam ŭbi
is spread to all the states of Gaul. For when

major atque illustrior res incidit, significant
a greater and more notable affair occurs, they indicate

per agros que regiones clamore; alĭi
(it) through the lands and territories by a shout; some

deinceps excipiunt hunc, et tradunt proxĭmis,
in succession receive this, and transmit (it) to the nearest

ut tunc accidit. Nam quæ gesta essent
as then happened. For what (things) had been done

Cenabi   sole   oriente (abl. abs.),[3]
at Cenabum [Orleans]   at sun   rise,

audita sunt   in   finĭbus   Arvernorum   ante
are heard   in   the territories of the Arverni before

primam   vigilĭam[4]   confectam,   quod est spatium
the first   watch   is completed,   which is   a space

          circĭter   centum   et   sexaginta   millĭum
[distance] of about   a hundred and   sixty   thousand

passŭum.
paces.

4. Ibi   simili   ratione   Vircingetorix,   Arvernus,
There   in like   manner   Vircingetorix,   an Arvernian,

filĭus   Celtilli,   adolescens   summæ   potentiæ,
the son   of Celtillus,   a young man   of the highest power,

(cujus   pater obtinuĕrat   principatum   totius Galliæ,
(whose   father   had held   the foremost place   of all   Gaul,

et   ob   ĕam   causam,   quòd   appetebat   regnum
and   for   this   reason,   that   he was seeking   sovereign

          interfectus ĕrat   ab   civitate),   sŭis clientibus
power   was put to death   ᵤᵧ   the state),   his   clients

          convocatis   facile   incendit   ĕos.   Ejus
having been called together   he easily   inflamed   them.   His

consilĭo   cognito   concurritur[5]   ad   arma.
design   having been known   they rush   to   arms.

Prohibĕtur   ab   Gobannitione   suo   patruo,   que
He was prevented   by   Gobannitio   his   uncle,   and

reliqŭis principibus, qui   non   existimabant
the other   chiefs,   who   were not   thinking   (that)

hanc fortunam   temptandam,   expellitur
this fortune [hazard]   ought to be attempted,   he is expelled

ex   oppĭdo   Gergoviâ.   Tamen   non
from   the town   (of) Gergovia.   However   he does not

desistit, atque in   agris   habet delectum
desist,   and   in   the fields [country]   holds   a levy

egentium ac perditorum.   Hâc   manu   coac-
of needy   and   desperate (men).   This   band   having

to,   quoscunque   ex   civitate   adit
been collected.   whomever   of   the state   he approaches

perducit in suam sententiam. Hortatur, ut
he brings over to his opinion. He exhorts, that

capiant arma causâ communis libertatis;
they take arms for the sake of the common liberty;

que magnis copiis coactis, expellit ex
and great forces having been collected, he expels from

civitate suos adversarios à quibus ejectus ĕrat
the state his adversaries by whom he had been evicted

paulò antè. Appellatur rex ab suis;
a little before. He is called king by his (followers);

dimittit legationes quoquoversùs; obtestatur ut
he sends embassies in every direction; he implores that

manĕant in fide. Celeriter adjungit sibi
they remain in faith. Speedily he attaches to himself

Senones, Parisios, Pictones, Cadurcos, Turones,
the Senones, the Parisii, the Pictones, the Cadurci, the Turones,

Aulercos, Lemovices, Andos, que omnes reliquos,
the Aulerci, the Lemovici, the Andes, and all the rest,

qui attingunt Oceanum. Imperium defertur
who border on the Ocean. The chief command is conferred

ad ĕum consensu omnium. Quâ potestate
on him by the consent of all. Which [This] power

oblatâ, impĕrat obsĭdes omnibus ĭis
having been obtained, he demands hostages from all these

civitatibus: jubet certum numĕrum militum
states: he orders a fixed number of soldiers

celerĭter adduci ad se; constituit quantum
speedily brought to him; he decrees what number

armorum quæque civitas effĭcĭat domi, que
of arms each state should prepare at home, and

ante quod tempus; in primis stŭdet equitatui.
before what time; especially he attends to the cavalry

Summæ diligentiæ addit summam severitatem
To the highest diligence he adds the highest severity

imperii; magnitudine supplicĭi cogit
of command; by the greatness of punishment he forces

dubitantes. Nam majore delicto commisso
the hesitating. For, a greater crime having been committed,

necat　　igni　atque　omnibus　　　　　tormentis;
he puts to death　by fire　and　　all　　(kinds of)　　tortures;

de　　leviore　causâ,　auribus　　desectis,　　　aut
for　a slighter　cause,　the ears　having been cut off,　or

singŭlis　oculis　　　　effosis,　　remittit
a single　eye　　(having been) put out,　he sends　(them)

domum;　ut　　sint　　documento　reliquis,　et
home;　that　they may be　(for) an example　to the rest,　and

perterrĕant　alios　magnitudiue　pœnæ.
may terrify　others　by the greatness　of the punishment.

5. Exercĭtu　　　coacto　　celerĭter　　his
An army　　having been assembled　quickly　by these

supplicĭis,　mittit　Lucterium　Cadurcum　hominem
punishments,　he sends　Lucterius　the Cadurcan　a man

summæ　　audacĭæ　cum　parte　copiarum　in
of the highest　daring　with　a part　of the forces　to

Rutenos;　ipse　proficiscitur　in　　Bituriges.
the Ruteni:　he himself　sets out　into　the Bituriges.

Ejus　adventu　Bituriges　mittunt　legatos　ad
On his　arrival　the Bituriges　send　ambassadors　to

Æduos,　(in　quorum　fide　ĕrant,)　rogatum
the Ædui,　(in　whose　alliance　they were,)　to ask for

subsidium,　　quo　　　possint　　facilius
aid,　　by which [that]　they may be able　the more easily

sustinere　copias　hostium.　Ædŭi　de　consilĭo
to resist　the forces　of the enemy.　The Ædui　by　the advice

legatorum,　quos　Cæsar　reliquerat　ad
of the lieutenants,　whom　Cæsar　had left　at [with]

exercitum,　mittunt　copias　equitatûs　que　peditatûs
the army,　send　forces　of cavalry　and　foot

Biturigibus;　qui　quum　venissent　ad　flumen
to the Bituriges;　who　when　they had arrived　at　the river

Ligerim,　quod　dividit　Bituriges　ab　Æduis,
Loire,　which　divides　the Bituriges　from　the Ædui,

morati　paucos　dĭes　ĭbi,　neque　ausi
having delayed　a few　days　there,　nor　having dared

transire　flumen,　revertunt　domum;　que　renunciant
to cross　the river,　they return　home;　and　they report

nostris   legatis   se   veritos   perfidiam
to   our   lieutenants   (that) they   having feared the treachery

Biturigum   revertisse;   quibus[6]   cognoverint
of the Bituriges to have [had] returned; to whom they had ascertained

id   consilii   fuisse,   ut   si   transissent
this   plan   to have [had] been,   that   if   they crossed

flumen,   ex   unâ   parte ipsi,   alterâ
the river,   on   the one side   they [the Bituriges]   on the other

Arverni   circumsisterent   se.   Ne   fecĕrint
the Arverni   would surround   them. Whether they did

id   de   ĕâ   causâ,   quam   pronunciârunt
this   from [for] this   reason,   which   they alleged

legatis,   an   adducti   perfidiâ,   quòd nihil
to the lieutenants, or   were induced by treachery. because nothing

constat nobis,   non videtur   esse ponendum
is evident to us.   it does not   seem (best) to be   put down

pro certo.   Biturges   ĕorum   discessu   statim
for certain.   The Bituriges on their   retreat   immediately

conjungunt   se   cum   Arvernis.
unite   themselves with   the Arverni.

6. His   rebus   nunciatis   Cæsari, in Italiam,
These   things having been reported to Cæsar, in   Italy,

quum   jam   ille   intelligĕret   urbanas   res
when   already he   understood   (that) the city   affairs

pervenisse in   commodiorem   statum   virtute[7]
had come   into   a more satisfactory state   by the conduct

Cn. Pompeii, profectus est in Transalpinam Galliam.
of Cn. Pompey,   he set out   for   Transalpine   Gaul.

Quum   venisset   eò   afficiebatur   magnâ
When   he had arrived there   he was affected   with the great

difficultate,   quâ   ratione posset pervenire
difficulty,   in [as to] what   manner he might reach

ad exercĭtum. Nam si   arcessĕret   legiones in
the army.   For   if   he should summon the legions into

Provinciam,   intelligebat   dimicatura
the province, he was understanding (that) they about to [must] fight

prœlio in   itinĕre,   se   absente;   si   ipse
in battle on   the march,   he being absent: if   he himself

contendĕret ad   exercĭtum,   videbat,   suam
should hasten   to   the army,   it was seeming (that)   his

salutem   rectè   committi   ne   ĭis,
safety   properly   to [could] be committed   not   to those,

quidem   qui   ĕo   tempŏre   viderentur
even   who   at this   time   were appearing   (to be)

pacati.
peaceable.

7.   Intĕrim   Lucterius   Cadurcus   missus
In the mean time   Lucterius   the Cadurcan   having been sent

in   Rutenos   conciliat   ĕam   civitatem   Arvernis.
to   the Ruteni   gains over   this   state   to the Arverni.

Progressus   in   Nitiobriges   et   Gabalos,   accipit
Having marched   into   the Nitiobriges   and   Gabali,   he receives

obsĭdes   ab   utrisque;   et   magnâ   manu   co-
hostages   from   each one: and   a large   band   having been

actâ,   contendit facĕre eruptionem   in   Provinciam
collected,   he hastens   to make   an invasion   into   the province

versus Narbonem.   Quâ   re   nunciatâ,
toward   Narbo.   Which [This]   thing   having been reported,

Cæsar   existimavit,   antevertendum   omnibus
Cæsar   thought,   that (it) to [must] be preferred   to all

consilĭis,   ut   proficisceretur   Narbonem.
(other)   plans,   that   he should set out   to Narbo.

Quum   venisset   eò,   confirmat timentes, constituᵼt
When   he had arrived there,   he encourages   the timid,   he places

præsidia   in   provincialibus   Rutenis,   Volcis
garrisons   among   the provincial   Ruteni,   the Volci

Arecomicis, Tolosatibus, que circum Narbonem, quæ
Arecomici,   the Tolosates,   and   about   Narbo,   which

loca ĕrant finitĭma hostibus; jubet partem copiarum
places were   near   the enemy;   he orders   a part   of the forces

ex   Provinciâ   que supplementum, quod   adduxĕrat
from   the province   and   the recruits,   which   he had brought

ex   Italiâ   convenire   in   Helvios   qui contingunt
from   Italy   to assemble   among   the Helvii   who   border on

fines   Arvernorum.
the territories   of the Arverni.

8. His   rebus   comparatis,   Lucterius   jam
These   things   having been arranged,   Lucterius   now

represso   et   remoto,   quòd   putabat
having been checked   and   removed,   because   he thought (it)

periculosum intrare   intra   præsidia,   pro-
dangerous   to enter   within [among]   the garrison,   he [Cæsar]

ficiscitur   in   Helvĭos.   Etsi   mons   Cebenna,
marches   into   the Helvii   Although   mount   Cevennes,

qui   discludit   Arvernos   ab   Helvĭis   impediebat
which   separates   the Arverni   from   the Helvii   was barring

iter   altissimâ   nive   durissĭmo   tempŏre
the road   with very deep   snow   at the severest   time [season]

anni;   tamen   nive   sex pĕdum in altitudinem
of the year: however   the snow   six   feet   in   height [depth]

discussâ,   atque   vĭis   ĭta   patefactis,
having been removed,   and   the roads   thus   having been opened,

pervenit   ad   fines   Arvernorum   summo
he arrives   at   the territories   of the Arverni   by the utmost

labore   milĭtum.   Quibus   oppressis,
labor   of his soldiers.   Who [They]   (having been) astounded,

inopinantibus, quòd   existimabant   se
taken unawares,   because   they were thinking   (that they) themselves

munitos   Cebennâ   ut   muro,   ac   ĕo
(were)   defended   by the Cevennes   as   by a wall,   and   in this

tempŏre   anni   semitæ   unquam   patuĕrant
season   of the year   the paths   never   had lain open

homini   ne singulari   quidem,   impĕrat
to a man   (not) by himself   even,   he [Cæsar] commands

equitĭbus,   ut   vagentur   quam   latissimè
the cavalry,   that   they should roam   as   far

possent,   et   infĕrant   quàm   maximum
as they could,   and   should occasion   the very   greatest

terrorem   hostĭbus.   Hæc   celerĭter perferuntur
fear   to the enemy.   These (things) are quickly   announced

ad Vercingetorigem   famâ   ac   nuncĭis;   quem
to   Vercingetorix   by report   and   messengers;   whom

omnes   Arverni   perterriti   circumsistunt   atque
all   the Arverni   alarmed   beset   and

obsecrant　ut　consulat　sŭis　fortunis,　neu
entreat　that　he look out　for their　property,　nor

patiatur　se　diripi　ab　hostibus,
suffer　themselves　to be plundered　by　the enemy

præsertim　qŭum　vidĕat　omne bellum　trans-
especially　when　he sees (that)　all　the war　was trans-

latum ad　se.　Percibus　quorum[8]　per-
ferred　to　themselves.　By the entreaties　of whom　having been

motus　ille　movet　castra　ex　Biturigibus
stirred　he　moves　(his)　camp　from　the Bituriges

versus in　Arvernos.
towards　the Arverni.

9. At　Cæsar　moratus　bidŭum　in　īis　lŏcis
But　Cæsar　having delayed　two days　in　these　places

quod[9]　præceperat　opinione,　hæc
because　he had anticipated　in [through] surmise,　(that) these

ventura　usu　de　Vercingetorige,
(things)　would come　in use [fact]　regarding　Vercingetorix,

discedit　ab　exercĭtu　per　causam　cogendi
he departs　from　the army　(as) for　the cause　of raising

supplementi　que　equitatûs;　præfecit　Brutum,
recruits　and　cavalry;　he placed　Brutus,

adolescentem,　īis　copĭis;　monet　hunc,　ut
a young man,　over these　forces;　he instructs　him,　that

equites　pervagentur　quàm latissimè　in
the cavalry　should range about　as　far　as possible　in

omnes　partes,　se　daturum　opĕram
all　directions,　(that) he　about to [would] take　care

absit　ab　castris　ne　longiùs
(that) he may be absent　from　the camp　no　longer　(than)

tridŭo.　His　rebus　constitutis,　pervenit
three days.　These　things　having been arranged,　he arrived

Viennam　maxĭmis　itineribus quàm　potest,
at Vienna [Vienne]　by as great　marches　as　he was able,

sŭis　inopinantibus.　Ibi　nactus　recentum
his (men)　not expecting (him).　There　having found　the fresh

equitatum, quem　præmiserat　ĕò　multis
[newly enrolled]　cavalry,　which　he had sent　there　many

diebus   antè   itinĕre   intermisso   neque
days   before   the march   having been interrupted   neither

diurno neque nocturno   contendit   per   fines
by day   nor   by night   he hastens   through   the territories

Æduorum   in   Lingones,   ŭbi   dŭæ   legiones
of the Ædu   into   the Lingones,   where   two   legions

hiemabant,   ut   si   etiam   quid   consilĭi   de
were wintering,   that   if   also   any   plan   respecting

suâ salute   iniretur   ab   Æduis   præcurreret,
his   safety   was entered into   by   the Ædui   he might anticipate

celeritate.   Quum   pervenisset   eò   mittit
(it),   by (his) quickness.   When   he had arrived   there   he sends

ad   reliqŭas legiones,   que   cogit   omnes   in   unum
to   the other   legions,   and   gathers   all   into   one

lŏcum,   priùs   quàm   possit   nunciari
place,   before   (that)   it was possible [could]   (to) be announced

Arvernis   de   ejus   adventu.   Hâc   re
to the Arverni   concerning   his   arrival.   This   thing

cognitâ,   Vercingetorix   rursus   reducit
having been known,   Vercingetorix   again   marches back (his)

exercĭtum   in   Bituriges,   atque   inde   profectus
army   to   the Bituriges,   and   thence   having set out

Gorgobinam,   oppidum   Boiorum,   quos
to Gorgobina,   a town   of the Boii,   whom   (having been)

victos   Helvetico   prœlio,   Cæsar   collocaverat
conquered   in the Helvetian   battle,   Cæsar   had placed

ibi,   que   attribuĕrat   Æduis;   instituit   oppugnare.
there,   and   had assigned   to the Ædui;   he resolved   to assault (it).

10. Hæc   res   afferebat   magnam   difficultatem
This   affair   was causing   great   perplexity

Cæsari   ad   capiendum   consilĭum,[10]   si   contin-
to Cæsar   for   taking [forming]   a plan,   if   he should

ĕret   legiones in ŭno loco   rĕliquam   partem
keep together   the legions in one place   the remaining   part

hiemis,   ne,   stipendiariis   Ædui   expugnatis,
of the winter,   lest,   the tributaries   of the Ædui   having been stormed,

cuncta Gallia   deficĕret,   quòd   videretur
all   Gaul   might revolt,   because   it would seem   (that)

nullum præsidium   positum esse   in   ĕo
no   protection   about to [could] be placed in   him

amicis;   sin   educĕret   maturiùs   ex
for (his) friends;   but   if he should lead   too early   from

hibernis,   ne   laboraret   ab   re frumentariâ,
winter quarters,   lest   he be troubled   by   the grain supply,

subvectionibus (pl.)   duris.   Visum est præstare
transportation   (being) difficult. It seemed to be better

tamen   perpeti   omnes difficultates, quàm   tantâ
however   to endure   all   difficulties,   than   so great

contumeliâ   acceptâ,   alienare   voluntates
an insult   having been received,   to alienate (the) good will

omnium suorum.   Itaque   cohortatus   Æduos
of all   his (allies).   Therefore   having exhorted   the Ædui

de   supportando commeatu   præmittit ad   Boios,
about   transporting   provisions   he sends before to   the Boii,

qui   doceant   de sŭo adventu, que
(those) who   may inform (them)   of   his   arrival,   and

hortentur   ut   maneant   in   fide,   atque
he exhorts   (them) that   they remain in   alliance,   and

sustineant impĕtum   hostium   magno   anĭmo.
resist   the attack   of the enemy with great courage [spirit].

Dŭabus legionibus,   atque   impedimentis   totius
Two   legions,   and   the baggage   of the entire

exercitûs   relictis,   Agendici,   proficiscitur
army   having been left,   at Agendicum [Sens],   he marches

ad   Boios.
to   the Boii.

11. Quum altĕro   die   venisset ad Vellaunodunum
When on the next day he had come to   Vellaunodunum

oppidum Senonum, ne   relinquĕret quem
[Beaune]   a town   of the Senones, lest   he might leave   any

hostem   post   se,   instituit   oppugnare,
enemy   behind   him,   he resolved   to attack (it),   (and)

quo   uteretur   expeditiore   re frumentariâ;   que
what he   might use   more easily   the grain supply,   and

bidŭo   circumvallavit id,   tertĭo   die   legatis
in two days   he invested   it,   on the third day   ambassadors

missis   ex   oppĭdo   de   deditione,
having been sent   from   the town   concerning   a surrender,

jubet   arma   proferri,   jumenta   produci,
he orders   the arms   to be brought out,   the cattle   to be produced,

sexcentos obsides   dari.   Relinquit C. Trebonium,
six hundred   hostages   to be given.   He leaves   C.   Trebonius,

legatum,   qui   conficeret   ĕa.   Ipse
(his) lieutenaut,   who   should execute   these things.   He himself

proficiscitur,   ut   facĕret   iter   quam   primùm
sets out,   that   he may make   the march   as   soon as possible

Cenabum   Carnutum;   qui,   nuncĭo   de
to Cenabum   of the Carnutes;   who,   the information   of

oppugnatione   Vellaunoduni   tum   primùm
the siege   of Vellaunodunum   then   first [immediately]

allato,   comparabant   præsidĭum   causâ
having been brought,   were preparing   a garrison   for the purpose

tuendi   Cenabi,   quod   mitterent   eò   quum
of defending   Cenabum,   which   they might send   there   as

existimarent   ĕam   rem   ire   ductum
they thought   this   affair   was   to be drawn out

longiùs.   Pervenit   huc   biduo.   Castiis
longer.   He arrived   there   in three days.   The camp

positis   ante   oppĭdum,   exclusus
having been placed   before   the town,   (being)   prevented

tempŏre   diei,   differt   oppugnationem   in
by the time   of day,   he defers   the attack   to

postĕrum;   imperat   militibus   quæque
the next   (day);   he demands   from the soldiers   whatever

sint   usŭi   ad   ĕam   rem;   et   quòd   pons
may be   of use   for   this   affair;   and   as   the bridge

flumĭnis   Ligĕris   continebat   oppĭdum   Cenabum;
of the river   Loire   was joining   the town   (of)   Cenabum;

verĭtus   ne   profugĕrent   ex   oppĭdo   noctu,
having feared   lest   they might flee   from   the town   at night,

jubet   dŭas   legiones   excubare   in   armis.
he orders   two   legions   to keep watch   under   arms.

Cenabenses   egressi   ex   oppĭdo   silentio
The people of Cenabum   having departed   from   the town   in silence

paulò ante mediam noctem cœperunt transire
a little before mid night began to cross

flumen. Quâ re nunciatâ per
the river. Which [This] thing having been announced by

exploratores, Cæsar, portis incensis
the scouts, Cæsar, the gates having been set afire

intromittit legiones, quas jussĕrat esse
sends in the legions, which he had ordered to be

expeditas, atque potītur oppido (abl.); perpaucis[11]
ready, and seizes the town; very few

ex numĕro hostium desideratis quin
from [of] the number of the enemy having escaped but that

cuncti caperentur, quòd angustiæ (pl.) pontis
the whole were taken, because the narrowness of the bridge

atque itinerum intercluserant fugam multitudinis.
and of the roads had cut off the flight of the multitude.

Dirĭpit atque incendit oppidum; donat prædam
He pillages and burns the town, he gives the booty

militibus; transducit exercĭtum Ligerim, atque
to the soldiers; he leads his army over the Loire, and

pervenit in fines Biturigium.
arrives in the territories of the Bituriges.

12. Vercingetorix, ŭbi cognovit de adventu
Vercingetorix, when he learned of the arrival

Cæsaris, desistit oppugnatione, atque proficiscitur
of Cæsar, desists from the siege, and marches

obviâm Cæsari. Ille instituĕrat oppugnare
to meet Cæsar. He [Cæsar] had begun to besiege

Noviodunum, oppidum Biturigum, positum
Noviodunum [Saucerre] a town of the Bituriges, situated

in viam. Ex quo[12] oppido quŭum legati
on the road. From which town when ambassadors

venissent ad ĕum oratum ut ignosceret sibi,
had come to him to entreat that he would pardon them,

que consuleret sŭæ vitæ (sing.), ut conficĕret
and would spare their lives, that he might accomplish

reliquas res celeritate, quâ pleraque
the remaining affairs with the speed, by which the most

ĕrat consecutus, jubet arma proferri
had been effected, he orders the arms to be brought forth

equos produci, obsides dari. Parte
the horses to be produced, (and) hostages to be given. A part

obsĭdum jam transdită, quum reli-
of the hostages now having been surrendered, while the other

qua administrarentur, centurionibus et paucis
things were being executed, the centurions and a few

militum intromissis, qui conquirerent
of the soldiers having been introduced, who should collect

arma que jumenta, equitatus hostium est
the arms and the horses, the cavalry of the enemy was

visus procul, qui antecesserat agmen
seen at a distance, which had proceded the army

Vercingetorigis; quem[13] atque sĭmul oppidani
of Vercingetorix; which as soon as the townsmen

conspexerunt, atque venerunt in spem auxilĭi
had seen, and had come to the hope of aid,

clamore sublato cœperunt capĕre arma,
a shout having been raised they began to take arms,

claudĕre portas, complere murum. Centuriones
to shut the gates, (and) to fill the walls. The Centurions

in oppĭdo, quum intellexissent ex significatione
in the town, when they had understood from the signals

Gallorum aliquid novi consilĭi iniri ab
of the Gauls (that) some (of) new plans was formed by

ĭis, gladĭis districtis occupaverunt
them, their swords having been drawn they took possession of

portas, que receperunt omnes sŭos incolŭmes.
the gates, and received all their (men) safe.

13. Cæsar jubet equitatum educi ex castris,
Cæsar orders the cavalry to be led from the camp,

que committit equestre prœlĭum. Sŭis jam
and joins in a cavalry battle. His (men) being now

laborantibus submittit circĭter quadringento
hard pressed he sends about four hundred

Germanos equĭtes, quos ab initĭo instit-
German horsemen, whom from the beginning he had

uĕrat	habere	cum	se.	Galli	potuerunt
determined	to keep	with	himself.	The Gauls	could

ron	sustinere	eorum	impĕtum;	atque		conjecti
not	sustain	their	attack;	and		having been thrown

in	fugam,	receperunt	se	ad	agmen,	multis
into	flight,	betook	themselves	to	the army,	many

amissis.	Quibus	profligatis,	oppidani
having been lost.	Who [These]	having been routed,	the townsmen

rursus	perterriti,	perduxerunt	ad	Cæsarem	eos
again	alarmed,	led out	to	Cæsar	those

	comprehensos	quorum	operâ	existimabant
(having been) arrested		by whose	means	they were thinking

	plebem	concitatam,	que	dediderunt	sese
(that)	the people	were incited,	and	surrendered	themselves

ei.	Quibus	rebus	confectis,	Cæsar
to him.	Which	things	having been accomplished,	Cæsar

profectus	est	ad	oppĭdum	Avarĭcum,	quod
marched		to	the town	(of) Avaricum [Bourges],	which

ĕrat	maximum	que	munitissĭmum	in	finibus
was	the largest	and	best fortified	in	the territories

Biturĭgum,	atque	fertillissimâ	regione	agri,
of the Bituriges,	and	in a most fertile	district	of country

quòd	ĕo	oppido	recepto,	confidebat
because	this	town	having been taken,	he was confident

	se	redacturum	civitatem	Biturigum
(that)	he	about to [would] reduce	the state	of the Bituriges

in	potestatem.
into (his)	power.

14. | Vercingetorix, | tot | | continuis | incommodis |
|---|---|---|---|---|
| Vercingetorix, | so | many | continual | reverses |

Vellaunoduni,	Cenabi,	Novioduni,	ac-
at Vellaundunum,	Cenabum,	(and) Noviodunum,	having been

ceptis	convocat	suos	ad	concilium;	docet
received	calls	his (followers)	to	a council;	he shows

"bellum	gerendum esse	longè	aliâ
(that)	"the war	to [must] be carried on	with a far	different

ratione,	atque	sit	gestum	antĕa,	huic	rĕi
plan,	than	it had been	carried on	before,	to this	thing

studendum omnibus modis, ut Romani
it must be attended by all means, that the Romans

prohibeantur pabulatione, et commeatu :
should be prohibited from foraging, and from provisions: (that)

id esse facĭle, quŏd ipsi abundent equitatu,
this to be [was] easy, because they abound in cavalry,

et quŏd sublevêntur tempŏre anni ;
and because they are assisted by the season of the year ;

pabŭlum posse non secari ; hostes
(that) forage could not (to) be cut ; (that) the enemy

dispersos necessariò petere ex ædificĭis ;
dispersed (must) necessarily (to) seek (it) from the buildings ;

omnes hos posse quotidie deleri ab
(that) all these could daily (to) be destroyed by

equitĭbus. Prætereă causâ salutis commoda
the horsemen. Moreover for the sake of safety the advantages

familiaris rĕi (sing.) negligenda ;
of private affairs to [must] be disregarded ; (that)

oportere vicos atque ædificĭa incen-
to be [it was] necessary (for) the villages and houses to be

di, hoc est, spatio à Boiâ quoquoversùs,
burnt, that is, in a space from Boia in every direction,

quò videantur posse adire causâ
where (the Romans) might seem to be able to go for the purpose

pabulandi. Harum rerum suppetĕre copiam
of foraging. Of these things there is at hand an abundance

ipsis, quòd, in quorum finibus bellum
for themselves, because, in whose territories war

geratur, eorum opibus subleventur ;
may be waged, by their means they would be assisted ; (that)

Romanos aut non laturos[14] inopiam,
the Romans either not to be about to [would not] bear privation,

aut progressuros longiùs à
or (that they) to be about to [would] proceed farther from

castris cum magno pericŭlo ; neque inter-
the camp with great danger; nor to be [was it] any

esse, ne interficiant ipsos ne exŭant
difference, if they kill them or strip away

impedimentis, quibus amissis, bellum possit
(their) baggage, which having been lost, war can

non geri. Præterĕa, oportere
not (to) be waged. Moreover, (that it) to be [was] necessary

oppida incendi, quæ sint non tuta ab
(for) the towns to be burnt, which were not safe from

omni pericŭlo munitione et naturâ loci;
all danger by fortifications and by the nature of the place;

neu sint suis receptacula ad
that neither they may be for our (people) retreats for

detrectandam militiam neu proposita Romanis
evading military service nor offered to the Romans

ad tollendam copĭam commeatûs que prædam.
for taking away an abundance of provisions and plunder.

Si hæc videantur gravĭa aut acerba, debere(inf.)
If these (things) seemed severe or cruel, they ought

æstimare, illa multò graviùs
to consider, (that) those things (are) much more severe (that

libros conjuges abstrahi in
(their) children (and) wives to [should] be dragged into

servitutem, ipsos interfici; quæ
slavery, (and they) themselves (to be) slain; which

sit necesse accidĕre victis.
would be certain to befall the conquered.

15. Hâc sententiâ probatâ consensu
This opinion having been approved by the consent

omnium, uno die amplius viginti urbes Biturigum
of all, in one day more than twenty cities of the Bituriges

incenduntur. Hoc idem fit in reliquis civitatibus.
are burned. This same is done in the remaining states

In omnibus partibus incendia conspiciuntur; quæ
In all parts conflagrations are seen; which

etsi omnes ferebant cum magno dolore, tamen
although all were bearing with great grief, yet

proponebant sibi hoc solaci,
they were placing before themselves this (as) a consolation,

confidebant quòd se, victoriâ prope
they were trusting that they, the victory being nearly

exploratâ, celerĭter   recuperaturos   amissa.
assured,   quickly   about to [would] recover (their) losses.

Deliberatur   in   communi concilĭo   de   Avarĭco,
It was deliberated in   general   council about Avaricum,

placeat,   incendi
(whether)   it was pleasing,   (that it) (to)   [should] be burnt

an   defendi.   Bituriges   procumbunt
or   (to) be defended.   The Bituriges   fell

ad   pedes   omnibus   Gallis,
at   the feet (of)   all   the Gauls,   (that)

ne   cogerentur   succendĕre   sŭis
they   should not be forced   to set fire   with their own

manĭbus   pulcherrimam urbem propè totius Galliæ,
hands   (to) the most beautiful town   nearly of all   Gaul,

quæ sit et   præsidĭo   et   ornamento civitati;
which was both (for) a protection and   an ornament to the state;

dicunt   se   defensuros   facile
they say   (that)   they   about to [would] defend (it)   easily

naturâ   loci,   quòd   circumdata propè
by the nature of the place, because (it was) surrounded almost

ex omnibus partibus flumĭne et palude;   habĕat
on   all   sides   by the river and by a marsh; (that) it had

ŭnum   et   perangustum adĭtum.   Venĭa
one [a single] and   very narrow   entrance.   Permission

datur petentibus, Vercingetorige primò dissuadente,
is given to those petitioning, Vercingetorix at first opposing.

post   concedente et   ipsorum   percibus et
afterwards conceding   both because of their entreaties and

misericordiâ   volgi.   Idonei defensores
because of compassion to [for] the multitude. Suitable defenders

deliguntur   oppĭdo.
are selected   for the town.

16. Vercingetorix subsequĭtur   Cæsarem minoribus
      Vercingetorix   follows near   Cæsar   by lesser

itineribus,   et   deligit lŏcum   castris   munitum
marches,   and   selects a place for the camp defended

paludibus que silvis, longè ab   Avarĭco quindĕcim
by marshes and woods, distant from Avaricum fifteen

millĭa   passŭum.   Ibi   cognoscebat   per   certos
thousand   paces   There   he was learning   by   faithful

exploratores in singŭla tempŏra (pl.) diĕi   quæ
scouts   at   each   time [hour] of the day what things

agerentur (pl)   ad   Avarĭcum;   et   imperabat
were done   at   Avaricum.   and   he was commanding

quid   vellet   fieri;   observabat omnes nostras
what   he wished   to be done :   he watched   all   our

pabulationes   que   frumentationes,   que   quum
foragings   and   corn-raids   and   when

necessariò   procedĕrent   longiùs,   adoriebatur
they had necessarily   proceeded   rather far.   he was attacking

dispersos,   que   afficiebat   magno incommodo
(them)   dispersed   and   was inflicting   great   injury ,

(dat.);   etsi   occurrebatur ab nostris
although (this)   was obviated   by   our   (men)

quantum   potĕrat   provideri   ratione,   ut
as much as   (it) could   (to) be provided against by foresight that

irĕtur (pass. sing.)[15]   incertis   temporibus   que
they should go   at uncertain   times   and

diversis   itineribus.
by different   routes

17. Castris   positis   ad   ĕam   partem
The camp   having been pitched   at   this   part

oppidi,   quæ   intermissa   à   flumĭne   et
of the town.   which   having been left   by   the river   and

palude, ut   diximus   supra,   habebat   angustum
marsh,   as   we have said   above.   was having   a narrow

adĭtum,   Cæsar   cœpit   apparare   aggerem,   agĕre
approach,   Cæsar   began   to prepare   the mound.   to move

vinĕas,   constitŭere   dŭas   turres;   nam
the shelters.   (and)   to construct   two   towers.   for

natura   lŏci   prohibebat   circumvallare.
the nature   of the place   was preventing   to blockade [investment].

Non   destitit adhortari Boios atque Ædŭos   de
He did not   cease   to exhort   the Boii   and   Ædui   about

frumentariâ re;   altĕri   quorum,   quòd   agebant
the corn supply: the latter   of whom.   because   they acted

nullo studĭo, adjuvabant non multùm; altĕrı non
with no   zeal,   were assisting   not   much ;   the others   not

magnis facultatibus, quòd civitas ĕrat exigŭa et
with great   means   because   the state was   small   and

infirma, consumpserunt celerĭter quòd habuerunt.
weak.   they consumed   quickly   what   they had.

Exercĭtu affecto summâ difficultate
The army   (having been) afflicted   with the greatest   want

frumentarie rĕi, tenuitate Boiorum, indiligentiâ
of provisions,   by the poverty   of the Boii.   by the negligence

Æduorum, incendĭis ædificiorum, usquє
of the Ædui,   (and)   by the burning   of the buildings,   even

eo[16] ut milĭtes caruĕrint frumento
Ꞇo this [so]   that   the soldiers   wanted   corn   (for)

complures dies, et pecŏre adacto è
many   days,   and   cattle   having been driven   from

longinquioribus vicis, sustentarent extremam
the more distant   villages,   they satisfied   the extreme

famem; tamen nulla vox audita est ab iɪs
hunger;   yet   not   a word   was heard   from   them

indigna majestate Romani popŭli et
unworthy   the majesty   of the Roman   people   and   (their)

superioribus victorĭis. Quin ĕtiam quum Cæsar
former   victories.   Moreover   also   when   Cæsar

appellaret singŭlas legiones in opĕre, et dicĕret
addressed   the several   legions   at   work   and   said

se dimissurum oppugnationem, si ferrent
(that)   he   would abandon   the siege,   if   they borє

iopĭam acerbiùs; universi petebant ab
the want   too severely ;   all to a man   were begging   from [of]

ĕo ne facĕret id; "se siє
him   that he would not   do   this;   "they themselves   so

meruisse complures annos, illo imperante,
to have [had] served   very many   years.   he   commanding,

ut accipĕrent nullam ignominĭam nunquam
that   they should suffer   no   dishonor   never

discederent, re infectâ; se
had they withdrawn,   the thing   (having been) unaccomplished: they

laturos　　　　hoc　　　lŏco　ignominia,　si
about to [would] bear　this　(as)　an occasion　of dishonor,　if

relinquissent　oppugnationem　inceptam;　præ-
they should abandon　　the siege　　commenced.　to be [it

stare　　perferre omnes acerbitates, quâm
was] preferable　to endure　all　　hardships.　than　(that)

non parentarent Romanis civibus,　qui
they should　not　avenge　the Roman　citizens.　who

interissent　perfidiâ　Gallorum　Cenabi.　Hæc
had perished　by the perfidy　of the Gauls　at Cenabum.　These

ĕadem　　　　mandabant　centurionibus que
same　(things)　they were consigning　to the centurions　and

tribunis,　ut　per　ĕos　　deferrentur
tribunes,　that　through　them　they might be communicated

ad　Cæsarem.
to　Cæsar.

18. Quum　turres　jam　appropinquassent muro,
When　the towers had already　approached　the wall,

Cæsar cognovit　ex　captivis　　Vercingetorigem,
Cæsar ascertained　from　the prisoners (that)　Vercingetorix,

pabŭlo　　consumpto,　　　movisse
the forage　having been consumed.　to have [had] moved　(his)

castra propiùs Avarĭcum, atque　　ipsum,　cum
camp　nearer to　Avaricum,　and　(that)　he.　with

equitatu　que　expeditis,　qui　consuêssent
the cavalry　and　the light armed,　who　were accustomed

prœliari inter　equites,　causâ　insidiarum
to fight　among　the horsemen,　for the purpose　of ambuscades

profectum　ĕo,　quò　arbitrabatur
to have [had] marched　thither.　where　he was thinking　(that)

nostros　venturos　pabulatum　postĕro
our　(men) about to [would] come　to forage　on the following

die. Quibus　rebus　cognitis　profectus
day.　Which [These]　things　having been known　having set out

silentio mediâ nocte pervĕnit ad　castra　hostium
in silence at mid　night,　he arrived　at　the camp　of the enemy

manè.　　　Illi,　adventu　Cæsaris celerĭter
early in the morning.　They,　the arrival　of Cæsar　speedily

cognito per exploratores, abdiderunt
having been learned through scouts, concealed

carros que sŭa impedimenta in arctiores silvas,
the wagons and their baggage in the thicker woods,

instruxĕrunt omnes copĭas in edito
(and) drew up all (their) forces on an elevated

atque aperto lŏco. Quâ re nunciatâ,
and open place. Which thing having been announced,

Cæsar celerĭter jussit sarcinas conferri,
Cæsar quickly ordered the packs to be collected together,

arma expediri.
(and) the arms to be got ready.

19. Erat collis leniter acclivis ab infĭmc.
There was a hill gently sloping from below.

Difficĭlis atque impedĭta palus cingebat hunc
A difficult and impassable swamp was surrounding this

ex ferè omnibus partibus, non latior
on nearly all sides, not wider than

quinquaginta pedibus. Hoc colle, pontibus
fifty feet. On this hill, the bridges

interruptis, Galli continebant se,
having been broken down, the Gauls stationed themselves

fiducia loci; que distributi generatim
in confidence of the place, and, arranged in tribes

in civitates, obtinebant omnia vada
according to their states, they were holding all the shallows

ac saltus ejus paludis certis custodibus; sìc
and passes of this swamp by trusty guards; thus

parati animo, ut, si Romani conarentur
prepared in mind, that, if the Romans should attempt

perrumpĕre ĕam paludem, premerent,
to break through this swamp, they would crush (them),

ex superiore lŏco, hæsitantes; ut
from the higher station, while sticking fast: so that

qui vidĕrent propinquitatem lŏci,
those who should see the nearness of the position

existimarent paratos ad dimicandum
would think (that) they were prepared for fighting

prope   æquo   Marte ;   qui   perspicĕrent
almost on equal terms ;   (but) those who perceived

iniquitatem   conditionis,   cognoscĕrent
the disadvantage of the condition [place], would understand (that)

sese   ostentare   inani   simulatione.   Cæsar
they (to) make show with an empty pretense.   Cæsar

edocet   milĭtes   indĭgnantes,   quòd   hostes
shows   the soldiers indignant,   because the enemy

possent   ferre   sŭum conspectum,   tantulo   spatio
could   endure   their   sight,   so small   a space

          interjecto,   et   exposcentes   signum
(having been) interposed.   and earnestly demanding the signal

prœlii,   quanto   detrimento,   et   morte
of [for] battle, with how great   loss,   and with the death

quot   fortium   virorum   sit   necesse
of how many brave   men   it would be necessary

constare   victoriam ;   quos[17]   quum   vidĕret   sic
to assure   the victory ;   whom   since   he saw   so

paratos   animo,   ut   recusarent   nullum   pericŭlum
prepared in mind, that they refused   no   danger

pro   sŭâ   laude, se debere   condemnari   summæ
for   his   glory, he ought to be condemned for the greatest

iniquitatis,   nisi   habĕat   ĕorum   vitam   cariorem
injustice,   unless he holds   their   lives   dearer

      sŭâ   salute.   Consolatus   milĭtes   sic,
than   his   safety.   Having consoled the soldiers thus,

reducit   in   castra   ĕodem   dĭe ;   institŭit
he returns to the camp on the same day ;   he undertook

administrare   reliqua,   quæ   pertinebant   ad
to perform   the other things, which were belonging to

oppugnationem   oppidi.
the siege   of the town.

20. Vercingetorix, quum   redisset   ad sŭos
    Vercingetorix, when he had returned to his (men)

insimulatus proditionis,   quòd   movisset   castra
was accused   of treason, because he had moved (his) camp

propiùs   Romanos,   quòd   discessisset   cum omni
nearer   to the Romans because he had departed with all

equitatu ;   quòd   relinquisset   tantas   copĭas   sĭne
the cavalry;   because   he had left   such great   forces   without

imperĭo ;   quòd   ejus   discessu   Romani   venissent
a command;   because   on his   departure   the Romans   had come

tantâ   opportunitate,   et   celeritate ;   omnia
with so great   timeliness,   and   celerity;   (that)   all

hæc   potuisse   non   accidĕre   fortuitò,   aut
this   could   not   (to) happen   accidentally,   or

sine   consilĭo ;   illum   malle[18] habere   regnum
without   design;   (that) he   to prefer   to have   the sovereignty

Galliæ   concessu   Cæsaris,   quàm   ipsorum
of Gaul   with the permission   of Cæsar,   than   by their

beneficĭo.   Accusatus   tali   modo,   respondit
favor.   Having been accused   in such   manner,   he replied

ad hæc   "Quod   movisset   castra,   factum
to   these (things)   "That   he had moved   the camp,   it was done

inopiâ   pabŭli,   ipsis   etiam hortantibus, quòd
by want   of forage,   they themselves   even   urging,   that

accessisset   propiùs   Romanos,   persuasum
he had approached   nearer   the Romans,   he was induced

opportunitate   lŏci,   qui   defendĕret,   se ipsum
by the advantage   of the place,   which   would protect,   its own self

munitione ;   verò   opĕram   equĭtum
by the defence;   (that) indeed   the service   of the horsemen

debuisse (inf.) neque   desiderari   in   palustri   lŏco,
ought   not   to be wanted   in   a marshy   place,

et   fuisse   utilem   illic,   quò
and   they to have been   [were]   useful   there,   where

profecti sint ;   se   consultò   discedentem
they had gone;   (that) he   on purpose   (when)   departing

tradidisse   summam   imperĭi   nulli,   ne
to have [had] conferred   the chief   command   on no one,   lest

is   impelleretur   ad dimicandum   studio   multi-
he   might be driven   to   fighting   by the zeal   of the

tudinĭs ;   cui   rĕi,   vidĕret   omnes   studere,
multitude;   to which   thing,   it seemed   all   to be [was] eager,

propter   mollitiem[19]   animi,   quòd   possent
on account of (their)   weakness   of mind,   because   they could

non diutiùs ferre laborem. Si Romani
no longer endure labor. If the Romans

intervenerint casu gratĭam habendam
had come up by chance, that, thanks must be given

fortunæ, si vocati indicio alicujus, huic,[20]
to fortune, if invited by the information of any one to him,

quòd et potuĕrint cognoscĕre ĕorum paucitatem
because they could both (to) perceive their small number

ex superiore lŏco, et despicĕre
from the higher ground, and (could) (to) despise

virtutem qui non ausi dimicare turpĭter
the courage (of those) who not having dared to fight basely

recepĕrint se in castra. Se desiderare (inf.)
had betaken themselves into camp. He desires

nullum imperĭum à Cæsare per proditionem,
no sovereign power from Cæsar by treason,

quòd posset habere victoriâ, quæ esset
because he was able (to) have (it) by victory, which was

jam explorata sibi ac omnibus Gallis; quin
now certain to himself and to all the Gauls; but

ĕtĭam remittĕre ipsis, si videantur tribuere
even he to [would] resign to them, if they seemed to confer

honorem sibi magìs, quàm accipĕre (inf.)
honor on him rather, than (that) they had received

salutem ab se." Inquit, "ut intelligatis
safety from himself." He said, "in order that you may know

hæc pronunciari sincerè à me, audite
these things to be [are] announced truly by me, hear

Romanos milĭtes." Prodŭcit servos quos
the Roman soldiers." He brings forward slaves whom

excepĕrat in pabulatione, paucis diebus antè,
he had captured in foraging, a few days before,

et excruciavĕrat et fame que vincŭlis.
and had tortured both by hunger and chains.

Hi edocti jam antè, quæ pronunciarent
They having been taught already before, what they should declare

interrogati, dicunt se esse legionarios,
(when) interrogated, say that they were legionary soldiers

adductos   fame   et   inopiâ
(and)   (having been)   led   by hunger   and   want

exisse   clam   ex   castris si   possent
to have [had] gone out   secretly   from   camp   if   they were able

reperire   quid   frumenti aut pecŏris in
[could]   (to)   find   any   (of) corn   or   cattle   in

agris ;   omnem exercĭtum   premi
the fields ;   (that)   all   the army   to be [was] oppressed

simili inopiâ; nec   vires   cujusquam jam
by a like   want ;   nor   (does) the strength   of any one   now

sufficere, nec   posse   ferre laborem
(to)   suffice,   nor   to be [are they] able   to bear   the labor

opĕris.   Itaque imperatorem   statuisse,   si
of the work.   Therefore   the commander   to have [had] resolved,   if

profecissent   nihil   in   oppugnatione   oppĭdi,
he accomplished   nothing   in   the siege   of the town.

deducĕre   exercĭtum   tridŭo.   "Hæc beneficĭa,"
to withdraw   (his)   army   in three days   "These   benefits,"

inqŭit Vercingetorix,   "habetis   à   me,   quem
said   Vercingetorix,   "you have   from   me.   whom

insimulatis proditionis,   cujus   opĕrâ videtis tantum
you accuse   of treason.   by whose   means   you see   so great

victorem   exercĭtum   pænè   consumptum   fame,
a conquering   army   nearly   destroyed   by hunger.

sine   vestro sanguine; quem,   turpĭter recipientem
without   your   blood ,   which,   disgracefully   betaking

se   ex   hâc   fugâ,   provisum est   à   me,   ne
itself   on   this   flight   it had been provided   by   me,   not

qua   civĭtas   recipĭat   sŭis   finibus."
any   state   shall receive   in its   territories."

21. Omnis   multitudo   conclamat   et   concrepat
     All   the multitude   shout   and   rattle

armis   suo   more,   quod   consueverunt
with (their) arms   in their   manner,   which   they are accustomed

facĕre   in   ĕo   cujus   orationem   approbant,
to do   for   him   whose   speech   they were approving.

"Vercingetorigem   esse   summum   ducem,   nec
"Vercingetorix   to be [is]   the greatest   general.   nor

dubitandum   de   ejus   fide,   nec
must it be doubted concerning his   faithfulness, nor

posse   bellum   administrari   majore
to be possible [could] the war   (to) be carried on with greater

ratione."   Statŭunt   ut   dĕcem   millĭa   homĭnum
judgement."   They decree that   ten   thousand   men

delecta   ex   omnibus   copĭis   snbmittantur   in
selected   from   all   the forces   should be sent   into

oppidum;   nec   censent   communem   salutem
the town;   nor   do they think   the general   safety

committendum   Biturigibus   solis,   quòd
to [must] be committed to the Bituriges   alone,   because

intelligebant   summam   victoriæ
they were understanding (that) the completeness of the victory

constare   pænè   in   eo,   si   retinuissent
would depend almost   upon   this,   if   they should hold

oppidum.
the town.

22. Consilia   cujusque   modi   Gallorum   occurrebant
    The plans   of every   kind   of the Gauls   were opposing

singulari   virtuti   nostrorum   militum,   ut   est (sing.)
the uncommon bravery   of our   soldiers,   as   they are

genus   summæ   sollertiæ,   atque   aptissimum   ad
a nation of the greatest ingenuity,   and   very apt   for [at]

imitandi   atque   efficienda,   quæ   traduntur
imitating   and   making   (things),   which   are imparted

ab   quoque.   Nam   avertebant   falces   laqueis,
by   any one.   For   they were turning the hooks with nooses,

quos[21]   quum   destinaverant,   reducebant   introrsus
which   when   they had caught, they were hauling within

tormentis,   et   subtrahebant   aggerem   cuniculis,
by engines,   and   they were undermining the mound by tunnels,

eò scientiùr,   quòd   apud   eos   sunt   magnæ
the more skilfully, because   among   them   are   great

ferrariæ,   atque   omne   genus   cuniculorum   est   notum
iron mines,   and   all   kinds   of tunnels   are   known

atque   usitatum.   Autem   contabulaverant   totum
and   employed.   Moreover   they had fortified   the entire

murum   ex omni parte   turribus,   atque intexerant
wall   on all parts   with towers,   and had covered

has   coriis :   tum   crebris   diurnis que nocturnis
these with hides : also in (their) frequent daily and nightly

eruptionibus,   aut   inferebant   ignem   aggeri,
sallies,   either they were setting fire to the mound,

aut adoriebantur   milites occupatos in opere ; et
or were attacking   our soldiers occupied in the work , and

adæquabant   altitudinem   nostrarum   turrium,
they were equaling   the height   of our   towers,

quantum   agger   quotidianus   expressĕrat   has,
as much as the mound   daily   raised   them.

malis   suarum turrium   commissis ;   et
the masts of their towers   having been joined [spliced] ; and

morabantur   apertos cuniculos præustâ et
they were retarding (our) open   tunnels by burnt and

præacutâ materiâ, et fervefactâ pice, et saxis
very sharp stakes, and by boiling pitch, and by stones

maximi   ponderis, que   prohibebant   (us from)
of very great weight, and they were checking

appropinquare (inf.) mœnibus.
approaching   the walls.

23. Autem hæc est   ferè   forma omnibus Gallicis
     Moreover this is generally the form of all the Gallic

muris. Directæ trabes perpetuæ in longitudinem,
walls   Straight beams continuous in   length,

binos pedes distantes paribus intervallis inter
two   feet   distant   at equal intervals   between

se[22]   collocantur in   solo.   Hæ revinciuntur
themselves are placed   on the ground. These are made fast

introrsus,   et   vestiuntur   multo   aggere.
within,   and are covered with much mound-filling.

Autem   ĕa   intervalla,   quæ   diximus
But   those intervals,   which we have mentioned,

effarciuntur in   fronte grandibus saxis. Iis
are filled up in   front with great stones. These

collocatis   et   coagmentatis,   alius   ordo
having been placed and united together.   another row

adjicitur insuper,   ut   illud   idem   intervallum
is put   above,   so that,   this   same   interval

servetur,   neque   trabes contingant   inter
may be observed,   nor   the beams may touch   among

se,[23]   sed   intermissæ   paribus   spatiis,   singulæ
themselves,   but   are separated   by equal   spaces,   each

contineantur (pl.)   artè   singulis   interjectis   saxis:
kept in place   closely   by the several   interposed   stones,

sic   deinceps   omne   opus   contexitur,   dum
so   successively   the whole   work   is bound together,   till

justa   altitudo   muri   expleatur.   Quum   hoc
the proper   height   of the wall   is completed.   Not only   this

opus est   non   deforme   in   speciem   que varietatem
work   is   not   unsightly   in   appearance   and   variety

alternis   trabibus   ac   saxis,   quæ   servant   suos
by the alternate   beams   and   stones,   which   preserve   their

ordines   rectis   lineis,   tum   habet   ad utilitatem,
order   in straight   lines,   but also   it has   for   utility,

et   defensionem   urbium   summam   opportunitatem,
and   defence   of cities   great   advantage,

quòd   et   lapis   defendit   ab   incendio,   et
because   both   the stone   protects   from   fire,   and

materia   ab   ariete,   quæ
the wood-work   from   the battering-ram,   which   (having been)

revincta   introrsùs   trabibus   plerumque   perpetuis
fastened   internally   by beams   mostly   continuous   (for)

quadragenos   pedes,   potest   neque   perrumpi,
forty   feet,   can   neither   be broken through,

neque   distrahi.
nor   rent apart.

24.   Oppugnatione   impeditâ   tot   iis
The siege   having been impeded   by so many   these

rebus,   quum   milites   tardarentur   tŏto
[such]   things,   though   the soldiers   were retarded   the whole

tempore   luto,   frigore,   et   assiduis   imbribus,   tamen
time   by mud,   cold,   and   continual   rains,   yet

superaverunt omnia   hæc   continenti   labore,
they overcame   all   these (things)   by their continual   labor,

et   viginti   quinque diebus,   extruxerunt   aggerem
and   in twenty   five   days,   they constructed   a mound

trecentos   et   triginta pedes latum,   octoginta
three hundred   and   twenty   feet   wide,   (and)   eighty

pedes altum.   Quum   is   pænè contingeret
feet   high.   When   this   (mound)   had nearly touched

murum   hostium,   et   Cæsar   excubaret ad   opus
the wall   of the enemy,   and   Cæsar   kept watch   at   the work

consuetudine,   que   exhortaretur   milites,   quod   ne
by his custom,   and   encouraged   the soldiers,   that   no

tempus omnino intermitteretur   ab   opere,   paulo
time   at all   should be lost   from   the work   a little

ante   tertiam   vigiliam,   est animadversum
before   the third   watch,   it was observed   (that)

aggerem   fumare (inf.),   quem   hostes   succendĕrant
the mound   (to) smoked,   which   the enemy   had fired

cuniculo; que   eodem   tempore clamore   sublato
by a mine;   and   at the same   time   a shout   having been raised

toto   muro,   eruptio   fiebat   duabus   portis   ab
on all   the wall,   a sally   was made   from two   gates   on

utroque latere   turrium.   Alii   eminus   jaciebant
each   side   of the towers.   Some   from a distance were throwing

faces   atque   aridam   materiem   de   muro   in
torches   and   dry   material   from   the wall   on

aggerem;   alii   fundebant picem   que reliquas   res,
the mound,   others   were pouring   pitch   and   other   things,

quibus   ignis   potest   incitari;   ut   ratio posset
by which   the fire   might   be encouraged,   so that   a plan   could

vix   iniri,   quò primum   occurreretur,[24]   aut
scarcely   be adopted,   where   first   they should obstruct.   or

cui   rei   auxilium   ferretur;
to which   affair [predicament]   aid   should be brought;

tamen   quòd,   instituto   Cæsaris, duæ legiones
however   as,   by the arrangement   of Cæsar,   two   legions

semper excubabant   pro   castris,   que plures   partitis
always   were watching   before   the camp,   and   many   at alloted

temporibus erant   in   opere,   celeriter factum est,   ut
times   were   at   work,   it was quickly managed,   that

alli resisterent eruptionibus, alli reducĕrent
some should oppose the sallies, others should draw back

turres que interscindĕrent aggerem; verò
the towers and cut off the mound; and indeed

omnis multitudo concurrent ex castris ad
(that) a whole multitude should run from the camp to

restinguendum.
extinguish (the fire).

25. Quum pugnaretur[25] in omnibus lŏcis,
When it was fought in all places,

reliquâ parte noctis jam consumptâ, que
the remaining portion of the night now having been spent, and

spes victoriæ semper redintegraretur hostibus(dat.),
the hope of victory continually was renewed in the enemy,

magìs eò quòd videbant pluteos turrium
the more so because they were seeing the coverings of the towers

deustos, animadvertebant apertos nec
burnt off. (and) were observing (that we) unprotected not

facilè adire ad auxiliandum, que ipsi
easily to go [approached] for aiding, and they

recentes semper succedĕrent defessis (dat.),
fresh all the time were succouring the wearied,

que arbitrarentur omnem salutem Galliæ
and (they) were judging (that) all the safety of Gaul

positam[26] in illo vestigio tempŏris, accidit
(was) placed in that instant of time, there happened

nobis inspectantibus quod visum dignum
to us observing (that) which seemed (to be) worthy

memoriâ existimavimus non prætermittendum.
(of) memory we have thought to [it must] not be passed over.

Quidam Gallum ante portam oppidi, qui è
A certain Gaul before the gate of the town, who from

regione turris projiciebat glebas sevi ac
the locality of the tower was throwing lumps of tallow and

picis in ignem, transditas per manus (pl.);
pitch into the fire, passed along by hand,

transjectus ab dextra latere scorpione, que
having been pierced on the right side by the cross-bow, and

exanimatus   concidit;   unus   ex   proximis
struck lifeless   fell,   one   from [of]   the nearest

transgressus   hunc   jacentem   fungebatur   illo
having stepped over   him   lying prostrate,   was discharging   that

eodem   manere;   eâdem   ratione   altero   exani-
same   duty;   in the same   manner   the other   having been

mate   ictu   scorpionis,   tertius   successit,
killed   by a stroke   of the cross-bow,   a third   succeeded,

et   quartus   tertio;   nec   ille   locus   relictus est
and   a fourth   to the third;   nor   that   place   was left

vacuus   à   propugnatoribus,   priùs   quàm   aggere
vacant   by   the defenders,   before   (that)   the mound

restincto   atque hostibus   submotis
(having been) extinguished   and   the enemy   having been repulsed

omni   parte,   finis   factus est   pugnandi.
on every   side,   an end   was made   of the fighting.

26.   Galli   experti   omnia,   quod   nulla   res
The Gauls   having tried   all things,   because   no   thing

successerat,   postero   die ceperunt consilium profugere
had succeeded,   on the next   day   adopted   the plan   to flee

ex   oppido, Vercingetorige hortante   et   jubente.
from   the town,   Vercingetorix   advising   and   commanding.

Sperabant,   conati   id   silentio   noctis
They were hoping,   having attempted   it   in the silence   of the night

sese   effecturos   non   magnâ
(that)   they   about to [would] accomplish   (it)   with no   great

jacturâ   suorum,   propterea   quòd   castra
loss   of their (men),   because   (that)   the camp

Vercingetorigis   aberant   neque longè   ab   oppido,
of Vercingetorix   was distant   not   far   from   the town,

et   perpetua   palus,   quæ   intercedebat,   tardabat²⁷
and   a continuous   marsh,   which   was intervening,   would retard

Romanos   ad   insequendum.   Que   jam
the Romans   for [in]   following.   And   already

apparabant   facere hoc   noctu,   quum   matres
they were preparing   to do   this   by night,   when   the mothers

familias   repentè procurrerunt   in   publicum,
of families [matrons]   suddenly   ran out   into   public.

que flentes projectæ   ad pedes suorum
and weeping having thrown (themselves) at the feet of their

petierunt omnibus precibus, ne
(husbands) they begged with all entreaties, that they would not

dederent se et communes liberos hostibus
give up themselves and (their) common children to the enemy

ad supplicium, quos natura, et infirmitas
for punishment, whom nature, and the weakness

virium (pl.) impediret ad capiendam fugam.
of (their) strength prevented for [from] taking flight.

Ubi viderunt eos perstare (inf.) in
When they saw (that) they persisted in (their)

sententiâ, quòd plerumque in summo periculo
design, because generally in the greatest danger

timor recipit non misericordiam, cæperunt conclamare,
fear admits not mercy, they began to cry out,

et significare de fugâ Romanis;
and to give warning concerning the flight to the Romans;

quo timore Galli perterriti, ne viæ
by which fear the Gauls having been alarmed, lest the road

præoccuparentur ab equitatu Romanorum destiterunt
should be preoccupied by the cavalry of the Romans they desisted

consilio.
from (their) design.

27. Cæsar, postĕro die turri pro-
Cæsar, on the next day the tower having been

motâ, que operibus directis, quæ
moved forward, and the works having been arranged, which

instituĕrat facĕre, magno imbri coorto,
he had determined to make, a great storm having arisen,

arbitratus est hanc tempestatem non inutilem ad
thought this time not unsuited for

capiendum consilium, quòd videbat custodias
carrying out the plan, because he was seeing the guards

in muro dispositas paulò incautiùs; que
on the wall arranged a little more carelessly; and

jussit suos versari in opere langui-
he ordered his (men) to be occupied in the work rather

diùs,   et   ostendit   quid   vellet   fiĕri.
sluggishly, and   showed   what   he wished   to be done.

Cohortatus   legiones   expeditas   in   occulto
Having exhorted the legions prepared   in   a concealed place

intra   vineas,   ut   aliquando   percipĕrent   fructum
within the sheds, that at length   they would receive the fruit

victoriæ pro   tantis   laboribus, proposuit   præmia
of victory for such great   labors,   he offers   rewards

ĭis,   qui   primi   ascendissent murum, que   dedit
to those, who   first   should scale the wall, and   gave

signum   militibus.   Illi   subitò   evolaverunt   ex
the signal to the soldiers. They   suddenly flew out   from

omnibus partìbus, que celeriter complêrunt murum.
all   sides,   and quickly   filled   the wall.

28. Hostes   perterriti   novâ   re,
The enemy   having been alarmed   by the sudden affair

            dejecti   muro   que turribus,
[action], (having been) driven   from the wall   and towers,

constiterunt cuneatim   foro   ac patentioribus
they drew up   as a wedge   in the square   and more open

lŏcis,   hôc animo, ut si ex quâ pârte   venire-
places, with this idea, that if on any side (any one) should

tur[28] contra obviam depugnarent   acie
come   against   they might fight   with a line of battle

instructâ. Ubi   viderunt   neminem demittere
drawn up.   When they saw (that)   no one   lowered

sese in   æquum locum, sed   undique   circum-
himself into the level place,   but   on every side they were

fundi   toto   muro,   veriti   ne   omnino
spread around on the whole wall,   having feared lest altogether

spes   fugæ   tolleretur,   armis
the hope of flight   might be taken away,   (their) arms

        abjectis   petiverunt   ultimas   partes
having been thrown away   they sought   the farthest parts

oppidi   continenti   impetu; que ĭbi   pars,
of the town with a continuous rush;   and there a part,

quum ipsi premerent   se   angusto   exitu
as   they crowded   themselves in the narrow passage

portarum, interfecta est à militibus, pars
of the gates, was killed by the soldiers, (and) a part

jam egressa portis, ab equitibus; nec
already having passed the gates, by the horsemen; nor

fuit quisquam qui studeret prædæ. (Having
was there any one who was attending to plunder.

Incitati sic et cæde Cenabensi,
been) excited so much both by the slaughter at Cenabum,

et labore opĕris perpecerunt non
and by the labor of the work they spared neither (those)

confectis ætate, non mulieribus non infantibus.
worn out with age, nor women nor children.

Denique ex omni ĕo numero, qui fuit circiter
Finally out of all this number, which was about

quadraginta millium, vix octingenti, qui primo
forty thousand, scarcely eight hundred, who, the first

clamore audito, ejecerant se ex
shout having been heard, had thrown themselves from

oppido, pervenerunt incolumes ad Vercingetorigem;
the town, came safe to Vercingetorix;

quos ille, nocte jam multâ, excepit
whom he, the night (being) now much [late], received

sic ex fugâ silentio (veritus ne qua seditio
thus from the flight in silence (having feared lest some sedition

oreretur in castris ex eorum concursu, et
might arise in the camp from their gathering, and

misericordiâ volgi) ut suis familiaribus, que
from the compassion of the throng) that his friends, and

principibus civitatum, dispositis procul
the chiefs of the states, having been located at a distance

in viâ curaret disparandos que
on the road he took care (that) they should be seperated and

deducendos ad suos, quæ[29] pars castris
be conducted to their (own people). which part of the camp

obvenerat cuique civitati ab initio.
had fallen to each state from the beginning.

29. Postero die concilio convocato,
On the following day a council having been called.

consolatus   que   cohortatus est   "ne
he consoled   and   exhorted,   " they should not be

admodum demittĕrent se animo,   neve perturbarentur
too much   cast down   in mind,   nor   troubled

incommodo: Romanos   non   vicisse   virtute
by (their) loss ;   (that)   the Romans   had not   conquered   by bravery

neque   in   acie,   sed   quodam   artificio   et
nor   in   a battle-line,   but   by a certain   skill   and

scientiâ   oppugnationis,   cujus   rei   ipsi   fuerint
by the science   of siege,   of which   thing   they   were

imperiti;   errare, si   qui   expectent   in bello
unskilled;   (those)   err,   if   they   expect   in war

omnes eventus   rerum   secundos;   nunquam
all   results   of affairs   (to be)   prosperous;   never

placuisse   sibi   Avaricum   defendi,
had it pleased   him   (that)   Avaricum   to [should] be defended,

ejus   rĕi   haberet   ipsos   testes;   sed
of which   thing   he had   themselves   as witnesses;   but

factum   imprudentiâ   Biturigum   et
to have been (it was) done   by the imprudence   of the Bituriges   and

nimiâ   obsequentiâ   reliquorum,   uti   hoc
by the too great   compliance   of the rest,   that   this

incommodum acciperetur;   tamen   se   sanaturum
disaster   was received;   however   he   would remedy

id   celeriter   majoribus   commodis.   Nam   civitates
this   quickly   by greater   advantages.   For   the states

quæ   dissentirent   ab   reliquis Gallis,   has   suâ
which   dissented   from   the other   Gauls,   these   by his

diligentiâ adjuncturum,   atque unum consilium totius
exertion   would be united,   and   one   counsel   of all

Galliæ   effecturum,   cujus consenui (dat.)   orbis
Gaul   would be effected.   whose   union   the whole

terrarum quidem   possit   ne   obsistere;
world   indeed   would be able [could]   not   (to)   oppose;

que   se   habere   prope   jam   effectum   id.
and   he   to have [had]   nearly   already   effected   this

Intereă   esse   æquum   impet.
In the mean time   to be [it was]   just   (that) to [it shou]d

rari   ab   ĭis   causâ   communis salutis,
be obtained   from   them   for the sake of the general safety,

ut   instituĕrent   munire   castra,   quo
that   they should decree to fortify   their camp,   so that

          possent   faciliùs   sustinere
they would be able [could]   the more easily   (to)   resist

repentinos impetus   hostium."
the sudden   attacks   of the enemy. "

30. Hac oratio fuit non   ingrata   Gallis,   quòd
    This speech was not disagreeable to the Gauls, because

ipse   non defecĕrat animo,   tanto incommodo
he himself had not   failed   in courage, so great   a loss

     accepto,   neque abdidĕrat   se   in occultum,
having been received, neither had he hid   himself in   secret,

neque   fugerat   conspectum   multitudinis :   que
 nor   fled   the sight   of the multitude :   and

existimabatur   providere   et   præsentire,   plus
he was thought   to foresee   and   to forecast,   more

animo   quòd,   re   integrâ,   con-
in mind   because,   the matter (being) not begun,   he ha l

suĕrat   primo   Avaricum   incendendum,
decided   first   (that) Avaricum   to [should] be burnt

pòst   deserendum.   Itaque ut adversæ
afterwards (that) it to [should] be deserted. And so as   adverse

res   minuunt auctoritatem reliquorum imperatorum ;
affairs   diminish   the authority   of other   commanders ;

sic ex contrario   dignitas   hujus incommodo
so   on   the contrary the authority of this one   a loss

     accepto,   augebatur   in   dies :
having been sustained,   was increased   (from day) to   day :

simul   vinebant   in,   spem,   ejus
at the same time   they were coming into,   the hope,   of his

affirmatione, de adjungendis reliquis civitatibus ; que
 assertion,   of   uniting   the other   states ,   and

primùm   Galli   eo   tempore instituerunt munire
 first   the Gauls at this   time   undertook   to fortify

     castra ;   et   sic homines   insueti   laboris
their   camp ;   and   so   men   unaccustomed to labor

confirmati sunt   animo,   ut   existimarent   omnia
were encouraged   in mind,   that   they sought   (that)   all

quæ   imperarentur   patienda   sibi.
(things) which   were commanded   must be endured   by them.

31. Nec Vercingetorix   laborabat   minùs animo
Nor   Vercingetorix   was exerting himself   less   in mind

quam   pollicitus est,   ut   adjungeret   reliquas
than   he had promised,   that   he might attach   the other

civitates, atque   alliciebat   eorum principes   donis
states,   and   he was enticing   their   chiefs   by presents

que   pollicitationibus.   Deligebat   idonĕos   homines
and   promises.   He selected   suitable   men

huic   rei,   aut   subdolâ   oratione aut   amicitiâ
for this   affair,   either   by the wily   speech   or   friendship

quorum   quisque   posset   facillime   capi.
of whom   each   (chief)   might   most easily   be gained.

Qui   refugĕrant   Avarico   expugnato,
Those who   had escaped,   Avaricum   having been stormed,

curat   armandos   que vestiendos.   Simul
he takes care   should be armed   and   clothed.   At the same time

ut   diminutæ   copiæ   redintegrarentur,   imperat
that   his diminished   forces   might be renewed,   he orders

certum   numerum   militum   civitatibus,   quem,   et
a certain   number   of soldiers   from the states,   whom,   and

ante   quam diem,   velit   adduci   in   castra;
before   what   day,   he wishes   to be brought   into   the camp;

que   jubet   omnes   sagittarios,   quorum   erat
and   he orders   all   the archers,   of whom   there was

permagnus numerus   in Galliâ,   conquiri,   et mitti
a very great   number   in   Gaul,   to be sought,   and   sent

ad   se.   His   rebus,   id   quod   deperierat
to   him.   By these   means,   this   which   he had lost

Avarici   celeriter   expletur.   Interim
at Avaricum   was speedily   replaced   In the mean time

Teutomatus,   filius Olloviconis,   rex   Nitiobrigum,
Teutomatus,   the son   of Ollovicon,   king   of the Nitiobriges,

cujus pater   appellatus erat   amicus   ab nostro Senatu,
whose   father   had been called   friend   by   our   Senate,

pervenit ad eum, cum magno numero suorum equitum,
came　to him,　with　a great　number　of his　cavalry,

et　　　quos conduxerat　ex　Aquitaniâ.
and (those) that　he had hired　from　Aquitania.

32. Cæsar commoratus complures dies Avarici,
　　Cæsar　having delayed　several　days　at Avaricum,

que　nactus　ibi　summam copiam frumenti et
and having obtained there the greatest supply　of corn　and

reliqui commeatus, refecit exercitum ex labore
of other provisions,　refreshed　his army　from　labor

atque inopiâ. Hieme　jam　prope confectâ,
and　want. The winter having been now nearly ended,

quum tempore ipso anni vacaretur ad
when by the season itself of the year he was at leisure for

gerendum bellum, et constituisset proficisci
carrying on　war,　and　he had determined　to march

ad hostem, sive elicere eum ex paludibus
against the enemy. either to entice him from the marshes

que silvis, sive posset premere obsidione,
and woods,　or　that he might　crush　by a siege,

legati principes Æduorum veniurt ad eum
ambassadors chiefs of the Ædui come to him

oratum ut maxime necessario tempore
to entreat that in an especially necessary [critical] time

subveniat civitati; "rem esse in summo
he should assist the state; "their affairs to be [are] in extreme

periculo; quòd quum singuli magistratus cre-
danger; that whereas single magistrates had been

ari antiquitùs, atque consuêssent obtinere
appointed of old,　and were accustomed to possess

regiam potestatem annum; duo gerant magistratum,
a kingly power for one year, two hold the magistracy,

et uterque eorum dicat se creatum esse
and each of them asserts (that) he was appointed

legibus. Horum alterum esse Convictrolitavem
by the laws. Of these the one was Convictrolitavis

florentem et illustrem adolescentem, alterum Cotum
a distinguished and illustrious young man, the other Cotus

natum   antiquissimâ   familiâ, atque ipsum hominem
sprung   from a most ancient   family,   and   himself   a man

summæ   potentiæ,   et   magnæ cognationis, cujus
of the highest   power,   and   of great   connections,   whose

frater   Valetiacus   gesserit   eundem   magistratum
brother   Valetiacus   had held   the same   magistracy

proximo   anno;   omnem   civitatem   esse   in   armis;
the last   year;   the whole   state   was   in   arms;

senatum   divisum,   populum   divisum,   suas
the senate   was divided,   the people   divided,   their

clientelas[30]   cujusque   eorum: quod   si   controversia
partisans   of each   of them: that   if   the dispute

alatur   diutiùs,   fŏre   utì   pars   civitatis
is formented   longer,   it would happen   that   a part   of the state

confligat   cum   parte;   id   ne accidat
would collide   with   a part;   (that)   this   may not happen

positum   in ejus diligentiâ atque auctoritate.
was placed [rested]   in   his   exertion   and   authority.

33. Cæsar,   etsi   existimabat   detrimentosum
Cæsar,   although   he thought it   injurious

descedere   à   bello   atque   hoste;   tamen non
to depart   from   the war   and   the enemy;   yet   not

ignorans   quanta   incommoda consuêssent   oriri
being ignorant   how great   wrongs   were wont   to arise

ex   dissensionibus;   ne   tanta   civitas   et   tam
from   dissensions;   lest   so great   a state   and   so

conjuncta   Romano   populo,   quam ipse semper
connected   with the Roman   people,   which   he   always

aluisset,   que ornâsset omnibus rebus, descendĕret
had cherished,   and   honored   in all   things,   should resort

ad   vim   atque ad   arma; atque   ĕa   pars   quæ
to   violence   and   to   arms,   and   this   part   which

confidĕret   minùs   sibi   accerseret   auxilia   à
might confide   least   in him   should call for   assistance   from

Vercingetorige; existimavit   huic   rĕi   præ-
Vercingetorix;   he thought   (that)   this   action   ought

vertendum;   et   quòd   legibus   Æduorum,
to be anticipated;   and   because   by the laws   of the Ædui.

iis   qui   obtinĕrent   summum   magistratum
to these   who   possessed   the chief   magistracy

non lĭceret   excedere   ex   finibus;   ne
it was not allowed   to depart   from (their) territories ,   lest

videretur   deminuisse   quid   de   eorum
he should seem   to have curtailed   any thing   respecting   their

jure   aut   legibus,   ipse   statuit   proficisci   in
authority   or   laws,   he himself   resolved   to set out   to

Æduos,   que   evocavit   omnem   senatum,   et
the Ædui,   and   he summoned   all   the senate,   and (those)

intra   quos   controversia   esset,   ad   se
among   whom   the controversy   might be,   to   (meet)   him

Decetiam.   Quum   propè   omnis   civitas
at Decetia   [Decize].   When   nearly   the whole   state

convenisset   eò,   que   doceretur   fratrem
had assembled   there.   and   he was informed   (that)   a brother

renunciatum   à   fratre,   paucis   clàm vocatis,
had been proclaimed   by a brother,   a few   having been secretly called,

alio   lŏco,   alio   tempŏre,   atque
in another   place,   (and)   at another   time,   than

oportuĕrit;   quum   leges   non   solùm   vetarent
was proper,   when   the laws   not   only   were forbidding

dūos   ex   unâ   familiâ,   utroque   vivo,   creari
two   of   one   family,   both   being alive,   to be chosen

magistratus,   sed   etĭam   prohibĕrent   esse   in
magistrates,   but   also   were forbidding (them)   to be   in

senatu ;   coëgit   Cotum   deponere   magistratum;
the senate ;   he compelled   Cotus   to resign   the magistracy

jussit   Convictolitavem,   qui   esset   creatus   per
he ordered   Convictolitavis,   who   had been   chosen   through

sacerdotes   more   civitatis,   magistratibus
the priests   after the custom   of the state,   the magistracy

intermissis,   obtinere   potestatem.
having lapsed,   to hold   the power [office].

34. Hôc   decreto   interposito,   cohortatus
This   decree   having been delivered,   he exhorted

Æduos   ut   obliviscerentur   controversiarum
the Ædui   that   they should forget   (their)   controversies

ac dissensionum, atque omnibus rebus   omis-
and   dissensions,   and   all   things   having been

sis,   servirent   huic bello, que exspectarent
laid aside, they should attend to this war, and might expect

ĕa præmia, quæ meruissent,   ab   se, Galliâ
those rewards, which they should merit, from him, Gaul

      devictâ,   que   mitterent   omnem
having been conquered, and (that) they should send all

equitatum, et decem millia   peditum celerĭter
the cavalry, and ten thousand footmen speedily

sibi, quæ disponĕret in præsidiis causâ
to him, whom he might place in garrisons for the sake

rĕi frumentariæ; divisit   exercitum in duas
of the grain supply; he divided (his) army into two

partes; dedit quatuor legiones Labieno ducendas
parts; he gave four legions to Labienus to be led

in Senones que Parisios; ipse duxit sex in
into the Senones and Parisii; he himself led six into

Arvernos ad oppidum Gergoviam secundùm flumen
the Arverni to the town (of) Gergovia down the river

Elaver: attribuit partem equitatûs illi,
Allier: he gave a part of the cavalry to him (Labienus)

reliquit partem sibi. Quâ re cognitâ,
he left a part for himself. Which thing having been known

Vercingetorix, omnibus potibus ejus fluminis
Vercingetorix, all the bridges of this river

      interruptis, cœpit facĕre iter ab
having been demolished, began to make his march on

alterâ parte fluminis.
the other side of the river.

35. Quum uterque exercitus exisset in conspectu
When each army led out in view

que utrimque ponebant castra ferè è
and on each side they were pitching a camp almost over

regione castris. Exploratoribus   dispositis,
against a camp. Scouts   having been stationed,

      necubi Romani, transducerent copias,
(so) that in no place the Romans, could lead across the forces

ponte	effecto;		res		erat
a bridge	having been built;		(this) thing	[condition]	was

	Cæsari	in	magnis	difficultatibus,	ne	imped-
	to [placed] Cæsar	in	great	difficulties,	lest	he should

iretur	flumine,	majorem	partem	æstatis,
be hindered	by the river,	for the greater	part	of the summer,

quòd	Elaver	soleat	non	transiri	vado
because	the Allier	is wont	not	to be crossed	by fording

	ferè	ante	autumnum.	Itaque	ne	id
	(till) nearly	before	autumn.	Therefore	lest	this

accidĕret,	castris	positis	silvestri	lŏco
might happen,	the camp	having been pitched	in a woody	place

è regione	unius	eorum	pontium,	quos	Vercin-
opposite	one	of these	bridges,	which	Vercin-

getorix	curaverat	rescindendos,	postĕro	die
getorix	had provided	should be destroyed,	on the next	day

restitit	in	occulto,	cum	duabus	legionibus;
he remained	in	a concealed place,	with	two	legions;

misit,	ut	consuevĕrat	reliquas	copias
he sent,	as	he had been accustomed	the remaining	forces

cum	omnibus	impedimentis,	quibusque	quartis
with	all	the baggage,	each	fourth

cohortibus	demptis,	uti	numĕrus	legionum
cohort	having been removed,	so that	the number	of the legions

videretur	constare.	Iis	jussis	progredi
should seem	to agree.	These	having been ordered	to advance

quàm	longissimè	possent,	quum	jam	ex
as	far	(as) they could,	when	at last	from

tempore	diei	caperet	conjecturam	per-
the time	of day	he could make	the conjecture	(that) they

ventum	in	castra,	cœpit	reficere	pontem
had arrived	to [in]	camp,	he began	to rebuild	the bridge

iisdem	sublicis	inferior	pars	quarum	remanebat
on the same	piles	the lower	part	of which	was remaining

integra.	Opĕre	celerĭter	effecto,	que
entire.	The work	quickly	having been completed	and

legionibus	transductis,	et	idoneo	loco
the legions	having been led over,	and	a suitable	place

castris delecto, revocavit reliquas copias.
for a camp having been selected, he recalled the remaining forces.

Vercingetorix, re cognitâ, ne
Vercingetorix, the thing [event] having been learned, lest

cogeretur dimicare contra suam voluntatem,
he might be forced to fight against his will,

antecessit magnis itineribus.
preceded (him) by great [forced] marches.

36. Cæsar pervenit Gergoviam, ex ĕo lŏco,
Cæsar reached Gergovia, from this place,

quintis castris que levi equestri prœlio
on the fifth encampment and a slight cavalry battle

facto ĕo die, situ urbis
having been fought on this day, the situation of the town

perspecto, quæ posita in
having been reconnoitred, which (having been) placed on

altissĭmo monte, habebat omnes aditus
a very high mountain, was having all the approaches

difficiles, desperavit de expugnatione; constituit
difficult, he despaired of an assault; he determined

non agendum[31] de obsessione
(that) not to be [it must not be] acted respecting the siege

priùs quàm expedisset rem frumentariam. At
before (that) he had secured a grain supply. But

Vercingetorix castris positis prope oppidum,
Vercingetorix (his) camp having been placed near the town,

in monte, collocaverat copias singularum
on the mountain, had stationed the forces of each

civitatum separatim, circum se, mediocribus
state separately, around himself, at moderate

intervallis; atque omnibus collibus ejus jugi
intervals; and all the hills of this range

occupatis quà poterat despici,
having been occupied where it was possible to be viewed,

præbebat horribĭlem speciem: que jubebat
he was presenting a formidable appearance; and he was ordering

principes earum civitatum, quos delegerat
the chiefs of these states, whom he had selected

sibi   ad   capiendum   consilium,   convenire   ad
for himself   for   taking   counsel,   to come   to

se   quotidie   primâ   luce   seu   quid
him   daily   at first   light [early dawn],   whether   anything

videretur   communicandum,   seu   quid   minis-
might seem best   to be discussed,   or   anything   (to) be

trandum;   neque   intermittebat   ferè   ullum diem,
performed;   nor   was he omitting   scarcely   any   day,

quin   periclitaretur   quid   animi   ac   virtutis
but that   he was trying   what (of)   spirit   and   (of) courage

esset   in   quoque   suorum   equestri   prœlio,
might be   in   each   of his men   by cavalry   engagements,

sagittariis   interjectis.   Erat   collis   è
the archers   having been intermixed.   There was   a hill

regione   oppidi   sub   ipsis   radicibus   montis
opposite   the town   at   the very   roots [foot]   of the mountain

egregiè   munitus,   atque   circumcisus   ex   omni   parte
excellently   fortified.   and   precipitous   on   every   side

(quem   si   nostri   tenerent,   videbantur
(which   if   our men   could hold,   they would seem   (able)

prohibituri   hostes   et[32]   ex   magnâ   parte
to prevent   the enemy   both   in   great   part   (from)

aquæ (gen.),   et   liberâ   pabulatione);   sed   is
water,   and   from free   foraging);   but   this

lŏcus   tenebatur   ab   iis   præsidio   non nimis
place   was held   by   them   with a garrison   not   very

firmo;   tamen,   Cæsar   egressus   ex   castris
strong,   however.   Cæsar   having marched out   from   the camp

silento   noctis,   priùs   quàm   subsidium   posset
in the silence   of the night.   before   (that)   aid   could

venire   ex   oppido,   præsidio   dejecto,
come   from   the town.   the garrison   having been dislodged.

potitus   loco,   collocavit   duas legiones,   ibi,
having seized   the place.   he stationed   two   legions   there,

que   perduxit   duplicem   fossam   duodenûm pedum
and   led   a double   trench   (of)   twelve   feet

à   majoribus   castris   ad   minora,   ut
(wide) from   the greater   camp   to   the lesser.   (so) that

etĭam singuli   posset commeare   tutò   ab
even   a single (soldier) could   pass   safely   from [on]

repentino incursu   hostium.
the sudden   attack   of the enemy.

37. Dum   hæc   geruntur   ad   Gergoviam.
While   these things are passing   at   Gergovia.

Convictolitais,   Æduus,   cui   demonstravimus
Convictolitais,   the Æduan,   to whom   we have shown

magistratum abjudicatum à Cæsare   sollicitatus
the magistracy was adjudged by Cæsar   having been solicited

pecuniâ   ab   Arvernis colloquitur cum quibusdam
with money by   the Arverni   confers   with   certain

adolescentibus quorum Litavicus ĕrat princeps, atque
young men   of whom Litavicus was   the chief,   and

ejus fratres, adolescentes nati amplissimâ familiâ,
his brothers,   young men   born of most illustrious family,

communicat præmium cum ĭis,   que hortatur ĕos
he shares   the money with them, and exhorts   them

ut   meminerint   se   liberos, et natos
that they should remember (that) they (were) free,   and born

imperio: "esse unam civitatem Æduorum   quæ
for empire; "it was alone the state   of the Ædui   which

distineat certissimam victoriam Galliæ; reliquas
retards   the most certain   victory of the Gauls.   the rest

contineri ejus auctoritate, quâ   trans-
were restrained by its   authority.   which having been brough'

ductâ, non fŏre   lŏcum Romanis consistendi
over.   there would not be a place for the Romans   to stand on

in Galliâ, se esse affectum nonnullo beneficio
in Gaul,   he was affected by a considerable   benefit

Cæsaris tamen sic ut   obtinŭerit justissimam
of Cæsar however so that he had obtained   a most just

causam apud ĕum; sed   tribuere (inf.) plus
cause through him;   but   (he) assigns   more

communi   libertati. Enim cur   Ædui
to (their) common   liberty.   For   why should the Ædui

veniant ad Cæsarem disceptatorem de   suo   jure
come   to   Cæsar   as arbiter   about their rights

et	de	legibus	potiùs	quàm	Romani	ad
and	about	their laws	rather	than	the Romans	to

Æduos?"	Adolescentibus		deductis
the Ædui?"	The young men		having been brought over

celeriter,	et	oratione	magistratûs,	et	præmio,
speedily,	both	by the speech	of the magistrate,	and	the bribe,

quum	profiterentur,	se	vel	fŏre	principes
when	they promised,	that they	indeed	would be	leaders

ejus	consilii,	ratio	perficiendi	quærebatur,
of this	enterprise,	a plan	of executing (it)	was inquired into,

quòd	confidebant		civitatem	non	posse
because	they were confident	(that)	the state	could	not be

adduci	temerè	ad	suscipiendum	bellum.
induced	rashly	for [to]	undertaking	the war.

Placuit	ut	Litavicus	præficeretur	illis
It was resolved	that	Litavicus	should be appointed	to those

decem	millibus	quæ	mitterentur	Cæsari	ad	bellum,
ten	thousand	that	were to be sent	to Cæsar	for	the war,

atque	curarat	ducenda	ĕa,	que	ejus
and	should have charge	of conducting	them,	and (that)	his

fratres	præcurrent	ad	Cæsarem;	constituunt
brothers	should go before	(him) to	Cæsar,	they determine

quâ	ratione	placeat	agi	reliqua.
in what	manner	it may be well	to perform	the rest.

38. Litavicus,	exercitu,	accepto	quum
Litavicus,	the army,	having been received	when

abesset	circĭter	trĭginta	millia	passŭum	ab
he was distant	about	thirty	thousand	paces	from

Gergoviâ,	subitò	convocatis	militibus,
Gergovia,	having suddenly	called together	the soldiers,

*l*acrymans	inquit,	"Quo	milĭtes	proficiscimur|?
weeping	he said,	"Whither	O soldiers	are we going?

omnis	noster	equitatus,	omnis	nobilĭtas	interiit.
all	our	knights,	all	the nobility	have perished,

Eporedorix	et	Viridomarus	principes	civitatis
Eporedorix	and	Viridomarus	chiefs	of the state

insimulati	proditionis	interfecti sunt	ab
having been accused	of treason	have been killed	by

Romanis   causâ   indictâ.   Cognoscite hæc
the Romans   the case   not having been called.   Know   this

ab   iis,   qui fugerunt   ex   ipsâ   cæde.   Nam
from   these,   who have fled from the very massacre.   For

ego   fratribus atque omnibus meis propinquis
I   (my)   brothers   and   all   my   relations

interfectis   prohibeor dolore pronunciare quæ
having been killed   am prevented by grief from announcing what

gesta sunt."   Ii   producuntur, quos ille edocuerat,
has been done. "   Those   are produced,   whom he   had taught

quæ   vellet   dici,   atque   ĕadem, quæ   Litavicus
what he wished to be said,   and   the same, which Litavicus

pronunciavĕrat,   exponunt   multitudini: "omnes
had announced,   they explain   to the multitude: "all

equites   Æduorum interfectos, quòd   dicerentur
the knights   of the Ædui   were slain,   because   they were said

collocuti   cum Arvernis; ipsos occultasse   se
to have conspired with the Arverni ; they   had hid   themselves

inter   multitudinem milĭtum, atque profugisse ex
among   the multitude   of soldiers,   and   had fled   from

mediâ   cæde."   Ædui   conclamant,   et
the midst (of the) massacre. "   The Ædui   exclaim,   and

obsecrant Litavicum   ut   consulat   sibi,
conjure   Litavicus   that   he should deliberate for themselves,

"Quasi verò,"   inquit ille,   "res   sit
" As if   indeed,"   said   he,   " the thing   were (a matter)

consilii,   ac   non sit necesse nobis contendĕre
of [for] a plan,   and   it were not necessary for us   to hasten

Gergoviam et conjungere nosmet cum Arvernis?
to Gergovia   and   to unite   ourselves with the Arverni?

An   dubitamus,   quin,   nefario   facinŏre
Or can   we doubt,   but that,   so nefarious   a crime

admisso,   Romani   jam concurrant ad
having been committed,   the Romans   now   gather   for

interficiendos nos? Proinde si   est   quid animi
slaying   us?   Therefore if there is any   spirit

in nobis persequamur   ĕorum mortem, qui
in   us   let us follow   [avenge]   their   death,   who

interierunt indignissimè, atque interficiamus hos
have perished most ignobly, and let us slay these

latrones." Ostendit Romanos cives, qui ĕrant
robbers." He shows the Roman citizens, who were

unà fiduciâ ejus præsidii. Continuò diripit
with them in the confidence of his protection. He forthwith seizes

magnum numĕrum frumenti que commeatus;
a great quantity of corn and provisions;

interficit ipsos crudelĭter excruciatos;
he kills them (the Romans) having cruelly tortured (them);

dimittit nuncios totâ civitate Æduorum; permovet
he sends messengers in all the state of the Ædui; he excites

ĕodem mendacio de cæde
(them) with the same falsehood about the massacre

equitum et principum; hortatur ut simili
of knights and chiefs, he exhorts (them) that in like

ratione, atque ipse fecerit, persequantur suas
manner, as he had done, they should avenge their

injurias.
injuries.

39. Eporedorix adolescens natus summo lŏco,
Eporedorix a young man born in the highest rank,

et summæ potentiæ domi, et unà Viridomarus,
and of the highest power at home, and also Viridomarus,

pari ætate et gratiâ, sed dispari genĕre,
of equal age and influence, but of unequal lineage,

quem Cæsar perduxĕrat ad summam dignitatem
whom Cæsar had elevated to the highest dignity

ex humili lŏco, traditum sibi
from an humble station, he having been recommended to him

ab Divitiaco, convenĕrant in numĕro equitum,
by Divitiacus, had come in the number of the horsemen

evocati nominatim ab ĕo. Erat
(having been) called by name by him (Cæsar). There was

contentio his inter se de
a contest (with) these (two) among themselves concerning

principatu; et in illâ controversiâ magistratum
rank; and in that dispute of the magistrates

alter   pugnaverat   pro   Convictolitae   alter   pro
the one   had contended   for   Convictrolitais   the other   for

Coto   summis   opibus.   Ex   Iis   Eporedorix,
Cotus   with (their) greatest   resources.   Of   these   Eporedorix,

consilio   Lìtavici   cognito   defert   rem
the designs   of Litavici   ha ing been learned   announced   the thing

ad   Cæsarem   ferè   mediâ   nocte;   orat
to   Cæsar   about   mid   night;   he begs   (that)

ne patiatur   civitatem   pravis   consiliis
he would not suffer   the state   by the wicked   counsels

adolescentium   deficere   ab   amicitiâ   Romani
of young men   to fall   from   the friendship   of the Roman

populi,   quod   provideat   futurum,   si   tot   millia
people,   which   he foresaw   would be,   if   so many   thousands

hominum   conjunxĕrint   se   cum   hostibus,
of men   should have united   themselves   with   the enemy,

quorum   salutem   neque   propinqui
whose   safety   neither   (their)   relations   (could/

negligĕre   neque   posset   civitas   æstimare   levi
neglect   nor   could   the state   consider   (it)   of slight

momento.
importance.

40. Cæsar   affectus   magnâ   sollicitudine
    Cæsar,   (having been) affected   with great   anxiety

hoc   nuncio,   quod   semper   præcipuè
by this   intelligence,   because   he had always   particularly

indulserat   civitati   Æduorum,   nullâ   debitatione
favored   the state   of the Ædui,   no   delay

interposîtâ,   educit   ex   castris   quatuor
having been interposed,   led forth   from   the camp   four

expeditas   legiones,   que omnem   equitatum.   Nec
light-armed   legions,   and   all   the cavalry.   Nor

fuit   spatium   tali   tempŏre   ad   contrahenda
was there   an interval   at such   a time   for   contracting

castra,   quòd   res   videbatur   posita
the camp,   because   the matter   seemed   placed [depending]

in   celeritate.   Relinquit C. Fabium   legatum
on   speed [dispatch].   He leaves   C. Fabius   (his) lieutenant

tum   duabus   legionibus   præsidio   castris;
with   two   legions   for [as] a garrison   to the camp,

quum   jussisset   fratres   Litavici   comprehendi,
when   he had ordered   the brothers   of Litavicus   to be arrested,

reperit   profugisse   paulo   antè   ad   hostes.
he finds   (that)   they had fled   a little   before   to   the enemy.

Adhortatus   milites,   ne permoveantur
Having encouraged   (his)   soldiers,   (that) they should not be troubled

labŏre   itinĕris   necessario   tempŏre, omnibus
by the labor   of the march   at (so) necessary   a time,   all

cupidissimis,   progressus   viginti quinque
(being)   most eager,   having proceeded   twenty   five

millia   passŭum,   conspicatus agmen   Æduorum.
thousand   paces [miles],   having seen   the army   of the Ædui.

equitatu   immisso,   moratur atque
the cavalry   having been sent against (them),   he retards   and

impedit   ĕorum   iter;   que   interdicit omnibus,
impedes   their   march :   and   he forbade   all.

ne interficiant   quemquam.   Jubet   Eporedorigem
that they should not kill   any one.   He orders   Eporedorix

et Viridomarus,   quos ille existimabant interfectos,
and   Viridomarus,   whom they   were thinking   had been killed,

versari   inter   equites,   que   appellare   suos.
to mingle   among   the horsemen,   and   to address   their

Iis   cognitis,   et   fraude
(countrymen).   These   having been recognized,   and   the fraud

Litavici   perspectâ,   Ædui   incipiunt
of Litavicus   having been perceived.   the Ædui   began

tendĕre   manus   et   significare deditionem,   et
to extend   (their)   hands   and   to signify   submission,   and

projectis   armis   deprecari   mortem.
having thrown away   (their)   arms   to beg off   death.

Litavicus profugit Gergoviam,   cum   suis clientibus,
Litavicus   fled   to Gergovia,   with   his   clients,

quibus   est nefas,   more   Gallorum,   deserĕre
with whom   it is   a crime,   by the custom   of the Gauls,   to desert

patronos,   etĭam   in   extremâ   fortuna.
(their)   patrons,   even   in   extreme [bad]   fortune.

41. Cæsar, nunciis missis ad civitatem
Cæsar, messengers having been sent to the state

Æduorum, qui docĕrent conservatos suo
of the Ædui, who should show (that they) had been saved by his

beneficio, quos potuisset interficĕre jure belli,
favor, whom he could have killed by the right of war,

que tribus horis noctis datis exercitui
and three hours of the night having been given to the army

ad quietem, movit castra ad Gergoviam.
for rest, he moves the camp toward Gergovia.

Ferè medio itinĕre equites, missi à Fabio,
About the middle (of the) march horsemen sent by Fabius,

exponunt in quanto periculo res fuerit;
reveal in how great danger the affair shall have been

demonstrant castra oppugnata summis
[was]; they explain (that) the camp was attacked by very great

copiis, quum integri crebrò succederunt
forces, as fresh (men) frequently succeeded

defessis, que defatigarent nostros assiduo
the tired, and exhausted our (men) by the continual

labŏre, quibus (dat.)³³ propter magnitudinem
labor, by whom on account of the size

castrorum perpetuò permanendum esset
of the camp it must continually be remained [stationed]

vallo iisdem, multos vulneratos
on the rampart (by) the same. (that) many were wounded

multitudine sagittarum, atque omnis genĕris
by the multitude of arrows, and of every kind

telorum; ad sustinenda hæc tormenta
of weapons; for resisting these the hurling engines

fuisse mâgno usui; Fabium eorum dicessu,
were (of) great use; (that) Fabius on their departure,

duabus portis relictis obstruere
two gates having been left (open) was blocking up

cæteras, que addere pluteos vallo, et se
the rest, and adding breastworks to the wall, and (that) he

parare ad similem casum in posterum diem
was preparing for a like fate on the next day

Iis   rebus   cognitis,   Cæsar   pervenit   in
These   things   having been learned.   Cæsar   arrived   at

castra   ante   ortum   solis   summo   studio
the camp   before   the rising   of the sun   by the highest   exertion

militum.
of the soldiers.

42. Dum   hæc   geruntur   ad   Gergoviam,
While   these things   are going on   at   Gergovia,

Ædui,   primis   nunciis   a   Litavico   accep-
the Ædui,   the first   messages   from   Litavicus   having been

tis,   relinquunt   sibi   nullum   spatium   ad
received,   leave   to themselves   no   time   for

cognoscendum.   Avaritia   impellit   alios   iracundia
ascertaining.   Avarice   impels   some,   passion

et   temeritas alios,   quæ   est maximè   innata
and   rashness   others,   which (last) is   especially   natural

illi   genĕri   hominum,   ut   habĕant   levem
to that   kind   of men,   (so)   that   they hold   a slight

auditionem pro   re   compertâ.   Deripiunt   bona
hearsay   for   a thing   assured.   They plunder   the goods

Romanorum civium,   faciunt   cædes,   abstra-
of Roman   citizens,   they commit   murder,   they drag (them)

hunt   in   servitutem.   Convictolitavis   adjuvat
away   into   slavery.   Convictolitavis   advances

proclinatam   rem,   que   impellit   plebem   ad
the ruined   condition,   and   drives   the people   to

furorem,   ut   facinŏre   admisso
madness,   that   an enormity   having been committed,

pudeat   reverti   ad   sanitatem.
it may shame   (them)   to return   to   soundness of mind.

Educunt   ex   oppido   Cobillono M. Aristium
They drag out   from   the town (of) Cobillonus   M.   Aristium

tribunum   militum   facientem   iter   ad
a tribute   of the soldiers   making   (his)   way   to (his)

legionem,   fide   datâ;   cogunt   ĕos
legion,   a pledge   having been given :   they force   those

facĕre   idem,   qui   constiterant   ibi   causâ
to do   the same,   who   had sojourned   there   for the purpose

negotiandi.　　Continuo adorti　　　hos　　ĭn
of trading.　　Having continually attacked　these　on　(their)

itinĕre ,　exuunt　　omnibus　　　impedimentis ;
journey,　they strip　(them)　of all　(their)　baggage ;

obsident　　repugnantes diem　que　noctes (pl.);
they besiege　(those)　opposing　day　and　night ,

multos　utrimque　interfectis,　concitant　majorem
many　on both sides　having been slain,　they summon　a greater

multitudinem　ad　arma.
multitude　　to　arms.

43.　Intĕrim　nuntiis　allatis,　　　omnes
Meantime　news　having been brought,　(that)　all

ĕorum　milĭtes　　teneri　in　potestate Cæsaris,
ef their　soldiers　to be [were] held　in　the power　of Cæsar

concurrunt　ad　Aristium,　demonstrant　　nihil
they gather　to　Aristium,　　they show　(that) nothing

factum publĭco consilio; decernunt　quæstionem
(was)　done　by public　design ;　they decree　an investigation

de　　bonis　　direptis;　publicant　bona
concerning　the goods　plundered ,　they confiscate　the goods

Litavici　que　　fratrum;　mittunt　legatos　ad
of Litavicus　and　(his)　brothers ,　they send　ambassadors　to

Cæsarem　gratiâ　purgandi　sui .　　Hæc,
Cæsar　for the sake of　clearing　themselves.　These things,

faciunt　gratiâ　recuperandorum　suorum ;
they do　for the sake　of recovering　　their　(soldiers);

sed contaminati　facinŏre　et　capti　compendio
but　implicated　in the crime　and　taken　by the income

ex　direptis　bonis,　quod　ĕa　res　pertinebat
from　the plundered　goods,　because　this　matter　was relating

ad multos et　　exterriti　timŏre　pœnæ,
to　many　and　having been alarmed　by the fear　of punishment,

incipiunt　clam　inire　consilia　de　　bello
they begin　secretly　to entertain　plans　concerning　war

que　solicitant　legationibus　reliquas　civitates.
and　incite　with embassies　the remaining　states.

Quæ[34]　tametsi Cæsar intellegebat, tamen quam
Which things　although　Cæsar　was knowing,　yet　as

mitissime   potuit   appellat   legatos   "Nihil
mildly as   he was able   he addresses   the ambassadors   "In no wise

se judicare   graviùs   de   civitate   propter
he   judges   more severely   concerning   the state   on account of

inscientiam   que   levitatem   volgi,   neque
the ignorance   and   fickleness   of the common people,   nor

deminuere   de   sua   benevolentia   in   Æduos."
does he abate   from   his   good will   toward   the Ædui."

Ipse   expectans   majorem   motum   Galliæ,
He himself   apprehending   a greater   commotion   of Gaul,

ne   circumsisteretur   ab   omnibus   civitatibus,
lest   he should be surrounded   by   all   the states,

inibat   consilia,   quemadmoduin   discedĕret   à
was devising   plans,   as to what manner   he might depart   from

Gergoviâ   ac   rursus   contraheret   omnem
Gergovia   and   again   might draw together   all   (his)

exercitum,   ne   profectio   nata   à   timore
army,   lest   a departure   arising   from   fear

defectionis,   videretur   similis   fugæ.
of a revolt,   might seem   like   (to) a flight.

44 Facultas   gerendæ   rei   bene   visa est
An opportunity   of executing   the affair   well   seemed

accidere   cogitanti   hæc.   Nam   quum
to occur   (to him)   meditating   these (things).   For   when

venisset   in   minora   castra   causâ   perspiciendi
he had come   to   the smaller   camp   for the purpose   of inspecting

operis,   animadvertit   collem,   qui   tenebatur
the work,   he observed   (that)   the hill,   which   was held

ab   hostibus   nudatum hominibus,   qui   superioribus
by   the enemy   was bared   of men,   which   on former

diebus   vix   poterat   cerni   præ multitudine.
days   scarcely   could   be discerned   for   the multitude.

Admiratus   quærit   causam   ex   perfugis,   quorum
Surprised,   he inquires   the cause   of   the deserters,   of whom

magnus   numĕrus   quotidie   confluebat   ad   ĕum.
a great   number   daily   were pouring in,   to   him.

Constabat   inter   omnes,   quod   Cæsar   ipse
it was agreed   by   all,   which   [as]   Cæsar   himself

cognoverat   jam   per   exploratores,   dorsum
had known   already   through (his)   scouts,   (that) the back

ejus   jugi esse   prope   æquum,   sed silvestre
[summit]   of this   hill   was   nearly   level,   but   woody

et   angustum,   quà   esset   aditus   ad   alteram
and   narrow.   where   was   a passage   to   the other

partem   oppidi,   illos   timere   vehementer
part   of the town,   (that)   they   feared   exceedingly

huic   loco;   viderentur   jam   sentire nec   aliter,
for this   place,   they appeared   now   to feel   not   otherwise,

uno   colle   occupato   ab   Romanis,   si
one   hill   having been occupied   by   the Romans,   if

amisissent   alterum,   quin   circumvallati
they should lose   the other.   (but) that   they would be   surrounded

pæne,   atque   interclusi   omni   exitu et pabulatione;
nearly,   and   cut off   from all   egress and   foraging;

omnes   evocatos   à Vercingetorige ad muniendum
all   were called out   by   Vercingetorix   for   fortifying

hunc   locum.
this   place.

45. Hac   re   cognitâ,   Cæsar   mittit
This   thing   having been learned.   Cæsar   sends

complures   turmas   equitum   eò   de   mediâ
several   troops   of horsemen   thither   at   mid

nocte;   imperat   iis,   ut   pervagentur
night,   he commands   them,   that   they should range about

in omnibus locis   paulò   tumultuosiùs.   Primâ
in   all   places somewhat more tumultously [noisily]   At the first

luce   jubet   magnum   numerum
light   [early dawn]   [he orders   a great   quantity

impedimentorum   produci   ex   castris,   que
of baggage   to be brought forth   from   the camp.   and

mulorum,   que   stramenta   detrahi   iis,   que
of mules,   and   the pack-saddles   to be taken from   them,   and

muliones   cum   cassidibus   circumvehi   collibus
the muleteers   with   helmets   to go round   the hills

specie   ac   simulatione   equitum.   His
in the appearance   and   manner   of horsemen.   To these

addıt paucos equites, qui vagarentur latiùs
he adds a few horsemen, who might range more widely

causâ ostentationis. Jubet omnes
for the purpose of display. He orders (them) all

petere ĕasdem regiones 'longo circuiƚu. Hæc
to seek the same places by a long circuit. These

videbatur procul ex oppido, ut erat
things were seen at a distance from the town, as there was

despectus à Gergoviâ in castra; neque, tanto
a view from Gergovia into the camp, nor, at such

spatio, poterat explorari quid certi
a distance, could it be made out what of [to a] certainty

esset. Mittit unam legionem ĕodem jugo, et
it might be. He sends one legion on the same hill, and

constıtuit progressam paulum, inferiore
he stations (it) (having been) advanced a little in a lower

lŏco, que occultat silvis. Suspicio
place, and hides (it) in the woods The suspicion (of)

Gallıs augetur, atque omnes copiæ munitionum
the Gauls is increased, and all the forces of the fortifications

transducuntur ıllò. Cæsar conspicatus
are brought over thither Cæsar having perceived (that)

castra hostium vacua, insignibus suorum
the camp of the enemy was deserted. the insignias of his

tectis, que mılıtarıbus signis
(men) having been covered, and the mi'itary ensigns

occultatıs, transducit milites ex
having been concealed, he leads out (his) soldiers from

majorıbus castris in minora raros, ne animad-
the larger camp into the smaller in squads, lest they should

verterentur ex oppĭdo; que ostendit
be observed from the town, and he shows [explains]

legatis, quos præfecĕrat singulis legionıbus,
to the lieutenants whom he had appointed to each legion.

quid vellet fieri · in primis monet, ut
what he wishes to be done, especially he admonishes that

contineant mılıtes, ne progrediantur
they should restrain the soldiers, lest they should proceed

longiùs,   studio   pugnandi aut   spe   prædæ.
too far,   by the desire   of fighting   or   by the hope   of plunder.

Proponit   quid   incommodi   iniquitas
He explains   what   (of)   disadvantage   the unfavorableness

lŏci   habeat   hoc   posse   vitari
of the place   may have,   (that)   this   could   be avoided

celerĭte   unâ,   rem   occasionis, non
by quickness [speed]   alone, (that it is)   a matter   of opportunity,   not

prœli.   His   rebus   expositis,   dat   signum,
of battle.   These   things   having been stated,   he gives   the signal,

et   mittit   Æduos,   ĕodem   tempŏre,   ab   dextrâ
and   sends   the Ædui,   at the same   time,   from   the right

parte   alio   adscensu.
side [flank]   by another   ascent.

46. Murus   oppidi   aberat   mille   et   du-
The wall   of the town   was distant   a thousand   and   two

centos [MCC]   passus   ab planitie,   atque   initio
hundred   paces   from the plain,   and from   the beginning

adscensûs,   rectâ   regione,   si nullus anfractus
of the ascent,   in a straight   direction,   if   no   bend

intercederet.   Quidquid   accesserat   huic
should intervene.   Whatever   may have been added   to this

circuitûs   ad molliendum   clivum,   id   augebat
(of) circuit   for   easing   the slope [ascent].   this   increased

spatium   itineris.   Galli   præduxerant   murum
the length   of the route.   The Gauls   had extended   a wall

sex   pedum   ex   grandibus saxis,   ferè   à
six   feet   (high)   of   great   stones,   nearly   in

medio   colle   in   longitudine   ut
the middle   (of) the hill   on   the length   [lengthwise],   as

natura   montis   ferebat,   qui   tardaret
the nature   of the mountain   was allowing,   which   might retard

impetum   nostrorum;   atque omni inferiore spatio
the attack   of our men;   and   all   the lower   space

relicto   vacuo,   compleverant superiorem partem
having been left   vacant,   they had filled   the higher   part

collis   usque   ad   murum   oppidi   castris
of the hill   even   to   the wall   of the town   with camps

densissimis.   Milites,   signo   dato,
very close.   The soldiers, the signal   having been given,

celerĭter   perveniunt   ad   munitionem,   que
quickly   arrived   at   (this) fortification,   and

transgressi   ĕam,   potiuntur   trinis
having passed over   it,   take possession (of) three (separate)

castris.   Ac   tanta   fuit   celerĭtas   in   capiendis
camps.   And   so great   was   the speed   in   capturing

castris,   ut   Teutomatus,   rex   Nitiobrigum,
the camps,   that   Teutomatus,   king   of the Nitiobriges,

oppressus   subitò   in   tabernaculo,   ut
having been surprised   suddenly   in   (his)   tent,   as

conquieverat   meridie,   vix   eripĕret   se
he went to rest   at noon,   scarcely   saved   himself

ex   manibus   præedantium   milĭtum,   superiore
from   the hands   of the plundering   soldiers,   the upper

parte   corpŏris   nudatâ,   equo
part   of (his) body   (having been) naked,   (and his) horse

vulnerato.
(having been) wounded,

47. Cæsar   consecutus   id   quod   proposuĕrat
     Cæsar   having attained   that   which   he had proposed

animo,   jussit   receptui   cani,   que
in mind,   ordered   the retreat   to be sounded,   and   (the soldiers)

decimæ   legionis,   quâ   erat   tum   comitatus,
of the tenth   legion,   by which   he was   then   accompanied,

consistĕre   signa.   At   milĭtes   relĭquarum
stood [halted] at   the standards.   But   the soldiers   of the other

legionum,   non   exaudito   sono   tubæ,   quòd
legions.   not   having heard   the sound   of the trumpet,   because

vallis   satis   magna   intercedebat,   tamen
a valley   sufficiently [quite]   large   was intervening,   however

retinebantur   à   tribunis   militum   que
were kept back   by   the tribunes   of the soldiers   and

legatis,   ut   præceptum erat   à   Cæsar.
by the lieutenants,   as   (it) had been commanded   by   Cæsar.

Sed   elati   spe   celeris   victoriæ et   fugâ
But   elated   by the hope   of a speedy   victory   and   by the flight

hostium,   que   secundis   prœliis   superiorum
of the enemy,   and   the favorable   battles   of former

temporum existimabant   nihil   adeò arduum
times   they are thinking (that) nothing (was) so   difficult

sibi,   quod   possent   non   consequi   virtute;
for them,   which   they could   not   accomplish   by valor;

neque   fecerunt   finem   sequendi,   priùs
nor   did they   make   an end   of following,   before

quàm appropinquârunt   muro   que   portis   oppidi.
(that)   they had approached   the wall   and   the gates   of the town.

Vero tum clamore   orto   ex   omnibus partibus
But   then   a shout   having arisen   from   all   parts

urbis,   qui   aberant   longiùs   perterriti
of the town.   those who   were distant   farther   frightened

repentino   tumultu,   quum   existimarent   hostes
by the sudden   tumult,   as   they thought   the enemy

esse   intra   portas,   jecerunt   sese   ex
to be [were]   within   the gates,   threw   themselves   from

oppido.   Matres   familiâs   jactabant.
the town.   The mothers   of families [matrons]   threw

vestem   que   argentum   de   muro,   et
(their)   clothes   and   silver   from   the wall,   and

prominentes   nudo   pectŏre,   passis   manibus
bending forward   with naked   breast,   with outstretched   hands

obtestabantur Romanos,   ut   parcĕrent   sibi; neu
they implored   the Romans,   that   they should spare   them;   nor

sicut   fecissent   Avarici,   abstinerĕrent   ne
as   they had done   at Avaricum,   abstain from   [spare]   not

mulieribus   quidem   atque   infantibus.   Nonnullæ
the women   even   and   children.   Some

demissæ   de   muris   per   manus,
having let themselves down   from   the wall   by   their hands

transdebant   sese   militibus.   L. Fabius
were delivering   themselves   to the soldiers.   L. Fabius

centurio   octavæ   legionis,   quem,   constabat
a centurion   of the eighth   legion,   whom [who],   it appeared

dixisse   eo   die   inter   suos,   se
to have [had] said   this   day   among   his   (men, that)   he

excitari   Avaricensibus præmiis,   neque commissurum,
was excited   by the Avarican   rewards,   nor   would he allow,

ut   quisquam   adscenderet   murum   priùs,
that   any one   should mount   the wall   before   (himself),

nactus   tres   suos   manipulares   atque
having taken   three   (of)   his   company   and

sublevatus   ab   iis   adscendit   murum;
having been raised up   by   them   he mounted   the wall;

ipse   rursus   exceptans extulit   eos   in   murum,
he   in turn   taking up   drew   them   onto   the wall,

singulos.
one at a time.

48.   Interim   ĭi,   qui convenĕrant ad altĕram
       In the meantime   those, who   had assembled   at   the other

partem   oppidi,   ut demonstravimus supra   causâ
part   of the town,   as   we have shown   above for the purpose

munitionis,   primo   clamŏrc   exaudito,   inde
of fortifying,   the first   shout   having been heard,   afterward

etĭam   incitatı   crebris   nunciis,   oppidum
also   incited   by frequent   reports,   (that)   the town

teneri   ab   Romanis,   præmissis   equitibus,
was held   by   the Romans,   having sent forward   the horsemen,

contenderunt   ĕo   magno   concursu. Ut quisque
they hastened   there   in a great   throng.   As   each

ĕorum   primus venĕrat consistebat   sub   muro,
of them   first   came   he was halting   under   the wall,

que   augebat   numerum suorum   pugnantium.
and   was increasing   the number   of their (men)   fighting.

Quum   magna   multitudo   quorum   convenisset,
When   a great   multitude   of these   had assembled,

matres familiâs   quæ   paulò   antè
the mothers of families   [matrons]   who   a little   before

tendebant   manus   de   muro   Romanis,
were holding   (their)   hands   from   the wall   to the Romans,

cœperunt obtestari suos   et   Gallico   mŏre
began   to beseech   their (people)   and   in the Gallic   manne1

ıstentare   passum   capillum,   que   proferre
to show   dishevelled   hair.   and   to bring forth

liberos　　in　conspectum.　Contentio　ĕrat　æqua
the children　into　view.　　The contest　was　equal

Romanis　　nec　lŏco　nec　numĕro (sing.)　;simul
for the Romans　neither　in place　nor　in numbers ;　at the same time

defatigati　et　　cursu　et　spatio　　pugnæ,
fatigued　　both　by running　and　by the duration　of the fight.

non facilè sustinebat　　recentes atque integros.
they were not easily withstanding　(those) fresh　and　vigorous.

49. Cæsar　　cùm　videret　　　　pugnari
　　Cæsar　　when　he saw　　(it)　to be [was] fought

iniquo　　　lŏco,　que　copias　　hostium
in a disadvantageous　place,　and　the forces　of the enemy

augeri,　　præmetuens　suis　　mittit ad
to be [were] increased,　being anxious　for his (men)　he sends to

T. Sextum　legatum, quem reliquerat　præsidio
T. Sextius　(his) lieutenant. whom　he had left　for [as] a guard

minoribus　castris,　ut　　celeriter educeret
to the smaller　camp,　that　he should quickly lead forth

cohortes　ex　castris,　et　constitueret　　sub
the cohorts　from　the camp,　and　should station　(them)　at

infimo　　colle　ab　dextro latĕre　hostium ;
the lowest (part of)　the hill　on　the right　wing　of the enemy :

ut　si　vidisset　nostros　　depulsos　lŏco,
that　if　he should see　our　(men)　repulsed　from the place

terreret　　hostes　quò　insequerentur minùs
he might alarm　the enemy　so that　they would follow　less

liberè.　Ipse　　progressus　paulùm　ex　ĕo
freely.　He himself　having proceeded　a little　from　this

loco　cum　legione,　ubi　constiterat,　expectabat
place　with　the legion,　where　he had halted,　was awaiting

eventum　　pugnæ.
the issue　of the battle.

50. Quum　pugnatur[35]　accerimè　comminus,
　　While　it was fought　most violently　hand to hand.

hostes　confiderent　loco　et　　numero
the enemy　confided　in the place　and　(their)　number

nostri　virtute ;　Ædui　sunt　subito　visi,　ab
our men　in (their) courage ;　the Ædui　were　suddenly　seen.　by

nostris   aperto   latĕre, quos Cæsar miserat
our   (men) on the exposed flank, whom Cæsar had sent

ab dextrâ parte   alıo   ascensu,   causâ
from the right sıde [flank] by another ascent. for the purpose

distinendæ manus.³⁶ Hi vehementer perterruerunt
of cutting off the force. They very much   alarmed

nostros   similitudine   armorum;   ac   tametsi
our men   by the sımılarity of (their) arms ; and although

animadvertebantur   dextris humeris   exertis,
they were observed   with the right shoulder   uncovered,

quod consueverat esse   insigne   pacatis,
which was accustomed to be the sign (of those) ın peace,

tamen   milites   existimabant   id   ipsum
however the soldiers were thinkıng (that) this same

factum ab hostibus   causâ   fallendi   sui.
(was) done by the enemy for the sake of deceiving them.-

Eodem   tempore   centurio,   L. Fabius,   que
At the same time   the centurion, L. Fabius, and

qui   adscendĕrant   murum   unâ,
(those) who   had ascended   the wall together (with him),

circumventi   atque interfecti, præcipitabantuɪ
having been surrounded   and   slain.   were thrown

de   muro. M. Petronius,   centurio   ejusdem
from ɩhe wall. M. Petronius,   a centurion of the same

legionis, quum conatus   esset   exscindere portas,
legion. when he had   attempted to cut down the gates,

oppressus   à   multitudine, ac   desperans
overpowered by   the multitude, and despairing of safety

sibi,   jam   vulneribus   acceptis,   inquit
for himself, already wounds   having been received, said

suis   manipularibus   qui   secuti   ĕrant illum.
to his   comrades   who   had followed   him.

"Quoniam possum non servare   me   unâ vobiscum,
" Sınce   I can   not save   mıyself together with you,

quidem certè   prospiciam vestræ saluti,   quos,
indeed certainly I will provide for your safety,   whom,

I,   adductos cupiditate gloriæ   deduxi   in
I.   led   by the desire of glory, have brought into

periculum;   vos,   facultate   datâ   consulite
danger;   you,   an opportunity   having been given,   consult

vobis."   Simul   irrupit   in   medios
for yourselves"   At the same time   he threw himself   into   the midst

hostes,   que   duobus   interfectis,   submovit
of (the) enemy,   and   two   having been killed,   he drove back

reliquos paulùm   à   portâ.   Suis   conantibus
the rest   a little   from   the gate.   To his (men)   endeavoring

auxiliari   inquit,   "Frustra conamini subvenire meæ
to assist   he said.   "In vain   you try   to save   my

vitæ   quem   sanguis   que   vires   jam   deficiunt,
life   whom   blood   and   strength   now   fail,

proinde   abite   hinc,   dum   est   facultas,
therefore   go   from here,   while   there is   the chance,

que recipite   vos   ad legionem."   Pugnans   ita
and   get [betake]   yourselves to   the legion."   Fighting   thus

concidit   pòst   paulùm,   ac   fuit   saluti[37]
he fell   after   a little.   and   was   (for) a safety

suis.
to his (men).

51. Quum   nostri   premerentur   undique,
      As   our   (men)   were pressed   on every side,

quadraginta   sex   centurionibus   amissis,
forty   six   centurions   having been lost,

dejecti sunt   lŏco.   Sed   decima   legio,
they were driven   from the place.   But   the tenth   legion,

quæ   constiterat   pro   subsidio   paulò   æquiore
which   had taken stand   for   a reserve   on a little   more level

lŏco   tardavit   Gallos   insequentes   intolerantiùs.
place   checked   the Gauls   following   too eagerly.

Cohortes   decimæ tertiæ legionis,   rursus   exceperunt
The cohorts   of the thirteenth   legion,   in turn   supported

hanc,[38]   quæ   ednctæ   ex   minoribus   castris,
this,   that   having been led   from   the smaller   camp,

cum   T. Sextio,   legato,   cepĕrant   superiorem
with   T. Sextius,   the lieutenant,   had occupied   the higher

lŏcum.   Ubi   legiones   primùm attigerunt planitiem
ground.   When   the legions   first   reached   the plain

constiterunt,   signis   infestis   contra
they halted,   the standards   having been turned   against

hostes.   Vercingetorix   reduxit   suos   ab
the enemy.   Vercingetorix   led back   his   (men)   from

radicibus   collis   intra   munitiones.   Eo
the foot   of the hill   within   the fortifications.   On this

die   paulò   minùs   septingentis   milites
day   a little   less   (than)   seven hundred   soldiers

desiderati sunt.
were missing.

52. Postero   die,   Cæsar,   concione   advocata,
On the next   day,   Cæsar,   a council   having been called.

reprehendit   temeritatem   que   cupiditatem   militum,
censured   the rashness   and   avarice   of the soldiers,

quòd   ipsi   judicavissent   sibi,   quò   videretur
because   they   had judged   for themselves,   where   it seemed

            procedendum,   aut   quid   agendum,
(that they)   to [must] go   or   what   to [must] be done,

neque,   signo   recipiendi   dato,
neither,   the signal   for halting   having been given,

constitissent,   neque   potuissent   retineri   à
did they halt,   nor   could they   be restrained   by

tribunis   militum   que   legatis.   Exposuit
the tribunes   of the soldiers   and   by the lieutenants   He showed

quid   iniquitas   lŏci   posset,
what   the disadvantage   of position   would be able   (to effect),

quid   ipse   sensisset   ad   Avaricum,   quum,
what   (he) himself   had thought   at   Avaricum.   when,

hostibus   deprehensis,   sine   duce   et
the enemy   having been surprised.   without   a leader   and

sine   equitatu,   demisisset   exploratam   victoriam,
without   cavalry,   he had given up   a certain   victory.

ne   acciperet   modò   parvum   detrimentum   in
lest   he might receive   only   a small   injury   in

contentione,   propter   iniquitatem   lŏci.
the contest,   on account of   the disadvantage   of the place

Quantopĕre admiraretur eorum magnitudinem animi,
As much as   he admired   their   greatness   of soul

quos non munitiones castrorum, non altitudo
whom neither the fortifications of the camp, nor the height

montis, non murus oppidi potuisset
of the mountain, nor the wall of the town could

tardare, reprehendere tantopere licentiam que
retard, he censured so greatly (their) lawlessness and

arrogantiam, quòd existimarent se sentire
presumption, because they were thinking (that) they understood

plus quàm imperatorem de victoriâ atque
more than (their) commander about victory and

exitu rerum; se desiderare in milīte nec
the issue of affairs, (saying that) he desired in a soldier no

minùs modestiam et continentiam, quàm virtutem
less moderation and submission, than valor

atque magnitudinem animi."
and greatness of soul."

53. Hac concione, habitâ et ad extremum
This council, having been held and at the end

militibus confirmatis oratione, ne
the soldiers having been encouraged by (his) speech, that (they)

permoverentur animo ob hanc causam, neu
should not be disturbed in mind on account of this affair, nor

tribuĕrent id virtuti hostium, quod
should they attribute this to the valor of the enemy, which

iniquitas lŏci attulisset; cogitans
the disadvantage of position had brought on (them); thinking

ĕadem de profectione, quæ senserat
the same concerning a departure, which [as] he had felt

antè, eduxit legiones ex castris, que
before. he led forth the legions from the camp, and

constituit aciem idonĕo lŏco. Quum
drew up the battle-line in a favorable place. When

Vercingetorix nihĭlo magìs descenderet in æquum
Vercingetorix no more would descend into level

lŏcum, levi equestri prœlio facto,
ground a slight cavalry engagement having occurred,

atque ĕo secundo, reduxit exercitum
and this (being) favorable, he led back (his) army

in   castra.   Quum   fecisset   hoc   idem   postero
into the camp   When   he had done this same thing the next

die, existimans   satis   factum   ad minuendam
day,   believing   (that) enough was done for lessening

Gallicam   ostentationem,   que   confirmandos
the Gallic   arrogance,   and for   encouraging

animos   militum,   movit   castra   in
the minds of (his) soldiers. he moves (his) camp   into

Æduos.   Hostibus   ne   tum   quidem   insecutis,
the Ædui. The enemy not then even   having followed,

tertio   die   refecit   pontem   ad   flumen
on the third day he repaired the bridge over the river

Elaver, atque   transduxit   exercitum.
Allier,   and   led over   (his) army

54. Ibi   appellatus   à   Viridomaro atque
There,   having been waited on by Viridomarus and

Eporedorige   Æduis,   discit   Litavicus, cum
Eporedorix   the Æduans. he learns (that) Litavicus, with

omni   equitatu   profectum   ad sollicitandos   Æduos;
all   the cavalry   had set out for instigating   the Ædui,

et   esse   opus   ipsos   antecedere
and (that) it was necessary (that) they should go before

ad   confirmandam civitatem.   Etsi   Cæsar   jam
for   restraining   the state. Although Cæsar already

multis   rebus   habebat   perfidiam   Æduorum
in many things was having the unfaithfulness of the Ædui

perspectam   atque   existimabat   disessu
clearly understood and   he was thinking (that) by the departure

horum   defectionem   civitatis   admaturari;
of these the defection of the state to [would] be hastened,

tamen   censuit   eos   non retinendos,   ne
however he was of the opinion that they should not be detained, lest

videretur   aut   inferre   injuriam,   aut   dare
he might appear either to impose a wrong. or to give

aliquam suspicionem timoris.   His   discedentibus,
some   suspicion   of fear. To them departing,

breviter exposuit   sua   merita   in   Æduos,   quos
he briefly states   his   services to the Ædui, whom

accepisset   et   quàm humiles, compulsos   in
he had taken in charge and   how   humbled,   driven   into

oppìda,   multatos   agris,   omnìbus   copìis
their towns.   deprived   of their lands,   all   (their)   means

ereptis,   stipendio   imposito,
having been taken away,   a tribute   having been imposed,   (and)

obsidìbus   extortis   cum   summâ   contumeliâ,
hostages   having been exacted   with   the greatest   insult,

in   quam   fortunam,   que   in   quam amplìtudìnem
to   what   fortune,   and   to   what   greatness

deduxisset,   ut   non solum redissent   in
he had raised (them),   that   they had not only returned   to (their)

prìstinum   statum,   sed   viderentur   antecessisse
former   state,   but   they seemed   to have surpassed

dignitatem   et   gratiam   omnium   tempŏrum.   His
the dignity   and   influence   of all   times.   This

mandatis   datis,   dimisit   ĕos   ab
charge   having been given,   he dismisses   them   from

se.
his presence.

55. Novidunum   ĕrat   oppidum   Æduorum
Novidunum   [Nevers]   was   a town   of the Ædui

positum   opportuno   lŏco   ad   ripas   Ligeris.
situated   in an advantageous   place   on   the banks   of the Loire.

Cæsar   contulerat   huc   omnes   obsides   Galliæ,
Cæsar   had brought   hither   all   the hostages   of Gaul

frumentum,   publicam   pecuniam,   magnam   partem
the corn,   the public   money,   a great   part

suorum   impedimentorum,   atque   exercitûs.
of his   baggage,   and   (that)   of the army,

Misĕrat   huc   magnum   numĕrum   equorum
He had sent   hither   a great   number   of horses

coëmptorum   ìn   Italiâ   atque Hispaniâ,   causâ
bought   in   Italy   and   Spain,   for the purpose

hujus   belli.   Quum   Eporedorix   que   Viridomarus
of this   war.   When   Eporedorix   and   Viridomarus

venissent   ĕo,   et   cognovissent   de   statu
had arrived   there,   and   had learned   about   the condition

civitatis ;   Litavicum   receptum   ab
[attitude]   of the state;   (that)   Litavicus   was received   by

Æduis   Bibracte,   quod   est   oppidum   maximæ
the Ædui   in Bibracte,   which   is   a town   of the greatest

auctoritatis   apud   ĕos,   Convictolitavem
importance   among   them,   (that)   Convictolitavis

magistratum   que   magnam   partem   senatûs
the magistrate   and   a great   part   of the senate

convenisse   ad   ĕum,   legatos   publicè
had gone   to   him,   (that)   ambassadors   were openly

missos ad Vercingetorigem   de   conciliandâ pace
sent   to   Vercingetorix   concerning   procuring   peace

et   amicitiâ,   existimaverunt   tantum   commodum
and   alliance,   they thought   so great   an advantage

non prætermittendum.   Itaque custodibus Novioduni
must not (to) be neglected.   Therefore   the guards of Noviodunum

interfectis,   que   qui   convenĕrant   ĕò
having been killed.   and   those who   had assembled   there

causâ   negotiandi,   aut   itinĕris,   partiti sunt
for the sake   of trading,   or   travel,   they divided

pecuniam atque   equos   inter   se ;   curaverunt
the money   and   the horses   among   themselves;   they took care

obsides   civitatum   deducendos   Bibracte
(that)   the hostages   of the states   should be conducted   to Bibracte

ad   magistratum,   oppidum,   quòd   judicabant
to   the magistrate,   the town,   because   they thought   (it)

posse   non   teneri   ab   se,   incenderunt,   ne
could   not   be held   by   them.   they burned,   lest

esset   cui   usui   Romanis.   Avexerunt
it might be   (of) some   use   to the Romans.   They carried away

subĭtò   navibus   quod   potuerunt frumenti ;   corru-
suddenly   in ships   what   they could   of corn   they

perunt   reliquum   flumine   atque   incendio ;   ipsi
destroyed   the rest   in the river   and   by fire ;   they

cœperunt copĕre copias   ex   finitimis   regionibus,
began   to collect   forces   from   the neighboring   districts

disponere   præsidia   que   custodias   ad   ripas
to place   garrisons   and   guards   along   the banks

Legeris,   que   ostentare equitatum omnibus   lŏcis
of the Loire,   and   to display cavalry   in all   places

causâ   injiciendi tĭmŏris, si   aut   possent
for the purpose of exciting alarm,   ,°   either   they could

excludere Romanos   re frumentariâ, aut adductos
cut off   the Romans (from) a corn supply,   or   driven

inopiâ,   expellĕre   ex   Provinciâ;
by want,   could expel (them) from the province; (this)

adjuvabat   ĕos multùm ad quam spem,   quòd
was assisting them much   to such hope,   because

Liger   creverat   ex nivibus, ut   videretur
the Loire had swollen from snows,   so that it seemed

omnino   posse   non transiri   vador.
altogether (that) it could not be crossed by a ford.

56. Quibus rebus   cognitis,   Cæsar   censuit
    Which things having been known,   Cæsar was of the opinion

sibi   maturandum,³⁹   si   esset   periclitandum
(that) he must hasten,   if   he must   take the risk

in perficiendis pontibus,   ut   dimicaret   priùs
in building   the bridges,   so that he might fight before

quàm majores copiæ   coactæ   ĕo.   Nam   ut,
(that) greater forces   were collected   there. For   that,

consilio   commutato,   convertĕret   iter
(his) plan   having been changed,   he might alter (his) route

in Provinciam, existimabat   id   ne   tum
into the Province, he was thinking (that) this not then

quidem necessariò   faciendum,   quum   infamia
even   of necessity to [must] be done, not only the disgrace

atque indignitas   rĕi,   et   oppositus   mons
and   humiliation   of the thing, and the opposed   mount

Cebenna, que difficultas viarum   impediebat (sing.);
Cevennes, and the difficulty of the roads were preventing;

tum   maxime   quòd   cupiebat   vehementer
but also especially   because   he was desiring   very much

adjungi   Labieno,   atque iis   legionibus quas
to be united with Labienus, and   these   legions   which

miserat   unà.   Itaque   admodùm magnis
he had sent   together (with him).   Therefore very   long

itineribus   diurnis   atque   nocturnis,   confectis
marches   by day   and   by night.   having been made

pervenit   ad Ligerim,   contra   opinionem   omnium;
he arrived   at the Loire.   contrary   to the opinion   of all;

que   vado   invento   **per**   equites,   opportuno
and   a ford   having been found   by   the horsemen   suitable

pro necessitate   rěi;   ut   brachia   mŏdo,   atque
for   the urgency   of the case.   that   the arms   only   and

humeri   possent   esse   liberi   ab   aquâ   ad
the shoulders   might   be   free   from   the water   for

sustinenda   arma,   equitatu   disposito
supporting   (their) equipments,   the cavalry   having been stationed

qui   refringeret   vim   fluminis,   atque
(that)   they   might break   the force   of the river.   and

hostibus   perturbatis   primo   adspectu,
the enemy   (having been)   confounded   at first   sight

transduxit   exercitum   incolumen   que   nactus
he led over   the army   safe   and   having found

frumentum   in   agris,   et   copiam   pecŏris,
corn   in   the fields.   and   abundance   of cattle,

exercitu   repleto   ĭis   rebus,   instituit
the army   having been supplied   with those   things,   he determines

facěre   iter   in   Senones.
to make (his)   march   into   the Senones.

57. Dum   hæc   geruntur   apud   Cæsarem,
While   these things   are transacted   under   Cæsar,

Labienus,   ěo   supplemento,   quod   nuper   veněrat
Labienus,   this   contingent [addition].   that   had lately   come

ex   Italiâ   relicto   Agendici,   ut
from   Italy   having been left   at Agendicum [Sens],   that

esset   præsidio   impedimentis,   proficiscitur
it might be   (for)   a guard   to the baggage.   marches

cum   quatuor   legionibus   Lutetiam.   id   est
with   four   legions   to Lutetia [Paris]   This   is

oppidum   Parisiorum   positum   in   insulâ   fluminis
a town   of the Parisii   situated   on   an island   of the river

Sequanæ.   Cujus   adventu   cognito   ab
Seine.   Whose   arrival   having been learned   by

hostibus, magnæ copiæ convenerunt ex   finitimis
the enemy,   great   forces   assembled   from   the neighboring

civitatibus.   Summa   imperii transditur Camulogero
states.   The supreme   command   is given   to Camulogenus

Aulerco;   qui   propè   confectus   ætate,
the Aulercan;   who   (though) nearly   worn out   with age.

tamen evocatus est ad ĕum honorem   propter
yet   was called   to   this   honor   on account of (his)

singularem scientiam militaris rĕi.   Is,   quum
singular   knowledge   of military   affairs.   He,   when

animadvertisset   esse perpetuam paludem
he had observed   (that there)   was   a continuous   marsh

quæ   influeret   in   Sequanam, atque magnopere
which   opened   into   the Seine,   and   greatly

impediret omnem illum lŏcum, consedit   hic,   que
obstructed   all   that   place,   encamped   there.   and

instituit prohibere nostros   transitu.
resolved   to prohibit   our   (soldiers)   from passing.

58. Labienus primò   conabatur   agĕre   vineas,
Labienus   at first   was endeavoring   to work   the sheds,

explere   paludem   cratibus atque aggere, atque
to fill up   the marsh   with hurdles   and   a mound,   and

munire   iter.   Postquam animadvertit   id
to open   a road.   After   he observed   (that)   this

confieri   difficiliùs,   egressus
would be accomplished   with great difficulty,   having marched out

è   castris silentio   tertiâ   vigiliâ, pervenit
from (his) camp   in silence   on the third   watch,   he arrived

Metiosedum,[40]   ĕodem   itinĕre,   quo
at Metiosedum   [Melun]   by the same   road,   by which

venerat.   Id   est oppidum   Senonum   positum
he had come.   This   is   a town   of the Senones   situated

in   insulâ Sequanæ, ut   paulò   antè   diximus
on   an island   of the Seine,   as   a little   before   we have said

Lutetiam.   Circĭter quinquaginta navibus   depre-
(was) Lutetia.   About   fifty   ships   having been

hensis,   quer   conjunctis celerite, atque
seized,   and   (having been) joined together   quickly,   and

militibus   impositis   ĕò,   et   oppidanis
soldiers   having been placed   thereon,   and   the people of the town

perterritis   novitate   rĕi,   magna
(having been) alarmed   by the novelty   of the thing   a great

pars   quorum   erat   evocata   ad   bellum,
part   of whom   had   been called away   to   the war,

potitur   oppido   sine   contentione.   Ponte
he seizes   the town   without   a contest.   The bridge

refecto,   quem   hostes   resciderant
having been rebuilt,   which   the enemy   had destroyed

superioribus   diebus,   transducit   exercitum,   et
on the preceding   days   he leads over   (his)   army.   and

cœpit facĕre   iter secundo flumine ad Lutetiam.
began   to make   (his)   way   down   the river   to   Lutetia.

Hostes,   re   cognitâ   ab   ĭis   qui
The enemy,   the matter   having been learned   from   those   who

profugĕrant   à   Metiosedo,   jubent   Lutetiam
had fled   from   Metiosedum,   order   Lutetia

incendi   que   pontes   ejus   oppidi   rescindi;
to be burned   and   the bridges   of this   town   to be destroyed:

ipsi   profecti   palude,   considunt   in
they themselves   having left   the marsh,   place themselves   on

ripis   Sequanæ   è   regione Lutetiæ   contra
the banks   of the Seine   over   against   Lutetia   opposite

castra   Labieni.
the camp   of Labienus.

59. Jam   Cæsar   audiebatur   discessisse   à
Already   Cæsar   was heard   to have departed   from

Gergoviâ;   jam   rumores afferebantur de defectione
Gergovia;   already   reports   were brought   of   the revolt

Æduorum,   et   secundo   motu   Galliæ,   que
of the Ædui,   and   of the successful   rising   of Gaul   and

Galli   in   colloquis   confirmabant   Cæsarem
the Gauls   in   their conversations   were asserting   (that)   Cæsar

interclusum   itinere   et   Ligere,
cut off   from (his) route   and   from the Loire   (and)

coactum   inopiâ   frumenti,   contendisse   in
forced   by the want   of corn,   had marched   into

Provinciam. Autem Bellovaci, defectione Æduorum
the province. But the Bellovaci, the defection of the Ædui

cognitâ, qui antè ĕrant per se
having been learned. who before were of themselves

infideles, cœperunt cogĕre manus, atque apertè
unfaithful, began to collect forces. and openly

parare bellum. Tum Labienus, tantâ
to prepare (for) war. Then Labienus, in so great

commutatione rerum intelligebat longè aliud
a change of affairs thought (that) a far different

consilium capiendum sibi, atque senserat
plan to [must] be taken by him. than he had consiαered

antea. Neque jam cogitabat, ut acquireret
before. Nor now was he thinking. that he should acquire

aliquid, que lacesseret hostes prœlio, sed ut
anything. and should attack the enemy in battle. but that

reduceret exercitum incolumen Agendicum.
he should lead back (his) army safe to Agendicum.

Namque ex altĕrâ parte Bellovaci, quæ civitas
For on the one side the Bellovaci. which state

habet maximam opinionem virtutis in Galliâ,
had the greatest reputation of [for] bravery in Gaul,

instabant; altĕram Camulogenus tenebat
were pressing: the other (side) Camulogenus was holding

parato atque instructo exercitu; tum
with an organized and equipped army, also

maximum flumen distinebat legiones
a very large river was separating the legions (having been)

interclusas à præsidio atque impedimentis
cut off from the garrison and baggage.

Tantis difficultatibus subĭtò objectis,
Such great difficulties suddenly having been presented,

videbat auxilium petendum ab virtute[41]
he saw (that) aid to [must] be sought from strength

anĭmi.
of mind.

60. Itaque sub vespĕrum, concilio con‑
Therefore towards evening. a council having been

vocato,   cohortatus,   ut   diligenter   que
called,   he exhorted   (his soldiers),   that   diligently   and

industriè   administrarent   ĕa   quæ
industriously   they should execute [perform]   those   (things)   which

imperâsset;   naves,   quas   deduxerat   à
he should command;   the ships,   which   he had brought   from

Metiosedo,   attribuit   singulas   Romanis   equitibus;   et
Metiosedum,   he assigns   each one   to Roman   knights;   and

jubet,   primâ   vigiliâ   confectâ,
orders   (them),   the first   watch   having been completed,

progredi   quatuor   millia   passŭum secundo flumine,
to proceed   four   thousand   paces   down   the river,

silentio,   que   ibi   se expectari.   Relinquit
in silence,   and   (that)   there   he was to be awaited.   He leaves

quinque   cohortes,   quas   existimabat   esse   minimè
five   cohorts,   which   he considered   to be   least

firmas   ad   dimicandum,   præsidio   castris;
sturdy   for   fighting,   for [as] a guard   to the camp;

imperat   reliquas   quinque   ejusdem   legionis
he commands   the remaining   five   of the same   legion

proficisci   de   mediâ   nocte   cum   omnibus   impedimentis
to proceed   at   mid   night   with   all   (their) baggage

adverso   flumine   magno   tumultu.   Etĭam
up   the river   with a great   din.   Also

conquirit lintres;   has   mittit   in   ĕandem   partem,
he collects   boats;   these   he sends   in   the same   direction,

incitatas   magno   sonitu   remorum.   Ipse,   paulò
driven   by a great   sound [noise]   of oars.   He himself,   a little

pòst,   egressus   silentio   cum   tribus   legionibus,
after,   having marched out   in silence   with   three   legions,

petit   ĕum   lŏcum,   quò   jusserat   naves
seeks   this   place,   where   he had ordered   the ships

appelli.
to be brought.

61. Quum   esset   ventum⁴²   ĕo,   exploratores
      When   it was come   [he came]   there,   the scouts

hostium,   ut   dispositi ĕrant   omni   parte
of the enemy.   as   they were stationed   in every   part

flumĭnis,   inopinantes,   quòd   magna   tempestas
of the river,   not expecting,   because   a great   storm

subitò cŏorta erat,   opprimuntur   ab   nostris;
had suddenly arisen,   were overpowered   by   our   (men);

exercitus   que   equitatus   celerĭter transmittitur,
the infantry   and   cavalry   are speedily transported,

Romanis equitibus administrantibus,   quos
the Roman   knights   superintending,   whom   he (Labienus)

præfeceret   ĕi   negotio.   Ferè   uno
had appointed for   this   affair.   Nearly   at one   [the same]

tempŏre   sub   lucem   nunciatur   hostibus,
time   about   daylight   it was announced   to the enemy,

tumultuari   in   castris   Romanorum præter
(that)   there was confusion   in   the camp   of the Romans   beyond

consuetudinem,   et   magnum agmen   ire
custom,   and   (that)   a great   force   was going

adverso flumĭne,   que   sonitum   remorum
up   the river,   and   (that)   the sound [noise]   of oars

exaudiri   in   ĕâdem   parte,   et   paulò
was heard   in   the same   direction,   and   (that)   a little

infra   milĭtes   transportari   navibus.   Quibus   rebus
below   soldiers   were transported   in ships.   Which   things

auditis,   quòd   existimabant   legiones
having been heard,   because   they thought   (that)   the legions

transire   tribus lŏcis,   atque   omnes perturbatos
were crossing   in three places,   and   (that)   all   alarmed

defectione   Æduorum   parare   fugam,
by the defection   of the Ædui   were preparing   for flight,

quoque distribuerunt   suas   copias   in   tres   partes.
they also divided   their   forces   into   three   parts.

Nam,   præsidio   relicto   à regione   castrorum,
For,   a guard   having been left   opposite   the camp,

et   parvâ   manu   missâ   versùs Metiosedum,
and   a small   force   having been sent   toward   Metiosedum,

quæ   progrederetur   tantum   quantum   naves   pro-
which   should advance   only   as far as   the ships   had

cessissent, duxerunt reliquas copias contra Labienum,
proceeded,   they led   the remaining forces   against   Labienus.

62. Primâ luce   et   omnes nostri
At first   light [daylight]   both   all   our   (soldiers)

transportati ĕrant,   et   acies   hostium   cernebatur.
had been transported,   and   the army   of the enemy   was discerned

Labienus cohortatus   milites   ut   tenĕrent
[seen].   Labienus   exhorted   the soldiers   that   they should hold

memoriam   suæ   pristinæ   virtutis,   et   tot
the memory   (of) their   former   valor,   and   (of) so many

secundissimorum prœliorum, atque   existimarent
very successful   battles,   and   that they should think

Cæsarem ipsum,   cujus ductu   sæpenum-
(that)   Cæsar   himself,   under whose leadership   they had so

ero superâssent   hostes   adesse;   dat   signum
often conquered   the enemy,   was present;   he gives   the signal

prœli.   Primo   concursu, ab dextro cornu,   ubi
of battle.   On the first   encounter,   on the right   wing,   where

septima   legio   constiterat,   hostes   pelluntur,
the seventh   legion   stood,   the enemy   are repulsed,

atque conjiciuntur   in   fugam;   ab sinistro,
and   are thrown   into   flight;   on   the left   (wing),

quem   lŏcum   duodecima   legio   tenebat,   quum
which   place   the twelfth   legion   was holding,   when

primi   ordĭnes   hostium   concidissent   transfixi
the first   ranks   of the enemy   had fallen   transfixed

pilis,   reliqui   tamen   resistebant   acerrimè,   nec
by javelins,   the rest   yet   were resisting   most actively,   nor

quisquam   dabat   suspicionem   fugæ.   Dux
was any one   giving   suspicion   of flight.   The general

ipse   hostium   Camulogenus   aderat   suis,
himself   of the enemy   Camulogenus   was present   with his

atque   cohortabatur   ĕos.   At   exitu
(men),   and   was encouraging   them.   But   the issue

victoriæ   etiam   nunc   incerto,   quum
of the victory   even   now   (being)   uncertain,   when

nunciatum esset   tribunis   septimæ   legionis,
it was announced   to the tribunes   of the seventh   legion,

quæ   gererentur   in   sinistro   cornu,   ostenderunt
what   was transpiring   on   the left   wing,   they displayed

legionem   post   tergum   hostium,   que intulerunt
the legion   behind [on] the rear   of the enemy, and   advanced

signa.   Ne   ĕo   tempŏre quidem quisquam cessit
the standards. Not at this   time   even   did any one leave

lŏco,   sed   omnes   circumventi sunt   que
the place,   but   all   were surrounded   and

interfecti;   Camulogenus   tulit   ĕandem
slain;   Camulogenus   bore [met]   the same

fortunam.   At   ĭi   qui relicti ĕrant   præsidio
fortune [fate]. But   those   who   were left   for a garrison

contra   castra   Labieni,   quum   audissent
over against   the camp   of Labienus, when   they had heard

      prœlium   commissum, ierunt   subsidio
(that)   the battle   (had) commenced, went   for [as] an aid

suis,   que   ceperunt   collem, neque
to their [people], and   took   [occupied],   the hill,   nor

potuerunt sustinere impetum   nostrorum militum
could they   endure   the attack   of our   soldiers

victorum: sic permixti cum   suis   fugientibus,
(when) conquerors; so   mingled with their own (men) retreating.

quos   silvæ   que   montes   non texerunt
those whom   the woods   and   the mountains did not conceal

interfecti sunt   ab   equitatu.   Hoc negotio con-
were killed   by   the cavalry. This   affair   having

fecto,   Labienus revertitur Agedincum,   ŭbi
been completed. Labienus returned   to Agedincum,   where

impedimenta totius exercitûs relicta ĕrant;   inde
the baggage   of all   the army   had been left,   thence

pervenit ad Cæsarem cum omnibus   copiis.
he came   to   Cæsar   with   all   (his) forces.

63. Defectione Æduorum   cognitâ,   bellum
     The revolt   of the Ædui having been known, the war

augetur;   legationes circummittuntur in   omnes
is increased;   embassies   are sent about   in   all

partes; nituntur ad sollicitandas civitates quantum
directions; they strive to solicit   the states   as much as

valent   gratiâ,   auctoritate,   pecuniâ.
they may avail by favor,   by authority,   (or) by money.

Nacti   obsides,   quos   Cæsar   deposuerat
Having got   the hostages,   whom   Cæsar   had deposited

apud ĕos,   territant   dubitantes   supplicio
with them,   they frighten   the hesitating   by the punishment

horum.   Ædui   petunt   â Vercingetorige   ut
of these.   The Ædui   request   of Vercingetorix   that

veniat   ad   se,   que   communicet   rationes
he come   to   them,   and   communicate   the plans

gerendi   belli.   Re   impetratâ,
of carrying on   the war.   This thing   having been obtained,

contendunt,   ut   summa   imperii   tradatur
they maintain,   that   the chief   command   should be assigned

ipsis   et,   re   deductâ   in controversiam,
to them and,   the thing having been brought into   dispute,

concilium   totius   Galliæ   indicitur   Bibracte.
a council   of all   Gaul   is convoked   at Bibracte.

Frequentes   undique   conveniunt ĕodem;   res
Great numbers   from everywhere   assemble   there;   the matter

permittitur   suffragiis   multitudinis;   omnes ad unum
is consigned   to the votes   of the multitude;   all   to   one

probant   Vercingetorigem   imperatorem.
[a man]   approve of   Vercingetorix   (as)   commander.

Remi,   Lingones,   Treviri,   abfuerunt   ab
The Remi,   Lingones,   (and)   Treviri,   were absent   from

hôc concilio;   illi   quôd   sequebantur
this   council;   those [two first]   because   they were following

amicitiam   Romanorum;   Treviri   quôd
[observing]   the friendship   of the Romans;   the Treviri   because

longiùs   aberant,   et   premebantur ab Germanis;
they were far   distant,   and   were hard pressed by   the Germans;

quæ   fuit   causa   quare   abessent   toto
which   was   the reason   why   they were absent in   the whole

bello,   et   mitterent   auxilia   neutris.   Ædui
war,   and   were sending   auxiliaries   to neither.   The Ædui

ferunt   magno   dolŏre   se   dejectos
bear   with great   resentment   (that)   they   were deprived

principatu;   queruntur   commutationem   fortunæ,
of the leadership;   they lament   the change   of fortune

et requirunt Cæsaris indulgentiam in se;
and they miss Cæsar's indulgence toward themselves ;

neque tamen, bello suscepto, audent
nor however, the war having been undertaken, do they dare

separare suum consilium ab reliquis.
to separate their plan [course] from the rest.

Eporedorix et Viridomarus adolescentes summæ
Eporedorix and Viridomarus young men of the highest

spei (sing.) inviti parent Vercingetorigi.
expectations unwillingly obey Vercingetorix.

64. Ille imperat obsides reliquis
He [Vercingetorix] demands hostages from the other

civitatibus. Denique constituit diem ĕi rĕi;
states. Finally he appoints a day for this matter;

huc jubet omnes equites, numĕro
here he orders all the horsemen, to the number

quindecim millia, convenire celerĭter. Dicit
of fifteen thousand, to assemble quickly. He says

se fŏre contentum peditatu quem
(that) he would be content with the infantry which

habuerit antè; neque temtaturum fortunam, neque
he had before; nor would he tempt fortune, nor

dimicaturum acie;[43] sed, quoniam abundet
would he fight in the battle-line; but, since he abounds

equitatu, esse perfacile factu prohibere
in cavalry, it would be very easy in fact to check

Romanos frumentationibus que pabulationibus; mŏdŏ
the Romans from corn and forage; provided

ipsi æquo animo corrumpant sua
they themselves with a calm mind destroy their own

frumenta, que incendant ædificia; quâ
corn, and burn (their) houses; by which

jacturâ familaris rĕi videant se
loss of private property they may see (that) they would

consequi perpetŭum imperium que libertatem. His
obtain perpetual empire and freedom, These

rebus constitutis, imperat Æduis que
things having been arranged. he demands from the Ædui and

Segusianis,   qui   sunt   finitimi   Provinciæ,   decem
the Segusiani,   who   are   nearest   to the Province,   ten

millia   peditum;   huc   addit   octingentos
thousand   (of) infantry: to this   he adds   eight hundred

equites;   his   præficit   fratrem   Eporedorigis,
horsemen;   over these   he appoints   the brother   of Eporidorix,

que   jubet   inferre   bellum   Allobrogibus.
and   orders   (him)   to wage   war   with the Allobroges.

Ex   alterâ   parte   mittit   Gabalos   que   proxĭmos
On   the other   side   he sends   the Gabali   and   the nearest

pagos   Arvernorum   in   Helvios;   item   Rutenos,
cantons   of the Arverni   against   the Helvii;   likewise   the Ruteni,

que   Cadurcos   ad depopulandos   fines   Volcarum
and   the Cadurci   to   lay waste   the territories   of the Volcæ

Arecomicorum.   Nihilominùs   sollicitat   Allobroges
Arecomici.   Nevertheless   he solicits   the Allobroges

clandestinis nunciis que legationibus, quorum mentes
by secret   messages and   embassies,   whose   minds

sperabat   nondum   resedisse   à
he was hoping   not yet   to have [had] recovered   from

superiore bello. Horum principibus pollicetur pecunias,
the former   war.   To their   leaders   he promises   money,

autem   civitati   imperum totius Provinciæ.
but   to the state   the empire   of all   the Province.

65.   Ad   omnes hos   casus   præsidia
     Against   all   these contingencies [crises]   the protection

viginti et duarum cohortium   provisa ĕrant,   quæ
of twenty and   two   cohorts   had been provided,   which

     coacta   ex Provinciâ ipsâ ab L. Cæsare,
having been collected   from   the province itself by L. Cæsar,

     legato   opponebantur   ad   omnes   partes.
(his) lieutenant   were opposing   at [on]   all   sides.

Helvii,   suâ sponte   congressi   prœlio cum
The Helvii,   of their own   accord   having engaged   in battle with

finitimis,   pelluntur,   et   C. Valerio Donotauro,
their neighbors.   are defeated.   and   C   Valerius   Donaturus,

filio   Caburi,   principe civitatis, que compluribus
the son of Caburus,   a chief   of the state,   and   many

aliis   interfectis,   compelluntur   intra   oppida
others   having been killed,   they are driven   into   the towns

que   muros.   Allobroges   crebris   præsidiis
and   fortifications.   The Allobroges   frequent   guards

dispositis   ad   Rhodanum,   tuentur   suos
having been placed   at [along]   the Rhone,   defend   their

fines   cum   magnâ   curâ   et   diligentiâ.   Cæsar,
frontiers   with   great   care   and   diligence.   Cæsar,

quòd   intelligebat   hostes   esse
because   he was perceiving   (that)   the enemy   to be   [were]

superiores   equitatu,   et   omnibus   itineribus
superior   in cavalry,   and,   all   the roads

interclusis,   poterat   sublevari   nullâ   re
having been shut up,   he could   be assisted   in no   thing   [respect[

ex   Provinciâ   atque   Italiâ,   mittit   trans   Rhenum
from the   Province   and   Italy,   sends   across   the Rhine

in   Germaniam   ad   ĕas   civitates,   quas   pacaverat
into   Germany   to   these   states,   which   he had conquered

superioribus   annis,   que   arcessit   equites   ab   his,
in former   years,   and   demanded   cavalry   from   them.

et   pedites   levis   armaturæ,   qui   consuevĕrant
and   infantry   of light   armor,   that   were accustomed

prœliari   inter   ĕos.   Eorum   adventu,   quòd
to battle   among   them.   On their   coming,   because

utebantur   equis   minùs   idonĕis,   sumit   equos
they used   horses   less   suitable,   he takes   horses

à   tribunis   militum,   sed   ut
(not only)   from   the tribunes   of the soldiers,   but   also

Romanis   equitibus,   atque   evocatis,   que   distribuit
from the Roman   knights,   and   veterans,   and   distributes

Germanis.
to the Germans.

66. Interea   dum   hæc   geruntur,   copiæ
Mean time   while   these things   are transpiring,   the force

ex   Arvernis,   que   equites,   qui   imperati ĕrant
from   the Arverni,   and   the cavalry,   that   had been demandeᴅ

toti   Galliæ,   conveniunt.   Magno   numero   horum
of all   of Gaul.   assemble.   A great   number   of these

coacto,   quum   Cæsar   faceret   iter   in
having been collected,   when   Cæsar   made   (his)   way   into

Sequanos,   per   extremos   fines   Lingonum,
the Sequani,   through   the extreme   borders   of the Lingones,

quò   posset   faciliùs   ferre   subsidium   Provinciæ,
so that   he could   more easily   bring   aid   to the Province,

Vercingetorix   consedit,   trinis   castris,   circĭter   decem
Vercingetorix   halted,   in three   camps,   about   ten

millia   passŭum   ab   Romanis;   que   præfectis
thousand (of)   paces   from   the Romans;   and   the commanders

equitum   convocatis   ad   concilium,   demonstrat
of the cavalry   having been called   to   a council,   he shows (that)

tempus   victoriæ   venisse;   Romanos   fugĕre   in
the time   of victory   had come;   the Romans   were fleeing   into

Provinciam,   que   excedere   Galliâ;   id   esse   satìs
the Province,   and   were leaving   Gaul;   (that) this   was   enough

sibi   ad   obtinendam   præsentem   libertatem;
for them   for   obtaining   present [immediate]   freedom;

profici   parum   ad   pacem   atque   otium
(but it)   profited   little   for   the peace   and   repose

reliqui   tempŏris;   enim   majoribus   copiis
of the remaining   time;   for   greater   forces

coactis   reversuros   neque   facturos
having been collected   they would return   nor   would they make

finem   bellandi;   proinde   adoriantur
an end   of waring;   therefore   let them attack   (them)

impeditos   agmine.   Si   pedites   ferant auxilium
incumbered   on the march.   If   the infantry   bring   assistance

suis,   atque morentur   ĕo,   iter   posse
to their (men),   and   delay   for this,   (that) the march   could

non   confici;   sin,   id   quod   magìs
not   be performed;   but,   this   which   the rather [the more]

confidat futurum,   impedimentis   relictis,
he trusts   would be,   the baggage   having been abandoned,

consulant   suæ   saluti,   iri   spoliatum
if they may consult   their   safety,   they would   be   deprived

et   usu   necessariarum rerum,   et   dignitate.
both   of the use   of necessary   things   and   of their honor.

Nam   de   equitibus   hostium,   ne   ipsos
For   concerning   the cavalry   of the enemy,   not   they

quidem   debere   dubitare,   quin   nemo   ĕorum
even   ought   to doubt,   (but) that   no one   of them

audeat   mŏdò   progredi   extra   agmen.
would dare even   to advance   beyond   the marching-line.

Quo   faciant   id   majore   animo,   se habiturum
That they may do this with greater spirit,   he would hold

omnes   copias   pro   castras,   et   futurum
all (his)   forces   before   the camp,   and   would be

    terrori   hostibus.   Equites   conclamant
(for) a terror   to the enemy.   The cavalry   shout   (that)

oportĕre   confirmari   sanctissĭmo   jurejurando,
it was proper to confirm   (this) by a most sacred   oath,

    ne recipiatur   tecto,   habeat aditum
that he should not be received under a roof, (nor) have   access

ne   ad   liberos   ne ad parentes, ne   ad   uxorem,
either to   children   or to parents,   or   to   wife,

qui   non   bis   perequitâsset   per   agmen
who   had not twice   ridden   through   the army

hostium.
of the enemy.

67.   Re   probatá,   atque   omnibus
    The thing   having been approved,   and   all

    adactis   ad   jusjurandum,   postĕro   die
having been bound   to   an oath,   on the next   day

equitatu   distributo   in   tres   partes,   duæ
the cavalry having been divided into   three   parts,   two

ostendunt   se   à   duobus lateribus;   una   cœpit
  show   themselves on   the two   flanks;   one   began

impedire   iter   à   primo   agmĭne.   Quâ
to impede the march   on   the first   line [the front].   Which

re   nunciatâ,   Cæsar quoque jubet suum
thing having been announced,   Cæsar   also   orders   his

equitatum divisum   tripartitò   ire   contra hostem.
 cavalry   divided   into three parts to go   against the enemy

Pugnatur (pass. sing.)   unà   in   omnibus partibus
They fought   together on   all   sides.

Agmen   constitit.   Impedimenta recipiuntur
The marching-column halted.   The baggage   is received

inter   legiones.   Si in   quâ   parte   nostri
among   the legions. If in   any   part   our   (men)

videbantur laborare, aut   premi   graviùs,   ĕò
were seeming to labor.   or   be pressed more severely, there

Cæsar   jubebat   signa   inferri,   que
Cæsar   was ordering the standards to be borne,   and

aciem   converti;   quæ   res   et   tardabat
the battle-line to be turned; which thing both was retarding

hostes   ad   insequendum,   et   confirmabat
the enemy   for [from]   following,   and   was encouraging

nostros   spe   auxili.   Tandem   Germani
our   (men) with the hope of aid.   At length the Germans

ab   dextro   latĕre,   nacti   summum   jugum
on   the right wing,   having gained :the top of the hill

depellunt   hostes   lŏco;   persequuntur
force   the enemy   from the place;   they pursue

fugientes usque ad   flumen,   ŭbi   Vercingetorix
(them) fleeing even to   the river, where Vercingetorix

consedĕrat cum pedestribus copiis,   que interficiunt
had halted   with the foot   forces,   and they kill

complures.   Quâ   re   animadversâ,   reliqui
very many.   Which thing   having been observed, the rest

veriti,   ne   circumvenirentur,   mandant   se
afraid,   lest they might be surrounded, consign   themselves

fugæ.   Cædes   fit   omnibus   lŏcis.   Tres
to flight. Slaughter is made   in all   parts.   Three

nobilissĭmi Ædui   capti   perducuntur ad Cæsarem;
most noble   Æduans captured are led back to   Cæsar;

Cotus   præfectus   equitum,   qui   habuerat
Cotus   the commander   of the cavalry, who   had held

controversiam cum Convictolitave proxĭmis   comitiis;
the contest   with Convictolitavis in the late elections;

et   Cavarillus,   qui, post defectionem   Litavici
and   Cavarillus,   who, after the revolt   of Litavicus

præfuerat   pedestribus copiis,   et   Eporedorix,
had commanded the foot   forces,   and Eporedorix,

quo   duce,   ante   adventum Cæsaris,   Ædui
with whom as leader, before   the arrival of Cæsar,   the Ædui

contendĕrant   bello   cum   Sequanis.
had fought   in the war   with   the Sequani.

68. Omni   equitatu   fugato,   Vercingetorix
All   the cavalry   having been routed,   Vercingetorix

reduxit   suas   copias   ut   collocaverɛt   pro
led back   his   forces   as   he had placed (them)   before

castris;   que   protinus   cœpit   fɑcere   iter
the camp;   and   immediately   began   to make (his)   march

Alesiam,[44] quod   est   oppidum   Mandubiorum;   que
to Alesia,   which   is   a town   of the Mandubii;   and

jussit   impedimenta celerĭter   educi   ex   castris,
ordered   the baggage   quickly   to be brought from   the camp,

et   subsequi   se.   Cæsar,   impedimentis
and   to follow closely   after him.   Cæsar,   the baggage

deductis   in proximum collem, que   duabus
having been conducted   to   the next   hill,   and   two

legionibus   relictis   præsidio,   secutus,
legions   having been left   for [as] a guard,   having followed,

quantum   tempus   diĕi   passum est, circĭter   tribus
as far as   the time   of day   allowed,   about   three

millibus   hostium   ex novissimo agmĭne   inter-
thousand   of the enemy   in   the rear   line   having been

fectis,   altĕro   die   fecit   castra   ad
slain,   on the next   day   makes [pitches]   camp   at

Alesiam.   Perspecto   situ   urbis,   quɛ
Alesia.   Having reconnoitered the situation of the town,   and

hostibus   perterritis,   quòd   erant pulsi
the enemy   (having been) terrified,   because   they were beaten

equitatu,   quâ   parte   exercitûs   maximɛ
by the cavalry, in which   part [branch] of the army   especially

confidebant;   adhortatus   milites   ad   laborcm,
they were confiding; having exhorted the soldiers   to   the labor

instituit   cicumvallare Alesiam.
he determined   to invest   Alesia.

69. Oppidum   ipsum   ĕrat   in   summo   colle,
The town   itself   was   on   the top   (of)   a hill

lŏco   admodum edĭto,   ut   vĭderetur non posse ex-
the place   very high,   so that it seemed it could not (to)

pugnarı   nisi   obsıdıone.   Duo flumĭna ex
be captured   unless   by a blockade. Two rivers   on

duabus partĭbus   subluebant   radĭces cujus collıs.
two   sıdes   were washing the foot of this hill.

Ante   oppĭdum planĭties   patebat   cırcĭter trium
Before   the town   a plain   was extending about   three

mıllia   passŭum   in   longĭtudĭnem. Ex   omnĭbus
thousand   paces [miles]   in   length   On   all

relĭquis   partĭbus,   colles,   medĭocri   spatia
the remaining   sıdes.   hılls,   a moderate   distance

         interjecto   pari   fastigio
(having been) interposed   with equal   elevation   [degree]

altĭtudĭnis   cingebant   oppĭdum.   Sub   muro,
of height   were encircling   the town.   Under   the wall.

pars   collıs,   quæ   spectabat   ad   orientem,
the part   of the hill,   which   was looking   to   the east,

omnem hunc lŏcum   copıæ   Gallorum compleverant,
all   this   place   the forces of the Gauls   had filled,

que   præduxĕrant   fossam,   et   maceriam
and   had led [thrown] around   a ditch,   and   a cement wall

sex   pedum   in   altĭtudĭnem.   Circuitus   ejus
six   feet   in   height.   The circuit   of this

munĭtionis,   quæ   instĭtuebatur   ab   Romanis
fortıfication,   which   was undertaken   by   the Romans

tenebat   undecim   millia   passŭum.   Castra
was extending eleven   thousand   paces [miles]. The camp

posĭta ĕrant   opportunis   lŏcis;   que ĭbi   vigĭnti
was placed   in favorable   positions; and there   twenty

tria   castella   facta,   in   quibus interdiu stationes
three   fortresses   were made, in   which   by day   guards

disponebantur,   ne   qua irruptio   fieret   subĭtŏ.
were placed,   lest   any sally   might be made suddenly.

Hæc   ĕadem   tenebantur   noctu excubĭtorıbus,
These   same   were held [occupied]   at night by pickets,

ac   firmis   præsidiis.
and   strong   posts.

70.   Opĕre instĭtuto,   equestre   prœlium
         The work having been undertaken,   a cavalry   battle

fit   in   ĕâ   planitie,   quam,   demonstravimus
took place on   this   plain,   which,   we have shown

suprà, patere tria millia   passŭum in longitudinem,
above, extends three thousand   paces   in   length,

intermissam   collibus.   Contenditur (pass. sìng.)
   limited   by the hills.   They contended

    summâ   vi   ab   utrisque.   Cæsar
with the highest [utmost] vigor   by [on]   both sides.   Cæsar

submittit Germanos   nostris   laborantibus,   que
   sends   the Germans   to our men   hard pressed,   and

constituit legiones   pro   castris,   ne   qua irruptio
draws up   the legions before   the camp,   lest   any   sally

subitò   fiat   peditatu   hostium.   Præsidio
suddenly should be made by the infantry of the enemy. The protection

legionum   addito,   animus augetur   nostris;
of the legions having been added, courage   is increased in our men ;

hostes   conjecti   in   fugam,   ipsi   impediunt
the enemy   thrown   into   flight,   they   impede

   se   multitudine; atque coartantur angustioribus
themselves by their mass ;   and   are crowded   in the narrower

portis   relictis.   Germani   sequuntur
gates   left   (open).   The Germans   follow   (them)

    acriùs   usque ad   munitiones;   maga   cædes
more vigorously   even   to   the fortifications; a great   slaughter

fit;   nonnulli,   equis relictis,   conantur
is made ;   some,   the horses having been abandoned,   endeavor

transire   fossam,   et transcendĕre   maceriam.
to cross over   the ditch,   and   climb   the cement wall.

Cæsar   jubet   legiones,   quas   constituerat
Cæsar   orders   the legions,   which   he had drawn up

   pro vallo   promoveri   paulùm.   Galli,
before the rampart   to be moved forward   a little.   The Gauls

qui   ĕrant   intra   munitiones,   non   minùs
who   were   within   the fortifications,   no   less

perturbantur;   existimantes   veniri
were terrified ;   thinking   (our men)   were coming

confestim ad se, conclamant ad arma. Nonnulli
quickly to them. they call to arms. Some

perterriti ìrrumpunt in oppidum. Vercingetorix
panic stricken burst into the town. Vercingetorix

jubet portas claudi, ne castra nudentur.
orders the gates to be closed, lest the camp should be left bare.

Multis interfectis, compluribus equis
Many having been slain, (and) very many horses

captis, Germani recipiunt sese.
having been captured, the Germans return [retire].

71. Vercingetorix capit consilium dimi*t*tere à
Vercingetorix adopts the plan to send away from

se omnem equitatum noctu, priusquam munitiones
him all the cavalry by night. before the fortifications

perficiantur ab Romanis. Mandat discedentibus,
should be finished by the Romans He commands them departing,

ut, quisque ĕorum adeat suam civitatem, que
that, each one of them should go to their own state, and

cogant ad bellum omnes, qui per
(that) they should assemble for the war all, who by

ætatem possint ferre arma. Proponit sua
their age might be able to bear arms. He states his

merita in illos, que obtestatur, ut habeant
services toward them. and implores, that they should have

rationem suæ salutis, neu dedant se hostibus
a regard for his safety, nor deliver him to the enemy

in cruciatum, meritum optime de
for torture, having merited so well concerning

communi libertate; qui[45] si fuerint indiligentiores,
the common liberty; who if they should be somewhat remiss,

demonstrat octoginta millia delecta hominum
he shows (that) eighty thousand chosen men

interitura cum se; ratione inita,
would perish with him: a calculation having been entered [made],

se habere frumentum exiguè triginta dierum, sed
he had corn scarcely of [for] thirty days, but

posse tolerare etïam paulò longiùs parcendo.
he could endure even a little longer by sparing.

His   mandatis   datis,   dimittit   equitatum
These   orders   having been given,   he dismisses   the cavalry

silentio,   secundâ   vigiliâ,   quâ   mostrum   opus
in silence,   in the second   watch,   where   our   work

intermissum;   jubet   omne   frumentum   ferri   ad
ceased;   he orders   all   the corn   to be brought   to

se;   consiituit   pœnam   capitis[46]   iis,
himself;   he ordains   the punishment   of the head [of death]   to those

qui   non   paruĕrint;   distribuit   pecus,   cujus
who   should not   obey;   he distributes   the cattle,   of which

magna   copia   compulsa erat   ab Mandubiis,
a great   abundance   had been driven (there)   by the   Mandubii,

viritim;   instituit   frumentum   metiri
man by man;   he regulates   (that) the corn   to [should] be measured

parcè   et   paulatim;   recipit   omnes   copias,
sparingly   and   by little: he receives   all   the forces,

quas   collocavĕrat   pro   oppido,   in   oppidum.
which   he had placed   before   the town,   into   the town.

His   rationibus   parat   expectare   auxilia   Galliæ,
In this   manner   he prepares   to await   the aid   of Gaul,

et   administrare   bellum.
and   to carry on   the war.

72.   Quibus   rebus   cognitis   ex   perfugis
Which   things   having been known   from   deserters

et   captivis,   Cæsar   instituit   hæc   genĕra (pl.)
and   prisoners,   Cæsar   adopts   this   kind

munitionis.   Duxit   fossam   viginti   pedum
of fortification.   He constructed   a ditch   (of) twenty   feet

latam   directis   lateribus,   ut   ejus   solum
broad   with perpendicular   sides,   so that   its   bottom

pateret   tantundem   quantum   summa   labra   distabant.
might open   just as much   as   the upper   edges   were apart.

Reduxit   omnes   reliquas   munitiones   quadringentis
He drew back   all   the other   fortifications   (by) four hundred

pedibus   ab   ĕâ   fossâ;   id   hôc   consilio
feet   from   this   ditch: this   with this   design

(quoniam   tantum   spatium   necessariò   esset   complexus,
(since   so great   a space   necessarily   was   embraced,

totum	opus	nec	facilè	cingeretur
(that) the whole	the work	not	easily	could be surrounded

coronâ	militum),	ne	aut	multitudo	hostium
by a circle	of soldiers),	lest	either	a mass	of the enemy

advolaret	ad	munitiones	de	improviso	noctu,
should sally out	to	the works	of	a sudden	by night,

aut interdiu	possent	conjicĕre	tela	in
or by day	they might be able	to throw	weapons	against

nostros	destinatos	opĕri.	Hôc	spatio	inter-
our men	assigned	to the work.	This	space	having been

misso,	perduxit	duas	fossas	quindecim	pedes	latas,
left,	he forms	two	trenches	fifteen	feet	wide,

ĕâdem	altitudine;	intĕriorem	quarum	
with the same	depth;	the inner one	of which	(being)

campestribus	ac	demissis	lŏcis,	complevit	aquâ
in level	and	low	ground,	he fills	with water

derivatâ	ex	flumine.	Post	ĕas	extruxit
led	from	the river.	Behind	these	he constructed

aggĕrem	et	vallum	duodecim	pedum.	Huic
a mound	and	rampart	of twelve	feet.	To this

adjecit	loricam	que	pinnas,	grandibus	cervis
he added	a parapet	and	battlements,	with great	stag-horns

eminentibus	ad	commissuras (pl.)	pluteorum (pl.)
projecting	at	the junction	of the parapet

atque	aggĕris,	qui	tardarent	adscensum
and	the mound,	which	might hinder	the ascent

hostium;	et	circumdedit	turres	toto	opere,	quæ
of the enemy;	and	he put around	towers	on all	the work,	which

distarent	inter	se[47]	octoginta	pedes.
were distant	among	themselves	eighty	feet.

73. Erat	necesse	eodem	tempŏre	et
It was	necessary	at the same	time	both

materiari,	et	frumentari,	et	tantas
to bring wood,	and	to get corn,	and	(that) so great

munitiones	fieri,	nostris	copiis	dim-
fortifications	to [should] be made,	our	forces	having been

mutis,	quæ	progrediebantur	longiùs	ab
diminished.	that	were proceding	rather far	from

castris ;   et   Galli   nonnunquam   conabantur
the camp ;   and   the Gauls   sometimes   were endeavoring

tentar   nostra   opĕra,   atque   facĕre   eruptionem
to attack   our   works,   and   to make   a sally

ex   oppĭdo   summâ   vi   pluribus   portis.
from   the town   with the utmost   vigor   by several   gates

Quare   Cæsar   putavit   ad   hæc   rursus
Therefore   Cæsar   thought   to   these   again   (to) [there must]

addendum   opera,   quò   munitiones   possent
be added   works,   so that   the fortifications   might

defendi   minore   numĕro   militum.   Itaque   truncis
be defended   with a less   number   of men [soldiers].   Therefore   trunks

arborum,   aut   ramis   admodum   firmis   abscissis,
of trees,   or   branches   somewhat   stout   having been cut down,

atque   cacuminibus   horum   delibratis   atque
and   the tops   of these   having been peeled   and

preacutis ;   perpetuæ   fossæ   quinos   pedes   altæ
sharpened ;   continuous   ditches   five   feet   deep

ducebantur.   Huc   illi   stipites   demissi,   et
were cut.   Here   these   stakes   were put down,   and

revincti   ab   infimo   possent   ne   revelli,
fastened   at   the bottom   (so that)   they could not   be pulled up,

eminebant   ab   ramis.   Quini   ordines
they were projecting   by   their branches.   Every five   rows

ĕrant   conjuncti,   atque   implicati   inter   se,
were   united,   and   intertwined   among   themselves

quò   ipsi   qui[48]   intraverant,   induebant   se
where   they   who   might enter,   were impaling   themselves

acutissimis   vallis ;   appellabant   hos   cippos.
on very sharp   stakes ;   they were calling   these   cippi [boundary

Ante   hos   obliquis   ordinibus,
posts].   Before   these   in oblique   rows,   and (having been)

dispositis   in   quincuncem,   scrobes,   in   altitudinem
arranged   in   quincunx,   pits,   to   the depth

trium   pedum   fodiebantur   paulatim   angustiore
of three   feet   were dug   with a little   narrower

fastigĭo   ad   summum.   Huc   teretes   stipites   crassitudine
surface   at   the top.   Here   round   stakes   of the thickness

feminis,   ab   summo   præacuti   et   præusti,
of the thigh,   at   the top   very sharp   and   burnt,

demittebantur; ita   ut   non amplius   quatuor
were set in :   so   that   not   more   (than)   four

digitis   eminerent   ex   terrâ.   Simul
inches   might project   from   the ground.   At the same time

causâ   confirmandi   et   stabiliendi,   singuli⁴⁹
for the purpose   of strengthening   and   steadying,   each

pedes (pl.)   ab   infĭmo   solo   terrâ
foot   from   the lowest   ground   with earth

exculcabantur;   reliqua   pars   scrobis   integebatur
were trodden down ;   the remaining   part   of the pit   was covered

viminibus   ac   virgultis   ad   occultandas   insidias.
with osiers   and   twigs   for   concealing   the traps.

Octoni ordĭnes hujus genĕris   ducti,   distabant
Eight   rows   of this   kind   were set,   they were distant

ternos pedes inter   se.   Id,   ex   similitudine
three   feet   among themselves.   This,   from   the likeness

floris,   appellabant   lilium.   Ante hæc taleæ,
to the flower,   they were calling   a lily.   Before these,   stakes,

pedem longæ,   ferreis   hamis   infixis,   totæ
a foot   long,   with iron   hooks   fixed in,   all   [wholly]

infodiebantur   in   terram: que,   mediocribus
were sunk   into   the ground ;   and,   moderate

spatiis   intermissis, disserebantur omnibus
spaces   (having been)   interposed,   were planted   in all

locis,   quos   nominabant   stimulos.
places,   which   they were calling   spurs.

74.   His   rebus   perfectis,   secutus
These   things   having been completed,   having followed

regiones æquissimas, pro   naturâ   loci   quàm
localities   the most level,   for   the nature   of the place   that [as]

potuit,   complexus   quatuordecim   millia
he could,   (and)   having enclosed   fourteen   thousand

passuum,   perfecit   pares   munitiones   ejusdem
paces,   he completed   like   fortifications   of the same

generis,   diversas   ab   his,   contra   exteriorem
kind,   opposite   from   these,   against   an external

hostem;   ut   præsidia   munitionum   possent
enemy;   that   the guards   of the fortifications   could

circumfundi   ne   magna[50]   multitudine, quidem (si
be surrounded   not   by a great   multitude,   even   (if

accidat   ita,   discessu[51]   ejus).
it should happen   so,   by the departure   of it   [its, the cavalry's

Neu   cogerentur   egredi   ex
departure].   Nor   (that)   they should be forced   to go   from

castris cum periculo, jubet omnes habere pabulum
the camp with   danger,   he orders   all   to have   forage

convectum que frumentum triginta dierum.
collected   and   corn   for thirty   days.

75. Dum   hæc   geruntur   ad   Alesiam,
While   these   (things) are transpiring   at   Alesia,

Galli,   concilio   principum   indicto,
the Gauls,   a council   of the chiefs   having been convoked,

statuunt,   non   omnes   convocandos   qui
ordain,   (that) not   all   should be called out   who

possent ferre arma   (ut   Vercingetorix   censuit),
could   bear   arms   (as   Vercingetorix   decided),

sed   certum   numĕrum   imperandum   cuique
but   (that)   a certain   number   should be ordered   for each

civitati;   ne,   tantâ   confusâ multitudine
state;   lest,   in so great   (and)   mixed   a multitude

possent nec moderari, nec discernere suos
they could neither   govern,   nor   distinguish   their (men)

nec habere rationem frumentandi.   Impĕrant
nor   have   the means   of provisioning   They demand

triginta quinque   millia   Æduis   atque
thirty   five   thousand   from the Ædui   and

ĕorum clientibus, Segusianis, Ambivaretis, Aulercis,
their   clients,   the Segusiani,   the Ambivareti,   the Aulerci.

Brannovicibus,   (Blannoviis);   parem   numĕrum
the Brannovices,   (Blannovii),   a like   number

Arvernis,   adjunctis   Eleutetis,   Cadurcis,
from the Arverni,   united   with the Eleuteti,   the Cadurci,

Gabalis,   Vellaviis,   qui   consueverunt
the Gabali,   (and)   the Vellavii,   who   have been accustomed

esse   sub   imperio   Arvernorum :   Senonibus,
to be   under   the command   of the Arverni .   from the Senones,

Sequanis,   Biturigibus,   Santonibus,   Rutenis,
the Sequani,   the Bituriges,   the Santones,   the Ruteni,

Carnutibus,   duodena   millia ;   Bellovacis,   decim ;
the Carnutes,   twelve   thousand ;   the Bellovaci,   ten ;

totidem   Lemovicibus ;   octona   Pictonibus,   et
the same   from the Lemovices;   eight   from the Pictones,   and

Turonis,   et   Parisiis,   et   Helvetiis ;   sena
the Turoni,   and   the Parisii,   and   the Helveti ,   six

Audibus,   Ambianis,   Mediomatricis,   Petrocoriis,
from the Audes,   the Ambiani,   the Mediomatrici,   the Petrocorii,

Nerviis,   Morinis,   Nitiobrigibus ;   quina   milia
the Nervii,   the Morini,   the Nitiobriges ,   five   thousand

Aulercis   Cenomanis ;   totidem   Atrebatibus ;
from the Aulercis   Cenomani ;   the same number   from the Atrebates;

quatuor   Veliocassis ;   (Lexoviis   et)   Aulercis
four   from the Veliocassi;   (the Lexovii   and)   the Aulerci

Eburovicibus   terna ;   Rauracis   et   Boiis   bina.
Eburovices   three ;   from the Rauraci   and   Boii   two.

Decim   universis   civitatibus,   quæ   attingunt
Ten   from   all   the states,   which   border on

Oceanum,   quæque   eorum   consuetudine   appellantur
the Ocean,   and that   by their   custom   are called

Armoricæ,   in   quo   numĕro   sunt   Coriosolites,
Armoricæ,   in   which   number   are   the Coriosolites,

Redones,   Ambibarii,   Caletes,   Osismi,   Veneti,
the Redones.   the Ambibarii,   the Caletes,   the Osismi,   the Veneti,

Lexovii,   Venelli.   Ex   his   Bellovaci   non
Lexovii,   Venelli.   Of   these   the Bellovaci   did not

contulerunt   suum   numerum ;   quòd   dixerunt
contribute   their   number ;   because   they said   (that)

se   gesturos   bellum   cum   Romanis   suo
they   would carry on   war   with   the Romans   by their own

nomine   atque   arbitrio,   neque   obtemperaturos
name   and   will,   nor   would they obey

imperio   cujusquam.   Rogati   à   Commius,
the command   of any one.   Requested   by   Commius,

pro   ejus   hospitio,   tamen   miserunt
on account of   his   tie of hospitality,   however   they sent

duo   millia.
two   thousand.

76. Cæsar,   ita   ut   antĕa demonstravimus,   ĕrat usus
      Cæsar,   just   as   before   we have shown,   had used

fideli   atque   utili   opĕrâ   hujus   Commius,
the faithful   and   helpful   service,   of this   Commius,

superioribus annis   in Britanniâ;   pro quibus meritis
in former   years   in   Britain;   for   which   deserts

jusserat   ejus civitatem   esse immunem,
he had ordered   his   state   to be   exempt (from tribute),

reddiderat   jura   que leges; atque   attribuerat
had restored   the rights   and   laws;   and   had conferred

ipsi   Morinos. Tamen tanta fuit   consensio
on himself [him]   the Morini.   Yet   so great   was   the unanimity

universæ   Galliæ   vindicandæ   libertatis,   et
of the whole   of Gaul   of [for] establishing   liberty,   and

recuperandæ   pristinæ laudis belli,   ut
of [for] recovering   (their)   ancient   renown   in war,   that

moverentur   neque beneficiis, neque   memoriâ
they could be moved   neither   by benefits,   nor   by the memory

amicitiæ,   que omnes   incumberent   in   id
of friendship,   and   all   were devoting themselves   to   this

bellum   et   animo   et   opibus; octo
war   with both   mind [thought]   and   means;   eight

millibus   equitum,   et   circĭter   ducentis   et
thousand   cavalry,   and   about   two hundred   and

quadraginta   millibus   peditum   coactis.
forty   thousand   infantry   having been collected.

Hæc recensebantur   in   finibus   Æduorum;   que
These   were reviewed   in   the country   of the Ædui;   and

numĕrus   inibatur;   præfecti   constituebantur;
the number   was secured;   commanders   were appointed;

summa   imperii transditur Commius Atrebati,
the supreme   command   is conferred on   Commius   the Atrebatian,

Viridomaro   et   Eporedorigi   Æduis-
Viridomarus   and   Eporedorix   the Æduans,   [and

Vercassivellauno   Arverno,   consobrino   Vercinge-
Vercassivellauns   the Arvernan,   cousin-german   to Vercinge-

torigis.   Iis   delecti   ex   civitatibus
torix.   To them   (those)   selected   from   the states

attribuntur, quorum consilio bellum administraretur.
are assigned,   by whose   counsel   the war   should be conducted.

Omnes proficiscuntur ad Alesiam alacres et pleni
All   set out   to   Alesia   eager   and   full

fiduciæ.   Nec   erat   quisquam omnium, qui,
of confidence.   Nor   was there   any one   of all,   who,

arbitraretur   adspectum   mŏdŏ   tantæ
supposed   that   the sight   even   of so great

multitudinis posse   sustineri,   præsertim   ancipiti
a multitude   could   be endured,   especially   in a two-fold

prœlio; quum   pugnaretur[52]   eruptione   ex
battle;   when   it would be [they] fought   by [in] a sally   from

oppido,   et   foris   tantæ   copiæ   equitatûs   que
the town,   and   outside   so great   forces   of cavalry   and

peditatûs   cerneretur.
infantry   should be descerned.

77. At   ĭi   qui   obsidebantur   Alesiæ,   die
But   those   who   were besieged   in Alesia,   the day

præterita,   quâ   expectaverant auxilia suorum,
having passed,   on which they had expected   the aid   of their (allies),

omni   frumento   consumpto,   inscii   quid
all   the corn   having been consumed,   ignorant   what

geretur   in   Æduis,   concilio   coacto,
was passing   among   the Ædui,   a council   having been assembled

consultabant   de   exitu   suarum fortunarum.
they were deliberating   about   the issue   of their   fortunes.

Ac   variis sententiis   dictis,   quarum pars
And   various   opinions   having been expressed,   of which   a part

censebant   deditionem, pars eruptionem   dum
were recommending   a surrender,   a part   a sally   while

vires (pl.) suppeterent.   Oratio   Critognati
(their) strength   was sufficing.   The speech   of Critognatus

videtur   non prætereunda,   propter   ejus
it seems   ought not to be passed over,   on account of   its

singularem   ac   nefariam   crudelitatem.   Hic,   natus
singular   and   infamous   cruelty.   He,   born

summo   lŏco   in   Arvernis,   et   habitus
of the highest family   among   the Arverni, and   possessed

magnæ   auctoritatis,   inquit: "dicturus sum   nihil
of great   influence,   said: " I am about to say nothing

de   sententiâ   ĕorum,   qui   appellant
concerning   the opinion   of those,   who   call

turpissimam   servitutem   nomĭne   deditionis;
the basest   slavery   by the name   of surrender:

censeo   hos   neque   habendos   lŏco
I am of the opinion (that) these neither ought to be held in the place

civium,   neque   adhibendos   ad
[role]   of citizens,   nor   ought they to be admitted   to

concilium.   Res   est   mihi   cum   ĭis,   qui
the counsel.   The business is   for me with those,   who

probant eruptionem; in consilio quorum   consensu
sanction   a sally,   in   the advice of whom with the consent

vestrum omnium   memoria   pristinæ   virtutis
of you   all   the memory   of the old-time   valor

videtur residere.   Ista   est   mollities   animi   non
seems   to abide.   This   is   a weakness of mind   not

virtus,   non   posse   ferre   inopiam   paulisper.
courage,   not to be able to endure privation for a little time.

Qui   ultro   offerant   se   morti   faciliùs
(Those) who willingly   offer themselves to death more easily

reperiuntur, quàm   qui patienter ferant dolorem.
are found,   than (those) who patiently endure distress.

Atque ego   probarem   hanc   sententiam   tantum
And   I   would approve this   opinion,   so much

apud me dignitas potest),   si   viderem
with   me   honor   is able [avails]), if I could see (that)

nullam jacturam   fieri   præterquam nostræ
no   loss   would be made   except   of our

vitæ (sing.). Sed   in   capiendo   consilio,
lives.   But   in   taking [forming]   plans,

respiciamus omnem   Galliam,   quam   concitavimus
let us regard   all   Gaul,   which   we have aroused

ad nostrum auxilium.   Octoginta millĭbus hominum
to   our   assistance.   Eighty   thousand   men

interfectis,   uno   lŏco,   quid   animi existimatis
having been slain, in one   place,   what   (of) spirit   do you think

fore   nostris propinquis que consanguineis, si
(this) would be   to our   relatives   and   kinsmen,   if

cogentur   decertare   prœlio   pænè   in
they may be forced   to engage   in battle   almost   over   (our)

cadaveribus   ipsis?   Nolite spoliare hos   vestro
dead bodies   themselves?   Do not   deprive   those   of your

auxilio, qui   causâ   vestræ   salutis   neglexerint
aid,   who   for the sake   of your   safety   have disregarded

suum   periculum,   nec   vestrâ   stultitiâ   ac
their own   peril,   nor   by your   folly   and

temeritate,   aut   imbecillitate   animi   prosternere
recklessness,   or   imbecility   of mind   prostrate

omnem Galliam,   ac addicere   perpetuæ servituti.
all   Gaul,   and   consign (it) to perpetual   slavery.

An   quòd   non venĕrint   ad   diem
Why   because   they may not have come   at [on]   the day

dubitatis   de ĕorum   fide   que constantia?   Quid
do you doubt   of   their   fidelity   and   constancy?   What

ergo?   Putatis   Romanos   exerceri quotidie
then?   Do you suppose (that) the Romans   are training   daily

in   illis   ulterioribus munitionibus   ne   causâ
in   those   outer   fortifications   only   for the purpose

animi?[53]   Si   potestis   non   confirmari   nun-
of the mind?   If   you can   not   be strengthened   by the

tiis   illorum,   omni aditu   præsepto,
messages   of those,   all   access   having been prevented

utimini   iis   testibus   ĕorum adventum
use   these (as)   witnesses   (that)   their   arrival

appropinquare   exterriti   timŏre   cujus   re
draws near   alarmed   by the fear   of this   thing

versantur   diem que noctem in   opĕre.   Quid
they are busied   day   and   night   in   the works.   What

ergo   est   mĕi   consilii?   Facere   quod   nostri
therefore   is   my   advice?   To do   what   our

majores fecerunt nequaquam pari beilo Cimbrorum
forefathers did in the by no means equal war of the Cimbri

que Teutonum, qui compulsi in oppida, ac
and Teutones, who driven into towns, and

subacti simili inopiâ, toleraverunt vitam corporibus
forced by a like want, supported life by the bodies

eorum, qui ætate videbantur inutiles ad bellum,
of those, who by age seemed useless for war,

neque transdiderunt se hostibus. Si
nor did they surrender themselves to the enemy. If

haberemus non exemplum cujus rěi, tamen
we had nct the example of this thing, yet

judicarem pulcherrimum causâ libertatis
I should judge it most glorious for the sake of liberty

institui, et prodi posteris. Nam
to be established, and be handed down to posterity. For

quid fuit simile illi bello?[54] Galliâ
what was it like that war? Gaul (having been)

depopulatâ, que magnâ calamitate illatâ,
depopulated, and a great disaster (having been) inflicted,

Cimbri aliquando excesserunt nostris finibus, atque
the Cimbri at length departed from our territories, and

petierunt alias terras; reliquerunt nobis jura,
sought other lands; they left us the rights.

leges, agros libertatem. Verò Romani
the laws, the lands (and) liberty. But the Romans

quid aliud petunt, aut quid volunt, nisi
what else do they seek, or what do they wish, except

adducti invidiâ, considěre in agris que
induced by greed, to settle in the fields and

civitatibus horum, quos cognoverunt famâ
states of these (those) whom they have learned by report

nobiles que potentes bello, atque his
(are) noble and powerful in war, and on these

injungěre æternam servitutem? Neque enim
impose perpetual slavery? Nor even

unquam gesserunt bella aliâ conditione. Quòd
have they ever waged war on any other terms. For

si   ignoratis   ĕa   quæ   geruntur   in
if   you know not   those things   which   are carried on   in

longinquis nationibus,   respicite   finitimam Galliam,
distant   nations,   look ye [you] at neighboring   Gaul,

quæ   redacta   in provinciam,   jure   et   legibus
which reduced   to   a province,   (its) rights and   laws

          commutatis,   subjecta   securi-
(having been)   subverted   (having been) subjected   to the (lic-

bus   premitur   perpetuâ   servitute!"
tors') axes,   is oppressed   by perpetual   slavery!"

78. Sententiis   dictis,   constituunt,   ut
    The opinions   having been delivered,   they resolve,   that

        qui valetudine, aut ætate sunt inutiles bello
(those) who by sickness,   or   age are   useless for war

excedant   oppido,   atque   omnia   experiantur,
should leave   the town,   and   all things   should be tried,

priùs   quàm   descendant   ad   sententiam
before   (that)   they descend   to   the recommendation

Critognati; tamen utendum illo consilio, is   res
of Critognatus;   however   to use   his advice,   if the case

cogat, atque auxilia morentur,   potiùs quàm
compels,   and   aid   be delayed,   rather than   (that)

conditionem deditionis aut pacis   subeundam.
a condition   of surrender   or   of peace   should be endured

Mandubii, qui recepĕrant ĕos oppido coguntur
The Mandubii,   who had received them in the town were forced

exire   cum   liberis   atque   uxoribus.   Hi
to depart with   the children   and   wives.   These

quum   accessissent ad   munitiones Romanorum,
when   they had approached to the fortifications of the Romans,

flentes orabant omnibus precibus, ut   recep-
weeping   were praying   with all   entreaties,   that having been

tos   in   servitutem,   juvarent   cibo.
received into   slavery,   they would relieve (them) with food.

Hos Cæsar, custodiis   dispositis   in   vallo,
These   Cæsar,   sentinels   having been posted   on the rampart,

prohibebat   recipi.
was refusing   to be received.

79.   Interea   Comius,   et   reliqui   duces,
In the mean time   Commius,   and   the other   leaders,

quibus   summa   imperii   permissa ĕrant, perveniunt
to whom   the supreme   command   had been assigned,   arrive

ad Alesiam cum omnibus   copiis,   et   exteriore
at   Alesia   with   all   the forces,   and   an outer

colle   occupato,   considunt   non longiùs
hill   having been occupied,   they encamp   not   farther (than)

mille   passibus   à   nostris munitionibus.   Postĕro
a thousand   paces   from   our   fortifications.   The next

die,   equitatu   eḍucto   ex   castris,
day,   the cavalry   having been led forth   from   (their)   camp,

complent omnem ĕam planitiem, quam demonstravimus
they fill   all   this   plain,   which   we have shown

patere   tria   millia passŭum in longitudinem;
to extend [extends]   three   thousand   paces   in   length;

que constituunt pedestres copias paulùm   ab   ĕo
and   they station   the foot   soldiers   a little   from   this

lŏco,   abditas   in superioribus lŏcis (pl.).   Erat
place,   removed   on   higher   ground.   There was

despectus   ex   oppido   Alesiâ   in   campum.
a view   from   the town   (of) Alesia   over   the plain.

His   auxiliis   visis,   concurritur,
These   auxiliaries   having been seen,   there is running together

gratulatio   fit (sing.)   inter   eos, atque animi
congratulations   are made   among   them,   and   the souls

omnium excitantur ad lætitiam.   Itaque,   copiis
of all   are excited   to   joy.   Therefore,   (their) forces

productis   ante   oppidum,   considunt   et
having been drawn out   before   the town,   they take stand   and

integunt proximam fossam cratibus, atque explent
cover   the nearest   ditch   with hurdles,   and   fill (it)

aggĕre,   que comparant   se   ad eruptionem,
with dirt,   and   prepare   themselves   for   a sally,

atque omnes   casus.
and   all   chances.

80. Cæsar,   omni   exercitu   disposito   ad
Cæsar,   all   the army   having been stationed   at

utramque   partem   munitionum,   ut si usus
both   sides   of the fortifications,   (so) that if the need

veniat, quisque noverit   et teneat suum locum,
came,   each   might know and keep his own place,

jubet   equitatum   educi   ex   castris,   et
orders   the cavalry   to be led from   the camp,   and

committi prœlium.   Erat despectus ex omnibus
to join   battle.   There was a view from   all

castris,   quæ   undique   tenebant   summum
the camp.   which   everywhere   was holding   the highest

jugum,   atque   animi omnium   militum   intenti
ridge,   and   the minds of all   the soldiers   absorbed

exspectabant   eventum   pugnæ.   Galli
were anticipating   the issue   of the battle.   The Gauls

interjecerant inter   equites   raros   sagittarios,
had placed   among   the horsemen scattered   archers,

que expeditos levis armaturæ,[55] qui   succurrent
and ready soldiers lightly   armed,   who   might succor

auxilio   suis   cedentibus   et   sustinērent
by (their) aid their (men)   retreating   and   hold

impetum nostrorum equitum. Complures
the charge   of our   cavalry.   Many   (of our men)

vulnerati de improviso ab   his   excedebant
wounded   unexpectedly   by   these   were withdrawing

prœlio.   Quum   Galli   confidērent   suos
from the battle.   When   the Gauls   were trusting   (that) their

esse superiores   pugnâ,   et   vidērent
(men)   were   superior   in the fight,   and   were seeing

nostros   premi multitudine; ex om-
our   (men)   (to be) hard pressed by the throng, from [on]

nibus   partibus,   et   ii qui centinebantur
all   parts [sides],   both   those who   were retained

munitionibus,   et   ii   qui   convenerant   ad
within the fortifications,   and   those who   had come   for

auxilium,   confirmabant animos suorum clamore
aid,   were encouraging the souls of their men by a shout

et   ululatu.   Quòd   res   gerebatur   in   conspectu
and   yell.   As   the action was carried on in   the sight

omnium,   neque   factum   rectè   ac[56]
of all,   neither   (a thing)   done   rightly [nobly]   and [nor]

turpiter   potĕrat   celari,   et   cupidĭtas   laudis,
shamefully   could   be concealed,   both   the desire   of praise.

et   timor   ignominiæ   excitabat (sing.)   utrosque   ad
and   the fear   of disgrace   were inciting   both sides   to

virtutem.   Quum   pugnaretur   à   meridie
valor.   When   it was [they] fought   from   noon

propè   ad   occasum   solis   dubiâ   victoriâ,
nearly   to   the setting   of the sun   with a doubtful   victory,

Germani   in   unâ   parte   confertis   turmis   fecerunt
the Germans   on   one   side   in compact   troops   made

impetum   in   hostes,   que   propulerunt   eos.
an attack   on   the enemy,   and   routed   them.

Quibus   conjectis   in   fugam,
Whom   [These]   (having been)   thrown   into   flight,

sagittarii   circumventi sunt   que   interfecti.   Item
the archers   were surrounded   and   slain.   Also

ex   reliquis   partibus   nostri   insecuti
in   other   quarters   our men   followed   (those)

cedentes   usque   ad   castra,   dederunt
retreating   even   to   the camp,   (and)   gave

non   facultatem   colligendi   sui.   At
no   opportunity   of [for] collecting   their (men).   But

ĭi,   qui   processĕrant   ab   Alesià,   victoriâ
those,   who   had come   from   Alesia,   the victory

propè desperatâ,   receperunt   se
nearly (having been) despaired of   betook   themselves

mœsti,   in   oppidum.
sorrowful,   into   the town.

81. Uno   die   intermisso,   atque   hôc   spatio
One   day   having intervened,   and   in this   period

magno   numĕro   cratium,   scalarum,   harpagonum
a great   number   of hurdles,   ladders,   pole-hooks

effecto,   Galli,   mediâ   nocte,   silentio,
having been made,   the Gauls,   at mid   night,   (and) in silence,

egressi   ex   castris   accedunt   ad
having marched   from   (their)   camp   approach   to

campestres　　　　munitiones.　　Subĭto　　clamore
the field　[outside]　fortifications.　A sudden　shout

sublato,　　　　quâ　　significatione,　　　　qui
having been raised,　by which　signal,　　(those)　who

obsidebantur　in　oppido,　possent　cognoscere　de
were besieged　in　the town,　might　know　of

suo　adventu,　　　　projicĕre　crates　deturbare
their　arrival,　(they) (to)　throw out　the hurdles,　force

nostros　de　vallo　fundis,　sugittis　lapidibus,
our men　from　the rampart　by slings,　arrows (and)　stones,

que　administrare　relĭqua　quæ pertinent ad
and　(to)　perform　the other things　which　belong　to

oppugnationem.　　Eodem　　tempŏre,　_ clamore
an assault.　At the same　time,　the shout

exaudito,　Vercingetorix　dat　signum　suis
having been heard,　Vercingetorix　gives　the signal　to his men

tubâ,　atque　educit　　　　ex　oppĭdo.
by the trumpet,　and　leads　(them forth)　from　the town

Nostri,　ut　superioribus　diebus,　suas　lŏcus
Our men,　as　on the former　days,　his　place (having

attributus　erat cuique,　accedunt　ad　munitiones;
been)　assigned　to each one,　proceed　to　the fortifications;

perterrent　Gallos　fundis　libralibus[57]　que
they alarm　the Gauls　by slings　(of) pound-weight　and

sudibus,　quas　disposuĕrant　in　opĕre,　ac
stakes,　which　they had placed　in　the works,　and

glandibus.　Prospectu　　　adempto　tenebris,
by lead bullets　The view　(having been) prevented　by darkness,

multa　vulnĕra　accipiuntur　utrimque,　complura
many　wounds　are received　on both sides,　numerous

tela　conjiciuntur　tormentis.　At　M. Antonius,[58]
weapons　are thrown　by the engines.　But　M.　Antonius,

et　C. Trebonius,　legati,　quibus　ĕa　partes
and　C.　Trebonius,　the lieutenants,　to whom　these　parts

obvenĕrant　ad　defendendum,　ex　quâ
had fallen　for　defending,　on　what　[whatever]

parte　intellexerunt　　　nostros　premi,
side　they understood　(that)　our men　were hard pressed

submittebant   Iis   auxilio   deductos   ex
they sent   to them   for [as] aid   (those)   drawn [led] out   from

ulterioribus   castellis.
the more remote   fortresses.

82. Dum   Galli   aberant   longius   ab
While   the Gauls   were distant   rather far   from

munitione,   proficiebant,   plus   multitudine
the fortifications,   they were accomplishing,   more   by the multitude

telorum;   posteaquàm   successerunt   propriùs,
[mass]   of weapons;   after   they approached   nearer,

aut   ipsi   inopinantes   induebant   se   stimulis,
either   they   unawares   were impaling   themselves   on the spurs,

aut   delapsi   in   scrobes   transfodiebantur,   aut
or   having fallen   into   the pits   were transfixed,   or

interibant   transjecti   murialibus   pilis   ex
were perishing   pierced   by the wall   javelins (thrown)   from

vallo   et   turribus.   Multis   vulneribus   accep-
the rampart   and   towers.   Many   wounds   having

tis   undique, nullâ   munitione   perruptâ,
been received   on all sides,   no   fortification   having been forced

quum   lux   appeteret,   veriti   ne
when   (day) light   was approaching,   having feared   lest

circumvenirentur   ab   aperto   latĕre,   eruptione
they might be surrounded   on   the exposed   flank,   by a sally

ex   superioribus   castris,   receperunt se   ad   suos.
from   the higher   camp,   they retreated   to   their (people).

At   interiores,   dum   proferunt   ea
But   those within   (the town),   while   they bring out   these things

quæ   præparata   ĕrant   Vercingetorige   ad
which   had been   prepared   by Vercingetorix   for

eruptionem, explent priores   fossas;   morati
the sally,   fill up   the first   ditches;   having been delayed

diutius   in   administrandis   iis   rebus,   cogno-
rather long   in   performing   these   things,   they

verunt   suos   discessisse   priùs   quàm
learned   (that)   their men   had withdrawn   before   (that)

appropinquarent   munitionibus.   Ita,   re
they had got near   (to)   the fortifications.   Thus,   the thing

infectâ,   reverterunt   in
[design] having been unaccomplished, they returned   into

oppĭdum.
the town.

83. Galli   bis   repulsi   cum   magno
   The Gauls   twice   having been repulsed with   great

detremento, consulunt quid   agant.   Adhibent
   loss,   consult   what   they should do. They admit

peritos   lŏcorum (pl.). Cognoscunt   ab
(those) acquainted with the locality. They learn   from

his   situs   superiorum   castrorum   que
these the position of the higher   camp   and

munitiones.   Erat   collis   à   septentrionibus,
the fortifications. There was a hill on   the north,

quem[59] quia non potŭerant circumplecti   opĕre,
which because they could not   enclose   in the works,

propter   magnitudinem   circuitûs,   nostri pænè
on account of   the greatness   of the circuit, our men almost

necessariò fecerunt   castra   iniquo   lŏco,
necessarily pitched   (their) camp in an unfavorable place,

et   lenĭter   declivi.   C. Antistius Reginus, et
and gently descending. C. Antistius Reginus.   and

C. Caninius Rubilus,   legati,   obtinebant hæc
C. Caninius Rubilus, the lieutenants, were holding this

cum duabus legionibus. Regionibus   cognitis
with   two   legions.   The country having been explored

per exploratores,   duces   hostium   deligunt
by   scouts,   the leaders of the enemy   select

sexaginta millia   ex   omni   numĕro   ĕarum
  sixty   thousand from all the number of those

civitatum,   quæ   habeant   maximam   opinionem
  states.   which have   the greatest reputation

virtutis; occultè constituunt   inter se,   quĭd,
of [for] bravery; secretly they arrange among themselves, what,

que   quo   pacto   placĕat   agi.
and in what manner it pleases (them) to be done [to take action].

Definiunt   tempus   adeundi   quum   videatur
They determine   the time   of advancing   when   it may seem

esse   meridies.   Præficiunt   Iis   copiis
to be   noon.   They place over   these   forces

Vercassivellaunus   Arvernum,   unum   ex
Vercassivellaunus   the Arvernian,   one   from   [of]

quatuor   ducibus,   propinquum   Vercingetorigis.   Ille
the four   leaders,   a kinsman   of Vercingetorix.   He

egressus   ex   castris   primâ   vigiliâ   itinĕre
having departed   from   the camp   on the first   watch   the march

confecto   propè   sub   lucem,   occultavit
having been completed   nearly   about   (day) light.   concealed

se   post   montem,   que   jussit   milites
himself   behind   the mountain,   and   ordered   the soldiers

reficĕre   sese   ex   nocturnol abore.   Quum
to refresh   themselves   from [after]   (their) nocturnal labor.   When

jam   meridies   videretur   appropinquare,   contendit
now   noon   was seeming   to draw near,   he marched

ad   ĕa   castra,   quæ   demonstravimus   suprà,   que
to   this   camp,   which   we have mentioned   above,   and

ĕodem   tempŏre   equitatus   cœperunt   accedere
at the same   time   the cavalry   commenced   to approach

ad   campestres   munitiones,   et   reliquæ
to   the field   [outer]   fortifications,   and   the remaining

copiæ   ostendĕre   sese   pro   castris.
forces   to show   themselves   before   the camp.

84. Vercingetorix   conspicatus   suos,   ex
Vercingetorix   having beheld   his   (allies),   from

arce   Alesiæ,   egreditur   ex   oppĭdo,   profert
the citadel   of Alesia,   marches   from   the town,   he brings forth

è   castris   longurios,   muscŭlos,   falces,   que
from   the camp   long poles,   moveable sheds,   wall hooks,   and

reliqua,   quæ   paraverat   causâ   eruptionis.
other things,   which   he had prepared   for the purpose   of the sally.

Pugnatur[60]   uno   tempŏre,   omnibus   lŏcis,   atque
It was fought   at one   time,   in all   places,   and

omnia   tentantur.   Quæ   pars   visa   esse   minimè
all things   are attempted.   What   part   is seen   to be   least

firma,   huc   concurritur.   Manus   Romanorum
strong,   hither (they)   run together.   The force   of the Romans

distinctur   tantis   munitionibus   ne   facilè
is extended   in so great   fortifications   that not   easily

occurrit   pluribus   lŏcis.   Clamor,   qui   exstitit
it opposed   in many   places.   The din,   that   arose

post   tergum   pugnantibus,   valuit multùm ad
in   the rear   to [of] the combatants,   served   much   for

terrendo   nostros,   quòd   vident   suum
alarming   our men,   because   they see   (that)   their

periculum consistere in virtute   alienâ. Enim
peril   depends   on   the bravery (of)   others.   For

plerumque   omnia   quæ   absunt   perturbant
generally   all things   which   are absent   alarm

mentes   hominum   vehementiùs.
the minds   of men   more violently.

85. Cæsar   nactus   idoneum lŏcum, cognoscit
Cæsar,   having chosen   a suitable   place,   learns

quid   geratur in quâque parte, submittit
what   is done   in   every   part,   he sends   (aid)

          laborantibus.   Occurrit ad animum utrisque,
(to those)   hard pressed.   It occurs   to   the mind   to each,

          illud   esse   unum tempus,   quo conveniat
(that)   that   was   the one   time,   in which   it was fitting

          maximè   contendi.[61]   Galli.   nisi
to the greatest degree   to be fought [to fight].   The Gauls,   unless

perfregĕrint   munitiones,   desperant de omni
they break through   the fortifications,   despair   of   all

salute.   Romani,   si   obtinuĕrint   rem
safety.   The Romans,   if   they should gain   the affair [action]

expectant finem omnium   laborum. Maxìmè
expect   an end   of all   (their)   labor.   Especially

          laboratur   ad superiores munitiones, quò
it was [they] struggled   at   the higher   fortifications,   where

demonstravimus   Vercassivellaunum   missum.
we have shown   (that)   Vercassivellaunus   (had been) sent.

Exiguum fastigium   lŏci   ad   declivitatem,
The small   elevation   of the place   with   the slope,

habet magnum momentum. Alii conjiciunt tela,
has   great   importance.   Some   throw   weapons

alii testudine factâ, subeunt, integri
others a testudo having been made advance. fresh men

succedunt defatigatis invicem. Agger conjectus
relieved the wearied by turns. The materials thrown

ab universis in munitionem, et dat (sing.)
by all against the fortifications, both give

adscensum Gallis, et contegit (sing.) quæ
an ascent to the Gauls, and cover what

Romani occultavĕrant in terram. Nec jam
the Romans had concealed in the ground. Neither now

arma, nec vires suppetunt nostris.
arms, nor strength suffice for our men.

86. His rebus cognitis, Cæsar mittit
These things having been known. Cæsar sends

Labienum cum sex cohortibus laborantibus
Labienus with six cohorts (to those) struggling

subsidio. Imperat, si possit non
for [as] aid. He commands (him), if he could not

sustinere, cohortibus deductis, pugnaret
withstand, the cohorts having been drawn [led] out. he should fight

eruptione; non faciat id, nisi necessariò.
in a sally; not [nor] do this, unless necessarily.

Ipse adit reliquos; cohortatur ne
He goes to the rest; he exhorts (them) that they should not

succumbant labori; docet fructum omnium
succumb to the work; he shows (that) the fruit of all

superiorum dimicationum consistere in ĕo
(their) former battles depended on this

die atque horâ. Interiores campestribus
day and hour. Those within [The besieged] the level

lŏcis desperatis, propter magnitudinem
places having been despaired of, on account of the size

munitionum, tentant lŏca prærupta ex
of the fortifications, attempt the places steep in

adscensu; hŭc conferunt ĕa quæ para-
ascent; here they bring those things which they had

vĕrant, deturbant propugnantes ex turribus
prepared. they drive back the defenders from the towers

multitudine telorum; explent fossas aggĕre
by the multitude of weapons; they fill up the trenches with earth

et cratibus expediunt aditus; rescindunt
and fascines they prepare an approach; they tear down

vallum ac lorīcam falcibus.
the rampart and parapet with hooks.

87. Cæsar primò mittit Brutum, adolescentem,
    Cæsar at first sends Brutus, a young man,

cum sex cohortibus, pòst Fabium legatum cum
with six cohorts, afterwards Fabius (his) lieutenant with

septem alïis. Postremò ipse, quum pugnaretur[62]
seven others. At length he himself, when it is fought

vehementiùs, adducit intergos subsidio.
more desperately, leads up fresh (men) for aid.

Prœlio restituto, ac hostibus repul-
The battle having been renewed, and the enemy having been

sis, contendit ĕò quò miserat Labienum;
repulsed, he marches thither where he had sent Labienus;

educit quatuor cohortes ex proxĭmo castello;
he draws out four cohorts from the nearest fortress;

jubet partem equitum sequi se, partem
he orders a part of the cavalry to follow himself, a part

circumire exteriores munitiones, et adoriri
to go around the other fortifications, and to attack

hostes ab tergo. Labienus, postquàm
the enemy from [in] the rear. Labienus, after (that)

neque aggeres neque fossæ poterant sustinere
neither the mounds nor the trenches could resist

vim hostium, una de quadraginta cohortibus
the force of the enemy, thirty-nine cohorts

coactis, quas deductas ex proxĭmis
having been assembled, which drawn from the nearest

præsidiis, sors obtulit; fecit certiorem Cæsarem,
posts, chance offered; he informs Cæsar,

per nuncios quid existimet faciendum. Cæsar
by messengers what he thought must be done. Cæsar

accelerat ut intersit prœlio.
hastens that he may be present at the battle.

88. Ejus   adventu   cognito   ex   colore*
     His   arrival   having been known   from   the color

vestitûs,   (quo   insigni   consueverat   uti
of (his) robe, (which (as) an insignia he was accustomed to use

in prœliis),   que   turmis   equitum   et   cohortibus
in   battle),   both the troops of cavalry and   cohorts

        visis,   quas   jusserat   sequi   se,   ut de
having been seen, which he had ordered to follow him, as from

superioribus lŏcis hæc declivia et devexa
the higher   places these sloping and inclined (places)

cernebantur, hostes committunt prœlium. Clamore
were beheld, the enemy   join   battle.   A shout

    sublato   utrimque,   clamor   rursus excipit
having been raised on both sides, a shout   is again received

         ex   vallo   atque omnibus munitionibus.
[heard] from   the rampart and   all   the fortifications.

Nostri   pilis   omissis,   gerunt
:Our   (men) the javelins having been laid aside, carry on

rem   gladiis (pl.).   Equitatus repentè cernitur
the action with the sword.   The cavalry suddenly is seen

post tergum;   aliæ cohortes appropinquant
in   the rear (of the Gauls); other cohorts   advance;

hostes   vertunt   terga;   equites   occurrunt
the enemy   turn   (their) backs; the cavalry   meet

        fugientibus; magna cædes   fit.   Sedulius
(those)   fleeing;   a great slaughter is made. Sedulius

dux   et   princeps   Lemovicum   occiditur;
general and   chief   of the Lemovices   is slain;

Vercassivellaunus   Arvernus   comprehenditur vivus
Vercassivellaunus   the Arvernian   is taken   alive

in fugâ; septuaginta quatuor militaria   signa
in   flight;   seventy   four   military   standards

referuntur   ad Cæsarem; pauci   ex   tanto
are brought   to   Cæsar;   few   from [of]   so great

numero recipiunt se incolumes in castra. Conspicati
a number   return   safe   into the camp. Having beheld

ex oppĭdo   cædem   et   fugam   suorum,
from the town the slaughter and   flight   of their (people),
       * white.

ȝalute   desperatâ,   reducunt   copias
safety   having been despaired of,   they lead back (their)   forces

à   munitionibus.   Hâc   re   auditâ
from   the fortifications.   This   action   having becn heard

fuga   protĭnus   fit,   ex   castris   Gallorum;
a flight   immediately   is made,   from   the camp   of the Gauls;

        quod   nisi   milites fuissent defessi
as to [regarding] which [this]   unless   the soldiers had been   fatigued

crebris   subsidiis   ac   labore   totius
by the frequent   reinforcements   and   by the labor   of the whole

diei, omnes   copiæ   hostium   potuissent deleri.
day,   all   the forces   of the enemy   would have been destroyed.

De mediâ nocte equitatus   missus   consequi*ur
About mid   night   the cavalry   having been sent   overtakes

novissimum   agmen.   Magnus   numĕrus   capitur,
the rear   line.   A great   number   are taken,

atque interficitur; reliqui discedunt   ex   fugâ
and   killed;   the rest   escape   from   the flight [rovt]

in   civitates.
into   their states.

89. Postero   die,   concilio   convocato,
        On the next   day,   a council   having been called,

Vercingetorix demonstrat   se   suscepisse
Vercingetorix   shows   (that)   he   had undertaken

bellum non   causâ   suarum necessitatum(pl.), sed
the war   not   for the sake   of his own   necessity,   but

communis   libertatis,   et   quoniam   sit
of (their) common   liberty,   and   because   it must

cedendum   fortunæ,   offere   se   illis
be yielded   to fortune,   (that he) offered   himself   to them

ad   utramque   rem,   seu   velint
for   either   thing   [alternative],   whether   they wished

satisfacĕre Romanis   suâ   morte, seu   tradere
to satisfy   the Romans   by his   death,   or   to surrender

        vivum.   Legati   mittuntur   ad   Cæsarem
(him)   alive.   Ambassadors   are sent   to   Cæsar

de   his   rebus.   Jubet   arma
concerning   these   things.   He orders   (their)   arms

tradi,   principes   roduci.   Ipse
to be surrendered, (and their)   chiefs   to be led forth.   He

consedit   in   munitione   pro   castris: eŏ
seated himself   at   the fortification   before   the camp;   there

principes   producuntur.   Vercingetorix   deditur;
the chiefs   are led forth.   Vercingetorix   is surrendered

arma   projiciuntur.   Æduis   atque   Arvernis
the arms   are thrown down.   The Ædui   and   _ Arverni

reservatis,   si   per   ĕos   posset   recuperare
having been reserved,   if   through   them   he could   gain over

civitates;   ex   reliquis   captivis   distribuit
(their)   states;   from   the remaining   captives   he distributed

singula   capita   toto   exercitu   nomĭne
one   each   in the whole   army   under the name

prædæ.
of booty.

90. His   rebus   confectis,   proficiscitur
     These   things   having been accomplished,   he marches

in   Æduos;   recipit   civitatem   Eò
into   the Ædui;   he receives   the state.   Thither

legati   ab   Arvernis   missi   pollicentur
ambassadors   from   the Arverni   having been sent   they promise

se   facturos,   quæ   imperaret.   Imperat
(that)   they   would do,   what   he might command.   He orders

magnum   numerum   obsĭdum.   Mittit   legiones   in
a great   number   of hostages.   He sends   the legions   into

hiberna.   Reddit   circiter   viginti   millia
winter-quarters.   He restores   about   twenty   thousand

captivorum   Æduis   que   Arvernis.   Jubet
(of)   prisoners   to the Ædui   and   Arverni.   He orders

T. Labienum   proficisci   in   Sequanos   cum
T.   Labienus   to march   into   the Sequani   with

duabus   legionibus   et   equitatu.   Huic   attribuit
two   legions   and   the cavalry.   To him   he assigns

M. Sempronium Rutilum.   Collocat   C. Fabium
M.   Sempronius   Rutilus;   He places   C.   Fabius

et   L. Minucium Basilum   in   Remis   cum
and   L.   Minucius   Basilus   among   the Remi   with

duabus   legionibus,   ne   accipiant   quam
two   legions,   lest   they might receive   any

calamitatem   à   finitimis   Bellovacis.   Mittit
injury   from   the neighboring   Bellovaci.   He sends

C. Antistium   Reginum   in   Ambivaretos,
C.   Antistius   Reginus   among   the Ambivareti,

T. Sextium   in   Bituriges,   C. Caninum Rebilum
T.   Sextius   among   the Bituriges,   C.   Caninus   Rebilus

in   Rutenos,   cum   legionibus   singulis;   collocat
among   the Ruteni,   with   a legion   each,   he stations

Q. Tullium Ciceronem,   et   P. Sulpicium Cabiloni
Q.   Tullius   Cicero,   and   P.   Sulpicius   at Cabilo

et   Matiscone   ad   Ararim   in   Æduis
and   Matisco   on [near]   the (river) Saone   among   the Ædui

causâ   frumentariæ rei;   ipse   constituit
for the purpose   of the corn supply,   he himself   determines

hiemare   Bibracte.   His   rebus   cognitis
to winter   at Bibracte.   These   things   having been learned

litteris   Cæsaris   Romæ,   supplicatio   viginti
by letter   of Cæsar   at Rome,   a thanksgiving   of twenty

dierum   indicitur.
days   is decreed.

NOTES

FIRST BOOK

PAGE 1—**1** Latin order: - *Gallia est omnis divisa in partes tres; quarum unam incolunt Belgae,* Lit., Gaul is all divided into parts three; of which one inhabit Belgæ.

PAGE 2—**2** *eorum* i. e. the Germans. *eorum* in the next sentence refers to the Celts or Gauls, *tertiam,* above. **3** Meaning, on the same side of the river, i. e. west side. **4** The country slopes to the north.

PAGE 3—**5** Dative after verb of pursuading, used as direct object. **6** on one side, the Rhine a river very wide and very deep—on the other side the Jura (St. Cloude) a very lofty mountain—on the third side by Lake Geneva and the river Rhone.

PAGE 4—**7** Other text: - *qua ex parte,* and for this reason. **8** they were considering that they had narrow territories in consideration of the multitude of men, the glory of war and their bravery. **9** to make as great sowings as possible. **10** they decided two years' time would be sufficient to them for accomplishing these things.

PAGE 5—**11** Orgetorix is chosen for executing these things. **12** Whose father had held sway among the Sequani many years.

PAGE 6—**13** he assures (them) that he himself is about to secure the kingdom for them with his resources and his army **14** they hope that they may be able to get possession of all Gaul. **15** and brought together to the same place all his clients and debt bondsmen of whom he was having a great number; through whom he rescued himself from pleading his cause.

PAGE 7—**16** nor is suspicion wanting as the Helvetians think, that he had committed suicide **17** they might be more prepared for undergoing all dangers.

PAGE 8—**18** Literally, and they vote in the Boii, admitted to themselves, as their *(sibi)* allies. In English a double verb construction would be used, not the participle they take the Boii into their own number *(ad se)* and vote them in as allies. **19** They were thinking that they *(sese)* either would pursuade the Allobroges because they were seeming to be not yet in good feeling toward the Roman people, or would compel by force to suffer them to go through their territories.

PAGE 9—**20** by journeys as great as he was able.

PAGE 10—**21** to ask that it may be allowed them to do this with his good will [permission] **22** Because Cæsar was holding in memory that Lucius Cassius the consul had been slain (supply *esse* with *occisum*) and his army had been routed (supply *esse*) by the Helvetians and sent under the yoke, he was considering that it must not be granted, nor was he thinking that men of hostile spirit, an opportunity of making a way through the province having been given, would refrain from injury and damage. **23** that he himself was about to take a day for deliberating,— —

PAGE 11—**24** nineteen thousand paces i. e. nineteen Roman miles about seventeen and one half English miles. The work actually represented five short spans the remaining distance being naturally protected somewhat by bluffs and ravines **25** he denies that according to the custom and example of the Roman people he is able to grant a way to any through the province; and if they attempt to employ force he shows that he would prevent them (supply *esse* with *prohibiturum*) **26** Lit. : - ships having been joined and rafts having been made i. e. when ships had been joined together and rafts made,— — **27** where the depth of the river was least.

PAGE 12—**28** because he had taken in marriage,— — **29** and induced by a desire (lit., greed) for the throne, he was zealous for a revolution and was wishing to have as many states as possible attached to him by his beneficence.

PAGE 13—**30** and where the route was the nearest into farther Gaul,— —

PAGE 14—**31** and were ravaging their lands. **32** their children led off into captivity,— —

PAGE 15—**33** now that their fields are devastated they are

not easily checking the violence of the enemy from the towns
34 and show that there is nothing left to them besides the
soil of the land.

P<small>AGE</small> 16—**35** When Cæsar had been informed by scouts
that the Helvetians had already led over this river three parts
of their forces but that the fourth part had been left,— —

P<small>AGE</small> 17—**36** he takes care that a bridge should be made
on the Saone   **37** when they were understanding that he had
done in one day, — —

P<small>AGE</small> 21—**37a** and from the Ædui and from their allies

P<small>AGE</small> 22—**38** Meantime Cæsar daily demands from the Ædui
the grain —   Flagitare is a historical infinitive used as a
finite tense   **39** The emphasized word or phrase stands between *ne* and *quidem* and *quidem* throws its force back upon
the emphasized term.   **40** The Ædui put him off from day to
day (and) say that it is being gathered, that it is being brougnt,
that it is at hand.—*ducere* and *dicere* are historical infinitives.

P<small>AGE</small> 23—**41** their chiefs have been called together — —
42 especially when in a great degree (lit., from a great part)
he induced by their prayers had undertaken the war.   **43** that
there are some whose authority avails very much among the
common people.

P<small>AGE</small> 25—**44** he had both increased his family estate i. e.
his clanship, and provided great means for — —

P<small>AGE</small> 26—**45** and for the sake of this power he had married
his mother among the Bituriges to a man there, most noble
and most powerful, he himself had a wife from the Helvetians, he had given his sister on his mother's side and his kinswomen in marriage into other states.   That he favors and
wishes well to the Helvetians on account of this alliance, that
he hates (*odisse*, perfect with present sense) Cæsar and the
Romans by his own right (lit., name) because his power had
been diminished by their arrival   **45a** He favors and wishes
well to the Helvetians on account of this alliance; also he
hated Cæsar and the Romans on his own account (lit., from
his own name) because his power (lit, the power of him) had
been diminished by their arrival (lit., by the arrival of them),
and Divitiacus, his brother, restored into the ancient place of
favor and honor: if anything may happen to the Romans, he

entertains the highest hope of obtaining the Kingdom through the Helvetians. **46** he entertains the highest hope of obtaining the throne through the Helvetians if anything happens to the Romans. **47** he not only despairs of the throne.

PAGE 27—**48** since the most certain facts were substantiating these suspicions — — **49** he was deeming that there was enough cause why (wherefore) either he himself should punish him (lit., attend to him) or should order the state to punish him.

PAGE 28—**50** that he himself knows that these things are true nor does anyone take more grief from this thing than himself

PAGE 29—**51** which means and strength he was using not only for diminishing his (Divitiacus') influence but almost for his destruction. **52** from which thing it would come to pass that — —

PAGE 30—**53** he warns him to avoid all suspicions — — **54** he says that he himself forgives the past (offences) for (the sake of) his brother Divitiacus.

PAGE 31—**55** It was reported that it was easy. **56** At early dawn when the mountain summit (lit., highest) is held by Titus Labienus — —

PAGE 33—**57** This movement (lit., thing) is reported to the enemy by fugitives from Lucius Æmilius, captain of the Gallic horse,— — **58** or because they were trusting that our men could be cut off from the grain supply.

PAGE 35—**59** It was a great disadvantage to the Gauls in the battle.....nor since the left hand was hampered to fight conveniently enough.....and to fight with unprotected person (i. e., the body unshielded, lit., naked).

PAGE 36—**60** having assailed our men upon the march on (the exposed flank began) to surround (them). **61** So the fighting continued in a doubtful battle long and fiercely. **62** no one could see a routed enemy.

PAGE 37—**63** When the fighting had continued a long time our men got possession of the baggage and the camp. **64** and if they (lit., if who) should assist them he would hold them in the same light (or, position - *locus*) as *(quo)* the Helvetians

PAGE 38—**65** Some texts have: *legatos de ditione ad eum miserunt* - sent ambassadors to him concerning a surrender.

PAGE 39—**66** they were thinking that their flight would be either concealed or overlooked altogether,— — **67** When Cæsar discovered (other readings: *resciit*) this (lit., which) he ordered those through whose territories they had gone — **68** if they were wishing to be exculpated toward himself i. e. in his eyes. **69** When they were brought back he held them in the class of enemies i. e. they were either sold into slavery or more probably put to death. **70** because he was unwilling that this place whence the Helvetians had departed should be unoccupied

PAGE 40—**71** and they afterwards received them into an equal estate of law and liberty as were they themselves.

Page 41—**72** ambassadors of almost all Gaul, chiefs of the states, assembled for congratulating Cæsar.

PAGE 43—**73** Divitiacus the Æduan spoke for these (saying that) there are two factions of all Gaul, that the Æduans hold the chieftaincy of one, of the other the Averni.

PAGE 44—**74** The Ædui and their clients time and again have contended— — **75** nor would refuse that they should be forever under their sway and empire (lit., sway and empire of them)

PAGE 45—**76** because Ariovistus king of the Germans had settled in their territories (lit., borders)— — **77** We would compare the worse with the better and would say in English: for neither is the German land to be mentioned with the Gallic— —

PAGE 46—**78** if anything is not done at his nod and will— — **79** his demands (lit., commands) cannot be endured longer. Unless there may be some aid in Cæsar or the Roman people, the same thing must be done by all the Gauls— — **80** there is no doubt (lit., he not to doubt).

PAGE 47—**81** This speech having been delivered by Divitiacus — —

PAGE 49—**82** That the Germans moreover were accustomed little by little to cross the Rhine and that a great multitude of them came into Gaul, he was seeing was a perilous thing to the Roman people, nor was he judging that wild and barbarous men, when they had occupied all Gaul as the Cimbri and Teutones had done, would restrain themselves before— — **83** he was thinking he must meet these things (lit., which things) as early as possible

PAGE 50—**84** had taken upon himself so many airs (so great insolence) that it seemed he must not be borne.   **85** if anything was needful to him from Cæsar, he would have come to him   **86** nor could he gather an army into one place without great provisions and trouble, moreover it seemed wonderful to himself — —

PAGE 51—**87** that he should, though invited, be averse to come into a conferance nor should think that he must not speak nor learn corcerning a common matter, these are the things which he was demanding from him, that — —   **88** that it should be granted to the Sequani that it should be allowed with his consent to return to them (the Ædui) those whom they were holding — --

PAGE 53—**89** if he was not dictating to the Roman people in what manner it should use its right, it was not proper that he himself should be hindered by the Roman people in his right   **90** he himself would not return the hostages to the Ædui, nor would he bring war with damage upon them nor upon their allies if they would abide by that (lit., remain in that) which had been agreed upon and would pay (lit., weigh out) the tribute yearly, if they would not do this the fraternal name of the Roman people would be far away from them.

PAGE 54—**91** were ravaging their territories, they could not purchase peace of Ariovistus when even hostages had been given   **92** judged that he must hasten, lest if the new hand —.

PAGE 55—**93** it could be less easily opposed   **94** when he had gone athree days' course — —   **95** that Ariovistus with all his troops was hastening to seize Vesontio (lit., for occupying Vesontio)   **96** which were of use for war   **97** for prolonging the war.

PAGE 56—**98** so that the foot (lit., roots) of this mountain touches the bank of the river on either hand (lit., each part, i. e. the entire intervening space)   **99** hither Cæsar hastens by forced marches day and night.   **100** for the sake of grain and provisions   **101** that they themselves having oftentimes encountered them were not able to bear even their looks, and — —

PAGE 57—**102** one of whom for one cause, another for another having reported what he was declaring was necessary to him for setting out, was asking that it might be allowed him to depart with his consent — — **103** to avoid the suspicion of fear, were remaining.   **104** (Those) of them who were wishing that they might be th ought less fearful were saying that they did not dread the enemy but feared the straits of the way ....or the matter of corn that it could not be transported conveniently enough.

PAGE 58—**105** that the soldiers would not be obedient to the command nor would bear the standard on account of fear. **106** because they were thinking it should be inquired or considered into what part

PAGE 59—**107** Indeed he himself was persuaded that when his demands were known and the fairness of the conditions preceived he would reject neither— —   **108** was seeming to have deserved not less praise than the commander himself. (Supply *esse* with *meritus*).   **109** in the slave uprising — —. Many of the slaves were German captives taken by Marius **110** From which it can be judged how much good firmness was having in itself.....by this (trickery) (.....) not even he himself expected our army could be taken.

PAGE 61—**111** upon the pretence of the grain supply and the straits of the ways did this officiously   **112** These things were his care.   **113** that it is said (translate *dicantur* as if singular) that they are not going to be obedient to the command and are not going to bear the standard, he himself is disturbed in nowise by this thing, for he knew that to whomsoever an army has been disobedient at the command — —

PAGE 62—**114** his own integrity in his life throughout — —

PAGE 63—**115** and the highest alertness and eagerness for waging war was incited   **116** and assured (him) that it was most prepared for waging war.   **117** Their apology (lit., satisfaction) having been received and the way having been reconnoitered by Divitiacus   **118** he was informed — —

PAGE 64—**119** and he was thinking he could do this without danger. Cæsar did not reject the terms.   **120** and thought he had now returned to reason   **121** it would transpire (fore) that he would cease from his obstinacy

PAGE 65—**122** in another manner he himself would not come.

P·ge 66—**123** now he enrolls it among the horse (lit., to the horse) i. e. makes them "*equites*," horsemen or knights. **124** When they had come there.

P·ge 67—**125** were existing between them and the Ædui.

P·ge 69—**126** that he himself had not inflicted war upon the Gauls, but the Gauls upon himself **127** he himself did this for the sake of protecting himself and not of assailing the Gauls.

P·ge 70—**128** that he did not come except as he was asked and that he did not wage war but had defended himself. **129** Never before this time had an army of the Roman people gone out of the borders of the province of Gaul.

P·ge 71—**130** He ought to be suspicious (*suspicari*, passive voice) that while friendship is feigned, because Cæsar had an army in Gaul, he has it for the sake of crushing him. **131** that if he should kill him he himself would be doing a grateful thing — — **132** that he himself has this, an ascertained fact, from themselves through their messengers.

P·ge 72—**133** allies who have deserved the best, nor does he himself judge that Gaul is rather the possession — —**134** but if it is proper that the most ancient time in detail (lit., each most ancient time) be regarded — —

P·ge 73—**135** approached nearer the hillock and rode up to our men, threw stones and weapons against our men — — **136** yet he was thinking it must not be permitted that, the enemy having been repulsed, it could be said they had been tricked by himself treacherously (lit., contrary to faith) in a conference **137** the arrogance that Ariovistus had used in the conference and that he had interdicted — —

P·ge 74—**138** It did not seem to Cæsar that there was a cause for conferring, and so much the more that — —

P·ge 75 **139** and because the Germans had in him no cause of transgressing (lit., because there was not cause to the Germans of transgressing in him) — — **140** But when Ariovistus had beheld them — — (*Quos*, whom, translate, But....them).

P·ge 76—**141** were brought (*supportaretur* is singular, the English idiom requires the plural number) **142** the opportunity might not be lacking to him **143** in cavalry battle

P·ge 77—**144** if they must advance farther or retire more quickly anywhere.

PAGE 79—**145** to assault the lesser camp. There was fighting sharply on both sides until towards evening **147** that they reported *(dicere)* thus: "it is not permitted (was,— the divine law, or fate) that the Germans shall conquer, if they should join in battle before the new moon." **148** because he was less powerful in the mass (lit.. multitude) of legionary soldiers as compared with the number of the enemy.

PAGE 80—**149** Cæsar appointed lieutenants one each and a questor (quartermaster) for the several legions

PAGE 81—**150** The javelins thrown aside the fighting went hand to hand with swords. **151** because he was more free to act (lit., more unencumbered) than those who were involved in the battle-line he sent as a reinforcement the third battle -line to our toiling men

PAGE 82—**152** The term, woman, is inserted to show the gender of *una* and *Sueva.*

PAGE 84—**153** and the Ubii who dwell nearest the Rhine having pursued them panic-stricken — — To follow the English idiom render *quos* by a connective and relative as if it were *etque eos.*

SECOND BOOK

PAGE 85—**1** also he was informed by the letters of Labienus that all the Belgæ ..... were conspiring ..... and were giving hostages among themselves. That these were the causes of conspiring — —

PAGE 86—**2** who were having means for mustering men. **3** he himself as soon as there was beginning to be plenty of forage came to the army.

PAGE 87—**4** that they ascertain these things that are transpiring among the latter (lit., them) and inform him concerning these matters **5** then indeed he judged that he must not hesitate to set out to them (lit., that it must not be hesitated but that — —) **6** that they entrust themselves and their all to the good faith and power of the Roman people.

PAGE 88—**7** that they could not intimidate (lit., restrain by fear) even the Suessiones ..... from intriguing (lit., but that they should intrigue. Or, from conniving) with these.

PAGE 89—**8** and that it was they alone who in the memory of our fathers when all Gaul was harassed, checked the Teutones and Cimbri from entering within their territories. **9** The Bellovaci were the most powerful among them.

PAGE 91—**10** and having dismissed them (lit., followed, took leave of) generously in an address —— **11** lest he must come to blows (lit., it must be combatted) at one time with so great a multitude

PAGE 92—**12** he dismisses him from his presence (lit., from himself). **13** nor now were far distant.

PAGE 93—**14** For when so great a multitude were hurling stones and weapons, there was an opportunity for no one of standing on the walls.

PAGE 95—**15** favorable and suitable for drawing up the battle-line.

PAGE 96—**16** *subsido*, lit. for a relief.

PAGE 97—**17** *illis*, those (forces) i. e. the enemy. **18** *contendebatur*, lit. it was contended. **19** for carrying on the war. **20** and were cutting off our (men) from supplies. Other reading: - *que sustenebant nostros commeatu* - and were sustaining our (men) with provisions. **21** light armed Numidians

PAGE 98—**22** There was sharp fighting in that place **23** when they understood that they had deceived themselves in the hope both of storming the town and of crossing the river, —— **24** for defending those into whose borders — —

PAGE 99—**25** were approaching the borders —— **26** It was not possible to persuade these to delay longer and not to bring aid to their (countrymen) **27** had not yet seen clearly **28** at daybreak

PAGE 100—**29** to whom they came **30** as the period of the day permitted

PAGE 101—**31** he was not able to storm it **32** although few were defending. **33** of use for storming

PAGE 102—**34** they bring it to pass (lit., obtain) that they shall be preserved. **35** the chiefs of the state and two sons — — Cæsar received the Suessiones into surrender **36** and signify by voice that they come into his protection and power and are not contending in arms against the Roman people.

PAGE 103—**37** (saying) the Belovæi for all time had been in the confidence — — that they had been impelled by their chiefs who had said that the Ædui were reduced to slavery by Cæsar and bore all indignities and affronts; (saying) that they had both revolted from the Ædui and had waged war against the Roman people.

PAGE 104—**38** support themselves if any wars have arisen

PAGE 105—**39** there was no approach for merchants to them; that they suffered no wine and other things tending to luxury to be imported, because they judged their minds were enfeebled and their valor diminished by these things; that the men were fierce and of great valor — — that they chided and blamed the remaining Belgians — — that they affirmed that they would neither send ambassadors nor would receive any conditions of peace.

PAGE 106—**40** Dative after *persuadeo*.   **41** there might not be access for an army

PAGE 107—**42** nor was there any difficulty when the first legion had come into camp   **43** it would come to pass that the remaining legions would not dare to take stand in opposition.

PAGE 108—**44** into which it was not possible not only to make entrance (pass. voice) but even to be seen through. **45** so that it was possible to get sight (pass. voice) within.

PAGE 109—**46** For, because Cæsar was approaching the enemy according to his custom he was leading six legions light armed   **47** nor were our (men) daring to follow those yielding farther than to the limit which the extended and open places were reaching; the six legions meantime — —

PAGE 110—**48** and encouraged themselves

PAGE 111—**49** those who had advanced rather far for the sake of mound material must be summoned

PAGE 112—**50** for the sake of exhorting the soldiers   **51** he gave the signal for joining battle   **52** and so prepared the mind of the enemy for fighting that time failed not only for putting on the badges but even for donning the helmet and drawing off the coverings from the shields

PAGE 113—**53** since some legions in one position others in another were resting the enemy in various places and as very dense hedges were interposing, as we have shown before, the view was intercepted and neither were sure reserves able to be placed nor what might be useful in each position before seen nor all the commands given by one (person)

PAGE 114—**54** They did not hesitate to cross the river **55** the Veromandui having been routed with whom they had joined (battle), were fighting from the higher ground on the very banks of the river

PAGE 115—**56** and some panicstricken were borne in one direction, others in another **57** they announced to the state that the Romans had been routed and overcome; that the enemy possessed their camp and baggage — With *pulsos, superatos* and *potitos* supply *esse*, after verbs of saying.

PAGE 117—**58** and that they (the enemy) pressed on from either flank and that the case was in a crisis, and that there was no reinforcement which could be sent up

PAGE 118—**59** Hope being infused in the soldiers by his coming and their spirit restored, since each one was desiring to do his best for himself in the sight of the General, even in his extreme dangers, the attack of the enemy was checked a little. **60** and should direct against the enemy the standards turned about — i. e. right and left face. **61** when some were bringing aid to some, others to others — —

PAGE 119—**62** they left nothing undone for themselves as regards speed

PAGE 120—**63** these dead bodies having been thrown down and heaped up **64** so that it ought to be considered that not without reason (i. e· with hope of success) men of so great valor — —

PAGE 121—**65** and in recounting the calamity of the state they said that they themselves were reduced

PAGE 122—**66** *esse* understood with *usus.* **67** Since this (town) on all sides in its circumference had very high rocks and outlooks, on one side a gently sloping approach was left not more than two hundred feet in width. This *quum*-clause explains *egregie munitum.*

PAGE 123—**68** when sometimes they were waging war, at other time were repelling it when brought upon (them)

PAGE 124—**69** But when they saw that it was moved and that it approached the walls

PAGE 125—**70** they said that they give up themselves and all their possessions into their (the Romans') power; that they sought and begged one thing

PAGE 126—**71** but that there was no condition of surrender except when the arms had been delivered; that he himself would do — —

PAGE 127—**72** There was a rush thither from the nearest fortresses and the battle was fought by the enemy — —

THIRD BOOK

PAGE 131—**1** and this (which) village located in a valley a plain not large adjoining is hemmed in on all sides by very lofty mountains.

PAGE 133—**2** and they had pursuaded themselves that the Romans were endeavoring to occupy the peaks of the Alps **3** since neither the work of winter quarters nor the fortifications were fully completed nor was enough grain and other provisions secured, because, — —

PAGE 134—**4** neither was it possible (*posset*, understood) for anyone to come to their aid **5** for arranging and executing these things which they had decreed **6** Historical infinitives denoting rapid action are translated like finite tenses. The same is true of *conjicere, repugnare, mittere, occurrere, ferre, superari.* **7** Our men at first repulse them bravely while their strength is fresh

PAGE 135—**8** When now the fight was continuing unceasingly, — — **9** and as our men were becoming more faint, they began to, — —

PAGE 136—**10** who, we have said, was spent with many wounds, — — **11** that there is one hope of safety

PAGE 137—**12** nor of collecting themselves i. e. of recovering their senses **13** those (lit., these) who had come into the hope of getting possession of the camp, when they were surrounded on every side. **14** nor suffered them to take stand even in the places that are higher, *quidem* emphasizes *in locis.* **15** and remembered that he had come into winter quarters with one design and was seeing that he had met with other circumstances.

PAGE 138—**16** and so at the beginning of winter had set out into Illyricum **17** omit *mare* in translation.

PAGE 140—**18** they take oath among themselves through their chiefs that they would act in nothing (accusative of specification) except by common counsel and that they would bear, — —

PAGE 141—**19** ambassadors, a name, — — .... had been detained by them and cast into chains. Supply *esse* with *retentos* and *conjectos*

PAGE 142 **20** Supply *esse* - that navigation was hindered **21** longer, or rather long, i. e. any length of time. **22** supplies of grain

PAGE 143—**23** These were the difficulties of waging the war lit., of war to be waged.

PAGE 144—**24** *esse* understood, forming the perfect passive infinitive after verbs of saying

PAGE 145—**25** Pluperfect of defective verb, *cœpi,* used with the force of the imperfect - they were beginning to despair

PAGE 146—**26** in order that they may be able the more easily to take the shoals and ebb-tides (lit., ebb of the tide); **27** for enduring any force and buffeting; the benches were made from beams a foot in width fastened together with iron nails of the thickness of a thumb.

PAGE 147—**28** and so great fury of the winds could *(posse)* not be withstood and so great masses of ships governed by sails conveniently enough **29** Some texts read *adigebatur.* - nor was a weapon easily shot at them.

PAGE 148—**30** nor could *(posse)* he inflict injury (*noceri,* passive voice) upon them, he decided that the fleet mnst be awaited. **31** about two hundred and twenty of their ships the best equipped and most provided with every kind of armament (lit., arms) — —

PAGE 149—**32** for they had understood that they could not inflict injury by the beak (prow). Lit., *hostes* understood is subject of *posse*.   **33** With a form not unlike that of wall-hooks. — —

P*age* 150—**34** all advantage of their ships was lost at the same time i. e. all at once.   **35** after the barbarians perceived that this was done

P*age* 151—**36** and this condition (which thing) was especially favorable for completing the business   **37** since the battle continued   **38** in whom there was some counsel or dignity had gathered there; besides they had assembled in one place what ships had been everywhere

P*age* 152—**39** under the hammer i. e. at auction

P*age* 153—**40** an enthusiasm for fighting was [were] recalling, — —

P*age* 154—**41** because he was thinking that a battle ought not to be undertaken by a lieutenant......except on equal grounds or when some opportunity was given   **42** to go over to the enemy   **43** nor is it farther off than that on the next night Sabinus may lead out, — — and set out to Cæsar for the sake of bringing him aid.   When this report was heard all shout that the opportunity for carrying on the business well must not be lost that it is the proper thing to go to camp.

P*age* 155—**44** the want of food which had been provided by them without sufficient care.   **45** Induced by these things they do not release Viridovix and the other leaders from the council before that it has been granted by them to take arms and to hasten to the camp

P*age* 156—**46** at full speed, that as brief a period as possible might be given the Romans for assembling and arming themselves, and arrived out of breath.   **47** It came to pass   **48** and our soldiers with fresh strength having pursued them (*quos*, translated by and....them) encumbered slew a great number of them

P*age* 157—**49** for undertaking wars, so their mind is soft and by no means sturdy [resistant] for bearing misfortunes.

P*age* 158—**50** There was fighting long and sharply   **51** that the security of the entire Aquitania was placed in their valor (Supply *esse* with *positam*)

P*age* 159—**52** that it should be seen what they could

accomplish without the general, — — The clause: *quid possent.....duce* is subject of *perspici*, and the whole construction is the object of *caperent*. **53** and when they were bravely resisting, — — One of the many instances in which an ablative absolute may be rendered best in English by a subordinate clause.

PAGE 160—**54** commit suicide **55** and the fighting there was violent

PAGE 161—**56** however he obtained from Crassus to enjoy (English idiom, the enjoyment of) the same condition of surrender. **57** because they had learned that a town ..,.... had been stormed (supply *esse*) in the few days in which (the Romans) had come there.

PAGE 162—**58** he considered that he must not delay settling the issue (but that he should settle the issue) in battle. **59** that all thought the same thing, — —

PAGE 163—**60** when the plan had been approved by their generals, although the troops of the Romans were drawn up, they were keeping themselves in camp. **61** that it was befitting them not to wait longer but that they should be off to the camp; having exhorted his men, all filled with eagerness, he hastens to the camp of the enemy.

PAGE 166—**62** far into the night

PAGE 167—**63** nor had ever sent ambassadors to him about peace. **64** and when Cæsar had arrived at the margin of these forests and had decided to fortify a camp nor meantime had an enemy been seen, — —

PAGE 168—**65** therefore all their fields (lit., all the fields of them) having been laid waste (or, when all their fields had been laid waste and their villages and buildings burned,) — —

FOURTH BOOK

PAGE 171—**1** from each of which they lead yearly a thousand armed men out of their territories. **2** but for the most part on milk and beef (lit., cattle) and are often (lit., much) in huntings; [in the chase]; and this condition (lit., which thing) — —

Page 173—**3** and fight on foot (lit., battle on the feet)   **4** therefore however few they dare to approach (to) any number whatever of saddled horsemen.   They do not permit wine to be imported — —   **5** because they think that by this thing men are enfeebled for enduring labor and are effeminated.   **6** are said to be unoccupied from the Suevi on one side; the Ubii come next in the other direction (lit., at the other part).

Page 175—**7** they arrived at the Rhine, the localities which the Memapii were inhabiting   **8** they were checking the Germans from crossing over — —   **9** they pretend that they are returning to their own habitations and countries — — **10** who have been informed of the departure of the Germans by spies

Page 176—**11** before (lit., before that) this part of the Memapii which was on this side of the Rhine was informed.

Page 177—**12** and very many answer fictions according to the wish of these.   **13** lest he might encounter a severer war. Sometimes rendered: - a rather severe war   **14** he learned that these things had been done which he suspected would be, that ambassadors had been sent by some states to the Germans and that they had been requested to depart (lit., that they should depart) from the Rhine — —   Supply *esse* with *facta missas* and *invitatos*.   **15** and the Germans induced by this *(Qua)* hope — —

Page 178—**16** When he was distant a few days' journey from them — —   **17** whose speech was as follows: (lit., these things).   **18** nor yet do they refuse to contend in arms if they are attacked.

Page 181—**19** forming many great islands (lit., many and great) — —

Page 182—**20** if their chiefs and senate would give pledge (lit., give faith) by oath they were showing that they themselves would use those terms that were offered by Cæsar (lit., this condition, let him give them (themselves) a period of three days for accomplishing these things.

Page 183—**21** let them assemble hither on the next day as numerously as possible that he might learn concerning their demands (lit., the requests of them)   **22** But as soon as (*ubi primum.* lit., when first) the enemy beheld our cavalry — —

Introduce the noun into the subordinate clause in English
and supply a pronoun as *ii* or *illi*, as subject of *perturbaverunt*,
the principal verb several lines below **23** some texts have
induciis.

PAGE 185—**24** to whom he was judging no time at all
should be given (lit., nothing of time) for taking counsel (lit.,
counsels). as well, (*simul*, correlative of *simul* below)

PAGE 186—**25** as it was said, for the sake of exonerating
themselves **26** (contrary to what (lit., as) had been declared
[said] and to what they themselves had sought — — **27**
Cæsar rejoicing (lit., having rejoiced) ordered them when
they were presented to him to be detained. Change the *quos*
clause to the English idiom. The fate of these people is
mention in the last few lines of Chapter 15.

PAGE 187—**28** *qui*, and they — — **29** time (lit., space)
having been given neither for forming plans nor for taking
arms **30** When their (lit., whose, or of whom) panic was
indicated — —

PAGE 189—**31** of which (cause) this (that) was the most
justifiable (lit., most just) **32** In addition also that portion
of the cavalry — —

PAGE 190 **33** when Cæsar had sent messengers to them
34 if he should judge that it was not just that the Germans
should cross the Rhine into Gaul, when he was unwilling, why
should he demand that any of his empire or power should be
across the Rhine.

PAGE 191—**35** since Ariovistus was routed and this last
battle fought — — an ablative absolute denoting cause, it is
best rendered in English by a subordinate clause

PAGE 192—**36** which having been separated and held fast
in opposite directions — —

PAGE 193—**37** at the lower part of the river — — i. e.
down stream.

PAGE 198—**38** the countries having been explored in so far
as opportunity could (*potuit*, was able) be given to him — —

PAGE 199—**39** concerning the project of the former season
(lit., time).

PAGE 200—**40** And when they were brought to him (lit.,
whom having been brought) he received them into alliance

PAGE 201—**41** since this was executed by these (lit., by whom) a little more slowly [rather slowly] — —

PAGE 202—**42** as the method of military affairs and especially as maritime movements (lit., thing) demand (as these (*quæ*) have a quick and unsteady motion).

PAGE 203—**43** moreover the soldiers both must leap down at the same time from the ships and must take stand in the waves and must fight with the enemy — — (lit., it must be leaped down by the soldiers — —) **44** while they (*illi*, the enemy) — — **45** when Cæsar perceived this (which) — —

PAGE 205—**46** there was sharp fighting by both sides.

PAGE 207—**47** he said he would pardon their indiscretion (lit., ignorance)

PAGE 208—**48** the fourth day after he had come into Britain (lit., it was come); when they were approaching to Britain — — **49** *quæ* translate as if *hæ*, these, subject of *complerentur*.

PAGE 209—**50** (in which Cæsar had caused (lit., had provided, or taken care,) the army to be transported) — —

PAGE 210—**51** and all things were lacking which were of use for repairing the ships and because it was evident to all that it was expedient to winter in Gaul (since) corn had not been provided in these places against the winter. **52** some texts have *ad ea facienda quæ Cæsar jusserat* for these (things) to be done which Cæsar had ordered i. e. for doing these things which Cæsar had ordered

PAGE 212—**53** he brought it to pass that they could make a sailing (*navigari*, passive voice, lit., to be sailed) easily in the rest. Some texts read: *satis commode*, quite easily.

PAGE 213—**54** and disorder the ranks generally by the very terror of the horses (lit., terror itself) — —

PAGE 214—**55** and battle on foot (lit., on the feet)

PAGE 215—**56** having thought the time unsuited for attacking the enemy and for joining battle — — **57** a short time having passed (lit., having been interposed) **58** the rest (i. e. the Britains) who were in the fields departed. **59** how great an opportunity was presented (lit., given) for (of) making plunder and of freeing themselves forever — —

PAGE 217—**60** he was thinking that the passage (lit., voyage) must not be incurred in winter (lit., exposed to win-

ter) with weak ships — — **61** when about three hundred
soldiers had been landed from these (which) ships and were
hartening into camp — — **65** if they were unwilling to be
slain (lit., if they were unwilling themselves to be slain) — —

FIFTH BOOK

PAGE 220—**1** that they should take care in the winter (that)
ships as many as could be (lit., as they were able) should be
built and the old repaired. He shows their size and form.

PAGE 221—**2** because he had learned that the waves became
less great there on account of the frequent alterations of the
tides. **3** for transporting cargos and a multitude of beasts of
burden— —**4** and for this object (lit., for which thing) etc.
Res is a very indefinite term and requires translation according
to the connection. **5** He orders these (materials) which are of
use for rigging ships, (lit,, for ships to be rigged) to be brought
from Spain. **6** he demands soldiers from the states. *Impero*
takes the dative of the person and accusative of the thing.

PAGE 222—**7** he shows that he would proceed against the
state with war.

PAGE 223—**8** nor were they far from (wanting much from)
this condition of being possible (*possent*) to be launched (lit.,
led down) in a few days. **9** This state is by far the most
powerful of all Gaul in cavalry

PAGE 224—**10** were striving with one another (lit., among
themselves) concerning the chieftaincy. **11** he prepares war
(*parare*, historical infinitive)

PAGE 225—**12** that he himself withdrew from his own people and had been unwilling to come to him for this reason in
order that he might preserve the state more easily in its allegiance etc. **13** for what reason these things were said (i. e. his
jealousy of Cingetorix).

PAGE 226—**14** and this thing (which thing) he was not only
understanding should be done by himself because of his deserts
but also he was judging that it concerned him greatly that
the authority of this one (lit., the authority of him) should

prevail as much as possible among his own people, whose good will he had perceived was so excellent toward himself.

PAGE 227—**15** had not been able, infinitive after *cognoscit.*

PAGE 228—**16** Impossible to render exactly, lit:- It was approaching hither that etc. It happened in addition that etc. **17** *suis* - his, i. e. Dumnorix's — — **18** After he saw that this was denied him persistently (lit., obstinately)

PAGE 229—**19** (saying) that he was alarmed with the fear that not without reason it was done so that Gaul should be stripped of all the nobility etc. **20** he insinuated a pledge to the rest, demanded an oath etc. **21** because he was seeing that his madness had gone too far, he must look out (lit., it must be looked out) that (*ne*, lest) he should (*posset*) not injure himself and the state.

PAGE 230—**22** he was taking pains (lit., giving work) etc. **23** and he orders that he be dragged back; if he shows violence (lit., makes violence) nor obeys, he orders that he be killed having considered that he would do nothing like a sane man since he had disregarded his commands in his presence.

PAGE 231—**24** that he might take counsel in accordance with time and circumstances — — Plu. in English idiom for *re.*

PAGE 232—**25** An approach was made to Britain by all the ships nearly at noon time. **26** Nor was an enemy seen in this place etc.

PAGE 234—**27** and were preventing our men from penetrating within the fortifications.

PAGE 235—**28** Some texts have the term *literis* in parenthesis as given here although quite probably it should be omitted.

PAGE 236—**29** not the time of night even - *nocturnis* is emphasized by *quidem.*

PAGE 237—**30** The chieftaincy of the command and of the managing of the war i. e. the leadership of the command and the chief management. **31** The interior part of Britian is inhabited by those who, it is handed down by memory, (by tradition) have been born in (i. e. are native to) the island itself. *Esse* is understood with *proditum.* The subject of *proditum esse* is the clause *quos natos (esse) in insula.*

PAGE 238—**32** *examinatis*, lit., weighed.

PAGE 240—**33** in *circuitu*, - all around. **34** and they have long hair.

PAGE 243—**35** Add to this etc.   See note 16 — — **36** and
some were relieving some, others others in succession

PAGE 244—**37** so that they were not keeping back from
the standards and the legions.   **38** neither did they give the
opportunity of collecting themselves nor of halting.

PAGE 246—**39** and by this fear was hindering them from
roaming more widely.   It followed (lit., was left) that Cæsar
would not allow departure to be made (lit., it to be departed)
too far from the marching-line of the legions and that injury
should be inflicted upon the enemy (lit., it should be injured to
the enemy in) by ravaging the fields and making conflagrations
(lit., burnings) etc.

PAGE 248—**40** many (of the enemy) etc.

PAGE 250—**41** He prohibits and commands Cassivellaunus
not to injure Mandubracius nor the Trinobantes.   **42** *et*, omit
in translating

PAGE 251—**43** and (those) which Labienus had taken care
to be made etc.   **44** When Cæsar had awaited these (lit.,
which) etc.

PAGE 252—**45** of these legions (lit., from which legions)
he gave one etc.

PAGE 254—**46** by whose management (lit., work) he may
learn that Tasgetius had been killed.   Meantime he was informed by all the lieutenants and quæstors to whom he had
assigned legions that they had arrived in winter quarters and
that the place was fortified for the winter quarters.   This is an
impersonal construction and impossible to translate literally
(i. e. that it had been arrived into winter quarters etc.).   In
about fifteen days since they had come into winter quarters
(lit., from which it was come etc.).

PAGE 257—**47** that Gauls are not easily able to refuse Gauls,
especially when a design was seeming best to be adopted (lit.,
entered into) concerning the restoring of the common liber-
ties.   **48** he advises Cæsar for his kindness, he beseeches
Titurius for his hospitality — — **49** it is their plan (i. e. it is
for them to decide) whether they etc.

PAGE 258—**50** when he does this he (*sese*) both consults for
the state because it will be relieved from winter quarters and
returns a favor to Cæsar for his good offices (lit., merits, or
services).

PAGE 259—**51** that nothing must be performed rashly nor must they depart (lit., it to be departed) from winter quarters without the order of Cæsar. **52** The fact is a witness. **53** Meantime reinforcements would arrive both from the nearest winter quarters and from Cæsar.

PAGE 260—**54** Neither otherwise would the Carnutes have formed the design of killing Tasgetius nor would the Eburones have come etc.

PAGE 261—**55** The English idiom would require some such form as this: who would persuade himself, or, would be persuaded, regarding this etc. **56** In which (i. e. following that advice) if not present danger etc.

PAGE 263—**57** Everything is calculated why they may not remain without danger and why the danger is increased by the weariness and wakefulness of the soldiers. **58** They set out at early dawn from the camp in such a manner (lit., so) as they etc. **59** but by Ambiorix as a most faithful man.

PAGE 265—**60** was performing the duties of a general in summoning and encouraging the soldiers and of a soldier in the battle. **61** this seemed to be done etc.

PAGE 267—**62** that they could in nowise be injured (lit., it was possible as to nothing to be injured to them) because of the lightness of their arms and their daily exercise.

PAGE 268—**63** Then Titus Balventius has each thigh pierced with a javelin. **64** who had led the first century i. e. had been first centurion.

PAGE 271—**65** that there is no trouble, for the legion, having been suddenly crushed, which winters with Cicero to be slain etc.

PAGE 272—**66** as great as they are able — — **67** *necesse*, unavoidable (lit., necessary)

PAGE 273—**68** they (the Romans) had brought together etc.

PAGE 274—**69** *contabulantur*, i. e. are built up with stories. **70** *nocturnum* is emphasized by *quidem* in the regular text. **71** they exhibit Ambiorix for the sake of creating confidence (lit., of making faith). **72** *inveterascere*, lit., to become old **73** he himself hopes that they may obtain what they sought in view of his justice.

PAGE 277—**74** i. e. it was spread into every part of the

camp. **75** but no one scarcely even looked back and besides all were fighting most fiercely and most valiantly.

P<small>AGE</small> 279—**76** *pugnaretur*, lit., when it was fought etc. **77** "or what opportunity (lit., place) of proving thy valor dost thou await?" **78** Pullo's shield is pierced.

P<small>AGE</small> 283—**79** for the sake of passing (lit., bearing), the winter.

P<small>AGE</small> 284—**80** *reciderat*, lit., had fallen back.

P<small>AGE</small> 286—**81** and therefore was thinking he must relax with an easy mind from speed (lit., it must be relaxed)

P<small>AGE</small> 288—**82** and that there be confusion as much as possible in managing these things and that it be performed (*agi*) with a pretence of fear. The enemy having been tempted by all these things (lit., by all which things) etc. **83** they approach nearer i. e. the enemy approach.

P<small>AGE</small> 289—**84** after this time no longer would be the opportunity. **85** nor was he seeing that the place had been left with a trifling loss on their part.

P<small>AGE</small> 292—**86** without anxiety on the part of Cæsar etc.

P<small>AGE</small> 294—**87** they were not obedient to the command. It availed so much among barbarian men that some were found the leaders in waging war etc.

P<small>AGE</small> 295—**88** lost no time of the whole winter without sending ambassadors across the Rhine, inviting the states, promising money, (who) should say etc. **89** Nor yet was it possible to prevail upon any state of the Germans to cross the Rhine;

P<small>AGE</small> 298—**90** but was thinking he should not lose any opportunity for performing a matter well.

P<small>AGE</small> 299—**91** with many insulting words. **92** and enjoins, (lit., forbids), which refers to the part of the sentence below: *omnes peterent quemquam.*

SIXTH BOOK

P<small>AGE</small> 302—**1** *augeri* cannot be translated literally, i. e. to be increased, the idea being that the loss can not only be repaired but may be more than made good, *supplemented* approaches the meaning. **2** *proximis* and **3** *ulteriores* Germans or states is understood — — **4** they bind each other (*inter se*) by an oath. **5** *parari, esse, venire, communicare, solicitari,* are infinitives after *videret* (saw that), which are translated as finite past tenses.

PAGE 304—**6** and had united these states, (i. e. with the Senones,) but they were thought to have been absent from this council (the recent confederacy). *Hac re* this thing (the adjournment to Lutetia) etc.

PAGE 305—**7** for the sake of asking quarter.

PAGE 306—**8** Lit., not to be about to contend.

PAGE 307—**9** Lit., for the sake of peace to be sought.

PAGE 308—**10** at fifteen thousand paces (from Labienus).

PAGE 309—**11** Lit., at first light.

PAGE 310—**12** Lit., among themselves.

PAGE 312—**13** Lit., for the sake of themselves to be cleared

PAGE 313—**14** Lit., he becomes, or is made more certain.

PAGE 315—**15** from one another.

PAGE 316—**16** and forced them to swear pnblicly that they would enter (*esse* understood with *inituros,* lit., to be about to enter) into no design (lit., nothing of design) against the Sequani.

PAGE 317—**17** Lit., themselves to use — — **18** as it was perceived that they (*quos*) equaled the Ædui in favor etc.

PAGE 319—**19** Lit., they to whom it had been interdicted are held in the number etc.

PAGE 321—**20** Lit., to pass from some to others, — plural to correspond with pl. number of *animas,* not the form.

PAGE 322—**21** they vow that they will sacrifice them.

PAGE 323—**22** *depellere, tradere, tenere, regere,* are infinitives after *habent....opinionem.*

PAGE 324—**23** Supply *esse* with *proditum.*

PAGE 325—**24** according to the manner with slaves, i. e. torture. **25** Lit., to have been to the heart to them living.

PAGE 328—**26** as wide as possible.

PAGE 331—**27** they not themselves even compare etc., *se* is emphasized.

PAGE 337—**28** because he thought he must not contend in battle etc.

P<small>AGE</small> 340—**29** for devastating this locality, lit., for this locality to be devastated.

P<small>AGE</small> 348—**30** consciousness leaves Sextius, i. e. Sextius faints.

P<small>AGE</small> 350—**31** through the midst of the enemy etc.

P<small>AGE</small> 352—**32** would not have assaulted the camp etc.

P<small>AGE</small> 353—**33** Lit., for harassing the enemy. **34** Lit., it would seem it to be perished by these.

P<small>AGE</small> 355—**35** He inflicted death by flogging.

SEVENTH BOOK

P<small>AGE</small> 357—**1** Lit., at the peril of their head, like our term capital (head *caput*) punishment.

P<small>AGE</small> 359—**2** Lit., it is departed from the council.

P<small>AGE</small> 360—**3** Lit., the sun rising (abl. absolute) — — **4** i. e. between nine and ten P. M., viz., about sixteen hours. It must be kept in mind that many miles of the country were then uninhabited. **5** recourse is had to arms, lit., it is rushed to arms.

P<small>AGE</small> 363—**6** who they ascertain had made this plan etc. **7** *virtute*, i. e. vigor. Sometimes translated: thanks to Cneius Pompey.

P<small>AGE</small> 366—**8** Having been stirred by their entreaties etc. **9** because he had anticipated in his judgment that these things would come to pass as regards Vercingetorix, he departs from the army etc.

P<small>AGE</small> 367—**10** for undertaking a plan.

P<small>AGE</small> 370—**11** very few of the whole number of the enemy having missed, (or escaped), being captured etc. *Cuncti*, in sense, goes with *perpaucis ex numero*. **12** When ambassadors had come to him from this town etc.

P<small>AGE</small> 371—**13** as soon as the townsmen had seen it (*quem* i. ei *equitatum*) and entertained the hope of aid etc.

P<small>AGE</small> 373—**14** Supply *esse* with *laturos* and *progressuros*, that the Romans either would not bear privation or would proceed rather far from the camp, with great danger.

P<small>AGE</small> 376—**15** Lit., that it should be gone.

PAGE 377—**16** to such a degree that the soldiers etc.

PAGE 380—**17** since he saw them (*quos*) so prepared in mind etc.

PAGE 381—**18** that he prefers to have etc.   **19** feebleness of purpose.

PAGE 382—**20** *gratiam habendam*, thanks must be given, is understood before *huic*.

PAGE 384—**21** and when they had caught them (*quos*) etc.

PAGE 385—**22** at equal intervals apart (*inter se*) etc.

PAGE 386—**23** In this passage the same phrase (*inter se*) may be rendered one another, each other.

PAGE 387—**24** where first it should be thwarted (lit., it should be run to meet so as to frustrate or thwart).

PAGE 388—**25** When the battle was raging in all places etc. **26** was depending on that instant of time (lit., to be placed in that instant etc., *esse* being understood with *positam*).

PAGE 389—**27** Lit., was retarding the Romans for following

PAGE 391—**28** that if any advance to meet them (*obviam*) on any side they might fight with the battle line arrayed.

PAGE 392—**29** that part of the camp which had fallen to each from the beginning.

PAGE 397—**30** That is, each of them has his own (followers) adherents. might translate freely *suas eorum*, each of them has his own partisans.

PAGE 401—**31** he resolved that he must not act regarding a seige etc.

PAGE 402—**32** both in a large measure from water and from unrestricted (free) foraging etc.

PAGE 409—**33** who (*quibus*) on account of the size of the camp must remain continually on the wall without relief (lit., the same).

PAGE 411—**34** Although Cæsar was knowing these things (lit., which things — *quae*) etc.

PAGE 419—**35** While they are fighting (While the fighting proceeds) most violently etc.

PAGE 420—**36** *Manus*, force lit., band, i. e. the force of the enemy.

PAGE 421—**37** and was the salvation of his men.   **38** viz., the tenth legion.

PAGE 427—**38** Lit., it must be hastened by himself if it must be hazarded in building the bridges.

PAGE 429—**40** or Melodunum, accoring to some authorities.

PAG 431—**41** aid must be sought from his own mental resources (lit., by the courage of mind)

PAGE 432—**42** When he had come there etc.

PAGE 437—**43** in a pitched battle.

PAGE 443—**44** *Alesia*, the modern Alise - St - Reine where many relics of the seige have been excavated.

PAGE 446—**45** and if they should be rather heedless (dila tory) he shows etc.

PAGE 447—**46** *Poenam capitis*, capital punishment.

PAGE 448—**47** from each other eighty feet i. e. about four hundred of them.

PAGE 449—**48** where if any (*qui*) might enter — — **49** the foot lit., feet, of each (the several feet) in the ground at the bottom (from [on] the lowest ground) were trodden in with earth.

PAGE 451—**50** could be surrounded not by a multitude even great, *quidem* emphasizes *magna*. **51** (if it happens so through its withdrawal) i. e. the departure of the cavalry. This clause is generally omitted in translation.

PAGE 454—**52** when these would be fighting in a sally etc.

PAGE 456—**53** for the joy of it, i. e. for a mere idea.

PAGE 457—**54** For what was in (lit., to) that war like this ?

PAGE 460—**55** active (soldiers) of the light armed troops.

PAGE 461—**56** *ac* must be rendered as if *nec*, nor, i. e. neither a noble nor cowardly act could be concealed.

PAGE 462—**57** by one-pounder sling shots. **58** Mark Anthony, the triumvir.

PAGE 464—**59** and because they could not enclose it in the works on account of the extent of the surface, our men etc. (*quem*, *viz.*, and .. it)

PAGE 465 **60** There was fighting at the same time in all places,

PAGE 466—**61** in which it was fitting that they should fight to the uttermost.

PAGE 468—**62** when they are fighting more desperately etc.